# Dynamics of International Advertising

This book is part of the Peter Lang Media and Communication list.
Every volume is peer reviewed and meets
the highest quality standards for content and production.

PETER LANG
New York • Washington, D.C./Baltimore • Bern
Frankfurt • Berlin • Brussels • Vienna • Oxford

# BARBARA MUELLER

# Dynamics of International Advertising

THEORETICAL AND PRACTICAL PERSPECTIVES

SECOND EDITION

PETER LANG
New York • Washington, D.C./Baltimore • Bern
Frankfurt • Berlin • Brussels • Vienna • Oxford

**Library of Congress Cataloging-in-Publication Data**

Mueller, Barbara.
Dynamics of international advertising: theoretical
and practical perspectives / Barbara Mueller. —2nd ed.
p. cm.
Includes bibliographical references and index.
1. Advertising. I. Title.
HF5823.M829  659.1—dc22  2010046421
ISBN 978-1-4331-0384-1


Bibliographic information published by **Die Deutsche Nationalbibliothek.**
**Die Deutsche Nationalbibliothek** lists this publication in the "Deutsche
Nationalbibliografie"; detailed bibliographic data is available
on the Internet at http://dnb.d-nb.de/.

The paper in this book meets the guidelines for permanence and durability
of the Committee on Production Guidelines for Book Longevity
of the Council of Library Resources.

© 2011 Peter Lang Publishing, Inc., New York
29 Broadway, 18th floor, New York, NY 10006
www.peterlang.com

Printed in the United States of America

For Juergen and Sophie

# Table of Contents

# Preface

My objective in preparing this second edition of *Dynamics of International Advertising: Theoretical and Practical Perspectives* was to reflect the dramatic changes that have impacted the field over the past 5 to 10 years. The current economic downturn has caused advertising budgets to shrink, agencies to lay off advertising professionals, and many consumers in developed and developing markets alike to tighten their belts. In response to the shifting demographics in more advanced countries, international advertisers are increasingly looking to developing markets for larger and more youthful consumer segments. New media forms are evolving—forms no one could have predicted when the first edition was published. And advertisers are increasingly being expected to behave in a socially responsible fashion—not only towards their customers, their employees, and the environment—but also to society at large. This new edition utilizes the best examples of contemporary advertising from around the globe to demonstrate how agencies are responding to these changes. The latest statistics are incorporated into each and every table. And new insights from academic research are highlighted.

This book introduces the reader to the challenges and difficulties of developing and implementing communications programs for foreign markets. Although advertising is the major focus, I recognize that an integrated marketing communications approach is critical to competing successfully in the international setting. In order to communicate effectively with audiences around the globe, marketers must coordinate not only advertising, direct marketing, sales promotions, personal selling, and public relations efforts, but all other aspects of the marketing mix as well. Therefore, the basics of international marketing are briefly reviewed in the first several chapters of this text. The remainder of the book then focuses on international advertising.

Significant changes are incorporated throughout the text, but I have kept the basic structure of the first edition. The text comprises a total of ten chapters. In Chapter 1, factors influencing the growth of international advertising are examined. Chapter 2 highlights the role that product, price, distribution, and promotion, play in selling abroad. Domestic advertising and international advertising differ not so much in concept as in environment; the international marketing and advertising environment is outlined in Chapter 3. Chapter 4 is devoted to developing a sensitivity to the various cultural factors that impact international marketing efforts. Chapter 5 addresses the coordination and control of international advertising. Chapter 6 deals with creative strategies and executions for foreign audiences. Chapters 7–9 explore media decisions in the global marketplace, international advertising research and methods for obtaining the information necessary for making international advertising decisions, and, finally, regulatory considerations. Chapter 10 focuses on the social responsibility of international advertising agencies and multinational corporations in foreign markets.

Every attempt has been made to provide a balance of theoretical and practical perspectives. For example, the issues of centralization versus decentralization and standardization versus localization are addressed as they apply to the organization of international advertising programs, development and execution of creative strategy, media planning and buying, and advertising research. Readers will find that these are not black-and-white issues. Instead, they can be viewed as a continuum. Some marketing and advertising decisions can be centralized while others may not be. Similarly, depending on the product to be advertised and the audience to be targeted, some elements of the marketing and advertising mix may be standardized while others will be specialized.

First and foremost, *Dynamics of International Advertising: Theoretical and Practical Perspectives* is the ideal textbook for upper-division undergraduate and graduate students in specialized courses dealing with international advertising or marketing. It is also an effective supplemental text for introductory advertising, marketing, or mass communications courses seeking to expand coverage of the international dimension. The text should also prove useful to practitioners of international advertising, whether on the client side or within the advertising agency. Finally, researchers of international advertising and marketing will find it a valuable resource.

I am indebted to a number of individuals for the successful completion of this text. I am most grateful to the folks at Peter Lang Publishing. In particular, I'd like to acknowledge the editor of the first edition, Chris Myers. I wish that every author could have the kind of experience I had with Chris. He has the fine knack of making just about everything related to writing a textbook as painless and simple as it possibly can be. Many thanks to Mary Savigar, senior acquisitions editor, for encouraging the development of this second edition and for being such pleasure to work with. Bernadette Shade once again held my hand through the production process and oversaw the development of the eye-catching cover. On a personal note, this book—like my others—would not have been possible without the unconditional love and support of my husband, Juergen, and my daughter, Sophie. Both stood by me—as always—without complaint.

Barbara Mueller

# CHAPTER ONE

# Growth of International Business and Advertising

The keystone of our global economy is the multinational corporation. A growing number of corporations around the world have traversed geographical boundaries and become truly multinational in nature. As a result, consumers around the world write with Bic pens and wear Adidas running shoes, talk on Nokia cell phones and drive Toyota autos. Shoppers can stop in for a McDonald's burger in Paris or Beijing, and German and Japanese citizens alike increasingly make their purchases with the American Express Card. And, for most other domestic firms, the question is no longer, Should we go international? Rather, the questions relate to when, how, and where the companies should enter the international marketplace. The growth and expansion of firms operating internationally have led to the growth in international advertising. U.S. agencies are increasingly looking abroad for clients. At the same time, foreign agencies are rapidly expanding around the globe, even taking control of some of the most prestigious U.S. agencies. The United States continues to both produce and consume the bulk of the world's advertising. However, advertising's global presence is evidenced by the location of major advertising markets. In rank order, the top global advertising markets are the United States, Japan, the United Kingdom, Germany, China, France, Italy, Spain, Brazil, and South Korea. And today, 8 of the top 10 world advertising organizations are headquartered outside the United States (Johnson 2009). This chapter outlines the growth of international business and advertising.

## HISTORICAL OVERVIEW

There have been three waves of globalization since 1870. The first wave, between 1870 and 1914, was led by improvements in transport technology (from sailing ships to steam ships) and by lower tariff barriers. Further driving this first wave of modern globalization were rising production scale economies due to advancements in technology that outpaced the growth of the world economy. Product needs also became more homogenized in different countries as knowledge and industrialization diffused. Communication became easier with the telegraph and, later, the telephone. By the early 1900s, firms such as Ford Motor, Singer, Gillette, National Cash Register, Otis, and Western Electric already had commanding world market shares. Exports during this first wave nearly doubled to about 8 percent of world income (World Bank 2002, 326).

The trend to globalization slowed between 1914 and the late 1940s. These decades were marked by a world economic crisis as well as two world wars, which resulted in a period of strong nationalism. Countries attempted to salvage and strengthen their own economies by imposing high tariffs and quotas so as to keep out foreign goods and protect domestic employment. It was not until after the Second World War that the number of U.S. firms operating internationally again began to grow significantly.

The second wave of globalization was from 1945 to 1980. International tensions—whether in the form of cold war or open conflict—tend to discourage international marketing. However, during this period, the world was, for the most part, relatively peaceful. This, paired with the creation of the International Monetary Fund (IMF) and the General Agreement on Tariffs and Trade (GATT) at the close of World War II, facilitated the growth of international trade and investment. Indeed, during this period, tariffs among the industrialized nations fell from about 40 percent in 1947 to roughly 5 percent by 1980. In 1950 U.S. foreign direct investment stood at $12 billion. By 1965 it had risen to $50 billion, and by the late 1970s to approximately $150 billion (U.S. Bureau of the Census 1995, 870).

The third wave of globalization has been from approximately 1980 to the present. Spurring this third wave has been further progress in transport (containerization and air freight) and communication technology (falling telecommunication costs associated with satellites, fiber-optic cable, cell telephones, and the Internet). Along with declining tariffs on manufactured goods (currently under 4 percent), many countries lowered barriers to foreign investment and improved their investment climates. After the September 11 attacks in the United States, some economists worried that the year 2001 would mark a reversal of the current era of globalization. Recession, U.S. security concerns, and resentment abroad seemed aligned against the forces that drove companies abroad in the 1990s in search of new markets. However, according to a PriceWaterhouseCoopers survey of 171 business executives at large U.S. multinationals, commitment to international expansion actually rose in the year after the September 11 attacks. Of those surveyed, 27 percent planned some sort of geographic expansion during the following year, up from 19 percent prior to the attacks (Hilsenrath 2002). And it appears that the same forces that drove globalization in the past might in fact be intensifying. A 2009 *Fortune* magazine survey reports that the top 500 multinational companies alone generated almost $25 trillion in sales in 2008. The United States led all countries, with 140 companies on the list (down from 153 the previous year); Japan ranked second (68 companies), and Germany third (38) (*Fortune* 2009). See Table 1.1 for ranking of the top 25 global firms.

In addition to these large corporations, thousands of smaller firms are engaging in international marketing. In the United States, smaller firms account for an amazing 97 percent of the companies involved in direct merchandise exporting. Indeed, smaller firms are grabbing an ever-growing share of U.S. exports. American businesses without international subsidiaries accounted for 46 percent of sales abroad in 2005—up from 38 percent in 1999, according to the Commerce Department (Schlisserman 2007). Smaller firms thus represent the largest pool for potential growth in export sales. Microbreweries provide an excellent example. With production normally limited to fewer than 15,000 barrels a year, microbreweries would seem more local than global players. But the microbrewery industry is going through a transition in which exports make sense. With more than 33 regional specialty breweries and

424 microbreweries in the United States, the field has become too competitive. As a result, several of the most successful "craft" brewers are among a growing number of smaller U.S. companies looking to foreign markets to expand sales. Brewers have had the greatest successes in Sweden, Italy, and, to a lesser extent, Great Britain.

Corporations look abroad for the very same reasons they seek to expand their markets at home. Where economies of scale are feasible, a large market is essential. However, if a single market is not large enough to absorb the entire output, a firm may look to other markets. If production equipment is not fully utilized in meeting the demands of one market, additional markets may be tapped. Seasonal fluctuations in demand in a particular market may also be evened out by sales in another. During economic downturns in one market, corporations may turn to new markets to absorb excess output.

**TABLE 1.1:** World's 25 Largest Corporations, 2009 (in U.S. million $)

| RANK | COMPANY | COUNTRY | REVENUES |
|------|---------|---------|----------|
| 1. | Royal Dutch Shell | Netherlands | 458,361.0 |
| 2. | Exxon Mobil | U.S. | 442,851.0 |
| 3. | Wal-Mart Stores | U.S. | 405,607.0 |
| 4. | BP (British Petroleum) | Britain | 376,053.0 |
| 5. | Chevron | U.S. | 263,159.0 |
| 6. | Total | France | 234,674.1 |
| 7. | Conocophillips | U.S. | 230,764.0 |
| 8. | ING Group | Netherlands | 226,577.0 |
| 9. | Sinopec | China | 207,814.5 |
| 10. | Toyota Motor | Japan | 204,352.3 |
| 11. | Japan Post Holdings | Japan | 198,699.8 |
| 12. | General Electric | U.S. | 183,207.0 |
| 13. | China National Petroleum | China | 181,122.6 |
| 14. | Volkswagen | Germany | 166,579.1 |
| 15. | State Grid | China | 164,135.9 |
| 16. | Dexia Group | Belgium | 161,268.8 |
| 17. | ENI | Italy | 159,348.5 |
| 18. | General Motors | U.S. | 148,979.0 |
| 19. | Ford Motor | U.S. | 146,277.0 |
| 20. | Allianz | Germany | 142,394.6 |
| 21. | HSBC Holdings | Britain | 142,049.0 |
| 22. | Gazprom | Russia | 141,454.7 |
| 23. | Credit Daimler | Germany | 140,327.9 |
| 24. | BNP Paribas | France | 136,096.4 |
| 25. | Carrefour | France | 129,133.9 |

*Source: Fortune* (2009), F1–F8.

Firms may also find that a product's life cycle can be extended if the product is introduced in different markets—products already considered obsolete by one group may well be sold successfully to another. In addition to the reasons noted, significant changes in the United States and around the globe have helped fuel this phenomenal growth in international business.

## SATURATED DOMESTIC MARKETS

As many markets reach saturation, firms look to foreign countries for new customers. Take the case of Starbucks. Starbucks began with 17 coffee shops in Seattle just two decades ago. Starbucks currently has over 11,500 stores in the United States alone. In Manhattan's 24 square miles, Starbucks has 124 cafes, which translates into 1 for every 12,000 New Yorkers. In coffee-crazed Seattle, there is a Starbucks outlet for every 9,400 people, and the company considers that the upper limit of coffee-shop saturation. Indeed, the crowding of so many stores so close together has become a national joke, eliciting quips such as the headline in *The Onion*, a satirical publication: "A New Starbucks Opens in Restroom of Existing Starbucks" (Holmes 2002, 101). The company had been blessed with extraordinary growth in both store traffic and same-store sales until quite recently, when this trend reversed itself. While the reversal may be attributable to the U.S. economic slowdown, some investors fear that weak growth figures could indicate saturation in the U.S. market. Indeed, Starbucks closed 600 under-performing locations in 2006—apparently an admission that cannibalization seems to be a major problem, To keep up the growth, Starbucks realized it had no choice but to export its concept aggressively. In 1999, Starbucks had just 281 stores abroad. Today it has about 5,000 outlets in more than 40 countries—and it is still in the early stages of a plan of globalization. Starbucks expects to eventually increase the number of its stores worldwide to 40,000. Canada and the United Kingdom are currently Starbucks's strongest markets abroad (some 69 percent of foreign revenues). However, India, Russia, and China represent key areas of focused future expansion.

## HIGHER PROFIT MARGINS IN FOREIGN MARKETS

For the typical Fortune 500 company today, domestic revenues account for just 62.5 percent of total sales—a figure that is bound to shrink even further as globalization continues to advance. For an ever-growing number of firms, foreign revenues as a percentage of total revenues are well over 50 percent. Consider McDonald's, which gets almost two-thirds of its revenue from overseas. For the quarter that ended September 30, 2007, it reported that sales at restaurants open at least 13 months grew 5.1 percent in the United States, 6.5 percent in Europe, and 11.4 percent in Asia/Pacific, the Middle East, and Africa (Pender 2007). General Motors Chairman Rick Wagoner estimates that foreign markets will soon account for 75 percent of the auto maker's global sales, a testament to the booming growth in Asia, Russia, and far-Eastern Europe, as well as the fierce competition and market share erosion in the developed markets of the United States and Western Europe (Howes 2008). Examples of other firms that derive more than half of their revenues from abroad include: Hewlett-Packard (65 percent), Exxon Mobil (69 percent), Coca-Cola (72 percent), and Intel (79 percent). This trend toward higher profit margins in foreign markets is clearly not limited to U.S. firms. Nokia sells over 97 percent of its products outside the home market, and Toyota sells more vehicles in the United States than it does in Japan. Analysts figure that almost two-thirds of the company's operating profits come from the United States.

## INCREASED FOREIGN COMPETITION IN DOMESTIC MARKETS

Over the past decades, foreign products have played an increasingly significant role in the United States. Classic examples include the phonograph, color television, video- and audiotape recorders, telephone, and integrated circuit. Although all were invented in the United States, domestic producers accounted for only a small percentage of the U.S. market for most of these products—and an even smaller share of the world market. For example, in 1970, U.S. producers' share of the domestic market for color televisions stood at nearly 90 percent. By 1990 it had dropped to little more than 10 percent. The decline in sales of United States-produced stereo components was even more serious—from 90 percent of domestic sales to little more than 1 percent during the same time span. Brand names such as Sony and Panasonic became household words for most American consumers.

Foreign companies continue to play a prominent part in the daily lives of Americans today, and domestic firms face competition in nearly every sector. While McDonald's, Burger King, KFC, and Subway dominate the fast food scene, they face competition from every corner of the globe. Pollo Campero reigns from Guatemala. The chain has 52 U.S. locations to date, but has plans for 200 by 2014. It offers chicken so good KFC couldn't beat it in Central America. Jollibee, from the Philippines, started out in California in 1998 and in 2009 added locations in New York and Las Vegas. The fast food restaurant serves everything from burgers with pineapple to spaghetti. Nando's, a South African firm, serves up Afro-Portuguese chicken with a spicy "peri-peri" sauce. Nando's has two locations in Washington, D.C. And British import Wagamama offers diners cheap ramen at three locations in Boston, with more coming to D.C. by 2010 (Demos 2009). When a U.S. consumer buys new tires, shops for the latest best-seller, or purchases a jar of mayonnaise, chances are increasingly good that the supplier will be a local subsidiary of a company based in Japan, Europe, or elsewhere outside the United States. For example, both Firestone Rubber and CBS Records were acquired by Japanese firms, and Macmillan Publishing and Pillsbury are owned by British firms (Shaughnessy and Lindquist 1993). Switzerland's Nestlé and the Anglo-Dutch giant Unilever moved into the U.S. market to grow their businesses. Unilever set the pace, paying $20.3 billion for Bestfoods, whose brands include Hellmann's Mayonnaise and Skippy Peanut Butter, as well as acquiring Slim-Fast, a diet-supplement firm, and Ben & Jerry's Ice Cream. Meanwhile, Nestlé acquired pet food manufacturer Ralston Purina, best known for its Purina Dog Chow brand. It was a logical move, as the pet food market is growing faster than Nestlé's traditional, matured businesses—particularly in the United States, where animal owners are buying higher margin products that promise both dietary and health benefits for their pets (Bernard 2001). This "selling of America" has caused a good deal of concern among the business community as well as the general public. The United Kingdom is the biggest investor in the United States by far, followed by Japan, Germany, and Canada. Increased foreign competition on domestic soil is not unique to the United States, but rather is occurring both in developed countries and in emerging economies. Regarding developed markets, the United States remains the largest recipient of FDI, followed by the United Kingdom, France, Canada, and Germany.

Worldwide, foreign direct investment (FDI) fell in 2008 to an estimated $1.4 trillion, down from an all-time high of $1.8 trillion in 2007. This was due largely to the economic and financial crisis that dampened investors' appetites to pour money abroad, including into the United States. Developed economies so far have been the hardest hit, as FDI was cut by an estimated one-third in 2008. Direct foreign investment flow to the United States slowed by just over 5 percent to $220 billion, while Japan captured 23 percent less FDI ($17.4 billion). FDI in Britain slumped from $224 billion in 2007 to an estimated $109.4 billion in 2008. Eastern and Central European economies suffered mixed fortunes with a slip in FDI for Poland and Hungary, but growth for the Czech Republic, Romania, and Russia. Developing countries managed to hold on to some growth in inward direct investment in 2008. China (up 10 percent, $82 billion) and India (up 60 percent, $36.7 billion) attracted more FDI in 2008. But Indonesia (minus 21 percent, $5.5 billion) Singapore (minus 57 percent, $10.3 billion), and Thailand (minus 4 percent, $9.2 billion) were the exceptions in Asia with declines. The United Nations Conference on Development (UNCTAD) suggested that poorer countries had been sheltered so far from the worst impact of the economic crisis and warned that they could suffer from an overall decline in foreign investment in the coming year (Agence France-Presse 2009). Overall, the trend continued in 2009, with FDI slipping to a little more than $1 trillion, as leading companies continued to cut costs and investments due to the poor economic outlook. Fortunately, the United Nations Conference on Trade and Development sees a moderate recovery by the end of 2010 and expects the economy to gain momentum in 2011 (Schlein 2010).

## THE TRADE DEFICIT

Exports are considered a central contributor to economic growth and well-being for a country. In 2008, U.S. exports increased 12 percent to $1.84 trillion. However, imports climbed 7.4 percent to $2.52 trillion. The trade deficit is the shortfall between what a country sells abroad and what it imports. In 2006, the U.S. trade deficit was a whopping $765 billion and was referred to as the "Grand Canyon" of trade deficits. In 2007, for the first time since 2001, it dropped to $708.5 billion. It further decreased in 2008, to $677.1 billion. The long-term trends that pushed the trade deficit to record highs in the first place still persist, and much of the improvement in recent quarters reflects slower import growth and the fact of a weakening economy (Weller and Wheeler 2008). Indeed, in 2009, the U.S. trade deficit shrank to just $390.1 billion. But the net improvement came entirely on the import side, as America's purchases of foreign goods and services shrank by more than 23 percent. Exports shrank, too—by just 15 percent. But because their fall-off was smaller, the deficit narrowed (Tonelson 2010). Amadeo (2010) provides an excellent analogy: "an on-going deficit is detrimental to the nation's economy over the long term because it is financed with debt. In other words, the United States can buy more than it makes because the countries that it buys from are lending it the money. It is like a party where you've run out of money, but the pizza place is willing to keep sending you pizzas and put it on your tab. Of course, this can only go on as long as there are no other customers for the pizza and the pizza place can afford to loan you the money. One day the lending countries may decide to ask the United States to repay the debt. On that day, the party is over." Table 1.2 presents U.S. trade with selected countries. Note that the United States exports much to its neighbors to the north and south.

## THE EMERGENCE OF NEW MARKETS

### European Union

The emergence of new markets has stimulated interest in international business. On December 31, 1992, many physical, fiscal, and technical barriers to trade among the 12-nation European Union (EU) began to disappear, giving birth to something akin to the United States of Europe. The original "European 12" (Belgium, Denmark, France, Germany, Greece, Ireland, Italy, Luxembourg, the Netherlands, Portugal, Spain, and the United Kingdom) were joined by Sweden, Finland, and Austria in 1999, bringing the total population to 375 million with an average per capita gross domestic product of $23,500. And in 2004, 10 additional countries joined the union, making a new "Mega-Europe" of 25 states and more than 450 million consumers. The newcomers were Poland, Hungary, the Czech Republic, Slovakia, Slovenia, Lithuania, Latvia, Estonia, Cyprus, and Malta. Most recently, in 2007, Bulgaria and Romania also joined the EU. In terms of GDP growth forecasts and average per capita income among the majority of member states, mega-Europe's economy is on a par with that of the United States. Many companies have already approached Europe as a single market—rather than as a group of distinct countries—by realigning their product lines and developing strategies that can be employed throughout the EU. For example, Nike, which has been marketing its "Just do it" slogan since 1988, is trying out a new softer catchphrase on young European women: "Here I am." Crafted by the Amsterdam office of the independent Wieden + Kennedy agency, the pan-European campaign includes five short animated web films about the life stories of five top European female athletes. One shows tennis player Maria Sharapova's rise from a childhood in Siberia to the number-one-ranked player in the world. The spots highlight the criticism and negativity that Maria had to overcome. "You're just another pretty face," critics in the spot say. "You won't be agile enough. You won't stay on top for long." At the end, the animated Sharapova morphs into the real Sharapova, who forms the "I" in "Here I am." The aim of the campaign is to deliver the message that there is more to sports than getting fit or competing. It's about building self-esteem. The idea for the slogan came out of research commissioned by Nike that found that university-aged women in Europe aren't as competitive about sports as men. "To appeal to them, agency copywriters decided they needed a different slogan from the 'Just do it' message," noted Mark Bernath, creative director for Nike at Wieden + Kennedy. "Here I am" promoted the personal benefit of exercise without being aggressive, he said (Patrick 2008). Nike executives liked the slogan because they thought it would be understood in English across Europe. Underscoring how marketers can use the Internet, particularly with younger consumers, Nike also paid for the spots to appear on Facebook, Bebo, and other social-networking sites popular with young women. In addition, Nike booked time for the ads on video screens in gyms and university student unions across Europe, including the U.K., France, Italy, Germany, and Russia. The campaign also

**TABLE 1.2:** U.S. Trade with Selected Countries 2009 (in U.S. million $)

| RANK | COUNTRY | TOTAL TRADE WITH U.S. | EXPORTS | IMPORTS |
|------|---------|----------------------|---------|---------|
| 1. | Canada | 429.6 | 204.7 | 224.9 |
| 2. | China | 366.0 | 69.6 | 296.4 |
| 3. | Mexico | 305.5 | 129.0 | 176.5 |
| 4. | Japan | 147.1 | 51.2 | 95.9 |
| 5. | Germany | 114.6 | 43.3 | 71.3 |
| 6. | United Kingdom | 93.2 | 45.7 | 47.5 |
| 7. | South Korea | 67.9 | 28.6 | 39.2 |
| 8. | France | 60.0 | 26.5 | 34.0 |
| 9. | Netherlands | 48.4 | 32.3 | 16.1 |
| 10. | Taiwan | 46.8 | 8.4 | 28.4 |

*Source:* U.S. Bureau of the Census (2010).

**Figure 1.1:** Ad from Nike's "Here I Am" campaign.

included traditional television and print ads, on-line banners, and even a collection of athlete stories on the Nikewoman.com Web site (see Figure 1.1), as well as a gallery-worthy coffee table book featuring 22 young international female athletes.

## Commonwealth of Independent States

With the failed coup of August 1991, the subsequent resignation of President Mikhail Gorbachev, and the relegation of the former Soviet Union to official oblivion, trade and investment opportunities in the newly formed Commonwealth of Independent States (CIS) increased dramatically. Corporations around the globe eyed the CIS, with its population of over 275 million, as the next marketing frontier. The CIS was officially formed in December 1991 by Belarus, Russia, and Ukraine, when the leaders of the three countries signed a Creation Agreement on the dissolution of the Soviet Union and the creation of the CIS as a successor entity to the USSR. On 21 December 1991, eight additional former Soviet Republics (Armenia, Azerbaijan, Kazakhstan, the Kyrgyz Republic, Moldova, Tajikistan, Turkmenistan, and Uzbekistan) joined the CIS. Georgia joined two years later, bringing the total number of participating countries to 12. The three Baltic states—Estonia, Latvia, and Lithuania—decided not to join, preferring to pursue membership in the European Union. The Creation Agreement remained the primary constituent document of the CIS until January 1993, when the CIS Charter was adopted. This charter formalized the concept of membership in that it defined a member country as one that ratifies the CIS Charter. It is of interest to note that Turkmenistan has not ratified the charter and changed its standing to associate member in 2005, and Ukraine, one of the three founding countries,

**TABLE 1.3:** Demographic Profile of the Commonwealth of Independent States, 2008

| REPUBLIC | POPULATION | GDP 2007 | % GROWTH OVER 2006 | PER CAPITA |
|---|---|---|---|---|
| Armenia | 3,002,271 | 9,177,274,353 | 43.69 | 3,057 |
| Azerbaijan | 8,467,171 | 31,248,521,184 | 48.93 | 3,691 |
| Belarus | 9,688,796 | 44,773,406,221 | 21.13 | 4,621 |
| Georgia | 4,395,420 | 10,175,826,838 | 31.38 | 2,315 |
| Kazakhstan | 15,421,864 | 104,143,432,632 | 28.57 | 6,753 |
| Kyrgyz Republic | 5,316,544 | 3,745,000,489 | 32.14 | 704 |
| Moldova | 3,793,603 | 4,394,888,125 | 28.95 | 1,158 |
| Russia | 142,498,534 | 1,289,582,151,445 | 30.93 | 9,050 |
| Tajikistan | 6,735,996 | 3,737,572,699 | 32.06 | 555 |
| Turkmenistan | 4,965,275 | 7,253,230,940 | 11.38 | 1,461 |
| Ukraine | 46,205,379 | 141,177,227,723 | 31.02 | 3,055 |
| Uzbekistan | 27,372,256 | 19,274,619,012 | 12.87 | 704 |

*Source:* http://unstats.un.org/unsd/snaama/selectionbasicFast.asp.

has never ratified the CIS Charter and is thus not legally a member. Further, following the South Ossetian war in 2008, Georgia's President Saakashvili announced that his country would leave the CIS, and the Georgian Parliament voted unanimously to withdraw from the regional organization. Georgia's withdrawal became effective on 17 August 2009. The population of the CIS is a heterogeneous one, and while the official language is Russian, there are more than 200 languages and dialects (at least 18 with more than 1 million speakers). Table 1.3 presents basic demographic information for the CIS. Note that Russia, with its 142 million consumers, is by far the largest of the republics, and also boasts the wealthiest consumers in terms of per capita income.

The Commonwealth's economy has experienced somewhat of a roller coaster ride over the past two decades. Immediately after the fall of the "Iron Curtain," a multitude of Western companies moved into this newly formed marketplace. For instance, Procter & Gamble signed a joint venture agreement in August 1991 with Leningrad State University to begin marketing and distributing consumer products such as Wash & Go shampoo (the European name for Pert Plus) throughout Ukraine and Baltics. Philip Morris signed agreements with the Russian republic to supply more than 20 billion cigarettes—the largest order in the company's history, but still only 5 percent of the market for cigarettes in the CIS. And, in late 1991, Visa became the first credit card available to the general public in the CIS. However, by late 1998, an overriding feeling of uncertainty replaced the rosy glow of optimism regarding marketing opportunities in the Commonwealth. Political and economic chaos in the region brought many marketing activities to a slowdown, if not an actual halt. Ruble values plummeted, inflation jumped, per capita income dropped, and the gap in income levels between the rich and poor increased. To make matters worse, crime and corruption flourished. According to a survey for the American Chamber of Commerce, nine out of ten companies significantly reduced their advertising budgets at the time. Nearly all shifted their emphasis to less expensive product lines to compete with domestic goods, and a few companies even suspended sales of products. For example, General Motors suspended sales of its Chevy Blazer, despite having just kicked off a new ad campaign for the vehicle. Fortunately the Commonwealth's economy rebounded by the turn of the century. For example, Russia's GDP between 1997 and 2000 reportedly rose almost 38 percent to $623.1 billion. The U.S. Department of Commerce reported that the GDP for the United States, by comparison, was nearly $10 trillion in 2000, up about 20 percent from its level in 1997. Inflation in Russia also dropped, from 36.5 percent in 1999 to 20 percent in 2000, and down to about 14 percent in 2001 (Bertagnoli 2001, 1). Russia's middle class grew to somewhere between 12 to 30 million people, or about 8 to 20 percent of that country's population. The list of Western companies that had made investments in Russia was a veritable Who's Who of multinational businesses. Ikea, the Swedish furniture manufacturer, had a vision of placing the firm's simple shelves, kitchens, bathrooms, and bedrooms in millions of Russian apartments that had not been remodelled since Soviet days. On the day that Ikea opened its first store in Moscow in 2000, the wait to get in was an hour. Highway traffic backed up for miles, and more than 40,000 customers crammed into the store and picked the shelves clean. Based on this phenomenal success, Ikea opened a second store in Moscow and, at the close of 2002, unveiled a "megamall" with two kilometers of shop fronts and 150,000 square meters of retail and restaurant space. The center is expected to attract between 25 to 40 million customers per year. The mall was built around a 31,000-square-meter Ikea store and a 24,000-square-meter hypermarket run by the French retailing group Auchan. The hypermarket sells over 40,000 items and requires more than 100 truck deliveries a day to keep its shelves stocked. A further 250 shops include international brand names such as Tommy Hilfiger, Reebok, Wolford, and Levi's, together with restaurants, a skating rink, and Russia's biggest multiplex cinema (FT.com 2002). Given the success of Ikea, and in particular Auchan, French rivals Carrefour and Casino, as well as the U.S. giant Wal-Mart, are also studying the market. Russia ended 2008 with GDP growth of 6 percent, following 10 straight years of growth averaging 7 percent annually since the financial crisis of 1998. During the past decade, poverty and unemployment declined steadily, and the middle class continued to expand. However, these "positive trends began to reverse yet again in the second half of 2008. Investor concerns over the Russia-Georgia conflict, corporate governance issues, and the global credit crunch in September of that year caused the Russian stock market to fall by roughly 70 percent. The economy took a further nosedive after the price of oil, its key export, collapsed, and investors pulled billions of dollars out of the country. The end result was growing unemployment, wage arrears, and a severe drop in production" (U.S. Central Intelligence Agency 2010). Officials had forecast earlier that Russia's GDP would decline by only 2.2 percent in 2009, but analysts expect an even sharper fall in GDP. Current estimates are that the economy contracted 7.9 percent in 2009 (Reuters.com 2009). What continues to make this an attractive market is that while the Russian population's propensity to consume is comparable to that of Western countries, the critical difference is that consumer needs are far from being satisfied. Indeed, Russian Prime Minister Viktor Zubkov expressed concern over rising imports of consumer goods, which have soared nearly 500 percent since 2000. Zubkov notes that imported products account for about 49 percent of consumer goods sold in Russia (Guerrero 2008).

## China

As recently as 1977, the total volume of two-way trade between the People's Republic of China and the United States was under $400 million. Less than two years later, China began to experiment with open markets and continued to liberalize trade laws. In 1979 Coca-Cola became the first American product available in China when the company was awarded the sole privilege of selling soft drinks to the Chinese market. That same year, for the first time, Chinese authorities permitted domestic product advertising in newspapers. By 1988 two-way trade between the United States and China had jumped to almost $17 billion. Despite the events in Tiananmen Square in June 1989, U.S. businesses continued to knock on China's door. In 1992, in a joint venture with a Chinese state-owned company, McDonald's opened a restaurant in Beijing, with 700 seats and 29 cash registers—the biggest McDonald's in the world, slightly bigger than the one that opened in Moscow in early 1990. At the close of the first day of business, the restaurant had registered 13,214 transactions—representing approximately 40,000 customers—setting a one-day sales record for any McDonald's in the world.

With over 1.3 billion consumers, China is the world's largest single-country market. More than 22 million new consumers are added each year. With 273 of its cities home to more than 1 million inhabitants (compared with fewer than 10 in the United States), China is more like dozen of countries sprawled across five time zones and 22 provinces. It is a land of youth—almost 50 percent of the population is under age 24. The average family size ranges from 3.7 individuals in the Beijing municipality to 5.2 in the Yunnan and Qinghai provinces. In just the past two years, the average gross domestic product per capita has passed $2,000 and is now close to $2,500. That average lumps together 250 million affluent and "rising affluent" urban residents with another 500 to 600 million people living in rural areas (and whose income may or may not exceed a dollar a day). Another several hundred million more Chinese are somewhere in between. That core of 250 million Chinese consumers—especially in coastal cities—actually earns closer to $10,000 a year on average. Given their modest living expenses, they are left with considerable disposable income that they are eager to spend. Though China has one of the higher personal savings rates in the world (over 40 percent), this does not so much reflect a wariness to spend as much as the absence of things to buy. That is now changing. According to a McKinsey survey, the Chinese love to shop and spend 9.8 hours per week doing so. In contrast, the average American shops just 3.6 hours per week. Forty-one percent of Chinese said that shopping was their preferred leisure activity (Karabell 2008). Such statistics have foreign companies climbing over one another to get a piece of the market. Indeed, many perceive China as the new gold rush. For example, Yum! Brands, owner of Kentucky Fried Chicken and Pizza Hut, has expanded aggressively in China. "We are extremely bullish on China," chief executive Dave Novak told analysts. "It's an absolute gold mine for us" (Gu 2003). In the United States and Germany, the company is barely growing and has anemic margins. In contrast, KFC in China is hugely popular and growing more than 25 percent a year. It now has more than 2,000 outlets that constitute a fraction of KFC's global presence, but account for a staggering 20 percent of the company's total profits (Karabell 2008).

But China's potential is not limited to chicken wings and pizza. Zheng Xinli, vice minister of the Communist Party's central policy research office, estimated that 55 percent of China's population will be middle class by 2020, with 78 percent of city dwellers and 30 percent of those in rural areas reaching that status. ("Middle class" is currently defined as having an annual household income of between $8,700 and $29,215.) In 2008 prices, the annual disposable income per household will be $14,900 in 2020 (ZenithOptimedia 2001). China is already the world's largest mobile phone market, signing up about 4 million wireless users every month—or about the population of Kentucky—to its 200 million cell-phone user base. Mobile handsets maker Motorola Inc. now sells 13 percent of its products in China. China recently displaced Japan to become the No. 2 market for computers and Internet use, helping computer manufacturers, as well as chip makers. It is also an important market for cars, beer, cigarettes, and even luxury goods. Despite the weak economy, sales of luxury goods in China grew 12 percent in 2009—to $9.6 billion. China is now the second-biggest consumer of luxury goods behind only the United States (Japan ranks third) and accounts for an amazing 27.5 percent of the global market. In the next five years, China's luxury spending is expected to increase to $14.6 billion, making it the No. 1 luxury market globally (Madden 2010). Coach is among the luxury brands trying to carve out growth in Asia to make up for lagging U.S. sales. Coach has opened dozens of new stores in China, Hong Kong, and Macau, invested in advertising, and even created product lines specifically for the Chinese market, such as a special handbag to celebrate *Elle* magazine's 20th anniversary in that country. For an increasing number of firms, China is their best-performing market and top cash generator.

China's economic policies over the past few years have borne remarkable fruit. In 2001, China gained admission to the World Trade Organization (WTO). China has long held "most favored nation" trading status with the United States, which grants it the same tariff rates that many other foreign countries receive. China's admission to the WTO will now force places like the European Union, Mexico, and Taiwan to lower trade barriers against a host of Chinese products. At a time when growth stalled in most other parts of the world, China's growth rates for 2003–2005 were recorded at around 10 percent per year in real terms, and despite efforts to cool the overheating economy, the officially recorded GDP growth rate was 11.4 percent in 2007 (Zhiming 2008). In 2008, the global economic crisis began to reduce China's growth rate somewhat, and it is expected to have slowed to 8.7 percent in 2009. Economists predict that sometime in the next 10 to 15 years China may well surpass the economic might of Europe. China's advantages are numerous. Its wage rates are one-third of Mexico's and Hungary's, and 5 percent of those in the United States or Japan. China's investments in education and training have attracted research facilities from companies such as IBM, Motorola, and Microsoft. The critical mass of factories, subcontractors, and specialized vendors has created a manufacturing environment in which few can complete. But China is not simply an export platform. Its large and ever-expanding domestic market is another attraction. Mushrooming investment reflects the obsession of many global CEOs to lower production costs by outsourcing whatever they can to large-scale specialists. Indeed, estimates suggest that 50 percent of all manufacturing could be outsourced to China by 2010 (Garten 2002). Today China mainly manufactures goods that are labor-intensive. It makes 60 percent of the world's bicycles, including 85 percent of those sold in the United States, and is also dominant in the production of shoes, toys, clothing, and furniture. It is only a matter of time before China is also a big factor in capital-intensive industries, such as high tech. High tech manufacturing will have become centered in Asia and China by the 2006–2010 period (Bauder 2003). The dark cloud on the horizon is that the world economy may be growing increasingly reliant on these factories.

## WORLD TRADE

World economic growth, as measured by total production, or gross domestic product (GDP), has slowed significantly over the past few years. World trade growth slid from 3.5 percent in 2007 to 1.7 percent in 2008. Growth in 2008 was the slowest since 2001 and well below the 10-year average rate of 2.9 percent. The financial market turbulence has considerably reduced economic growth projections for the major developed markets. Developed economies managed a meager 0.8 percent growth in 2008, compared with 2.5 percent in 2007 and an average rate of 2.2 percent between 2000 and 2008. In contrast, developing economies expanded their output in 2008 by 5.6 percent, down from 7.5 percent in 2007—but still equal to their average rate for the 2000–2008 period (World Trade Report 2009). The rate of future growth will largely depend on how soon developed countries can shake off the financial turmoil currently dogging the markets.

The United States was once considered the "hub" of world trade. While it remains a major player, U.S. participation in world trade, measured as a portion of world market share, has declined drastically. Whereas in 1950 the United States accounted for nearly 25 percent of the world trade flow, its current share is less than 10 percent. It is not that U.S. exports have actually dropped during this period; rather, these figures reflect the entrance of other trading partners into the picture. *Fortune's* 2009 list of the Global 500 shows the fewest U.S. businesses since *Fortune* began keeping its Global 500 count in 1995, confirming the rising prominence of the emerging markets. Less than 10 years ago Russia, India, and Mexico posted only one company on the Global 500. The 2009 list includes eight from Russia, seven from India, and four from Mexico. But China appears to be stealing the show. Joining petrochemical giant Sinopec—China's highest-ranking company at No. 9—are nine new arrivals, and the rest are climbing the ranks. With an unprecedented total of 37 companies on the list (up from 29 the previous year), China has more companies than Italy, Spain, and Australia combined. "In terms of size, speed, and directional flow, the transfer of global wealth and economic power now underway—roughly from West to East—is without precedent in modern history." Who says so? The U.S. Government. In a report called Global Trends 2025, the National Intelligence Council, a federal agency that does strategic analysis for the intelligence community, says, "If current trends persist, by 2025 China will have the world's second largest economy" (Gunther 2009). American corporations have slowly come to realize

**TABLE 1.4:** Global Advertising Spending in Measured Media

|  | 2008 | 2009 (F) | 2010 (F) |
|---|---|---|---|
| North America | | | |
| Yoy% | 169,007 (-1.0) | 155,797 (-7.8) | 149,640 (-4.0) |
| Latin America | | | |
| Yoy% | 22,712 (10.6) | 24,307 (7.0) | 26,860 (10.5) |
| Western Europe | | | |
| Yoy% | 122,121 (-1.7) | 106,520 (-12.8) | 104,848 (-1.6) |
| Emerging Europe | | | |
| Yoy % | 21,220 (12.5) | 17,364 (-18.2) | 18,455 (6.3) |
| Asia Pacific (ALL) | | | |
| Yoy% | 127,329 (5.8) | 126,818 (-0.4) | 133,583 (5.3) |
| North Asia | | | |
| Yoy% | 47,740 (18.1) | 50,202 (5.2) | 55,388 (10.3) |
| ASEAN | | | |
| Yoy% | 9,845 (10.2) | 10,480 (6.5) | 11,694 (11.6) |
| Middle East & Africa | | | |
| Yoy% | 13,780 (20.9) | 13,802 (0.2) | 14,744 (7.0) |
| WORLD | | | |
| Yoy% | 476,169 (1.8) | 444,609 (-6.6) | 448,159 (0.8) |

*Source:* American Association of Advertising Agencies Press Release (2009).

**TABLE 1.5:** Total Advertising Expenditures by Country (in U.S. million $)

| 2007 RANK | EXPENDITURE | 2010 RANK | EXPENDITURE |
|---|---|---|---|
| 1. U.S. | 179,251 | 1. U.S. | 194,063 |
| 2. Japan | 41,528 | 2. Japan | 43,875 |
| 3. U.K. | 23,320 | 3. U.K. | 27,861 |
| 4. Germany. | 21,676 | 4. China | 24,266 |
| 5. China | 15,023 | 5. Germany | 22,678 |
| 6. France | 12,881 | 6. Russia | 17,205 |
| 7. Italy | 11,227 | 7. Brazil | 14,223 |
| 8. Spain | 9,847 | 8. France | 13,486 |
| 9. Brazil | 9,703 | 9. Italy | 12,319 |
| 10. South Korea | 9,701 | 10. South Korea | 11,796 |

*Source:* ZenithOptimedia (2008).

that the United States is no longer an isolated, self-sufficient national economy but rather just another player in the global marketplace.

## GROWTH IN ADVERTISING EXPENDITURES WORLDWIDE

Patterns in the growth of international advertising mirror those of international business. At the end of World War II, the bulk of advertising activity was domestic, and 75 percent of recorded advertising expenditures worldwide were concentrated in the United States. Since then, the growth in advertising expenditure worldwide has been phenomenal. In 1950, estimated advertising expenditure totaled $7.4 billion worldwide, including $5.7 billion in the United States alone. By the late 1970s the advertising expenditure had swelled to nearly $72 billion worldwide, including $38 billion in the United States. Table 1.4 presents global ad spending for the period 2008–2010. Global figures in 2008 were $476 billion, according to the latest 70-country forecast by GroupM. GroupM's forecast for North America was rather gloomy for 2009, with a predicted fall of almost 8 percent in ad spending, and a mild recovery expected in 2010. Global ad spending in 2010 is expected to fall just 0.8 percent to $448 million. The so-called BRIC nations (Brazil, Russia, India, and China) are expected to lead the recovery, while ad spending in the United States and G7 nations (Canada, France, Germany, Italy, Japan, the United Kingdom, and the United States) will probably lag behind, according to the report, which is part of GroupM's media and marketing forecasting series drawn from data supplied by parent company WPP's worldwide resources in advertising, public relations, market research, and specialist communications. It appears that the global prospects for a limited ad recovery in 2010 are improving (American Association of Advertising Agencies Press Release 2009).

The role of advertising varies significantly from country to country, as the figures in Table 1.5 suggest. Table 1.5 lists countries with over $1 billion in advertising expenditures in 2007 and also provides projections for 2010. Countries spending the most on advertising are primarily the rich industrialized nations, such as the United States, which spent more on advertising than the next nine countries

**TABLE 1.6:** Top 25 Global Marketers by Measured Media, 2008 (in U.S. million $; Measured Worldwide

| RANK | MARKETER | HEADQUARTERS | 2008 AD SPENDING | % CHANGE FROM 2007 |
|------|----------|--------------|------------------|--------------------|
| 1. | Procter & Gamble | Cincinnati | 9.731 | 0.0 |
| 2. | Unilever | London/Rotterdam | 5,715 | 1.8 |
| 3. | L'Oréal | Clichy, France | 4,040 | 10.0 |
| 4. | General Motors Corp. | Detroit | 3,674 | 5.4 |
| 5. | Toyota Motor Corp. | Toyota City, Japan | 3,203 | -3.2 |
| 6. | Coca-Cola Co. | Atlanta | 2,673 | 13.5 |
| 7. | Johnson & Johnson | New Brunswick, NJ | 2,601 | 4.5 |
| 8. | Ford Motor Co. | Dearborn, Michigan | 2,448 | -14.0 |
| 9. | Reckitt Benckiser | Slough, Berkshire, U.K. | 2,369 | 13.0 |
| 10. | Nestlé | Vevey, Switzerland | 2,314 | 1.0 |
| 11. | Volkswagen | Wolfsburg, Germany | 2,309 | 15.4 |
| 12. | Honda Motor Co. | Tokyo | 2,220 | 4.6 |
| 13. | Mars Inc. | McLean, VA | 1,998 | 5.0 |
| 14. | McDonald's Corp. | Oak Brook, IL | 1,968 | 6.9 |
| 15. | Sony Corp. | Tokyo | 1,851 | -3.3 |
| 16. | GlaxoSmithKline | Brentford, Middlesex, U.K. | 1,831 | -3.2 |
| 17. | Deutsche Telecom | Bonn, Germany | 1,812 | 7.7 |
| 18. | Kraft Foods | Northfield, IL | 1,792 | -2.7 |
| 19. | Nissan Motor Co. | Tokyo | 1,716 | -9.7 |
| 20. | Walt Disney Co. | Burbank, CA | 1,586 | -2.0 |

*Source: Advertising Age (2009).*

combined. The United States has traditionally been the world leader in total advertising expenditures, contributing 50 percent or more of the total figure year after year.

For the most part, the developing countries tend to be light advertisers. However, economic development is not the sole predictor of advertising expenditure. Some relatively rich countries, such as Canada or Austria, are not even on this list, while countries such as South Korea are. This suggests that other variables, such as culture, must be considered in attempting to understand the role of advertising in a particular country. Nor do the figures in the table reflect the relative costs of media time/space in each of the countries. It should be noted that media costs in many developing countries tend to be rather low, and this factor should be taken into consideration when making comparisons. It is of interest to note that for 2010, China moves up in the rankings, from fifth place to fourth, while Russia, previously not on the list, ranks sixth.

The leading 20 advertisers, based on total worldwide media spending, are listed in Table 1.6. Procter & Gamble Co. heads the list with worldwide media spending at $9.73 billion, followed by Unilever and L'Oréal. *Advertising Age* ranks marketers by total worldwide media spending in more than 90 countries, from Algeria to Zambia. A company must advertise on at least three continents to qualify as "global" regardless of its headquarters. Overall, the top 100 spent $117.9 billion in 2008—with 62 percent of their measured media budgets spent outside the United States. Eleven of the 44 U.S.-based companies among the Global 100 rely so heavily on international sales that they do more than half their ad spending abroad. For example, Procter & Gamble, the world's largest advertiser since overtaking Unilever in 2002, devotes 65 percent of its spending to international markets, slightly ahead of the 61 percent of P&G revenue that comes from outside the United States. The biggest marketers are investing ad dollars wherever they can find revenue or potential growth in a tough global economy—and increasingly, that's China. Some 39 of the Global 100 had measured media spending in China in 2008. Five of them invest more than 10 percent of their budgets there—Yum! Brands, Pernod Ricard, Avon Products, Colgate-Palmolive Co., and P&G. Overall, China represents 3.4 percent of total ad spending for the Global 100. In contrast, the United States accounted for 35 percent of worldwide media spending. Overall, total measured ad spending for the Global 100 increased 3.1 percent in 2008. The crucial question is when spending will return to the 5–6 percent growth rate considered normal. Projections suggest it won't be until 2012 (Wentz 2009).

## TREND TOWARD INTERNATIONAL AGENCIES

Around the turn of the 20th century, in order to better service clients who were beginning to market their products internationally, advertising agencies also moved abroad. The first U.S. agency to establish itself overseas was J. Walter Thompson, which opened an office in London in 1899 to meet the needs of its client General Motors. By the early 1920s both J. Walter Thompson and McCann-Erickson had large overseas networks with offices in Europe, India, and Latin America. Overall, however, agency movement to foreign soil was rather slow prior to 1960.

A study of 15 large American multinational agencies revealed that in the 45 years between 1915 and 1959, these agencies had opened or acquired only 50 overseas branch offices. Yet in the subsequent 12-year period, 210 overseas branch offices were opened or acquired—a fourfold increase (Weinstein 1974, 29).

When firms began to expand to foreign markets, their advertising agencies were faced with the following options: (1) allow a local agency abroad to handle the account, (2) allow a U.S. agency with an established international network to service their client, or (3) open or acquire an overseas branch. Initially, when multinational clients were the exception rather than the rule, the second alternative was the most common practice. However, allowing another agency to handle a client's international business became rather risky. For example, when D'Arcy, the agency handling advertising for Coca-Cola, was unable to provide service to Coca-Cola's overseas branches, the client turned to McCann-Erickson to handle its international account. Shortly thereafter, Coca-Cola dropped D'Arcy altogether, giving McCann-Erickson both its international and domestic accounts (Tyler 1967, 366).

The 1960s were characterized by rampant expansion abroad by U.S. advertising agencies. Agencies began to see many advantages to joining their clients in foreign markets. By moving abroad, these agencies could not only service their domestic clients but also compete for the foreign accounts of other U.S.-based multinational firms and for the accounts of local foreign firms. Thus, as domestic advertising volume began to taper off, foreign markets looked increasingly appealing. In addition, there was the attraction of potentially higher profits. Overseas salaries of advertising staff members in the 1960s were as much as 70 percent lower than in the United States, while average agency profits were often twice what

**TABLE 1.7:** World's Top 25 Agency Companies, 2009; Ranked by 2009 worldwide revenue for companies' agencies and related services (in U.S. million $)

| RANK | AGENCY COMPANY | HEADQUARTERS | WORLDWIDE REVENUE |
|------|----------------|--------------|-------------------|
| 1. | WPP | London | 13,598 |
| 2. | Omnicom Group | New York | 11,721 |
| 3. | Publicis Groupe | Paris | 6,287 |
| 4. | Interpublic Group of Cos. | New York | 6,028 |
| 5. | Dentsu | Tokyo | 3,113 |
| 6. | Aegis Group | London | 2,109 |
| 7. | Havas | Suresnes, France | 2,010 |
| 8. | Hakuhodo DY Holdings | Tokyo | 1,522 |
| 9. | Acxion Corp. | Little Rock, AR | 750 |
| 10. | MDC Partners | Toronto/New York | 546 |
| 11. | Alliance Data Systems (Epsilon) | Plano, TX | 514 |
| 12. | Asatsu-DK | Tokyo | 451 |
| 13. | Edelman | Chicago | 440 |
| 14. | Media Consulta | Berlin | 401 |
| 15. | Photon Group | Sydney | 366 |
| 16. | Sapient Corp. (SapientNitro) | Boston | 356 |
| 17. | Groupe Aeroplan (Carlson) | Montreal | 351 |
| 18. | IBM Corp. (IBM Interactive) | Chicago | 322 |
| 19. | Cheil Worldwide | Seoul | 312 |
| 20. | Grupo ABC (ABC Group) | Sao Paulo | 277 |
| 21. | inVentive Health | Westerville, OH | 272 |
| 22. | Huntsworth | Londo | 245 |
| 23. | Aspen Marketing Services | West Chicago, IL | 225 |
| 24. | LBi International | Stockholm | 224 |
| 25. | Markle | Columbia, MD | 223 |

*Source: Advertising Age (2010).*

they were in the United States (*Business Week* 1970, 48). Setting up offices overseas had the additional benefit of freeing U.S. agencies from a total dependency on the performance of the U.S. economy as a whole. For example, during the 1970 recession, domestic advertising agency billings declined 1 percent while the foreign billings of multinational agencies increased 13 percent (*International Advertiser* 1971).

In contrast to the 1960s, the 1970s was a period of consolidation and retrenchment for many U.S. advertising agencies. While the combined annual billings of multinational agencies continued to increase, many smaller multinational agencies with a limited presence overseas were forced to withdraw from foreign markets. Many realized that in order to compete successfully, they had to maintain offices in almost all of the important countries of Europe, Latin America, and the Far East—a commitment that only the largest multinational agencies were prepared to make. In 1970 *Advertising Age* listed 58 agencies that had international billings; by 1977 that number had dropped to just 36.

In the late 1980s, the profile of the industry changed substantially. In 1986, BBDO International, Doyle Dane Bernbach, and Needham Harper Worldwide announced a three-way merger to create the world's largest advertising firm, the Omnicom Group. At about the same time, a small London-based agency, Saatchi & Saatchi, purchased three U.S. agencies—Dancer, Fitzgerald, Sample; Backer & Spielvogel; and Ted Bates—and immediately surpassed Omnicom as the world's largest advertising organization. In 1989 the British WPP Group brought two of U.S. advertising's most glamorous names—J. Walter Thompson and the Ogilvy Group—into its "family" via hostile takeovers. Madison Avenue, it was said, was being invaded by an army speaking the Queen's English (Rothenberg 1989, 14). French agencies, too, looked to U.S. soil. In 1988, Publicis Group formed the first big Franco-American alliance with Chicago-based Foote, Cone & Belding Communications. In 1989, Della Femina became a subsidiary of Eurocom, France's top agency. In 1990, Paris-based Boulet Dru Dupuy Petit bought 40 percent of Wells, Rich, Green. Then, in 1994, Publicis Group acquired Bloom FCA, with offices in New York and Dallas (Toy and Lindler 1990, 74). Two Japanese agencies, Dentsu (Japan's largest agency) and Hakuhodo, also opened offices in the United States. As part of Dentsu's plan to establish majority-owned advertising and sales promotion networks in the world's major markets, the agency opened Nova Promotion Group in New York (Kilburn 1991, 3).

Over the past decade, the United States has lost its unchallenged grip on hucksterism—not only at home but abroad as well. European, Japanese, Australian, and Brazilian agencies have expanded or merged operations with agencies in other countries in order to meet the needs of their clients. Today, many of the largest multinational agencies have regrouped, and regrouped again, into multimillion- and multibillion-dollar multiservice transnational mega-advertising organizations. Today, the top three holding companies, WPP, Omnicom, and Publicis, together control over one-third of the world's advertising agencies. Table 1.7 lists the world's top 25 advertising organizations. *Advertising Age* notes that an advertising organization may be either an agency or agency holding company and qualifies for the ranking if it owns 50 percent or more of itself. This table ranks advertising organizations by worldwide revenues. Only 10 of the top 25 agencies have their headquarters solely in the United States, and the top agency is British-based WPP, the parent of global ad networks such as Ogilvy & Mather and J. Walter Thompson, as well as other marketing, media, and public relations firms such as Wunderman, Mindshare, and Burson-Marsteller. Three agencies are headquartered in London, and two are based in Japan. Beyond their sheer size, such mega-advertising organizations offer a number of benefits to their clients. They can present clients with a significantly larger pool of talent, and the potential for service synergies exists as well. In addition, clients have the ability to shift portions of accounts from one agency to another without going through the time-consuming process of an agency review. On the downside, clients must contend with potential conflicts with competing accounts.

## SUMMARY

The growth of international business has paralleled the growth of international advertising. Before turning our attention to the development of effective advertising programs for foreign markets, it is essential to understand the role that advertising plays in the international marketing mix and the challenges posed by the international marketing environment. These topics are the subject of Chapters 2 and 3.

## REFERENCES

*Advertising Age.* 2009. Top 100 global advertisers heap their spending abroad. 30 November, 1, 11.

———. 2010. Agency report. 26 April, 22.

Agence France-Presse. 2009. Global investment flow slows sharply in 2008: UNCTAD. 20 January. <http://abs-cbnnews.com/business/01/19/09/global-investment-flow-s...>. Retrieved 29 May 2009.

Amadeo, Kimberly. 2010. The U.S. trade deficit. About.com Guide. <http://useconomy.about.com/od/tradepolicy/p/Trade_Deficit.htm>. Retrieved 14 May 2010.

American Association of Advertising Agencies Press Release. 2009. GroupM forecasts global ad spending recovery to begin in 2010. 8 December. <http://www2.aaaa.org/news/agency/Pages/120909_recovery.aspx?PF=1>. Retrieved 14 May 2010.

Bauder, Don. 2003. China factor involves hefty helping of angst. *San Diego Union-Tribune,* 19 February, C-1.

Bernard, Bruce. 2001. Food firms fight for world market. *Europe,* June, 16.

Bertagnoli, Lisa. 2001. To Russia with...reservations. *Marketing News,* 9 April, 1, 11.

*Business Week.* 1970. Madison Avenue goes multinational. 12 September, 48–51.

Demos, Telis. 2009. Fast, foreign food. *Fortune,* 31 August, 16.

*Fortune.* 2009. Fortune global 500. 20 July, F1–F8.

FT.com. 2002. Ikea is building a shopping center on a scale Russia has not seen before. 26 April. *Financial Times* (London). <http://80-proquest.umi.com.webgate.sdsu.edu:88/pgdweb?Did=0000001161046768fmt=3>.

Garten, Jeffrey. 2002. When everything is made in China. *Business Week,* 17 June, 20.

Gu, Wei. 2003. U.S. companies in China find the silk road. *San Diego Union-Tribune,* 23 February, H-3.

Guerrero, Antonio. 2008. Russia's retail therapy. *Global Finance* (New York) 22(6): June, 42–48.

Gunther, Marc. 2009. China Inc. takes off. *Fortune,* 20 July, 131–134.

Hilsenrath, Jon E. 2002. Globalization efforts will see revival—search for new consumers, low cost suppliers, power expansion abroad. *Asian Wall Street Journal,* 2 January, 1.

Holmes, Stanley. 2002. To keep up the growth it must go global quickly. *Business Week,* 9 September, 100–110.

Howes, Daniel. 2008. Auto-makers lust after emerging markets. *Detroit News,* 15 January, A-1.

*International Advertiser.* 1971. International agencies. 12(3): 44.

Johnson, Bradley. 2009. U.S. revenue rises 3.7% (but watch out for '09). *Advertising Age,* 27 April, 1.

Karabell, Zachary. 2008. Thank God for the Chinese consumer. *Wall Street Journal* (Eastern Edition), 8 August, A-15.

Kilburn, David. 1991. Dentsu opening U.S. promo shop. *Advertising Age,* 8 July, 3, 34.

Madden, Normandy. 2010. Luxury sales in China grew 12% in 2009. *Advertising Age,* 19 May. <http://adage.com/print?article_id=143946>. Retrieved 19 May 2010.

Patrick, Aaron. 2008. Softer Nike pitch woos Europe's women. 11 September. <http://online.wsj.com/article/SB122108023306820723.html?mod=h...>. Retrieved 8 June 2009.

Pender, Kathleen. 2007. Overseas markets in your sights? Try big U.S. firms. *San Francisco Chronicle,* 30 October, C1.

Reuters.com. 2009. World Bank cuts Russia GDP forecast to -7.9 percent in 2009. 24 June. <http://www.reuters.com/article/idUSLO68247420090624>. Retrieved 14 May 2010.

Rothenberg, Randall. 1989. Brits buying up the ad business. *New York Times Magazine,* 2 July, 14–38.

Schlein, Lisa. 2010. Foreign direct investment falls sharply in 2009. VOA News.com, 19 January. <http://www1.voanews.com/english/news/economy-and-business/Fore...>. Retrieved 14 May 2010.

Schlisserman, Courtney. 2007. Smaller companies grab bigger share of surging U.S. exports. 23 November. <http://www.bloomberg.com/apps/news?pid=20670001&sid=aXW>. Retrieved 25 May 2009.

Shaughnessy, Rick, and Diane Lindquist. 1993. Foreign investment in the United States drops 47 percent. *San Diego Union-Tribune,* 9 June, C2.

Tonelson, Alan. 2010. 2009 trade deficit reduction masks serious US competitiveness deficiencies. 22 February. <http://americaneconimicalert.org/view_art.asp?Prod_ID=3413>. Retrieved 14 May 2010.

Toy, Steward, and Mark Lindler. 1990. And now, rue de Madison. *Business Week*, 21 May, 74–75.

Tyler, Ralph. 1967. Agencies abroad: New horizons for U.S. advertising. In *World marketing*, ed. John K. Ryans and J. C. Baker. New York: Wiley, 366–380.

U.S. Bureau of the Census. 1995. *Statistical history of the United States*. New York: Basic Books.

———. 2010. Top trading partners. <http://www.census.gov/foreign-trade/statistics/highlights/top/top0912...>. Retrieved 14 May 2010.

U.S. Central Intelligence Agency. 2010. *The world factbook*.

Weinstein, Arnold K. 1974. The international expansion of U.S. multinational advertising agencies. *MSU Business Topics*, 22(3): 29–35.

Weller, Christian, and Holly Wheeler. 2008. Nothing to brag about. U.S. trade deficit remains high priority despite recent improvements. 26 March. <http://www.americanprogress.org/issues/2008/03/high_priority.html>. Retrieved 20 May 2009.

Wentz, Laurel. 2009. Top 100 global advertisers heap their spending abroad. *Advertising Age*, 30 November, 1.

World Bank. 2002. *World development indicators*.

World Trade Report. 2009. The trade situation in 2008–09. World Trade Organization. 1–3.

ZenithOptimedia. 2001. *Advertising expenditure forecasts*. 1–10. 11 March 2009. <http://www.euromonitor.com/Chinese_consumers_in_2020_A_look_into_the_future>. Retrieved 20 March 2009.

———. 2008. ZenithOptimedia ad forecast: Boom in developing markets, gloom in West. 2 April. <http://www.marketingvox.com/zenithoptimedia-ad-forecast-boom-in-developing-markets-gloom-in-west-037754/>.

Zhiming, Xin. 2008. WB: China's GDP to slow to 7.5% in 2009. *China Daily*, 28 November. <http://www.chinadaily.com.cn/bizchina/2008-11/25/content_72379>.

# CHAPTER TWO

# The International Marketing Mix

The primary focus of this text is international advertising. However, because an advertising campaign is part of an overall marketing strategy and must be coordinated with other marketing activities, the role of the other marketing mix elements will be reviewed. Companies operating in one or more foreign markets must decide whether to adapt their marketing mix to local conditions, and if so, to what degree. The concept of a marketing mix, popularized by Jerome McCarthy, includes the following four P's:

- Product: includes a product's design and development, as well as branding and packaging;
- Place (or distribution): includes the channels used in moving the product from manufacturer to consumer;
- Price: includes the price at which the product or service is offered for sale and establishes the level of profitability;
- Promotion: includes advertising, personal selling, sales promotions, direct marketing, and publicity. Broadly defined, it also includes sponsorships, product integration, and even trade fairs. (McCarthy 1960)

## GLOBALIZATION VERSUS LOCALIZATION OF THE MARKETING MIX

Experts disagree over the degree to which firms should globalize, or standardize, their marketing programs across markets. At one extreme are companies that support the use of a fully standardized approach. Marshall McLuhan coined the term "global village" to describe an emerging world tightly linked through telecommunications. Many marketers believe that these advances in telecommunications, along with cheaper air transportation and the resulting increase in international travel, have created increasingly international consumers, making the world ripe for global marketing—at least for selected products.

This concept is not new. Debates regarding the viability of global marketing surfaced as far back as the late 1960s (Buzzell 1968). However, the concept was popularized by Harvard marketing professor Theodore Levitt, who suggested that people everywhere want goods of the best quality and reliability

**Figure 2.1:** Print ad from Gillette's "The Moment" campaign.

at the lowest price; and that differences in cultural preferences, tastes, and standards are vestiges of the past, because the world is becoming increasingly homogenized (Levitt 1983, 92). With a global approach to the marketing mix, a firm utilizes a common marketing plan for all the countries in which it operates—essentially selling the same product in the same way everywhere in the world. Major benefits associated with such standardization include lower production, distribution, management, and promotion costs. Yet the number of firms with the potential to standardize the majority of their marketing mix elements are indeed few.

Gillette is one such advertiser. Its line of male grooming products includes Gillette Fusion, Gillette Series Shave Gels, Gillette Styling, Gillette Clinical Strength Ultra Comfort anti-perspirant and deodorant, and Gillette Hydrating Body Washes. For a number of years, Gillette employed the global theme "The Best a Man Can Get" in communicating with the more than 600 million men worldwide who start each day with the brand. In 2009, the company debuted a new global brand campaign. Building on the brand's recent introduction of men's hair styling and personal care products, the campaign is part of Gillette's strategy to expand the brand beyond shaving and strengthen the emotional bond among men. The new campaign, entitled "The Moment," was developed from a deep understanding of men. Gillette conducted extensive global research among thousands of men and learned that even the most confident guys have doubts at many moments throughout their lives. Also revealed was that men are looking for products that give them the confidence they want and need to step up; perform; and look, feel, and be their best. The campaign features everyday guys as well as the Gillette Champions Tiger Woods, Roger Federer, and Derek Jeter experiencing moments of doubt and showing how they overcome them to succeed. A 30-second television spot depicts the doubt faced by every guy, whether it be the moment he steps on the doorstep before a date, just before he delivers a presentation, or giving a "best man" toast at a wedding, and the role Gillette's high-performance grooming products play in helping him gain the confidence to succeed in that moment (*Entertainment Newsweekly* 2009). See Figure 2.1 for a sample of this global campaign.

At the other extreme are companies committed to localization, or specialization. They argue that because consumers and marketing environments in different countries vary so greatly, it is necessary to tailor the marketing mix elements to each foreign market. Although such a customized approach typically results in higher costs, marketers hope that these costs will be offset by greater returns and a larger market share. Wal-Mart serves as an excellent example of the specialized approach.

Wal-Mart became an international company when it opened a Sam's Club near Mexico City in 1991. Today, Wal-Mart International is the fastest-growing part of Wal-Mart's overall operations. However, expansion into foreign markets has not always been easy. In markets such as Germany, South Korea, and Japan, where the giant retailer lost more than $1 billion, its troubles came in part from underestimating the local competition, battling labor unions, and failing to grasp the local culture. For Wal-Mart, China represents the biggest frontier since it conquered America, and when it entered the market in 1996, it vowed not to make the same mistakes. But success in China required more than replicating the company's formula of cheap, steep, and deep. It required the kind of flexibility Wal-Mart has rarely shown: it required going native. One of the biggest cultural changes for Wal-Mart has been its acceptance of organized labor in China. Domestically, Wal-Mart fiercely fights unions, and it took the same hard-line approach in its first eight years in China. Analysts suspect that Wal-Mart initially failed to appreciate the role unions play in China. In contrast to the United States, unions in China don't bargain contracts. Rather, they are an arm of the state, providing funding to the Communist Party, and—in the government's view—securing social order. In 2004, Wal-Mart softened and agreed to accept unions, but required workers to ask for representation. Finally, seeing organized labor as a cultural and political imperative in China, the company accepted the first union into its stores in 2006 (Naughton 2006).

The differences between Wal-Mart's presence in China and elsewhere don't stop there. At store grand openings—such as one in Chongqing, on the upper reaches of the Yangtze River—there are fire-breathing Sichuan opera dancers at the entrance who perform the traditional lion dance. The eye of a lion's head is painted to bring good luck. Inside the store, things get even more exotic. While Wal-Marts in China have stopped slaughtering poultry on the premises since the SARS epidemic in 2003 and no longer offer rabbits or snakes, customers can purchase spicy chicken feet and stinky tofu. Shoppers with nets typically mob the serve-yourself tanks swimming with grass fish, crabs, clams, and eels. Also available are turtles and live bull frogs the size of soccer balls. Wal-Mart in China also offers "retail-tainment." Stores provide space for local school groups to perform, and they organize daily activities for the elderly (Chandler 2005). Though store shelves are stocked with U.S. brands such as Crest toothpaste, Clairol shampoo, and Johnson's Baby Oil, these products sit alongside moisturizers infused with sheep placenta, which the Chinese swear reduces wrinkles. Wal-Mart buyers have even learned to chart the Chinese calendar. They stocked up on diapers in the Year of the Monkey because it's considered a lucky year to bear children. The Pampers flew off the shelves (Naughton 2006). And now, after more than a decade of ingratiating itself to Chinese consumers by adopting their customs and culture, Wal-Mart is making its move from a minor player to a dominant force. To date, the company's Web site boasts 266 Wal-Marts in China.

A great deal of confusion surrounds the issue of standardization versus specialization, in part because of the various terms employed. Marketing standardization has also been called globalization, while marketing specialization has been referred to as localization as well as customization. Regardless of the terminology, too often the issue of standardization versus specialization of international marketing is perceived as an either/or proposition. In fact, standardization versus specialization of the marketing mix may be seen as the end points on a continuum, with many possible approaches between these two extremes. A company may choose to standardize one element while customizing another. For example, Visa Inc. operates the world's largest retail electronic payments network, providing processing services and payment product platforms including consumer credit, debit, prepaid, and commercial payments. Visa enjoys unsurpassed acceptance around the world, and Visa/Plus is one of the world's largest global ATM networks, offering cash access in local currency in more than 170 countries. In 2009, the company unveiled its new campaign, "More people go with Visa." The campaign enables Visa to align its worldwide marketing under a single theme and highlights the superior value Visa delivers versus cash and checks—including more security, more control, and more convenience. Visa notes that the "More people go with Visa" platform is relevant across all geographic regions and demographic groups and will be used to promote the vast product choices that Visa offers, as well as the brand itself. But while the campaign establishes a single global marketing message, it will be executed locally for maximum relevance. In the United States, two national spots have appeared, one of which, entitled "Aquarium," celebrates moments in which Visa's debit product, the Visa Check Card, allows cardholders to experience the beauty of every day. In this spot, viewers are told the story of a father-daughter trip to the aquarium viewed through the eyes of a child. Visa's international markets launched with a television commercial named "Gofesto." The spot, which was customized by each Visa region, takes viewers on a journey across the globe showing people from different places enjoying what the world has to offer—from experiencing the great outdoors to taking simple trips to the supermarket. The

**Figure 2.2:** "More People Go With Visa" print advertisement appearing in the United States.

spot reminds cardholders that life is not about collecting possessions but, more important, about collecting experiences (*Business Wire* 2009). Both traditional and new media are employed to deliver the message to Visa's target audience around the globe. See Figure 2.2 for an example of Visa's print ads in the United States.

The issue of marketing standardization versus specialization, as it pertains to product, price, and distribution, will be addressed in this chapter. Globalization versus localization of advertising will be discussed in detail in Chapters 5 and 6.

## PRODUCT

The American Marketing Association defines a product as "anything that can be offered to a market for attention, acquisition, use, or consumption that might satisfy a want or need" (American Marketing Association 1960). A product can be thought of in terms of three levels. These three levels, as outlined by Philip Kotler and Gary Armstrong (Kotler and Armstrong 1990, 221), are illustrated in Figure 2.3.

The *core product* refers to the bundle of benefits the consumer expects to receive from purchasing the item. These benefits can be functional, psychological, social, or economic in nature. For example, consumers may purchase an automobile for purposes of transportation (functional benefit), select a specific style because it is currently in fashion among their group of friends (social benefit), opt for a stick shift over an automatic because it provides better mileage (economic benefit), and choose the color red because it's their favorite (psychological benefit).

**Figure 2.3:** Three levels of a product.

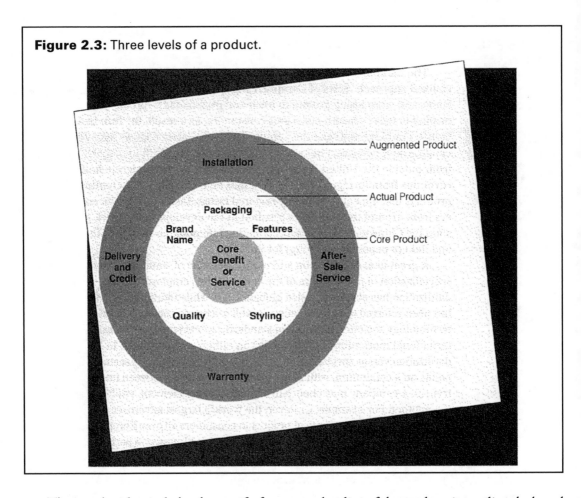

The *actual product* includes the specific features and styling of the product, its quality, the brand name, and its packaging; and the *augmented product* refers to product installation, delivery and credit provided to consumers, warranty, and postpurchase servicing.

Most products can be classified as durable goods, nondurable goods, or services. *Durable goods* are major products, often high-ticket items that tend to last for an extended period of time and, as a result, are purchased rather infrequently. Automobiles, appliances, and furniture are examples of durable goods. *Nondurable goods* are typically lower in price, consumed in a relatively short period of time, and thus purchased frequently. Examples of nondurable goods are food products and personal care items such as shampoos and toothpaste. *Services* are defined as activities or benefits offered by one party to another that are essentially intangible and do not result in the transfer of ownership of any kind. Obtaining health insurance, getting a haircut, or having an auto repaired are examples of services that consumers may purchase.

Products can be further distinguished between consumer goods and industrial goods. *Consumer goods* are items purchased by the end consumer for personal consumption. In contrast, *industrial goods* are items a firm purchases so that it may engage in business. Industrial goods include raw materials that actually become part of the end product (for example, in the garment industry, textiles purchased by a garment manufacturer that become part of its line of clothing), goods such as equipment and machinery used in the manufacturing process itself (for instance, industrial-quality sewing machines purchased to enable the creation of the fashions), and supplies and services (such as photocopier paper and long-distance telephone service).

Product planning in the international setting requires that marketers explore the needs and wants of consumers in different markets and determine how those needs and wants might be satisfied by the firm's products. In addition to deciding which products should be offered, the international marketer must determine whether product modifications are necessary.

## PRODUCT STANDARDIZATION

One option available to the international marketer is to sell exactly the same product abroad as is sold in the home market—what is known as product standardization. The advantages of this strategy are numerous. Selling an identical product in a number of markets eliminates duplication of costs related to research and development, product design, and package design. Consider the case of Black & Decker, a classic example of the benefits of product standardization. In 1982, Black & Decker operated 25 plants in 13 countries on 6 continents, which led to considerable duplication of effort. Indeed, Black & Decker produced 260 different motor sizes before it undertook global restructuring of its operations. Employing the same raw materials, equipment, plants, and processes typically leads to manufacturing economies of scale. A standardized product also increases the potential for economies of scale related to promotional efforts. Coca-Cola, Kellogg's Corn Fakes, Perrier bottled water, Pond's cold cream, Mitsubishi autos, Gillette razor blades, Birkenstock sandals, and Colgate toothpaste are examples of products that are available in the same form in markets around the globe.

Studies have revealed that the feasibility of product standardization may depend on the specific product category. Among consumer goods, nondurables generally are believed to require greater customization than durable goods because they appeal more directly to tastes, habits, and customs, which tend to be country-specific (Douglas and Urban 1977, 53; Hoevell and Walters 1972, 69). Some research has indicated that industrial products are more amenable to standardization than are consumer goods (Boddewyn et al. 1986, 69; Cahn and Mauborgne 1987). Product standardization also may be effective for markets with highly similar target audiences (Sheth 1986, 9; Kale and Sudharshan 1987, 60). For example, the youth market around the world is said to be surprisingly similar. Marketers of jeans, records, and soft drinks find that they can sell essentially identical products to teens in Peoria and Paris. And marketers of "global village products"—essentially goods and services targeted to international travelers, such as hotels and rental cars—also find similarities in their target audience. Teresa Domzal and Lynette Unger propose that product standardization appears most feasible when products approach either end of the "high-tech/high-touch" spectrum:

> Consumers around the world who are interested in high-tech products share a common language, in bytes or other technical features, which enable global strategies to be successful. The hypothesized success of global marketing of "high-touch" products is more difficult to explain beyond the fact that products such as fragrance, fashion, or jewelry, for example, simply touch on universal emotional themes or needs. The high-tech/high-touch hypothesis appears to be borne out in the recent success of certain global products. High-tech products such as personal computers, video and stereo equipment and automobiles, and high-touch categories such as health food, fitness clothing, mineral water and fragrances are popular the world over. (Domzal and Unger 1987, 23)

## PRODUCT ADAPTATION

Although product standardization is the less costly approach, the international marketer may choose to engage in product adaptation for a variety of reasons. Marketing environments vary from country to country, and as a result, a product designed and developed for consumers in one market may not match needs in another.

*Mandatory Product Adaptation:* Mandatory adaptation refers to situations in which the international firm adapts its products because it literally has no other choice. Differing levels of technical sophistication may necessitate product simplification. For example, frozen foods cannot be marketed in countries where retailers do not have freezer storage facilities. Likewise, if consumers in these markets typically do not own refrigerators, demand for frozen foods is likely to be quite limited. Variations in electrical systems from one country to the next (and even within countries) must also be considered when marketing consumer or industrial electrical appliances. A television designed for the U.S. market simply will not run in Mexico or Germany because of differences in both the frequency and voltage of the electrical power supply and the broadcast standards in these countries. In addition, the United States still relies on the American/British measurement system, while almost every other country has converted to the metric system. Any American firm attempting to sell a product abroad for which measurement is an important variable must go metric. For example, as Louis Kraar recounts, Hewlett-Packard had little choice—and lots of incentive—but to modify one of its products for the Asian market:

> The firm introduced its first Japanese-language computer printer. The Japanese version of the popular DeskJet 500 machine was followed by similar models with built-in software to print in Chinese characters and the Hankul alphabet of Korea. Localizing products is well worth the trouble and considerable expense. Hewlett-Packard's sales of $2 billion in Asia and the Pacific that year represented 16 percent of the corporate total. (Kraar 1991, 133)

Governmental regulations often present formidable barriers to product standardization. These regulations relate to product standards as well as testing and approval procedures. Each country has different product requirements designed to protect its citizens and its environment. For years, the Kellogg Co. has attempted to sell the same cereal across Europe, but the company has hit obstacle after obstacle in its efforts to persuade regulators to allow the U.S. cereal maker to sell the same vitamin-fortified cereals throughout Europe. Denmark doesn't want vitamins added, fearing that cereal eaters who take multi-vitamins might exceed recommended daily allowances, which some experts say can damage internal organs. Netherlands officials don't believe either Vitamin D or folic acid is beneficial, so it doesn't want them added. Finland wants more Vitamin D than other countries to help Finns make up for sun deprivation. And the list goes on. So Kellogg, of Battle Creek, Michigan, has to manufacture four varieties of corn flakes and other cereals in its plants in Manchester, England, and Bremen, Germany (Sims 2005).

Despite a "unified" European Union, persistent national differences continue to saddle companies with extra costs and hinder expansion. Examples abound. The German government long had strict guidelines regarding the purity of beers sold in that country, which prevented many brands from entering the market. Similarly, the United States has very specific safety restrictions on auto emissions that must be met by both foreign and domestic automobiles sold in this country. If such government-mandated standards force international firms to spend additional time and money modifying products, they can function as a non-tariff barrier and, in discouraging imports, help protect domestic manufacturers.

When faced with technical differences or governmental restrictions, the international firm has little choice but to adapt its product. In other instances the decision to standardize or adapt is not nearly so clear-cut. In these cases the international marketer must explore differences in consumption patterns, such as whether the product is purchased by relatively the same consumer income group from one country to another, whether most consumers use the product or service for the same purpose, and whether the method of preparation is the same for all target countries. In addition, the marketer must consider the psychosocial characteristics of consumers, such as whether the same basic psychological, social, and economic factors motivate the purchase and use of the product in all target countries; and whether the advantages and disadvantages of the product or service in the minds of consumers are basically the same from one country to another. Finally, the marketer must take into account more general cultural criteria, such as whether some stigma is attached to the product or service, or whether the product or service interferes with tradition in one or more of the targeted markets (Britt 1974, 32).

Campbell's Soup has clearly learned valuable lessons from its early mistakes. The firm would have benefited from a more in-depth analysis of both consumption and psychosocial factors when it initially moved overseas in the late 1950s. During the decade that followed, the company recorded some $30 million in losses in its overseas operations. The firm's difficulties stemmed mainly from its failure to adapt its product to suit local preferences (Ricks et al. 1974, 16; *Sales Management* 1967, 31). England comprised Campbell's most important foreign market. A primary mistake was the failure to explain to the English housewife how to prepare the soup. The English, accustomed to the ready-to-eat Heinz soups but unfamiliar with the concept of condensed soups, were unable to justify the cost of the smaller Campbell's soup can compared to the larger Heinz can. It took two years for Campbell's to provide the necessary explanations and to promote the idea of condensed soups. Failure to adapt the taste of their soups to local palates was another problem. The taste of established local varieties of tomato soup so differed from Campbell's that it was not until Campbell's made significant changes in its flavors that sales picked up. As a result, Campbell now creates new products to appeal to distinctly regional tastes. Taste-testing with consumers from around the world has resulted in the development of duck gizzard soup for Chinese consumers, *creama de chile poblano* soup for Mexicans, and *flaki* (a peppery tripe soup) for Poles (Weber 1993, 52).

McDonald's has successfully marketed its fast food worldwide for decades. While the restaurant provides its customers with a nearly identical eating experience wherever the Golden Arches appear, it also pays very close attention to local tastes and customs. For example, McDonald's first adapted its menu to European tastes when it began to offer beer in many of its German restaurants in the 1980s. Today, a separate food factory in Munich is assigned the task of coming up with new menus for the differing tastes in the 41 European countries, including Russia. In Portugal, McDonald's offers soup, and in France the menu includes "cheese saga" burgers with French cheeses. Also designed to appeal to French consumers is Croque McDo—a ham and melted Swiss cheese on toast. In the Netherlands, a popular item is the McKroket—a deep-fried patty of beef ragout. Such variation has become the norm, belying McDonald's monolithic image as a big American corporation that serves standard fare around the world. In catering to Singaporeans' penchant for spaghetti and preference for chicken, McDonald's launched McSpaghetti—a pasta-based meal served in a tangy chicken pomodoro sauce. Retailing for $2.20 and including a garlic McMuffin, McSpaghetti is served at all McDonald's island-wide, along with traditional McDonald's fare. This follows other product innovations such as the savory breakfast item chicken SingaPorridge. Porridge is a popular local breakfast item and is widely considered a comfort food in Singapore. Research clearly paid off for McDonald's, given that weekend breakfast now accounts for half of the chain's entire business across Singapore's 126 outlets. Menu tailoring is not unique to Singapore. In Japan, teriyaki burgers often appear alongside the Big Mac, and in Hong Kong, McDonald's has begun offering customers a rice-based alternative (see Figure 2.4). Tailoring its offerings appears to have paid off for the restaurant chain. Its worldwide operations are now far bigger than its U.S. domestic business, and they are growing substantially faster (Gumbel 2008).

**Figure 2.4:** In Hong Kong, it's McRice.

Regardless of the source of pressure for product modification, the international marketer must attempt to measure the costs and revenues associated with marketing a standardized product and compare them with the costs and revenues expected in a product adaption strategy. Further complicating the decision to standardize or adapt is the fact that this formula may vary on a market-by-market basis. As a case in point, two years after Mattel allowed its Japanese affiliate to "Japanize" Barbie Doll's features, sales blossomed from near zero to 2 million units. Interestingly, Barbie sold well without modification in 60 other countries (Kotler 1986, 13).

## NEW PRODUCT DEVELOPMENT

Too often marketers have attempted to export products that, while appropriate to the home market, are not particularly well suited to the needs of consumers in other countries without significant modifications. In some instances product modifications may be so extensive that it is no longer profitable to market the item. Here marketers may find that creating a completely new product is the best way to meet the needs of a foreign market. For example, Martha Stewart found great success catering to Japanese tastes. Pairing with local retailer Seiyu, she has opened more than 200 outlets and annually sells over $1 million worth of products to women who want to bring a piece of New England to their crowded Japanese apartments. But products intended for the American market did not appeal to Japanese consumers. Towels targeted at American women in reds and browns, for example, were deemed "muddy." Instead, Martha sold linens in vibrant colors, along with chopsticks in pastels, square frying pans for making traditional cube-shaped omelettes, and bedroom slippers—a must in every Japanese home (Dawson and Brady 2002). P&G employs what it calls "reverse engineering" in selling to consumers in emerging countries. Rather than create an item and then assign a price to it—as in most developed markets—the company first considers what consumers need and what they can afford. For example, running water is in short supply for many low-income Mexican consumers. In response, P&G developed a fabric softener called Downy Single Rinse. It can be added to a load of laundry along with the detergent, eliminating an entire rinse cycle in the semiautomatic machines typically used there (Byron 2007).

## COUNTRY-OF-ORIGIN EFFECT

Consumers base their product evaluations on a variety of criteria, including the country in which the product is produced. Marlboro is an American cigarette, Chanel No. 5 is a French perfume, Buitoni is an Italian pasta, and Johnny Walker is a Scotch whiskey. Each of these brands has national credentials, and anyone attempting to market worldwide a Scottish pasta or an Italian whiskey probably would have serious credibility problems because of this country-of-origin effect (Shalofsky 1987, 88). Some countries have particularly positive associations with specific product categories. For example, Germany and Japan are stereotypically seen as producing high-quality autos, France and Italy are typically associated with fine wines, and Russia is the home of vodka. A plausible national base or home market appears to be an important characteristic of the overall product and may influence perceptions of the product's quality. Figure 2.5 shows an example of an advertisement highlighting the country of origin.

In some instances a firm may wish to downplay a product's country of origin. It appears that Coca-Cola, McDonald's, and Colgate-Palmolive are among the blue-chip U.S. brands that are taking a beating when it comes to how well liked they are around the world, according to a study by GfK Roper Consulting, in part because of their country of origin. Attitudes toward Americans and their culture are increasingly negative, notes Jennifer James, senior consultant at Roper. "Our foreign policy has contributed." The Roper study tracked the so-called likability of 60 major brands, about half of them American. According to Roper, which has been conducting the study for a decade, American brands have been losing popularity in developed regions for several years. What was different in this most recent survey was that developing markets were also eschewing American classics. "This past year we're starting to see consumer favorability waning in the developing markets in Asia, Latin America and Central Europe," Ms. James said. "That's why we're seeing slippage." American companies posted four of the five biggest drops in likability, and Coca-Cola tumbled the furthest, nearly 40 percent. The biggest gainers were all foreign: Germany's BMW, Mercedes, and Volkswagen, along with Japan's Sony and Honda (York 2007). Marketers should be ready to drop the flag if national or global sentiment suddenly drops based on negative news. Of course, the reverse likely holds true as well.

Given our increasingly multinational corporate world, it is often difficult to determine exactly where a product comes from. According to a recent study from Anderson Analytics, most U.S. college consumers are not sure where their favorite products come from. For instance, only 4.4 percent of college students surveyed knew that Nokia is Finnish, while 53.6 percent guessed the brand was Japanese. Lego, LG, Samsung, and Adidas faced similar problems, with fewer than 10 percent of students knowing their respective countries of origin as Denmark, Korea, Korea, and Germany, instead guessing, also respectively: United States, United States, Japan, and the United States Not surprisingly, retail brand Ikea did comparatively well with this segment—likely because its stylish but inexpensive furniture is a college staple—with 31.2 percent correctly guessing Sweden. But even so, another 23.6 percent thought Ikea was a U.S. brand (Bulik 2007). And some manufactures are really products of a number

**Figure 2.5:** Ad for Stolichnaya Russian vodka noting it's "Fresh from the Motherland."

of countries. Because they build their products all over the globe, companies like IBM, Mitsubishi, and Siemens AG are in fact American, Japanese, and German in name only. For example, IBM manufactures products in more than a dozen countries, and an IBM personal computer stamped "Made in U.S.A." might be assembled in Raleigh, North Carolina, yet contain a floppy disk drive from IBM's Japanese plants, a monitor from Korea, and a mixture of imported and domestic computer chips (*San Diego Union-Tribune* 1992a). "Almost any one product weighing more than 10 pounds and costing more than $10 these days is a global composite, combining parts or services from many different nations," notes Robert B. Reich, political economist and former secretary of labor (*San Diego Union-Tribune* 1992b).

## BRANDING AND TRADEMARK DECISIONS

Branding decisions are an important part of international product marketing strategy. A brand is any name, term, sign, symbol, or design—or combination of these—intended to differentiate the goods or services of one seller from those of another. A trademark is a brand or part of a brand that is given legal protection. Registering a trademark protects the seller's exclusive rights to the use of that brand name. From the consumer's perspective, trademarks help to identify the origin of the product and provide a guarantee of consistent quality.

Protection of successful and well-known trademarks, while challenging in the home market, is doubly so internationally. Most countries offer some system of trademark registration and protection for both foreign and national firms. There are two basic systems of trademark registration:

**Priority in registration:** In Europe and elsewhere, the first firm to register a trademark is considered the rightful owner of that trademark.

**Priority in use:** In the United States and Britain, rights to a trademark are established and maintained through use. In order for a brand to be protected, it must both be registered and have, in fact, been sold in that particular country. "Use" is defined legally and varies from one country to the next. In some countries, the export sale of several cases of a product is sufficient to be defined as use; in others, the product might have to be manufactured locally.

When looking to register an international trademark, the registrant has several options. The three most common are outlined below.

1.  Single International Trademark Application: The Madrid Protocol for International Registration of Trademarks allows a marketer to obtain international protection of a trademark in one or more of the 70 countries that are members of the Protocol. Under this system a U.S. applicant, for example, can file an application with the U.S. Patent and Trademark Office. The applicant indicates on the form the countries belonging to the Madrid Protocol in which it wants protection. The form can be submitted in French or English, eliminating the need for applying in multiple languages. The Patent and Trademark Office then forwards the application to the World Intellectual Property Organization (WIPO), and WIPO sends out an international registration for the mark. WIPO then sends the application to the relevant countries, where trademark examiners analyze the application. Each country may take 18 months to make a final decision—or longer if the application is opposed. If the trademark is approved, the Madrid Protocol gives it a lifespan of 10 years plus one renewal, for which the owner must pay a renewal fee. It is an easier, cheaper, and more efficient way for trademark holders to secure worldwide protection than submitting separate applications to each country

involved. For small companies and independent inventors, the rule makes it feasible to invest in international trademarks by significantly reducing the red tape, local agents, language, and fees involved. For example, in 2000 the U.S. government estimated that a U.S. trademark owner who wanted to register his mark in 10 countries faced $14,000 in fees for 10 separate applications. The Madrid Protocol brings that cost down to about $4,700. But the new rule means that trademark applicants will have to search not only U.S. trademark archives but an international register of archives from all Madrid Protocol countries when checking whether the mark they want already belongs to someone else (Chartrand 2002).

2.  Community Trademark Application: A second alternative is the Community Trademark Application, a single application that covers all countries of the European Union. Community Trademarks are administered through a central office located in Spain.

3.  Individual Trademark Registration in Each Market: Multinational marketers can file individual applications in each country in which they seek a trademark. For trademarks in countries that are not members of the Madrid Protocol, this is the only avenue for obtaining a trademark.

In some countries the international marketer is required to renew registration rights periodically and pay a renewal fee. Registration fees are typically modest, but the associated legal fees can raise costs significantly. Given the costs and efforts required to register trademarks, the international marketer must carefully evaluate each market in order to determine whether to seek protection. The marketer must also continually monitor the foreign markets in which it operates to ensure that trademark infringement does not become a problem.

The international marketer must also decide whether to promote a single product brand world-wide—commonly referred to as a *global brand*—or to promote different brands for different regions or even individual markets. Certain advantages are associated with registering a single brand in all countries in which the firm operates. There is often a certain level of prestige associated with an international brand. Brands aren't usually listed on corporate balance sheets, but they can go further in determining a company's success than a new factory or technological breakthrough. That's because nurturing a strong brand, even in bad times, can allow companies to command premium prices. A strong brand also can open doors when growth depends on breaking into new markets (Khermouch 2002, 93). A recent survey of the world's most valuable brands, conducted annually by *Business Week,* found Coca-Cola to be the top brand worldwide. To determine which global brands are the most valuable, *Business Week* and Interbrand, a unit of Omnicom Group Inc., ranked brands by dollar value, based on the idea that strong brands have the power to lift sales and earnings. Interbrand attempts to figure out how much of a boost each brand delivers, how stable the boost is likely to be, and how much those future earnings are worth today. The value that is assigned is strictly for the products with the brand on them, not for others sold by the company. Therefore, Coca-Cola—with a value approaching $70 billion—is ranked just on those products carrying the Coke name, not Sprite or Powerade. Table 2.1 lists the top 25 global brands.

It is clearly less costly to prepare advertising campaigns and promotional literature for a single brand than for several. A single brand also allows the marketer to utilize international media and reap the benefits in places where media spill over national borders, such as in Europe. With increasing international travel, a single trademark will ensure that consumers recognize a firm's products, thereby eliminating brand confusion.

Collectively, however, local brands still account for the overwhelming majority of consumers' purchases. Of more than 10,000 brands in a database complied by market research firm Millward Brown, only 3 percent show up in seven or more countries (Pfanner 2009). Certain factors may necessitate modification of the brand name or trademark. Some brand names simply do not translate well. In other cases, a brand name in one market may mean something entirely different in another. Consider the case of the Japanese car manufacturer Mitsubishi Corp., which wanted to name one of its models Pajero. In certain Latin American countries, the term is slang for compulsive sexual behavior. Instead Mitsubishi adopted the name Montero for most markets around the world (Asher 2001). Also, different countries often prefer different types of brand names. For example, there is a pronounced difference in the names Americans and Japanese give to their cars. Whereas the Japanese lean toward pastoral names or names of girls—Bluebird, Bluebonnet, Sunny, Violet, Gloria—American cars have names such as Mustang, Cougar, and Thunderbird. The first sports car Nissan sent to the United States was named

**TABLE 2.1:** World's 25 Most Valuable Brands, 2009 (in U.S. billion $)

| RANK | BRAND | 2009 BRAND VALUE | COUNTRY OF OWNERSHIP |
|------|-------|------------------|----------------------|
| 1. | Coca-Cola | 68,734 | U.S. |
| 2. | IBM | 60,211 | U.S. |
| 3. | Microsoft | 56,647 | U.S. |
| 4. | General Electric | 47,777 | U.S. |
| 5. | Nokia | 34,864 | Finland |
| 6. | McDonald's | 32,275 | U.S. |
| 7. | Google | 31,980 | U.S. |
| 8. | Toyota | 31,330 | Japan |
| 9. | Intel | 30,636 | U.S. |
| 10. | Disney | 28,447 | U.S. |
| 11. | Hewlett-Packard | 24,096 | U.S. |
| 12. | Mercedes Benz | 23,867 | Germany |
| 13. | Gillette | 22,841 | U.S. |
| 14. | Cisco | 22,030 | U.S. |
| 15. | BMW | 21,671 | Germany |
| 16. | Louis Vuitton | 21,120 | France |
| 17. | Marlboro | 19,010 | U.S. |
| 18. | Honda | 17,803 | Japan |
| 19. | Samsung | 17,518 | S. Korea |
| 20. | Apple | 15,443 | U.S. |
| 21. | H&M | 15,375 | Sweden |
| 22. | American Express | 14,971 | U.S. |
| 23. | Pepsi | 13,706 | U.S. |
| 24. | Oracle | 13,699 | U.S. |
| 25. | Nescafé | 13,317 | Switzerland |

*Source: BusinessWeek (2009).*

the Datsun Fair Lady. Nissan's head of sales for the western United States was so convinced that such a name would not sell cars in this country that he replaced it with one using the company's internal name for the car, the 240Z. The auto went on to become a big seller for Nissan (Johnston 1988, 33).

Governmental restrictions may prohibit the use of a brand name. For example, in marketing Diet Coca-Cola to a number of European countries, the Coca-Cola company encountered restrictions regarding use of the word "diet." As shown in Figure 2.6, Coca-Cola solved the problem by changing the product name to Coca-Cola Light. However, packaging and graphics are standardized, so despite the name change, the product is quite familiar and reassuring to U.S. consumers travelling abroad.

Target audience preferences may also influence the brand name selected. The Coca-Cola Light name was also used for the Japanese market because Japanese consumers tend not to be overweight and do not like to admit they are dieting by purchasing products labeled as dietetic. Accompanying this new brand name was a shift in promotional strategy, which emphasized "figure maintenance" rather than "weight loss."

## BRAND PIRACY

A problem that many well-known brands face in foreign markets is brand piracy. There are three distinct forms of piracy: imitation, faking, and preemption. *Imitation* involves producing a virtually identical copy of an established brand. For instance, LaCoste, manufacturer of the popular jerseys with the alligator logo, must combat knockoffs of its product sold in numerous countries. *Faking* refers

**Figure 2.6:** Diet Coca-Cola renamed Coca-Cola Light for the European market—here an outdoor advertisement in Germany.

to identifying the fraudulent product with a symbol, logo, or brand name that is very similar to the famous brand. For example, preference for foreign brands in Vietnam has led to knockoffs such as Volgate toothpaste and Lix soap. Coca-Cola, which manufactures the soft drink Sprite, asked a South Korean court to ban the production and sale in South Korea of Sprint, which was introduced with a name, logo, and taste much like Sprite's. *Preemption* of brand names occurs in those countries where the law permits wholesale registration of brand names. In such countries a person may register, in his or her name, a large number of well-known brand names and then sell them either to those interested in counterfeiting or—better still—to the multinational when it is ready to move into that country. China, for example, maintains a first-to-file system that generally grants protection to the first party to file a mark. In attempting to set up business in China, a number of large multinational corporations such as Starbucks, Dell, and Disney discovered that third parties had already registered their marks (or at least Chinese-language translations of their marks), often in hopes of extracting exorbitant sums. Yet trademark law in China does recognize an owner's prior right to a mark in some cases. If an owner discovers that his or her trademark has been preemptively registered, the owner may file a request with the Trademark Review and Adjudication Board to have the mark cancelled, as long as the request is filed within five years of the registration date of the disputed mark. If the owner's mark qualifies as "well known" under Chinese law, the cancellation action is not subject to the five-year limitation. The "well known" determination focuses on the reputation of the mark in the Chinese market, its duration of use, and other factors. According to one report, more than 400 trademarks have been recognized as well known in China so far, including foreign brands such as McDonald's and Ferrari (Perlman and Timaru 2008).

According to the International Chamber of Commerce, approximately 7 percent of world trade is in counterfeit goods. Some 40 percent of the counterfeited brands are the same 25 names (Brand Papers 2006). Counterfeiting is costing the U.S. economy more than $250 billion a year. According to U.S. Customs and Border Protection, this translates into more than 750,000 lost jobs. However, it is not just multinational firms that bear the costs. Consider the following:

- Governments bear much of the financial cost through loss of tax revenues.
- Consumer health and safety are threatened, especially with the widespread counterfeit production of pharmaceuticals, as well as aircraft and motor parts.
- Research and innovation efforts are stymied.
- Recent intelligence from Interpol shows that piracy and counterfeiting are increasingly used to fund organized crime.
- Low priorities for intellectual property rights in a country have a direct negative impact on foreign direct investment and economic growth.
- Counterfeit products pose the biggest problem to economies in Africa (particularly in Morocco, Kenya, and South Africa), the Commonwealth of Independent States (Kazakhstan and Russia), and the majority of Eastern European and Asian countries (International Chamber of Commerce's Commission on Commercial Law and Practice 2005).

There appear to be several reasons why brand piracy is at epidemic levels today. First and foremost is the economy. London-based intellectual property firm Marks & Clerk found that 97 percent of senior brand officials in the United Kingdom fear that the recession will increase counterfeiting activity. Further, 80 percent of executives consider brands to be at greater risk because of a combination of the recession and e-commerce. These two forces acting in concert have made the counterfeiting problem particularly intractable. "In the current climate, low-priced fake goods will be of increased interest to consumers looking to make their money go further," says Marks & Clerk attorney and intellectual property expert Pamela Withers. "Add the Web as a limitless, unregulated vehicle to do that," Withers says, "and you've got a runaway train for counterfeits" (Klara 2009). Most upscale brands have little hope of foiling the sale of an item made in China and purchased by a customer in California from a Web site based in Estonia. Another contributing factor appears to be the fact that some brands are shifting some or all of their manufacturing to developing markets (in particular, China, where 81 percent of the world's counterfeit goods now originate, according to the Department of Homeland Security). When a brand entrusts its production to a factory in Asia, it obviously saves money. But it also furnishes the factory owner with all the know-how he needs to produce knockoffs. It's no wonder that many fake goods look so authentic; they are made in the same factory as the real ones—the so-called third shift. Some marketers have taken aggressive measures to confront the counterfeiting problem. Louis Vuitton, for example, conducted more than 7,600 anti-counterfeiting raids globally in 2007. The company's lawyers initiated more than 24,000 lawsuits, and its e-investigators successfully shut down more than 750 Web sites trading in fake Vuitton merchandise (Klara 2009). Others have chosen to focus their efforts on those who purchase counterfeit products, as it is ultimately consumer demand that drives counterfeiting. Swiss watches have also been hit hard by the counterfeiting plague. The Federation of Swiss Watches estimates that over 40 million fake Swiss watches are made each year (compared with exports of almost 26 million authentic Swiss watches in 2007) and that they generate net profits of around $1 billion. This illicit trade, whose main victims are the most prestigious Swiss brands, is equivalent to about 6 percent of total Swiss watch exports in 2007. FHS recently unveiled "Fake Watches Are for Fake People," a global campaign running in various media (see Figure 2.7 for a sample ad). While luxury goods have long been counterfeited, knockoffs are turning up in the most mundane product lines: Duracell batteries, Head & Shoulders shampoo, extension cords with the UL-tested safety seal—anything with a recognized brand (Orr 2007).

Many multinational marketers have high expectations for the passage of the Anti-Counterfeiting Trade Agreement (ACTA). In talks since 2006, ACTA

> aims to establish international standards for enforcing intellectual property rights among member nations—which include the U.S. and 27 member states of the European Union—including civil and criminal enforcement, border protection, and significantly, copyright infringement and the sale of counterfeit items on the Internet. The plurilateral agreement represents the best hope yet for a global policing of the counterfeit trade, but many hurdles remain. Though more countries have entered the talks since the 2006 preliminary session, one essential nation—China—is not among them. Nonetheless, ACTA is a start, and proponents are optimistic about its passing. (Klara 2009, 9)

## PACKAGING AND LABELING DECISIONS

*Packaging* refers to the design and production of product containers or wrappings. Packaging includes the immediate container (for example, the tube surrounding Crest toothpaste), a secondary package that is discarded after purchase (the cardboard box that a tube of Crest is sold in), and any packaging necessary to ship the product to retailers (such as a cardboard carton containing dozens of packages of Crest toothpaste). Labeling is also considered part of the packaging, and consists of printed information appearing on or along with the packaging.

Packaging has both protective and promotional aspects. In determining whether the same packaging can be used for foreign markets, marketers must consider a variety of marketplace conditions. Packaging must allow the product to reach its destination without damage. Markets with long, slow,

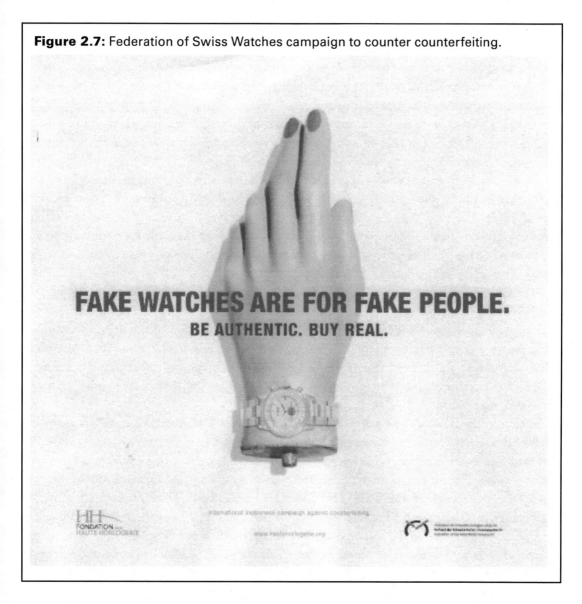

**Figure 2.7:** Federation of Swiss Watches campaign to counter counterfeiting.

or poor distribution channels may require sturdier packaging. Climatic extremes may necessitate packaging modifications. For example, Quaker Oats adopted special vacuum-sealed tins to protect its products in hot and humid climates. Consumption rates directly influence storage time and may vary from one market to the next.

Packaging is often determined by the income level of a market. Unilever attempted to reach consumers in emerging markets by both modifying its packaging and using less expensive formulations. Using a concept with the code name "Project Everyman," Unilever added new customers too poor to regularly buy standard versions of the company's detergent or shampoo. For example, in Brazil, Unilever's research revealed that many Brazilians could not afford washing machines or Unilever's Omo brand of detergent, which was way beyond their financial means. Instead, many poorer Brazilians purchased bars of soap to wash clothes in rivers and lakes. The lack of washing machines made a simpler soap formula an option. And, because many consumers washed their clothes in rivers, the powder was packaged in plastic instead of paper that would get soggy. The newly developed detergent, named Ala, was also produced locally to cut transportation costs, further lowering its price. Within three months of its launch, Ala had captured at least 15 percent of the test market. Developing and emerging markets account for about 40 percent of total Unilever sales (up from just 16 percent in 1985) (Byron 2007).

Lower per capita income usually translates into lower usage rates and smaller purchase amounts, and it might even suggest that products such as razor blades, chewing gum, and cigarettes be individually packaged, so that consumers with limited incomes can afford them. Coca-Cola, for example, began testing 200-milliliter bottles in several rural areas. Coke's standard bottle is 300 milliliters, and the lower price for the smaller bottle aimed to increase consumption.

Smaller sizes may also be more appropriate for countries where consumers shop daily or have smaller homes and thus fewer storage facilities. For example, superconcentrated versions of laundry detergents (Fab Ultra and Wisk Power Scoop) introduced into the U.S. marketplace have sold successfully for well over a decade in Europe and Japan, where space in both the supermarket and the home is at a premium. Larger packages are appropriate for markets where shopping is conducted on a weekly basis and storage space is ample.

The type of retail outlet in which the product is sold may further influence the packaging. Self-service retailing, which plays an increasingly important role in most developed countries, dictates that packaging perform a multitude of promotional functions as well—from attracting the consumer's attention, to describing product features, to making the ultimate sale. In markets with predominantly small retail outlets, with limited floor or shelf space, it may be appropriate to modify the packaging. In terms of legal restrictions, some countries do not allow the promotional tactics commonly employed in other markets.

Customer preferences, often shaped by culture, may influence whether packaging is persuasive to consumers in various markets. Utilizing the same or similar packaging employed in the home market may prove ineffective. It could be that a particular visual resonates well with consumers in one market but not another. For the introduction of cholesterol-lowering Benecol margarine, designers created a package that included a mountain scene to communicate cross-culturally that the product's key ingredient is natural. But designers left considerable room for differences in the product shot to accommodate local needs. For example, in the U.S. market the package for the spread featured an English muffin, as opposed to Europe, where rolls, which are more commonly consumed, were depicted (Asher 2001). Even the color of a product's packaging may prove problematic for a marketer. For example, while white connotes purity and cleanliness in many regions and cultures, in the Far East it is also associated with mourning. Likewise, red is a positive color in Denmark as well as many Asian countries, but it represents witchcraft and death in a number of African nations. Using the colors of the national flag may be perceived as patriotic in some countries, yet disallowed in others.

In many countries—both developing and developed—the usefulness of the packaging plays a greater role. Often the package will be kept and reused as a container. Lego, the Danish toy manufacturer, employed a standardized marketing philosophy in over 100 countries to sell its building blocks. In recent years, however, Lego has encountered stiff competition from look-alike and lower-priced rival products from Japan, the United States, and elsewhere. The *Harvard Business Review* describes Lego's dilemma—and its response:

> In the United States, where the competition has been the fiercest, Tyco, a leading competitor, began putting its toys in plastic buckets that could be used for storage after each play. This utilitarian approach contrasted with Lego's elegant see-through cartons standardized worldwide. But American parents seemed to prefer the functional toys-in-a-bucket idea over cartons. Seeing a potential for serious damage, Lego's alarmed U.S. management sought permission from Denmark to package Lego toys in buckets. The head office flatly refused the request. The denial was

based on seemingly sound arguments. The bucket idea could cheapen Lego's reputation for high quality. Moreover, the Lego bucket would rightly be seen as a "me too" defensive reaction from a renowned innovator. Finally, and perhaps most important, buckets would be a radical deviation from the company's policy of standardized marketing everywhere. Even U.S. consumer survey results comparing buckets favorably with cartons weren't considered a good enough reason for change from the global concept. Two years later, however, headquarters in Billund reversed itself. The impetus was a massive loss of U.S. market share to competitive goods sold in buckets. Soon after, the American subsidiary began marketing some of its toys in a newly designed bucket of its own. Now to the delight of many in Billund, the buckets are outselling the cartons, and the share erosion has reassuringly halted. The bucket was introduced worldwide and became a smashing success. (Kashani 1989, 91)

Ecological concerns are an additional variable that must be considered in evaluating product packaging. In some countries certain forms of packaging are either banned or not condoned by consumers, or else there is a market preference for specific packaging materials, such as glass instead of aluminum or tin, or paper rather than plastic. In Denmark, for instance, soft drinks may be sold only in glass bottles with refundable deposits, and in the United States consumers' criticism of styrofoam packaging used by fast food outlets led to burgers and sandwiches wrapped in foil. Virtually all deodorant manufacturers have done away with the secondary cardboard packaging to cut down on unnecessary packaging material. Consumers in many foreign markets are not accustomed to the elaborate packaging so common in the United States, considering it quite wasteful. For example, 80 percent of British consumers say it is important that the brands they buy are committed to acting in a way that can be considered socially aware or environmentally responsible. More than three-quarters of Brits say minimal packaging, as well as packaging that is biodegradable or recycled, is an important consideration in terms of the brands they buy (Ridgley 2008). Indeed, in many countries shoppers bring their canvas or string totes to the grocery store in order to carry home purchases. Carrefour, the first supermarket in Spain to join the green movement, has introduced a campaign that equates plastic bags to excrement. The concept is straightforward, simple, and easy to remember: "Plastic bags = shit." The campaign, created by Publicis Madrid, informed consumers that "Plastic bags take 400 years to decompose. Shit = bags. 400 years. 400 shits. We must do something." The supermarket also suggested replacing plastic bags with a different kind of material, such as raffia, cotton, or biodegradable starching. "Carrefour is heading down a path that will soon become the only choice for stores and supermarkets. In 2008, the Spanish government approved the Plan Nacional Integrade de Residuos, or National Integrated Plan of Waste Materials, a set of rules aimed at restricting and eventually banning the use of plastic bags by 2015. Spain is the third-largest consumer of plastic bags in Europe. Spaniards use an average of 238 bags per year and supermarkets are a big provider" (Vescovi and Rocca 2009). In France, reusable plastic bags now account for more than half of the market. Taiwan has banned plastic bags, and a threat of fines of up to $300 has resulted in a 70 percent reduction in their use and a 25 percent cut in landfill waste. Interestingly, Bangladesh was the first country to ban plastic bags. A movement against them began in the 1980s in Dhaka, where bags clogged drains in the monsoon rains, causing flooding (Ridgley 2008). In just the past few years, an increasing number of American retailers have joined the trend and begun selling reusable shopping bags. San Francisco was the first city in the United States to ban plastic bags altogether.

Government regulations may affect labeling with regard to a product's origin, name of the producer, weight, description of contents and ingredients, use of additives and preservatives, and dietetic information. Twice a year, the European Union issues "Designation of Origin" labels. To qualify, products must come from a specific geographic region. For example, only cows that graze within 75 miles of Parma can provide the raw materials for "real" Parmesan cheese. Bresse chickens must come from France's Bresse region, and Jamon Serrano (ham) can only be cured in Spain's Serrano. Supporters argue that the labels safeguard against fraud, such as when the Dutch sell grated Gouda cheese as Parmesan. In addition, the labels also allow small-scale "artisan" producers to stay in business. "We want to protect traditional foods against imitators," noted Martine Poudelet, the European Union's food label director (Echikson 1998). To enforce the laws, the government created a division of the Ministry of Agriculture called the Institut National d'Appellations d'Origine (INAO).

The EU is working on the creation of a global register of geographically defined products that would ban producers from outside the traditional regions from using these names. A particularly bitter trademark problem involved the United States. "Americans can call any fizzy white wine 'Champagne,' any white wine 'Chablis,' and any red wine 'Burgundy.' They must stop or we'll take legal action," noted Poudelet. The threats were serious. Major U.S. food and wine producers countered that the changes were unreasonable and didn't come with reciprocal promises to protect U.S. designations, such as Idaho potatoes (Locke 2003). The EU, however, is not alone in its attempts at protecting regionally produced goods. India is keen to protect Darjeeling tea, Sri Lanka its Ceylon tea, Guatemala its Antigua coffee, and Australia its wines. In the United States, some fresh produce has used origin labeling as advertising for a number of years—for example, Vidalia onions from Georgia and orange juice from Florida. In 2002, a Country of Origin Labeling (COOL) law mandated that retailers were required to notify customers of the country of origin (including the United States) of raw beef, veal, lamb, pork, chicken, goat, wild and farm-raised fish and shellfish, fresh and frozen fruits and vegetables, peanuts, pecans, and macadamia nuts. But lobbying by the grocery stores and large meatpackers led Congress to delay the U.S. Department of Agriculture's implementation of it. Seafood labeling was phased in first in 2005, and the other categories followed in 2008. The new guidelines allow those who want to buy local (or who prefer, say, Chilean grapes and New Zealand lamb) to more easily exercise their purchasing power. However, the real benefit is that it provides a more comprehensive system for tracing food items during outbreaks. So, for example, the next time tomatoes are suspected of food poisoning, consumers may be able to tell investigators they bought only ones grown in a certain region, thereby speeding the probe (Neergaard 2008).

Regardless of governmental restrictions, the label must be written in a language that local consumers will understand—and this typically means different labels for different markets. Marketers may attempt to get around this by printing multilingual labels. Many companies are trying to maximize profits by selling the same product in the same package in as many different countries as they can. Product information on a package of Procter & Gamble's (P&G) Ariel Futur laundry detergent, sold across the European continent, now appears in 10 languages, with English at the bottom of the list. As a result, it takes 10 times as many words to convey information to consumers. However, a package of P&G's Pampers diapers contains information in up to 20 languages, ranging from Hungarian to Hebrew. P&G has tried to ease the pressure on space by substituting pictograms for some of the information (Tomkins 2000). In some instances, bilinguality is legally mandated. For instance, products destined for Canada must carry product information in both English and French.

Differing levels of literacy may necessitate greater use of visuals rather than extensive copy. This commonplace practice proved to be quite perplexing for one major marketer. As David Ricks explains, the firm attempted to sell baby food to the indigenous peoples of one developing country by using its regular label showing a baby and stating the type of baby food in the jar. "Unfortunately, the local population took one look at the labels and interpreted them to mean the jars contained ground-up babies. Sales, of course, were terrible" (Ricks 1983, 34).

# PLACE

Once foreign markets have been selected, the international marketer must determine the appropriate channels of distribution. These channels essentially connect the producer of the goods with the end consumer. Firms operating internationally must determine appropriate channels between nations—commonly called market entry channels—which involve movement of the product to the borders of foreign countries, as well as channels within nations—those that move the product from the foreign entry point to the final consumer. Channels between nations include indirect export, direct export, and manufacture abroad (which includes licensing, franchising, management contracting, foreign assembly, joint ventures, and direct investment). Channels within nations involve decisions regarding wholesalers and retailers.

## Channels between Nations: Indirect Export

Exporting is the most common as well as the simplest means of foreign market entry. Firms lacking the resources to build or acquire factories abroad can penetrate foreign markets through this method, in which all goods are produced in the home market, and the international marketer may or may not choose to modify the product for consumers abroad. In indirect export the firm works with independent international marketing middlemen who are responsible for the distribution process. Because a wide variety of middlemen providing these services exists, only the most common methods of indirect exporting will be discussed.

Firms unwilling or unable to establish their own export departments may opt to enter foreign markets with the assistance of domestic sales organizations, better known as *export management companies* (EMCs). EMCs produce no goods of their own; instead they act as export departments for several manufacturers of unrelated products. They may operate in one of two ways: (1) functioning as a distributor for the manufacturer or (2) serving as an agent of the domestic firm. As a distributor the EMC actually purchases products (takes title) from the domestic firm and then operates abroad on its own behalf. In an agency capacity the EMC's role is limited to establishing foreign contacts and developing foreign marketing strategies. As a distributor the EMC assumes greater risk but also has the opportunity to reap greater profits than it does acting as an agent. Because EMCs service a variety of clients, their mode of operation may vary from one domestic client to the next. Payment for services is made through commission, salary, or retainer plus commission. EMCs often specialize in a particular geographic area, enabling them to offer expertise to domestic corporations.

Firms planning to conduct business abroad may also deal with *international trading companies*, which buy, sell, transport, and distribute goods. They may also provide financing, assist in the development of joint ventures, provide technical assistance, and even produce goods. They are typically the major suppliers of goods to the markets they serve. Trading companies hail from a number of different countries, including Japan, the United States, and even the CIS. Some of these trading companies were designed primarily for export, while others were originally developed to supply import services. Among the most famous export trading companies are the *sogo shosha* of Japan. Contrary to what most Americans believe, these firms actually import more into Japan from the United States than they export from Japan to the United States. Mitsui and Mitsubishi alone account for well over half of all Japan's imports. Some trading companies are region-specific, handling commodities produced in only one geographic area. Others are product-specific, handling only a limited variety of goods. Still others are industry-oriented, handling only goods specific to a particular industry, such as pharmaceuticals or chemicals.

There are certain advantages associated with utilizing the services of independent middlemen. A firm commits neither time nor money to set up an overseas sales force, and it can rely on the established contacts and marketing know-how of the middlemen operating within foreign markets. And because the indirect approach involves a good deal less investment on the part of the exporting company, it faces considerably less risk. On the downside, the exporter typically has little or no control over the distribution process. Should a product more profitable to the marketing middleman come along, the manufacturer's product may simply be dropped. Also, should sales in a market expand significantly, the exporting firm may find itself without the services of an EMC.

## Channels between Nations: Direct Export

In contrast to indirect export, when a firm engages in direct export it does so without the assistance of intermediaries. The manufacturer is responsible for conducting any necessary market research; identifying, evaluating, and selecting foreign markets as well as agents or distributors to represent the firm in those markets; setting product prices; handling international shipping and insurance and preparing export documentation; and coordinating international promotional activities. While both the investment and the risk involved in direct export are greater, the marketer also has more control over the distribution process, which typically results in increased sales and higher profits. For example, bottlers of Equil, Indonesia's only natural mineral water, export their product to Singapore and even Australia. The water is bottled at the source from a spring at the foot of a West Java mountain. Marketed in both sparkling and still varieties, the water is claimed to be free of contaminants and undergoes no processing. The product is said to have particular appeal among expatriates.

## Channels between Nations: Manufacture Abroad

A variety of circumstances may prevent the international marketer from engaging in direct export. For example, tariffs or quotas may prevent a firm from selling its products in specific countries, or transportation costs may make products noncompetitive. Positive factors may also encourage a firm to produce its goods abroad. For instance, the size of some markets may justify setting up a plant in a foreign country, or local manufacture may allow the marketer to better respond to local market needs, or manufacturing costs may be lower in foreign markets. Foreign production can take the form of licensing, management contracting, foreign assembly, contract manufacturing, joint ownership, and direct investment.

*Licensing:* One method of market entry is licensing, in which a company offers a licensee in the foreign market rights to a trademark or patent, the use of a manufacturing process, technical advice, or marketing skills. In exchange for the rights or know-how provided by the licensor, the licensee produces and markets the product and pays the licensor a fee or royalty, typically related to the sales volume of the product. Franchising is a particular type of licensing agreement in which the franchisee typically operates under the name of the franchisor, who provides the franchisee with not only trademarks and know-how but also management and financial assistance. Table 2.2 lists the world's top 20 franchises.

Matthew Shay, president of the International Franchise Association, notes: "From a business perspective, the most important consideration is finding a partner who understands the culture, the customs and the consumer" (Gibson 2006). In late 2009, with some 31,800 locations around the globe, Subway is racing to match the 32,158 total restaurants of McDonald's (York 2009a). And Subway is just starting to get aggressive in its international development. "You pick some good ones, you pick some that aren't so good," Patricia Demarais, director of international operations for Subway, says of the company's experience in finding partners in more than 80 countries. Trusting a surrogate becomes vital because, she notes, "we're very much into delegating decisions. But, while we want them to be really aggressive and believe in the brand, we don't want them to reinvent it" (Gibson 2006). To establish its fast food chain in India, Subway relied on two Indian brothers who has been educated in the United States. Manpreet and Gurpreet Gulri were responsible for finding franchisees and helping them open stores while overseeing the brand's operations across India. To date, the Gulris have signed up 35 franchisees who operate a total of 60 restaurants in major cities (see Figure 2.8 for a Subway located in Hyderabad, India). Although Manpreet Gulri was experienced in Indian commerce, it nonetheless took two years of negotiating to win the necessary approvals to open India's first Subway outlet. Obtaining supplies proved a challenge as well—in particular finding flour suitable for making sandwich bread. The quality of the flour in India apparently was not on a par with the flour in the West. The Gulris also encountered a problem that Subway franchisees in other markets were unlikely to face: Indians are not a bread-eating community. So the two brothers had to continuously educate prospective customers

**TABLE 2.2:** Top 20 Global Franchises

| RANK | FRANCHISE |
|------|-----------|
| 1. | Subway  (Submarine sandwiches & salads) |
| 2. | McDonald's (Hamburgers, chicken, salads) |
| 3. | Liberty Tax Service (Income tax preparation) |
| 4. | Sonic Drive-in Restaurants (Drive-in restaurant) |
| 5. | InterContinental Hotels Group (hotels) |
| 6. | Ace Hardware Corp.  (Hardware & home improvement store) |
| 7. | Pizza Hut (pizza, pasta, wings) |
| 8. | UPS Store, The/Mail Boxes Etc. (Postal, business & communication services) |
| 9. | Circle K (Convenience store) |
| 10. | Papa John's Int'l. Inc. (Pizza) |
| 11. | Jiffy Lube Int'l. Inc. (Fast oil change) |
| 12. | Baskin-Robbins USA Co. (Ice cream, frozen yogurt) |
| 13. | KFC Corp. (Chicken) |
| 14. | Jani-King (Commercial cleaning) |
| 15. | Dairy Queen (Soft-serve dairy products and sandwiches) |
| 16. | Super 8 Worldwide (Hotels) |
| 17. | Arby's (Sandwiches, chicken, salads) |
| 18. | Jan-Pro Franchising Int'l. Inc. (Commercial cleaning) |
| 19. | Taco Bell Corp. (Quick-service Mexican restaurant) |
| 20. | Hampton Inn/Hampton Inn & Suites (Mid-price hotels) |

*Source: Entrepreneur Magazine* (2009).

on the merits of their products. And, to win over the vegetarian multitudes, five meatless sandwiches were introduced (Gibson 2006). The Gulri brothers' understanding of the Indian has proven invaluable in breaking into this marketplace.

A number of advantages are associated with licensing. It offers a quick and easy means of entry into foreign markets. It requires neither capital investment nor an in-depth understanding of the foreign market. In some instances licensing permits entry into markets that might otherwise be closed to imports or direct foreign investments. It can negate high transportation costs, which may make exports noncompetitive. Finally, it offers an alternate means to enter markets with high duty rates or import quotas. For many firms, licensing serves as an intermediate step on the road toward internationalization by providing a means to test foreign markets without an actual outlay of capital or management time.

However, licensing also entails potential disadvantages. The manufacturer has little control over the licensee or its production, distribution, or marketing of the product. From a revenue standpoint, licensing is unlikely to be as profitable as the returns that could be generated from a firm's own operations, as license fees are typically only a small percentage of sales—generally 3–5 percent. Licensing in no way guarantees a basis for future expansion into a market. In fact, when a licensing agreement expires, a firm may find it has created a competitor not only in the markets for which agreements were made but possibly in other markets as well. Firms intending to engage in licensing agreements also need to be aware that licensing regulations vary dramatically from country to country. Finally, there

**Figure 2.8:** Subway located in Hyderabad, India. Outside Asia, bread and toppings is an almost universal food.

may be variations in restrictions regarding registration requirements, royalty and fee payments, and applicable taxes.

*Management Contracting:* A firm may choose to enter a foreign market through management contracting. Here the domestic firm supplies the management know-how to a foreign firm willing to invest the capital. The domestic firm is compensated through management fees, a share of the profits, and sometimes the option to buy some share in the managed firm at a later date. Management contracting is a low-risk means of market entry that requires no capital investment, capitalizes on the domestic firm's management skills, and assures a quick return. Here, the local investor has a greater say in how the investment is managed. Profits, however, are not likely to be as great as if the firm were to undertake the entire venture. Management contracting is most commonly used in the following sectors: public utilities, tourism (hotels, for example), and agriculture in developing countries.

*Foreign Assembly:* In foreign assembly, a firm produces all or most of the product's components or ingredients domestically and then ships them to foreign markets for final assembly. Many products may be more easily shipped broken down, and transportation costs may also be lower as a result. In some instances tariffs prevent a firm from shipping a fully assembled product. By forcing assembly in the local markets, foreign governments increase local employment.

*Contract Manufacturing:* Another option is contract manufacturing, which involves the actual production of a firm's product in a foreign market by another producer. Typically, the company placing the contract retains full control over both distribution and marketing of the goods. Benefits associated with contract manufacturing include limited local investment, potentially cheaper local labor, and the positive image associated with being locally produced. A marketer may also manufacture goods in one foreign country to be sold in another. Consider the case of Hennes & Mauritz (H&M), the Swedish retailer. H&M began its international expansion in 1976, the year it opened its store in London. By 2009, H&M boasted 1,840 stores in 27 countries, 175 of which are located in the United States. Even more stores are planned. Karl-Johan Persson, the retail chain's new chief executive, notes that H&M will focus most of its near-term expansion on the United States, United Kingdom, Germany, France, Spain, China, and Japan. It is the world's third-largest fashion chain by revenue, behind U.S.-based Gap Inc. and Spain's Inditex SA (Kinnander 2009). The stores are geared toward young, fashion-conscious females. H&M's formula for success is that it keeps its fashions fresh and affordable. H&M generates "buzz" and drives shoppers into its stores through tie-ins with big-name designers and celebrities. Britain's Matthew Williamson, who has dressed such celebrities as Keira Knightley and Gwyneth Paltrow, designed the summer 2009 collection. Previous collaborators included Rei Kawakubo (of Comme des Garçons fame), Roberto Cavalli, Stella McCartney, and Karl Lagerfeld (see Figure 2.9 for an H&M ad running in Spain). All merchandise is designed in-house. To keep costs down, the company outsources manufacturing to a network of 900 garment shops located in 21 mostly low-wage countries, primarily Bangladesh, China, and Turkey. H&M constantly shifts production to ensure that it gets the best deals on manufacturing (Capel and Khermouch 2002, 106). On the downside, it may prove difficult in some cases to locate a foreign firm that has the capability of manufacturing the product to the domestic firm's specifications. Extensive technical training of the subcontractor may be necessary, and even then, the firm has limited control over product quality. Here, too, at the end of a contract, the subcontractor may become a competitor. Types of products generally involved in such arrangements include electronics, textiles, and clothing.

*Joint Ownership:* When two or more firms in different countries join forces to create a local business in which they share ownership and control of management, manufacturing, and marketing, they have joint ownership. An international firm may purchase interest in a foreign company, or the two parties may form an entirely new business venture. In some joint ventures each partner holds an equal share; in others, one partner holds the majority share. Equity can range anywhere between 10 and 90 percent.

Joint ownership offers the potential for greater profits, as compared to contract manufacturing or licensing, and may also afford the international marketer greater control over production, distribution, and marketing activities. The national partner in a joint venture can offer the international marketer valuable knowledge about the local marketplace. The joint venture may also lead to better relationships with local organizations—government, local authorities, or labor unions. Finally, it may be the preferred option if 100 percent foreign equity ownership is not permitted by foreign governments. Mexico and India have traditionally been particularly restrictive about foreign firms owning more than 50 percent of any venture in their countries. In instances where political or other uncertainties call for some limitation of investment risks, joint ventures may be an appropriate entry method.

Ford provides an excellent example. In late 2009, Ford Motor Co. began building a new plant in China's southwestern city of Chongquing, primarily to produce the next-generation Focus car. Covering about 100 hectares with a total investment of $490 million, the plant is being built jointly by the Changan Ford Mazda Automobile Co. Ltd., a joint venture of Ford; the Chongqing-based Chana Auto Co., Ltd.; and Japan's Mazda Motor Corp. The plant, the second in Chongqing and third in China, will have an annual output of 150,000 cars after completion in 2012. "China is one of Ford's most important markets in the world and also the fastest growing market," noted Ford's CEO Allan Mulally at the foundation stone-laying ceremony of the new Ford plant. Notes Xu Liuping, board chairman of Changan, "I believe that with concerted efforts from all sides, Chanan Ford Mazda cars will win consumers' favour with excellent products and services, and the joint venture will become a model for China's auto market" (BBC Monitoring Asia Pacific 2009). The new plant is part of a broader effort to overcome Ford's late start in China and to catch up with key competitors in China—Volkswagen AG, General Motors Co., Hyndai Motor Co., and Toyota Motor Corp., the top-four car concerns in China's fast-growing auto market.

Certain drawbacks are associated with joint ownership. When compared with contract manufacturing or licensing, there is a greater investment of capital and management resources, as well as an increased level of risk. And, as with any partnership, the potential for conflict of interest always exists. The two parties may disagree about any or all of the marketing mix elements, as well as management style, research and development, personnel requirements, and the accumulation and distribution of profits. What is good for the national firms may not always be beneficial to the international company, and vice versa.

*Direct Investment:* The greatest commitment a firm can make to a foreign market is direct investment, which involves entering a foreign market by developing foreign-based manufacturing facilities. The international firm has the option of obtaining foreign production facilities by acquiring an existing foreign producer or by establishing its own facilities. Acquisition is typically a quicker way for a firm to move into a new market, and it also offers the firm benefits such as built-in political know-how and expertise. For example, when Procter & Gamble first entered the Japanese market by absorbing a soap company, it also acquired a well-trained Japanese sales staff. Because it had, in fact, saved the Japanese firm from bankruptcy, P&G immediately established good relations with not only the staff but also the Japanese government. However, establishing a new facility may be preferable if the international firm

**Figure 2.9:** Advertisement for H&M featuring Karl Lagerfeld appearing in the Spanish-language edition of *Cosmopolitan.*

is unable to find a national company willing to sell, or if the national government prohibits the sale of domestic companies. Establishing a new facility also allows the international firm to incorporate the most up-to-date technology and equipment.

Regardless of how acquired, foreign production facilities offer numerous advantages. Complete ownership means that 100 percent of the profits goes directly to the international firm. The firm keeps full control over its investment, and there is no possibility for conflict with a national partner. Foreign direct investment also allows corporations to sidestep trade barriers or tariffs and operate abroad as a domestic firm. Nationalism may also lead foreign customers to prefer locally produced goods and services. And, while some governments limit foreign investments, others actually offer incentives to international firms. For example, many governments are under increasing pressure to provide jobs for their citizens. As compared to direct or indirect exporting, the international firm may benefit from lower costs or increased availability in terms of natural or human resources. Mineral or agricultural resources may be more available in some foreign markets, and/or their costs may be lower than they are domestically. Similarly, a skilled work force may be more readily available and/or less costly.

The major disadvantage associated with direct investment is that it requires substantial investment in terms of capital and management resources. This factor typically prevents smaller firms from engaging in this mode of market entry. The international firm also faces increased risks, such as devalued currencies or even expropriation, which is more likely to happen to wholly owned firms. The international environment is growing increasingly hostile toward full ownership by multinational companies. A major concern is equitable profit repatriation. Therefore, many governments insist that foreign firms engage in licensing or even joint ventures as a means of sharing in the profits obtained in the local market.

## Channels within Nations: Distribution to Consumers

The particular market entry strategy a firm selects will impact its decisions about distribution channels within nations. On the one hand, firms that make their products available in foreign markets via indirect exporting and some forms of direct exporting must rely on the distribution channels selected by their intermediaries. Firms engaging in joint ventures or direct investments, on the other hand, will be responsible for evaluating and selecting from among the available channels of distribution within those nations. The specific distribution channels a firm selects within a particular country will impact many of the other marketing elements. For example, product prices will need to reflect markups allowed to middlemen; where and how the product is available to the end user will impact promotional tactics. Channel decisions also involve long-term commitments to foreign organizations that are often difficult to change.

In some instances the international marketer will be faced with distribution channels that are a good deal more complex than those in the home market. For example, a U.S. company marketing in Japan will need to deal with a frustrating maze of middlemen. Larry Rosenberg explains that, historically, Japan has been a country of numerous small retailers, typically located in residential areas and near train stations where local people could shop daily for food and other necessities. Dependency relationships developed between consumers and retailers, and patronage was rewarded by guarantees of a constant supply of high-quality products and good service. Each retailer obtained goods from a long chain of middlemen, who in turn assured retailers of personalized service in exchange for continued patronage. Thus, dependency relationships developed along the entire chain from producer to consumer. The number of wholesalers and retailers is five times greater than in the United States. The sheer number of middlemen, in addition to the dependency relationships that have developed among them, makes it very difficult for foreigners to distribute goods in Japan (Rosenberg 1980, 47).

At the other extreme, an international marketer operating in a less developed country may well find that channels taken for granted in the home market simply do not exist. Or channels may have already been contracted on an exclusive basis to competitors. Under such circumstances the foreign investor may choose to lure away distributors by offering extra-high margins or other financial incentives. Other options include buying out local distributors or even building up parallel distribution channels from scratch. Finally, an international marketer may be forced to develop original methods of distribution.

Within-country channels of distribution—both wholesaling and retailing—vary greatly from one market to the next. These channels have typically evolved over many years and reflect differences not only in economic development but in culture as well. Each country poses a unique situation, and no general rules can be applied. The international marketer must carefully analyze the established distribution systems in order to uncover differences in the number, size, and types of middlemen, as well as the services they provide.

## Channels within Nations: Wholesaling Abroad

Wholesaling patterns are typically reflective of the cultures and economies in which they operate. As a general rule, industrialized countries have many large-scale wholesaling organizations serving a large number of retailers. In contrast, in developing countries wholesaling is likely to be far more fragmented—smaller firms with fewer employees serving a limited number of retailers.

The spectrum of services offered by wholesalers typically relates to the size of their operations: the larger the wholesaler, the greater the variety of services it can provide. Larger wholesalers also generally have larger staffs available to assist the international firm. If it is necessary to utilize the services of a smaller wholesaler, this typically translates into greater responsibility for the international firm. Smaller wholesalers tend to carry less inventory, are less likely to provide adequate promotional efforts, and offer more limited geographic coverage than their larger counterparts.

## Channels within Nations: Retailing Abroad

Differences in retailing from one international market to the next are at least as extensive as those in wholesaling. Here, too, the international marketer must carefully analyze each country to assess retailing opportunities as well as constraints. As with wholesaling, there is great variation in the number and size of retail operations in foreign markets and in the services they provide. Overall, the more developed the country, the more likely it is to have larger retail outlets. For example, supermarkets and department stores are the norm in the United States, while hyper-markets—huge facilities stocked with thousands of products—are popular in many European countries. Up to seven acres in size, hypermarkets sell everything from groceries to auto supplies to refrigerators. Carrefour, a French retailer that once had plans to open ten such hypermarkets in the United States, closed a number of locations in the early 1990s (Denitto 1993). Wal-Mart has also experimented with them, finding greater success. By the end of 2009, the company was operating 2,612 such "Supercenters." Wal-Mart's Supercenters average about 187,000 square feet in size (though some are upward of 230,000 square feet). However, Supercenters are just too large for some U.S. consumers. In response to weary shoppers who complained that the size of such stores made it too difficult to run in and grab just one item, Wal-Mart built 49 "neighborhood markets"—grocery and general merchandise outlets covering a mere 39,000 square feet. Neighborhood markets are quick-stop stores with additional checkouts and nearby parking. Other retailers, including Home Depot and Staples, are also following suit. Another reason retailers are scaling down the size of their stores in the United States is that the number of good locations in which to position oversize outlets is disappearing in many major markets. Also, in some areas there may not be a large enough customer base to support the superstore concept (Green 2003).

Typically, the number of retail outlets per capita in developed countries is limited. However, even here there is variation. The United States and Germany both have approximately 6 shops per 1,000 people, while France has about 11 and Japan has 13. Developing countries have a much larger number of overall outlets, but these tend to be significantly smaller in size. In emerging markets, Procter & Gamble estimates that 80 percent of people buy their wares from mom-and-pop stores no bigger than a closet. Crammed with food and a hodgepodge of household items, these retailers serve as the pantries of the world's poorest consumers, for whom both money and space are tight. P&G calls such locally owned bodegas, stalls, and kiosks "high-frequency stores" because of the multiple times shoppers visit them during a single day or week. It is estimated there are about 20 million high-frequency stores worldwide (Byron 2007). Table 2.3 shows some sample data on the number of retail outlets in both developed and developing markets. These numbers demonstrate the significant variation in retailing from market to market.

In most developed countries, international firms can expect to receive the following services from retailers: stocking the product, displaying and promoting the merchandise, extending credit to customers, providing service, and gathering market information. Because retail outlets are significantly smaller in developing countries, they typically carry very limited inventories. This may mean that the international firm cannot sell its full range of products, that adequate display of products may be a challenge, and that the use of point-of-purchase displays will be limited. The smaller the retailer, the less likely it is to be able to offer customers credit or to service the product.

An ever-increasing number of retailers are operating at an international level. Although Woolworth's and Sears are considered the "old-timers" of international retailing, in recent years Wal-Mart, Home Depot, Safeway, Target, and others have also ventured overseas. Table 2.4 lists the world's top 25 retailers, ranked by sales.

As of 2009, Wal-Mart was the largest retailer in the world. Wal-Mart operates 7,873 stores around the globe, with more than 3,000 of them outside the United States, where the company has increased its presence at an average annual rate of 30 percent between 2005 and 2008. Indeed, the company's Web site boasts that Wal-Mart serves more than 49 million international customers weekly. Wal-Mart

**TABLE 2.3:** Total Number of Retail Outlets in Developed and Developing Markets, 2000

| DEVELOPED MARKETS | NO. OF MARKETS | DEVELOPING MARKETS | NO. OF MARKETS |
|---|---|---|---|
| Canada | 104,844 | Brazil | 1,595,062 |
| France | 369,609 | China | 19,306,801 |
| Germany | 419,229 | Egypt | 509,366 |
| Japan | 1,240,237 | India | 10,537,079 |
| United Kingdom | 311,844 | Mexico | 737,895 |
| United States | 685,367 | Vietnam | 727,269 |

*Source: Euromonitor* (2002a); and *Euromonitor* (2002b).

operates international locations of its Wal-Mart and Sam's Club stores, as well as other retail stores and supermarkets. Of its 3,121 international locations, 7 percent are in China, 9 percent in Canada, 10 percent in the United Kingdom, 10 percent in Japan, 15 percent in Central America, 16 percent in South America, and 33 percent in Mexico. In 1997, international sales represented just 5 percent of Wal-Mart's revenue, but within a decade that figure had increased to 22 percent (Dunn 2007). In 2009, Wal-Mart's international locations generated $98.6 billion in revenue, a 9.1 percent increase over 2008. As the company begins to slow its square-footage growth in the United States, it is expected to turn to its international locations to continue its growth. Indeed, Wal-Mart plans to add 550 to 600 new international stores in 2010.

In its most recent expansion efforts, Wal-Mart has moved into India. Under Indian rules governing foreign retailers, Wal-Mart and its joint-venture partner, Bharti Enterprises Ltd., cannot sell directly to consumers but will instead operate a cash-and-carry business selling 10,000 products to licensed store owners, schools, hospitals, hotels, and other institutions. Wal-Mart's efforts are targeted at a retail industry worth more than $350 billion a year, and made up almost entirely of small merchants. The more than 10 million tiny retailers in India are both the company's greatest challenge and opportunity. If Wal-Mart is successful in winning them over, they are likely to become the retailer's biggest customers. Though the government welcomes the investment and the jobs it will create, there is also concern about the effect Wal-Mart will have on small merchants, an issue that accompanied the firm as it expanded in the United States as well (Bellman 2009).

Foreign retailers are also exploring U.S. soil, as U.S. consumer familiarity with brands like Benneton, Laura Ashley, and Ikea indicates. European grocery chains are also conquering the United States. France's Carrefour and the United Kingdom's Tesco have both set up shop on American soil, as has Germany's Aldi, dubbed "the next Wal-Mart." Much like the Arkansas-based giant, Aldi boasts awesome margins, huge market clout, and seemingly unstoppable growth, including an estimated sales increase of 8 percent a year since 1998. It focuses relentlessly on efficiency, matching—or even beating—Wal-Mart stores in its ability to strip out costs (*BusinessWeek* 2004). Aldi opened its first U.S. store in Iowa in 1976, and by 2008, the nearly 1,000 stores in 28 states boasted sales of $7 billion (Rohwedder and Kesmodel 2009). In comparison, Wal-Mart has nearly $375 billion in U.S. sales. A typical Aldi has only about 1,300 different items, compared with more than 50,000 at a typical supermarket, or the more than 150,000 at a Wal-Mart Supercenter. Aldi stores average 10,000 square feet, much smaller than the 50,000 to 60,000 square feet of a standard, full-service supermarket (see Figure 2.10 for a typical Aldi store). The grocer is aggressive in driving down prices on branded consumer packaged goods through strongly negotiated deals with manufacturers. More important, it has created a wide range of store-brand products that keep the price of the average shopping basket down. While store-brand goods generally make up 22 percent of U.S. food sales in terms of unit volume at Aldi, 95 percent of the goods are the retailer's own brands, according to research by Nielsen Co. It purchases in bulk from suppliers and commissions them to make its own store brand of groceries cheaper than that of rivals. In the Midwest, for example, its prices are between 15 and 20 percent less than Wal-Mart and 30 to 40 percent less than regional grocery store chains (Rohwedder and Kesmodel 2009). The limited selection simplifies shipping and handling.

Aldi designs its stores to run lean. A typical store has five to ten employees and can open with as few as two people and up to a maximum of five working at one time. Shoppers who want to use a cart at Aldi must pay 25 cents to pull one from the storage rack, although they get their money back when they return the cart to the rack. There are no carts left in the parking lot, so the store doesn't have to pay staffers to round them up and bring them back. Aldi's longstanding policy on shopping bags is similarly frugal: bring your own or pay for one at the checkout. Finally, Aldi won't take checks or credit cards, a practice that also holds down expenses. Customers pay in cash or with debit cards (Hajewski 2008). Trader Joe's Co., a specialty grocer owned by a family trust that Aldi co-founder Theo Albrecht created for his sons, has become the hottest thing in U.S. retailing by extending the Aldi concept to upscale products like grappa and goat cheese.

## Distribution Standardization versus Specialization

An international marketer will need to determine whether factors favor the utilization of uniform distribution patterns in foreign markets or whether a more specialized approach will be more profitable. A standardized approach may offer certain economies of scale. For example, if markets are sufficiently similar, the international marketing manager's skills in one market may be transferred to another. However, given the variation in the number, size, and nature of wholesalers and retailers described previously, a specialized approach may be the only viable option. And, if the market entry approaches vary from one market to another, the international marketer may have little choice but to adapt distribution efforts. For example, Kentucky Fried Chicken (KFC) was the first fast food outlet to enter the Japanese market. KFC and Mitsubishi established a 50–50 joint venture and opened the first KFC in 1970 at the Osaka Exposition; several additional restaurants were opened shortly thereafter. However, within a year after opening its doors, the local chain almost went bankrupt. KFC had made the mistake of locating its outlets in the suburbs and on highways, mimicking the U.S. model, only

**Figure 2.10:** Aldi in America: foreign retailers attempt to conquer the United States.

to learn that few Japanese had cars at the time. Only after putting aside the American distribution approach and opening downtown outlets did KFC experience steady growth.

In moving into foreign markets, Domino's Pizza faced a number of distribution challenges. In the Philippines, locations of stores were chosen using feng shui, the Chinese art that positions buildings according to spiritual flow. In Japan, Domino's had to modify its delivery procedures, because addresses in Japan often aren't sequential but instead are determined by the age of the building. And,

**TABLE 2.4:** World's 25 Largest Retailers Ranked by Retail Sales, 2007

| SALES RANK | COMPANY NAME | COUNTRY | SECTOR | (IN U.S. MILLION $) |
|---|---|---|---|---|
| 1. | Wal-Mart | U.S. | Discount Store/Wholesale Club | 374,526 |
| 2. | Carrefour | France | Hypermarket | 112,604 |
| 3. | Tesco | U.K. | Supermarket/Hypermarket | 94,740 |
| 4. | Metro AG | Germany | Diversified | 87,586 |
| 5. | The Home Depot | U.S. | Home Improvement | 77,349 |
| 6. | Kroger Co. | U.S. | Supermarket | 70,235 |
| 7. | Schwarz Unternehmens Treuhand KG | Germany | Discount Store/Hypermarket | 69,346 |
| 8. | Target Group | U.S. | Discount Store | 63,367 |
| 9. | Costco | U.S. | Wholesale Club | 63,088 |
| 10. | Aldi, GMBH | Germany | Food/Discount Store | 58,487 |
| 11. | Walgreen | U.S. | Drug Store | 53,762 |
| 12. | Rewe-Zentral AG | Germany | Diversified | 51,929 |
| 13. | Sears Holding Corp. | U.S. | Discount Department Store | 50,703 |
| 14. | Groupe Auchan | France | Discount Store | 49,295 |
| 15. | Lowe's Companies, Inc. | U.S. | Home Improvement | 48,284 |
| 16. | Seven & I Holdings Co. Ltd. | Japan | Department Store/Hypermarket | 47,891 |
| 17. | CVS Caremark Corp. | U.S. | Drug Store | 45,087 |
| 18. | Centres Distributeurs E. Leclerc | France. | Diversified | 44,686 |
| 19. | Edeka Zentrale AG & Co. | Germany | Diversified | 44,609 |
| 20. | Safeway | U.S. | Supermarket | 42,286 |
| 21. | AEON Company Ltd. | Japan | Diversified | 41,339 |
| 22. | Woolworths Ltd. | Australia | Discount Department Store | 41,021 |
| 23. | ITM Development International | France | Discount Store | 40,692 |
| 24. | Best Buy Co. Inc. | U.S. | Electronics Specialty | 40,023 |
| 25. | Koninklijke Ahold N.V. | Netherlands | Discount Store/Hypermarket | 38,589 |

*Source:* Deloitte (2009).

on the Caribbean island of Aruba, the company found that using motorcycles to deliver pizzas was too dangerous because of the island's strong winds; small trucks solved the problem (Gibson 2006).

## PRICE

In pricing products, international marketers must determine whether to standardize prices in markets worldwide or to differentiate prices among countries. In setting a standard worldwide price, a firm establishes a uniform price for its product all around the world. However, that price may be too high for consumers in less-developed countries. For example, Western brands are usually priced higher than domestic brands in transition economies. A pair of glasses at VisionExpress in Russia costs consumers about $60—half of what it costs in the United States, but more than 60 times what government stores charge (Alon and Banai 2000, 104). When Starbucks opened its first store in Mexico at the beginning of the decade, a major challenge was getting Mexican consumers to pay U.S.-style prices for coffee. A small cup of coffee at Starbucks's Mexico City store cost 16 pesos ($1.60), and specialty coffee drinks ran more than 50 pesos ($5). Mexicans were accustomed to far lower prices, with a cup of coffee at a corner café usually costing less than 50 cents. Mexico's minimum wage at the time was 43 pesos [$4.30] per day (Weissart 2002). Despite a high degree of price sensitivity in many developing markets, foreign brands nonetheless often remain competitive because of the high level of perceived quality and status that is associated with Western goods.

At other times the price may not be high enough for consumers in wealthier countries with higher levels of income. Here a marketer may opt to use a *differentiated pricing strategy*, in which price is based on a number of factors and not determined in isolation from the other marketing mix elements. For example, the prices of well-known household brands vary significantly across Europe, according to a major European study. The Internal Market Scoreboard Survey looked at 11 branded products in 15 European Union countries. British consumers spent 70 percent more for a tube of Colgate toothpaste than did shoppers in Portugal and Spain, and they paid 80 percent more for Nivea shaving foam than did the French. In Denmark, which along with Sweden is one of the most expensive European Union countries for grocery items, a Mars chocolate bar cost double what people paid in Belgium, and a bottle of Coca-Cola cost double the price in Germany. Heinz ketchup was twice as expensive in Italy as in Germany, and a bottle of Evian water cost four times as much in Finland as in France. The introduction of the euro has only highlighted these differences. No country was consistently expensive or cheap, but overall, Spain ranked the cheapest, followed by the Netherlands, Germany, and France. The United Kingdom was one of the more expensive countries, but Kellogg's Corn Flakes was a real bargain there, costing half what it did in Greece. In general, the richest countries tended to charge the most. However, Germany and the Netherlands, both with high per capita incomes, were exceptions. The survey found that prices were strongly influenced by what type of retail outlet has a big market share. Countries such as Spain, France, and Germany, in which hypermarkets had a relatively high market share, charged less. While variables such as market size, consumer tastes, landscape, and climate explained some of the discrepancies, the survey concluded that the price differences were too large to be explained away by natural factors. Instead, the survey claimed that the very large price differences for specific items suggested that producers exploit market fragmentation by operating different pricing policies in different national markets. There is still considerable scope for price convergence in the European Union (Bowes 2002).

A classic investigation found that, among U.S. multinational corporations, over two-thirds of consumer-nondurables marketers and almost 50 percent of industrial-products manufacturers adapted pricing to local conditions (Boddewyn 1976, 1). This adaptation is justified on the grounds that local market considerations play such a significant role in setting product prices. Among the factors influencing pricing are corporate objectives, competition, consumer demand, and governmental and regulatory considerations.

## Pricing Objectives and Strategies

International marketers may adjust pricing objectives based on the specific conditions of the markets they enter. Typical pricing objectives include profit maximization, return on an investment, and increases in total sales volume or market share. In pursuing pricing objectives, a firm may select from a variety of pricing strategies. The pricing strategy adopted will, in turn, impact the other marketing factors. A firm might engage in a market penetration strategy, which entails establishing a relatively low price with the goal of stimulating consumer interest. The firm accepts a lower per unit return in hopes of capturing a large share of the market and discouraging competition. Once a satisfactory level of market share is obtained, the firm typically raises prices to increase profitability. Penetration pricing is commonly employed with low-cost consumer products and tends to be most effective with price-sensitive consumers and in countries with significant manufacturing economies of scale.

In a situation in which no competitors—or very few—exist, or in which consumers are willing to pay a high price, perhaps because a product is unique or innovative, marketers may opt to "skim the cream" from the market. The aim of a *market skimming* strategy is to obtain a premium price for a product—at least initially. This approach allows marketers to recoup research and development costs quickly, as well as to generate profits. Prices are typically reduced once competitors enter the market or in order to attract more price-conscious consumers.

If competitors already exist in a given market or if a product is essentially indistinguishable from the competition, a firm may engage in *competitive pricing*. Here, a manufacturer sets product prices at or just below those of competitors. This approach requires constant monitoring of competitors' prices so that the marketer can prominently display a lower price in promotional messages. In contrast, with a *prestige pricing* strategy, product prices are set high and remain high. Promotional messages are aimed at a select clientele who can afford to pay the higher prices, and product quality and service are highlighted.

Clearly, the actual cost involved in manufacturing, distributing, and promoting a product will play a role in the price charged. The actual costs may vary from country to country. If specific markets require product modifications, these will need to be factored in to the price of the product. The manufacturer will also need to factor in any additional operational costs related to the export operation, such as transportation and insurance costs. Further, costs incurred in entering the foreign market—including taxes, duties, and tariffs—must also be taken into account. Finally, wholesaler and retailer markups must be considered.

The number and nature of competitors' manufacturing similar products or providing similar services will influence pricing decisions. The fewer the competitors, the greater the pricing flexibility. The intensity of demand for a certain product also impacts its price. Higher prices may be charged where demand is buoyant, and lower prices charged where demand is weak—even if production costs are the same in both instances. Total demand for a product is the net result of the combination of (1) consumer satisfaction derived from the product's "bundle of benefits," (2) the size of the market, and

(3) the market's ability to purchase the product. Not only must consumers be willing to purchase a product, they must also be able to.

## Governmental Influences on Pricing

Pricing is often one of the most heavily regulated areas in international marketing. Host countries have a variety of means to influence pricing. International marketers frequently encounter specified price markups, price ceilings, price freezes, restrictions on price changes, restrictions on acceptable profit margins, and government subsidies. The international marketer may also encounter governmental monopolies that control all international selling and buying. Further, tariffs and other government-controlled barriers force prices up for selected goods. Drug prices are often cheaper in Canada than in the United States—even for drugs produced by U.S. manufacturers. This is because pharmaceutical prices are governed by a governmental price ceiling. For example, Vioxx, a popular arthritis pain treatment, sells for 43 percent less in Canada. As a result, for the past few years, bands of renegade U.S. shoppers have piled onto buses to stock up on medications across the border. This has raised the issue of permitting drugs from U.S. manufacturers to be literally reimported into the United States from Canada, and the debate over whether reimportation would, in fact, reduce costs without compromising safety (Calfee 2002).

## Export Pricing

When U.S. firms export products to international markets, costs associated with freight and shipping, insurance, tariffs, taxes, storage fees, documentation costs, and middleman margins must all be added to the domestic price of the product. These costs typically inflate the final price to a level significantly higher than the price charged in domestic markets for the same product, in what is commonly known as price escalation. This higher price for the product may mean that it is out of line with domestically available substitutes—which, in turn, may have a negative impact on consumer demand. In some instances this may be offset by the fact that the foreign goods are perceived as exclusive. For example, U.S. consumers generally pay more for French perfumes, German beers, and Italian leather shoes than for their domestic counterparts, yet demand still remains high.

On the other hand, a variety of factors may lead to a situation in which the imported product costs less than domestic goods. As noted previously, a desire to price products competitively may result in lower prices. In some instances, overproduction may necessitate moving product inventories; storage space may not be available, or products may be perishable. This may result in a price lower than that charged in the home market.

Numerous international firms also have been accused of dumping goods on foreign markets. *Dumping* refers to the selling of goods in foreign markets for less than they are sold in the home market or to setting the product price below the cost of production. In some cases this may be unintentional on the part of the international marketer. Some firms, however, intentionally sell at a loss in foreign markets in order to increase their market share. In many countries, including the United States, domestic firms may petition their governments to impose antidumping measures on imports alleged to be dumped—for example, imposing additional import duties. Often, however, antidumping actions feed retaliatory responses. A generous attitude by one country to requests for antidumping actions triggers a similar attitude in the other markets. Indeed, dumping accusations have become somewhat of a trend in the current economic climate. Indonesia provides an interesting case. More than 20 countries have accused Indonesia of dumping its export products on the international market. Countries that have lodged reports include India, South Africa, Thailand, New Zealand, Australia, the Philippines, several countries in the European Union, Malaysia, the United States, Turkey, Canada, Peru, Argentina, Egypt, Brazil, Colombia, and South Korea. A list of 20 products Indonesia has been accused of dumping includes paper, toilet paper, stationery, aluminum, dry batteries, tires, steel, textiles, ready-to-wear garments, synthetic fibers, pharmaceuticals, bicycles, and motorcycles. Indeed, between 1995 and 2008, 180 accusations of dumping were lodged against Indonesia. However, 85 of these were dismissed because there was no proof. The country addressed another 76 of the complaints and is currently processing 19 others. Recently, the Indonesian government was urged by domestic manufacturers to take Australia to the World Trade Organization after it imposed anti-dumping duties on Indonesian tissue paper. However, the government is first analyzing all necessary legal aspects of the case before making such a decision (*Jakarta Post* 2009).

## Pricing and Manufacture Abroad

When goods are both produced and distributed within the foreign country, the various marketing objectives and strategies discussed previously apply as well. The marketer must take into account consumer demand and the competitive environment. However, firms must take additional factors into consideration in pricing goods. When goods are manufactured abroad, foreign labor and material costs may be lower or higher than those in the home market, directly affecting overall production costs and, ultimately, product price.

Foreign governments in both developed and developing countries may impose price controls on goods produced within their borders. Should a firm wish to raise product prices, it typically must apply for a price increase and provide documentation supporting the request, which may or may not be granted. Such price controls can jeopardize not only the financial well-being but even the survival of a company. For example, Gerber began operations in Venezuela in the 1960s. Unprofitable operations forced the firm to close its doors in 1979. Gerber blamed price controls for its failure in the market—some of Gerber's products were still being sold at prices set more than 10 years earlier because the Venezuelan government had refused repeated requests for price increases.

Inflation rates around the world vary dramatically. In many foreign countries the rate is similar to that in the United States, or perhaps even lower. According to Bespoke Investment, the U.S. inflation rate is about 4.3 percent, while the inflation rate of Italy is 3.6 percent, and Japan's inflation rate is a mere 0.8 percent. However, in other countries, double-digit inflation rates are not uncommon. In Indonesia inflation stands at 10.3 percent, in Russia 15.1 percent, and in Venezuela an unbelievable 31.4 percent (Global Inflation Rates 2008). Firms operating in such markets face a definite challenge in terms of pricing products. In countries with no price controls, pricing strategy involves raising prices frequently enough to keep pace with inflation. The situation becomes even more problematic when price controls are also imposed.

# PROMOTION

Promotion is the fourth and final component in the marketing mix. Promotion includes advertising, sales promotion, public relations and publicity, and personal selling. In addition, the areas of direct marketing, sponsorships, trade fairs, and product integrations will be addressed.

## Advertising

Advertising, according to the Definitions Committee of the American Marketing Association, "is any paid form of non-personal presentation and promotion of ideas, goods or services by an identified sponsor" (*Journal of Marketing* 1948, 202).

Several aspects of this definition deserve further explanation. The "paid" aspect refers to the fact that the advertiser must purchase time and space for the message. "Non-personal" indicates that the message appears in the mass media, which means there is little opportunity for feedback from the message receiver. Because of this, advertisers utilize research to determine how a specific target audience might interpret and respond to a message prior to its distribution. Finally, the "identified" aspect refers to the fact that the media require sponsors to identify themselves.

The role that advertising plays in a society differs from one market to the next. In Chapter 1 we examined countries in terms of their total advertising expenditures. In comparing the role of advertising in various nations, it is also useful to examine per capita advertising expenditures. Table 2.5 presents this measure for 2007—the most recent year for which data were collected. These figures demonstrate the significant variation from one country to the next. Advertising expenditures per capita range from a high of $923 for Hong Kong and $533 for the United States, to a low of $5.40 per person in India and a mere 10 cents per person in Yemen.

As with the other marketing mix elements, advertising can be standardized (whereby the same advertising theme is employed for each foreign market) or specialized (whereby the messages are adapted for local markets). Agencies and advertisers alike are divided over the issue. While some agencies have jumped on the "globalization bandwagon," others remain committed to localization. Both Saatchi & Saatchi and BBD&O are believers in the global approach. Grey Advertising, on the other hand, suggests that each world business challenge is unique and, as a result, espouses "global vision with a local touch." Views regarding the effectiveness and practicality of the global approach to marketing messages are mixed. Exxon's "Put a tiger in your tank" theme, employed in many different markets, provided the firm with a uniform positioning across markets. Marlboro cigarettes have also been advertised in much the same fashion around the globe. Other marketers, due to a variety of constraints, opt to modify their advertising campaigns. Often, themes or appeals used in the home market may not be appropriate for specific foreign audiences. In a classic example, Pepsodent attempted to sell its toothpaste in a remote area of Southeast Asia via a message that stressed how the toothpaste helped whiten teeth. Unfortunately, this campaign had little effect, as this was an area where many local people deliberately chewed betel nut in order to achieve darkly stained teeth—a sign of prestige. A variety of other factors may also limit the feasibility of standardized campaigns. The issue of standardization versus specialization of advertising will be dealt with in greater detail in Chapters 5 and 6. It should be noted here, however, that of all the elements of the marketing mix, advertising is generally acknowledged to be the most difficult to standardize (Boddewyn et al. 1986, 69).

In addition to strategic decisions, such as whether to standardize or specialize campaigns, the international marketer must decide on the appropriate message content. Advertising is effective only if it is able to both gain the attention of the target audience and communicate the product benefits clearly. Creative considerations will be addressed in Chapter 6. If the target audience is to receive the advertising message, it must appear in the appropriate medium. Media decisions include whether to employ local or international media. Advertising media will be discussed in Chapter 7. Research guides both whom the advertising should be targeted to and what the content of the message should be. Creative appeals may be evaluated prior to dissemination to help predict whether the message appeals to the correct

**TABLE 2.5:** Per Capita Advertising Expenditures in Selected Countries

| COUNTRIES WITH HIGHEST SPENDING | PER CAPITA (IN U.S. $) | COUNTRIES WITH LOWEST SPENDING | PER CAPITA (IN U.S. $) |
|---|---|---|---|
| Hong Kong | $923.40 | Yemen | .10 |
| United States | 533.70 | Pakistan | 2.70 |
| Australia | 513.40 | India | 5.40 |
| United Kingdom | 492.10 | Indonesia | 16.60 |
| Switzerland | 447.40 | Turkey | 33.90 |
| Canada | 343.80 | Romania | 48.80 |
| Japan | 300.80 | China | 56.10 |
| United Arab Emirates | 296.00 | Malaysia | 59.70 |
| Germany | 294.20 | Russia | 60.90 |
| France | 236.60 | South Africa | 67.70 |

*Source:* World Advertising Research Center (2008).

audience. Research is also undertaken after a campaign has run to determine whether objectives have been met. Research in the international setting is the focus of Chapter 8.

## Sales Promotion

Sales promotion consists of a variety of techniques designed to support and complement both advertising and personal selling. The goal of sales promotion is to stimulate immediate consumer purchasing or dealer effectiveness. Cents-off coupons, premiums, samples, and point-of-purchase displays may induce trial purchase of products as well as maintain consumer loyalty. Sweepstakes and contests can create interest in and excitement about a company's product or service and increase the likelihood that its advertising campaigns will receive attention. See Figure 2.11 for a British advertisement for Paul Mitchell hair care products incorporating a sweepstakes. To celebrate the release of the film *He's Just Not That Into You*, Paul Mitchell teamed up with Entertainment Films to offer readers of *Glamour* (Britain's number-one women's magazine) the chance to win a trip to Hollywood. Price deals, trade shows, and contests are typical trade promotion activities that may be directed at wholesalers, distributors, and retailers. The overall use of sales promotion efforts appears to be on the increase worldwide.

Here are just a few examples of successful, award-winning promotions from around the world:

- Marketers hit Brazilian bars and clubs to promote Johnnie Walker, the country's best-selling whisky. In addition to on-premises samples, they placed an alphanumeric pager at each table. Every 30 minutes, calls were made to the pagers, awarding prizes to some Johnnie Walker drinkers and telling others to wait for a chance to win. The four-month promotion also used e-mail to spread the word about participating bars, a Web site with screensavers, virtual postcards, event photos, and a blind-date service that electronically matched up cybersurfers' profiles. The promotion generated 7,000 e-mail addresses and increased consumption levels by as much as 120 percent.

- Another successful brand-building promotion was Coca-Cola's 2005 and 2006 "Win a Player" scheme to back its sponsorship of the English Football League and Scottish Premier League. British football (soccer) fans could text the name of their favorite team to a number promoted on 80 million Coke packs. The team with the most votes won £250,000 (approximately $500,000) to buy a player, while entrants who voted for that team stood to win £10,000 ($20,000) in a prize draw.

- To create awareness for the relaunch of Philips's Softone colored light bulbs while boosting trials among young homeowners and generating repair purchases, marketers distributed two million "Yes Please" promotional bags to British households. The bags contained a glossy, 16-page brochure, a coupon, a questionnaire, and a creative offer for a free Softone light bulb. Recipients filled out the questionnaire, which included a spot for them to select one of the seven colored bulbs. They then hung the bag and questionnaire outside their front door. The next morning, the questionnaire was withdrawn from the bag and the desired light bulb—a short-life, 10-hour bulb made just for the promotion—was left behind. The 700,000 bulb requests resulted in a 35 percent response rate. Another 8 percent of respondents redeemed the coupon, and 27 percent filled out the survey, supplying Philips with solid marketing information on a crop of new prospects. Brand awareness increased from 9 to 82 percent.

- While many companies effectively utilize sales promotion tools to help sell their products in foreign markets, marketers must be aware of potential pitfalls. Because of cultural differences among consumers, promotional incentives that have proven successful in the home market may not be as effective in foreign markets. For example, when Procter & Gamble mailed 580,000 free samples of Vidal Sassoon Wash & Go shampoo to consumers in Warsaw in the early 1990s, it never expected an adverse reaction. The samples were in such demand that some Poles wrecked mailboxes to steal them. Following what was believed to be the first mass mailing of free samples in Poland, about 2,000 mailboxes—mostly in large urban areas—were broken into by people who wanted the samples either to use or to sell. The samples turned up at open markets, selling for 60 cents each. P&G assured the Polish post office that it would pay for the damages (Gajewski 1991).

Differing legal restrictions and regulations from one country to the next may render some promotional efforts impossible while requiring that others be modified significantly. Such restrictions often mean that marketers must develop separate promotions for each country. Over the past few years, marketers and their agencies have experienced increasing frustration at the complex web of regulations regarding sales promotions in Europe. For example, in Germany, considered one of the most restrictive of the European Union nations, "buy one get one free" offers are illegal, as are mail-in offers and self-liquidating premiums. In France, on-pack premiums are restricted to 7 percent of the product's value. Italy does not allow cash rebates. And, the Netherlands, Belgium, Ireland, Sweden, and France prohibit or seriously restrict sweepstakes. Some countries, such as Spain and Italy, require pre-authorization from government for certain sales promotions. The idea of creating an internal market for sales promotion, allowing advertisers to run identical promotions across the EU, was first presented as a draft proposal in 2001. After four years of clashing over the guidelines, the proposal was jettisoned by the European Commission after member states failed to reach a consensus. The proposed regulation would have brought the countries with the most restrictive promotions laws, such as Germany, France, and Belgium, into line with the more liberal countries, such as the United Kingdom. It remains to be seen whether member states can hammer out an agreement regarding pan-European promotion guidelines

**Figure 2.11:** Advertisement for Paul Mitchell's "Win a Trip to Hollywood" sweepstakes.

in the future. The following are perceived to be quite liberal with regard to the regulation of premiums, gifts, and competitions: Australia, Canada, France, Hong Kong, Ireland, Malaysia, New Zealand, the Philippines, Singapore, Spain, Sweden, the United Kingdom, and the United States. In contrast, Austria, Belgium, Denmark, Germany, Italy, Japan, Korea, Mexico, the Netherlands, Switzerland, and Venezuela are seen as significantly more restrictive. Because both industrialized and developing countries appear on each list, any attempt to generalize is useless.

Because distribution channels in foreign markets generally are different from those in the United States, promotions that rely heavily on retailer involvement and cooperation may not be effective. For example, while U.S. retailers commonly handle processing of coupons and the display of point-of-purchase materials, international marketers cannot assume that this level of assistance exists in foreign markets. In the United States, 70 percent of dollars spent on consumer promotions go into coupons. This is not the case in many foreign markets. Coupons are far less common—or even nonexistent—in some countries simply because the cultures don't accept them. Also, retailers in many foreign markets may be smaller in size or greater in number, and as a result it may be more difficult to contact them. With regard to promotions directed at both consumers and the trade, international marketers must study each country separately.

## PUBLIC RELATIONS

Public relations involves a variety of efforts to create and maintain a positive image of an organization with its various constituencies. Corporate public relations typically focuses on an organization's noncustomer constituencies, such as employees, stockholders, suppliers/distributors, governmental agencies, labor unions, the media, and various activist groups, as well as with the public at large. When the focus is specifically an organization's interactions with current and potential consumers, this marketing-oriented aspect of public relations is called marketing public relations, or MPR. MPR is defined as "the process of planning, executing and evaluating programs that encourage purchase and consumer satisfaction through credible communication of information and impressions that identify companies and their products with the needs, wants, concerns and interests of consumers" (Harris 1993, 12). In short, MPR supports marketing's product and sales focus by increasing the brand and company's credibility with consumers.

MPR is often further delineated as involving either proactive or reactive public relations (Goldman 1984, 16). *Proactive MPR* is offensively rather than defensively oriented and opportunistic rather than remedial. Proactive MPR is a tool for communicating a brand's merits and is typically used in conjunction with advertising, sales promotion, and personal selling. Proactive MPR is typically employed when introducing a new product and announcing product revisions. Unilever provides an excellent example of proactive MPR. The company markets Cif, a household cleaning product, in 52 countries. In introducing Cif to the Argentine market, the manufacturer demonstrated the product's effectiveness by scrubbing clean the 35-year-old planetarium located in the city of Buenos Aires. Nueva Comunicacion, the brand's press and public relations agency, organized the event. It included a print campaign. "Imagine what you can do in your home," the ads boasted below a picture of a sparkling-clean planetarium.

In contrast, *Reactive MPR* is undertaken as a result of pressures and challenges that might be brought on by competitive actions, shifts in consumer attitudes, changes in government policy, or other influences. Reactive MPR generally deals with changes that have negative consequences for a company. An unanticipated marketplace event or faulty product can place an organization in a vulnerable position, requiring reactive MPR (Shimp 2003, 569). Consider the case of Toyota. As far back as March 2007, Toyota began receiving complaints of gas pedals being slow to rise after being stepped on. Engineers fixed the problem in the Tundra pickup in 2008, but troubles persisted in other models. Toyota had adopted the practice of using the same part on several models, saving vast sums of money but exposing itself to the risk that a defect could cause global mayhem for the company (Foster 2010). The result: unintended acceleration was linked to at least 34 deaths by the U.S. National Highway Traffic Safety Administration (NHTSA). In early 2010 Toyota recalled more than 7.5 million vehicles in the United States alone, plus many more in Europe and China, for problems not only with the accelerators, but also the floor mats that could trap the gas pedal. Further, for a period of time, the sales and production of eight models were suspended in the United States. The NHTSA levied a $16.4 million fine against Toyota for "knowingly hiding" safety concerns from regulators. The company subsequently became the subject of negative global publicity for weeks. Further, the automaker was faulted for communicating too little, too late; however, it did ultimately launch an aggressive print, television, and social-media campaign featuring Toyota's U.S. President-Chief Operating Officer Jim Lentz. (See Figure 2.12 for a newspaper ad in which Lentz updates customers about the recall.)

Toyota's unprecedented recall cost it dearly in terms of both dollars and consumer attitudes. The financial impact on Toyota from the global recall was expected to total more than $5 billion over a one-year period due to increased incentive campaigns (post-recall, Toyota offered customers 0 percent interest, five-year loans, and competitive lease prices and free maintenance across 80 percent of its vehicle line-up), litigation costs, and marketing efforts (Sanchanta and Takahashi 2010). Regarding consumer attitudes, according to a *USA Today*/Gallup Poll, a majority (55 percent) of Americans believed that Toyota failed to respond quickly enough to the safety defects, and a significant minority (31 percent) felt it was unsafe to drive a Toyota or Lexus (Healey 2010). A Kelley Blue Book study showed that consideration of the Toyota brand was cut nearly in half, from 29 percent prior to the recall to 18 percent afterward. But the study also offered some good news for Toyota, showing that consumers believed that the world's leading automaker would learn from the crisis. Over 30 percent of those surveyed believed that, despite the current situation, Toyota would offer better products in the future, and another 28 percent noted that Toyota has had fewer recalls than other car manufacturers and that this recall "doesn't change the fact that they produce great products." Notes James Bell, VP-executive market analyst at Kelley Blue Book:

> What you have here is the perfect storm of a corporate culture within Toyota that is very methodical, reasoned and conservative in its steps, which has served them exceptionally well and allowed them to build a stellar reputation and be profitable and successful. But it seems like they didn't have a play in their playbook for this. A company that is as wealthy from a financial and talent perspective like they are should have grabbed this problem in the first hour and thrown up their hands and said they know about the situation and here's what we are going to do to fix it. The recall would have seemed a bit crazy two months earlier, but it would have averted the trouble Toyota is having today.... They will recover and come out of this a better and smarter company, but the reputation they have nurtured for 30 years is severely stained. (Bush 2010)

Clearly, even seemingly invincible brands aren't immune to disaster. And when a major crisis strikes, judicious public relations strategies are essential to saving the brand's image. A mismanaged crisis brings on the dreaded "Seven Plagues of Unhappy Repercussions": extended duration/negative press, angry customers and shareholders, lawsuits, government investigations, public interest groups, low employee morale/productivity, and a drop in stock price and earnings (Cohn 2000, 16).

Each plague begets another. The longer the story is covered, the bigger the hit to a company's reputation and bottom line. While a company doesn't necessarily get off scot-free when it manages a crisis well, the damage is relatively short-term in contrast to damage caused by a problem that is poorly managed.

*Publicity*, as part of the broader function of public relations, involves seeking favorable comments on the product/service or firm itself via news stories, editorials, or announcements in the mass media. In contrast to advertising, publicity is not directly paid for by the company, nor does the company have control over the content or frequency of the coverage. The advantages of such "free publicity" are both credibility and message length. Information conveyed through non-advertising media are generally considered more credible by the public. In addition, a news or feature treatment of an issue is typically longer than a 30-second spot or an advertisement in the print media. While publicity is an important communication technique employed in public relations, public relations practitioners have a number of additional tools at their disposal, such as newsletters and other publications, press conferences, company-sponsored events, and participation in community activities.

Public relations often plays a more critical role for a firm operating abroad than it does domestically. Clearly, international marketers face fewer problems if their firm is perceived positively in the country in which it operates. A variety of groups, including local governments, local media, and the general public, for example, may feel threatened by the presence of a foreign multinational in their country. Thus it is the responsibility of public relations personnel to position the firm as a good corporate citizen that is involved with and concerned about the future of the host country. This is often best accomplished via community involvement. Company management and employees may contribute to the community's social and economic development through participation in a variety of activities: civic and youth groups, cultural or recreational activities, charitable fundraising events, and so on.

## Personal Selling

Personal selling involves individual, personal contact with the customer, with the intent of either making an immediate sale or developing a long-term relationship that will eventually result in a sale. Personal selling can take a variety of forms, including sales calls at a customer's place of business or a consumer's home, or customer assistance at a retail outlet. As such, it is often the most expensive element in the promotion mix on a per customer basis. In addition to such face-to-face contact, personal selling may also include contact through some form of telecommunication, such as telephone sales, which can help to reduce costs. Personal selling generally involves a greater degree of feedback than advertising, as the impact of the sales presentation often can be assessed directly through consumers' reactions. This provides a sales representative with the opportunity to tailor the presentation.

The international marketer may choose to utilize a traveling sales force based at the company headquarters or perhaps to manage a team of expatriates based abroad. This approach tends to be expensive and is often challenging. While the global marketplace has somewhat narrowed the differences in business culture between the United States and the rest of the world, key differences remain for salespersons. U.S.-based salespersons operating overseas must often contend with longer sales cycles in nearly every country. Even within the European continent, there are variations, which tend to delay the closing of sales. For example, German customers tend to need strong reassurances in everything. They don't like risk. Notes Ute Zimmerman, president and founder of euroPResence, a public relations firm with offices in Frankfurt and Boston:

> Forget about pointing out the product's new bells and whistles. Germans only want to hear about three product
> features: its bottom line benefits and how it will make life easier; that there will be strong service support for the

**Figure 2.12:** Toyota advertisement updating consumers about the massive recall.

# There's been a lot of talk about the recall. Here are the facts for our customers.

Over the past few days, there has been a lot of speculation about our sticking accelerator pedal recall. Our message to Toyota owners is this — if you are not experiencing any issues with your accelerator pedal, we are confident that your vehicle is safe to drive. If your accelerator pedal becomes harder to depress than normal or slower to return, please contact your dealer without delay.

At Toyota, we take this issue very seriously, but I want to make sure our customers understand that this situation is rare and generally doesn't occur suddenly. In the instances where it does occur, the vehicle can be controlled with firm and steady application of the brakes.

**Here's the latest update on the recall:**

1. We're starting to send letters this weekend to owners involved in the recall to schedule an appointment at their dealer.

2. Dealerships have extended their hours — some of them working 24/7 — to fix your vehicle as quickly as possible.

3. Trained technicians have begun making repairs.

We've halted production of these models this week to focus fully on fixing this problem for the vehicles that are on the road.

Our entire organization of 172,000 North American employees and dealership personnel has been mobilized. And we're redoubling our quality control efforts across the company.

Ensuring your safety is our highest priority. I will continue to update you with accurate and timely information about the status of the recall in the days and weeks ahead.

Sincerely,

*Jim Lentz*

Jim Lentz
President and Chief Operating Officer
Toyota Motor Sales, U.S.A., Inc.

product; and that the product is guaranteed. Germans are also fanatical when it comes to references. Instead of the two or three checks that an American executive would typically seek, Germans demand four, five, or six. As for closing a sale, all contracts are thoroughly reviewed by lawyers for both sides. In contrast, further south, in Spain and Italy, a salesperson should expect to spend more time on the social aspects of selling. U.S. salespeople may find themselves schmoozing not only the company decision maker, but his spouse, perhaps the children, and possibly even the extended family members, such as siblings, parents, aunts and uncles. (Bertagnoli 2001)

Because it typically involves both communication and personal contact, personal selling is closely linked to national or even regional cultural characteristics. As a result, personal selling activities are often conducted on a national basis. Most companies, regardless of their size, prefer to use sales representatives from the host country to staff their sales force. Even in the European Union, personal selling is slow to cross national borders. With few exceptions, a German salesperson will not be particularly effective in Holland, nor will a French salesperson have much luck persuading a Swiss consumer. Nationals are quite simply more readily accepted than foreigners, and they are also more familiar with their country. The challenge in utilizing a national sales force lies in recruitment and training, as well as in adapting personal selling activities to fit the local market.

Personal selling often plays a greater role in foreign than in domestic markets. Government restrictions on advertising, limitations in available media, and low literacy rates may cause marketers to turn to personal selling as a means of communicating with foreign customers. Lower wages in many developing countries may make personal selling a more cost-efficient method of selling as well. However, in other instances, personal selling, and in particular door-to-door sales, may be less acceptable abroad. Amway distributes home and personal care products in more than 80 countries, normally via its door-to-door sales force. However, in China, Amway was forced to employ a different approach. Amway first entered China in 1995, but in 1998 the company was shut down by the Chinese government. Officials claimed that direct sales companies like Amway were providing cover for illegal pyramid schemes, which were widespread in the 1990s and resulted in thousands of people losing their life savings. After months of lobbying, Amway negotiated a compromise. It would survive in China by opening up retail shops—the only such ones in the world—and would make all sales representatives direct employees, garnering wages only for their sales and not their recruits. In 2005, as part of its World Trade Organization commitments, the Chinese government eased restrictions by allowing limited home-to-home sales. More than a decade after the original ban, Amway has learned to adjust to the new regulations by bending the rules. The vast majority of sales at Amway retail stores are to its salespeople, who use them as distribution centers. Special cards are required to purchase products in the stores—cards only sales representatives possess. If customers off the street come into the store to make a purchase, they are told to contact their sales representative. The company has also worked out a way to circumnavigate the recruitment incentive ban. It gives employees a bonus linked to performance—the bonus happens to be 40 percent of their recruit's sales. Amway sells its cosmetics, nutritional, and personal care products in nearly 200 outlets throughout China, and its 2008 sales jumped 28 percent to $2.5 billion. Today Amway counts 6,000 direct employees and an estimated 200,000 sales representatives across the country. Beijing now sees Amway as a model company that helps the Chinese government by increasing domestic consumption on a grand scale (Calinoff 2009).

## Direct Marketing

Traditionally, direct marketing has not been considered an element in the promotions mix. However, because of the increasingly important role direct marketing plays in the communications programs of many different kinds of organizations, it is included here. Indeed, direct marketing is currently growing faster than virtually any other form of promotion. The reasons for this are numerous. The widespread use of credit cards and the convenience of toll-free numbers have made it significantly easier for consumers in most markets to respond to direct-marketing offers. From the marketer's perspective, the desire for greater accountability of the effectiveness of a promotional effort has encouraged the use of this approach. In most instances, messages are sent to a known individual, making it possible to track whether that customer did or did not respond. This is clearly a benefit that most advertising and promotions cannot offer. But probably the most significant recent advance has been the ability of firms to collect massive amounts of information about their customers via computer databases. The data are used to help marketers understand who their customers are and determine their likes and dislikes and when they are most likely to purchase. Such information, of course, helps to increase the likelihood that those receiving a direct marketing offer will indeed respond.

Direct marketing refers to a way of doing business—one in which the marketer attempts to sell goods directly to the consumer without the aid of a wholesaler or retailer. Messages are designed to solicit a measurable response or transaction from the target audience. Direct marketing is seen as much more personal than advertising because it incorporates a degree of two-way communication. Direct marketers may employ a variety of media, placing such messages on the Internet, on radio and television, and in newspapers and magazines. Procter & Gamble, for example, launched a general-interest women's magazine in the French market, demonstrating the household giant's intention to diversify product advertising away from mass-media campaigns and toward greater use of direct marketing. P&G has mailed out 2.7 million copies of the new 52-page French-language magazine entitled *Mieux* (Better). It has announced tentative plans to publish the magazine twice yearly. Editorial content in *Mieux* mimics the conventional subjects of women's magazines, with articles on children, decoration, entertaining, and the kitchen. The magazine is heavy on product placement (which will be discussed in the following pages), with frequent mention of leading P&G brands such as Ariel, Dash, Mr. Clean, Swiffer, and Tampax. A coupon booklet distributed with the magazine offers about $20 of savings on P&G products, which provides ample opportunity for follow-up on the effectiveness of the mailing. "We definitely want to see how many of the coupons were used, for which products, and where," notes P&G Communications Director Christian Vivier de Vaugouin. "This is the sort of information that allows us to move toward more of a one-to-one relationship with our consumers" (*Advertising Age Global Daily News* 2001).

Direct selling, direct mail, telemarketing, and catalog sales are also commonly employed in direct response campaigns. Otto Versand is the world's largest mail-order retailer, with subsidiaries and affiliates in Europe, Asia, South America, and the United States. Based in Hamburg, Germany, Otto Versand's numerous catalog businesses in 20 countries include Grattan and Freemans in the United Kingdom, 3 Suisses in France, and Heine, Schwab, and the flagship Otto in Germany. Otto Versand offers its customers a variety of ordering methods, including print and CD-ROM catalogs, as well as options via online services and the Internet. In the United States, Otto Versand acquired Spiegel Inc., known for its flagship Spiegel catalog, in the early 1980s. And in 1998, the company acquired a majority stake in Crate & Barrel, which sold primarily through its chain of more than 60 home furnishing stores but which also sold via catalog. Crate and Barrel agreed to the deal in order to tap into the deep pockets of its new parent for expansion; it also hoped that Otto Versand's mail-order expertise could bolster its catalog operation.

While direct-marketing techniques may be quite sophisticated in many markets, in others they may play a minimal role or even be nonexistent. For example, direct marketing is a relatively new and as yet underdeveloped promotional tool in the Middle East. One of the real obstacles to the growth of direct marketing in the Middle East is the problem of names. Some Arabs don't use surnames in the Western sense; others describe themselves one way for ordinary purposes but use other names, including tribal connections and family antecedents, for official purposes. Another challenge relates to mailing lists. While there are many list owners in the region (such as shops, banks, airlines, and conference organizers), not much effort is put into updating or cleaning files. Although direct mailing to the general public may still be some way off as a viable promotional tool, it appears that business-to-business offers a significant opportunity. Directories of businesses and chamber of commerce membership lists are a good deal easier to come by than data on individual consumers.

## Sponsorships

Sponsorships are one of the fastest-growing forms of marketing today. Indeed, Mediaedge:cia, the WPP media agency, issued a report that forecasts significant global growth in the sector. At a time when ad budgets are shrinking, the report predicts that spending on sponsorships would climb worldwide by 15 percent in 2009, to $44 billion (McClellan 2009). A number of reasons have been given for this tremendous growth in sponsorship activities: the escalating costs of traditional advertising media, the fragmentation of media audiences, the growing diversity in leisure activities, and the ability to reach targeted groups of people economically. In addition, by attaching their names to special events and causes, companies are able to avoid the clutter inherent in traditional advertising media.

> Sponsorship involves two main activities: 1) an exchange between a sponsor (such as a brand) and a sponsee (such as a sporting event) whereby the latter receives a fee and the former obtains the right to associate itself with the activity sponsored and 2) the marketing of the association by the sponsor. Both activities are necessary if the sponsorship fee is to be a meaningful investment. (Cornwell and Maignan 1998)

The objectives of sponsorships include increasing the awareness of a company and its brands, enhancing the corporate or brand image, and showing corporate responsibility. While the primary audience of current and potential consumers may be valuable, even more important may be the secondary audience. Sponsorships can be a powerful public relations tool. The company sponsoring an event may also be communicating with stockholders, community leaders, and employees.

The benefits of sponsorships were examined in a recent global study by Mediaedge:cia. The survey polled 12,000 consumers in 18 countries by telephone and over the Internet. Respondents were asked how much they notice sponsorships, whether they are influenced by them, and what their perceptions are about companies that do sponsorships. Fifty-three percent of male respondents said sports sponsorships strongly influence their buying habits; only 26 percent of women concurred. However, nearly 70 percent of women said they would buy a product if its maker sponsored a good cause, compared with 46 percent of men. Age also played a role. Slightly more than 40 percent of people aged 25–34 cited sports sponsorships as influencing purchases, and nearly 35 percent in that age group said sponsors are a factor in buying decisions. By contrast, 25 percent of respondents aged 35–44 and only 18 percent aged 45–55 said sponsorships were an influencing factor for them. Income was also a differentiator. Half of the respondents in households with incomes of more than $50,000 were aware of sponsors. However, mid-market households ($40,000–$50,000) were most likely to act on that awareness, with 40 percent indicating they would purchase products in response to a sponsorship (Kaplan 2002).

Sponsorships can take a variety of forms. The bulk of sponsorship dollars goes to sporting events. According to the sponsorship agency IEG, sports accounts for 68 percent of the $17 billion North American sponsorship market, and global sports sponsorships have doubled in the past 10 years to about $30 billion annually (Toms 2009). Sports sponsorships include golf and tennis tournaments, motor sports, professional sports leagues or teams, and, of course, the Olympics. Twelve companies (including Coca-Cola, Visa, McDonald's, and Samsung Electronics) paid $866 million, or an average of $72 million apiece, to sponsor the Turin and Beijing Olympics. That's almost one-third more than the $633 million total paid to back the Salt Lake City and Athens Games in 2002, and up from the $579 million for the Nagano and Sydney games in 1998 and 2000. Rowland Jack, a senior bid consultant in the sports marketing and sponsorship team at Hill & Knowlton, noted that the attractiveness of the Beijing Games was probably a big factor in the jump in sponsorship fees, as so many companies were interested in bidding. Yet some research suggests that few consumers even notice who is backing the games. In a survey of 1,500 Chinese city dwellers by London's Fournaise Marketing Group, only 15 percent could name two of the 12 global sponsors, and just 40 percent could name just one sponsor: Coca-Cola. Adding to the confusion for consumers were the 21 additional national-level sponsors, including Adidas and Volkswagen (Balfour and Jana 2008). This highlights two of the primary drawbacks of sponsorships in general. First, sponsorships can be quite costly, even in instances where events are cosponsored. Second, while cosponsoring an event may prove less expensive, a marketer must then contend with clutter. Indeed, some events have so many sponsors that no single sponsor's message ends up standing out.

Sponsors may also support entertainment attractions (rock concerts, for example, or the theater) or festivals, fairs, and annual events (such as the Macy's Thanksgiving Day Parade). Or companies may choose to form an alliance with a nonprofit organization. This is also known as *cause-related marketing*. Cause-related marketing allows firms to enhance their brands' images and sales while allowing nonprofit partners to obtain additional funding by aligning their causes with corporate sponsors. While the sponsored event or organization may be nonprofit, cause-related sponsorships are not the same as philanthropy. Philanthropy is support of a cause without any commercial incentive. Cause-related marketing is used to achieve specific commercial objectives.

Though there are several varieties of cause-related marketing, the most common form involves a company contributing to a designated cause every time a customer undertakes some action (such as buying a product or redeeming a coupon) that supports the company and its brands (Varadarajan and Menon 1988, 58). A fashionable brand of cosmetics provides an excellent example. M-A-C cosmetics, a unit of Estée Lauder, has distributed money to charities assisting people living with HIV/AIDS since the 1990s. As a by-product of its AIDS efforts, M-A-C has a best-selling lipstick known as Viva Glam. All proceeds from Viva Glam sales, including counter reps' commissions, go to the M-A-C AIDS Fund, which to date has raised more than $130 million—a tie M-A-C also promotes in its advertising. "We definitely believe the reason Viva Glam is our best seller is because it supports a charity," notes a M-A-C executive. "People care about being able to make a difference, even if they're just choosing one lipstick over another. As the face of AIDS has evolved, M-A-C now spends more time on the crisis outside the United States, targeting young people with education and prevention messages" (Bittar 2002, 18). In 2008, songstress Fergie became the M-A-C VIVA GLAM VI spokesperson, announcing 11 new grants aimed at preventing the spread of HIV among young people aged 15 to 25, who account for more than half of all new infections. Although cause-related marketing was initiated in the United States during the early 1980s, marketers around the globe have become active participants in supporting causes.

Regardless of the form that a sponsorship takes, successful sponsorships require a meaningful fit among the brand, the event or cause, and the target market. Avon provides an excellent example. The world's leading direct seller of beauty and related products, with $10 billion in annual revenues, Avon currently markets to women in more than 130 countries through 5.4 million independent sales representatives. Avon is committed to women through programs such the Avon Worldwide Fund for Women's Health, the Avon Global Women's Walking-Running Wellness Program, and Avon's Breast Cancer Crusade. The mission of the Crusade is to raise funds and awareness for advancing access to care and finding a cure for breast cancer, with a focus on the medically underserved. From its launch in 1992 through 2007, the multifaceted initiatives of the Avon Breast Cancer Crusade have raised and awarded more than $525 million to the breast cancer cause worldwide. Funding is awarded in five areas: breast cancer education and awareness, screening and diagnosis, access to treatment, support services, and scientific research. Avon now supports programs for breast cancer in some 50 countries around the world. The Crusade raises funds through many initiatives, including year-round sale of special Crusade "pink ribbon" products by Avon independent sales representatives around the world; special events, walks and runs worldwide, including the U.S. Avon Walk for Breast Cancer series and the global Walk Around the World; and direct online donations. See Figure 2.13 for an ad encouraging readers to register for the Avon Walk for Breast Cancer.

## Trade Fairs

Trade fairs or trade shows, as they are also known, are a temporary forum (usually lasting from several days to up to a month) for sellers of a product category to exhibit and demonstrate their wares to prospective buyers. Thousands of trade fairs are conducted annually around the world. Trade fairs play an even larger role abroad than they do in the United States—indeed, some of the world's largest trade fairs take place overseas. (The Paris Air Show is an example.) Trade fairs account for up to one-third of a typical European firm's marketing budget. *Business America* publishes an annual listing of international trade fairs where U.S. manufacturers can exhibit their products. Trade fairs have many functions, including:

- servicing present customers
- identifying prospects
- introducing new or modified products
- gathering information about competitors' new products
- taking product orders
- enhancing the company's image (Kerin and Cron 1987)

In addition, at the international level, trade fairs can prove invaluable to firms in the early stages of internationalizing their business, such as in exporting, as they offer a means of checking out foreign markets. Exhibiting at trade fairs provides firms with a chance to explore market possibilities before making a commitment to an export country—particularly a developing country. Also, many countries offer subsidies to firms participating in joint sales efforts (de Mooij 1994, 371). Potential distributors and agents are also likely to attend such fairs.

There are two main types of trade fairs. Some are broad, general exhibitions, such as the China Import and Export Fair. This fair is so large it is held in three phases over a three-week period, boasting 55,000 exhibitors offering everything from consumer electronics to building materials to heath-related products. Figure 2.14 shows an advertisement promoting the 106th Canton Fair at the China Import and Export Fair Complex in Guangzhou. These are considered "horizontal" trade fairs. In contrast, "vertical" trade

**Figure 2.13:** Invitation to join the Avon Walk for Breast Cancer.

fairs are often sponsored by a specific industry group or field (such as food products, automobiles, or toys). For example, at the Frankfurt Book Fair, over 400,000 titles are on display each year. The fair typically occupies about a dozen floors of five huge halls. In 2008, the space housed more than 7,000 exhibitor booths, with more than half the exhibitors from abroad, and well over 250,000 visitors in attendance (Boos 2008). Trade fairs are not the only means of exhibiting products overseas. Manufacturers may also rent space in trade centers to display their merchandise on a more permanent basis.

A recent innovation is the online trade fair or digital trade fair. "The traditional trade show is typically conducted at a convention center in a major city. As noted in the example above, representatives for the multitude of exhibitors along with hundreds, if not thousands, of potential customers travel to the trade show site to participate in the event. Needless to say, millions of dollars are invested in renting space, setting up exhibits, travelling, lodging, dining, and so on. The online trade show eliminates most of these expenses, a significant benefit. On the downside, such online trade fairs lack the opportunity for physically inspecting products and interacting with trade-show exhibitors on a personal, one-to-one basis. Online trade shows will not eliminate their traditional counterparts, but this would appear to be a growth area" (Shimp 2003, 514).

## Product Integration

Heralded by many as the next big development in marketing, consumer-product integration into media content, such as television, films, video games, and even music, is showing increasingly positive results. Originally known as product placement, the tactic is now beginning to go under the moniker of "product integration" (Fitzgerald 2003). In the United States, product placement in television dates back to the 1940s, when shows such as *Texaco Star Theatre* and *The Colgate Comedy Hour* were funded by advertisers. Back then, there were no separate commercials. Instead, the star of the show would break off to plug the sponsor's product. The system worked well as long as there were only three television networks, because advertisers were rewarded with enormous viewing figures. But as more channels were created, the economics of solo sponsorship were undermined by fragmenting audiences and rising production costs. Eventually the networks took over program production and introduced the concept of the multi-advertiser commercial break. Now, economics are undermining the system again. With hundreds of channels being created, heavy demand for programming is raising the cost of advertising while audiences per channel decline. As a result, the financially squeezed networks are having to rethink the rules that until recently kept advertisers out of programs (Tomkins 2002).

Product placement is also being driven by advertisers' concerns. Advertisers' confidence in the effectiveness of the traditional 30-second spot is waning, based in good part on the findings of a Roper poll. The survey revealed that 39 percent of Americans said they "often" switch to another channel when ads come on, a figure that is up 25 points from 1985. Another 19 percent said they turn down the television or mute it, a 10-point increase. In fact, one of the fastest growing gadgets respondents said they can't live without is the remote control, which 44 percent consider a necessity (only 23 percent did in 1992). And 76 percent feel advertising is "shown in far too many places now, you can't get away from it," a response that jumped 10 points since just 1998 (Ebenkamp 2001). Sprinkled into the mix is the fear of new technology that allows viewers to eliminate television commercials altogether. TiVo and and others in the United States have introduced digital videocassette recorders with internal hard drives instead of cassette tapes, allowing commercials to be skipped or eliminated with a click or two of the remote control. By 2007, an estimated 20.8 million U.S. homes had a DVR, compared to just over 15 million the year before. With around 112 million television homes in the country, this translates into a DVR

**Figure 2.14:** Ad promoting the Canton Fair at the China Import & Export Fair Complex.

penetration of under 20 percent. Interestingly, people in the United Kingdom are more likely to have a DVR than in any other country, relatively speaking. A recent Ofcom survey found that 30 percent of respondents in the United Kingdom said they owned a DVR, compared to one in five in the United States, Canada, or Italy. The figure in France was 17 percent, compared to 13 percent in Japan and just 11 percent in Germany (Digital Video Recorders 2008). By 2006 product placement worldwide was worth $2.21 billion, and, according to a report by PQ Media, the market will grow to nearly $7.6 billion by 2010, largely driven by advertising within dramas, sports, and reality programs. The United States is the world's biggest market for product placement, valued at $1.5 billion. Of that figure, $941 million was spent on television and $500 million on film. Brazil and Australia are the next biggest markets, owing to fewer regulatory controls, with $285 million and $104 million spent respectively. France is ranked fourth at $57 million, primarily due to product placement in its films, and Japan completes the top five at $53 million (Product Placement Set to Triple 2006). EU countries lag behind the rest of the world because of strict rules regarding advertising on television. Interestingly, while product placement on television was banned until quite recently in the United Kingdom, OFCOM announced in September 2009 that the ban would be lifted in an effort to raise funds for commercial broadcasters. However, the ban would remain in force in children's television and on the BBC (Product Placement for TV Approved 2009). While it is expected that the United States will still be the largest market for product placement in 2010, it will likely be overtaken by China as the fastest-growing market for the practice.

The Federal Communications Commission's (FCC) code requires television broadcasters to acknowledge any paid promotions. Brand-name products can appear in television shows without acknowledgment only if the manufacturer has not paid for airtime and if the products are "reasonably related" to the content of the show (Jacobson and Mazur 1995, 71). But advertisers have found ways to get around the rules. In ABC's version of the British quiz show *Who Wants to Be a Millionaire?* for example, AT&T sponsored the program and bought advertising spots during the commercial breaks. Host Regis Philbin even invoked "our friends at AT&T" when contestants phoned a friend for help in answering a question, and an AT&T clock timed the 30-second call. A coalition of 31 groups reported that paid placements rose 13 percent in 2007—totaling 26,000 in the top 10 U.S. television shows. The Campaign for a Commercial-Free Childhood (CCFC) counted about 160,000 placements on cable programs, including placements for Big Macs, Doritos, and Cheerios (Trosclair 2008). According to Nielsen Media Research, television programs with the greatest number of product placements for the period 11/07—11/08, in rank order, are *The Biggest Loser* (6,248), *American Idol* (4,636), *Extreme Makeover Home Edition* (3,371), *America's Toughest Jobs* (2,807), *One Tree Hill* (2,575), *America's Next Top Model* (2,241), *Last Comic Standing* (1,993), *Kitchen Nightmares* (1,853), and *Hell's Kitchen* (1,807). As a result of this deluge, parental, consumer, and writers' groups are demanding better product placement disclosures than those currently employed, which are written in small type and displayed with the credits at the end of the show. Currently, the FCC is examining whether the placement notices should be written in larger print and displayed for a defined period of time.

Some advertising agencies are not only placing products in television programs but are also involved in making the programs. In an effort to gain control over how products are integrated into shows, one of the world's largest advertising agencies and a major producer of reality television are teaming up to make programs on behalf of sponsors and sell them to networks. They hope the networks, facing intense economic pressure and eroding audiences, will be willing to buy the shows—in good part because they should cost less. Under the venture, RDF Media, which makes *Wife Swap* and *Secret Millionaire*, has taken over management of Omnicom Media Group's Full Circle Entertainment, a firm formed in 2004 to develop television programs to showcase advertisers' products. Omnicom's clients include major sponsors Pepsi, McDonald's, and Visa. "The prime-time economic model is under increasing pressure," media analyst Larry Gerbrandt said. "If they bring advertisers in on the ground floor then that might offset some of the production costs. That also means these shows can be profitable even with lower ratings." At the same time, Gerbrandt noted, Omnicom and RDF will have to be careful about turning the programs they produce on behalf of advertisers into thinly disguised informercials. "To work, the show still has to stand on its own," he said (James 2009). For more than half a century, the networks have produced the programming, controlled the content, and invited advertisers to participate. The shows produced by this venture would flip that relationship by putting the advertisers in the driver's seat and the networks more in the passenger's role.

Product placements have also appeared in films for decades. However, until relatively recently, product plugs were the result of an informal barter system between advertisers and film producers. In exchange for featuring a particular brand of auto in a movie, for example, the auto manufacturer would provide wheels for the film's stars during the shoot. However, paid product placements were pioneered in the 1980s, and Steven Spielberg's 1982 film *E.T.* is widely credited with starting the trend—a trend that turned out to be quite profitable to the advertiser. When the alien in *E.T.* nibbled on Reese's Pieces onscreen, sales of the candy soared by over 60 percent. While in the past a film might have had one or two such "sponsors," today's films boast literally dozens. In *Sex & the City: The Movie*, viewers were exposed to 26 different clothing and accessory designers; 8 stores and services; 7 electronic gadgets (including Carrie's Apple computer, an iPhone, and a BlackBerry); 7 publications; 7 drinks and snacks; 5 beauty products; and 8 places or transportation brands (such as American Airlines, Mercedes Benz, and the Four Seasons Hotel).

But for many companies seeking to reach a global audience, an international box office smash can prove far more effective and efficient than domestically produced ads. Today there are dozens of agencies—both in the United States and abroad—that arrange cash deals between filmmakers and corporate sponsors. A corporation will typically retain a product-placement agency for an annual fee, then pay for each placement in a film. Placement fees vary according to the prominence of the plug. Variables include whether the product is used in the background or foreground, whether a character in the program touches the product, wears the product, or talks about the product, and whether it is featured in a product-centered episode. Clearly, the more prominent the placement, the greater the impact on brand-name awareness and recall.

A number of factors are driving the trend toward product integration in Latin America and Asia. but these factors vary on a market-by-market basis. For example, in Argentina, ad spending is down, and broadcasters are having trouble paying for programs to fill their schedules. In this economy, branded content ideas are inspired by survival as much as by a commitment to innovation. Brazil is using product placements in television shows to hype products for export to other countries. The idea is to use Brazil's soap operas, which are shown around the world, to promote Brazilian coffee and soft drinks, clothing, and even jet planes. The soap opera *Esperanca* (Portuguese for "hope") incorporated the quality of Brazilian coffee in its plot, and the program was slated for international sales. The cost of such initiatives is split between industry trade associations and the government's Agency of Export Promotion.

Marketers in India face an entirely different challenge. Here, many rural consumers lack television reception, making it difficult to reach them with this medium. However, the country boasts the world's largest movie industry, with more than 1,000 films being produced each year. Thus it makes sense for marketers to focus on placement in films. In 2001 Publicis Group's Leo Burnett Worldwide opened Leo Entertainment, specializing in creating ads to promote films and arranging product placement in movies. One of Leo Entertainment's first big projects was the film *Kaante* (Hindi for "thorns"). It was a natural fit for Burnett client Coca-Cola Co., which had been looking for ways to enhance the macho image of Thums Up, India's leading cola brand. *Kaante*, in which a gang of six Indians plans the perfect bank robbery in Los Angeles, has the image Thums Up wanted. Thums Up has a more macho, rugged appeal than Coca-Cola or Pepsi. During the movie, the bank robbers drink Thums Up, the cola's logo is visible on a tote bag used in the heist, and the robbers use the "thumbs up" gesture. According to Leo Entertainment, "it is very subliminal, very natural in the film," (Britt 2002, 18). So far, the blurring of advertising with programming worldwide is in its infancy, but all indications suggest that consumers will be seeing a lot more product integration in the future.

## Integrated Marketing Communications

Until quite recently, most firms planned and managed their marketing and promotions functions separately. Increasingly, however, companies are moving toward integrated marketing communications. The American Association of Advertising Agencies defines integrated marketing communications (IMC) as:

> a concept of marketing communications planning that recognizes the added value of a comprehensive plan that evaluates the strategic roles of a variety of communication disciplines, e.g., general advertising, direct response, sales promotion and public relations—and combines these disciplines to provide clarity, consistency and maximum impact. (Duncan and Everett 1993, 30)

A major benefit associated with IMC is synergism, "meaning that the individual efforts are mutually reinforced with the resulting effect being greater than if each functional area had selected its own targets, chosen its own message strategy, and set its own media schedule and timing" (Novelli 1989/1990, 7).

However, even this view of IMC is too narrow. Researchers and practitioners alike have noted that the messages consumers receive about a company and its products are not limited to advertisements, direct-marketing efforts, publicity, and sales promotions. Rather, as Don Schultz and colleagues claim, "almost everything the marketer does relates to or provides some form of communication to customers and prospects, from the design of the product through the packaging and distribution channel selected. These product contacts communicate something about the value and the person for whom the product was designed" (Schultz et al. 1994, 45).

The kind of customer service that is provided after the product is purchased also sends a message to consumers. Thus the other elements of the marketing mix—which have typically been isolated from the communication strategy—are, in fact, sources of information for the consumer as well. In addition, the target audience may gather information about a product or service from conversations with friends, relatives, and co-workers. Even retailers and the media have something to say about a manufacturer's product. According to Schultz and colleagues, "The marketer has very limited control over much of the information and data that the consumer receives.... That's why it's so critical for marketers to maintain some sort of control over the communication they initiate or influence" (Schultz et al. 1994, 45).

IMC, then, is all about managing the various contacts a firm has with its customers, since each of these contacts potentially influences consumer behavior. In order to better manage these contacts, the firm actively solicits responses from consumers. Response solicitation devices may include a telephone call, a direct-mail flyer, a purchase warranty card, or some other form through which the consumer can engage in two-way communications with the manufacturer. Response information is then stored in a database (along with demographic and psychographic data), providing the marketer with the necessary feedback to adjust future communications.

Schultz and colleagues note: "In short, marketing is communication and communication is marketing. The two are inseparable. And, for that reason, the proper integration of all marketing messages is that much more important" (Schultz et al. 1994, 45).

Because IMC was developed in the United States, it was initially practiced predominantly by innovative American firms such as IBM and Eastman Kodak. Today, an ever-increasing number of marketers are exploring the benefits that IMC has to offer. Indeed, integrated marketing communications was ranked as U.S. senior marketers' top priority for the second year in a row, according to a 2008 survey by the Association of National Advertisers (ANA), followed by marketing accountability and aligning marketing organization with innovation (World Federation of Advertisers 2008a). Another ANA study found that fully 74 percent of U.S. marketers now employ IMC campaigns for most of their brands. However, significant challenges to achieving optimal IMC performance remain, with only one-quarter of marketers giving their firms' IMC efforts a "very good" or "excellent" rating. Key barriers to effective IMC as cited in the study are: the existence of function silos (59 percent), the lack of strategic consistency across communication disciplines (42 percent), insufficient marketing budget (36 percent), lack of standard measurement process (36 percent), lack of needed skill sets among marketing staff (33 percent), and need to develop the "big creative idea" that can be leveraged across different media disciplines (32 percent) (World Federation of Advertisers 2008b).

Despite the challenges associated with implementing a fully integrated marketing communications program, most marketers today consider themselves proponents of the approach, and the benefits of IMC are just as applicable when operating in the global marketplace as in the domestic marketplace. In *Communicating Globally: An Integrated Marketing Approach*, authors Don Schultz and Philip Kitchen outline an eight-step integrated global marketing communication planning process:

*Step 1:* Global Customer/Prospect Databases. The authors note that a key ingredient in this approach to developing effective and efficient global marketing communication programs is substantive, continually updated knowledge about customers and prospects. Such information typically comes from databases that the organization maintains. Of particular value is capturing and using information that describes or illustrates the relationship the corporation has with a customer (this includes data on purchases, inquiries, responses to promotions, and any other behavioral data).

*Step 2:* Customer Prospect Valuation. Ideally, an organization should invest its finite resources in cultivating its best prospects. Thus some means of valuing each prospect is essential, and Schultz and Kitchen propose that the best way to value such potential consumers is financially. If the marketer has a sense of how much income a prospect might generate in the future, it can determine how much it is willing to invest to acquire that prospect and turn him or her into a customer.

*Step 3:* Contact Points and Preferences. The marketer should attempt to audit and value the various ways in which customers come into contact with an organization. Such contacts can come about not only through traditional advertising, but also through employees, channel partners, or other means. Then each of those contact points can be viewed as useful methods of communicating in the future.

*Step 4:* Brand or Organization Relationships. The authors note a common practice on the part of many global organizations of treating every customer as if he or she were the same—for example, by preparing a single advertisement and, using a variety of media, sending it out to everyone in the target audience. But relationships with customers vary, so the astute marketer will understand these differing relationships and apply this information in developing effective marketing communication programs.

*Step 5:* Message and Incentive Development and Delivery. At the heart of integrated marketing communication is the premise that you can't develop effective communications unless you understand the audience you are trying to communicate with. And these messages must be communicated via appropriate delivery systems—which may be the traditional forms of media (print, broadcast, direct mail, and so forth), but should be looked at more broadly to include unique forms of delivery as well.

*Step 6:* Estimate on Return on Customer Investment. A marketer's next step is to estimate what type of return or response might be generated from the firm's marketing activities. Clearly, the better the customers or prospects the marketer chooses to invest in, the better the return will be. By knowing the value of the prospects (Step 2) and what the investments in communications are, it becomes possible to estimate what type of return might be generated.

*Step 7:* Investment and Allocation. The next step in the process is the actual determination of financial investment the firm plans to make in customers and prospects. This involves matching up the costs of various marketing communication activities and testing them against estimated returns. For example, if a message needs to be delivered to a specific group, the marketer must determine whether media advertising, direct-marketing approaches, or in-store point-of-purchase efforts will provide the best returns on investment.

*Step 8:* Marketplace Measurement. The final step is to set up systems of measurement to determine marketplace results. This involves determining what the marketer got back for its investment in various prospects and just how long it took to achieve those returns. This information is then input back into the customer/prospect database. Schultz and Kitchen note that this closed-loop, circular system is what really differentiates the integrated marketing communication approach. "Only by using actual marketplace results as the basis for our next planning cycle can we truly become a learning organization. Knowing what worked and what didn't work, knowing what performed up to expectations and what didn't enables us to become better, more effective integrated global marketing communication managers. We can't succeed unless we close the loop" (Schultz and Kitchen 2000, 85).

It has been said that Starbucks's immense popularity is partly the result of its integrated marketing communication initiatives. The Starbucks brand signifies much more than just coffee in the minds of its various stakeholders: it represents a sense of community and shared ideals among employees, customers, and the world at large. Starbucks's marketing efforts include internal marketing, engaging in sustainable development projects, and encouraging customer participation (Storace 2009). The company's positive brand image is partly a manifestation of its efforts with its employees. Both part- and full-time "partners" qualify for a comprehensive package that includes healthcare benefits and stock option grants. Each partner participates in an extensive training program that facilitates strong coffee knowledge, product expertise, and a commitment to customer service. Baristas are encouraged to greet regulars by name and remember their beverage of choice. And customer satisfaction is guaranteed. Headlines from Starbucks's current print campaign read: "If your coffee isn't perfect, we'll make it over. If it's still not perfect, make sure you're in a Starbucks," and "This is what coffee tastes like when you put your heart into it." All bear the tagline: "It's not just coffee. It's Starbucks." The company's brand image is further enhanced through its commitment to sustainable development products. Starbucks realizes that the success of the farmers with whom it does business is intrinsically linked to the sustainability of its business, and it has adopted an integrated and sustainable model based on six fundamental principles:

- Making it their goal to pay premium prices to help farmers make profits and support their families;
- Encouraging participation in C.A.F.E (Coffee and Farmer Equity) Practices, including social and environmental guidelines for producing, processing, and buying coffee;
- Purchasing conservation (shade-grown) and certified coffees, including organic and Fair Trade Certified;
- Providing funds for farmers to access affordable credit so that they can invest in their farms and receive assistance to help them through cash shortages during crop cycles;
- Investing in social development projects in coffee-producing countries;
- Collaborating with coffee producers globally on coffee quality, production, processing, and research through their team of experts at the Starbucks Coffee Agronomy company, located in Costa Rica.

Customers feel that by supporting Starbucks they are helping the world at large. These efforts have helped Starbucks to successfully create a brand image with meaning that transcends tangible product and service benefits, resulting in both client satisfaction and retention. Finally, Starbucks is conscious of how increasing customer participation in its brand can result in heightened loyalty. In introducing Via—the instant coffee product that took 20 years to develop—Terry Davenport, Starbucks's senior VP of marketing, notes: "Instead of selling something at them, we ask them to participate with us" (York 2009b). Starbucks sent its 4 million Facebook friends invitations to participate in taste tests of the new product. The chain expected between 8 and 10 million consumers to visit its 7,500 company-run cafes in the United States and Canada to give the new product a try. Taste-test participants received a "thank you" card good for a free coffee on their next visit, and $1 off their purchase of Via at any Starbucks. Further, Starbucks has questionnaires in all of its stores urging customers to submit feedback about their experiences. These steps, among many others, have helped Starbucks to become one of the most recognized and respected brands in the world.

## SUMMARY

Although the focus of this text is on advertising, the international marketer must realize that decisions relating to advertising in the international arena cannot be made without regard to other promotions efforts or the remaining elements of the marketing mix. From the international marketer's perspective, the elements of the marketing mix are generally seen as the "controllable elements" of the marketing decision. This is the case with both domestic and international marketing. However, international marketers must also deal with a number of elements outside their control when they enter a foreign market. Product, price, distribution, and promotion decisions must be made within a framework of several uncontrollable elements of the specific marketplace—what is commonly known as the marketing environment. Although marketing principles are universally applicable, the environment within which the marketer must implement the marketing plan can and usually does change dramatically from country to country. Thus we turn our attention to this topic in Chapter 3.

## REFERENCES

*Advertising Age* Global Daily News. 2001. P&G launches women's magazine in France. 10 January. <www.adageglobal.com/cgi-bin/daily.pl?daily_id=4187&post_date=2001–01–10>.

Alon, Ilan and Moshe Banai. 2000. Executive insights: Franchising opportunities and threats in Russia. *Journal of International Marketing.* 8(3),: 104-119.

American Marketing Association. 1960. *Marketing definitions: A glossary of marketing terms.* Compiled by the Committee on Definitions, Chicago.

Asher, Jonathan. 2001. Global branding: Same but different. *Brandweek,* 9 April, 25.

BBC Monitoring Asia Pacific. 2009. Ford begins construction of new car factory in China. 25 September. <http://proquest.umi.com.libproxy.sdsu.edu/pqdweb?index=2&did=1>. Retrieved 28 September 2009.

Balfour, Frederik, and Reena Jana. 2008. Are Olympics sponsorships worth it? *BusinessWeek,* 31 July. <http://businessweek.com/globalbiz/content/jul2008/gb200807>. Retrieved 2 October 2009.

Bellman, Eric. 2009. Corporate news: Wal-Mart exports its deep-discounting concept to India. *The Wall Street Journal Asia* (Hong Kong), 29 May, 4.

Bertagnoli, Lisa. 2001. Selling overseas complex endeavor. *Marketing News,* 30 July, 4.

Bittar, Christine. 2002. Seeking cause and effect. *Brandweek,* 11 November, 18–24.

Boddewyn, J. J. 1976. American marketing in the European Common Market 1963–1973. In *Multicultural product management.* Cambridge: Marketing Science Institute, 1–25.

Boddewyn, J. J., Robin Soehl, and Jacques Picard. 1986. Standardization in international marketing: Is Ted Levitt in fact right? *Business Horizons,* 29: November/December, 69–75.

Boos, Juergen. 2008. The 60th Frankfurt Book Fair shows how people and their ideas are at the heart of both print and digital media. Speech held by the Director of the Frankfurt Book Fair at the Preview Press Conference, September 10, in the Literaturhaus, Frankfurt, Germany.

Bowes, Elena. 2002. Where's the cheapest Coke in Europe? EC study investigates. *Advertising Age Global Daily News,* 30 May. <www.adageglobal.com/cgi-bin/daily.pl?daily_id= 7663&post_date=2002–05–30.>

Brand Papers. 2006. Piracy: Faking it can be good. *Brand Strategy* (London), 8 May, 30.

Britt, Bill. 2002. Content, commerce deals offer answers in overseas markets. *Advertising Age,* 21 October, 18.

Britt, Stuart Henderson. 1974. Standardizing marketing for the international market. *Columbia Journal of World Business* 9: Winter, 32–40.

Bulik, Beth Snyer. 2007. Ditch the flags; kids don't care where you come from. *Advertising Age,* 78(23): 4 June, 1.

Bush, Michael. 2010. Consumer consideration, interest in Toyota falls sharply amid recall. *Advertising Age,* 3 February. <http://adage.com/print?article_id=141905>. Retrieved 4 February 2010.

*BusinessWeek.* 2004. The next Wal-Mart? 26 April. <http://businessweek.com/magazine/content/04_17/b3880010.htm>. Retrieved 14 November 2009.

———. 2009. 100 best global brands. 28 September.

*Business Wire.* 2009. Visa introduces first global advertising campaign, entitled "More people go with Visa." 2 March. <http://proquest.umi.com.libproxy.sdsu.edu/pqdweb?index=428&did>. Retrieved 25 September 2009.

Buzzell, Robert D. 1968. Can you standardize multinational marketing? *Harvard Business Review* 6: November/December.

Byron, Ellen. 2007. P&G has big plans for the shelves of tiny stores in emerging nations. *Wall Street Journal Asia* (Hong Kong), 17 July, 16.

Cahn, Kim, and R. A. Mauborgne. 1987. Cross cultural strategies. *Journal of Business Strategy* 7: Spring, 31.

Calfee, John. 2002. Why drugs from Canada won't cut prices. *Consumer's Research Magazine,* November, 10.

Calinoff, Jordan. 2009. China's makeover considered an "evil cult" a few years ago, Amway is now seen in China as a model company. *Pittsburgh Post-Gazette*, 10 May, G1.

Capell, Kerry, and Gerry Khermouch. 2002. Hip H & M. *Business Week*, 11 November, 106–110.

Chandler, Clay. 2005. The great Wal-Mart of China. 25 July. <http://money.cnn.com/magazines/fortune/fortune_archive/2005/07/25>. Retrieved 21 October 2009.

Chartrand, Sabra. 2002. After 13 years of ruminating, the U.S. agrees to join a global trademark system. *New York Times*, 16 December, C-16.

Cohn, Robin. 2000. Crisis readiness: Insurance for your reputation. *Directorship*, September, 16.

Cornwell, Bettina, and Isabelle Maignan. 1998. An international review of sponsorship research. *Journal of Advertising*, 27(1): Spring, 11.

Dawson, Chester, and Dianne Brady. 2002. Land of the rising glue gun. *Business Week*, 7 January, 14.

Deloitte. 2009. Feeling the squeeze: Global powers of retailing. January. <www.deloitte.com/consumerbusiness>. Retrieved 12 September 2009.

de Mooij, Marieke. 1994. *Advertising worldwide*. 2nd ed. New York: Prentice Hall.

Denitto, Emily. 1993. Hyper markets seem to be big flop in U.S. *Advertising Age*, 4 October, 20.

Digital video recorders are most popular in the U.K. 2008. 20 November. <http://informitv.com/news/2008/11/20/digitalvideorecorders/>. Retrieved 2 October 2009.

Domzal, Teresa, and Lynette Unger. 1987. Emerging positioning strategies in global marketing. *Journal of Consumer Marketing*, 4(4): Fall, 23–40.

Douglas, Susan P., and Christine Urban. 1977. Lifestyle analysis to profile women in international markets. *Journal of Marketing*, 61(3): July, 53–54.

Duncan, Thomas R., and Stephen E. Everett. 1993. Client perceptions of integrated marketing communications. *Journal of Advertising Research*, 33(3): May/June, 30–39.

Dunn, Brian. 2007. Wal-Mart global expansion could surpass pace of U.S. *WWD* (New York), 193(59): 21 March, 12.

Ebenkamp, Becky. 2001. Return to Peyton placement. *Brandweek*, 4 June, S-10.

Echikson, William. 1998. When cheese is not just cheese: Getting picky about origin. *Christian Science Monitor*, 22 January, 1.

*Entertainment Newsweekly*. 2009. Gillette launches new global brand marketing campaign. 17 July, 34.

*Entrepreneur Magazine*. 2009. Top global franchises. <www.entrepreneur.com/franzone/listings/topglobal>.

*Euromonitor*. 2002a. International marketing data and statistics. 408.

———. 2002b. European marketing data and statistics. 266.

Fitzgerald, Kate. 2003. Growing pains for placements. *Advertising Age*, 3 February, S-2.

Foster, Malcolm. 2010. Japan Inc.'s image takes a hit. *San Diego Union-Tribune*, 1 February, A-1.

Gajewski, Maciek. 1991. Samples: A steal in Poland. *Advertising Age*, 4 November, 54.

Gibson, Richard. 2006. Franchises abroad need to break the mold; Local mores include long days, feng shui; taking on euro risk. *The Wall Street Journal* (Europe), 26 September, 4.

Global Inflation Rates. 2008. 22 June. <http://seekingalpha.com/article/82217-global-inflation-rates>. Retrieved 28 September 2009.

Goldman, Jordan. 1984. *Public relations in the marketing mix*. Lincolnwood, IL: NTC Business Books.

Green, Frank. 2003. Retail trend: Not-so-superstores. *San Diego Union-Tribune*, 22 February, C-1.

Gumbel, Peter. 2008. Big Mac's local flavor. *Fortune*, 5 May, 115–121.

Hajewski, Doris. 2008. Aldi wins converts: No-frills grocery chain attracts shoppers, steps up its expansion plans. *McClatchy-Tribune Business News* (Washington), 27 July. <http://proquest.umi.com.libproxy.sdsu.edu/pqdweb?index=0&did=1>. Retrieved 28 September 2009.

Harris, Thomas. 1993. *The marketer's guide to public relations.* New York: Wiley.

Healey, James. 2010. *USA Today*/Gallup poll: 55% say Toyota too slow to act. *USA Today*, 2 March. <http://iphone.usatoday.com/Money/1532600/>. Retrieved 26 March 2010.

Hoevell, P. J., and P. G. Walters. 1972. International marketing presentations: Some options. *European Journal of Marketing*, Summer, 69–79.

International Chamber of Commerce's Commission on Commercial Law and Practice. 2005. Fake goods pose major threat to business worldwide, survey reveals. 15 February. <http://www.iccwbo.org/policy/law/iccdebd/index.html>. Retrieved 20 October 2009.

Jacobson, Michael, and Laurie Ann Mazur. 1995. *Marketing madness: A survival guide for consumer society.* Boulder, CO: Westview Press.

*Jakarta Post.* 2009. RI widely accused of price dumping. 10 March. <http://proquest.umi.com.libproxy.sdsu.edu/pqdweb?index=2&did=1>. Retrieved 28 September 2009.

James, Meg. 2009. RDF Media, Omnicom's full circle team to place products. *Los Angeles Times*, 23 March. <http://articles.latimes.com/2009/mar/23/business/fi-cotown-fullcircle23>. Retrieved 2 October 2009.

Johnston, Jean. 1988. Japanese firms in the U.S.: Adapting the persuasive message. *Bulletin for the Association for Business Communications*, 51(3): September, 33–34.

*Journal of Marketing.* 1948. Report of the Definitions Committee. 12 October.

Kale, Sudhir, and D. Sudharshan. 1987. A strategic approach to international segmentation. *International Marketing Review*, 4(2): Summer, 60–71.

Kaplan, David. 2002. How to play the name game with women, men. *Adweek*, 9 September, 3.

Kashani, Kamran. 1989. Beware the pitfalls of global marketing. *Harvard Business Review*, 67(5): September/October, 91–98.

Kerin, Rover A., and William Cron. 1987. Assessing trade show functions and performance. *Journal of Marketing*, 51(3): July, 88.

Khermouch, Gerry. 2002. The best global brands. *Business Week*, 5 August, 92–99.

Kinnander, Ola. 2009. H&M net up 4.1%; ambitious expand. *Wall Street Journal* (Eastern Edition), 25 September, B-4.

Klara, Robert. 2009. Copying machines. *Adweek*, 50(26): 29 June, AM6.

Kotler, Philip. 1986. Global standardization—Courting danger. *Journal of Consumer Marketing*, 3(2): Spring, 13–15.

Kotler, Philip, and Gary Armstrong. 1990. *Marketing: An introduction.* Englewood Cliffs, NJ: Prentice Hall.

Kraar, Louis. 1991. How Americans win in Asia. *Fortune*, 7 October, 133–140.

Levitt, Theodore. 1983. The globalization of markets. *Harvard Business Review*, May/June, 92–102.

Locke, Michelle. 2003. European effort to protect food names leaves bad taste. *San Diego Union-Tribune*, 13 August, C-4.

McCarthy, Jerome. 1960. *Basic marketing: A managerial approach.* Homewood, IL: Irwin.

McClellan, Steve. 2009. MEC Forecasts rise in sponsorships. *Adweek*, 1 June. <http://www.adweek.com/sw/content_display/news/media/e3ic05077>. Retrieved 2 October 2009.

Naughton, Keith. 2006. The great Wal-Mart of China. *Newsweek*, 30 October. <http://www.newsweek.com/id/45140>. Retrieved 20 October 2009.

Neergaard, Lauren. 2008. Labels to identify country of origin. *Daily Herald* (Arlington Heights, IL), 6 October, 4.

Novelli, William D. 1989/1990. One-stop shopping: Some thoughts on integrated marketing communication. *Public Relations Quarterly*, 34(4): 7–9.

Orr, Deborah. 2007. Pirate's ball. *Forbes*, 179(7): 9 April, 49.

Perlman, Ed, and Octavian Timaru. 2008. *Intellectual Property & Technology Law Journal* (Clifton, NJ), 20(2): February, 17.

Pfanner, Eric. 2009. Being local replaces going global: On advertising. *International Herald Tribune*, 12 January, 10.

Product placement for TV approved. <http://news.bbc.co.uk/1/hi/entertainment/8252901.stm>. Retrieved 2 October 2009.

Product placement set to triple. 2006. 17 August. <http://news.bbc.co.uk/2/hi/entertainment/4801135.stm>. Retrieved 2 October 2009.

Ricks, David. 1983. *Big business blunders: Mistakes in multinational marketing.* Homewood, IL: Dow Jones-Irwin.

Ricks, David A., Marilyn Fu, and Jeffrey S. Arpan. 1974. *International business blunders.* Columbus, OH: Grid, Inc.

Ridgley, Marie. 2008. Ethical packaging: The dash to bag a green image. *Marketing Week* (London), 6 March, 28.

Rohwedder, Cecilie, and David Kesmodel. 2009. German discounter Aldi invades Wal-Mart turf. *Wall Street Journal* (Brussels), 14 January, 5.

Rosenberg, Larry. 1980. Deciphering the Japanese cultural code. *International Marketing Review*, Autumn, 47–57.

*Sales Management.* 1967. The $30 million lesson. 1 March, 31–38.

*San Diego Union-Tribune.* 1992a. With multinational ties, it's difficult to tell where products really came from. 2 February, A36.

———. 1992b. Made in America gets tougher to determine. 2 February, A33.

Sanchanta, Mariko, and Toshio Takahashi. 2010. Toyota's recall costs could top $5 billion. *Wall Street Journal* (online ed.), 10 March. <http://proquest.umi.com.libproxy.sdsu.edu/pqdweb?index=7&did=1...>. Retrieved 30 April 2010.

Schultz, Don E., and Philip J. Kitchen. 2000. *Communicating globally: An integrated marketing approach.* Lincolnwood: IL: NTC Business Books.

Schultz, Don E., Stanley L. Tannenbaum, and Robert E. Lauterborn. 1994. *The new marketing paradigm: Integrated marketing communications.* Lincolnwood, IL: NTC Business Books.

Shalofsky, Ivor. 1987. Research for global brands. *European Research*, May, 88–93.

Sheth, Hagdish. 1986. Global markets or global competition? *Journal of Consumer Marketing*, 3(2): Spring, 9–11.

Shimp, Terence A. 2003. *Advertising, promotion & supplemental aspects of integrated marketing communications.* Mason, OH: Thompson-Southwestern.

Sims, G. Thomas. 2005. Europe's market anything but unified. *San Diego Union Tribune*, 5 November, A-12.

Storace, Ottavio. 2009. Starbucks's marketing mojo. 15 July. <http://marketingpr.suite101.com/article.cfm/starvucks_marketing_mojo>. Retrieved 5 October 2009.

Tomkins, Richard. 2000. Laundry, with a minor in linguistics: Once informative, product packaging has gone global and now offers lessons in a dozen different languages. *Financial Times* (London), 10 June, 13.

———. 2002. As television audiences tire of commercials, advertisers move into programs. *Financial Times* (London), 5 November, 21.

Toms, Pete. 2009. Sports marketing is the recession's new shipping boy. 5 March. <http://www.bizofbaseball.com/index.php?option=com_content&view>. Retrieved 2 October 2009.

Trosclair, Carroll. 2008. America's television product placement rules. 30 June. <http://tv-advertising.suite101.com/article.cfm/tv_product_placement_...>. Retrieved 2 October 2009.

Varadarajan, P. Rajan, and Anil Menon. 1988. Cause-related marketing: A coalignment of marketing strategy and corporate philanthropy. *Journal of Marketing*, 52(3): July, 58–74.

Vescovi, Valentina, and Aixa Rocca. 2009. In Spain, Carrefour equates plastic bags with excrement. *Advertising Age*, 15 October. <http://adage.com/print?article_id=139713>. Retrieved 15 October 2009.

Weber, Joseph. 1993. Campbell: Now it's M-m global. *Business Week*, 15 March, 52–56.

Weissart, Will. 2002. Starbucks set for Mexico debut. *San Diego Union-Tribune*, 6 September, C-2.

World Advertising Research Center. 2008. World advertising trends, 24–25.

World Federation of Advertisers. 2008a. Integrated marketing top of mind for U.S. marketers. 4 August.

———. 2008b. US: Integrated marketing embraced by marketers but internal structures limit uptake. 22 May. <http://www/wfanet.org/globalnews.cfm?id=72>. Retrieved 2 October 2009.

York, Emily Bryson. 2007. U.S. weakly: American brands take hits. *Advertising Age*, 78(34): 27 August, 3.

———. 2009a. Subway set to overtake McD's in omnipresence. *Advertising Age*, 21 September, 3.

———. 2009b. Starbucks marketing push for Via begins with taste tests. *Advertising Age*, 28 September. <http://adage.com/print?article_id=139319>. Retrieved 5 October 2009.

# CHAPTER THREE

# The International Marketing and Advertising Environment

Demographic and geographic characteristics, and economic and political-legal factors, all are important not only in evaluating a country's potential as a market but also in designing and implementing the marketing mix for a specific market. Thus, each of these environmental factors will be analyzed in this chapter. The international marketer must consider demographic characteristics (size of the population, rate of population growth, education, population density, and age structure and composition of population), economic factors (GNP per capita, income distribution, and rate of GNP growth), geographic characteristics (size of the country, topographical characteristics, and climate conditions), and the political-legal environment (political stability, laws and regulations, and the degree of nationalism). Clearly, cultural characteristics also play an influential role. However, this aspect of the international marketing and advertising environment will be dealt with separately in Chapter 4. Figure 3.1 shows the relationship of these environmental factors to the marketing mix.

The international marketer generally has very limited, if any, control over these environmental factors. The marketer's task is to assess these factors in order to identify potential barriers to doing business. Firms operating in affluent markets are accustomed to having extensive secondary data available, but obtaining similar data in developing markets can prove quite a challenge. Often, data are inaccurate or simply not available. If no insurmountable barriers are detected, the research on these uncontrollable environmental elements will provide information that allows the international marketer to adapt the marketing mix to the specific market.

**Figure 3.1:** Relationship of environmental factors to the marketing mix.

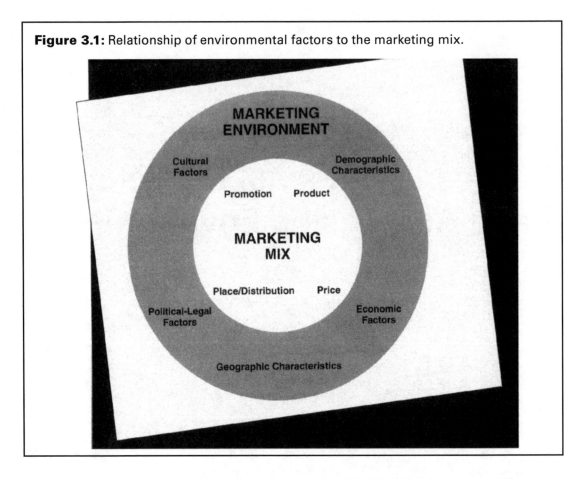

## DEMOGRAPHIC CHARACTERISTICS

Just as the demographic characteristics of various segments within the U.S. population make them more or less appealing to marketers, so, too, do demographic characteristics of foreign countries—such as market size, population growth and distribution, and education—influence a marketer's decision regarding whether and how to enter a market.

### Market Size

The current world population is estimated at 6.8 billion—already more than twice the 1950 figure. It is expected to grow to 7 billion as early as 2012, and to surpass 9 billion people by 2050, according to recently released United Nations projections (United Nations 2009). How these 6-plus billion potential consumers are distributed around the globe is of intense interest to the international marketer. Knowing a market's size is essential in determining whether to enter a market, and a country's population provides one basic indicator of market size. Generally, the larger the population of a market, the greater its potential, all other things being equal. However, population figures alone are usually not a sufficient guide to market size. Population size must typically be combined with many other factors, such as population growth rates, distribution patterns, and available income.

There is enormous variation in the population of countries around the globe, as Table 3.1 shows. The table reveals that well over half the people in the world live in only 10 countries and that the world's largest nation has a population approximately *10,000* times the population of some of the smallest countries.

**TABLE 3.1:** 2007 Population Figures (in millions)

| COUNTRY | POPULATION | COUNTRY | POPULATION |
|---|---|---|---|
| China | 1,318 | Zimbabwe | 13 |
| India | 1,124 | Guatemala | 13 |
| United States | 301 | Greece | 11 |
| Indonesia | 225 | Zambia | 11 |
| Brazil | 191 | Czech Republic | 10 |
| Pakistan | 162 | Belgium | 10 |
| Russian Federation | 142 | Portugal | 10 |
| Japan | 127 | Sweden | 9 |
| Mexico | 105 | Bolivia | 9 |
| Philippines | 87 | Dominican Republic | 9 |
| Germany | 82 | Austria | 8 |
| Egypt | 75 | Switzerland | 7 |
| Thailand | 63 | Israel | 7 |
| United Kingdom | 61 | Libya | 6 |
| France | 61 | Denmark | 5 |
| Italy | 59 | Finland | 5 |
| South Korea | 48 | Jordan | 5 |
| South Africa | 47 | Norway | 4 |
| Colombia | 44 | Ireland | 4 |
| Spain | 44 | Lebanon | 4 |
| Argentina | 39 | New Zealand | 4 |
| Kenya | 37 | Costa Rica | 4 |
| Canada | 33 | Singapore | 4 |
| Venezuela | 27 | United Arab Emirates | 4 |
| Malaysia | 26 | Puerto Rico | 3 |
| Saudi Arabia | 24 | Panama | 3 |
| Yemen | 22 | Oman | 2 |
| Australia | 21 | Mongolia | 2 |
| Sri Lanka | 20 | Slovenia | 2 |
| Netherlands | 16 | Kuwait | 2 |
| Ecuador | 13 | Trinidad & Tobago | 1 |

*Source:* World Bank (2009).

## Population Growth

Most international marketers are also concerned with population growth rates. The world's population is currently growing at a rate of 1.17 percent per year. A number of countries have particularly high rates of growth: Liberia (4.50 percent), Afghanistan (3.85 percent), Niger (3.49 percent), and Uganda (3.24 percent). Other countries' growth rates are more moderate, such as Malaysia (1.69 percent), India (1.46 percent), Mexico (1.12 percent), and China (0.58 percent). Some countries even report declining growth rates: Japan (-0.02 percent), Hungary (-0.29 percent), Russia (0.51 percent), and Ukraine (-0.76 percent) (United Nations 2006). Overall, wealthier countries tend to have more stable populations, while developing countries have rapidly expanding populations.

From the perspective of the international marketer, high population growth rates may indicate the formation of new households, and therefore increased demand for a variety of consumer goods. However, rapidly expanding populations also may have a negative effect on per capita income, translating into more limited purchasing power. Even in countries with stagnant or declining population growth rates, potential exists for the international marketer.

## Population Distribution

Along with population growth rates, the international marketer will need to evaluate the distribution of the population. Three important population distribution characteristics are density, age and age structure, and household size.

*Density:* As with population size, there is a great deal of variation in population density among nations. In 2007, for example, the United States had a population density of 33 persons per square kilometer, as compared to the 4 persons per square kilometer in Canada. Note, however, that most Canadians live within 150 miles of the U.S. border and that the population density is actually much lower in the predominantly uninhabited Yukon and Northwest Territories. On the high end of the scale, Bangladesh has an almost unbelievable 1,118 persons per square kilometer, and Singapore a staggering 6,660 persons per square kilometer (World Bank 2009, 14).

*Age:* One important aspect of age is the average life expectancy of consumers in various markets. In most Western countries, the average life expectancy is quite similar (for example, 77 for the United States, 77 for France, 80 for Canada, and 82 for Japan). In contrast, most people living in developing nations have a relatively short life expectancy (for example, 61 in Pakistan, 50 in South Africa, and 46 in Nigeria) (*Euromonitor* 2005).

Markets also vary in their age structure. Markets with varying age groupings reflect consumers with both differing needs and differing levels of purchasing power. The lower life expectancy in many countries also means their populations are comparatively young. As Table 3.2 shows, a significantly larger percentage of the population in many lower-income countries falls into the 0–14 age grouping than in the higher-income ones. However, even within these groupings, variation exists.

Nearly half of Uganda's population is currently under 14 years of age. One-third of India's population and one-fifth of China's population are currently 14 or younger. Savvy marketers keep an eye to the future—in 15 to 20 years, these citizens will be in their late 20s to late 30s, the prime earning and spending years, which makes these countries particularly appealing to international marketers. However, a profound trend is sweeping the industrialized world: due to plunging birth rates, an ever-increasing percentage of the population is graying. In virtually all countries of the more developed regions, fertility is currently below the replacement level of 2.1 children per woman—the level needed to ensure that a population will replace itself in the long run. The birth rate in European countries has dropped significantly—in Germany, the fertility rate is 1.3, and in southern and central Europe it is 1.2. The pattern is just as dramatic in Japan and Korea, and to a lesser extent in the United States. This

**TABLE 3.2:** Economic Development and Age Structure (percentage 0–14 years)

| LOW-INCOME ECONOMIES (39%) | | LOWER-MIDDLE INCOME ECONOMIES (27%) | | UPPER-MIDDLE INCOME ECONOMIES (24%) | | HIGH-INCOME ECONOMIES (18%) | |
|---|---|---|---|---|---|---|---|
| Uganda | 49 | Philippines | 35 | Venezuela | 31 | United States | 20 |
| Nigeria | 44 | India | 32 | Brazil | 27 | France | 18 |
| Uzbekistan | 32 | China | 21 | Russia | 15 | Germany | 14 |
| Vietnam | 28 | Georgia | 18 | Poland | 15 | Japan | 14 |

*Source:* World Bank (2009).

shift is expected to continue. A few decades hence, even large developing nations like Russia, Brazil, and Thailand will see a surge of retirees. According to United Nations forecasts, by 2050, the average age will go up from 35.6 to 41.3 in the United States, and from 39 to 48.5 in the European Union (De La Dehesa 2004). On the plus side, these older consumer segments tend to be more affluent—having reached the peak of their earning potential. Over-50s are more likely to be mortgage- and debt-free and have savings—translating into money to spend on discretionary items. Ad agencies devoted to appealing to the over-50 segment have begun to crop up around the world, for example, Older & Wiser in Los Angeles and Millennium in London. Over-50s already control 80 percent of the wealth and 60 percent of the savings in the United Kingdom, according to the Henley Centre, a WPP-owned forecasting unit. By 2020, more than 50 percent of the adults in the United Kingdom will be 50 or older, according to the Office of National Statistics. Fiona Hought, managing director of Millennium, says, "This is not a niche audience anymore, but they are not being catered to. Our survey shows that 86 percent of the over-50s don't relate to the advertising they see. On average, over-50s think of themselves as 15 years younger than their actual age, so 50 is the new 35. They hate being stereotyped, and they hate being patronized" (Hall 2008). Increasingly both products and messages will be tailored to meet the needs of this growing segment. However, there are negative implications to this aging trend, as well. Reports reveal that the dependency ratio—defined as the number of people over 65 as a percentage of the number of people 20 to 64 years old—will rise by 2050 to 37 percent from 22 percent in the United States, but will jump to 52 percent from 26 percent in the EU (Brooks 2005). Who will do the work in geriatric societies? Who will support the burgeoning class of pensioners? And what will happen to growth? After all, in addition to productivity, a rising labor force is the key ingredient of economic expansion (Baker 2002, 138).

*Household Size:* A *household* refers to all persons, both related and unrelated, who occupy a housing unit (Engel and Blackwell 1982, 20). The term means very different things in different countries. A household in a developing market typically consists of an extended family, with grandparents and grandchildren, aunts and uncles, and cousins all living under one roof. For example, the average household in Pakistan consists of 7.2 individuals, and 5.2 in India. Also, in many parts of the world, households pool their incomes, which slightly distorts per capita income figures. The typical household in the United States, in contrast, is generally limited to the nuclear family. Average household size in the United States is 2.5, and the figure is even lower for Germany: 2.1. While population figures in many developed countries remain stable, the number of households has increased while the average household size has decreased.

This can be attributed to two factors: increases in both the divorce rate and the number of sole-survivor households. Smaller-sized households have direct implications for the marketers of consumer goods. For example, package sizes may need to be smaller or prepackaged for single servings. This, in turn, impacts advertising message content.

*Education:* Another demographic variable of interest to international marketers is education. The education information available is largely limited to the national enrollments in the various levels of education—primary, secondary, and university or college. A fairly close relationship seems to exist between economic development and educational attainment, with individuals in the more developed countries generally completing more years of education. As one might expect, education is also highly correlated with literacy. From an international marketer's standpoint, consumers must be able to read advertising messages and product labels as well as understand warranty and guarantee information. If large percentages of consumers are illiterate in certain markets, advertising programs and product packaging may need to be modified. Level of education is also of interest because it reflects the degree of consumer sophistication. Complex messages and products that require instructions may need to be adapted depending on educational trends in a particular country. Table 3.3 lists sample rates of literacy by country.

**TABLE 3.3:** Literacy Rates by Country

| COUNTRY | MALE | FEMALE | COUNTRY | MALE | FEMALE |
|---------|------|--------|---------|------|--------|
| Niger | 43 | 15 | Philippines | 93 | 94 |
| Chad | 43 | 21 | Malaysia | 94 | 90 |
| Bangladesh | 59 | 48 | Mexico | 94 | 91 |
| Pakistan | 68 | 40 | Chile | 97 | 96 |
| Mongolia | 69 | 43 | Argentina | 98 | 98 |
| Egypt | 75 | 58 | Hungary | 99 | 99 |
| India | 77 | 54 | Italy | 99 | 99 |
| Guatemala | 79 | 68 | Russia | 100 | 99 |
| Uganda | 82 | 66 | Poland | 100 | 99 |
| S. Africa | 89 | 87 | Ukraine | 100 | 100 |

*Source:* World Bank (2009).

## ECONOMIC FACTORS

In addition to demographic information, international marketers require economic data in order to assess market potential. This is because the attractiveness of a market goes beyond sheer numbers of people—a nation's current and future attractiveness is also based on the willingness and ability of those people to spend. A clear understanding of a host country's economic environment, including type of economy, per capita income, and level of urbanization, is also essential in developing an appropriate marketing and communications strategy.

## Classification Systems

Classifications of economic systems vary depending on the originator of the classification system as well as its intended use. The following system is commonly employed in the marketing literature:

*Subsistence economies:* includes countries in which the vast majority of citizens are engaged in agriculture. They tend to consume much of what they produce and to barter any excess production. Overall, market opportunities here are still rather limited.

- *Raw-material–exporting economies:* includes countries that are rich in one or more natural resources but considered poor in most other ways. Their revenues generally come from exporting these resources—for example, Saudi Arabia (oil) and Zaire (copper and coffee). Such countries tend to be good markets for heavy machinery and tools.
- *Industrializing economies:* includes countries in which manufacturing accounts for roughly 10–20 percent of the national economy—for example, Brazil, Egypt, and the Philippines. As manufacturing increases, these countries may require imports of raw materials and heavy machinery. Industrialization often creates a new rich class as well as a growing middle class, both of which demand a variety of consumer goods.
- *Industrial economies:* includes countries that are major exporters of manufactured goods as well as investment funds. Industrial economies trade goods among themselves as well as export them to industrializing and raw-material–exporting economies. Industrial economies generally have large middle classes, making them ideal for most categories of consumer goods.

Historically, industrial economies have represented the greatest marketing opportunities for corporations, because consumers in these countries typically have the capacity to purchase goods offered by international marketers. In addition, the communications, transportation, financial, and distribution networks necessary to conduct business are in place. However, such markets also tend to have stable or—as noted previously—even shrinking population bases, and as a result, markets for many goods and services may already be saturated. Thus, marketers are increasingly turning to less developed nations, which tend to have expanding populations and therefore potentially greater growth opportunities. For Unilever, the poor already are a huge market. The consumer goods giant has made an art of selling its products in tiny packages costing a few cents each. The conglomerate's Indian subsidiary, Hindustan Lever Ltd., knew that many Indians could not afford to buy a large bottle of shampoo—a product typically used only on special occasions, anyway. So it created single-use packets (in three sizes, according to hair length) that go for a few cents—and now sells 4.5 billion of them a year (Murphy 2002, 169). The strategy has gone global. Unilever's Rexona brand deodorant sticks sell for 16 cents and up. They are big hits not only in India, but also in the Philippines, Bolivia, and Peru—where Unilever has grabbed 60 percent of the deodorant market. A nickel-size Vaseline package and a tube containing enough Close Up toothpaste for 20 brushings sell for about 8 cents each. In Nigeria, Unilever sells 3-inch-square packets of margarine that don't need refrigeration (Kripalani and Engardio 2002, 112).

## Income

A statistic commonly used to describe the economic condition of a country is per capita income, a widely accepted indicator of a country's economic development as well as the potential purchasing power of its individuals. Per capita income is often stated in relation to a country's total income, or gross national product (GNP). The World Bank Atlas method of calculating gross national product

**TABLE 3.4:** 2007 GNI per Capita and Purchasing Power Parity

| COUNTRY | GNI PER CAPITA | PURCHASING POWER PARITY |
|---|---|---|
| Switzerland | $60,820 | $44,410 |
| United States | 46,040 | 45,840 |
| United Kingdom | 40,660 | 34,050 |
| Germany | 38,990 | 34,740 |
| Singapore | 32,340 | 47,950 |
| China | 2,370 | 5,420 |
| India | 950 | 2,740 |
| Bangladesh | 470 | 1,330 |
| Niger | 280 | 630 |
| Ethiopia | 220 | 780 |

*Source:* World Bank (2009).

(also known as GNI, for gross national income) per capita converts national currency units to dollars at prevailing exchange rates, adjusted for inflation and averaged over three years. Because those rates do not always reflect differences in prices, purchasing power parities are united to convert GNI per capita estimates into international dollars. An international dollar buys the same amount of goods and services in a country's domestic market as one dollar would buy in the United States. Table 3.4 shows the wide range in the per capita income figures (both GNI per capita and purchasing power parity) among nations of the world. For example, in 2007, Switzerland had a GNI per capita of U.S. $60,820, while Ethiopia has a GNI per capita of little more than U.S. $220.

Note that per capita figures are averages and give no indication of income distribution. Typically, the more developed the country, the more even the distribution of income. In many developing countries, however, there is a bimodal distribution of income—a very rich segment of the population and a very large, very poor segment with literally no middle class. The following serves as a useful classification system:

- *Very low family incomes:* subsistence economies characterized by rural populations in which consumption relies on personal output or barter. Some urban centers may provide markets.
- *Mostly low family incomes:* economies that are beginning to industrialize. Most goods are produced domestically.
- *Very low, very high family incomes:* economies that exhibit strongly bimodal income distributions. The majority of the population may live barely above the subsistence level, while a minority provides a strong market for imported or luxury items. The affluent are truly affluent and will consume accordingly.
- *Low, medium, and high family incomes:* economies in which industrialization has produced an emerging middle class with increasing disposable income. However, due to traditional social class barriers, the very low—and very high—income classes tend to remain.

*Mostly medium family incomes:* advanced industrial economies with institutions and policies that reduce extremes in income distribution. The result is a large and comfortable middle class able to purchase a wide array of both domestic and imported products and services. (Kotler 1988, 383)

Household income may be a more telling statistic than GNP per capita. In many developing countries, the extended family rather than the nuclear family is the norm. For example, in Latin American countries the typical household includes aunts, uncles, cousins, grandparents, and sometimes even great-grandparents. Several family members may be wage earners, directly impacting the buying power of the family unit. And while the nuclear family is still the norm in the United States, today that unit typically includes two wage earners. As a result, international marketers often pair household income with household size in analyzing a market's willingness and ability to spend. Clearly, available income directly influences what individuals are capable of purchasing. Table 3.5 reveals the varying degrees to which consumers possess various goods in both developed and developing countries.

As can be seen from the figures above, there is a great deal of variation in the ownership of durable goods. Automobile ownership ranges from 93 cars for every 100 households in the United States to just 3 cars per 100 households in China—one of the lowest rates in the world. Indeed, for years most cars in China were sold to state institutions and companies, or ended up in taxi fleets. This is now changing. China's vehicle market has grown dramatically in recent years, overtaking Japan in 2006 to become the world's second largest by annual sales. And in January 2009, monthly auto sales in China surpassed those in the United States for the first time (China's Monthly Auto Sales 2009). Every major international auto manufacturer is now present in the Chinese market. Chrysler, whose U.S. sales slumped 30 percent in 2008, saw its sales double in the Chinese market. Toyota Motors, the Japanese auto giant, sold 17 percent more vehicles in China in 2008. Its rival, Honda Motors, posted an 11.7 percent gain during the same year. And Europe's largest auto-maker, Volkswagen AG, reported a 12.5 percent jump in China sales in 2008—to more than 1 million vehicles, building on its successful sponsorship for the Beijing Olympics (Auto Giants 2009). The number of Chinese car owners is expected to surge fivefold

**TABLE 3.5:** Possession of Goods (per 100 households)

| | SHOWER | WASHING MACHINE | REFRIGERATOR | AUTO | TELEPHONE | PERSONAL COMPUTER |
|---|---|---|---|---|---|---|
| Argentina | 93.6% | 49.5% | 83.8% | 58.9% | 69.8% | 26.6% |
| Canada | 99.6 | 85.7 | 99.1 | 86.4 | 88.7 | 59.1 |
| China | 42.7 | 2.6 | 6.7 | 3.0 | 27.1 | 15.7 |
| India | 42.7 | 4.9 | 14.7 | 0.6 | 17.3 | 1.0 |
| Japan | 99.7 | 99.3 | 97.7 | 81.8 | 87.4 | 49.1 |
| Mexico | 68.7 | 41.0 | 68.7 | 23.0 | 31.1 | 9.2 |
| Philippines | 84.2 | 8.1 | 43.8 | 7.8 | 12.2 | 3.1 |
| Singapore | 99.6 | 95.4 | 99.4 | 43.4 | 96.7 | 63.7 |
| South Africa | 59.8 | 26.3 | 80.4 | 9.4 | 29.3 | 8.9 |
| Thailand | 67.0 | 5.0 | 70.4 | 35.4 | 29.7 | 9.8 |
| U.S. | 99.7 | 82.3 | 99.5 | 93.2 | 85.9 | 72.7 |
| Venezuela | 92.3 | 39.6 | 83.1 | 47.5 | 42.7 | 13.0 |

*Source: Euromonitor (2006).*

in the next decade, touching an average of 148 cars per 1,000 residents by 2020 (Foreign Carmakers Gung-ho 2009). Ultimately, China has the potential to become the largest car market in the world.

Critics of globalization note that free trade and cross-border investment have benefited the rich at the expense of the poor. They argue that the ranks of the poor are growing, and that the disparity between rich and poor has grown. However, recent research has shown that, contrary to popular belief, it is precisely during the recent period of increased globalization of the world economy that poverty rates and global income inequality have most diminished. Global poverty measured at the $1.25 a day poverty line has been decreasing since the 1980s. The share of the population living on less than $1.25 a day fell 10 percentage points, to 42 percent in 1990, and then fell nearly 17 percentage points between 1990 and 2005. The number of people living in extreme poverty fell from 1.9 billion in 1981 to 1.8 billion in 1990 and to about 1.4 billion in 2005. This substantial reduction in extreme poverty over the past quarter century, however, disguises significant regional variation. For example, the greatest reduction in poverty occurred in East Asia and the Pacific, where the poverty rate declined from 78 percent in 1981 to 17 percent in 2005, and the number of people living on less than $1.25 a day dropped more than 750 million. Much of this decline was in China. In contrast, the poverty rate fell only slightly in Sub-Saharan Africa—from less than 54 percent in 1981 to 51 percent in 2005. But the number of people living below the poverty line nearly doubled (World Bank 2009). Nonetheless, corporations have continued to operate in just such markets. Coca-Cola has been operating in Africa for almost 60 years, though the entire continent still brings in only 3 to 4 percent of its profits. To make the product as affordable as possible in African markets such as Zimbabwe, Coke uses local inputs and distribution, offers a break on the price of the formula to operations, and reduces recurring costs, such as packaging (Coke uses returnable glass bottles in most poor markets, for example).

Many multinationals, driven by conscience, have signed on to the idea that they have to do more in poor countries than slurp up profits and spit them out back home in the form of dividends (Murphy 2002, 164). London's Freeplay Energy Group proves that good corporate citizenship can also be good business. In 1996, Freeplay helped to pioneer the windup radio, which can be charged by cranking a handle. In the West, where they sell for up to $100, they are especially popular among campers. But Freeplay has found a much more rewarding market in sub-Saharan Africa, where only 30 percent of homes have electricity, and per capita incomes are $100 to $300 a year, prohibiting the regular purchase of batteries. Here Freeplay sells its radios at a discount to aid agencies and governments, so that Africans can listen to public-service broadcasts of health and agriculture information and school lessons. In Rwanda, Freeplay's radios went to 65,000 teenagers who are heads of their households because their parents died in civil strife. A private company, Freeplay says its radio business is profitable (Kripalani and Engardio 2002, 112). Corporate social responsibility will be addressed in greater detail in Chapter 10.

## Urbanization

One of the most telling economic indicators is the degree to which a country is urbanized. Table 3.6 shows the degree of urbanization for the world's four broad economic groupings. The averages for these groupings reveal a strong correlation between degree of urbanization and level of economic development. However, even within the broad economic groupings, there is significant variation. Typically, the more urbanized markets tend to be more appealing to international marketers. Developing countries are generally much less urbanized and, as a result, tend to be less attractive markets, particularly for consumer goods. Even less developed countries, however, may contain sizable pockets of high-income consumers. Products targeted to the urban markets in such countries may need only minimal changes

**TABLE 3.6:** Economic Development and Urban Population (as percentage of total population), 2007

| LOW-INCOME ECONOMIES | 32% | UPPER-MIDDLE INCOME ECONOMIES | 75% |
|---|---|---|---|
| Ethiopia | 17% | South Africa | 60 |
| Bangladesh | 27 | Malaysia | 69 |
| Vietnam | 27 | Mexico | 77 |
| Pakistan | 36 | Brazil | 85 |
| **LOWER-MIDDLE INCOME ECONOMIES** | 42% | **HIGH-INCOME ECONOMIES** | 77% |
| India | 29% | Hungary | 67% |
| Thailand | 33 | United States | 81 |
| China | 42 | United Kingdom | 90 |
| Philippines | 64 | Singapore | 100 |

*Source:* World Bank (2009).

from those marketed in developed countries. However, if the marketer is attempting to reach both the rural and urban populations in developing countries, a greater degree of product specialization is likely to be required (Hill and Still 1984, 62). In any case, whether consumers live in predominantly urban or rural areas directly influences the media selected to disseminate advertising messages.

## GEOGRAPHIC CHARACTERISTICS

Geography, which refers to the earth's surface, climate, continents, countries, and available resources, is an uncontrollable environmental element that the international marketer cannot ignore. Topography and climate are of particular interest here. A market's physical characteristics may affect the international marketer's appraisal of a market and may well influence a number of the marketing mix factors.

Topography refers to the surface features of a country—its rivers, lakes, deserts, forests, and mountains. These characteristics are of interest to the international marketer in that they may impact product distribution. For example, large mountain ranges or bodies of water may complicate the physical distribution of products. In contrast, predominantly flat surface areas typically translate into easy transportation by road or rail, and navigable rivers likewise enable economical transportation. Further, the topography may serve to separate groups within the larger market. For example, consumers living in the highland regions of a country may display differing consumption behavior from those living in the valleys or flatlands.

Altitude, humidity, and temperature are all features of a country's climate. The climate and its degree of variation throughout the year can potentially impact what products a firm offers for sale, how they are distributed, and even how they are priced. The products that consumers may need will vary, depending on whether they live in tropical, temperate, desert, or arctic regions. For example, whether an automobile manufacturer equips vehicles with air conditioners or heaters depends on where those autos are being shipped.

## THE POLITICAL-LEGAL ENVIRONMENT

International marketers must have a good understanding of the political systems as well as the laws and regulations of the market in which they operate. Both the political system and local laws shape a given country's business environment and may directly impact various aspects of the marketing program, including whether a product can be sold in a particular country and how it will be distributed, priced, and, in particular, advertised. Legal and political constraints can be particularly challenging for the international marketer to overcome. A variety of factors influence the political-legal relationship between an international firm, its home country, and the host country in which it hopes to operate.

### Political-Legal Environment of the Home Country

The political environment in most countries typically provides support for the international marketing efforts of firms located in that country. Governments may engage in efforts to reduce trade barriers or to increase trade opportunities. The United States, for example, has traditionally had a liberal attitude toward exports and imports. In other instances, however, foreign policy or national security concerns may result in constraints on free trade.

*Trade Sanctions:* Governmental actions that restrict the free flow of goods and services between countries are known as *trade sanctions.* Sanctions often are used during times of war as a means of forcing countries to behave peacefully. In the 1992 Gulf War, for example, the United States imposed severe trade sanctions against Iraq and encouraged other countries to do the same. Trade sanctions may also be employed in the hopes of changing a nation's government or its policies. Reasons for the imposition of trade sanctions have varied, ranging from violations of human rights to terrorist activities and even nuclear armament. For instance, in 1994, President Bill Clinton lifted a 19-year trade embargo against Vietnam. In anticipation of the lifting of the ban, at least six advertising agencies moved to establish relationships in the market. U.S. businesses cheered because the move immediately created sales opportunities for companies hungry to catch up with their foreign competitors in Vietnam, a market of over 70 million potential consumers. Much like the advertising agencies, many U.S. corporations, including Motorola, Microsoft, Coca-Cola, and Caterpillar had already laid the groundwork during the embargo. The company's plans included building roads and sewage systems. Caterpillar had opened two sales offices and even began taking orders—but was forbidden from actually making transactions until after the embargo was lifted. With regard to South Africa, against which the United States imposed economic sanctions in 1988, Steven Burgess, a marketing professor at the Witwatersrand University School of Business Economics, noted: "If we have a nonracial government here tomorrow morning, South Africa becomes a boom town" (Barnes 1993). Burgess's prophecy has proven correct. Multinational firms returned to South Africa in record numbers since the fall of apartheid and the subsequent lifting of the economic sanctions. For example, PepsiCo, which divested in protest against apartheid in the mid-1980s, is again selling its products in this nation. Following the decision by Pepsi to re-enter South Africa, its worldwide lead agency, BBD&O, also announced its return. BBD&O was one of South Africa's biggest shops until it was liquidated when the ban was imposed (Koenderman 1994). Multinationals such as General Motors, Honeywell, IBM, Procter & Gamble, and Sony see this nation of 35 million potential consumers as an appealing starting point for the rest of southern Africa.

The United States currently prohibits firms from dealing with Cuba. The United States instituted a trade embargo against Cuba in 1962 when dictator Fidel Castro seized power. The embargo was codified into law in 1992 with the purpose of maintaining sanctions on the Castro regime so long as it continued to refuse movement toward democratization and greater respect for human rights. But the Trade Sanctions Reform and Export Enhancement Act of 2000 permited shipments of humanitarian cargo such as food and medicine. So, in November 2001, when Hurricane Michelle devastated parts of Cuba, the United States responded with aid. Thus the United States's first commercial shipment of food to Cuba in nearly 40 years was delivered—nearly 96,000 metric tons of food. Many marketers expressed hope that this signalled a shift in U.S. policy. By the end of 2001, the U.S. Congress began allowing food and agricultural exports. "The trade door was opened a crack, and now products are flowing through that crack," said Steve Appel, vice president of the American Farm Bureau. "We expect that crack to grow wider and wider" (Case 2003). Indeed, purchases have continued and grown since then. By 2007, the United States was the largest food supplier of Cuba and its fifth-largest trading partner. Nonetheless, at present, the embargo, which limits American firms from conducting business with Cuban interests, is still in effect, and violators are faced with severe penalties. Criminal penalties for violating the embargo can include up to ten years in prison, $1 million in corporate fines, and $25,000 in individual fines. This is the most enduring trade embargo in modern history and, it should be noted, has been condemned by much of the international community.

Clearly, if trade with certain countries or regions is cut off, the international firm may incur significant loss of business. Therefore, international firms must actively monitor the political climate in the countries in which they do business in order to anticipate potential sanctions and prepare for the consequences.

*Export and Import Controls:* Two additional governmental activities that may directly impact the international marketer are export controls and import controls. *Export controls* are usually designed to prevent adversaries from acquiring strategically important goods, or at least to delay their acquisition. In the United States, exporters of defense-related equipment, for example, must obtain a license from the U.S. Department of Commerce permitting shipment. In fact, in order for any good, service, or idea to be exported from the United States, the exporter must obtain an export license from the Department of Commerce, which administers the Export Administration Act (Springer 1986, 10). The Department of Commerce has a list of commodities available whose export is considered sensitive. Goods may be ranked high on this list due to concerns over national security, foreign policy, limitations in supply, or nuclear proliferation. An additional list ranks countries according to their political relationship with the United States.

If an industry—particularly a strategic industry—faces strong competition from imports, it may pressure government for protection against foreign goods. It is often argued that such protection is necessary to save jobs and that increased imports may further worsen the U.S. balance of payments. In response to such pressure, minimum prices may be set for imported goods. While import barriers often encourage foreign firms to invest in the domestic market, resulting in capital inflows, all too often consumers bear the brunt of protective measures—paying higher prices for goods and finding fewer choices available.

## Political-Legal Environment of the Host Country

In evaluating a host country, the international marketer also must gauge its degree of economic, as well as political, stability. Because entering a foreign market generally translates into a long-term commitment, firms seek assurance of relatively stable governmental policies regarding foreign business. In most countries, the political environment is relatively stable. However, a glance at world headlines in recent years, and even recent months, reveals that political environments can change rapidly. In 1990 the Soviet Union was a socialist country; today, Russia and most of the republics are taking steps toward capitalism. Similarly, East Germany no longer exists, and the nations of Eastern Europe are evolving before our very eyes from Soviet satellites to viable political and economic entities—as members of the European Union.

## Political Risk

Should a firm choose to operate in a country where the political risk is high, it may face civil disturbances, terrorism, and possibly even warfare. Political unrest is often associated with an anti-industry element, making the company and its employees potential targets for violence. Even when such violence seems unlikely, the international marketer may still be faced with adverse governmental actions, which include expropriation, confiscation, domestication, and a variety of other impediments to trade.

*Expropriation* refers to the takeover of a foreign investment by the host government. While it does not relieve the host government from providing some compensation to the former owners, compensation negotiations are often protracted and often result in settlements unsatisfactory to the owners. Moreover, if expropriation occurs, it can ward off other foreign firms. *Confiscation* is similar to expropriation in that ownership of the firm is transferred to the host country. However, when a firm is confiscated, no compensation is forthcoming. Certain industries are more prone than others to expropriation or confiscation—particularly those considered by the host nation to be critical to national defense or national wealth. Many countries, however, are turning from expropriation and confiscation to *domestication*. Here, the host government demands partial transfer of ownership and management responsibility and imposes regulations to ensure that a large share of the product is locally produced and a large share of the profit is retained in the country.

Restrictions affecting imports can be classified as tariff and nontariff barriers. A *tariff* is simply a tax imposed by a government on goods entering its borders. A tariff may be imposed either to generate revenues or to discourage the importation of goods in an attempt to protect domestic products from being outpriced by cheaper imports. As such, tariffs can serve as a very effective form of protectionism. Worldwide, tariffs range from minimal to quite hefty. Virtually every significant trading economy around the world has permanent tariff systems—with the exception of Hong Kong and Libya, which have none, and Singapore, which imposes tariffs only on beets and a local liquor called samsu. The World Bank calculates the average worldwide tariff on manufactured goods at about 7 percent. Typically, the tariff on agricultural goods is somewhat higher. In most developed countries, average tariffs are less than 10 percent, and often less than 5 percent. The average U.S. tariff is about 3 percent. Developing countries, as a group, have higher average tariff rates than developed countries. But for many countries that have recently joined the World Trade Organization, tariffs have been reduced substantially in order to gain entry. In addition, the United States, as well as many other countries, has laws that, under special circumstances, impose temporary tariffs above permanent rates. The most commonly used is the anti-dumping tariffs, a five-year penalty intended to compensate for the "below-cost" sale of goods.

*Nontariff barriers* are equally serious impediments to trade. One form of nontariff barrier is the *quota*—a numerical or dollar limit applied to a specific category of goods. Quotas are not something only other countries do. The automobile industry provides a classic example. In the early 1980s, the United States government imposed quotas on Japanese auto imports in order to reduce the number of autos shipped to this country. Standards are another form of nontariff barrier. Whether imposed by design or accident, stringent requirements affecting the product, its packaging and labeling, and testing methods serve to restrict the entry of foreign goods. Bureaucratic red tape (such as customs guidelines or extensive documentation) also may effectively serve to discourage imports.

In addition to controlling the movement of goods across borders, host countries also influence the movement of capital into and out of their markets. *Exchange controls* may be employed by host governments that face a shortage of foreign currency; such controls can make it difficult for the international firm to remove its profits and investments from a country. When a country's balance of payments is unfavorable or unstable, it will not want precious capital to cross its borders. Thus, for instance, rather than originally selling Pepsi to the former Soviet Union, PepsiCo engaged in barter—trading Pepsi for vodka.

Foreign countries may also exercise control over exchange rates. Currency needed to purchase foreign luxuries often carries high exchange rates while necessities receive more favorable rates. Such controls may be implemented in an effort to reduce the importation of goods that are considered unnecessary. Countries may also raise the tax rates applied to foreign investors in an effort to control the firms and their capital. Such tax increases may result in much-needed revenue for the host country, but they can severely damage the operations of the foreign investors.

In order to reduce the risk of adverse governmental actions, the international firm must demonstrate genuine concern for the welfare of the host country and not simply for its own profits. International firms can convey this message in a variety of ways. They can employ locals, particularly in management and decision-making positions, and offer fair pay and favorable working conditions. Local production of goods, production utilizing local materials, and the use of local suppliers all help to strengthen the image of the firm as a good corporate citizen.

*Political Risk:* While international marketers may still find it profitable to do business with an unstable country, the situation will certainly affect how business is conducted. International marketers must assess the economic and political risk of each country the firm considers entering and, once operations have been set up, must continually monitor the risk level.

A few major corporations have a separate office or staff assigned to evaluating risk in foreign markets they plan to enter, as well as dealing with crises in countries in which they already operate. However, for most small-and medium-sized companies, such an undertaking is unrealistic because of the cost, expertise, and resources required. These firms have a number of alternatives. One option is to hire a firm specializing in this area. For a fee (often ranging upward of $10,000), such firms advise their clients on the risks of doing business abroad as well as provide training for executives on how to protect themselves, cope with potential kidnapping and extortion, and guide their employees in political crises. Another alternative is to utilize one of a number of risk-assessment reports available to assist such international marketers in determining which countries are likely to prove most hazardous. Some of these measurement techniques focus very narrowly on whether a country has an open or closed political system. A political system is considered open "when non-governmental actors can shape events by voicing their approval or discontent in the form of voting, protests, boycotts, and so on. In closed systems, a government does not allow these forms of expression publicly and the repression of the populace can lead to violent encounters" (Onkvisit and Shaw 1997, 150). Others are broader, examining not only the political risk, but the country risk in general. For example, to obtain an overall country risk score, *Euromoney* magazine assigns a weighting to a variety of categories in addition to political risk: economic performance, debt indicators, credit ratings, access to bank finance, access to short-term finance, and access to capital markets (O'Leary 2002, 208). Countries regularly ranked as least risky include Luxembourg, Norway, Switzerland, Denmark, Sweden, Ireland, Austria, Finland, the Netherlands, and the United States. Countries posing the greatest risk include the Sudan, Cuba, Iraq, Afghanistan, North Korea, Liberia, Somalia, Libya, and Ethiopia. Another valuable resource is the country credit rating, which is prepared by *Institutional Investor* magazine. This report is based on a survey of 100 leading international banks concerning a country's credit worthiness and the chance of payment default. As an alternative to subscribing to such reports, major banks can provide assistance to clients in assessing business risks overseas. Bank of America, for example, uses a ranking system based on a common set of economic and financial criteria to evaluate eight countries for business risk.

*Nationalism:* The degree of nationalism a foreign market exhibits may make it more or less appealing to the international marketer. Some nations are quite receptive to foreign firms and may actively encourage investment from abroad, while others are quite hostile. It is a fact that there are more Barbie dolls in the United States than people. However, she has not been so warmly embraced in a number of nations. She is banned in Saudi Arabia as a symbol of Western decadence. A ban was proposed in Russia because of her "harmful effects on the minds of young girls," and in Malaysia on the grounds that Barbie "does not encourage creativity since she is ready-made." In Iran, the importation of toys from the West has been discouraged for more than a decade. In particular, top Iranian officials have warned about the "destructive" cultural and social consequences of importing Barbie dolls. Barbie has been called a "Trojan horse—sneaking in Western influences such as makeup and revealing clothes" (Iranian Official 2008). Barbie is sold wearing swimsuits and miniskirts in a society where women must wear headscarves in public and men and women are not allowed to swim together. Iran has introduced its own competing dolls—the twins Dara and Sara—who were designed to promote traditional values with their modest clothing and pro-family stories. But the dolls proved unable to stem the Barbie tide.

Firms will clearly receive a better reception from a host country that has positive relations with its own country. A wide spectrum of factors can impact these relations. For example, if a host country is critical of some aspect of the foreign policy of the international firm's home country, the firm may be subject to fallout from this criticism. Another factor is whether the home country has particularly friendly or antagonistic relations with either the host country or even other nations. In such a case, a number of elements of the marketing mix may require modification. For example, products might be adapted, and commercial messages may play down rather than emphasize the advertised product's country of origin. McDonald's provides an excellent example. During most of the 78-day air war against Yugoslavia in the fall of 1999, McDonald's kept the burgers flipping while NATO kept the bombs dropping. Vandalized at the outset by angry mobs, McDonald's Corp. was forced to temporarily close its 15 restaurants in Yugoslavia. But when local managers again opened their doors, they accomplished an extraordinary comeback using an unusual marketing strategy: they put McDonald's U.S. origins on the back burner.

> To help overcome animosity toward a quintessential American trademark, the local restaurants promoted the McCountry, a domestic pork burger with paprika garnish. As a national flourish to evoke Serbian identity and pride, they produced posters and lapel buttons showing the golden arches topped with a traditional Serbian cap called the sajkaca (pronounced shy-KACH-a). They also handed out free cheeseburgers at anti-NATO rallies. The basement of one restaurant in the Serbian capital even served as a bomb shelter. Once the war was over, cash registers began ringing at prewar levels. In spite of falling wages, rising prices and lingering anger at the United States, McDonald's restaurants around the country were thronged with Serbs hungry for Big Macs and fries. (Block 1999)

Though they are registered as local businesses, every restaurant in the former Yugoslavia is in fact 100 percent owned and operated by McDonald's. Key to the success of the campaign was presenting McDonald's as a Yugoslav company.

Nationalism is often cyclical. Back in the early 1990s, everything Western was embraced in Russia. President Boris Yeltsin even complained to the Russian Duma about the "Snickerization" of his country's economy, referring to the phenomenal success Mars Inc. had in penetrating the market. A newspaper poll in 1994 revealed that fully 85 percent of Russians had sampled a Snickers bar. Amaretto, a novelty liqueur from the West, was the "in" drink in bars, and everyone watched the latest Sylvester Stallone movie. At the time it was very uncool to be Russian. But with the rise in political nationalism under President Vladimir Putin, consumer nationalism also began to rise. Radio stations began to play all-Russian rock, and the "made-in-Russia" labels became increasingly common in supermarkets. Russian bars promoted domestic beer, and kerchiefed babushkas starred in cutting-edge music videos. The trademark onion domes of Russian churches decorated labels for chocolate bars and dumplings. Marketing surveys confirmed how dramatic the turnabout was. Before 1998, according to the firm Comcon, only 48 percent of Russians said they preferred to buy domestic goods when considering quality and not just price. By 1999, that figure had jumped to 90 percent (Glasser 2001).

The striking change was clearly accelerated by the 1998 ruble devaluation that made many imported goods inaccessibly expensive for Russians. But some say the change suggests something deeper—perhaps the wounded pride of an ex-superpower struggling to reassert itself. Western companies once found it easy to sell anything with English on the package. Now, if a product isn't *nasha*—Russian for "ours"—it's simply harder to sell. "The most successful products today are local ones created by Western companies and promoted using Western techniques—but aimed at Russian patriotism," noted Alexander Gromov, managing director of the Moscow office of the ad agency Saatchi & Saatchi. "They are talking to Russians speaking their language—but using all the tricks of western advertising" (Glasser 2001).

Mars responded successfully to this "Russification." When the U.S. confectionary giant introduced a new candy bar in the country, they named it Derzhava—a politically loaded word that translates literally as "power" and is the unofficial slogan of Russia's strong-state crowd. The Derzhava television ad campaign appeals directly to Russians who believe they have been left behind by capitalism: a husband, his wife, and her mother sit at their modest country dacha watching in disgust as their nouveau-riche neighbors haul in tacky statues to adorn their glitzy new palace. As the husband bites into his chocolate, he reassures the tea-drinking mother and daughter: "Forget about money; taste is everything."

## International Law

A variety of international laws and agencies regulate business across national boundaries.

*The International Monetary Fund (IMF):* Marketers typically exchange goods and services for money. Either gold or an internationally acceptable currency is necessary for this exchange. Currently, U.S. dollars are the most widely used medium of exchange in international trade, followed by the euro and the yen. There is some speculation that the euro—or possibly some other currency—has the potential of replacing the U.S. dollar as the world's major currency. The IMF, created at the end of World War II, works to foster global monetary cooperation, secure financial stability, facilitate international trade, promote high employment and sustainable economic growth, and reduce poverty. It works to diminish the degree of nationalistic actions taken by countries, thereby decreasing financial barriers to international trade. The IMF also lends money to member countries facing deficits in their international debt payments, allowing them to continue trading on the world market, until they can correct their payment problems. At present the fund has over 186 member countries, accounting for over 80 percent of total world production and 90 percent of world trade.

*World Bank:* Membership in the World Bank is open to all members of the IMF, and the bank is owned and controlled by its 186 member governments. Each member country subscribes to shares for an amount reflecting its relative economic strength. The United States is the bank's largest shareholder. The primary purpose of the bank is to provide both financial and technical assistance to developing countries. The World Bank's goal is to help raise the standard of living in poor countries. The bank provides loans for a variety of projects related to agriculture, rural development, education, population planning, electrical power, transportation, telecommunications, and water supply. The bank evaluates the prospects for repayment before granting loans. Loans are usually repayable over a 20-year period.

*General Agreement on Tariffs and Trade (GATT):* The General Agreement on Tariffs and Trade was initially set up in 1948 as a temporary body to ensure that the discriminatory trade practices of the 1920s and 1930s would not again plague international business. The United States and 22 other countries signed this agreement. The multinational, intergovernmental treaty, which operated within the framework of the United Nations, had approximately the same membership as the IMF. GATT's rules governed trade relations between member countries, the goal of which was the reduction of trade barriers and the further liberalization of world trade. The growth achieved during the past quarter century in the world economy is due in no small part to the efforts of GATT.

*World Trade Organization (WTO):* Even though GATT was successful in reducing tariff barriers around the globe, the increased use of nontariff barriers such as quotas and subsidies went largely ignored. GATT also focused primarily on manufactured goods, and yet trade in services—such as banking, insurance, and accounting—has also increased globally. Further, a number of countries have become increasingly concerned about the lack of intellectual property protection and the lax enforcement of existing patent, trademark, and copyright laws. Using GATT as its foundation, the World Trade Organization was created in 1995 in order to address these issues (Terpstra and Russow 2000). Initially GATT and WTO coexisted, but GATT ceased to exist after 1996. WTO, being more permanent than GATT, will have greater authority to settle trade disputes and will serve along with the IMF and the World Bank to monitor trade and resolve disputes. The WTO currently has 159 members representing more than 95 percent of total world trade. Headquarters are located in Geneva, Switzerland.

# SUMMARY

The international marketing environment contains a variety of elements: demographic characteristics (market size, population growth and distribution, education), geographic characteristics (topography and climate), economic factors (per capita income, GNP, distribution of income, household income, education), and the political-legal system (tariff and nontariff barriers, exchange controls, political risks, degree of nationalism). Acquiring and interpreting marketplace information relating to each of these areas are of fundamental importance to the development of marketing and advertising strategies. The one key area that we have not yet addressed is the cultural environment. Chapter 4 will be devoted to exploring this topic.

**REFERENCES**

Auto giants report rising sales in China. 2009. China Economic Net, 14 January. <http://en.ce.cn/Industries/Auto/200901/14/t20090114_17953359.shtml>. Retrieved 6 November 2009.

Baker, Stephen. 2002. The coming battle for immigrants. *Business Week,* 26 August, 138–140.

Barnes, Kathleen. 1993. Big marketers poised to flood into South Africa. *Advertising Age,* 17 May, 11.

Block, Robert. 1999. How big mac kept from becoming a Serb archenemy. *The Wall Street Journal,* 3 September, B-1.

Brooks, David. 2005. A tale of two systems. *The New York Times,* 4 January, A-19.

Case, Brendan. 2003. Exports to Cuba a booming business for U.S. farmers, ranchers. *Knight Ridder Tribune News Service,* 17 February, 1.

China's monthly auto sales overtake US for 1st time. 2009. *The Economic Times,* 11 February. <http://economictimes.indiatimes.com/News/International_Business/C...>. Retrieved 6 November 2009.

De La Dehesa, Guillermo. 2004. Europe's social model will crumble without reform. *Financial Times* (London), 15 September, 21.

Engel, James F., and Rodger E. Blackwell. 1982. *Consumer behavior.* Chicago, IL: Dryden Press.

Euromonitor. 2005. *World consumer lifestyle databook.*

———. 2006. International Marketing Data and Statistics.

Foreign carmakers gung-ho on China. 2009. China Economic Net, 17 July. <http://en.ce.cn/Industries/Auto/200907/17/t20090717_19560567.shtml>. Retrieved 6 November 2009.

Glasser, Susan. 2001. Patriotism, selling like hot cakes. *Washington Post,* 9 May, C-1.

Hall, Emma. 2008. Ad agency with focus on over-50s opens in U.K. *Advertising Age,* 24 May, 124.

Hill, John, and Richard Still. 1984. Effects of urbanization on multinational product planning: Markets in lesser developed countries. *Columbia Journal of World Business,* 19: Summer, 62–67.

Iranian official tries to stem the rising tide of Barbie dolls. 2008. *San Diego Union-Tribune,* 29 April, A-2.

Koenderman, Tony. 1994. Pepsi, BBD&O thirst for S. Africa. *Adweek,* 4 July, 12.

Kotler, Philip. 1988. *Marketing management.* Englewood Cliffs, NJ: Prentice Hall.

Kripalani, Manjeet, and Pete Engardio. 2002. Small is profitable: What will work in developing world is a focus on inexpensive, downsized, simple-to-use products. *Business Week,* 26 August, 112–114.

Murphy, Cait. 2002. The hunt for globalization that works. *Fortune,* 28 October, 163–176.

O'Leary, Michael. 2002. Analysts take an optimistic view. *Euromoney,* September, 208–215.

Onkvisit, Sak, and John Shaw. 1997. *International marketing: Analysis and strategy.* Upper Saddle River, NJ: Prentice Hall.

Springer, Jr., Robert. 1986. New export laws and aid to international marketers. *Marketing News,* 3 January, 10, 67.

Terpstra, Vern, and Lloyd Russow. 2000. *International dimensions of marketing.* Cincinnati, OH: Southwestern College Publishing.

United Nations. 2006. *United Nations world population prospects.* Rev. ed. Table A.8. <http://www.un.org/esa/population/publications/wpp2006/WPP 2006_Highlights_rev.pdf>. Retrieved 18 November 2009.

———. 2009. Press release, World population to exceed 9 billion by 2050. 11 March.

World Bank. 2009. *World development indicators.*

# CHAPTER FOUR

# The Cultural Environment

The final aspect of the marketing and advertising environment that the international marketer must consider is the culture of a particular country. Marketers have traditionally examined a potential market's demographic and geographic characteristics, as well as economic and political factors, in order to determine if and how they might impact the marketing mix. However, only in recent years has greater attention been paid to the cultural environment. Each country exhibits cultural differences that influence consumers' needs and wants, their methods of satisfying them, and the messages they are most likely to respond to. The international business literature reveals hundreds of blunders that have resulted from miscalculating—or simply ignoring—the cultural environment. This chapter explores the concept of culture and its various elements, and discusses tools potentially useful to international marketers attempting to analyze foreign cultures and penetrate foreign markets.

## CONCEPT OF CULTURE

Culture can be conceptualized in many ways. Indeed, in the early 1950s, Kroeber and Kluckhohn (1952) identified well over 160 different definitions of culture in the anthropological literature. Of course, many new definitions have appeared since. A classic definition is provided by E. B. Taylor, who defined culture as "a complex whole, which includes knowledge, beliefs, art, morals, law, custom, and any other capabilities and habits acquired by individuals as members of a society" (Taylor 1871, 1). Adamson Hoebel referred to culture as the "integrated sum total of learned behavioral traits that are manifest and shared by members of society" (Hoebel 1960, 168). Culture has also been defined as a "learned, shared, compelling, interrelated set of symbols whose meaning provides a set of orientations for members of a society" (Terpstra and David 1991, 12).

Even the three definitions provided here reveal some commonalities. It is generally agreed that culture is not inherent or innate, but rather is learned. Learning typically takes place in institutions such as the family, church, and school. Samovar, Porter, and Stefani (1998, 39) note that, in addition to these formalized institutions, we also learn culture from more invisible instructors, such as proverbs, folktales, legends, art forms, and, of course, the mass media. Most definitions of culture also emphasize that culture is shared by members of a group. It is this shared aspect that enables communication between individuals within that culture. Because culture is shared, it defines the boundaries between different groups. Cross-cultural communication is so difficult, in large part, because of the lack of shared symbols. Finally, all facets of culture are interrelated—if one aspect of culture is changed, all else will be influenced as well. As Edward T. Hall notes, "you touch a culture in one place and everything else is affected" (Hall 1976, 13).

## Self-Reference Criterion and Ethnocentrism

When we examine other cultures, we tend to view them through "culturally tinted glasses." For example, if our own culture places a high value on education or cleanliness, we may assume—correctly or incorrectly—that other cultures share these same values. James Lee terms this unconscious reference to one's own culture the *self-reference criterion* (Lee 1966, 47). Because of this unconscious reference to one's own cultural values, marketers operating abroad may behave in a culturally myopic fashion.

Ethnocentrism poses another obstacle to understanding foreign cultures. Literally defined, *ethnocentrism* means "culturally centered"; it refers to people's tendency to place themselves at the center of the universe and not only evaluate others by the standards of their own culture but also believe that their own culture is superior to all others. A fundamental assumption of ethnocentric people is that their way of doing things is right, proper, and normal, and that the ways of culturally different people are wrong and inferior (Ferraro 1990, 34). Not surprisingly, this tendency toward an "us versus them" mentality is universal. People in all cultures, to some degree, display ethnocentric behaviors. Ethnocentrism limits our ability to accept cultural differences, which diminishes the chance of developing effective marketing programs. Gap experienced significant challenges in moving abroad. Sales in Gap's 525 international stores were so poor that the firm cut international store growth by 50 percent. Gap's failing may have been in believing that just because its merchandising and marketing were effective in the United States, they would surely be equally effective everywhere else. For example, in Japan the tags on Gap clothing were in English, and Gap employees cheerfully greeted customers with the casual Japanese version of "hi," an unaccustomed informality for the mannerly Japanese (Barron and Ito 2001, 62). The best defense against ethnocentrism is an awareness of the tendency toward ethnocentrism.

## Subcultures

While the focus of this text is international in scope, it is important to recognize that variations within cultures may be even greater than variations among cultures. In each culture there exist *subcultures*—groups of people with shared value systems based on common experiences. People belonging to various nationality groups (Italian, Polish, and Scandinavian Americans), religious groups (Protestants, Jews, Catholics), ethnic groups (blacks, Asians, Hispanics), political groups (Democrats, Republicans, socialists), and geographic groups (westerners, easterners, southerners) may well exhibit characteristic patterns of behavior that serve to distinguish them from other subgroups within a country. The same can be said about people who belong to specific age or income groups. Clearly, an individual can belong to more than one subculture. To the extent that these patterns of behavior impact wants and needs, these subcultures can be targeted by marketers.

**TABLE 4.1:** U.S. Population Growth

| POPULATION (IN MILLIONS) | 2005 POPULATION | 2050 ESTIMATED POPULATION |
| --- | --- | --- |
| Ethnicity | 296% | 438% |
| White, non-Hispanic | 67% | 47% |
| Hispanic | 14% | 29% |
| Black | 13% | 13% |
| Asian | 5% | 9% |

*Source:* Pew Research Center (2008).

The U.S. population is expected to become increasingly diverse over the coming decades. Table 4.1 presents population percentages for 2005 and projections for 2050 for Hispanic Americans, African Americans, and Asian Americans. All told, these three groups currently comprise about 32 percent of the U.S. population and, by 2050, they are projected to make up over half of the total U.S. population. In short, minorities will become the new majority. Each of these groups is currently more youthful than the general population. According to 2010 Census projections, 80 percent of people age 65-plus will be white non-Hispanics. But just 54 percent of children under age 18 will be white non-Hispanics. And whites are expected to account for fewer than half of births by 2015 (Johnson 2009). Over the coming decade, the multicultural population will not only continue to grow but will also be at its wage-earning peak and have income equal to or even greater than that of the general market. These developments, combined with the aging demographics of the white population, will make multicultural consumers of increasing interest to marketers.

Hispanics are not only the nation's largest, but also its fastest-growing, minority. The Hispanic population in the United States is expected to have increased by 118.9 percent between 1990 and 2010. That rapid population growth translates directly into economic clout. Hispanic buying power totaled $800 billion in 2006, according to the Selig Center for Economic Growth at the University of Georgia. By 2011, Hispanic buying power will hit $1.2 trillion, representing 9.5 percent of all U.S. buying power (Liesse 2008). A fundamental error made by marketers trying to reach the Hispanic audience is to view the Hispanic community as homogeneous. Over 80 percent of Hispanics say they identify themselves by their country or origin or as Latino or Hispanic. But when asked which term they used first or exclusively, more than half chose their country of origin, while only a quarter used the terms Latino or Hispanic. Thus, while members of the U.S. Hispanic population understand themselves to be part of a common ethnic group, most have a stronger identification with their nationality (Marketing to Hispanics 2005). Because Hispanics emigrated from different countries at different times and for different reasons, demographics of specific subgroups based on country of origin can be quite different. Effective marketing and advertising to Hispanic Americans means reaching a deeper understanding of these various subgroups—Mexicans, Puerto Ricans, Cubans, Dominicans, Central Americans, and South Americans—in terms of heritage, values, customs, and preferences. And while there is no such thing as pure Spanish, it is important to note that the Spanish language is a factor that unifies these subgroups.

According to George San Jose, president of The San Jose Group of Chicago—ranked 19th of the top 50 Hispanic ad agencies by *Advertising Age* (*Advertising Age* 2009b, 44)—there are two trends marketers need to keep in mind as they begin to figure out how to tap the Hispanic marketplace. First, many Hispanics are still comfortable with Spanish as the language of choice. "The grandparents may still speak Spanish exclusively, while their children may be bilingual, and the 20-something generation may speak primarily English while still being fluent in Spanish," San Jose says. Indeed, according to the research of Synovate and Nielsen, a global marketing research corporation, 44 percent of Hispanic consumers say that at home they speak Spanish only or more often than English; 25 percent say they are equally bilingual; and 31 percent use English only—or more often than—Spanish. Among second-generation consumers, 93 percent say they are bilingual or English dominant (*Americano* 2009). San Jose suggests that Spanish-language television, radio, and newspapers are especially good avenues for reaching this audience. The second factor to understand is how much family is integral to the Hispanic lifestyle. Not only does the burgeoning younger generation tend to have more children than does the general U.S. population, making baby and family products a big seller, but many also have extended families throughout Latin America, offering even more opportunities. For example, San Jose shared the story of the Midwest airline that was unsuccessful in selling to the Hispanic market. The problem, he says, was that the airline's slogan was "Use Our Airline to Get Away!" But Latino families don't want to "get away"; instead they want to meet up with their extended families and vacation together. A new slogan, "The Official Airline of Family Vacations," worked wonders (Strauss 2007). See Figure 4.1 for an example of Nestlé's efforts to target Hispanics. Note that Nescafé is extremely popular with Hispanic consumers, as it was in countries such as Mexico.

African Americans are the second-largest segment of the multicultural market. Though many marketers are focusing on how the 2010 Census will show growth in the Hispanic population, a new study argues that the African American community presents another great opportunity. The report, commissioned by BET and based on U.S. Census Bureau data, shows that black Americans are both more well-off and more suburban than previously thought. The report, entitled "African Americans in 2010," finds that the black population is growing 34 percent faster than the population as a whole. When the census finishes tallying its numbers in 2011, demographers expect it to show that there are about 50 million Hispanics in the United States and around 42 million African Americans. But although there are fewer African Americans, the population is changing in ways that make such consumers more attractive to marketers, namely:

- African Americans are nearly six years younger than all consumers; 47 percent are between 18 and 49 years old, which is considered the top-spending age demo by marketers.
- Black households making $75,000-plus annually have increased 47 percent in the last five years—1.5 times faster than the general population.
- If current trends continue, more than half of all black Americans will live in the suburbs by 2015.
- Although their population is smaller, there are more African American households in the United States than Hispanic households, because the latter tend to have larger families (Wasserman 2010).

It is forecast that the buying power of the African American market in the United States will hit $1.2 trillion by 2013, and that this number will translate into nearly 9 percent of the nation's estimated buying power. In his "Guide to Marketing to African American Consumers," Matt Alderton (2010) recommends the following four steps, among others: (1) Customize your products: Mattel, for example, found success launching a new line of Black Barbie dolls in 2009. The "So in Style" dolls have fuller lips, a wider nose, and more pronounced cheek-bones. The dolls reflect varying skin tones—light brown, chocolate, and caramel, and some feature curlier hair. Barbie designer Stacey McBride-Irby, who is black and has a young daughter, noted that she wanted to create dolls for young black girls that looked like them

**Figure 4.1:** Nescafé Targets Hispanic Consumers in the United States.

and were inspirational and career-minded (Scott 2009). (2) Advertise in African American media: On average, African Americans are more than twice as likely to trust black media over mainstream media. Also, 81 percent of all African Americans ages 13–74 watch black-interest television channels weekly (Miley 2009). (3) Be relevant to your customers: Carol Sagers, director-marketing at McDonald's USA, notes that "African-Americans have nuances in lifestyle and nuances in language and culture that should be used to leverage communication. McDonald's believes in speaking to all our customers, and speaking to them directly" (Miley 2009). Indeed, the McDonald's "I'm Lovin' It" campaign was rooted in hip-hop culture but had messaging that transcended race and ethnicity and gained popularity around the world. (4) Hire African American employees: African Americans like doing business with other African Americans; they're most likely to spend their money with companies that hire more African Americans and in more prominent positions. McDonald's has a strong reputation for its commitment to the African American community. *Black Enterprise* ranked McDonald's as one of the "40 Best Companies for Diversity," and *Essence* listed it as one of "25 Great Places to Work" for African American women. In fact, 17 percent of its U.S. officers are African American, 20 percent of its U.S. employees are African American, and 13.5 percent of its Owner/Operators are African Americans. See Figure 4.2 for a McDonald's advertisement targeting black consumers. The copy reads: "At McDonald's our support of entrepreneurs means that with a lot of hard work and determination, you could one day join a fraternity of more than 1,200 African-American owned restaurants—generating billions of dollars annually." Take note of the logo in the lower right-hand corner.

The Asian American segment of the U.S. multicultural market is not only smaller, but also more diverse in language and culture than the Hispanic and African American segments. The term Asian American is a bit of a misnomer in that it suggests a single monolithic group. Nothing could be further from the truth. Asian Americans reflect the influence of well over 15 distinct ethnic groups and national origins, including Bangladeshi, Cambodian, Chinese, Filipino, Indian, Indonesian, Japanese, Korean, Laotian, Malaysian, Pakistani, Sri Lankan, Taiwanese, Thai, and Vietnamese. Chinese Americans are the largest segment, followed by Filipinos and Indians. While there is certainly a cultural divide among the different Asian segments, there are also similarities that they share to some degree. The Cultural Access Group notes that the five main values that Asian Americans share include a group orientation, an emphasis on family, respect for elders and the community, and the importance of saving money and education (Desjardins 2006). Indeed, overall, Asian Americans tend to be more affluent and more likely to be college educated than other population groups in the country.

- Asian Americans' purchasing power in 2007 was $459 billion and is projected to total nearly $700 billion by 2012.
- Median household income for Asian Americans was $64,000 in 2006—more than $11,000 ahead of Caucasian Americans and $15,000 ahead of the total population.
- Asians have the highest percentage of households in the upper income ranges: 43 percent earn more than $75,000 per year (index of 143 against the total population) and 31 percent earn $100,000 + (index of 160 against the total population).
- Asian Americans have the highest mean home values of all groups (including non-Hispanic whites) in 48 out of 50 states in the United States.
- 48 percent of Asians hold a BA degree or higher (vs. non-Hispanic white: 30 percent; African Americans: 17 percent; Hispanics: 12 percent) (*Adweek Media* 2008).

As multicultural markets continue to grow in scope and buying power, an ever-increasing number of marketers will attempt to reach these consumers. According to a 2008 study conducted by the

**Figure 4.2:** McDonald's targets African American consumers in the United States.

Association of National Advertisers (ANA), over 77 percent of U.S. marketers (surveyed among ANA members) have multicultural initiatives, and 66 percent of survey participants responded that their company's efforts in this area increased over the past few years. Over half (55 percent) of the respondents preferred to work with specialized multicultural ad agencies (*Gravity Media* 2010). Multicultural advertising agencies understand the opportunities as well as the difficulties associated with reaching ethnic consumers. Marketing to African Americans, Hispanics, and Asian Americans means much more than simply replacing a Caucasian model with an ethnic model. Much as with marketing to Caucasian consumers, advertisers that succeed in multicultural marketing tailor their messages to their audience and integrate advertising, public relations, promotions, direct marketing, sponsorships, and community events. Research has consistently shown that multicultural consumers respond best to messages and images that reflect a deep insight into their culture and the unique ways they perceive and use a product. Table 4.2 lists the top multicultural agencies by gross income.

LatinWorks was selected by *Advertising Age* as its multicultural agency of the year for 2010. One of the agency's hallmarks is work that is highly creative and effective in the Hispanic market but eschews stereotypes and transcends ethnicity. Despite a disastrous 2009 economy, LatinWorks increased its revenue by 13 percent and came up with strategic solutions to drive business for its clients' brands. While other shops had to resort to layoffs, LatinWorks's staff grew by 15 percent, to 106 people. In a slow year for new business, the agency won pitches for Bacardi and Burger King, now its biggest client, and took home the U.S. Hispanic market's only trophy from the Cannes Lions International Advertising festival. The winning ad was a Starburst commercial in which a llama faces a young man as they both chew contentedly, then with a hand and hoof feed each other more Starburst candies, sending the message that the intensely juicy treat is one that people—and their llamas—love to share. After a double-digit decline in Hispanic sales (down 27.7 percent in 2008), Starburst's Hispanic sales shot up 14.8 percent within three months of the launch of LatinWorks's campaign. The spot was so successful that it crossed over from the Hispanic market to general-market television and into popular culture in 2009, as fans posted their own spoofs on YouTube and tweeted, "I wanna eat Starburst with a llama" (Wentz 2010).

An understanding of subcultures is essential, because the failure to recognize distinctive subcultures can lead to an illusion of sameness within a market that simply does not exist. Additionally, understanding a subculture in one country may also help the marketer to understand a similar subculture in a foreign market. Knowing what motivates a New York businessman who earns $100,000 annually may well assist in the understanding of his counterpart abroad. A Paris businesswoman is likely to be much more similar to her colleague across the ocean than she is to a fellow French woman who works in the vineyards of Burgundy.

## CULTURE AND COMMUNICATION

Many cultural differences, and their impact on elements of the marketing mix, are obvious. Clearly, if one wishes to communicate with consumers in Kenya, language differences must be taken into account, and all promotional materials must be translated into the local tongue. Many cultural differences are, however, quite subtle. For example, one American shoe manufacturer promoted its product through advertisements with photos of bare feet. Although such a message would pose no problem in most countries, the campaign failed miserably in Southeast Asia, where exposure of the foot is considered an insult. The problem of communicating to people in diverse cultures has been called one of the greatest challenges in marketing communications (Ricks 1988, 11). International marketers, if they are to be

**TABLE 4.2:** Top Multicultural Agencies, 2008 (dollars in thousands)

| AMERICANS MARKETING TO HISPANIC AMERICANS | | | MARKETING TO AFRICAN AMERICANS | | |
|---|---|---|---|---|---|
| **RANK** | **AGENCY** | **U.S. REVENUE** | **RANK** | **AGENCY** | **U.S. REVENUE** |
| 1. | Dieste [Omnicom] | 44,900 | 1. | GlobalHue | 25,900 |
| 2. | Vidal Partnership | 35,000 | 2. | UniWorld Group [WPP] | 25,668 |
| 3. | Bravo Group [WPP (Y & R)] | 31,500 | 3. | Carol H. Williams Advertising | 23,900 |
| 4. | GlobalHue | 28,178 | 4. | Burrell Communications Group [Publicis] | 22,000 |
| 5. | Lopez Negrete Communications | 24,150 | 5. | Sanders/Wingo | 14,350 |
| 6. | Zubi Advertising Services | 21,500 | 6. | Fuse | 9,351 |
| 7. | Bromley Communications [Publicis] | 21,100 | 7. | Images USA | 9,253 |
| 8. | Conill [Publicis (Saatchi)] | 19,900 | 8. | Footsteps [Omnicom] | 7,000 |
| 9. | LatinWorks [Omnicom] | 17,440 | 9. | Matlock Advertising & Public Relations | 5,107 |
| 10. | Alma DDB [Omnicom (DDB)] | 14,800 | 10. | Moroch Partners | 5,000 |

| MARKETING TO ASIAN AMERICANS | | |
|---|---|---|
| **RANK** | **AGENCY** | **U.S. REVENUE** |
| 1. | Kang & Lee Advertising [WPP (Y & R)] | 15,500 |
| 2. | Admerasia | 10,250 |
| 3. | InterTrend Communications | 10,245 |
| 4. | IW Group [Interpublic] | 9,085 |
| 5. | AdAsia Communications | 7,059 |
| 6. | Time Advertising | 5,800 |
| 7. | PanCom International | 5,103 |
| 8. | Global Advertising Strategies | 5,000 |
| 9. | ES Advertising | 4,486 |
| 10. | Aaaza | 3,000 |

*Source: Advertising Age* (2009a, 16).

successful in their efforts, must become culturally sensitive—that is, tuned to the nuances of culture. Indeed, they must become students of culture.

Among the important elements of culture that marketers must take into consideration are verbal communication (both spoken and written) and the various forms of nonverbal communication (among them gestures, space, time, and other signs and symbols).

## Verbal Communication

In deciding which markets to enter and how to enter them, the international marketer must speak with governmental and business leaders in foreign countries as well as with potential employees and suppliers. Marketers probably will deal with the local language when collecting market data. Also, in attempting to communicate with potential customers, marketers are faced with choosing a brand name, selecting copy or text to be included on product packaging, developing advertising slogans, and creating advertising messages.

Because language plays such a central role in international marketing, it is crucial to understand the close relationship between culture and language. Culture and communication are inextricably linked. It has been said that it is impossible to truly understand a culture without understanding the language spoken by its people (Whorf 1956, 212). Conversely, a language cannot be fully understood outside its cultural context. As Gerhard Maletzke explains:

> The art and manner in which one understands the world is determined to a large extent by language; but language, at the same time, is an expression of a specific group-experiencing of the world, and therefore may itself be shaped by the Weltanschauung as well as the wishes, expectations, and motivations of the group using it. (Maletzke 1976, 74)

Put more simply, culture both influences and is influenced by language.

Linguists claim that up to 5,000 different languages are spoken around the globe—some spoken by millions, others by no more than several hundred. Table 4.3 lists the leading languages spoken around the world. Chinese tops the list as the most spoken language, but although the written language is uniform, there are literally hundreds of local dialects in China. Multilingual societies constitute the majority of the world's nations. For example, Zaire has over 100 different tribal languages, and in India over 200 languages and dialects are spoken. Any country in which a number of different languages are spoken undoubtedly will also have a number of different cultures. Consider Canada, where citizens speak predominantly English or French; or Belgium, where French and Flemish are spoken. In both Canada and Belgium, the differing linguistic groups have clashed on occasion. In Zaire and India, such confrontations have even resulted in violence.

A debate continues regarding whether English can be considered the world's first genuinely global language. To be worthy of the designation "global," a language needs to be present in every country in the world. English now probably is; it is the first language for about 340 million people, mainly in the United States, Canada, Britain, Ireland, Australia, New Zealand, and South Africa. It has achieved special status as a second language spoken by another 375 million people in more than 70 countries, such as China, Nigeria, India, Singapore, and Vanuatu. And in most—perhaps all—of the remaining countries, it is the foreign language children are most likely to learn at school. Foreign English language learners may now exceed 1 billion. Although estimates vary greatly, some 1.5 billion people are thought to be competent communicators in English. That is one-quarter of the world's population. The question is, how can English be a global language when three out of four people never use it? The answer is that English is now the dominant tongue in international politics, banking, the press, news agencies, broadcasting, the recording industry, movies, travel, science and technology, knowledge management, communications—and, of course, advertising (Crystal 1999, 4).

But even English is not universally embraced. The French have a long reputation for being monolingual and quite defensive about their language. French officials have been waging an increasingly aggressive war against English creeping into common usage. French, as well as international, advertisers have come under fire for using English words in advertising copy. The advertising standards regulator

**TABLE 4.3:** Languages Spoken Around the World

| LANGUAGE | HUB | COUNTRIES | SPEAKERS (MILLIONS) |
|---|---|---|---|
| Chinese, Mandarin | China | 16 | 873 |
| Hindi | India | 17 | 370 |
| Spanish | Spain | 43 | 350 |
| English | United Kingdom | 104 | 340 |
| Arabic | Saudi Arabia | 26 | 206 |
| Portuguese | Portugal | 33 | 203 |
| Bengali | Bangladesh | 9 | 196 |
| Russian | Russia | 30 | 145 |
| Japanese | Japan | 26 | 126 |
| German | Germany | 40 | 101 |

*Source: Ethnologue (2005).*

(BVP) argues that only 35 percent of the population speak enough English to be able to understand English language slogans such as Nike's "Just do it." So, in line with a 1994 law, advertisers are supposed to include a French translation equal in size and prominence and with exactly the same meaning. But the BVP notes that the rules are often bent, and "English first" appears to be the order of the day (King 2000, 18). France is not alone in its mission to protect its language. In Kaliningrad, Russia's western-most province, local authorities are cracking down on advertisers that violate the "purity" of the Russian language. In 2005, a federal law was passed that forbids the use of foreign-language words or expressions when Russian equivalents are available. Advertisements on buildings, billboards, and shops should be in the Russian language. Thus, the once-ubiquitous English-language "sale" signs in store windows in Kaliningrad, as well as other major Russian cities, have begun to disappear. Currently there is no fine in place for language violations, so ads are simply torn down (Adelaja 2008). Iran has a law dating back to 1996 that aims to preserve the Farsi language. It appears that recently there have been considerable violations of this law, so officials have begun to confront the problem. In a warning issued through official media, the Advertising Bureau of the ministry noted that the law—which applies to the press and printed ads, television commercials, billboards, and shop signs—stipulates that Farsi letters have to be more than double the size of any non-Farsi letters used. Violators risk receiving a written warning, temporary closure, or even a ban on business activity (Middle East Online 2004).

It appears that the number of English-language advertisements in Europe is on the increase. For example, in the Netherlands, where most people speak English as a second language, it is estimated that 40 percent of advertising slogans contain English words. Apparently, bilingual populations understand the words, and employing English slogans lends consistency to global campaigns and saves on translation costs. But according to a study from RSM Erasmus University in Rotterdam, people who speak more than one language respond more acutely to marketing messages delivered in their mother tongue. An experiment was carried out in Belgium with Flemish-French bilinguals. Half the participants had Flemish as a native language, the others French. Emotionally oriented slogans were presented, including one for a florist ("See the face you love light up in a brilliant smile") and one for a hotel chain ("When you are here, you are family. We will leave the light on for you"). The participants were asked to rate how emotional the slogans made them feel. Those delivered in a participant's native tongue were perceived to be far more emotional than those in a second language. Clearly, this does not seem to be a question of understanding, since all those who took part were bilingual. Rather, it is thought to be linked to the way in which people connect words with memories. Theory suggests that we associate certain words with our experiences. Reading or hearing a word subconsciously reminds us of these memories, generating an emotional response. It stands to reason that consumers will have had more personal experiences linked to words in their native language compared with those learned later in life. So messages delivered in a first language are more emotional than those in a second language. The message to international marketers is that if you want your ads to resonate with consumers, speak to them in their mother tongue (Ford 2008).

While language helps to define a cultural group, as Table 4.3 reveals, the same language can be spoken in a number of different countries. For example, Spanish is spoken in Spain, Mexico, Argentina, and Peru. English is spoken in the United States, England, much of Canada, Australia, and Ireland. Nonetheless, marketers must use caution when employing the same language in two or more markets. For example, there are significant differences between American English and British English. Often the same word or phrase may mean different things. A billion means a thousand million to an American, but a million million to a Brit. Also, different words may be used to mean the same thing, as Table 4.4 illustrates.

Further, a word that is perfectly acceptable in one market can cause regulators to clamp down in another. The British Advertising Clearance Center ordered the slang term "bloody" stricken from an Australian tourism campaign designed to lure Britons Down Under with a television commercial featuring bikinis, beer, and the Great Barrier Reef. The commercial closes with the question, "Where the bloody hell are you?"—or at least it does outside Britain. British viewers were informed that they would hear a version in which the offending word was expertly excised. The regulatory body raised no objections to any other words in the commercial—not even "hell." Print and Internet ads were not affected by the ruling (see Figure 4.3 for the print version of the campaign). Fran Bailey, Australia's tourism minister, echoed what many Australians had been thinking since the storm broke: that profanity was introduced to Australia by convicts shipped there by Britain in the 19th century. "The British have seen it before in their advertising, and I don't think a lot has changed—it's not as if they have become more precious or stuffy overnight," Bailey said. "After all, it was the British who brought the word 'bloody' to our shores. To not be able to use the phrase as we now invite them to come back for a holiday is a bit of a joke." Scott Morrison, managing director of Tourism Australia, the government-funded authority responsible for the campaign, noted: "We are being a bit cheeky about it, in a fun, good-humored way. It's about delivering a uniquely Australian invitation." The *Bloomsbury Dictionary of Contemporary Slang* defines "bloody" as an adjective that is "now considered fairly mild, but which was held to be taboo in

**TABLE 4.4:** American English vs. British English

| AMERICAN | BRITISH | AMERICAN | BRITISH |
|----------|---------|----------|---------|
| aisle | gangway | baby carriage | pram |
| bacon | gammon | checkers | draughts |
| diaper | nappy | druggist | chemist |
| elevator | lift | flashlight | torch |
| French fries | chips | lawyer | solicitor |
| line | queue | mail box | pillar box |
| radio | wireless | second floor | first floor |
| sidewalk | pavement | toilet | W.C. |
| truck | lorry | two weeks | fortnight |
| underwear | smalls | vacation | holiday |

many circles until the later 1960s." What constitutes offense for viewers changes with time. "But it is also true that what is commonplace language for many is extremely distasteful for others," according to the British Advertising Clearance Center. Yet Tourism Australia is having the last laugh. Since the British newspapers reported the flap, traffic on its site has more than tripled (Kirka 2006).

Languages differ in their levels of formality. In English, there is only one word for "you." In contrast, the French use the informal *tu* for family and friends, and the formal *vous* for people they do not know well. Similarly, Germans use *du* for informal and personal settings, and *Sie* in formal settings. In Vietnamese, there are 18 words for "you" depending on whether you are addressing one person or several, young or old, formally or informally.

This situation is significantly more complicated in Japanese. In the Japanese language the level of formality depends on the gender and status of the speaker and listener as well as the context of the conversation. This has a number of implications for marketing communications. For example, the language used by the seller is much more deferential than that of the buyer—the buyer is always placed in the position of superior status. Moreover, the female speaker is always required to use more polite, deferential language. As a result, saleswomen or female characters in broadcast advertisements tend to give a product a "feminine" image. While this association may be beneficial for certain kinds of products, such as household items, for others it may hurt sales (Shane 1988, 155).

*Language and Context.* The concept of high and low context provides an understanding of different cultural orientations and explains how communication is conveyed and perceived. As defined by Edward T. Hall, low-context cultures place high value on words, and communicators are encouraged to be direct, exact, and unambiguous. What is important is what is said, not how it is said or the environment in which it is said. In contrast, high-context cultures consider verbal communications to be only a part of the overall message, and communicators rely much more heavily on contextual cues. Edward and Mildred Hall wrote: "Context is the information that surrounds an event and is inextricably bound up with the meaning of that event. The elements that combine to produce a given meaning—events and context—are in different proportions depending on culture" (Hall and Hall 1987, 7). Thus, messages in high-context cultures tend to be a good deal more implicit and ambiguous, with

**Figure 4.3:** Australian ad offends the British with the slang term "Bloody."

communicators relying much more on nonverbal behavior, the physical setting, social circumstances, and the nature of interpersonal relationships. The Halls further explain that "a high context communication or message is one in which most of the information is already in the person, while very little is in the coded, explicit, transmitted part of the message. A low-context communication is vested in the explicit code" (Hall 1976, 16). Cultures typically are not perceived as either high- or low-context but, as Figure 4.4 shows, are arranged along a continuum. Note that this continuum should not give the impression of equal intervals. In part, contextuality of communication is related to whether the language itself expresses ideas and facts more or less explicitly. As Jean-Claude Usunier explains:

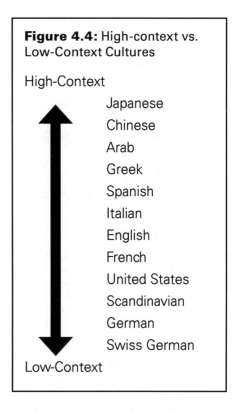

**Figure 4.4:** High-context vs. Low-Context Cultures

High-Context

Japanese
Chinese
Arab
Greek
Spanish
Italian
English
French
United States
Scandinavian
German
Swiss German

Low-Context

> Japanese, for instance, is on average less precise than English or French. For example, personal pronouns are often not explicitly expressed in Japanese, and the number of tenses is largely reduced (especially in comparison to French). In Japanese, both spoken words (that is sounds) and written words (based on *kanjis*, that is pictograms) often have multiple meanings, so that the listener needs some kind of contextual clarification. Sometimes, Japanese people write the *kanjis* (ideographs) briefly on their hand to make clear what they are saying. Naturally it would be a mistake to say that certain languages are vague and others precise. The real world is more complex. This has to be strongly nuanced when one looks more carefully at the structure of the language. For instance, German has many verbs that have quite different meanings according to context. It is easy to discover such examples just by consulting a German English dictionary. For instance, the verb *absetzen* means, according to context, to deposit or deduct a sum, to take off a hat, to dismiss an official, to depose a king, to drop a passenger, to sell goods, to stop or pause, or to take off (a play). The same holds true for the Finnish language, even though the Finns may have a reputation, like many northern Europeans, for their explicitness in communication. Finnish has a very special language structure which renders the use of context useful in communication, that of Finno-Ugrian languages, really only shared with Estonia and Hungary. The Finnish language uses sixteen cases which virtually replace all prepositions used in other languages. Even proper nouns can be declined using these cases. (Usunier 1966, 371)

The differences between communications styles in high- versus low-context cultures have direct implications for the international advertiser. Messages constructed by writers from high-context cultures might be difficult to understand in low-context cultures because they do not come to the point. Similarly, messages constructed by writers from low-context cultures may be difficult to understand in high-context cultures because they omit essential contextual material (Wells 1987, 18). For example, the United States is considered to be a low-context culture while Japan is considered a high-context culture. American marketers tend to be more logical, scientific, and oriented toward data, systems, and procedures, while Japanese marketers tend to be more intuitive, subjective, and oriented toward communications and human relations (Lazer 1985, 69). As might be expected, the advertising messages created in these two markets differ dramatically. American consumers are known for their interest in product information and precise details (Biswas et al. 1992, 73).

Consumers in the United States look to advertising messages for just such information. Thus commercial communications tend to emphasize the merits of the product clearly, logically, and reasonably by directly presenting information, facts, and evidence related to the product (Hong et al. 1987, 55).

A number of studies have documented that Japanese ads, both broadcast and print, contain fewer information cues than ads appearing in the United States and many other countries (Lin 1992, 1; Ramaprasad and Hasegawa 1990, 1025). Japanese advertising is less likely to focus on the product's merits; the direct or hard-sell approach so common in American advertising seems to leave the Japanese consumer cold (Mueller 1992, 22). Comparative claims, a mainstay in American advertising, are almost unheard of in Japan. Instead, note Edward and Mildred Hall, "Japanese advertising evokes a mood and is designed to appeal to emotions, produce good feelings, and create a happy atmosphere. The approach is soft-sell" (Hall and Hall 1987, 139). Indeed, much of Japanese advertising is so soft-sell that it is often difficult to determine what the product is from viewing an advertisement. For example, a quick glimpse at the Japanese advertisement in Figure 4.5 would probably not reveal that this is a message promoting mayonnaise. Indeed, even reading the copy probably wouldn't help much. The headline (in English) reads: "One Bedroom, One Bath. There is a Deli in Your Neighborhood." The copy reads: "When I was a student, I used to live in Chelsea in Manhattan. A real estate agent who primarily dealt with rental apartments found a room for me with one bedroom and one bath for $1,200. There was an Italian delicatessen in the neighborhood and every morning at around 7 a.m. they baked Focaccia bread. It was beautiful. They used only the highest quality ingredients. Yesterday, I happened to find an apartment ad that says it's close to a deli. I recalled a salad served at that deli in Chelsea and a younger version of myself who used to walk around that neighborhood." The ad simply tells a story. The only hint that this is a commercial message for Kewpie mayonnaise is the trade figure in the lower right-hand corner of the ad. The suggestion that salads be prepared with Kewpie mayonnaise is merely implied.

*Translations:* No discussion of language in international commercial communications would be complete without addressing the importance of translations. Errors in the translation of brand names, packaging copy, and advertising messages have cost businesses millions of dollars, not to mention damaging their credibility and reputation. It is not enough for translators merely to be familiar with the native tongue. In order to avoid translation blunders, translators must also be familiar with nuances, idioms, and slang. Consider the following:

- The American Dairy Association experienced tremendous success with the campaign "Got Milk?" (see Figure 4.6). It was decided to extend the ads to Mexico. Unfortunately, the Spanish translation was "Are you lactating?"
- Coors translated its slogan "Turn it loose" into Spanish, where it was read as "Suffer from diarrhea."
- Bacardi concocted a fruity drink with the name "Pavian" to suggest French chic…but "Pavian" means "baboon" in German.
- When Kentucky Fried Chicken entered the Chinese market, it discovered to its horror that the slogan "finger lickin' good" came out as "eat your fingers off."
- When Vicks first introduced its cough drops in the German market, it was chagrined to learn that the German pronunciation of v is f—which in German is the vulgar equivalent of "sexual penetration."
- In Italy, a campaign for "Schweppes Tonic Water" translated the name into the much less thirst-quenching "Schweppes Toilet Water."
- Puffs tissues proved challenging to introduce into the German market because "Puff" in German is the colloquial term for a whorehouse. The English weren't too fond of the name either, as it is a highly derogatory term for a homosexual.

**Figure 4.5:** Ad crafted in a high-context culture: Kewpie mayonnaise.

- Ford introduced the Pinto in Brazil. After watching sales go nowhere, the company learned that "Pinto" is Brazilian slang for "tiny male genitals." Ford pried the nameplates off all the cars and changed them to read "Corcel," which means horse.

One useful technique in revealing translation errors is called back-translation (Miracle 1988, RC-51). One individual is responsible for the initial translation of the message. A second individual then translates the message back into the original language. If the message does not translate back, it's likely that there is a translation problem. While back-translation is a helpful tool, it's no guarantee against translation bloopers. Hiring only native speakers of the language into which the message is to be translated also helps to reduce problems, as does acknowledging that some words and phrases simply cannot be translated. Translation techniques will be discussed in greater detail in Chapter 6. A final caution with regard to language: international marketers must recognize that writing and reading rules differ from culture to culture as well. Americans simply take it for granted that when they read or write, they move from left to right. Failure to recognize that this is not the case everywhere can result in marketing disasters. For example, a print ad for a laundry detergent appeared in the United States and featured a classic product demonstration. Laundry detergent was poured onto soiled clothing, which was soaking in a washing machine. After laundering, the clothing looked clean as new. The execution was so straightforward that the New York agency team responsible for it sent it directly to their Arabic agency's traffic person—suitably translated—for placement in local media. Unfortunately, the American advertising professionals were unaware that Arabic is read from right to left. The result: the ad showed laundry becoming soiled as a result of the detergent being added (Caporimo 1995, 16).

## Nonverbal Communication

We communicate not only through spoken language but also through nonverbal language. Indeed, it has been estimated that approximately 70 percent of all communication between two individuals within the same culture is nonverbal in nature. Nonverbal communication, often referred to as the silent language, can pose serious problems for international marketers and advertisers.

A number of classification systems of nonverbal language exist, some containing up to 24 different categories of behaviors (Hall 1976; Condon and Yousef 1975). Most classification systems include facial expressions, eye contact and gaze, body movement (such as hand gestures and posture), touching, smell, space usage, time symbolism, appearance or dress, color symbolism, and even silence. It is important to note that nonverbal methods of communication are no more universal than verbal methods.

Nonverbal communication regulates human interaction in several important ways: (1) it sends messages about our attitudes and feelings, (2) it elaborates on our verbal messages, and (3) it governs the timing and turn-taking between communicators (Ferraro 1990, 34). A thorough discussion of all of the aspects of the silent language, as it is often called, is beyond the scope of this text. However, because of their importance to the international marketer, four areas will be addressed briefly: gestures, space usage, time symbolism, and signs and colors.

*Gestures:* Thousands of cross-cultural examples prove that the meaning of gestures shifts from culture to culture. Gestures refer to any movement of the fingers, hands, or arms. Just as one word can mean different things in different countries, so, too, nonverbal cues vary in their meaning. The American "OK" gesture communicated by making a circle with one's thumb and index finger means zero or worthless in France and signifies money in Japan and Korea. In Greece and Brazil, it carries a quite vulgar connotation. However, in Arab countries, paired with a baring of the teeth, it suggests extreme

**Figure 4.6:** The "Got Milk?" campaign got into trouble in Mexico.

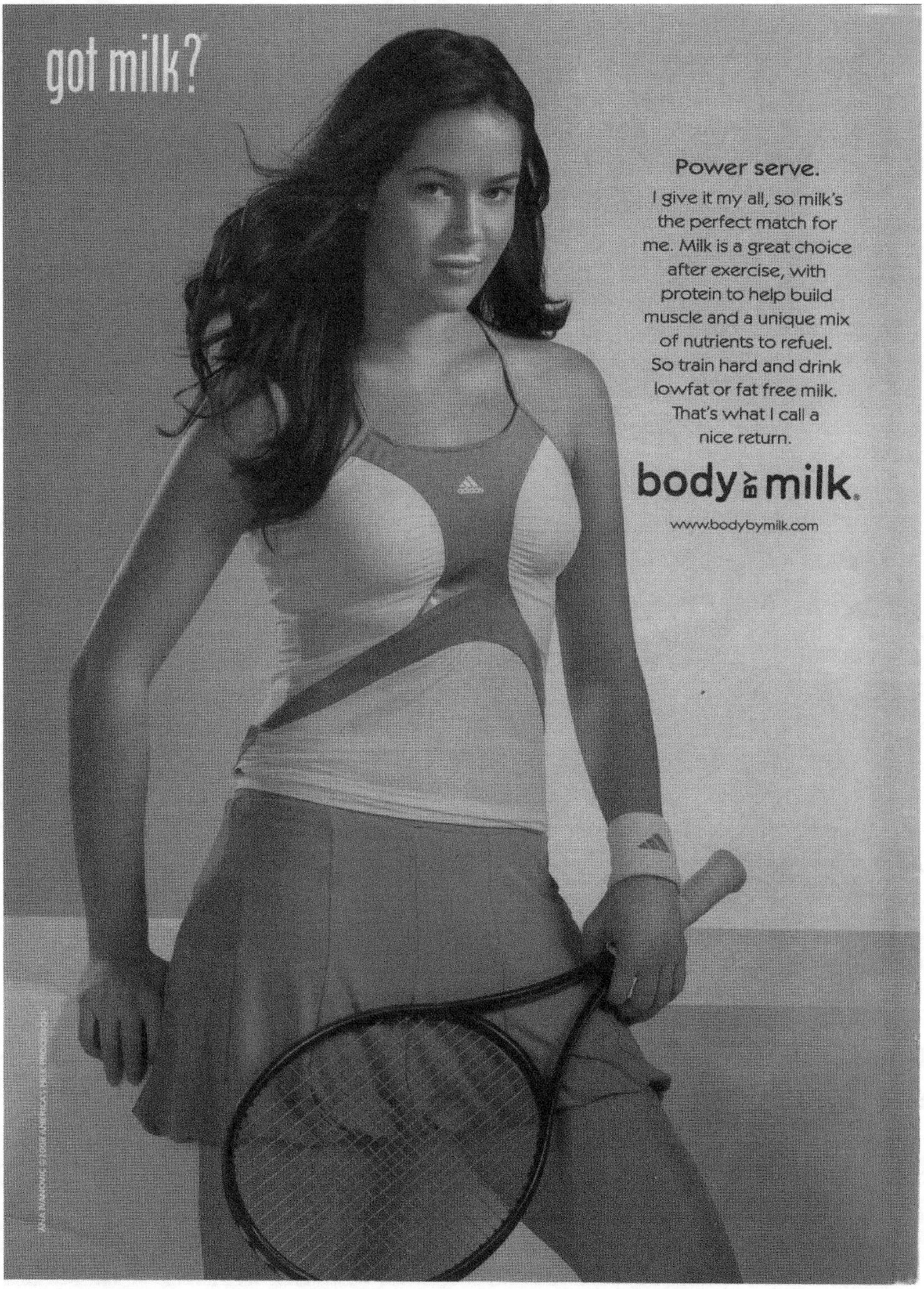

hostility. Caution is advised using this gesture in Tunisia, because there it means "I'll kill you." The "thumbs up" sign used in an AT&T campaign presented a problem when it had to be translated into other languages. For most Americans this gesture signifies positive affirmation. But to Russians and Poles, because the palm of the hand was visible, it gave the print advertisement, produced by N. W. Ayer, an entirely different—even offensive—meaning. YAR Communications, an agency specializing in translations, was engaged to reshoot the graphic element of the advertisement so that only the back of the hand was seen, thereby conveying the intended meaning (Davis 1993, 50).

There are also different gestures that convey the same message from market to market. Consider how men in different parts of the world show their appreciation of an attractive female through gestures:

- *The waist curve* (common in English-speaking cultures): hands sweep down to make the curvaceous outline of the female body.
- *The cheek screw* (Italy and Sardinia): the forefinger is pressed into the cheek and rotated.
- *The hand on the heart* (South America): the right hand is placed over the heart, signifying a heart throb.
- *The eye touch* (Italy and South America): a straight forefinger is placed on the lower eyelid and pulled down slightly.
- *The cheek pinch* (Sicily): a man pinches his own cheek.
- *The breast cup* (Europe in general): both hands make a cupping movement in the air, simulating the squeezing of the woman's breast.

Gestures used in greetings also vary from one culture to the next. In the United States, the hand wave is a common form of greeting. Hence, at McDonald's restaurants across the country, life-size Ronald McDonald statues have their hands raised in a friendly wave. However, operators of McDonald's restaurants in Thailand were required to modify the figure to display the unique Thai greeting gesture, the "Wai." The traditional greeting consists of the palms of both hands placed together and raised in front of the head as a sign of humility and respect. This is the first time that Ronald McDonald—the fast food chain's mascot—has displayed a culture-specific gesture such as this one. Usually, the rather neutral and internationalized statue is distributed from the United States to franchises around the globe. In this case, Thai operators had to custom-manufacture the molded fiberglass and resin stature. The end result? The mascot has become genuinely Thai (*Advertising Age* 2002).

There are also cultural differences regarding the amount and size of gestures employed during communication. Some cultures are quite animated. Middle Easterners, South Americans, Greeks, and, in particular, Italians employ a wide variety of gestures quite frequently. Indeed, there is even a stereotype that suggests Italians would be unable to explain themselves if their hands were tied behind their backs. Other cultures—Americans and Northern Europeans, for example—are more restrained in their gestures. These cultures place a higher value on verbal communication and consider excessive gesturing to be overly emotional or irrational.

*Space Usage:* How humans use space is referred to as *proxemics.* Edward and Mildred Hall suggest that "each person has around him an invisible bubble of space which expands and contracts depending on his relationship to those around him, his emotional state, and the activity he is performing" (Hall and Hall 1987, 12). Based on his observations of North Americans, Edward Hall developed four categories of distance in human interactions:

*Intimate distance:* ranging from body contact to 18 inches, this distance is used for personal contact, comforting, and protecting. Here, olfactory and thermal sensations are at their highest.

*Personal distance:* from 18 inches to 4 feet, depending on the closeness of the relationship, in this distancing mode people have an invisible "space bubble" separating themselves from others.

*Social distance:* from 4 to 12 feet, this distance is used by acquaintances and strangers in business meetings and classrooms.

*Public distance:* from 12 to 25 feet, at this distance recognition of others is not mandatory, and the subtle shades of meaning of voice, gesture, and facial expression are lost. (Hall 1966, 177)

However, the use of space is culture-bound—members of different cultures do not necessarily conform to Hall's four categories of distance. Americans are said to demonstrate a particularly high level of territoriality when compared with members of other cultures. In contrasting Europeans and Americans, Hall and Hall note:

> In Northern Europe the bubbles are quite large; moving south to France, Italy, Greece and Spain, the bubbles get smaller and smaller so that the distance that is perceived as intimate in the north overlaps personal distance in the south, which means that Mediterranean Europeans get too close to the Germans, Scandinavians, English, and Americans of northern European ancestry. (Hall and Hall 1987, 113)

Imagine the diversity when we compare how space is used in Africa or Asia. For example, most Americans feel quite uncomfortable when trapped on a crowded commuter train or in a full elevator. However, space is used differently by members of Japanese society. Japanese tend to stand and sit much closer together than Americans and appear to endure crowded conditions in public areas without much discomfort. As further evidence that Japanese and Americans use space differently, consider that in the United States top executives are typically separated from their employees—often inhabiting the top floor of the company building or, at the very least, sequestered in private offices. Because the Japanese are a group-oriented people, top executives rarely occupy private offices, preferring instead to work shoulder to shoulder with their employees. Clearly, each culture develops its own set of rules for space, and proper use of space must be employed when developing visuals for advertising messages destined for foreign markets. Space usage also has implications for personal selling. A salesperson who does not understand the appropriate use of space in a given market may find it difficult to sell his or her product line.

*Time Symbolism:* Just as the use of space is culturally influenced, so, too, is our use of time. A culture's concept of time refers to the relative importance it places on time. Edward T. Hall noted that "two time systems have evolved—monochronic and polychronic. "Monochronic time means paying attention to and doing only one thing at a time. Polychronic time means being involved with many things at once. Like oil and water, the two systems do not mix" (Hall 1966, 16). In a *monochronic* time (M-time) system, schedules often take priority over everything else and are treated as sacred and unalterable. Planes and trains must always run on time. Individuals raised in M-time systems constantly check their calendars and watches, worry about being prompt for appointments, and take it as an insult if kept waiting by others. Although this may seem natural and logical, it is merely a learned product of northern European culture. Hall explains that M-time systems grew out of the Industrial Revolution in England, wherein the factory labor force was required to be on hand and in place at the appointed hour. While examples of purely monochronic societies are rare, it can safely be said that Western cultures, in particular the United States, Switzerland, Germany, and Scandinavia, are dominated by M-time.

*Polychronic* time (P-time) systems are the antithesis of M-time systems. P-time is characterized by the simultaneous occurrence of many things and by a much greater involvement with people. In P-time systems, schedules and agendas mean very little, and appointments are often forgotten or rearranged at the last minute. No eyebrows are raised if one arrives at a meeting 45 minutes late. Middle Eastern and Latin American cultures often exhibit P-time behaviors. Indonesians have an expression for polychronic time: they call it *jam karet* or "rubber time"— flexible, stretchable meeting times, schedules, and agendas. Indonesians tend to place a higher value on human relationships than on arbitrary schedules and deadlines.

What does all this mean for businesses operating in the international arena? Consider the agency–client relationship—and the confusion that might result if each participant in the relationship is operating on a different time system. A Western client might rush to ensure arriving on time for a meeting with a Middle Eastern agency executive—and feel quite irritated if left sitting for nearly an hour in an outer office. Consider the potential impact on advertising message content. A telephone company did not take time orientation into account when developing a television spot for its Latin American audience. In the ad, the wife told her husband to "run downstairs and phone Mary. Tell her we'll be a little late." In fact, this commercial contained two major cultural errors. First, almost no Latin American would feel obligated to phone to warn of tardiness because it is expected. Second, Latin American wives seldom dare to order their husbands around (Ricks 1983, 70). It is impossible to estimate how much business has been lost because marketers failed to take into account differences between monochronic and polychronic peoples.

*Colors and Other Signs and Symbols:* International marketers may encounter problems with the connotative meanings of colors and other signs and symbols as they vary from culture to culture. Laurence Jacobs and colleagues note: "Like language, marketers in a particular nation often take color for granted, having experienced certain color associations all their lives, and do not even question whether other associations may exist in different societies" (Jacobs et al. 1991, 21). However, the significance of and meanings associated with specific colors vary from culture to culture. For example, while black signifies mourning in many Western cultures, white is the color most associated with death in Japan, Hong Kong, and India. White lilies are the appropriate flower for funerals in England, Canada, and Sweden, yet in Mexico white flowers are said to lift the spirits. Yellow flowers connote death in both Mexico and Taiwan, while purple is the color of death in Brazil and purple flowers are considered most appropriate for funerals. In the former Soviet Union, yellow flowers are considered a sign of disrespect to a woman, and in Taiwan, wearing a green hat signifies an unfaithful wife. Red is considered a positive color in Denmark but associated with the occult in many African countries.

International marketers need to know what associations a culture has in terms of colors and how they might affect product design, packaging, logos, advertisements, and other collaterals. When color meanings are similar across markets, a standardized strategy may be viable. A recent study by Madden, Hewett, and Roth (2000) found that blue, green, and white tend to be well liked across many countries and have similar meanings. However, the meanings associated with black and red varied considerably. Despite such generalizations, a thorough understanding of how colors are perceived in each country a marketer is planning to enter is clearly advisable. When the meaning associated with a color is different across cultures, marketers benefit from pursuing a customized strategy. David Ricks points out that the "choice of package and product coloring is very tricky. Sometimes companies have failed to sell their products overseas and have never known why. Often the reason was a simple one; the product or its container was merely an inappropriate color" (Ricks 1983, 32). For example, a number of years ago a leading U.S. golf ball manufacturer targeted Japan as an important new market for its product. However, sales of the company's golf balls were well below average. As it turned out, the firm had offered its product in white packaging—a color often associated with mourning. To make matters worse, it had packaged the balls in groups of four—the number signifying death in Japan (Glover 1994, 2). While the number 4 sounds like the word "death" in both Japanese and Chinese, it also happens to sound like "loin" in other languages. Numbers and shapes both mean different things to different peoples. While Americans associate misfortune with the number 13, it has no particular meaning in most other cultures. The number 7 is considered bad luck in Kenya and good luck in the former Czechoslovakia, and it has magical connotations in Benin.

Even the use of animals can prove problematic. The owl in both the United States and United Kingdom symbolizes wisdom; in France the bird is considered to have rather limited intelligence, while in the Middle East it is seen as a bad omen. Not knowing the symbolism associated with a particular animal in various cultures can directly affect the bottom line. German Electronics retailer MediaMarkt encountered problems in the use of animals in an ad campaign in Turkey. The firm employed billboards portraying human bodies with the heads of animals and asked if people were foolish enough to over-pay for electronics. The campaign insulted Turkish consumers—many of whom are Muslim—on two levels: first by using animals' heads on the bodies of humans, and second by questioning the audience's intelligence (Egrikavuk 2009). In another example of an advertising *faux pas* involving animals, a print ad for a men's cologne pictured a male model with his dog in a rural American setting. This ad worked well in the United States, yet failed in Northern Africa. The advertiser simply assumed that "man's best friend" was loved everywhere and failed to recognize that Muslims usually consider dogs to be either signs of bad luck or symbols of uncleanliness. But marketers should note that not all animals are forbidden in ads appealing to Muslim consumers: camels, for example, are perceived as a gift from God. They help people survive, and huge parts of the planet would not be livable without them (Kelley 2009).

## THE INFLUENCE OF CULTURE ON MARKETING AND ADVERTISING

### Religion, Morals, and Ethical Standards

Robert Bartels notes that "the foundation of a nation's culture and the most important determinant of social and business conduct are the religious and philosophic beliefs of a people. From them spring role perceptions, behavior patterns, codes of ethics and the institutionalized manner in which economic activities are performed" (Bartels 1982, 5). As such, knowledge of the moral and religious traditions of a country are essential to the international marketer's understanding of why consumers behave the way they do in a particular market.

Although numerous religious groups exist in the world today, Buddhism, Christianity, Hinduism, Islam, and Shinto are considered the major religions in terms of numbers of adherents. The influences of religion on international marketing are manifold. In some countries references to God or religion are taken very seriously. In cultures practicing Islam, it is considered highly inappropriate to use quranic quotations, the Prophet's name, God's name, or pictures of Islamic shrines on products or in promotional materials (Hashmi 1987). In a marketing blunder tied to religion, a shipment of Nike shoes featured a logo that resembled the word "Allah" in Arabic script. Allah is Islam's word for God. Nike said the logo (see Figure 4.7) was meant to look like flames, for a line of shoes to be sold during the summer with names such as Air Bakin', Air Melt, Air Grill, and Air-B-Que. When Nike's Eastern European office discovered that the original logo could be insulting to Muslim consumers, it immediately changed the design—but not before the Islamic Council loudly criticized the product (Abu-Nasr 1997, A-11). Other marketers tread lightly when it comes to religion. When Hyatt Hotels enters a new market, it takes religious customs very seriously. In Singapore, ceiling arrows point in the direction of Mecca. The Grand Hyatt in Bangkok boasts both a house god and a house temple. In Bali, Hyatt asked religious leaders for help in approving the artwork before the hotel opened. Artifacts the hotel had purchased to be placed near the restaurant were repositioned elsewhere when company officials were informed that the artifacts were too holy to be close to an area where people eat (Greenberg 1993, F4).

Religion directly impacts the way its adherents feel about work and the value they place on material goods. At the heart of Buddhism, for example, is the belief that suffering is caused by attachment to material possessions and selfish enjoyment of any kind. Islam also considers an emphasis on material wealth immoral. Such views stand in direct contrast to the Protestant work ethic, wherein acquisition of wealth is a measure of achievement. The doctrine "for the good of all" is at the heart of the Shinto religion, practiced extensively in Japan. This doctrine is reflected in the Japanese work ethic: to live is to work and to work is to be conscientious and to make everyone proud. The Japanese dedication to hard work has resulted in twelve-hour work days, often six days per week.

Religious traditions may forbid altogether the sale, or at least the advertising, of various products. There are about 320 million consumers in North Africa and the Middle East, and most do not consume alcoholic beverages for religious reasons. In some countries, such as Saudi Arabia, alcohol is even outlawed. For most brewers this would seem an insurmountable obstacle. However, Heineken and Carlsberg, two international brewers, have found it quite lucrative to sell nonalcoholic beers to consumers in such markets (Mortimer 2003, H-2). In Egypt, two Heineken products have become particularly successful. Each year, the company sells over 11 million gallons of Fayrouz, a fruit-flavored malt beverage that produces a head of foam when poured into a glass but contains no alcohol. A second product does nearly as well: over 9.2 million gallons of Birell, a beer-flavored nonalcoholic drink, are sold to consumers each year.

While some product categories such as alcoholic beverages and cigarettes obviously have the potential to cause difficulties in foreign markets, sometimes quite benign products come up against obstacles related to religion as well. Gillette faced quite a challenge in promoting its razors to consumers in Iran, because Islam discourages followers from shaving. As Laurel Wentz relates, in attempting to obtain media space for Gillette's Blue II advertisements, a representative from an affiliate agency went from one paper to the next. Finally, he came across a newspaper advertising manager without a beard and noted that "shaving is not just for your face…if you have a car accident and someone has to shave your head, Gillette Blue II is the best" (Wentz 1992, 140). Using this argument, the newspaper advertising manager consulted his clergyman and returned with permission to run the ad. Other products that are banned in this market because of the very conservative application of Islamic teachings include cigarettes, lighters, and even candy and chocolates. Islam also forbids the consumption of pork, while followers of the Hindu religion don't eat beef. An advertising blunder occurred some years ago when an appliance manufacturer ran an advertisement depicting an open refrigerator containing a centrally placed chunk of ham. Ads often feature a refrigerator stocked with delicious food, and because such photos are rather difficult to shoot, they generally are used for as many promotional purposes as possible. Unfortunately, the company used the stock photo in an ad headed for the Middle East. Locals considered the portrayal of pork to be insensitive and unappealing.

Religion may influence male/female roles, which may, in turn, impact various aspects of the marketing program—everything from the product to be promoted, to marketing research, and even creative

**Figure 4.7:** Nihad Awad, executive director of the Islamic Council, displays Nike shoes he says are insulting to Muslims.

expression. The Arabic culture, which is grounded in the Islamic religion, provides an excellent example. Under the concept of halal, which means "lawful" in Arabic, pork and its by-products, alcohol, and animals not slaughtered according to Quranic procedures are all forbidden. Many Muslim women feel they are violating Islam's teachings if they use skin creams with alcohol or pig residues. Apparently, fatty acids and gelatin used in moisturizers, shampoos, face masks, and lipsticks, as well as other items, are often extracted from pigs. A senior cleric at the United Arab Emirates' Dar al Iftaa, which issues fatwas, or religious edicts, noted that "if any cosmetic products contain pig derivatives or alcohol they should not be used because this is contaminated and one does not want to apply contaminated products on one's body" (*Jakarta Globe* 2009). To resolve this problem for Muslim women, a Canadian makeup artist who converted to Islam introduced a line of religiously correct "halal" cosmetics. Layla Mandi sells OnePure—cosmetics with the luxury feel of international brands minus the elements banned under Islamic law—in small boutiques, on Saudi Airlines, and via online stores in Malaysia, Jordan, and Britain. Mandi also has plans to launch a line of cosmetics for men. In attempting to gather market information on female consumers in the Middle East, one marketer planned to conduct a series of focus group interviews. But because of the very secluded role of women in this society, which is a direct outgrowth of the dominant religion, the marketer had to invite husbands and brothers to the focus group sessions instead. Similarly, hiring men to conduct face-to-face interviews with or even telephone surveys of women, or addressing mailed questionnaires to women for the purpose of collecting market data, would be considered highly inappropriate (Hashmi 1987). Even though the guidelines provided in the Quran may not be strictly followed by all Arabs, public expectations about modesty are still strongly influenced by it, and advertisers are not advised to deviate from these public expectations. In Arabic advertising today, female models are only portrayed if their presence relates directly to the product category (such as cosmetics or household products), and when they do appear, they are appropriately dressed. Showing any part of the body other than the face, hand, or foot may be regarded as a sexual stimulant and is thus considered inappropriate for public presentation. Indeed, many international advertisers have been forced to modify their print campaigns by superimposing long dresses on any scantily clad models. Even cartoon characters need to be appropriately dressed.

What is considered moral behavior is also directly influenced by religion. Warner Lambert had its share of marketing problems in the late 1960s when it attempted to introduce Listerine to Thai consumers. In Thailand, Warner Lambert produced commercials fashioned after a well-known American television spot showing a young man and woman kissing and otherwise expressing affection. Sales remained minimal, and company executives were puzzled by the turn of events. Finally, the problem was discovered: such public portrayals of male–female relationships was objectionable to the Thai people. The commercial was quickly reshot to show two young women instead. The ad caught on, and increased sales confirmed the effectiveness of the modifications (Diamond 1969, 50). In developing commercial messages for the Muslim world, human nudity is to be avoided at all costs, as it is regarded as highly offensive. In other countries, such as France and, increasingly, the United States, nude models in advertisements hardly raise an eyebrow.

Many major holidays are also closely tied to religion. We are all familiar with the fervor with which American businesses gear up for the Christmas season. As early as September, many retailers begin to decorate their stores and shops with garlands and Christmas trees to stimulate holiday shopping. In December retailers generally extend their business hours in response to dramatic increases in consumer purchases. In many countries where Christianity plays a major role, Sundays are considered a type of holiday, and no or very few business establishments are open for business. In the Muslim world the entire month of Ramadan is a religious holiday, and Muslims are required to fast from dawn to dusk. Because of the rigors of such fasting, there is a marked drop-off in productivity during this period. At the same time, Ramadan is a significant holiday in terms of marketing and advertising because, at the end of the holiday, Idul Fitri is celebrated, and every man, woman, and child receives a gift of clothing. Religious holidays can present real marketing opportunities to savvy international marketers. Consider the following example. The Hindu festival Kumbh Mela takes place every three years, rotating among four locations. However, the Kumbh Mela at Allahabad, at the confluence of three of India's holiest rivers (Ganges, Yamuna, and Saraswati) is considered the most important and is known as the Maha Kumbh Mela. A holy dip in the Ganges at Prayag is believed to wash the bather of all sins and grant salvation. Indians from all over the country join the pilgrimage, and the religious event is regularly attended by upwards of 50 million participants over the three-month festival. Companies providing pilgrims with a "brand experience" have included international marketers such as Unilever, SmithKline Beecham, Coca-Cola Co., PepsiCo, and Colgate-Palmolive. Specialist rural marketing agencies, such as Interpublic Group of Cos.' Linteractive and WWP Group's HTA Rural and Ogilvy Outreach, have helped clients reach Indian consumers at the event. They mounted product sampling blitzes and product demonstrations, and flaunted brands using novel ad media such as rail stations, kiosks, hoardings, giant screens, glow signs, handcarts, and even boats. HTA Rural coordinated stalls for product sales and demonstrations. To reinforce brand recognition for the Unilever cream Fair 'N Lovely, a logo game was included, and consumers who bought a large tube at the stall got a free photo of themselves with the brand and the event as a backdrop. The photo was processed on the spot and provided a permanent reminder of the brand's tie to the event. Ogilvy Outreach conducted "live" product demos for Hindustan Levers's Lifebuoy soap. Villagers tended to wash in muddy water and they were shown how Lifebuoy kills germs while mud multiplies them. Branded handcarts then moved around the Mela selling products at a discount (*Advertising Age* 2001). For global marketers seeking a deeper rural penetration into the Indian market, the Mela is indeed a blessing.

## EXPRESSIONS OF CULTURE

Geert Hofstede proposed that the four basic expressions of culture are symbols, heroes, rituals, and values. These expressions are depicted by Hofstede much like the layers of an onion, suggesting that symbols represent the most superficial and values the deepest manifestations of culture, with heroes and rituals falling in between. Marieke de Mooij (1994, 123) does a fine job of defining these layers.

*Symbols* can be words, gestures, pictures, and objects that carry a specific meaning recognized only by members of a particular culture. Included here are the latest status symbol, the newest fashion trend, and the hippest hairstyle. New symbols are quickly developed, and old ones fade away. Often, the symbols from one cultural group are adopted by another. For these reasons, symbols are shown in the outer, most superficial layer of the diagram. *Heroes* are persons, alive or dead, real or imaginary, who possess characteristics prized in a particular culture. Thus heroes serve as models for members of a society. Political figures (from Abraham Lincoln to George W. Bush) can be upheld as heroes by a specific group, as can film and television stars (such as Brad Pitt and Angelina Jolie). Even cartoon characters can be perceived as heroes (whether it be Superman or Snoopy). *Rituals* are collective activities considered essential within a culture. Social and religious ceremonies, business and political meetings, even sporting events, are all rituals. Consider the ritualistic behavior associated with football games in the United States. Tickets are purchased months in advance. Fans often paint themselves with the team's colors to show support in the stands. Before the event itself, tailgate parties take place in the stadium parking lot. Symbols, heroes, and rituals are intersected with the term *practices*. While practices are visible to nonmembers of a culture, their cultural meaning is invisible. The true meaning of practices lies in how they are interpreted by members of the culture. At the core of culture lie *values*. Values are broad tendencies to prefer certain states of affairs over others, and typically embody contrasts (what is good versus what is evil, what is beautiful versus what is ugly) (Hofstede 1990). Because cultural values are of critical importance to the international marketer and advertiser, they will be discussed in greater detail below.

## VALUES

Values go much deeper than behavior or attitudes, and they determine, at a basic level, people's choices and desires. Behavior changes with amazing speed in response to outside forces of all kinds, such as whether a person had a good night's sleep or how long the line at the grocery store was. Although slower to change, attitudes are also prone to external forces, such as the beliefs of one's peer group. Core values, however, are intrinsic to a person's identity. By appealing to people's inner selves, it is possible to influence their outer selves—their purchase behavior (Miller 1998, 11).

Milton Rokeach provides a classic definition of a value: "an enduring belief that a specific mode of conduct or end state of existence is personally and socially preferable to an opposite or converse mode of conduct or end state of existence" (Rokeach 1973, 27). Put more simply, Edward C. Steward states that values "represent a learned organization of rules for making choices and for resolving conflicts" (Steward 1972, 74). Articles on values and consumer behavior in scholarly journals suggest that values may indeed be one of the most powerful explanations of and influences on consumer behavior (Rokeach 1968).

While an examination of value systems can prove quite beneficial to a marketer, it is often fraught with problems. A major stumbling block in analyzing value systems is that many nations are multicultural. The United States, though often called a cultural melting pot, is an example of a particularly heterogeneous culture. If we state that a particular value is characteristic of the United States, it is not to say that each and every member of this society will possess that value. Rather, the concept of values should be used to assist in identifying the primary differences among consumers in different societies. Thus it is possible to make broad statements regarding the value systems that tend to dominate in a particular society.

An examination of cultural values can do more than assist marketers in segmenting consumers. With regard to the relationship between values and advertising, values may be among the major influences on human behavior. As noted in *Social Values and Social Change*, "Value-linked advertisements may animate affect, creating an affective response closer to the value-induced affect than to the product or advertisement without the value link. To the extent that affective advertisements are more influential than bland ads, values may be a mechanism to explore when trying to understand the sources of affect" (Kahle 1983). Indeed, numerous empirical studies have found that advertisements reflecting local cultural values are, in fact, more persuasive than those that ignore them (Gregory and Munch 1997; Taylor and Wilson 1997; Han and Shavitt 1994). If marketers hope to formulate more effective messages for foreign markets, they must become sensitive to the core values of a given country.

*Classifying and Assessing Values:* Several classification systems have been devised for assessing the dominant values of a culture. For example, Rokeach developed a means of quantifying personal value systems (Rokeach 1968). As shown in Table 4.5, the Rokeach value survey identifies 18 terminal and 18 instrumental values. Terminal values concern desired end states of existence that are socially and personally worth striving for. Instrumental values relate to modes of conduct and represent beliefs that are socially and personally preferable in all situations with respect to all objects. Value systems are identified by having individuals complete a survey that asks them to arrange all 36 values in order of their importance as guiding principles in their lives. Like many academics examining values, Rokeach assumes (a) that the total number of values an individual possesses is relatively small; (b) that people everywhere possess the same values, but to varying degrees; (c) that values are organized into value systems; and (d) that the antecedents of people's values can be traced to the culture, society, and its institutions (Anaudin et al. 2005).

**TABLE 4.5:** Terminal and Instrumental Values

| Terminal Values | Instrumental Values |
| --- | --- |
| A comfortable life (a prosperous life) | Ambitious (hardworking, aspiring) |
| An exciting life (a stimulating active life) | Broadminded (open-minded) |
| A sense of accomplishment (a lasting contribution) | Capable (competent, effective) |
| A world at peace (free of war and conflict) | Cheerful (lighthearted, joyful) |
| A world of beauty (beauty of nature and the arts) | Clean (neat, tidy) |
| Equality (brotherhood, equal opportunity for all) | Courageous (standing up for your beliefs) |
| Family security (taking care of loved ones) | Forgiving (willing to pardon others) |
| Freedom (independence, free choice) | Helpful (working for welfare of others) |
| Happiness (contentedness) | Honest (sincere, truthful) |
| Inner harmony (freedom from inner conflict) | Imaginative (daring, creative) |
| Mature love (sexual and spiritual intimacy) | Independent (self-sufficient) |
| National security (protection from attack) | Intellectual (intelligent, reflective) |
| Pleasure (an enjoyable leisurely life) | Logical (consistent, rational) |
| Salvation (saved, eternal life) | Loving (affectionate, tender) |
| Self-respect (respect, admiration) | Obedient (dutiful, respectful) |
| Social recognition (respect, admiration) | Polite (courteous, well-mannered) |
| True friendship (close companionship) | Responsible (dependent, reliable) |
| Wisdom (mature understanding of life) | Self-controlled (restrained, self-disciplined) |

*Source:* Rokeach (1973), 28

Rokeach's list of values has been used in a multitude of cross-cultural marketing and advertising studies. However, Rokeach is an American researcher who based his list on typically American values. According to de Mooij (1998, 101–102), there are some serious consequences of employing value studies developed in one culture for other cultures. Among them, certain relevant values of one culture may not exist in another. A list of values developed by a Belgian scholar reveals values not mentioned by Rokeach, including "having your own house, a place in the sun," and "Progeny, having decendents" (Vyncke 1992). Similarly, in Rokeach's list of values, two important Asian values are not reflected: thrift and perseverance. Another issue is that some values cannot be translated, so using a single value list for cross-cultural research will likely result in errors. Values might be incorrectly translated, or in the translation process become different values, and as a result the data may be incomparable. DeMooij provides an excellent case in point: International Research Associates INRA reported the results of a world survey

> which was based on questions related to such values as responsibility and respect for others. What caused great doubt about the reliability and meaning of the whole survey was the remark that "the organizers had been confronted with translation difficulties." The example given was that the English word *imagination* was translated as *verbeelding* in Dutch, which means conceitedness. Indeed, this is one of the two words provided in the dictionary, meaning "you think you are more than you are." It illustrates a relevant value of Dutch feminine culture, that one should not show off. However, the word that should have been used is *fantasie*, another translation possibility, which does not reflect negatively on the value found and better compared with the English concept of imagination. (de Mooij 1998, 102)

Also of concern is that values considered to be instrumental in one culture might be deemed terminal in another. For example, obedience is listed by Rokeach as an instrumental value. However, in Asian countries, where respect for elders, parents, or any higher-placed person is ingrained in the culture, it is likely considered a terminal value.

## Internationally Based Frameworks for Examining Cultural Variation

To date, several internationally based frameworks have been developed that allow for the examination and comparison of cultural variation from one market to the next. These frameworks outline a number of cultural dimensions that attempt to explain a significant portion of country-to-country variance. Two classification systems, which report data from a large number of countries, will be discussed here. The first, developed by Hofstede, identifies five value dimensions based on fundamental problems that all societies face. The second framework—entitled GLOBE—offers a new alternative. Drawn from organizational and management science, GLOBE outlines nine cultural dimensions and differentiates between societal values and societal practices.

## Hofstede's Dimensions of Culture

One of the most important frameworks for understanding the influence of culture is Geert Hofstede's typology of cultural dimensions (Hofstede 1980). Hofstede outlined four fundamental problems that all societies face: (1) the relationship between the individual and the group; (2) social inequality; (3) social implications of gender; and (4) handling of uncertainty inherent in economic and social processes. Work-related values and behaviors among matched samples of IBM employees at subsidiaries around the globe were examined. Based on 117,000 questionnaires collected between 1968 and 1972 from 88,000 respondents in 20 languages and reflecting 66 countries, Hofstede delineated four important dimensions that can be used to classify countries. They are *power distance*, societal desire for hierarchy or egalitarianism; *individualism*, society's preference for a group or individual orientation; *masculinity versus femininity*, a sex-role dimension; and *uncertainty avoidance*, a culture's tolerance for uncertainty. Later research resulted in the addition of a fifth dimension, *long-term orientation* (Hofstede and Bond 1988), the cultural perspective on a long-term versus short-term basis. Each of the five dimensions is measured on a scale from 0 to 100. The scores indicate the relative differences between cultures. An increasing number of marketing and advertising researchers have recognized the potential applicability of Hofstede's dimensions to marketing research problems (for example, Albers-Miller 1996; Caillat and Mueller, 1996; Taylor, Miracle, and Wilson, 1997; and Diehl, Terlutter, and Weinberg, 2003). As with time orientation and context, differences in the following five dimensions impact both the content of commercial messages and the creative strategies most likely to be employed.

## Power Distance

*Power Distance* in Hofstede's typology focuses on the degree of equality or inequality among people in a country's society. Cultures with a high power distance index (PDI) tend to be more accepting of hierarchies and autocratic leadership. Everyone has a rightful place in the social hierarchy, and the acceptance and giving of authority is considered normal. Individuals tend to obey the recommendations of authority figures such as parents, teachers, or bosses. Dependency is also an element of hierarchical relationships among people. Dependency can be used to a marketer's advantage, as the following example related to personal selling shows. An export manager for an Australian manufacturer of manhole covers, while visiting Malaysia (ranked high in PDI), never raised the issue of business when calling on prospective or regular clients. Rather, he ascertained whether there were relatives living in Australia or children pursuing studies there. On his return to Australia, he would contact these relations or students and look after them so as to create obligations. These obligations would be discharged by the Malaysian firms placing orders with his company without his ever having to solicit business (Fletcher and Melewar 2001, 10). In high power distance markets, commercial messages should avoid egalitarian appeals. Consumers in such cultures are more likely to expect clear directions in communications. Zandpour and Campos (1994) found that testimonials by a celebrity, a credible source, or a user of the product were a distinct feature of ads in cultures with high power distance.

In cultures ranking lower on the power distance index, such as the United States, authority has a negative connotation. Low power distance cultures stress equality and opportunity for everyone. In the United States, for example, it is assumed that superiors and subordinates are basically equal, and employees will quite readily approach and even contradict their bosses. Americans avoid becoming dependent upon others and don't want others to become dependent upon them. Indeed, children in the United States are raised to be independent at a relatively young age (de Mooij 1998). In low power distance cultures, there is little tolerance for authority, and consumers are more likely to make their decisions on the basis of facts and reasoning.

## Individualism versus Collectivism

Hofstede's *individualism versus collectivism* dimension pertains to the importance of the group rather than the individual. A high individualism ranking indicates that individuality and individual rights are paramount within the society. Ties between individuals are loose, and all are expected to look after themselves. Laws, rules, and regulations are institutionalized to protect the rights of the individual.

Americans are considered highly individualistic. Indeed, it is said that both the best and worst features of American culture can be attributed to individualism. Proponents of individualism have argued that it is the basis of liberty, democracy, and freedom, and serves as a protection against tyranny. On the other hand, individualism has been blamed for alienation from others, loneliness, selfishness, and narcissism. Research has shown that advertisements containing only a single person are quite common in countries that rank high on the individualism index, whereas portrayals of a person alone in an ad are infrequent in countries scoring low on individualism (Frith and Sengupta 1991). As one might expect, advertisements in individualistic cultures place a high value on individuality (or being unique), independence, success, and self-realization. As an example of such an orientation, consider the advertisement in Figure 4.8. The copy in the ad for Hennessy cognac reads: "Never blend in."

A low individualism ranking indicates that a country tends to be collectivistic. In collectivistic societies, social ties are much tighter. One owes one's lifelong loyalty to one's in-group, and breaking this loyalty has dire consequences. The supreme value is the welfare of the group. Japan is considered a collectivistic society wherein the concern for belonging plays a critical role. Japanese belong to reference groups, which vary from small to large, formal to informal, and intimate to impersonal. In identifying themselves, the Japanese stress their position in a social frame rather than their individualistic attributes. The Japanese approach to the group role is to perceive oneself as an integral part of the whole. The individual does not interact as an individual, but as the son in a parent-child relationship or as a worker in an employee-employer relationship.

**Figure 4.8:** Hennessy Cognac ad touting individualism.

A high value is placed on the harmonious integration of group members and on consensus. It is emphasized that opinions should always be held unanimously. The Japanese see all decisions and actions as part of group consensus. The individual is not held morally responsible for such decisions. When a person commits a wrongful act, it is the group that is embarrassed and, in the final analysis, responsible for the misdeed. Among the Japanese, this generates pressure for conformity to group norms and pressure to be like everyone else. The sense of identity anchored to in-group belongingness is sustained by going along with peers. There is a restraint from expressing disagreement with whatever appears to be the majority opinion.

This strong sense of belongingness as a state of self-identity calls for the individual's total commitment and loyalty to the group. This also means that the group is responsible for taking care of all the needs of its members. Mutual obligations of loyalty and total protection are established in Japanese employment practices. Although the current economic crisis in Asia has challenged the concept of lifetime employment, promotion and wage-rank based on length of service, and paternalistic relationships between employer and employee, most companies still try to provide employees with basic needs such as housing, medical care, education, and recreational facilities.

Japanese advertising, as well as advertising in other collectivistic cultures, reflects this group orientation. The majority of ads in such cultures tend to show people in groups rather than as individuals. "We" and "us" are popular pronouns. Message content tends to emphasize interdependence, family, group well-being, and concern for others. It is important to note that the group orientation dominates—between 70 and 80 percent of the world's population is more or less collectivistic.

## Masculinity versus Femininity

Cultures that rank high in *masculinity* emphasize stereotypical "masculine" traits—achievement, assertiveness, dominance, success, competition, and heroism. Those ranking low on masculinity emphasize "feminine" traits—a preference for relationships, modesty, caring for the weak, and quality of life. A fundamental issue addressed by this dimension is the way in which a society allocates social (as opposed to biological) roles to the sexes. Masculine societies tend to strive for maximum social differentiation between the sexes. The norm is that men are given the more outgoing, assertive roles, and women the caring, nurturing roles. Minimum social-differentiation societies, in comparison to maximum social-differentiation societies, permeate their institutions with a quality-of-life–oriented mentality. Such societies become "welfare societies," in which caring for all members, even the weakest, is an important goal for men as well as women (Milner and Collins 2000).

Venezuela has one of the highest masculinity rankings in Latin America. This indicates that the country experiences a high degree of gender differentiation of roles. Even today, males play the dominant role in society. Sweden, in contrast, has one of the lowest masculinity rankings. For more than two decades, Swedish women have earned as much as 90 percent as their male counterparts. And more than one-third of parliamentary seats are held by women. Whether masculine or feminine values dominate in a particular culture is reflected in a country's advertisements. For example, traditional sex roles do not play well in Swedish ads. Figure 4.9 is a Swedish ad for Knorr sauce mixes. Note the inset at the top left side of the page—the male partner is setting the table rather than the female. Examining television ads from a range of countries that Hofstede designated as either masculine or feminine, Milner and Collins (2000) found that ads produced for consumers in countries at the feminine end of the continuum also feature a greater proportion of characters in relationships than those at the masculine end. The researchers propose that this finding has practical implications for determining the types of ad appeals that might be appropriate in a specific country. For instance, a firm providing cellular phone service might find it effective to develop messages that show cell phones being used in nurturing relationships in Sweden (for example, developing closer bonds between grandparents and grandchildren), whereas it might use nonpersonal situations (such as dial-ups to a financial news provider) in the United States, which tends to be a more masculine country. Further, in cultures characterized as predominantly masculine, winning, achievement, performance, success, and status are much used in advertising appeals, and comparison advertising is common.

## Uncertainty Avoidance

Uncertainty avoidance focuses on the degree to which society reinforces or does not reinforce uncertainty and ambiguity. People in countries low in uncertainty avoidance are relatively comfortable

**Figure 4.9:** Differentiation between the sexes is minimized in this Swedish ad for Knorr sauce mixes.

Lyxa till det med något enkelt

På finare restauranger finns det speciella kockar som enbart ägnar sig åt att laga olika såser. En stor konst i sig själv med andra ord.

Nu kan du också lyxa till det hemma med en riktigt god sås. Utan att anlita en speciell såskock. Prova Sauce Raffinesse, en ny serie smakrika såser av hög kvalitet. Sauce Raffinesse finns i sju varianter, alla är lika enkla att laga, alla lika välsmakande till både fest och vardag.

*Knorr* Mer smak på livet

with ambiguity and are tolerant of others' behaviors and views. Weak uncertainty avoidance cultures feel that there should be as few rules as possible. They believe more in generalities and common sense, and exhibit less ritual behavior. Conflict and competition are not threatening. Consumers in such cultures more readily accept change and take on greater risks.

Where uncertainty avoidance is high, there is a need for rules, regulations, and controls. Formality and structure are central. This often translates into a search for truth and a belief in experts. The implication for communication is that uncertainty reduction requires explicit, logical, and direct information on the part of the communicator. Conflict and competition are avoided. People in strong uncertainty avoidance cultures have higher levels of anxiety, and the show of emotion is accepted. People living in such societies are likely to build up tension and stress that must be released. This is done in different ways: They may talk louder, use their hands while speaking, drive more aggressively, or embrace more emotionally (de Mooij 1998).

Consumers in high uncertainty avoidance cultures are likely to be drawn to products that emphasize low risk or safety features. In terms of creative strategy, the "argument" provides an audience with facts and reasons why they should purchase the advertised product or service. Zandpour and Campos (1994) found arguments and explicit conclusions to be the strategy of choice among cultures with a low tolerance for ambiguity and uncertainty. Uncertainty reduction requires explicit, logical, and direct information on the part of the communicator. In contrast, "symbolic association" as an advertising strategy (utilizing subtle presentations linking the product to a symbol with minimal and implicit information about the product) was found to be uncommon in high uncertainty avoidance cultures.

## Long-Term/Short-Term Orientation

Hofstede identified his four cultural dimensions using a survey developed from a Western perspective. To examine culture from an Eastern perspective, a group of researchers, the Chinese Culture Connection (1987), developed a survey based on Chinese values. This instrument revealed a fifth cultural dimension: *long-term/short-term orientation.*

A high long-term orientation ranking indicates that the country prescribes values of long-term commitment and respect for tradition. This is thought to support a strong work ethic where long-term rewards are expected as a result of today's hard work. A low long-term orientation ranking indicates that the country does not reinforce the concept of long-term traditional orientation. In this culture, change can occur more rapidly as long-term traditions and commitments do not become an impediment to change.

In general, people from East Asian countries, such as China, Japan, and Korea, tend to score high on the long-term index. Those with a long-term orientation value tradition and history and tend to look to the past for inspiration. By comparison, many Westerners, such as Americans and northern Europeans, are said to have a short-term orientation. People with a short-term orientation are more likely to perceive that the past is over and done with. The old is easily discarded, the new is quickly embraced, and there is an emphasis on planning for the future.

Of late, Hofstede's work has come under some scrutiny. The description of countries on a mere four or five dimensions is seen as insufficient, with several important dimensions missing. Hofstede (1980, 313) himself admitted: "It may be that there exist other dimensions related to equally fundamental problems of mankind which were not found...because the relevant questions simply were not asked." Another area of criticism focuses on cultural homogeneity. Hofstede's study assumes that a national domestic population is a homogenous whole. Yet, as has been discussed previously, most nations are groups of ethnic units (Myers and Tan 1997; Nasif et al. 1991). Others argue that the sample is not representative. One company comprised primarily of middle-class employees, the reasoning goes, cannot provide information about entire national cultures (McSweeney 2002; Sondergaard 1994). They question whether IBM, which has a powerful U.S.-derived organizational culture, may have socialized its employees to the point where their values do not reflect aspects of local national cultures. Some criticize that nations are not the best-suited unit for studying cultures, as cultures are not necessarily bound by borders. Indeed, research has found that culture is instead fragmented across group and national lines (DiMaggio 1997). Another weakness is that the IBM data is old and therefore considered obsolete (Mead 1994). Critics propose that because of globalization younger people in particular are converging around a common set of values. Finally, because Hofstede measured work-related behaviors among employees, transfer of his results to other groups (such as consumers) or other areas (such as marketing or advertising) and the use of his results to discriminate national cultures in general, are at best speculative. Hofstede stated: "The values questions found to discriminate between countries had originally been chosen for IBM's internal purposes. They were never intended to form a complete and universal instrument for measuring national cultures" (Hofstede 2001, 493).

Despite all the criticism, Hofstede's typology of cultural values, because of its contribution to the understanding of culture, the large pool of country scores available for a variety of cultures, and the lack of alternative frameworks at the time, has been applied extensively in cross-cultural research for the last 25 years.

## The GLOBE Study

A recent body of work entitled the GLOBE project (Global Leadership and Organizational Behavior Effectiveness Research Program) (House et al. 2004) offers an alternative to Hofstede's framework of cultural dimensions. As with Hofstede's framework, GLOBE reports data on cultural variables from a large number of countries. Data are provided for 62 cultures, based on a survey of 17,300 middle managers in 951 organizations. Managers were drawn from three industries: financial services, food processing, and telecommunications. Given that data collection began after 1994, the GLOBE framework is based on relatively current information, especially when compared with the data provided by Hofstede. Over 170 researchers from different cultural backgrounds worked together on defining, conceptualizing and measuring the dimensions. In most countries/cultures analyzed in the GLOBE project, data collection was carried out by natives of the country or by researchers with extensive experience in those markets.

GLOBE provides data on the societal level and explicitly differentiates between cultural *values* and cultural *practices*. Values are the individuals' or society's sense of what "ought to be" as distinct from "what is." They primarily reflect what "*should be.*" In contrast, practices refer to the behaviors of a culture and mainly reflect the "*what is.*" The distinction made between values and practices is similar to de Mooij's (2005) distinction between "desirable" and "desired" values. The "desirable" refers to social norms that are held in a culture and by an individual (corresponding to the "should be" or GLOBE values), whereas the "desired" refers to individuals' choices (corresponding to the "what is" or GLOBE practices). Both values and practices (the desirable and the desired) are often contradictory in a culture and are therefore seen as paradoxical values, which are found in many cultures. An example provided by de Mooij (2005, 2) may help clarify the distinction: "We don't want to be fat, we should eat healthy food, yet we do eat chocolate or drink beer, and we get fat." Given the fact that values and practices in a society may be inconsistent and sometimes even contradictory, it is a major strength that GLOBE clearly distinguishes between both levels of cultures. Hofstede, in contrast, often confused values and behaviors (practices) in his dimensions, which is a further weakness of his framework.

GLOBE outlined nine cultural dimensions:

(1) *uncertainty avoidance*, the extent to which members of a society strive to avoid uncertainty by relying on established social norms and practices;

(2) *power distance*, the degree to which members of a society expect and accept that power is distributed unequally;

(3) *collectivism I (institutional collectivism)*, the degree to which societal institutional practices encourage and reward collective distribution of resources and collective action, as opposed to individual distribution and individual action;

(4) *collectivism II (in-group collectivism)*, the extent to which members of a society express pride, loyalty, and cohesiveness in their groups, organizations, or families;

(5) *gender egalitarianism*, the degree to which a society minimizes gender role differences while promoting gender equality;

(6) *assertiveness*, the degree to which individuals in societies are assertive, confrontational, aggressive, and straightforward;

(7) *future orientation*, the degree to which members of a society engage in future-oriented behaviors such as planning, investing, and delaying gratification;

(8) *performance orientation*, the degree to which a society encourages and rewards group members for performance improvement and excellence; and

(9) *humane orientation*, the extent to which a society encourages and rewards its members for being fair, altruistic, friendly, generous, caring, and kind to others.

Several of the GLOBE dimensions sound quite similar to those of Hofstede. Indeed, GLOBE scales measuring uncertainty avoidance, power distance, and collectivism dimensions were designed to reflect Hofstede's dimensions of uncertainty avoidance, power distance, and individualism. However, analyses conducted by the GLOBE researchers revealed that the dimension of collectivism should be divided into two sub-dimensions: institutional collectivism and in-group collectivism. Institutional collectivism reflects the degree to which laws, social programs, or institutional practices are designed to encourage collectivistic behavior. Cultures with high scores on institutional collectivism practices tend to emphasize group performance and rewards, whereas cultures that report comparatively low scores tend to emphasize individual rewards. In-group collectivism reflects the degree to which individuals take pride in and are loyal toward their families.

The GLOBE researchers also found weaknesses with Hofstede's masculinity dimension and introduced two new cultural dimensions: gender egalitarianism and assertiveness. Societies that report higher scores on gender egalitarianism practices tend to have more women in positions of authority, have higher female literacy rates, and have similar levels of education for men and women. Societies that report lower scores tend to have fewer women in decision-making roles, have more occupational sex segregation, and have a lower level of education on average for women vs. men. As a point of interest, none of the 62 societies participating in the GLOBE project reported scores reflecting a truly egalitarian society (House et al. 2010). Yet, according to a recent survey, while women remain far behind men in economic and political power, the Nordic countries come closest to closing the gender gap (Lederer 2009). Four Nordic countries—Finland, Iceland, Norway, and Sweden—have topped the Global Gender Gap Index since it was first released in 2006 by the Geneva-based World Economic Forum. They did so again in 2010, although Iceland replaced Norway at the top of the list with a score of 82.8 percent, meaning it came closest to 100 percent gender equality. At the bottom of the list were Qatar, Egypt, Mali, Iran, Turkey, Saudi Arabia, Benin, Pakistan, Chad, and Yemen. The United States dropped from 27th to 31st place in the rankings as a result of minor drops in the participation of women in the economy and improvements in the scores of previously lower-ranked countries.

Prior to the GLOBE Study, there were no frameworks focusing specifically on assertiveness as a cultural dimension. Societies that score high on assertiveness practices tend to value tough, dominant, and assertive behavior for everyone in society, value direct communication, have sympathy for the strong, have a "can-do" attitude, and value what you do more than who you are. Societies that score low on assertiveness tend to have sympathy for the weak, value modesty and cooperation, speak indirectly and emphasize "face saving," and value ambiguity and subtlety in language and communication (House et al. 2010). A preliminary investigation by Terlutter et al. (2005) focused on the dimension of assertiveness. Prior to this investigation, no study had ever explored the dimension of assertiveness in the context of international advertising. This is surprising, given that assertiveness is an appeal commonly employed in commercial messages (see the example of a print advertisement employing an assertive appeal in Figure 4.10). The researchers found that assertiveness is a positively held value in many countries and can therefore be seen as an appeal type suitable for cross-cultural advertising campaigns. In a follow-up study, Terlutter and colleagues (2010) surveyed subjects from the United States, Germany, Great Britain, Austria, and Argentina, five countries that differed in their societal values and practices in terms of assertiveness, according to GLOBE. The authors hypothesized that the levels of assertiveness practices and values in each culture would influence the perception and evaluation of a standardized ad featuring an assertive appeal. Their findings suggest that in assertive markets, stronger assertive cues may be required if consumers are to perceive the ads as assertive in nature. In less assertive countries, more subtle cues may be sufficient to obtain the same level of perceived assertiveness.

Future orientation reflects the past, present, or future orientation of the majority of the population in the society and is based on the work of Kluckhohn and Strodtbeck (1961). This dimension has some similarities with, but also some distinctions from, Hofstede's long-term orientation. Societies reporting higher scores on this dimension show a propensity to save for the future, have individuals who are more intrinsically motivated, value the deferment of gratification and place a higher priority on long-term success, and view material success and spiritual fulfilment as an integrated whole. Societies reporting comparatively lower scores on this dimension have a propensity to spend now, have individuals who are less intrinsically motivated, see material success and spiritual fulfilment as dualities requiring trade-offs, and value instant gratification (House et al. 2010).

Performance orientation is associated with the construct of need for achievement (McClelland 1985). Societies that score high on performance orientation tend to value training and development, emphasize results more than people, expect demanding targets, and have a sense of urgency. These societies may favor performance-appraisal systems that emphasize achievement. In contrast, societies that score lower on this dimension tend to value relationships, have high respect for quality of life, emphasize seniority and experience, regard being motivated by money as inappropriate, emphasize tradition, and have a low sense of urgency (House et al. 2010). Diehl and colleagues (2008) examined responses from consumers in the United States, Germany, France, Spain, and Thailand to performance-oriented appeals in commercial messages. An important finding of the study is that it is not consumers from the country with the highest performance orientation scores who perceive the highest level of performance orientation in an advertisement. Instead, countries with higher performance orientation in terms of societal practices, in fact, perceive lower levels of performance orientation in the ad, and vice versa. The authors

**Figure 4.10:** Example of U.S. print advertisement incorporating an assertive appeal.

concluded that advertisers employing a standardized approach in their international efforts must be aware that an ad incorporating performance-oriented appeals may well be perceived differently from one country to the next, depending on the role that performance orientation plays in that particular market (see Figure 4.11 for a sample of an ad incorporating performance-related appeals).

Finally, humane orientation is derived from Kluckhohn and Strodtbeck's (1961) dimension of "human nature as good" vs. "human nature as evil," as well as from work by Putnam (1993) and McClelland (1985). Societies that score high on humane orientation tend to place importance on others (i.e., family, friends, community); believe people are motivated by the need for belonging and affiliation; give high priority to values of altruism, benevolence, love, kindness, and generosity; expect people to promote patronage norms and paternalistic relationships; and believe that children should be obedient and should be closely controlled by their parents. Societies scoring low on this dimension believe that self-interest is important; power and material possessions motivate people; people are expected to solve personal problems on their own; formal welfare institutions replace paternalistic norms and patronage relationships; the state sponsors public provisions and sectors; and children should be autonomous and independent (House et al. 2010).

While GLOBE provides data on the societal level, it does not do so on the individual level. The items used in the GLOBE project are designed to reflect societal values and practices, not individual values and practices. However, as individuals are socialized through values that are held and behaviors that are practiced in their cultures, it is very likely that they adopt values and practices that are shared among members of their society (Markus and Kitayama 1991). The values held and practices exhibited by members of a culture influence individual values and practices, as they enable the individual to behave according to social norms and rules and in a manner that is rewarded by other members of that group.

Much like Hofstede's framework, the GLOBE study also has its weaknesses. A major limitation is its relatively small sample, with an average of only about 250 subjects per culture. GLOBE researchers report that the number of respondents ranged from 27 to 1,790, though more than 90 percent of the cultures investigated had sample sizes of 75 respondents or greater. While 17,300 total respondents is indeed a large figure, it is still a small sample for describing societal values and practices in 62 different cultures. Hofstede's framework is based on a significantly larger sample. A second serious limitation is that respondents were middle managers in corporations. As with the Hofstede study (where IBM employees were surveyed), a single group within each culture was analyzed in the GLOBE project, as well. Transfer to other groups (for instance, consumers) remains speculative and requires empirical testing.

## INFLUENCE OF CULTURE ON CONSUMER BEHAVIOR

The culture of a society affects the kinds of products that are consumed as well as when and how they are consumed, by whom they are purchased and consumed, and how much is consumed.

### Why Consumers Buy

Anthropologists, psychologists, and sociologists all have been attempting to explain why individuals engage in consumption behavior. It is difficult enough to answer this question in the domestic market, but it becomes truly challenging in the international environment. In attempting to understand consumers, both domestic and foreign, marketers may look at the needs that motivate purchase behavior. A useful theory of human motivation was developed by Abraham Maslow (1964), who hypothesized

**Figure 4.11:** Example of a U.S. ad incorporating performance-oriented appeals.

that people's needs can be arranged in a hierarchy reflecting their relative potency. At the base of the hierarchy are physiological needs. As humans, our need for food, water, and shelter from the elements dominates our behavior. As these fundamental or "lower" needs are met, higher needs emerge, such as the need for safety— for security and protection from dangers in the environment. Once this need has been provided for, social needs arise—for affection from family and friends and to belong to a group. Higher-order needs include the need for esteem (self-respect, prestige, success, and achievement) and, finally, the need for self-actualization (self-fulfillment). People are not, however, locked into a particular level; clearly, an individual attempting to fulfill esteem needs also must address basic physiological needs.

Maslow's model has relevance to the international marketer in that the needs that dominate a particular culture are closely tied to that country's level of development. Apparently, the more highly developed the market, the greater the proportion of goods and products devoted to filling social and esteem needs as opposed to physiological needs. An examination of American advertisements reveals this to be the case in this country. Consider the many products promoted as status-enhancing goods— from automobiles to clothing to bottled water. The advertising appeals employed in cultures at different stages of economic development are likely to be quite different. While Maslow's hierarchy of needs is a useful tool, and presumably applies to consumer buying behavior in many different countries, caution should be exercised when employing it in a cross-cultural setting. The hierarchy is a theory based on Western behavior and has not been proven applicable to non-Western or developing countries.

## What Consumers Buy

People around the globe purchase goods and services to meet the various needs outlined in Maslow's model above. But as Terpstra and Russow (2000) note, the exact contents of the particular market basket will differ from country to country. Of concern to international marketers is whether their product can find a place in the market basket of a particular group of foreign consumers. It should come as no great surprise that because they are dictated by culture, consumption habits vary greatly from one market to the next. While there are numerous examples of products that have been sold successfully around the globe, other products face nearly insurmountable challenges. Our preferences for specific foods is very much culturally determined. Nestlé, for example has created 19 unique flavors for its Kit Kat chocolate bars that are available only in Japan. Besides the regular chocolate variety, which must seem mundane to the Japanese, Nestlé has come up with variations that reflect the local produce and palate of each region. There are some staple flavors like miso, soy sauce, and green tea, but the list doesn't end there. Kit Kat varieties now range from yubari melon and baked corn from Hokkaido Island, to green beans and cherries from Tohoku in northeastern Japan, to yuzu fruit and red potatoes from Kyushu Island at the southernmost tip of the country. The Kanto region, including Tokyo, contributes the sweet potato, blueberry, and kinako (soybean) flavors. The soy sauce Kit Kat is the most popular flavor nationwide (Madden 2010). As Andrew Zimmern notes in his Travel Channel television program *Bizarre Foods*, "one man's weird is another man's wonderful" (see the advertisement for this program in Figure 4.12).

There is no shortage of examples of how culture directly impacts consumption. Laundry-product manufacturers have had little success in introducing dryer-activated fabric softeners in many European countries because of the custom of hanging out clothes to dry on a clothesline. Demand for products that a marketer fails to provide can cause headaches as well. For example, after successfully opening a park in Tokyo, Disney decided to expand to the European market, opening Euro-Disney just outside Paris. Just as with the parks in the United States and Tokyo, all alcoholic beverages were banned. However, Disney failed to consider the European penchant for drinking wine and beer with meals. In addition,

**Figure 4.12:** With regard to which foods we find appealing, "One man's weird is another man's wonderful."

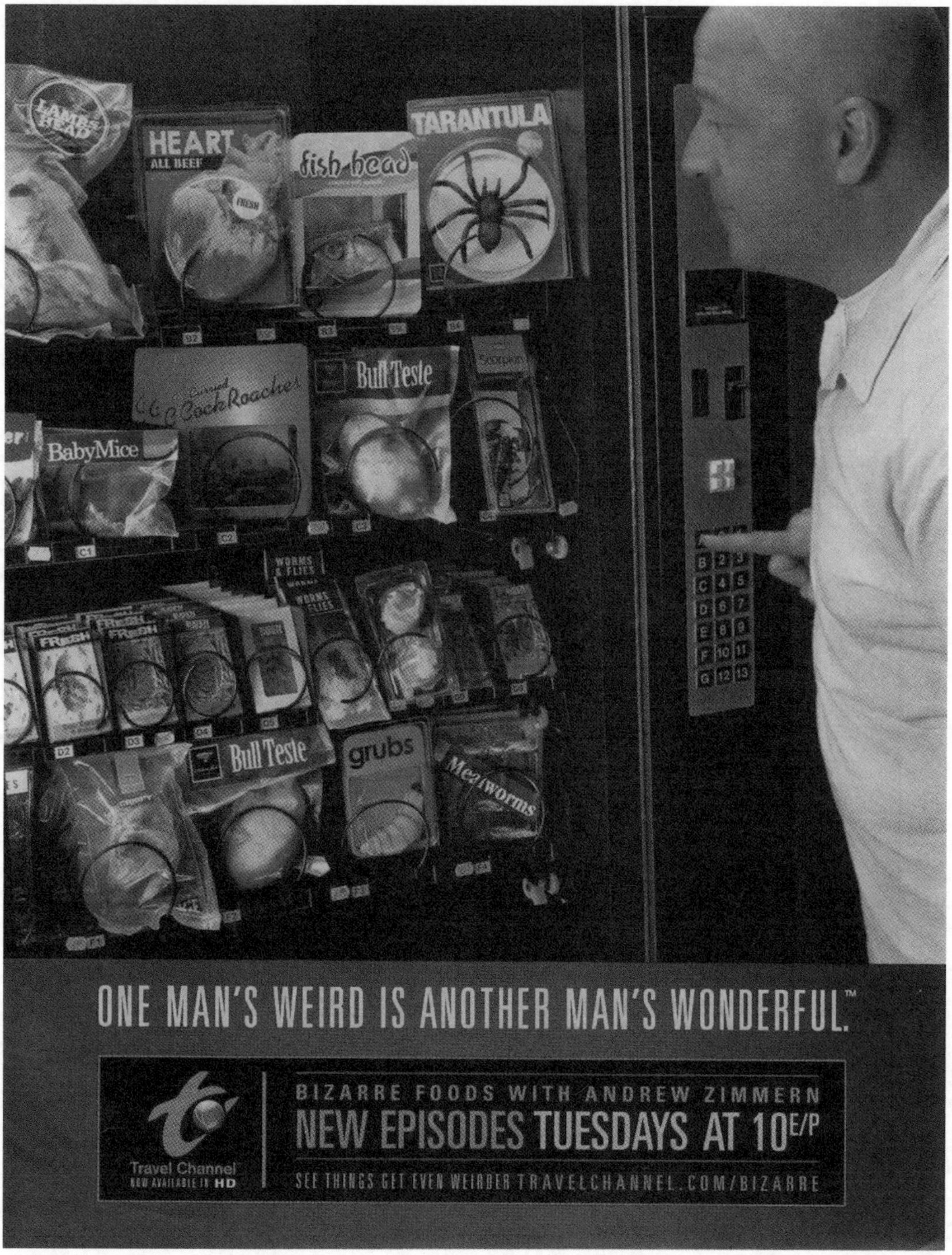
TARANTULA
HEART
fish head
Bull Teste
BabyMice
Bull Teste
grubs
Mealworms
ONE MAN'S WEIRD IS ANOTHER MAN'S WONDERFUL™
Travel Channel
NOW AVAILABLE IN HD
BIZARRE FOODS WITH ANDREW ZIMMERN
NEW EPISODES TUESDAYS AT 10E/P
SEE THINGS GET EVEN WEIRDER TRAVELCHANNEL.COM/BIZARRE

the park did not offer sufficient restaurant seating for European customers, who expected to sit down at the accustomed dining time and enjoy a leisurely meal. Disney was criticized strongly for sticking too closely to its homogeneous "It's a Small World After All" philosophy. Euro-Disney estimated that it would lose almost $350 million during its first year of operations. Disney has since introduced both beer and wine at all park restaurants (Wentz & Crumley, 1993, p. 1).

## Who Makes Purchase Decisions

The marketer must know who in the family is the primary decision maker, and for which products. In some cultures the female holds the purse strings, while in others it is the male. In Japan, for example,

> [the] housewife makes most of the major purchases for the family and buys the family's food, household supplies and clothing. Usually, she receives her husband's paycheck, manages the household budget, and allocates funds for different categories of expenses, including savings for children's education, vacations, leisure activities, and retirement. She is the person advertisers must try to reach. (Hall and Hall 1987, 137)

In contrast, in many fundamental Islamic markets, such as Libya, household purchasing is most often undertaken by men.

In the United States, for an increasing number of product categories, children, teens, and young adults are the primary decision makers. There are currently 50 million children age 11 or under (25 million aged 0–5 and more than 24 million aged 6–11) in the United States, and another 24 million between the ages of 12 and 18 (America's Children in Brief 2008). In 2002, children aged 4–12 spent $30 billion—money saved from gifts, allowances, and odd jobs. Those aged 12–17 spent $170 billion during the same time, an average of $101 per week per teen. Further, children under 12 influence another $500 billion in expenditures—either directly ("I want that Shrek DVD") or indirectly ("I know Sophie would love this American Girl doll"). Kids even influence what were once considered adult purchases. As the resident technology experts in many homes, they often help parents select computer hardware and software. And when parents decide on a vacation destination, or even a specific brand of vehicle, their children heavily influence those decisions as well. The Cayman Islands Department of Tourism buys ads on Nickelodeon, a children's cable channel, promoting expensive holidays. Beaches Resorts, a hotel chain, has teamed up with Sesame Street to make its resorts more appealing to children. Hummerkids.com offers games and coloring pages to teach children about the joys of owning a colossal sport utility vehicle. And Honda, another carmaker, launched an ad campaign on Disney's ABC Kids channel (*Economist* 2006). Simple math explains why advertisers spent a whopping $15 billion advertising to young consumers in 2007: they will get $700 billion in return sales (Kendle 2007).

## How Much Consumers Buy

Even the amount or quantity of a product that consumers in different cultures purchase is not constant. In the United States, shoppers typically purchase the economy size of products, as shopping is typically done on a weekly basis. In both Europe and Japan, where shopping is often done on a daily basis and where household storage space is more limited, consumers tend to purchase smaller-sized packages. Once Philips introduced a smaller version of its coffee makers to fit into smaller-sized Japanese kitchens, sales took off. Two-liter bottles of Coca-Cola failed to move from retail shelves in Spain, because few consumers had refrigerators with large enough compartments to store the beverage container. In contrast, in Mexico Campbell sells its soup in cans large enough to serve four or more, as families in this market are typically larger. Even deodorant consumption varies dramatically (*Advertising Age* 1992). Americans consume almost twice as much deodorant as the French and nearly four times as much as Italians. Consumers in the United States are perceived by much of the rest of the world as quite fanatical with regard to personal hygiene.

Consumption patterns clearly have importance for advertisers in deciding how to introduce a brand. Where a group of products enjoys widespread acceptance, the message will likely be directed toward obtaining the largest share of the market. Where consumption is low or nonexistent, the marketing communications will have an educational character. With regard to breakfast cereal, for example, U.S. citizens consume 9.3 pounds per person annually, while the British consume 12.9 pounds and the Irish a whopping 13.3 pounds. When Kellogg runs ads for Frosted Flakes and Corn Flakes in these markets, it is competing with other brands of cereals. In contrast, the German and Japanese cereal markets are comparatively undeveloped. Per capita cereal consumption is a mere 1.6 pounds in Germany and an almost negligible 0.1 pounds in Japan. Traditionally, Germans eat bread with cheese or meat in the mornings or, occasionally, a type of whole-grain cereal, while the Japanese eat primarily rice-based breakfasts. It is also important to note that many Japanese suffer from lactose intolerance, which further complicates the promotion of a breakfast consisting of cereal and milk. Kellogg initially faced quite a challenge in marketing its cereals in Germany and, in particular, in Japan, where it is only now making a serious breakthrough. Early messages for both Frosted Flakes and Corn Flakes tended to be predominantly educational in nature. Interestingly, even in the 1960s, Western-style soups had little trouble making it to the Japanese table—even the breakfast table. George Fields notes: "It was easier for soup to be served for the Japanese breakfast than cereal, because, traditionally, Japanese bean-paste soup (misoshiru) was always served for breakfast; thus, when breakfast started to turn Western, with toast and margarine, etc., Western-style soup had no conceptual problems being positioned. In a traditionally salt-oriented Japanese breakfast, cereals with milk and sugar had problems in this respect" (Fields 1989, 115).

## CULTURAL UNIVERSALS

Much attention has been given in this chapter to the differences between cultures. Some suggest focusing instead on the similarities between cultures. Theodore Levitt, often called the global marketing guru, proposes that the "world is becoming a common marketplace in which people—no matter where they live—desire the same products and life-styles. Global companies must forget idiosyncratic differences between countries and cultures and instead concentrate on satisfying universal drives" (Lynch 1984, 49).

Cultural universals are defined as modes of behavior common to all cultures. George Murdock (1945) developed a list of cultural universals that includes athletics, bodily adornments, calendars, cooking, courtship, education, etiquette, family, folklore, funeral rites, gestures, gift giving, incest taboos, joking, kin groups, law, magic, marriage, mealtimes, mourning, mythology, property rights, religious rituals, tool making, and weather control. Proponents of globalization argue that, to the extent that some aspects of the cultural environment may be perceived as universal as opposed to unique to each distinct society, it may be possible for international marketers and advertisers to standardize various aspects of the marketing mix.

Granted, as human beings, we all share basic biological similarities. For example, all humans sense hunger, and the eating of food to ensure survival is a universal behavior. However, just how we respond to this biological drive—what we eat, as well as when, how, where, and with whom we eat—is shaped by culture. Beyond biological drives, humans are confronted with universal needs, as outlined by Maslow above. But once again, the manner in which consumers in different markets address these needs can vary substantially. While consumers in the United States and Japan both experience "social needs," Americans nonetheless identify themselves as individuals, whereas Japanese identify themselves by their associations with various groups. This is not to suggest that standardization of the marketing mix is not possible or not desirable. The benefits associated with this approach are many, and examples of successful global products speak to its viability. Rather, this should serve as a warning that what might appear to be a cultural universal is often no more than an illusion of similarity. Prior to attempting to sell the same product in the same fashion abroad, the international marketer must carefully examine the various elements of the marketing environment (demographic, economic, geographic, political-legal, and cultural) for potential pitfalls.

# TOOLS FOR UNDERSTANDING CROSS-CULTURAL COMMUNICATION

Many firms, especially smaller ones, or those entering foreign markets for the first time, do not have the resources, time, or personnel required to assess all the elements of the marketing environment that might potentially influence the marketing mix. Nevertheless, the international marketer can draw on various tools in comparing the foreign market with the firm's domestic market for the purpose of making promotional decisions.

## Market Distance

The concept of market distance has its origins in early international trade theory as an explanation for why trade tended to be concentrated in foreign markets most similar to domestic markets. Migration patterns are at the core of this concept. When migrant groups settle in foreign countries, they carry with them their culture—their language, religion, values, and learned behaviors—all of which affect the goods and services they tend to purchase. Marketers in the host country thus acquire knowledge with regard to these consumption styles and habits, and this information influences their views on other foreign markets. Foreign markets are then seen as more or less similar to what the marketers know about their home market. In turn, this perceived similarity influences managerial preferences and choices of foreign markets, the international expansion strategies firms select, and the magnitude and direction of international trade (Reid 1986, 22).

**Figure 4.13:** Cross-cultural communications model.

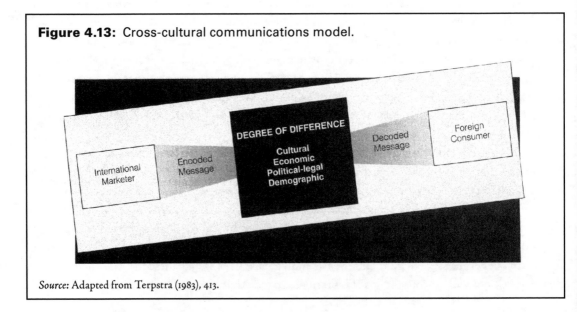

*Source:* Adapted from Terpstra (1983), 413.

In communicating with consumers in foreign countries, regardless of perceived market distance, messages encoded in one country must be decoded in another. However, when messages are communicated cross-nationally between similar markets, the decoding effect of the receiver produces results more nearly like those intended in the original message encoding by the sender. Conversely, when messages are communicated cross-nationally between highly dissimilar—or distant—markets, the decoding effect of the receiver may not produce the intended results. The model of cross-cultural communication outlined in Figure 4.13 incorporates economic, political-legal, and demographic differences in addition to cultural differences. This model is useful in that it refers to the degree of homogeneity or heterogeneity between markets in general. Clearly, the greater the degree of homogeneity, the greater the potential for a standardized approach. Greater heterogeneity suggests that one or more of the elements of the marketing mix (the product, price, distribution, and promotion) may require modification.

Larry Samovar and Richard Porter propose that the degree of similarity or dissimilarity between senders and receivers may be viewed on a continuum of compared cultures, as shown in Figure 4.14. The authors explain the scale as follows:

**Figure 4.14:** Continuum of compared cultures, subcultures, and subgroups.

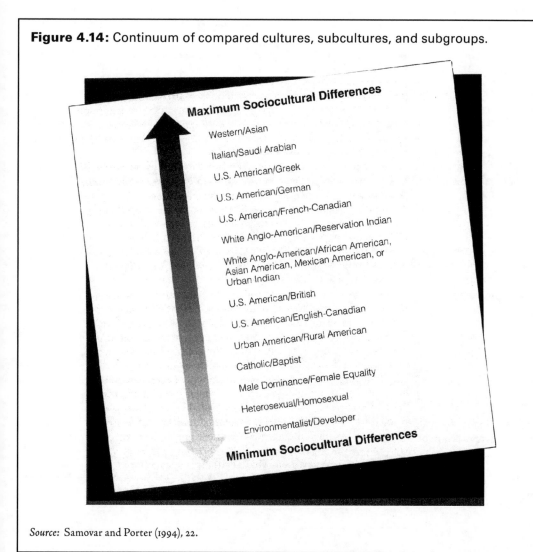

Maximum Sociocultural Differences

Western/Asian

Italian/Saudi Arabian

U.S. American/Greek

U.S. American/German

U.S. American/French-Canadian

White Anglo-American/Reservation Indian

White Anglo-American/African American, Asian American, Mexican American, or Urban Indian

U.S. American/British

U.S. American/English-Canadian

Urban American/Rural American

Catholic/Baptist

Male Dominance/Female Equality

Heterosexual/Homosexual

Environmentalist/Developer

Minimum Sociocultural Differences

*Source:* Samovar and Porter (1994), 22.

If we imagine differences varying along a minimum-maximum dimension, the degree of difference between two groups depends on their relative social uniqueness. Although this scale is unrefined, it allows us to examine intercultural communication acts and gain insight into the effect cultural differences have on communication. To see how this dimensional scale helps us understand intercultural communication we can look at some examples of cultural differences positioned along the scale.

The first example represents a case of maximum differences—those found between Asian and Western cultures. This may be typified as an interaction between two farmers, one who works on a communal farm on the outskirts of Beijing in China and the other who operates a large mechanized and automated wheat, corn and dairy farm in Michigan. In this situation we should expect to find the greatest number of diverse cultural factors. Physical appearance, religion, philosophy, economic systems, social attitudes, language, heritage, basic conceptualization of self and the universe, and the degree of technological development are cultural factors that differ sharply. We must recognize, however, that these two farmers also share the commonality of farming, with its rural life-style and love of the land. In some respects, they may be more closely related than they are to members of their own cultures who live in large urban settings. In other words, across some cultural dimensions, the Michigan farmer may have more in common with the Chinese farmer than with a Wall Street securities broker.

Another example nearer the center of the scale is the difference between American culture and German culture. Less variation is found: Physical characteristics are similar, and the English language is derived in part from German and its ancestor languages. The roots of both German and American philosophy are found in ancient Greece, and most Americans and Germans share some form of the Judeo-Christian tradition. Yet there are some significant differences. Germans have political and economic systems that are different from those found in the United States. German society tends toward formality while in the United States we tend toward informality. Germans have memories of local warfare and the destruction of their cities and economy, of having been a defeated nation on more than one occasion. The United States has never lost a war on its own territory.

Examples near the minimal ends of the dimension can be characterized in two ways. First are variations found between members of separate but similar cultures—for instance, between U.S. Americans and English-Canadians. These differences are less than those found between American and German cultures, between American and Greek cultures, between American and British cultures, or even between American and French-Canadian cultures, but greater than generally found within a single culture. Second, minimal differences also may be seen in the variation between co-cultures, within the same dominant culture. Socio-cultural differences may be found between members of the Catholic church and the Baptist church; environmentalists and advocates of further development of Alaskan oil resources; middle-class Americans and the urban poor; mainstream Americans and the gay and lesbian community; the able and the disabled; or male dominance advocates and female equality advocates.

In both these categorizations, members of each cultural group have more in common than in the examples found in the middle or at the maximum end of the scale. They probably speak the same language, share the same general religion, attend the same schools, and live in the same neighborhoods. Yet, these groups to some extent are culturally different; they do not fully share the experiences, nor do they share the same perception. They see their worlds differently. (Samovar and Porter 1994, 22).

# SUMMARY

To operate effectively in foreign markets, international marketers and advertisers must recognize the pervasive influence of culture. Failure to understand the cultural environment can lead and has led to misunderstandings, miscommunications, and marketing failures. In this chapter we examined only a few of the more prominent elements of culture—including verbal language, nonverbal communications, signs and symbols, needs and values, religion, and customs—as they impact consumer behavior. In addition, we outlined a number of tools for assessing foreign cultures. In the next chapter we turn to the standardization-versus-specialization controversy.

## REFERENCES

Abu-Nasr, Donna. 1997. Muslim group demands apology from Nike. *San Diego Union-Tribune*, 10 April, A-11.

Adelaja, Tai (2008). Kaliningrad bans signs in English. *The St. Petersburg Times*. <http://www.sptimes.ru/story/25164>. Retrieved 26 March 2010.

*Advertising Age.* 1992. Orbit international database. 27 April, I30.

———. 2001. Marketing to the masses: Unilever, Pepsi among those targeting 70 m pilgrims at Hindu event. 17 January. www. adageglobal.com/cgi-bin/daily.pl?daily_id=4215&post_ date=2001–01–17.

———. 2002. Ronald McDonald statues greet customers in true Thai style. Agency Report. 20 September, S-12. <www. adageglobal.com/cgi-bin/daily.pl?daily_id=8410&post_date=2002–09–20>.

———. 2009a. Top U.S. agencies in ten specialties. Agency Report 2009. 27 April, 16.

———. 2009b. Hispanic fact pack—Annual guide to Hispanic marketing and media.

*Adweek Media.* 2008. Marketing to Asian Americans. <http://www.adweekmedia.com/aw/content_display/custom-reports/>. Retrieved 29 March 2010.

Albers-Miller, Nancy. 1996. Designing cross-cultural advertising research: A closer look at paired comparisons. *International Marketing Review,* 13(5): 59–75.

Alderton, Matt (2010). Guide to marketing to African American consumers. <http://www/work.com/marketing-to-african-american-consumers-1341>. Retrieved 26 March 2010.

*Americano.* 2009. Marketers poised to make Hispanic market top priority. 6 November. <http://theamericano.com.2009/11/06/marketers-poised-to-make-hispanics…>. Retrieved 26 March 2010.

America's children in brief: Key national indicators of well-being. 2008. <http://childstats.gov/americaschildren/demo.asp>. Retrieved 16 September 2008.

Anaudin, Virginie Villeneuve, Stephane Manin, and Alain Ramsamy. 2005. Managing the dream reality dilemma in advertising. ANZMAC Conference: Consumer Behavior, 7–12.

Barron, Kelly, and Shiyori Ito. 2001. Culture gap. *Forbes,* 19 March, 62.

Bartels, Robert. 1982. National culture—Business relations: United States and Japan contrasted. *Management International Review,* 22(2): 5.

Biswas, Abhigit, Janeen Olsen, and Valerie Carlet. 1992. A comparison of print advertisements from the United States and France. *Journal of Advertising,* 21(4): December, 73–81.

Caillat, Zahna, and Barbara Mueller. 1996. The influence of culture on American and British Advertising: An exploratory comparison of beer advertising. *Journal of Advertising Research,* 36(3): 79–88.

Caporimo, James. 1995. Worldwide advertising has benefits, but one size doesn't always fit all. *Brandweek,* 17 July, 16.

Chinese Culture Connection. 1987. Chinese values and the search for culture-free dimensions of culture. *Journal of Cross Cultural Psychology* 18(2),: 143-64.

Condon, John, and Merrill Rathi Yousef. 1975. *Introduction to intercultural communication.* Indianapolis, IN: Bobbs-Merrill.

Crystal, David. 1999. English as she is spoke in the world: Why our tongue qualifies as the first ever global language. *Financial Times* (London), 6 December, 4.

Davis, Riccardo. 1993. Many languages—I ad message. *Advertising Age,* 20 September, 50.

de Mooij, Marieke. 1994. *Advertising worldwide.* 2nd. ed. New York: Prentice Hall.

———. 1998. *Global marketing and advertising: Understanding cultural paradoxes.* Thousand Oaks, CA: Sage Publications.

Desjardins, D. 2006 . Multi-Asian sector has buying power. *Drug Store News,* 26 June, 113.

Diamond, R. S. 1969. Managers away from home. *Fortune,* 15 August, 50.

Diehl, Sandra, Ralf Terlutter, and Barbara Mueller. 2008. The influence of culture on responses to the GLOBE dimension of performance orientation in advertising messages: Results from the US, Germany, France, Spain and Thailand. *Advances in Consumer Research,* 35: 269–275.

Diehl, Sandra, Ralf Terlutter, and Peter Weinberg. 2003. Advertising effectiveness in different cultures: Results of an experiment analyzing the effects of individualistic and collectivistic advertising on Germans and Chinese. *European Advances in Consumer Research*, 6: 128–136.

DiMaggio, P. 1997. Culture and cognition. *Annual Review of Sociology*, 23(1): 263–287.

*Economist*. 2006. Buybabies: Marketing to kids. 9 December. <http://www.commercial freechildhood.org/news/buybabies. htm>. Retrieved 1 April 2010.

Egrikavuk, I. 2009. Ads criticized for insulting Turkishness with animal heads on humans. <http://www.hurriyetdailynews. com/n.php?n=did-animals-really-insult-turkishness-2009-10-2>.

*Ethnologue: Languages of the world*. 2005. 15th ed. Dallas: International Academic Bookstore.

Ferraro, Gary P. 1990. *The cultural dimension of international business*. Englewood Cliffs, NJ: Prentice Hall.

Fields, George. 1989. *Gucci on the Ginza: Japan's new consumer generation*. Tokyo: Kodansha International.

Fletcher, Richard, and C. Melewar. 2001. The complexities of communicating to customers in emerging markets. *Journal of Communication Management*, 6(1): September, 9–23.

Ford, Emily. 2008. First in line foreign language advertising. *The Times* (London), 29 December 43.

Frith, Katherine Toland, and S. Sengupta. 1991. Individualism and advertising: A cross-cultural comparison. *Asian Mass Communication Research and Information*, 18(4): 191–197.

Glover, Katherine. 1994. Do's and taboos: Cultural aspects of international business. *Business America*, 8(15): 2–6.

*Gravity Media*. 2010. A new look at multicultural online trends: Gravity Media investigates. 3 March. <http://www.media-gravity.com/news/new-look-multicultural-online-trends>. Retrieved 26 March 2010.

Greenberg, Peter. 1993. Cultural sensitivity is becoming new aim for international hotels. *San Diego Union-Tribune*, 3 October, F4.

Gregory, Gary, and James Munch. 1997. Cultural values in international advertising: An examination of familial norms and roles in Mexico. *Psychology & Marketing*, 14(2): March, 99–119.

Hall, Edward T. 1966. *The hidden dimension*. Garden City, NY: Anchor Press/Doubleday.

———. 1976. *Beyond culture*. New York: Doubleday.

Hall, Edward T., and Mildred Reed Hall. 1987. *Hidden differences: Doing business with the Japanese*. New York: Anchor Books.

Han, Sang, and Sharon Shavitt. 1994. Persuasion and culture: Advertising appeals in individualistic and collectivistic societies. *Journal of Experimental Social Psychology*, 30(4): July, 326–350.

Hashmi, Mahmud S. 1987. Marketing in the Islamic context. Presented to the 6th annual Conference on Languages and Communication for World Business and the Professions, 8 May. Ann Arbor, MI.

Hoebel, Adamson. 1960. *Man, culture and society*. New York: Oxford University Press.

Hofstede, Geert. 1980, 2001. *Culture's consequences: International differences in work-related values*. Beverly Hills, CA: Sage Publications.

———. 1990. Expressions of culture at different levels. Working paper 90–006, University of Limburg, Netherlands.

Hofstede, Geert, and Michael H. Bond. 1988. The Confucius connection: From cultural roots to economic growth. *Organizational Dynamics*, 16: Spring, 5–21.

Hong, Jae W., Aydin Muderrisoglu, and George Zinkhan. 1987. Cultural differences and advertising expression: A comparative content analysis of Japanese and U.S. magazine advertising. *Journal of Advertising*, 16(1): 55–68.

House, Robert J., P. J. Hanges, M. Javidan, P. W. Dorfman, and V. Gupta. 2004, eds. *Culture, leadership, and organizations*, Thousand Oaks, CA: Sage.

House, Robert J., Narda Quigley, and Marry Sully de Luque. 2010. Insights from Project GLOBE: Extending global advertising research through a contemporary framework. *International Journal of Advertising*, 29(1): 111–139.

Jacobs, Laurence, Charles Keown, and Kyung-Il Ghymn. 1991. Cross-cultural color comparisons: Global marketers beware. *International Marketing Review*, 8(3): 21–30.

*Jakarta Globe*. 2009. Muslim women get Halal cosmetics. 31 March. <http://thejakartaglobe.com/muslim-women-get-halal-cosmetics>. Retrieved 30 March 2010.

Johnson, Bradley. 2009. New U.S. census to reveal major shift: No more Joe Consumer. *Advertising Age*, 12 October. <http://adage.com/print?article_id=139592>. Retrieved 12 October 2009.

Kahle, Lynn R., ed. 1983. *Social values and social change: Adaptions to life in America*. New York: Praeger.

Kelley, L. 2009. In the name of God, most gracious, most merciful. <http://www.submission.org/Camels.html>.

Kendle, Jeanine. 2007. About children: Ad media influence powerful with kids. *The Daily Record* (Wooster, OH), 108(169): 24 November, 1.

King, Samantha. 2000. Language police give billboards in English a pasting. *South China Morning Post*, 30 November, 18.

Kirka, Danica. 2006. British regulators edit "bloody" out of television ad. *San Diego Union-Tribune*, 16 March, A-2.

Kluckhohn, F. R., and F. L. Strodtbeck. 1961. *Variations in value orientations*, Evanston, IL: Row, Peterson.

Kroeber, A. L., and Kluckhohn, C. 1952. Culture: A critical review of concepts and definitions. *Harvard University Peaboby Museum of American Archaeology and Ethnology Papers*, 47: 181.

Lazer, William, Shoji Murata, and Hiroshi Kosaka. 1985. Japanese marketing: Toward a better understanding. *Journal of Marketing*, 49: Summer, 69–81.

Lederer, Edith. 2009. Survey: Nordic countries closest to gender equality. *San Diego Union Tribune*. 28 October, A-20.

Lee, James A. 1966. Cultural analysis in overseas operations. *Harvard Business Review*, March/ April, 47.

Liesse, Julie. 2008. The face of the new general market. *Advertising Age*, 3 March, A-5.

Lin, Carolyn. 1992. Cultural differences in message strategies: A comparison between American and Japanese television commercials. Paper presented at the AEJMC Annual Conference, 8–11 April, Montreal.

Lynch, Mitchell. 1984. Harvard's Levitt called global marketing guru. *Advertising Age*, 25 June, 49.

Madden, Normandy. 2010. Soy-sauce-flavored Kit Kats? In Japan, they're No. 1. *Advertising Age*, 4 March. <http://adage.com/print?article_id+142461>. Retrieved 16 March 2010.

Madden, Thomas, Kelly Hewett, and Martin Roth. 2000. Managing images in different cultures: A cross-national study of color meanings and preferences. *Journal of International Marketing*, 8(4): 90–107.

Maletzke, Gerhard. 1976. Intercultural and international communication. In *International and intercultural communication*, ed. Heinz-Dietrich Fischer and John Calhoun Merrill. New York: Hastings House.

Marketing to Hispanics in the U.S. 2005. *Brand Strategy*, 6 October, 48.

Markus, H. R. and S. Kitayama. 1991. Culture and the self: Implications for cognition, emotion, and motivation. *Psychological Review*, 98 (2): 224–253.

Maslow, Abraham. 1964. A theory of human motivation. In *Readings in managerial psychology*, ed. Harold Leavitt and Louis Pondy, 6–24. Chicago: University of Chicago Press.

McClelland, D.C. 1985. *Human motivation*, Glenview, IL: Scott Foresman.

McSweeney, B. 2002. Hofstede's model of national cultural differences and their consequences: A triumph of faith—A failure of analysis. *Human Relations*, 55(1): 89–118.

Mead, R. 1994. *International management: Cross-cultural dimensions*. Oxford: Blackwell.

Middle East Online. 2004. Iran gets tough on foreign-language advertising. 6 October. <http://www.middle-east-online.com/english/?id=11488>. Retrieved 26 March 2010.

Miley, Marissa. 2009. Don't bypass African-Americans. *Advertising Age*, 2 February. <http://adage.com/print?article_id=134232>. Retrieved 29 March 2010.

Miller, Tom. 1998. Global segments from "strivers" to "creatives." *Marketing News*, 4 July, 11.

Milner, Laura, and James Collins. 2000. Sex-role portrayals and the gender of nations. *Journal of Advertising*, 29(1): Spring, 67–79.

Miracle, Gordon. 1988. An empirical study of the usefulness of the back-translation technique for international advertising messages in print media. In *Proceedings of the 1988 Conference of the American Academy of Advertising*, ed. John D. Leckenby. Austin, TX: American Academy of Advertising, RC-51.

Mortimer, Jasper. 2003. Breweries tap Mideast market. *San Diego Union-Tribune*, 16 February, H-2.

Mueller, Barbara. 1992. Standardization vs. specialization: An examination of westernization in Japanese advertising. *Journal of Advertising Research*, 32(1): January/ February, 15–24.

Murdock, George P. 1945. The common denominator of cultures. In *The science of man in the world crises*, ed. Ralph Linton, 123–42. New York: Columbia University Press.

Myers, M. D., and F. B. Tan. 1997. Beyond models of national culture in information systems research. *Journal of Global Information Management*, 10(1): 24–32.

Nasif, E. G., H. Al-Daeaj, B. Ebrahimi, and M. S. Thibodeaux. 1991. Methodological problems in cross-cultural research: An update. *Management International Review*, 31(1): 79.

Pew Research Center. 2008. *San Diego Union-Tribune*, 12 February.

Putnam, R.D. 1993. *Making democracy work: civic traditions in modern Italy*, Princeton, NJ: Princeton University Press.

Ramaprasad, Preponderant, and Kazumi Hasegawa. 1990. An analysis of Japanese television commercials. *Journalism Quarterly*, 67: Winter: 1025–1033.

Reid, Stan. 1986. Migration, cultural distance and international market expansion. In *Research in international marketing*, ed. Peter W. Turnbull and Stanley Paliwoda, 22–33. London: Croom Helm.

Ricks, David. 1983. *Big business blunders: Mistakes in multinational marketing.* Homewood, IL: Dow Jones–Irwin.

———. 1988. International business blunders: An update. *Business and Economic Review*, 34: January/February/March: 11–14.

Rokeach, Milton. 1968. *Beliefs, attitudes and values.* San Francisco: Jossey-Bass.

———. 1973. *The nature of human values.* New York: Free Press.

Samovar, Larry, and Richard E. Porter. 1994. *Intercultural communication: A reader.* 7th ed. Belmont, CA: Wadsworth.

Samovar, Larry, Richard Porter, and Lisa Stafani. 1998. *Communication between cultures.* 3rd ed. Belmont, CA: Wadsworth.

Scott, Megan. 2009. Mattel introduces black Barbies, to mixed reviews. Signon San Diego News, 8 October. <http://www.signonsandiego.com/v=news/2009/oct/08/us-fea-lifestyles>. Retrieved 10 November 2009.

Shane, Scott. 1988. Language and marketing in Japan. *International Journal of Advertising*, 7: 155–161.

Sondergaard, M. 1994. Hofstede's consequences: A study of reviews, citations and replications. *Organizational Studies*, 15(3): 447.

Steward, Edward C. 1972. *American cultural patterns: A cross cultural perspective.* Pittsburgh, PA: Intercultural Communications Network.

Strauss, Steve. 2007. To tap the Hispanic market, you first have to understand it. *USA Today*, 20 February. <http://www.usatoday.com/money/smallbusiness/columnist/strauss/20>. Retrieved 26 March 2010.

Taylor, Charles Raymond, Gordon E. Miracle, and R. D. Wilson (1997). The impact of information level on the effectiveness of US and Korean television commercials. *Journal of Advertising*, 26(1): 1–18.

Taylor, Eda, and Dale R. Wilson. 1997. Impact of information level on the effectiveness of U.S. and Korean television communication. *Journal of Advertising*, 20: Spring, 1–15.

Taylor, Edward B. 1871. *Primitive culture.* London: John Murray.

Terlutter, Ralf, Barbara Mueller, and Sandra Diehl. 2005. The influence of culture on the responses to assertiveness in advertising messages. In *Advertising and communication: Proceedings of the 4th International Conference on Research in Advertising (ICORIA)*, Saarbruecken, Germany, 183–192.

Terlutter, Ralf, Sandra Diehl, and Barbara Mueller. 2006. The GLOBE study: Applicability of a new typology on cultural dimensions for cross-cultural marketing and advertising research. In *International advertising and communication: Current insights and empirical findings*, ed. S. Diehl and R. Terlutter, 420–438. Wiesbaden, Germany: Gabler Editions.

———. 2010. The cultural dimension of assertiveness in cross-cultural advertising. *International Journal of Advertising*, 29 (3): 369–399.

Terpstra, Vern. 1983. *International marketing.* 3rd ed. Chicago: Dryden.

Terpstra, Vern, and Kenneth David. 1991. *The cultural environment of international business.* 2nd ed. Cincinnati, OH: South-Western.

Terpstra, Vern, and Lloyd Russow. 2000. *International dimensions of marketing.* 4th ed. Cincinnati, OH: South-Western College Publishing.

Usunier, Jean-Claude. 1996. *Marketing across cultures.* 2nd ed. New York: Prentice Hall.

Vyncke, P. 1992. *Imago-management: Handboek voor reclamestrategen*, 134. Ghent, Belgium: Mys & Breesch, Uitgevers & College Uitgevers.

Wasserman, Todd. 2010. Report shows a shifting African-American population. *Brandweek*, 12 January. <http://brandweek.com/fdcp?1269635066771>. Retrieved 26 March 2010.

Wells, William. 1987. Global advertisers should pay heed to contextual variations. *Marketing News*, 13 February, 18.

Wentz, Laurel. 1992. Smooth talk wins Gillette ad space in Iran. *Advertising Age*, 27 April, 140.

————. 2010. LatinWorks is Ad Age's multicultural agency of the year. *Advertising Age*, 25 January. <http://adage.com/print?article_id=141693>.

Wentz, Laurel, and Bruce Crumley. 1993. Magic doesn't travel during Euro-Disney visit. *Advertising Age*, 20 September, 1, 3.

Whorf, Benjamin Lee. 1956. *Language, thought, and reality*. Cambridge, MA: Technology Press of Massachusetts Institute of Technology.

Zandpour, Fred, and Veronica Campos. 1994. Global reach and local touch: Achieving cultural fitness in TV advertising. *Journal of Advertising Research*, 34(5): September/October, 35.

# CHAPTER FIVE

# Coordinating and Controlling International Advertising

Chapter 2 focused on the four P's of the marketing mix—product, price, place (distribution), and, briefly, promotion. In Chapter 3 we highlighted the importance of examining various characteristics of foreign markets—demographic and geographic characteristics, economic factors, and the political-legal environment—and in Chapter 4 we explored the cultural environment. Now we turn our attention to the coordination and control of international marketing communications. Once international marketers have developed a product that meets the needs of a specific group in a foreign market, have priced it properly, and have distributed it through the appropriate channels, they must still inform consumers abroad of the product's availability and benefits. Advertising's goal is to generate awareness, interest, desire, and, ultimately, action. In this chapter we will focus on centralized versus decentralized control of international advertising, advertising agency selection, and marketing and advertising strategy options.

## CENTRALIZED VERSUS DECENTRALIZED CONTROL OF INTERNATIONAL ADVERTISING

One of the first issues a company must address when it decides to communicate with consumers in the various markets in which it intends to do business is how to organize international promotional functions—including advertising, personal selling, direct marketing, publicity, and sales promotions. A critical question relates to the locus of decision making—will it be highly centralized at company headquarters, or will a more decentralized, collaborative, and participatory approach to marketing communications be adopted? It should be noted that there is a close relationship between the decision on centralization and the extent of advertising standardization ultimately employed. In international advertising, Tai and Wong (1998) propose that marketers have four basic options: (1) global approach (centralized decision process, standardized advertising approach), (2) local approach (decentralized decision process, differentiated advertising approach), (3) "regcal" approach (centralized decision process, regional advertising approach), and (4) "glocal" approach (decentralized decision process, standardized advertising approach).

## Global Approach (Centralized Decision Process, Standardized Advertising Approach)

Complete *centralization* of decision making related to international advertising implies a high level of head office control—advertising agency selection, campaign planning, creative strategy and message development, media strategy and selection, budgeting, and sales promotion efforts all are conducted in the country in which the firm's headquarters is situated. One of the major advantages associated with centralization is that it affords the marketer complete control over all promotional efforts. This degree of control is essential if the marketer is planning to integrate marketing communications. In addition, it eases coordination efforts in multiple markets.

A centralized approach is significantly more likely to be employed if the marketing environments of the message sender and receiver(s) are highly similar. In particular, centralization is commonly used if there is little variation in both the media available for advertising and the regulation of advertising from one market to the next. Depending on the foreign market, the international marketer may not feel that local managers possess the management skills necessary to conduct effective research and to develop coherent advertising strategies. Further, subsidiaries may lack the financial resources to produce advertising executions with high production values. In many instances foreign managers are quite relieved to turn over responsibility for advertising decisions to headquarters.

The centralized approach is highly correlated with the use of standardized advertising— employing virtually the same campaign in both domestic and foreign markets. Conversely, a low level of head office control (decentralization) suggests that local development of advertising campaigns is more likely to be employed (Kirpalani et al. 1988, 323). For example, Sharp Electronics has employed a standardized campaign to promote a new type of color technology available on its Aquos line of televisions. The campaign, crafted by mcgarrybowen (which Dentsu Advertising—the world's fifth-largest ad agency—acquired in late 2008), features George Takei, best known as Mr. Sulu from *Star Trek*, who stars as Dr. Q and explains how the television technology works. Takei appears in television and print ads (see Figure 5.1), as well as retail displays. As a pitchman he wears a white lab coat, carries a clipboard, and chuckles at the notion that anyone watching the spots on non-Aquos television can't see the difference the new technology makes. "At Sharp, our goal is to reproduce every color in the world on TV," Takei says in the television spot. He adds that the new technology "adds a fourth color—yellow—to the standard RGB system, creating a vast array of colors you can't see with your TV's three-color technology. But you can see this." Then he turns to look closely at the screen of the new television before exclaiming "Whoa," and his signature line, "Oh, my." The tagline doubles as an invitation to retail outlets: "You have to see it to see it" (McMains 2010). The campaign broke in the United States before spreading to Canada and Europe. Television spots are dubbed for foreign markets, and print ads are translated into the local language.

However, there are weaknesses associated with highly centralized control as well. For example, a firm employing such an organizational approach may find it lacks (1) the ability to sense changes in market needs occurring away from home, (2) the resources to analyze data and develop strategic responses to competitive challenges emerging in foreign markets, or (3) the managerial initiative, motivation, and

**Figure 5.1:** Global campaign for Sharp's Aquos televisions featuring George Takei (Mr. Sulu).

capability in its overseas operations to respond imaginatively to diverse and fast-changing environments (Bartlett and Ghoshal 1986, 87).

## Local Approach (Decentralized Decision Process, Differentiated Advertising Approach)

Complete *decentralization* of international advertising means that all, or nearly all, advertising decisions are made by local managers in the foreign markets. The philosophy here, according to Christopher Bartlett and Sumantra Ghoshal, is that international subsidiaries should not be mere "pipelines to move products. Their own special strengths can help build competitive advantage" (Bartlett and Ghoshal 1986, 88). A primary benefit of decentralization is that promotional programs are tailored to the specific needs of each market. Nationals may be perceived as knowing the local market best and thus better equipped to make necessary modifications to advertising campaigns as a result of differences in the local media scene, political-legal environment, or culture. An international marketer may also opt for a decentralized approach if markets are small or the volume of international business and advertising is too limited to warrant close attention from headquarters. Local managers are likely to be more highly motivated when given responsibility for the promotional programs in their market. In some instances this approach is employed because foreign managers can be resentful if the home office centralizes control over advertising functions and then mandates the specific messages to be used in their markets. Certainly, a degree of control over promotional efforts is relinquished if a decentralized approach is adopted. Tai and Wong note that many food brands engage in the local approach. One example is the U.S. company Welch Food Inc., where a team approach is used in order to take advantage of the expertise of both management at the Welch Food company and local distributors, as well as to ensure better coordination between both sides. All advertising decisions are made jointly by headquarters and local distributors. But apart from the target segment, which is kept consistent, all other advertising elements differ from the home market (Tai and Wong 1998, 319).

## Regcal Approach (Centralized Decision Process, Regional Approach)

Tai and Wong note that the regcal approach is made up of "reg" (regional) and "cal" (local); that is, it uses a combined approach of centralized decision making and regional—sometimes even local—adaptation. For example, an international or network agency may be designated as the lead agency, responsible for developing what is termed pattern advertising (Tai and Wong 1998, 320). Pattern advertising refers to centralization of the "what" of an ad campaign and regionalization or localization of the "how" (Roth 1982, 290). Thus the basic advertising strategy, general creative, and even media approaches are provided to each subsidiary; however, local managers are then free to select their own media and modify copy, visuals, or other elements of the message to meet regional or local needs. This approach allows for local input and adaptation while still permitting a degree of uniformity in a firm's international promotions. Nikon, for example, unveiled a pan-European campaign with the theme "I am Nikon." The campaign was rolled out in early 2010 in television, print, outdoor, and online formats, and was supported by a dedicated Web site as well as social media channels to encourage consumer interaction. The campaign played on the already-existing Nikon tagline "At the heart of the Image," and included real-life scenarios in which people show who they are with a Nikon camera. Various pop culture and historic moments were referenced in the television spots, including a scene likening a baby's real first steps to the historic first walk on the moon. Other footage shown included Robbie

Williams turning his camera on the crowd at his concert; a Spanish bride who allowed her final pre-wedding preparation to be filmed for the campaign; vacationers exploring the Egyptian pyramids; and people from across the globe interacting with each other using the Internet and their Nikon cameras (Fernandez 2010). However, the regcal approach is not without problems. A critical question is how much country-to-country autonomy is practical.

## Glocal Approach (Decentralized Decision Process, Standardized Approach)

Glocal is a combination of the "glo" (global) and "cal" (local) approaches. Here, the headquarters develops a global campaign, which local offices may or may not choose to follow, but most decisions are determined by local subsidiaries or distributors. McDonald's provides an excellent example of the glocal approach (Wilken and Sinclair 2007). In 2003, McDonald's moved to give all of its previously disparate global advertising a consistent theme, even while allowing for local variations in the creative work. "I'm Lovin' It" is now the company's most successful and longest-running campaign, surpassing the iconic "You deserve a break today" and "Food, Folks and Fun," both in longevity and sales gains. The campaign began as "Ich Liebe Es" when it was written by the agency Heye & Partner of Unterhaching, Germany (a member of DDB worldwide Communications Group). The first McDonald's worldwide campaign ever produced outside the United States, "I'm Lovin' It" was the culmination of a competition of ideas held among McDonald's top international advertising agencies to spark a new brand attitude and direction. "We challenged our agency partners to put aside everything they knew about us and come up with fresh, original thinking, all of it with today's consumers in mind," noted Larry Light, McDonald's Executive Vice President and Global Chief Marketing Officer. "I'm Lovin' It' represents the best of what we felt were a number of outstanding ideas" (McDonald's Press Release 2003). Once selected, the idea was developed centrally into a full-fledged ad campaign, with creative work handled on a global basis, but one in which local agencies were given the opportunity to tailor the campaign to suit each national market. Subsidiaries could opt to keep the English tagline, translate it exactly, or adapt it to work for their local culture (see Figure 5.2 for examples of U.S. outdoor ads incorporating the "I'm Lovin' It" slogan). Five "I'm Lovin' It" launch spots were shot in 12 languages and a variety of locations, including the Czech Republic, Brazil, South Africa, and Malaysia. They depict how consumers from around the world feel about the brand and the way McDonald's fits into their lives. For television spots, a "template," which included "green-screen segments," was created so that local agencies could insert local touches. While English-language spots featured the vocals of Justin Timberlake, vocals by award-winning pop superstars Eason Chan and Joey Yung were featured in Cantonese-language commercials. In 2004, Larry Light caused quite a stir in advertising circles by declaring that "the days of mass marketing are over." McDonald's had adopted an alternative approach, which Light referred to variously as creating "brand journalism" or a "brand chronicle"—that is, taking a narrative approach that "seeks to tell as many different stories in as many different ways as it takes to reach McDonald's 47 million consumers in 119 countries." According to Light, "a brand is multidimensional. No one communication, no one message can tell a whole brand story" (quoted in Cardona 2004). For Light, McDonald's "I'm Lovin' It" campaign has been a crucial element in this "brand journalism" approach, and it has been claimed to have "reinvented a brand that had lost its way." By 2010, after running for seven years, there was much speculation that McDonald's would scrap the campaign and start fresh. But the chain's marketing executives believed the campaign still had a lot of life left in it and so charged the chain's biggest agency partners with making it better. According to Mark Tutssel, global chief creative officer of Publicis Group's Leo Burnett "This advertising is expected to lift the bar on McDonald's creative around the world." As an example, Tutssel points to a Leo Burnett spot for the U.S. market sure to garner attention. The ad features a father bear treating his cub son to a McDonald's after getting all A's on his report card (subjects include fishing and mangling). For them, that means using the cub as a decoy to attract a passing car so the father can then scare the passengers away. The pair eats McDonald's French fries that the tourists had been munching on along their scenic drive. There's even a lesson: Papa Bear shakes the car to get a stray fry from the floorboard, and then tosses the vehicle. "There's always an extra fry at the bottom," he says. Recently, McDonald's reported second-quarter earnings that confounded Wall Street expectations—same-store sales grew 3 percent globally and surged a stunning 6 percent in the United States, clearly a sign that McDonald's advertising is doing what it's supposed to do (York 2010). The overall approach described above—a single global campaign designed for local adaptation—is indicative of the McDonald's philosophy of "think global, act local."

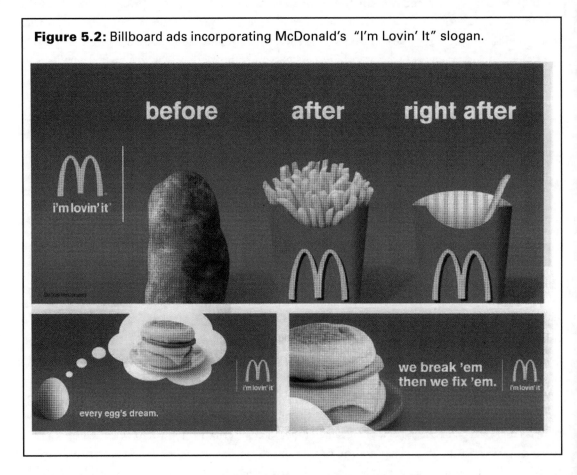

**Figure 5.2:** Billboard ads incorporating McDonald's "I'm Lovin' It" slogan.

## AGENCY SELECTION

Firms marketing their goods and services abroad must decide who should plan, prepare, and execute their promotional campaigns. International marketers have a variety of options, including (1) employing their domestic agency (and then exporting advertising messages), (2) using their domestic in-house agency or a foreign subsidiary's in-house agency, (3) calling on the services of an international agency with domestic and overseas offices, or (4) hiring a foreign advertising agency.

## Domestic and In-House Agencies

In some instances, firms may choose to simply export advertising campaigns originally created for the domestic market. Indeed, there are numerous examples of campaigns that have been exported quite successfully: the Marlboro man, conceived for the U.S. market, has travelled well all around the world—literally for decades. Other advertisers who have used this approach include IBM, Philips, and Waterman Pens. Firms may also choose to rely on their domestic advertising agency to prepare advertising messages for their foreign markets. A firm's domestic agency may well be affiliated with foreign shops capable of providing necessary translation services and assistance with media planning and buying. A domestic agency might also belong to an international network offering similar services. However, a very real danger of employing a domestic agency is that it may not be familiar with the many pitfalls associated with international advertising.

Some companies rely on their in-house advertising departments for foreign advertising assistance. On the plus side, the in-house agency is likely to be intimately familiar with the product or service to be promoted. Recently, there have been several examples of major advertisers who previously relied on international agencies shifting to in-house agencies. Prior to the firm's recall fiasco in early 2010, Toyota announced plans to axe its agencies and bring its advertising in-house. Toyota announced in July 2009 its intention of forming a domestic marketing company for Japan and a second company to coordinate global marketing activities for Toyota and its affiliates. Indeed, Toyota is set to hire a total of 250 employees in 2010 to handle its advertising needs. A statement released on the company Web site said the initiative was designed to bring Toyota's marketing closer to consumers and find ways to feed marketing activities back into product development. It remains unclear whether Toyota might continue to work alongside its agency partners—or fire the dozens of agencies that currently service the account. According to reports, Toyota did not notify roster agencies of its plans prior to the announcement, which caused a high level of confusion. This development follows a recent decision by Hyundai to transfer all creative duties to in-house agency Innocean (Blecken 2009). On the downside, domestic in-house agencies may lack the necessary experience in dealing with foreign markets. When international advertisers turn to a foreign subsidiary's in-house agency, they may gain familiarity with the local market but lose a degree of control over promotional efforts. Further, there is no guarantee that the quality of the work produced will live up to the firm's expectations.

## International Agencies and Global Networks

International firms leaning toward a centralized approach are three times more likely to employ an international agency or global network than they are to use a foreign agency (Kanso 1991, 129). Clearly, it is easier for international marketers to deal with a single international agency than with a separate agency in each market in which they operate. Although agency networks offer multicountry coverage, there is no guarantee that offices in each country will be equally strong. Clients may find agency work in one market of especially high quality, but less so in another market.

It can safely be said that Saatchi & Saatchi was the first of the truly global agencies. In an attempt to become the first advertising agency capable of meeting the needs of increasingly global clients, the London-based firm introduced its global orientation in 1984 in an advertisement headlined, "The New Opportunity for World Brands." The advertisement reflected the philosophy of global marketing outlined by Harvard Business School professor Theodore Levitt, who stated:

> The world's needs and desires have been irrevocably homogenized by technology. The global corporation accepts that technology drives consumers relentlessly towards the same common goals, i.e. the alleviation of life's burdens and the expansion of discretionary time and spending power.... Successful global companies sell the same things the same way everywhere and different cultural preferences, national tastes and standards are vestiges of the past. (Levitt 1983)

Not surprisingly, Levitt became a member of the Saatchi board. In late 1991 Saatchi & Saatchi further enhanced its global orientation by restructuring its North American and non–North American operations into a single unit. The agency even offered rewards to employees creating successful international campaigns, a practice reflecting its recognition that major clients, such as Procter & Gamble, look for advertising ideas that could run globally (Wentz 1991, 49).

Along with the globalization of the advertising business that has occurred since the 1980s has inevitably come consolidation, as agencies without the resources to compete on a full international footing have sought protection within ever-larger holding companies. Indeed, Saatchi & Saatchi, with its more than 130 offices in 80 countries, was acquired by Paris-based Publicis Group in 2000. Corporate clients include General Mills, Procter & Gamble, and Toyota.

By the mid-1990s, the top 10 agency networks' combined share of global advertising spending more than doubled, from 22.9 percent during the previous 10-year period to 48.3 percent. Driving this concentration of power was the assumption that ad agencies must have a global presence, enormous size, and a full range of marketing services to survive. This led to years of mergers and acquisitions, during which, for example, Omnicom bought more than 150 agencies. Interpublic grew from two U.S.-based ad agency groups to three worldwide ad agency networks: 30–40 smaller U.S.- and overseas-based ad shops, three global direct-marketing agencies, and 16–18 agencies focused on services such as public relations, health care marketing, entertainment and sports marketing, and consumer research.

Clearly, this alignment fever has spelled success for international agency networks, and today is undoubtedly the era of the advertising superpowers: superagencies with superclients. As revealed in Chapter 1 (Table 1.8), today the big four (WPP, Omnicom Group, Publicis Group, and Interpublic group of companies) dominate the international agency business. Dublin-based WPP, with worldwide revenues of $13.6 billion, ranked No. 1 in *Advertising Age*'s most recent listing (*Advertising Age* 2010a). WPP employs over 98,000 professionals worldwide. Table 5.1 presents WPP's agency family tree.

**Table 5.1:** WPP Group's Agency Family Tree.

### GLOBAL NETWORKS

| | |
|---|---|
| Young & Rubicam Brands | $2.65 billion |
| Y & R (Network Lead Agency) | 932 million |
| Sudler & Hennessey (Healthcare Agency) | 126 million |
| Landor Associates (Branding Consultancy) | 121 million |
| Cohn & Wolf (PR Agency) | 117 million |
| VML (Digital Agency) | 91 million |
| Bravo Group (Hispanic Ad Agency) | 29 million |
| Kang & Lee Advertising (Asian-American Ad Agency) | 16 million |
| SicolaMartin (Ad Agency) | 7 million |
| Robinson Lerer & Montgomery (PR Agency) | NA |

*Table continued on next page*

## GLOBAL NETWORKS

| | |
|---|---|
| WUNDERMAN (Marketing Services Agency and Network) | 828 million |
| Blast Radious (Vancouver-based Digital Agency in Wunderman Network) | 55 million |
| Zaaz (Digital Agency in Wunderman Network) | 25 million |
| RTC Relationship Marketing (Direct-Marketing Agency in Wunderman Network) | 25 million |
| DesignKitchen (Digital Agency in Wunderman Network) | |
| Burson-Marsteller (PR Agency & Network) | 385 million |
| Proof (Ad Agency/Burson-Marsteller Network) | 12 million |
| Ogilvy & Mather | $1.75 billion |
| OgilvyOne Worldwide (Marketing Services Agency) | 383 million |
| Ogilvy & Mather Advertising (Network Lead Agency) | 585 million |
| Bates 141 (Hong-Kong-based Marketing Communication Network) | 126 million |
| Ogilvy Public Relations Worldwide (PR Agency) | 122 million |
| Neo@Ogilvy (Digital Media Agency) | 103 million |
| Ogilvy Healthworld (Healthcare Agency) | 90 million |
| OgilvyAction (Marketing Services Agency) | 45 million |
| JWT | $1.12 billion |
| JWT (Network Lead Agency) | 1.07 billion |
| JWT Specialized Communications (Recruitment & Other Services) | 36 million |
| Malone Advertising (Marketing Services Agency) | 18 million |
| Grey Group | $912 million |
| Grey (Network Lead Agency) | 505 million |
| G2 (Marketing Services Agency) | 280 million |
| GHG (Healthcare Agency) | 110 million |
| Batey (Singapore-based Agency Network) | 8 million |
| Wing (Hispanic Ad Agency) | 8 million |
| United Group | $86 million |
| Berlin Cameron United (Ad Agency) | 15 million |
| Cole & Weber United (Ad Agency) | 11 million |

## OTHER AGENCIES

| | |
|---|---|
| Hill & Knowlton (PR Agency) | $330 million |
| CommonHealth (Healthcare Agency) | 156 million |
| Tapsa (Madrid-based Ad Agency) | 30 million |
| Brand Union (Ad Agency) | 13 million |
| WPP Digital | $221 million |
| 24/7 Real Media (Digital Ad Network) | 110 million |
| Bridge Worldwide (Digital Agency) | 49 million |

*Table continued on next page*

**GLOBAL NETWORKS**

| | |
|---|---|
| Schematic (Digital Agency) | 40 million |
| Blue Interactive Marketing (Singapore-based Digital Agency) | 11 million |
| HeathWallace (U.K.-based Web Design Firm—WPP owns 75%) | 8 million |
| Quasar Media (India-based Digital Agency—WPP owns 75%) | 4 million |
| Media Agencies | |
| Group M | $2.06 billion |
| Mindshare Worldwide (Media Agency) | 713 million |
| MEC (Media Agency) | 595 million |
| MediaCom (Media Agency) | 570 million |
| Group M Search (Search Marketing Agency) | 90 million |
| Maxus (Media Agency) | 90 million |
| Kinetic (Out-of-home Media Agency) | NA |
| Market Research | |
| Kantar (Market Research Group) | $3.60 billion |
| WPP Investments | |
| Asatsu-DK (Tokyo-based Ad Agency—WPP owns 24%) | $451 million |
| BPG Group (Bates PanGulf—Dubai-Based Agency Network—WPP owns 40%) | 50 million |
| Brierley & Partners (CRM Agency—WPP owns 20%) | 24 million |
| Chime Communications (London-based Agency Company—WPP owns 16%) | 193 million |
| HighCo (France-based Marketing Services Firm—WPP owns 34.1%) | 96 million |
| STW Group (Sydney-based Agency Company—WPP owns 20.6%) | 213 million |
| UniWorld Group (Multicultural Agency—WPP owns 49%) | 22 million |

*Source: Advertising Age (2010b).*

Such mega-groups clearly offer opportunities for synergy. They can deliver to their clients the ease of one-stop shopping for all of their marketing and promotional needs. They provide a multitude of marketing services alongside advertising, as they have aligned themselves with a wide variety of communication specialists in order to be able to offer integrated communication services to their clients. For example, networks also offer clients the services of interactive agencies, which have risen in importance as marketers attempt to deal with the mobile, Web, iPod, blog, BlackBerry, and consumer-generated advertising world. Today, non-advertising services (sometimes called below-the-line marketing) account for an ever-increasing percentage of annual revenue. At WPP, for example, advertising and media investments account for about 38.7 percent of revenues worldwide. Branding and identity, healthcare, and specialist communications account for 25.7 percent, consumer insight another 26.5 percent and public relations and public affairs about 9.2 percent. The change is being encouraged by marketers who are trying to reach consumers through a wide variety of communications channels. For example, Mary Kay Haben, group vice president of Kraft Foods North America, notes that at Kraft:

> we spend almost as much in other forms of marketing as we do on advertising. The goal is to simplify the development of integrated ideas. Agencies capable of providing integrated campaigns in a cost-efficient, time efficient manner have an opportunity for a big win. (Sanders and Cuneo 2002, 3)

Indeed, how holding companies handle the integration of these disciplines is expected to go a long way toward determining their performance level in years to come. Notes Lou Schultz, former chairman of Interpublic's Initiative Media Worldwide: "As marketers integrate more programs to communicate with their audiences, the distinction between advertising and below-the-line activities will blur" (Van der Pool and Rountree 2003, 9).

In addition to integrated marketing communications, conglomerates can also offer additional benefit to clients, including a means to consolidate and cut administrative expenses. Size is also of benefit when it comes to securing commodities. Media services is the term generally employed to describe the process of delivering an advertisement via the media. Broadly speaking, there are two aspects to this: media planning, which involves deciding where the advertisement should be placed in order to achieve maximum impact on its intended audience, and media buying, the process of negotiating with individual media owners over availability and price. Although some advertising agencies still offer media services in-house, as Lane and colleagues (2008) note, the major agency holding companies have created mega-media buying and planning agencies (also known as media services agencies) in order to be more efficient and cost effective—and thereby better able to attract global clients. As a result of the consolidation process, this part of the market is now dominated by global networks such as Mindshare, Carat, and Starcom MediaVest (SMV), each of which operates through 100 or more local offices around the world. The media function will be discussed in greater detail in Chapter 7.

On the downside, critics complain that the holding companies have become too large and too complex. (See Figure 5.3 for an "anti-conglomerate" ad.) The message for Seiter & Miller pokes fun at the mega-agency networks with a headline that asks: "Inter-Omni-PP.... Is your ad agency telling you to get lost?" The copy reads:

> How much bigger and bureaucratic can the public agencies get? At Seiter & Miller, there are no divisions, sub-divisions, subsidiaries, or sub-par work. Here you'll find smart, talented professionals all under one roof, and all dedicated to one mission—working hand in hand with you to build you business.

Many on both the creative and business sides of advertising contend that the expansion of agency companies has smothered originality under a blanket of conformity. Paul Cappelli, a refugee from the Interpublic agency McCann-Erickson, noted:

> You have a holding company dictating what can and can't be done, which stifles creativity, and the corporate culture numbs individuality. We call those agencies "notworks" instead of "networks" because if you're not one of the biggest clients, you get lost in the shuffle. (Elliott 2002, 3)

Another major drawback of such conglomerates is that sometimes an agency brand must be sacrificed to benefit another owned by the same holding company. Madison Avenue's history is replete with shuttered agencies whose doors carried the names of former giants—Lintas, Ayer, and Wells, Rich & Green. In October 2002, D'Arcy Masius Benton & Bowles, which began in 1906 and developed into the world's 14th-largest agency brand, was another victim of industry consolidation. Publicis, which became D'Arcy's parent after its merger with Bcom3 group, closed the agency and folded DMB&B's clients into the holding company's other agencies. A related disadvantage for holding companies is that as they continue to grow and expand, client conflicts become a critical issue. For example, Interpublic was unable to persuade PepsiCo that "walls" could be constructed in such a way as to insure there would be no leaks of confidential PepsiCo information among Interpublic's PepsiCo agency (Foote, Cone & Belding) and Interpublic's Coca-Cola Co. agencies (principally McCann-Erickson Worldwide and Lowe Lintas & Partners Worldwide). In the end, PepsiCo could not see a difference between the Interpublic shops (Kurz 2001, 22).

**Figure 5.3:** Anti-holding company advertisement for Seiter & Miller advertising agency.

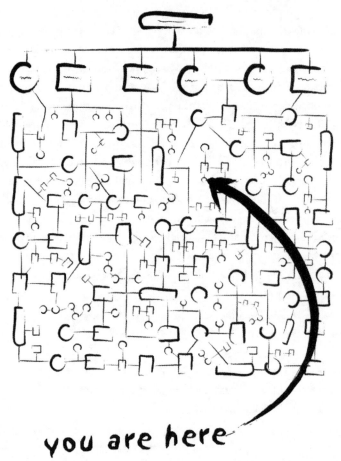

IS YOUR AD AGENCY TELLING YOU TO GET LOST?

(FIND YOURSELF AT A BETTER PLACE)

How much bigger and bureaucratic can the public agencies get? At Seiter & Miller, there are no divisions, subdivisions, subsidiaries, or sub-par work. Here, you'll find smart, talented professionals all under one roof, and all dedicated to one mission – working hand in hand with you to build your business. If you still remember why advertising used to be called a 'people business', call us.

Seiter & Miller

Contact Steve Seiter: 212-843-9900 or visit www.seitermiller.com

## Foreign (Local) Agencies

If the multinational firm adheres to decentralization, giving a good deal of autonomy to foreign managers, the advertiser is significantly more likely to select foreign (local) agencies to coordinate promotional activities for each market in which it operates. The selection of a local agency may even be left to overseas managers. Academics and practitioners who encourage the use of foreign (local) agencies argue that only such agencies can truly appreciate the local culture and, as a result, can develop messages best able to communicate with foreign consumers. A survey undertaken by *Advertising Age's* Clancy Shulman revealed that while Europeans regularly purchase brands from other countries, when it comes to advertising messages they prefer the home-grown variety (Giges 1992, 11). Foreign agencies thus can act as a cultural bridge between the international firm and the local market (Terpstra 1988, 159).

Because foreign agencies are often independent and typically smaller in size, they may demonstrate an innovativeness that agency networks cannot—and this may be just what a marketer is looking for. Pizza Hut, a division of U.S.-based Yum Restaurants International, has allowed its French division to create the first-ever "Made in France" advertising campaign for the introduction of a locally sourced specialty item—the Alpine-influenced Tartiflette Pizza. The television campaign, along with direct marketing and point-of-sale promotions, was the first solo effort for local independent K Agency, Paris, which until then had been responsible for adapting various U.S. campaigns to the French market. Pizza Hut assigned the local campaign with hopes that K Agency's locally sourced ads would tap into French consumers' love of regional cheeses and the national penchant for passing the winter holidays in the Alps, which was the hook behind the new pizza. La Pizza Tartiflette was the U.S. restaurant chain's bid to cash in on the winter ski fever that hits city dwellers, the principal customers at the chain's 140 French shops. The new product adapted the traditional Alpine Tartiflette recipe—a combination of potatoes, onions, ham, and local reblochon cheese—into a tasty pizza. Humorous television spots were set in a typical ski resort restaurant and depicted the pleasure skiers often take in munching down a Tartiflette after a hard day on the slopes...except that in this case, it was not a traditional version of the cheese dish, but a Pizza Hut Pizza (Speer 2003).

On the downside, utilizing a separate local agency for each foreign market makes coordinating worldwide campaigns quite challenging. International marketers must be aware, however, that the availability of advertising agencies in various markets varies greatly. Some countries, mostly in Africa, have just a single local agency. At the other end of the spectrum are countries such as the United States and the United Kingdom, each with well over 500 advertising agencies.

A major reason that foreign (local) agencies continue to prosper is nationalism. Many countries resent the role played by foreign firms in their economy and particularly the effect of foreign-produced messages on their culture. Increasingly, countries are mandating local production of advertising messages. For example, Canada, Australia, Malaysia, and Venezuela have laws banning commercials produced outside the native country, while Peru bans advertising messages containing foreign-inspired content or foreign models in an attempt to enhance its own national culture. Not only do such policies promote the local culture, but they also ensure the good health of the local advertising industry and provide employment for nationals.

## Agency Selection Criteria

In addition to considering the organizational approach (centralized, decentralized, or combined), the international marketer should focus on a number of additional criteria in selecting the best agency or agencies to help the firm achieve its set goals:

- *Market coverage:* The firm must determine whether the agency or network under consideration provides coverage for all relevant markets.
- *Quality of coverage:* The firm must assess the agency's or network's reputation in each market.
- *Market research, public relations, and other marketing services:* If the firm needs market research, public relations, or other marketing services in addition to advertising, it must compare what the different agencies offer.
- *Relative roles of the firm's in-house advertising department and agency:* Some firms have a large in-house staff that takes on significant portions of advertising campaign development. These firms require fewer services from an advertising agency than do companies that rely on an agency for almost everything relating to advertising.
- *Size of the firm's international business:* The smaller the firm's international advertising expenditures, the less likely it will be to divide up its expenditures among numerous agencies. A firm's advertising volume may determine agency choice to assure some minimum level of service. An advertising budget multiplied by a number of markets may be of interest to an international agency even if it is of little interest to a single agency in any one market.
- *Image:* The firm must decide whether it wishes to project a national or international image. Desire for local identification and good local citizenship might indicate that the firm should select a number of national agencies rather than one international one.
- *Level of involvement:* In joint-venture arrangements the international firm typically shares decision making. The foreign partner may already have established a relationship with a local agency, which would be the decisive factor. In the case of licensing agreements, the licensee is typically responsible for the advertising function. Selling through distributors also reduces the degree of control the international firm has over promotional efforts. Generally, international marketers can choose agencies only for the advertising paid for by their firms. If a firm is engaging in a cooperative program with its distributors, its influence in agency selection may be somewhat greater. (Terpstra 1987, 432)

## MARKETING AND ADVERTISING STRATEGY OPTIONS

Duncan and Ramaprasad (1995) note that the crux of the standardization debates used to be: "Should multinational advertising be standardized or localized?" Today the question is: "In what situations and to what extent should multinational advertising be standardized?" Their international study of advertising agency executives, conducted in the mid-1990s, focused on practitioners from the West (Europe and the Americas) as well as non-Western regions (Asia, including the Pacific Rim and Australia). Duncan and Ramaprasad distinguished between strategy (the creative selling proposition) and execution (the actual elements and their structure in an ad). In terms of the amount and type of standardization of multinational brands, the researchers found that 68 percent of the multinationally advertised brands used a standardized *strategy* in all the countries in which their advertising ran, 24 percent in some of the countries, and 7 percent not at all. Standardization of execution was surprisingly similar, with 54

**TABLE 5.2:** Mean* Importance of Reasons for Standardizing Multinational Advertising

| REASON | WESTERN | NON-WESTERN | TOTAL |
|---|---|---|---|
| Create a single brand image in all markets | 1.5 | 1.7 | 1.5 |
| Make full use of a proven, successful idea | 1.9 | 2.1 | 2.0 |
| Take advantage of the demographic/ psychographic similarity in target audience | 2.2 | 2.0 | 2.1 |
| Culture is similar between countries | 2.3 | 2.1 | 2.2 |
| Product usage is similar in all markets** | 2.2 | 2.7 | 2.4 |
| Research has shown that one campaign will work*** | 2.2 | 2.6 | 2.4 |
| Product is standardized | 2.3 | 2.7 | 2.5 |
| Pressure from client's headquarters | 2.6 | 2.9 | 2.7 |
| Saves money (one campaign costs less) | 2.7 | 2.9 | 2.8 |
| Pressure from other agency branches | 3.8 | 3.6 | 3.71 |
| Time pressure (one campaign takes less time) | 3.0 | 3.5 | 3.74 |

*A 5-point scale was used. A lower score indicates greater importance.

**$t = -2.76$; $df = 98$; $p < .01$.

***$t = -2.23$; $df = 98$; $p < .05$.

*Source:* Duncan and Ramaprasad (1995).

percent of the multinational brands using it in all countries, 36 percent in some countries, and 8 percent not at all. They found, however, the use of standardized language to be uncommon in all countries.

Table 5.2 highlights the most important reasons for standardizing multinational advertising. Note that in asking their questions, Duncan and Ramaprasad used a 5-point scale—a lower score indicates higher importance. The table reveals that practitioners consider a "single brand image" the most important reason to standardize. They consider reasons related to pressures the least important, and product- and audience-based reasons as having middling importance. The researchers note:

> Business efficacy reasons vary in importance, with "exploiting a successful idea" high on the list, "research backing" getting a middling position, and "saving money" placing lower. At the same time, "saving money" and "client pressure" are not unimportant; they have means below 3, suggesting above-average importance. Only "time pressure" and "pressure from other agency branches" have means above 3, indicating smaller importance. In sum, respondents consider creative and advertising fit reasons more important than external pressures. Interestingly, agencies in the western region consider similarity in product use and research backing as significantly more important than do agencies in the non-western region. (Duncan and Ramaprasad 1995, 61)

This research suggests that

> western region agencies, in general, used standardization more than did non-western agencies, but in an interesting reversal for specific elements, western agencies standardized strategy and execution more and language less than did non-western agencies. Interviews with respondents explained that standardization was more appropriate for western and highly industrialized markets and for markets that are contiguous. Apparently, it is more challenging to have a pan-Asian than a pan-European campaign because of the physical distances between Asian countries and their different levels of industrialization which has resulted in less assimilation and homogenisation. (Duncan and Ramaprasad 1995, 59)

The results of the Duncan and Ramaprasad (1995) research suggest the potential for standardization of advertising campaigns in the European Union. A uniform marketing strategy across the continent has long been advocated by both the business and academic worlds (Dibb et al. 1997; Whitelock et al. 1995). Optimism regarding the adoption of standardized stragegies across Europe has been justified by the benefits associated with a market of approximately 490 million consumers. As noted previously, there has been a trend toward the use of "pan-European" advertising campaigns by global marketers operating in the EU. For example, Yahoo and MSN reported that the number of multinational campaigns across Europe doubled during a 12-month period and included marketers such as Adidas, Apple, Levi's, and Nissan (*New Media Age* 2004). More than a decade after the Duncan and Ramaprasad investigation, Taylor and Okazaki (2006) raised the question: "Who standardizes advertising more frequently for the EU, and why do they do so?" The two researchers compare U.S. and Japanese subsidiaries' advertising practices in the "Common Market," as it is frequently called. Their first research question explores Japanese and U.S. managers' perceptions of EU markets. They examine the similarity of consumers and market conditions across Europe and consider the level at which the EU market as a whole is sought after by competitors. Their second research question pertains to the degree to which Japanese and U.S. subsidiaries standardize their advertising in terms of both strategy and execution in the EU. Finally, their third research question examines whether Japanese and U.S. firms believe that standardization is associated with specific benefits. They explore the extent to which the ability to create a global brand image, the achievement of cost savings, the ability to appeal to cross-national market segments, and improved coordination between headquarters and subsidiaries are perceived as benefits by the U.S. and Japanese firms. Table 5.3 presents the subsidiaries' responses to these three questions. Note that in this investigation a 7-point scale was used, ranging from "strongly disagree" to "strongly agree."

Regarding the perceptions of similarity of European markets, both the Japanese and U.S. firms gave neutral ratings (3.73 and 3.74) for similarity of the advertising infrastructure. In addition, the perceptions of similarity of market conditions across the EU did not differ significantly across the two countries (3.66 in Japan and 3.81 in the United States). Further, managers' perceptions of the level of competition across the EU did not vary across the Japanese and U.S. respondents—however, the means (5.90 in Japan and 5.79 in the United States) are notably high, suggesting that both groups of managers consider the EU market highly competitive. These findings indicate that, despite years of integration, Japanese and U.S. managers still perceive significant differences across the different EU markets. Notably, however, managers from both countries expressed strong agreement that competitive conditions are uniformly high across the EU.

Regarding the extent to which Japanese and U.S. firms standardize strategic elements of their advertising across the EU, firms in the United States responded somewhat more positively to this question than Japanese firms (4.68 in the United States and 4.12 in Japan). Japanese firms responded very close to the neutral point on the scale, but U.S. firms were only somewhat higher. In contrast, on the dimension of executional elements, the Japanese and U.S. firms responded similarly, with means of 4.17 and 4.36 respectively. Both responses were again toward the neutral part of the scale. It is of interest to note that although U.S. firms report being slightly more likely to standardize strategy than executions (4.68 versus 4.36), there is virtually no difference in the response for these variables in the Japanese sample (4.12 versus 4.17). Given the lukewarm perceptions of the EU as a single market, it is not surprising that firms do not indicate strong agreement related to standardizing advertising. The finding that the extent of ad standardization at the strategic level was somewhat higher among U.S.

**Table 5.3:** Mean* Perceptions of the EU and the Potential for Standardization

|  | U.S. FIRMS | JAPANESE FIRMS |
|---|---|---|
| **PERCEPTIONS OF SIMILARITY OF EUROPEAN MARKETS** | | |
| Perception of Advertising Infrastructure | 3.74 | 3.73 |
| Perception of Market Similarity | 3.81 | 3.66 |
| Perception of Level of Competition | 5.79 | 5.90 |
| **DEGREE OF STANDARDIZATION EMPLOYED** | | |
| Use of Standardized Advertising Strategies** | 4.68 | 4.12 |
| Use of Standardized Advertising Executions | 4.36 | 4.17 |
| **MOTIVATION FOR STANDARDIZATION** | | |
| Desire to Create a Uniform Brand Image*** | 4.83 | 4.22 |
| Importance of Cost Savings | 4.89 | 4.69 |
| Ability to Appeal to Cross-Market Segments | 4.75 | 4.41 |
| Centralized Decision Making | 4.29 | 4.81 |

* A 7-point scale was used, ranging from "strongly disagree" to "strongly agree." ** $t = 2.52$, $p = .013$.

*** $t = 2.71$, $p = .008$.

firms than among their Japanese counterparts is consistent with Duncan and Ramaprasad's (1995) suggestion that standardization of ads may be more of a Western phenomenon.

Taylor and Okazaki (2006) examined four primary advantages of standardization. Their results reveal a higher level of agreement with the need to create a uniform brand image among U.S. respondents (4.83) than among Japanese respondents (4.2). Means for subsidiaries from both countries were higher for cost savings than from uniform brand image, however. In contrast to the results for uniform brand image, the importance of cost savings was perceived similarly by Japanese (4.69) and U.S. (4.89) firms. It appears that firms in both countries believe it important to save costs through the use of standardization. Regarding the desire to appeal to cross-market segments, results show that Japanese and U.S. firms both gave ratings slightly above the midpoint of the scale (4.41 and 4.75 respectively). Finally, the researchers examined the degree to which managers perceived implementing centralized decision making as a key benefit of standardization. Again, the results show that the Japanese mean (4.81) and the U.S. mean (4.29) are above the midpoint of the scale. In this case, the Japanese mean is higher than that of the U.S. mean, indicating that Japanese subsidiaries are more likely to perceive headquarters' pressure to standardize advertising in the EU. Overall, the

> results suggest that the idea that the EU has become a uniform market in which firms can ignore cross-national differences in planning advertising strategy is too simplistic. Apparently, many firms from outside the EU believe that at least some cross-national differences related to the advertising infrastructure and market conditions remain and, thus, that some adaptation is necessary. Therefore, when assessing the extent to which they can standardize advertising, managers of firms operating in the EU should expect to monitor environmental conditions in the markets in which they operate. (Taylor and Okazaki 2006, 116)

The framework outlined in Table 5.4 can assist international marketers in assessing marketing and advertising strategy options. As the framework shows, marketers must examine each step in a marketing

**TABLE 5.4:** Analysis of Standardization and Specialization of the Marketing Mix and Advertising Program

| | STANDARDIZATION | | ADAPTION | |
|---|---|---|---|---|
| | **FULL** | **PARTIAL** | **FULL** | **PARTIAL** |
| Product Design | | | | |
| Brand Name | | | | |
| Product Positioning | | | | |
| Packaging | | | | |
| Distribution | | | | |
| Price | | | | |
| Personal Selling | | | | |
| Publicity | | | | |
| Sales Promotion | | | | |
| Advertising Strategy | | | | |
| Theme/Appeal | | | | |
| Copy/Dialogue | | | | |
| Music/Visuals | | | | |
| Models/Spokespersons | | | | |
| Media Planning | | | | |
| Media Buying | | | | |

program, taking into consideration the specific product to be marketed as well as the given marketing environment (characterized by its demographic, economic, political-legal, and cultural profile). Only then can the marketer evaluate the potential outcomes of steps taken toward the standardization or specialization end of the continuum. The framework can assist international marketers and advertisers in thinking globally with regard to marketing and advertising strategy, yet acting locally as market circumstances warrant.

Figure 5.4 provides an illustrative mixed strategy and highlights that globalization of both marketing and advertising should be viewed on a continuum.

## SUMMARY

Clearly, global marketing and the role of international advertising in selling products in foreign markets are complex issues. Marketers must decide whether to use a centralized, decentralized, or combination approach with regard to the coordination of promotional programs. A firm planning on selling products abroad may rely on its own in-house agency or on the in-house agency of a foreign subsidiary. Or a marketer may turn to the firm's domestic agency for assistance in preparing marketing communications for foreign markets. Use of a foreign (local) agency or an international agency/network

**Figure 5.4:** Strategic options in the marketing mix: an illustrative mixed strategy.

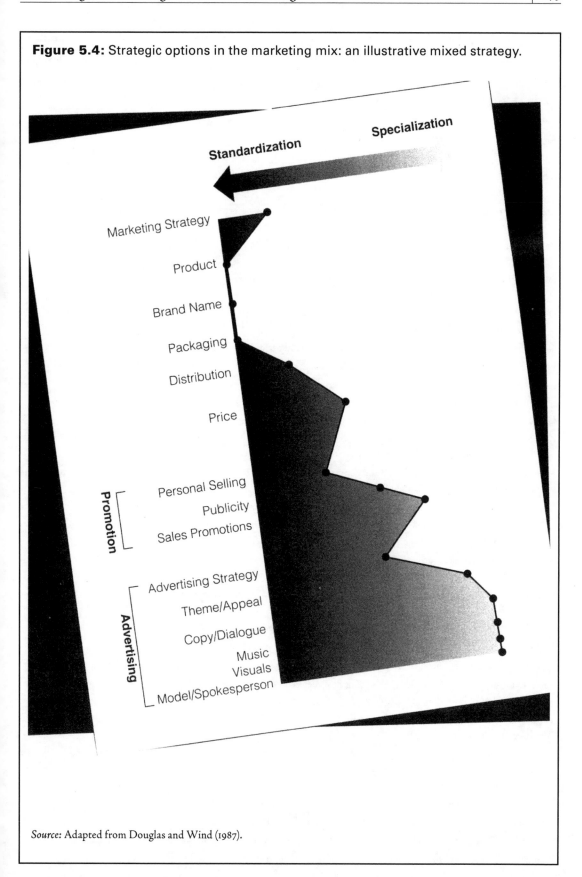

*Source:* Adapted from Douglas and Wind (1987).

are additional options. A framework outlining the strategic options in the marketing mix can assist the international marketer in making creative decisions for foreign markets—the focus of Chapter 6.

## REFERENCES

*Advertising Age.* 2010a. The Agency Issue, 26 April, 11.

———. 2010b. Profiles of the world's top 50 agency firms. <AdAge.com/agencyfamilytrees2010>.

Bartlett, Christopher A., and Sumantra Ghoshal. 1986. Tap your subsidiaries for global reach. *Harvard Business Review,* 64: November/December, 87–94.

Blecken, David. 2009. Toyota agencies downplay marketing overhaul. 6 August. <http://www.media.asia/Marketingarticle/2009_08?Toyota-agencies-...>. Retrieved 17 May 2010.

Cardona, M. M. 2004. Mass marketing meets its maker; McDonald's chief espouses "brand journalism" approach. *Advertising Age,* 1 June, 21.

Dibb, Sally, Yvonne Russell, and Lyndon Simkin. 1997. The EU marketing environment: Pharmaceuticals and Japanese strategy. *European Management Journal,* 15(2): 195–205.

Duncan, Tom, and Jyotika Ramaprasad. 1995. Standardized multinational advertising: The influencing factors. *Journal of Advertising,* 24(3): Fall, 55–69.

Douglas, Susan P., and Yoram Wind. 1987. The myth of globalization. *Columbia Journal of World Business,* 22(4): 19–29.

Elliott, Stuart. 2002. Advertising's big four: It's their world now. *New York Times,* 31 March, 3.

Fernandez, Joe. 2010. Nikon unveils pan-European ad campaign theme "I am Nikon." *MarketingWeek.* <http://www.marketingweek.co.uk/news/nikon-unveils-pan-european-...>. Retrieved 10 May 2010.

Giges, Nancy. 1992. Europeans buy outside goods, but like local ads. *Advertising Age,* 27 April, 11.

Kanso, Ali. 1991. The use of advertising agencies for foreign markets: Decentralized decisions and localized approaches? *International Journal of Advertising,* 10: 129–136.

Kirpalani, V. H., Michel Laroche, and Rene Darmon. 1988. Role of headquarters control by multinationals in international advertising decisions. *International Journal of Advertising,* 7: 323–333.

Kurz, Mitchell. 2001. Holding companies: Size is not a strategy. *Advertising Age,* 26 November, 22.

Lane, W. Ronald, Karen Whitehill King, and J. Thomas Russell. 2008. *Advertising Procedure.* 17th ed. Upper Saddle River, NJ: Pearson/Prentice Hall.

McDonald's Press Release. 2003. McDonald's unveils "I'm lovin' it" worldwide brand campaign in Hong Kong. <http://www.mcdonalds.com.hk/english/press/030923.htm>. Retrieved 12 May 2010.

McMains, Andrew. 2010. Sharp's bug push puts Aquos in focus. *AdWeek.* <http://www/adweek/aw/content_display/news/agency/e3i56ed4...>. Retrieved 14 May 2010.

*New Media Age.* 2004. Yahoo! and MSN plan for Pan-European ads growth. 14 September, 5.

Roth, Robert F. 1982. *International marketing communications.* Chicago: Crain Books.

Sanders, Lisa, and Alice Cuneo. 2002. 4A's chairman rues multiple assaults. *Advertising Age,* 22 April, 3, 61.

Speer, Lawrence J. 2003. Pizza Hut goes local in France with new menu item, ad campaign. 10 January. <www.adageglobal.com/cgi-bin/daily.pl?daily_id=9086&post_date=2-003-01010>.

Tai, Susan, and Y. H. Wong. 1998. Advertising decision making in Asia: "Glocal" versus "regcal" approach. *Journal of Managerial Issues,* 10(3): Fall, 318–339.

Taylor, Charles R., and Shintaro Okazaki. 2006. Who standardizes advertising more frequently, and why do they do so? A comparison of U.S. and Japanese subsidiaries' advertising practices in the European Union. *Journal of International Marketing,* 14(1): 98–120.

Terpstra, Vern. 1987. *International marketing.* 4th ed. Chicago: Dryden Press.

———. 1988. *International dimensions of marketing.* Boston: PWS-Kent.

Van der Pool, Lisa, and Dristen Rountree. 2003. Below-the-line goes above and beyond. *Ad-week,* 3 February, 9.

Wentz, Laurel. 1991. Saatchi thinks global with international bonuses. *Advertising Age,* 3 June, 49.

Whitelock, Jeryl, Carole Roberts, and Jonathan Blakeley. 1995. The reality of the Eurobrand: An empirical analysis. *Journal of International Marketing*, 3(3): 77–95.

Wilken, Rowan, and John Sinclair. 2007. Global vision, regional focus, "Glocal" reality: Global marketers, marketing communications, and strategic regionalism. Communications, Civics, Industry—ANZCA 2007 Conference Procedings, 1–11.

York, Emily Bryson. 2010. McDonald's unveils "I'm lovin' it" 2.0. *Advertising Age*, 22 April. <http://adage.com/print?article_id=143453>. Retrieved 23 April 2010.

# CHAPTER SIX

# Creative Strategy and Execution

Charles Frazer offers a generally accepted definition of *creative strategy*: "a policy or guiding principle which specifies the general nature and character of messages to be designed. Strategy states the means selected to achieve the desired audience effect over the term of the campaign" (Frazer 1983, 36). One of the most important strategic considerations is whether to globalize advertising worldwide or to adapt it to the specific needs of each market. Scholars and practitioners alike are divided with regard to the benefits and disadvantages associated with each strategic approach. It should be reiterated, too, that this debate carries a variety of labels. Globalized campaigns have also been referred to as standardized and universal in the literature; localized campaigns have been called specialized, adapted, and even customized. In this chapter we will use the terms interchangeably in examining globalization versus localization as it relates to creativity in advertising. We will also touch on the creative development and production of advertisements, examining the use of advertising appeals and both verbal and nonverbal aspects of commercial messages.

## STRATEGIC DECISIONS

### Globalization of Advertising

An increasing number of advertising and marketing executives agree that the needs and desires of consumers around the world are growing ever more homogenized. These experts contend that the world is one large market and that regional, national, and even international differences are at best superficial. Therefore, the consumer may well be satisfied with similar products and services. There's no arguing with the fact that, today, Campbell's soup, Crest toothpaste, and Camel cigarettes are at home in markets around the globe. Not only may consumers around the globe be satisfied with similar products, but advertisers can potentially sell them with similar messages (Levitt 1983, 92). Narrowly defined, *globalized advertising* refers to messages that are used internationally with virtually no change in theme, illustration, or copy—except, perhaps, for translation where needed.

Globalization of international campaigns generally takes one of two routes. One option is to adopt a campaign deemed successful in the national or domestic market for a firm's foreign markets. Esso's "Put a tiger in your tank" campaign is a classic example of a promotional effort that proved effective in the United States and was subsequently exported to numerous other countries. Another option is a preplanned effort to develop a campaign for use in multiple markets.

Advertisers and agencies alike perceive very real benefits associated with this approach. For one thing, coordination and control of marketing and promotional programs are greatly simplified, and, as a result, foreign campaigns can be implemented much more quickly. This simplification may assist in faster product roll outs. Anthony Rutigliano notes: "As product life cycles shrink, companies will be hungry for quicker worldwide product roll outs, leaving less time to develop scores of local or national advertising campaigns" (Rutigliano 1986, 27). Indeed, the speed of mega-brand launches can be staggering. Ogilvy & Mather introduced Pond's skincare line in 33 markets in a period of 18 months, and an American Express testimonial campaign in 18 new markets in 15 months. If the drive to market brands appears to be full throttle, it is because competitive conditions warrant it. "The days of testing brands regionally in a single market are practically over," notes Michael Sennott, vice-chairman and director of multinational accounts at McCann-Erickson in New York. "Because of the speed of technology, our clients realize they have to launch a brand globally or regionally to pre-empt their competition" (Kaplan 1994).

In addition, fewer marketing and advertising personnel are required at the local level to administer advertising campaigns developed at headquarters than are required to customize promotional efforts. Staff reductions lead to cost savings, and advertising production costs are reduced dramatically. It is certainly much less expensive to produce a single campaign for a number of markets than it is to produce a separate campaign for each specific market. Similarly, the cost associated with developing one television commercial for the European market, for example, and translating the dialogue or dubbing the spot into seven languages is significantly less than it is to develop seven separate television spots. McCann-Erickson claims to have saved Coca-Cola over $90 million in production costs over a 20-year period, during which the company was a staunch supporter of globalization, by producing worldwide commercials.

Further, good ideas can be exploited. If a campaign has proven successful in one market, there may be no need to "re-invent the wheel" in others. Kenneth Robbins, deputy chairman at Interpublic Group company SSC&B Lintas Worldwide, notes that really good ideas are extremely hard to find. As an example, he shares his experiences with Snuggle, introduced in Germany in 1970 as a liquid fabric softener that made clothes incredibly soft. The big idea was the use of a teddy bear as a spokesperson. Research revealed that the depth of feeling for teddy bears was enormous—the stuffed animals personified security, comfort, love, and, most important, softness. Within one year of completing national distribution, the brand claimed a 26 percent market share. The brand was subsequently introduced into 12 additional countries, and the teddy bear spokesperson was dearly loved throughout Europe and the United States (Bowes 1992, 129). Unilever launched Snuggle in Mexico in a bid to enter the country's $250 million fabric softener market—the third largest in the world. Mexican homes consume more than 10 liters of softeners a year, well above the Latin American average of 4 liters. And the Snuggle teddy bear played center stage in the television, magazine, and outdoor campaigns (Monjaras 2003). Clearly, a big idea introduced nearly four decades ago remains fresh.

**Figure 6.1:** Nespresso print ads featuring George Clooney—from Turkey and France.

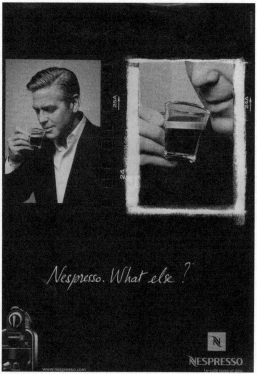

Finally, a consistent international brand or company image can be achieved. A uniform image serves to reduce message confusion in areas where there is media overlap or a good deal of cross-border travel, as is the case in many European countries. For example, across Europe, Nestlé has utilized spokesperson George Clooney to pitch its luxury coffee. The Nespresso coffee system allows users to make café-style espresso at home. Small pods of coffee are sold in tiny boxes much like expensive chocolates. The pods are placed in the Nespresso coffee maker (which ranges in cost from approximately $200 to $1,000), a button is pressed, and the hot water forced through, allowing the user to make a perfect cup of espresso, latte, or cappuccino. The pods are purchased through the company's Web site, over the phone, or from a very limited number of its own shops, which it prefers to call "boutiques." Clooney appears in both television and print messages. The series of television spots shows beautiful young women ignoring the actor as they reach past him for a cup of Nespresso. Nespresso has a strong base in Europe, which accounts for about 90 percent of its $2 billion annual sales. Based on this success, the Swiss food giant is mounting a major push into the United States. Unfortunately for Nestlé, Clooney's contract does not allow the company to show him in U.S. ads (Matlack 2009). See Figure 6.1 for two examples of Nespresso print advertisements—one appearing in Turkey and the other in France.

Numerous firms have adopted a globalized approach. L'Oréal provides an excellent example. L'Oréal has been in the beauty business since the early 1900s. A century later it has become the world's largest cosmetics company, with over $24 billion in annual sales and a long record of double-digit profit growth. Little more than a decade ago, the European market accounted for over 75 percent of its sales; today that figure has dropped to about 45 percent. North America, where L'Oréal is now market leader, now accounts for approximately one-quarter of turnover. In 2007, for the first time, "newer countries"

**Figure 6.2:** British ad for L'Oréal makeup featuring spokesperson Eva Longoria.

(in areas such as Asia, Latin America, and Eastern Europe), which L'Oréal calls "the rest of the world zone," comprised a larger market than North America (29.2 percent). Over the coming years, this zone is expected to make a major contribution to the increase in L'Oréal's profitability. Notes Sir Lindsay Owen-Jones, chairman of L'Oréal, "The globalization of cosmetics consumption is only just beginning" (*Beauty Packaging* 2008). The company has used a globalized approach to sell a wide variety of its products around the world. L'Oréal employs what has been dubbed the "Dream Team"—a stable of dozens of models and actresses to plug its products. The team has included supermodel Claudia Schiffer, Destiny's Child singer Beyoncé Knowles, and actresses Andie MacDowell, Heather Locklear, and Catherine Deneuve. In 2005 L'Oréal signed an exclusive worldwide contract with actress Eva Longoria, who had shot to fame playing former model Gabrielle Solis on the ABC hit series *Desperate Housewives*, to promote the company and its brands. See Figure 6.2 for a British print ad for L'Oréal's Roll On True Match makeup featuring Eva Longoria.

## Products Suitable for Globalized Advertising

Globalization of advertising is viewed by many marketers as a challenging task. Clearly, however, some international marketers are successfully employing this approach. Progress has been made in understanding under what conditions globalized advertising works best and for which products such campaigns are particularly well suited (Fannin 1984, 74).

*Products for Which Audiences Are Essentially Similar:* Cross-border consumer segments are emerging. Global youth is a ripe and growing group that is becoming increasingly homogenized. More than one in four persons in the world today are youth—defined as people between the ages of 10 and 24. In developing countries, youth make up about 29 percent of the total population, while in developed markets they constitute about 19 percent of the total population. The number of youth will keep rising in some parts of the world, offsetting declines in other regions. There will be about 72 million more youth in 2025 than at present (Ashford et al. 2006). Moreover, global youth represent $100 billion in spending power, certainly an appealing figure to international marketers. Teens are simultaneously plugging into two cultural channels: local and global. For global culture, they are a homogeneous target market. They are plugged into global culture via satellite television, Hollywood films, and the Internet. Teens around the world increasingly listen to the same music, eat at the same restaurants, drink the same soft drinks, and wear the same clothes. A 2009 TRU Global Teen Study asked nearly 16,000 teens in 15 countries to name their favorite brands. Teens in 11 countries named Coca-Cola and Nike as among their top three, while teens in 10 countries similarly honored Adidas. According to Riz Badr, TRU's global director, "this finding shows beyond a shadow of a doubt that teens around the world are not simply willing to accept global brands—they actively embrace them" (TRU 2009). Benetton has long employed global advertising campaigns to appeal to youth around the world (see Figure 6.3 for a Benetton ad appealing to young consumers in Mexico). In 2010, Benetton launched its first global interactive multimedia campaign. As part of the campaign, a global online casting session was conducted to choose faces from around the world for United Colors of Benetton's future advertisements. Global youth were invited to attend the casting session and illustrate their style and personality—the things that make them unique—through videos and photographs they could upload at no charge at Benetton's Web page and through a special YouTube page. According to Benetton, the new "It's My Time" campaign offers young people around the world a "means of sharing their opinions, as well as a place to be noticed and a dream to aspire to. Through the open culture of social media, the blogosphere, and citizen journalism,

**Figure 6.3:** Global Benetton campaign appealing to young consumers in Mexico.

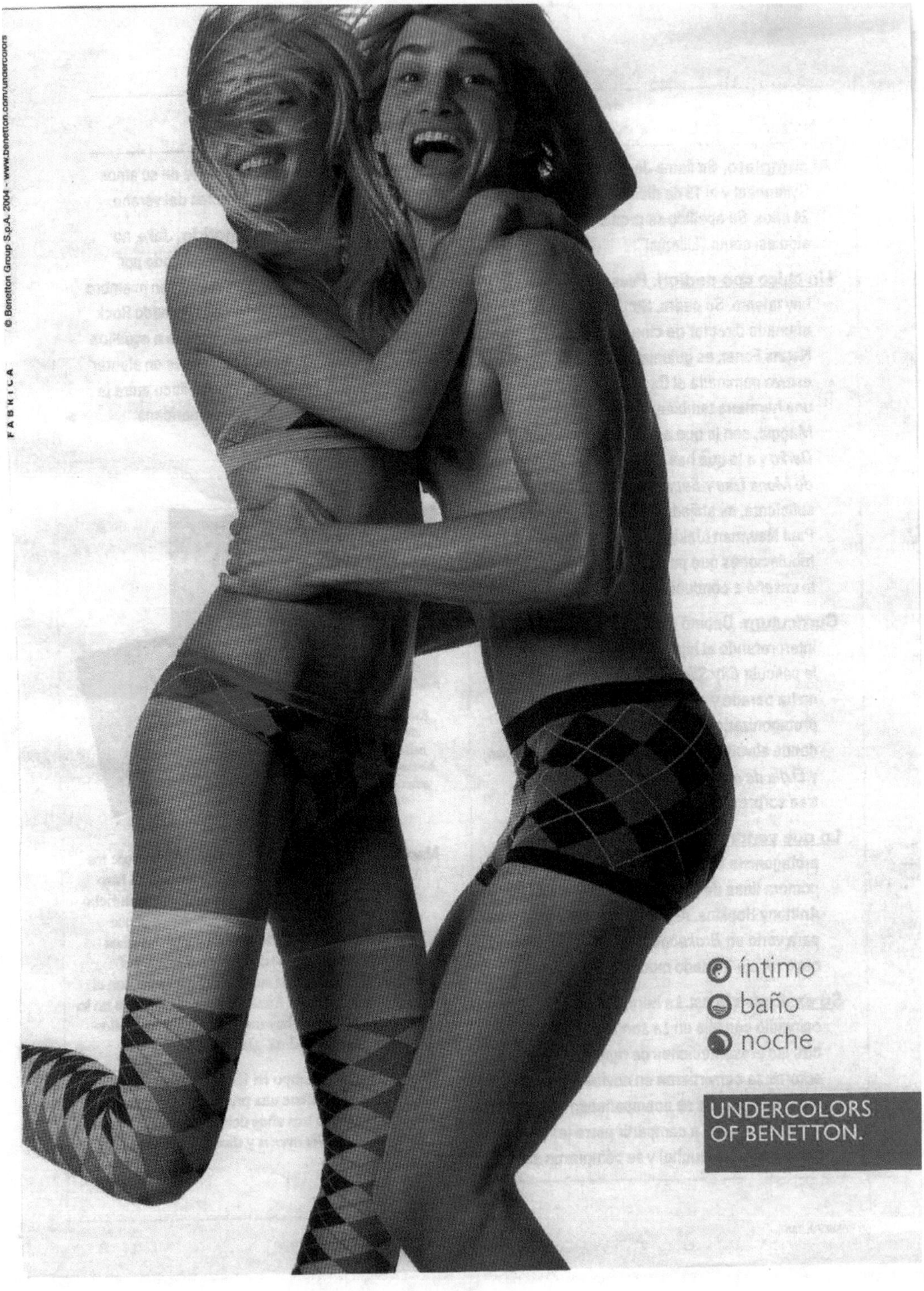
FABRICA
© Benetton Group S.p.A. 2004 - www.benetton.com/undercolors
íntimo
baño
noche
UNDERCOLORS
OF BENETTON.

**Figure 6.4:** Print ad from the global InterContinental Hotel campaign appearing in a German magazine.

DIE WERTVOLLSTE KUNSTSAMMLUNG UNSERER ZEIT: IHRE ERINNERUNGEN.

Außergewöhnliche Augenblicke und einzigartige Eindrücke – ist es nicht das, was das Reisen so besonders macht? Die Mitarbeiter der InterContinental Hotels & Resorts haben nur ein Ziel: dass Sie sich an viele solcher Momente erinnern. Sie helfen Ihnen dabei, jeden Ort authentisch zu erleben und selbst an bekannten Plätzen Neues zu entdecken. Streifen Sie in Wien mit den Tipps unseres Concierges durch unzählige Kulturschätze, zum Beispiel den Prunksaal der Nationalbibliothek mit seiner 30 Meter hohen Kuppel und Büchern von 1501 bis 1850.

*Do you live an InterContinental life?*

www.intercontinental-online.com
Tel.: 00800 1800 1800

INTERCONTINENTAL.
HOTELS & RESORTS

**Figure 6.5:** Ad for DKNY fragrance appearing in a South African magazine.

it promotes a radical freedom enabling them to make the leap from objects to subjects. "Benetton is giving an open invitation…to share their tastes…and find like-minded friends" (*Financial* 2010).

Shared sensibilities are also emerging among social classes across different countries, such as affluent consumers and international business travelers. Upper-class markets have long been targeted globally for upscale products such as jewelry, fine watches, and expensive cars. American Express has found that the market for its platinum card, aimed at wealthy consumers, responds to the same type of luxury message whether it is in Paraguay or Paris (Parmar 2002, 49).

McCann-Erickson's Michael Sennott argues that "a male middle executive in Italy has more in common with a male middle executive in the U.K. than with a farmer in Italy" (Kaplan 1994, 50). Global travelers are another group with much in common. InterContinental Hotels Group, which operates more than 4,400 hotels in 100 countries, recently introduced a global campaign for the upscale hotel chain featuring a new tagline that challenges its audience to answer the question: "Do you live an InterContinental life?" Notes the company's senior vice president for global brand management, Jenifer Zeigler, "At a time when other hotel brands are working to keep people in a bubble, InterContinental wants to provide our guests with memorable and unique experiences that will enrich their lives and broaden their outlook," (ASIATravelTips 2005). See Figure 6.4 for an InterContinental ad appearing in a German magazine. The visual portrays a couple walking through a museum. The headline reads: "The most valuable collection of our time: Your memories."

*Products That Can Be Promoted Via Image Campaign:*

> Many of the packaged goods products that account for much of the advertising dollars spent in the United States are difficult to differentiate on a functional…basis. Thus, creative strategy used to sell these products is based on the development of a strong, memorable identity or meaning for the brand through image advertising. (Belch and Belch 1993, 344)

Image advertising has been used successfully around the world to promote a variety of services and products, including airlines, financial services, liquor, soft drinks, clothing, and perfumes. For an example of a successful international image campaign, see the DKNY fragrance ad in Figure 6.5. The ad—identical to the campaign utilized in the United States—appeared in a South African magazine.

*High-Tech Products:* Globalized messages may be appropriate for products coming to the world market for the first time, because such goods are generally not steeped in the cultural heritage of a particular country. Examples of products in this category include DVD recorders, plasma screen televisions, and computer hardware and software. Research shows a definite trend toward standardization in advertising strategy for such products. Bob Nelson explains: "High tech products are purchased and used in the same manner everywhere, are most often standardized and utilitarian, share a common technical language and use information appeals" (Nelson 1994). Figure 6.6 shows an ad in a Turkish magazine for Sony's VAIO laptop computer.

*Products with a Nationalistic Flavor:* If a country has a reputation for producing high-quality goods of a certain type or in a specific field, those goods may well be sold via global advertising messages. Examples of this category include Beck's beer from Germany, Burgundy wine from France, the Lexus automobile from Japan, and Swiss cheese. (See Figure 6.7 for an ad promoting Swiss cheese in an Italian magazine.) Likewise, products from the United States have been sold on the basis of their country of origin—Levi's blue jeans, Coca-Cola, McDonald's food, and Marlboro cigarettes are all are promoted as fundamentally American.

**Figure 6.6:** Ad for a high-tech product appearing in a Turkish magazine: Sony's VAIO.

Note that the benefits of employing a standardized approach, whatever the product, accrue to the firm using that approach—not to its customers around the world. For example, consumers of laundry detergent in Bavaria, Germany, are not likely to be overly impressed that they are being exposed to the same television campaign as their counterparts in Beverton, Oregon. However, both groups do care about purchasing a detergent that will get their laundry clean.

**Figure 6.7:** Advertisement for Swiss cheese appearing in an Italian magazine.

## Localization of Advertising

While globalization has been hailed as the new wave in marketing and advertising by some, others contend that while people's basic needs and desires may well be the same all around the world, how they go about satisfying them may vary from country to country. The "global market" still consists of hundreds of nations, each with its own customs, lifestyles, economies, and buying habits, and marketers are urged to take these differences into account (Hornik 1980, 36; Green et al. 1975, 25). Advertising has been positioned as one of the most difficult of the marketing-mix elements to standardize. Skeptics note that it is impossible to ascertain whether the success of brands such as Coke, Pepsi, Marlboro, and McDonald's was due to their internationalism or not. The fact is, claims Greg Harris, "one cannot prove in any scientific way…the specific contribution that advertising integration has made to the international sales performance of these brands" (Harris 1984, 223). In other words, these brands might have been even more successful had the promotional messages been adapted for each market.

In the case of a fully adapted or "specialized" campaign, the advertiser localizes message content for several countries or even for each country in which the firm operates. Proponents of localization argue that by concentrating on similarities in geographically divided marketplaces, firms may ignore or oversimplify many significant differences. The primary benefit of localization is simply that it allows for differences in the international environment. In terms of demographics, for example, the proportion of individuals attending school or having completed various levels of education affects message development and the media employed to disseminate those messages. In many southern African nations, illiteracy rates are particularly high. In these markets an advertising medium was developed that would be considered quite foreign in the eyes of a Madison Avenue advertising executive: boats travel up and down rivers to broadcast product messages to folks standing on shore.

With regard to the political-legal environment, a variety of issues may present problems for the marketing communicator. For example, laws and regulations imposed on the advertising industry differ among nations. Legal and regulatory considerations will be addressed in detail in Chapter 9. For now, we will highlight just a few examples to demonstrate that the legal environment has a direct impact on the development of international advertising campaigns. In 1997, in the United States, the Food and Drug Administration relaxed the rules on pharmaceutical product promotion. As a result, U.S. consumers have been bombarded with a plethora of commercial messages for everything from allergy treatments to anti-impotence pills. It should be noted that the United States is on the cutting edge of this trend. At this time, pharmaceutical marketers may not target consumers in Europe—or almost anywhere else. That regulatory environments vary between markets such as the United States and Europe, for example, should come as no great surprise, but variation occurs even within markets. While major steps have been taken over the past few years to harmonize advertising regulation throughout the European Union, marketers still encounter differences in regulatory guidelines from country to country. For example, Sweden bans all television ads for viewers under the age of 12. In Norway, Austria, and the Flemish part of Belgium, advertising is not allowed around children's programs. Greece does not allow advertisements for toys to be screened between 7:30 A.M. and 10:00 P.M. British advertisers and agencies, however, are quite opposed to any ban on marketing to children.

The media that advertisers are permitted to employ can also vary widely. The media scene abroad may not resemble that in the domestic market. For instance, in the United States, commercial time on television is typically widely available, and on many stations, 24 hours a day. In other markets, however, because some or all of the stations may be state controlled and government operated, television advertising may be banned or severely restricted. In Germany, on some channels, commercial time is limited to 20 minutes per day and typically only in the evenings (5:00 P.M.–8:00 P.M.) in blocks of five to seven minutes. As in many other markets around the world, television advertisements do not interrupt programming—they either run prior to it or after. Television advertising content may also be much more closely controlled in foreign markets. An advertiser who wishes to air a television commercial on any of the three Malaysian networks must first submit the script and storyboard for approval to the Ministry of Information at Radio Television Malaysia. Once the script and storyboard have been reviewed by the Advertising Division, they are returned with comments and suggestions for changes to the advertiser or its agency. Only after the client and agency agree to the changes will the script and storyboard receive station approval and proceed to production.

As noted in previous chapters, cultural differences also can pose formidable hurdles to standardization. Eating habits vary from market to market and can inhibit the use of a globalized campaign for a food product. Kentucky Fried Chicken is one of the world's largest fast-food chains, owning and franchising more than 16,200 outlets in more than 100 countries. And while it rules the roost when it comes to serving chicken, poultry does not appeal to consumers in all of its outlets worldwide. Nearly all of the one billion people living in India eat meat only occasionally—or not at all. India is home to the Hindu religion, which preaches non-violence. Believers fear the karmic consequences of harming other creatures—thus approximately one in five Indians is vegetarian. Indeed, there are large regions in the north and west of India where virtually half of the population is vegetarian. This is a fact that Kentucky Fried Chicken failed to note when it entered the market in 1995. "KFC was guilty of a classic MNC [multinational corporation] mindset of just bringing its global products to India, expecting the consumer to accept them without any changes," notes Lulu Raghavan, client director at Landor, a brand consulting firm. "Indians expect the global corporations to provide the same international standards in service and ambience, but will not accept an alien food culture," explains Raghavan (Kar 2008). Not only were KFC's menu items all chicken based, but they were meant to be eaten without any other accompaniments, while Indians like their chicken with something. In 2004, KFC underwent a makeover. That year saw vegetarians order a tikka wrap 'n roll, a chana snacker, veg fingers, or potato fries, as their non-vegetarian friends feasted on chicken buckets coupled with vegetarian pulao and makhani curry. To reassure the vegetarians, the meat dishes came out of kitchens carefully segregated from the vegetarian section. The company's advertising and marketing campaigns consciously stayed away from its "fried chicken" image. Indeed, the brand's relaunch was quickly followed by a global renaming in 2006, from Kentucky Fried Chicken to KFC—a far more inclusive moniker without any of the connotations of "fried" or "chicken." This is perhaps the reason why it continues with it on a global basis, despite the fact that the brand reverted to its previous name in the United States in order to break through the clutter here.

If a specific product's brand name differs from one market to the next, the international marketer may have no choice but to employ a specialized approach to advertising. For example, the Japanese company Kao entered its first non-Asian detergent market with the introduction in Australia of the laundry product that led the Japanese market. The concentrated detergent was marketed as Attack in Japan, Singapore, Hong Kong, Taiwan, Malaysia, and Thailand, but it was renamed Bio-z for the Australian market. "Taking account of history, we felt the name Attack was not suitable for a Japanese product in Australia; we felt it might sound a little too aggressive. In any case, rights to that name are owned by another company in Australia," a Kao spokesman explained (Kilburn 1992). Western companies experience similar challenges. Unilever's detergent, known in North America as All, is sold in France under the name Skip, as Persil in the rest of Europe, in India as Surf Excel, and Omo in Brazil,

China, and Vietnam. Each brand operated independently, which resulted in locally entrenched marketing infrastructures. Switching to a single brand name was out of the question—in Brazil alone, Omo enjoys enviable name recognition and a 50 percent market share (Wong 2009). Procter & Gamble's global marketing officer Jim Stengel explains:

> Developing global brands is not an end in itself, but a means to an end. Our goal is a global brand leadership in the categories in which we choose to compete. Sometimes we can do that with one brand name and brand positioning and sometimes it takes several brands with different positionings. We got on a kick where we tried to go too far on global standardization with some of our brands, even to the point of changing names. Safeguard provides a case in point. Safeguard was a strong bar soap brand in Mexico under the Spanish name Escuda. As we were trying to standardize more, we changed it to Safeguard. Volume dropped precipitously. We changed it back and volume went back up. (Neff 2002, 53)

Finally, if a specific foreign market is in a different stage of market development than the U.S. market, a given product may find itself in a different stage of the life cycle in that country. Professional sport watch Tag Heuer is no stranger to the challenges of communicating its brand to different markets. Tag Heuer has subsidiaries in multiple countries, including the United States, the United Kingdom, France, Italy, Spain, Germany, Switzerland, Singapore, Hong Kong, Australia, Japan, and Malaysia. In those markets there are varying degrees of brand acceptance, requiring different approaches to marketing and advertising. Christian Viros, worldwide chief executive officer, notes:

> Where the brand is well established and there is a higher degree of brand awareness, there are more opportunities to carry out unconventional advertising. In those markets, the commercials can be more avant garde and above the typical campaign. However, in countries where the brand is just beginning to gain a foothold, a more straightforward and conventional advertising approach is used. (Banoo 1999)

See Figure 6.8 for an example of a Tag Heuer advertisement employing Brad Pitt as the spokesperson targeting German consumers. In some markets an international firm will compete against other international marketers; in other markets the competition may be purely national. Sound advertising strategy in one market will not necessarily be appropriate in another market with a different competitive environment.

A number of firms that had initially adopted the global approach have since soured on the concept. In the early 1980s, Parker Pen was manufacturing about 500 styles of pens in 18 plants. Local offices in over 150 countries were responsible for creating their own advertising and packaging. Putting Theodore Levitt's theory into practice, Parker consolidated to 100 pen styles manufactured in only eight plants. It also hired a single advertising agency to create a global advertising campaign, which was then translated into myriad local languages. However, Parker did not anticipate the resistance of local managers, who resented that the U.S. firm was mandating what the advertising should be and which advertising agency they should employ. Profits plunged almost immediately—Parker had a $12 million loss for fiscal 1985, and the firm almost went broke. By 1986 a group of its British managers had bought the pen business. The company once again became profitable, and local managers were allowed to select advertising for their own markets (Lipman 1988). Previously committed to a standardized approach, Colgate-Palmolive likewise shifted back to a country-by-country advertising strategy. As part of the move toward specialization, an approach intended to be a basic element of the firm's long-term growth plans, Colgate-Palmolive decided to decentralize the advertising function and turn over responsibilities to individual operating units. All future advertising will be tailored specifically to local markets and countries (Freeman 1990).

Since 2001, Coca-Cola has moved to an increasingly "think local, act local" approach. Coca-Cola's CEO Douglas Daft recognized that a single global strategy or single global campaign just didn't work,

**Figure 6.8:** Tag Heuer ad featuring Brad Pitt appeals to German consumers.

and locally relevant executions have since become an important element of Coke's global brand strategy. In Turkey, the firm launched Bibo, a flavored drink for children. Bibo is positioned as "an adventure drink to help children in their development." Ultimately, the product was also marketed in the rest of Eastern Europe and in South Africa (*Advertising Age* 2000). Coke sells Thums Up cola in India and Inca cola in Peru. In China, Coca-Cola introduced Xingmu (Smart), a line of carbonated fruit drinks that include green apple, watermelon, and coconut flavors. Not only are products increasingly customized; so too are the advertising messages. Coca-Cola launched a massive campaign across China to boost sales of its products during the Spring Festival—the most important holiday for the Chinese people. In an attempt to reflect Chinese culture, a special television commercial was produced featuring traditional Ah Fu clay dolls, symbols of good luck and fortune. Images of the painted Ah Fu dolls also appeared on special packaging (*Advertising Age* 2001). Also in 2001, after almost a decade of lagging behind rival Pepsi in the region, Coke re-examined its approach in an attempt to gain leadership in the Indian market and capitalize on significant growth potential, particularly in rural markets. The new brand localization strategy acknowledged that urban and rural India were two distinct markets. "India A" was the designation Coca-Cola gave to the market segment including metropolitan areas and large towns, representing a mere 4 percent of the population (Kaye 2004). This segment responded well to aspirational messages, celebrating the benefits of their increasing social and economic freedoms. "Life ho to aisi" (life as it should be) was the successful and relevant tagline used in Coca-Cola's commercial messages for this audience. "India B" included small towns and rural areas comprising the other 96 percent of the nation's population (Balakrishna and Sidharth 2003). This segment's primary need was out-of-home thirst-quenching, and the beverage category was virtually undifferentiated in the minds of rural consumers. Additionally, with an average Coke costing rural consumers the equivalent of one-tenth of their daily wages, the soft drink was perceived as a luxury few could afford. In order to offer Coke at a price within reach of rural Indians, Coca-Cola introduced a new 200 milliliter bottle—about one-third smaller than the traditional bottle sold in urban markets—and cut the price in half. The pricing strategy closed the gap between Coke and other refreshments, making the soft drink truly accessible for the first time. Coke's advertising and promotion strategy for this segment used local language and idiomatic expressions. "Thanda," meaning cool/cold, is also a generic term for cold beverages. The slogan "Thanda Matlab Coca-Cola" (Thanda means Coca-Cola) addressed both the primary need of the segment for cold refreshment while at the same time positioning Coke as a "Thanda" or generic cold beverage just like tea, lassi, or lemonade. The Thanda campaign attempted to embed Coca-Cola in a local tradition, rather than inserting a foreign one. Rather than highlighting "aspiration" for this market, the campaign focused on proximity to the familiar. These efforts contributed to the doubling of rural penetration in just a single year and the pushing of Coke ahead of its former rival (Businessline 2003). It appears that the most ubiquitous brand of all has left behind both cookie-cutter products and advertising.

## The Globalization-Localization Continuum

Examples of effective globalized campaigns clearly do exist, just as do examples of ineffective ones. Similarly, there are numerous examples of both more- and less-successful localized campaigns. The pros and cons of both approaches to international advertising will continue to be debated. Many companies have moved away from viewing globalization as an all-or-nothing phenomenon and instead have chosen to employ a modified approach—standardizing some elements of their promotional plan while customizing others. The question is, in fact, one of degree, with globalization and localization at opposite ends of a continuum, and with many shades of adaptation between the two extremes.

A classic example of this modified approach is a campaign developed by Coca-Cola. A good number of years ago, the firm's advertising agency, McCann-Erickson, created an award-winning commercial showing Pittsburgh Steeler football star "Mean" Joe Greene giving his jersey to a young boy who had offered him a bottle of Coke after a tough game. However, the advertisement could not be used outside the United States for two reasons. First, Joe Greene was unknown in foreign markets, and second, American football is not nearly so popular abroad as it is in the United States. Rather than abandon the concept, the agency adapted it to other countries by creating advertisements featuring stars of the more popular international sport of soccer. Advertisements in South America used the popular Argentinian player Diego Maradona, and those in Asia used Thai star Niwat as the heroes of the spots.

Nokia also employed the modified approach in selling its mobile phones in Asia. The campaign, created by Bates, Singapore, ran in China, Hong Kong, Taiwan, Singapore, Malaysia, Indonesia, Philippines, Thailand, Vietnam, India, Australia, and New Zealand. The overall objective of the campaign was to create brand awareness, and all messages emphasized the importance Nokia places on stylish design. However, elements were adapted to ensure local relevance. "At Nokia, we design products based on our observations of human behavior," noted Nigel Litchfield, senior vice president of Nokia Mobile Phones in Asia Pacific. "Over and above the single common need to be connected, consumers want products that adapt to their own lifestyles and respond intuitively to their personal needs." For example, one spot for China depicted two people who met for a soccer game thanks to the Chinese-language short messaging capabilities of Nokia phones. Another ad, for the Nokia 9110 Communicator, showed that even in the middle of a power failure, it was still possible to send and receive faxes and e-mails with Nokia's all-in-one communications tool. The ad campaign characterized the many ways in which Nokia's "human technology" simplifies technology, making it readily accessible to consumers in Asia through easy-to-use products that enhance their particular lifestyles (*Advertising Age* 1998).

## EXECUTION DECISIONS

If strategy refers to "what is said" in a campaign, then execution refers to "how it is said." The advertising strategy adopted for a specific international campaign thus guides the execution—the selection of advertising appeals as well as copy and illustrations (Kaynak 1989, 57).

### Advertising Appeals

According to George and Michael Belch, advertising appeals "refer to the basis or approach used in the advertisement to attract attention or interest consumers and/or to influence their feelings toward the product, service or cause" (Belch and Belch 1993, 344). The advertising appeals employed should be consistent with the values and tastes of the target audience. Indeed, one survey found that, on the whole, consumers seem to prefer domestically generated commercials. Foreign-produced advertisements did not appeal to more than half of European respondents in the three categories surveyed: taste, product differentiation, and likability. The English and French were rated as the most closed cultures toward foreign ads, while the Italians and Germans were rated as the most receptive (Giacomotti 1993). This reinforces the view that advertising carries its culture with it. It is not surprising, then, that commercial messages created in various markets differ significantly. Note Abhijit Biswas and colleagues:

> Cross cultural differences in advertising expression [are] a growing and important area of research, primarily because an understanding of these differences is needed in order to take on the creative challenge of communicating to people of diverse cultural backgrounds. (Biswas et al. 1992, 73)

As highlighted in the continuum of compared cultures shown in Figure 4.4, the United States and Japan fall at the "maximum socio-cultural differences" end of the scale. Japan also offers a prime example of a country that differs significantly from the United States in terms of creative message content. As previously noted, Japanese ads have traditionally tended to employ indirect communications and rely on soft sell. They also tended to make greater use of status appeals and demonstrate a greater respect for the elderly than did advertisements in the United States (Mueller 1987, 51). This contrasts sharply with the U.S. emphasis on rational appeals with a focus on presenting features and benefits in order to showcase a product's superiority. In Japanese messages, write C. Anthony Di Benedetto and colleagues:

> The goal is to transfer intended feelings to the consumer rather than detailing specific product attributes and quality. This is because the latter approach can be perceived as an insult to the consumer's intelligence concerning their ability to make a sound judgement about their company preference. (Di Benedetto et al. 1992, 39)

Recall the very soft-sell approach employed in the Japanese mayonnaise ad shown in Figure 4.5. Significant differences are also found in message content when comparing the advertising of European countries with that of the United States. While France and the United States have a good deal more in common, the ads produced in each country are quite distinct. One study found that French ads resorted to more emotional appeals and contained fewer information cues than did U.S. ads. Sex appeals were also employed more frequently—a finding consistent with the perception that France is a more sexually liberated country than the United States. Overall, French ads employed humor appeals to a greater extent than did their U.S. counterparts (Biswas et al. 1992, 73). Likewise, despite the many cultural similarities between the United States and United Kingdom, substantial differences between U.S. and British advertising exist. Researchers revealed that British ads tend to make frequent use of features inherent in British culture, such as the persistence of class divisions and the affection for eccentricity, and often employ understated humor. In addition, they generally contain less information, employ a softer-sell approach, and attempt to entertain rather than educate the consumer (Nevett 1992, 61). The findings of each of these studies should give pause to practitioners who advocate a complete standardization of commercial messages for international markets.

*Themes and Concepts: Universal versus Culture-Bound:* Clearly, globalization of advertising is possible with certain target groups, for certain product categories, and in certain market conditions. At the same time, commercial messages for some audiences require tailoring. Similarly, some products and some market conditions are less suited to the global approach. In terms of creative execution, it appears that there are themes and concepts that tend to have better success at crossing borders, while others are almost guaranteed to cause the marketer headaches. The following list of universal and culture-bound themes and concepts is adapted from de Mooij (1994).

*Universal: New or Improved Products:* Common among consumers around the globe is that they look for new products, new uses for old products, or improvements on old products. Power words that suggest newness have been proven to increase attention—such words include "now," "suddenly," "announcing," "introducing," "it's here," "improved," "at last," "revolutionary," "just arrived," and "important development" (Arens 2002, 15). See Figure 6.9 for a British ad for Lenor laundry detergent. The headline reads: "New and improved," and the copy highlights the fact that the fresh scent now lasts four times longer. Such words improve the "boom" factor of an ad and can effectively be employed to communicate with

**Figure 6.9:** British laundry detergent ad highlighting the improved features of the product.

consumers in different markets for a wide variety of consumer products, as well as industrial and business-to-business products.

*Universal: Basic Everyday Themes:* Typically, themes based on appeals such as hunger, thirst, affection, motherhood, pride, and jealousy can be used universally. See Figure 6.10 for a Hungarian ad for Amo body wash and soap. The visual of a mother and child after the bath is one that the audience can easily identify with. But even here there are potential land mines. A case in point: what could be wrong with a food commercial that shows hungry kids licking their lips in response to a tasty treat? Nothing—unless, of course, the message is aired in a third world country where exposing the tongue is considered obscene.

*Universal: The Made-In Concept:* Recall that in the discussion of products suitable for globalization, products with a nationalistic flavor were highlighted. The tendency for consumers to evaluate goods manufactured in some countries more favorably may encourage a marketer to highlight the country of origin when promoting those goods. The use of "made-in" appeals in advertising fall into three categories (Head 1988, 237):

1. *Appeals to the patriotism or national pride of consumers to motivate the purchase of products manufactured in the home country.* A Molson beer ad that ran in Canada provides an excellent example. To appreciate the success of this message, the reader must understand that many Canadians are frustrated with living in the shadow of the United States and with general misconceptions about their country. Proclaiming Canada as the "best part of North America," the 60-second television spot has an everyman Canadian defiantly expressing the rarely spoken sentiments of a nation that takes pride in its differences from its mighty southern neighbor. The ad consists of a young Canadian called Joe delivering what its creators call "the rant" in front of a large screen showing corresponding images. Dressed in a lumberjack shirt and jeans, Joe starts off slowly by quashing historical images of Canadians, saying: "I'm not a lumberjack or a fur trader. I don't live in an igloo, or eat blubber, or even own a dog sled." He pokes fun at typical misconceptions by Americans and other foreigners of the country's vastness. He notes that he says "about," not "aboot," and pronounces the letter "z" in the British way of "zed" instead of the American style "zee." "I have a prime minister, not a president. I speak English and French, not American," he says, his voice rising and gestures getting more pronounced. The ad ends with Joe raising his arms in triumph as he shouts: "Canada's the second largest land mass, the first nation of hockey and the best part of North America. My name is Joe and I am a Canadian." The spot has become so popular among Canadians that live performances have been scheduled in movie theaters and at sports events—resulting in audiences on their feet, cheering and clapping (Wroughton 2000). The commercial has also received numerous national and international creative awards.

2. *Appeals that highlight for the audience positive and usually stereotypic attributes of another country and then imbue the product or service originating from that country with those image-enhancing qualities.* For example, the Marlboro cigarette campaign portrays the image of the American cowboy and the freedom of the American West to consumers all around the world.

3. *Appeals that allude to a particular expertise that is associated with the country and that, if promoted in advertising messages, might instill confidence in the product.* For example, when we think of pasta, we typically associate it with the birthplace of this cuisine—Italy. Barilla, Italy's largest pasta maker, took advantage of this association. The company markets its products in more

**Figure 6.10:** Hungarian body wash/soap ad that plays up motherhood.

**Figure 6.11:** French ad for Dyson vacuum cleaners demonstrates how the product functions.

Cyclones intérieurs pour microparticules de poussière

Grille de séparation

Core separator pour petites particules de poussière

Cyclone extérieur pour grosses particules de poussière

1970: Sac en papier.

2008: Sac en polypropylène non-biodégradable.

## Le progrès, selon certains.

Depuis des décennies, les aspirateurs à sac perdent de l'aspiration: les pores des sacs se bouchent et l'aspiration chute.

## Le progrès, selon Dyson.

Les aspirateurs Dyson n'utilisent pas de sac, ils ne perdent donc pas d'aspiration. Les nouveaux DC22 et DC23 possèdent trois niveaux de technologie cyclone qui se servent de puissantes forces centrifuges pour séparer de l'air les microparticules de poussière, quelle que soit leur taille. C'est ça, le progrès.

Garantie 5 ans

dyson

L'aspirateur qui ne perd pas d'aspiration.

than 25 countries. It unveiled its first worldwide campaign with the unified ad slogan, "When you think of Italy, think of pasta. When you think of pasta, think of Barilla" (Lyman 2001).

*Universal: Product Demonstrations:* Typically straightforward in tone, demonstrations focus on how a brand works and its specific features. Products can be demonstrated in use, in competition with other products, or in before-versus-after scenarios. This technique often helps consumers visualize what the product can do for them. See Figure 6.11 for a French ad for the Dyson vacuum cleaner. The visual portrays the progression in the development of vacuums—and the diagram of the components of the Dyson explains how this product can function without a disposable filter.

*Universal: Heroes:* The reader may recall that in Chapter 4 we discussed heroes as an expression of culture, suggesting that they may be unique to a society. Traditionally, heroes have been culture-bound, for the most part. However, Hollywood has spread the faces of the silver screen around the globe—and many actors have become international heroes. Film stars are increasingly appearing in international advertising campaigns. Japan has demonstrated a particular fascination with Hollywood stars. Tokyo streets and television screens have been sprinkled with images of Peter Falk and Suntory whisky, Eddie Murphy and Saporro canned coffee, Sylvester Stallone and packaged ham, and Arnold Schwarzenegger and Cup o' Noodles. At one point, one out of every five Japanese television commercials featured a foreign actor or model. Long a guilty financial pleasure of the Hollywood A-list, the so-called "Only in Japan" ad emerged and bloomed during the 1970s and 1980s. Named because of strict deals forbidding distribution or publicity outside Japan, such ads offered a chance for mega-stars to blatantly cash in on their fame while maintaining loftier images at home, where top-grossing movie actors might pitch high-end perfume or elite watches, but rarely food or whiskey. Things changed after Japan's economic bubble burst in the early 1990s, leaving Japanese companies reluctant to shell out for Tinseltown's highest earners. A big name would appear occasionally, but the Japanese ad scene became mostly dominated by cheaper Hollywood B-listers as well as domestic celebrities. But the new millennium brought with it economic growth, and Japanese companies dusted off their ad budgets and began hiring big guns again. In 2006, Japanese companies spent an estimated $52 billion on domestic ad campaigns, the second-highest figure of the postwar era, according to Dentsu Inc., Japan's largest ad agency (Faiola 2007). Brad Pitt, Angelina Jolie, Scarlett Johansson, Kiefer Sutherland, and Cameron Diaz are among the American stars who have been hawking everything from cell phones to power bars in recent years. See Figure 4.12 for a Japanese ad featuring Cameron Diaz pitching cell phones. In the Internet age, it has become increasingly difficult for stars to keep their Japanese forays a secret. Vigilant users of YouTube, for example, posted Diaz's cell phone commercials for everyone with a modem to see.

The trend toward employing celebrities has spread to Europe, as well as much of the rest of the world. Recall the image of Brad Pitt in the German Tag Heuer ad (Figure 6.8.) and George Clooney in the Nespresso ads appearing in France and Turkey (Figure 6.1). Harrison Ford has sold Lancia cars in Italy, and Dustin Hoffman starred in a German ad for Audi. Evidently consumers around the globe are so seduced by the sight of a famous face that one in four of us profess that we will buy a product simply because a celebrity is promoting it. And more than half of consumers (55 percent) worldwide believe that a star makes a brand stand out, according to MEC's MediaLab global sensor report (Roberts 2009). Apparently marketers are paying attention, as literally one in four brands globally now use celebrity endorsements. The study, which asked more than 24,000 consumers around the world about celebrity endorsements, also revealed that many people believe too many products are being promoted by stars. While consumers still seem much in love with celebrities in a general

**Figure 6.12:** Cameron Diaz looms over Tokyo shoppers in an ad for a cell phone.

sense, the reliance of so many brands on selling themselves through famous faces appears to be eroding the value of such endorsements. Damian Thompson, head of consumer insight at MEC MediaLab, warns that many celebrities are being seen as over-exposed and that parts of both North America and Europe are becoming more cynical of endorsements. He goes on to note, "In countries such as China and India, it's a different story. There's a great degree of aspiration—people haven't had a chance to get bored of celebrity culture" (Roberts 2009). The report also suggested that local celebrities not be overlooked. Latin America and Asia are especially keen to see more of their local stars promote brands, with 52 percent of Latin Americans and 46 percent of Asian consumers wanting to see more famous faces relevant to their country. Overall, regardless of celebrity or market, endorsements must be part of a strategic integratred communications initiative.

*Universal: Lifestyle Concepts:* Research conducted by Charles R. Taylor and Eunju Ko has indicated that targeting consumers by lifestyle provides better results than targeting an audience on a country-by-country basis. The researchers examined U.S., Korean, and European female consumers' reactions to advertising campaigns run by Chanel in the Asian, European, and American editions of *Vogue*. In analyzing reactions to the ad campaign, findings proved lifestyle to be a more important segmentation criterion than the consumer's country of origin. The study identified four distinct fashion lifestyle segments of female fashion consumers that cut across cultures: conspicuous consumers, information seekers, sensation seekers, and utilitarian consumers. The authors suggest that while savvy fashion advertisers are already incorporating a significant degree of standardization into their advertising programs to establish brand image, the firms that successfully target the appropriate cross-national segments to whom their brands appeal will develop a sustainable competitive advantage (Taylor 2008).

**Figure 6.13:** Turkish Airlines promises German travelers the globe.

The lifestyle concept is not limited to fashion. Fast food and soft drink advertisers may target their products to young people. Similarly, airlines and hotels often feature the lifestyles of time-challenged business people in their messages. Figure 6.13 is a prime example of an ad that features a lifestyle—the message for Turkish Airlines targets consumers in Germany whose lifestyle revolves around world travel.

*Culture-Bound: Sex Appeals:* There is an old adage in the advertising business: sex sells. But cultural norms strongly influence what is considered appropriate in terms of the use of sex appeals in advertising messages. Consider the ad for a Scandinavian brand of soft drink called "Life" (Figure 6.14.) While this ad might not have raised eyebrows among Scandinavian consumers, audiences (and regulators) in other markets would likely have been outraged. For example, China's broadcasting watchdog has banned all sexually suggestive advertising on both television and radio. China's State Administration

**Figure 6.14:** Ad appearing in Scandinavian markets for a brand of soft drink called "Life."

of Radio, Film and Television announced that advertisements featuring suggestive language or scantily clad women were "socially corrupting and detrimental to society." Broadcasters not complying with the rules would face severe penalties. Within just two weeks of the report, about 2,000 ads judged to be sexually suggestive were dropped from television and radio broadcasts across China (Xinhua News Agency 2007). The question thus becomes: Does sex travel? When it comes to employing sex appeal in advertising messages intended for foreign audiences, marketers are urged to exercise caution. Often, because of increasing advertising clutter, copywriters hope that the use of sex will help their commercial message attract attention. It may well receive attention, but not necessarily the kind the advertiser intended. And what may be considered perfectly tame in one market can be perceived as downright indecent in another. For example, Leo Burnett Worldwide created a campaign for breast cancer awareness. In the ad, an attractive woman in a sundress draws stares from men on the sidewalk. "If only women paid as much attention to their breasts as men do," said the voice-over. The message was a big hit in Japan, where consumers felt it was a humorous way to draw attention to an important health issue. Surprisingly enough, the campaign flopped in France, despite the fact that in France full-frontal nudity in commercial messages hardly raises an eyebrow. Apparently, the use of humor to talk about a serious disease offended French sensibilities (Ellison 2000).

Sometimes the offending campaign will air only once or a few times prior to being pulled. In other instances, the results may be significantly more serious. The agency may be fired from the account, or even brought before a local advertising standards board. Land Rover ran a print campaign in South Africa depicting a seminude African woman whose artificially elongated breasts were blown sideways in the tailwind of a Land Rover Freelander. The campaign caused immediate public outcry. The African Advertising Standards Authority (ASA) subsequently ruled that the ad, created by TBWA Hunt Lascaris, was "irresponsible and exploitive, constituted racial stereotyping, violated human dignity, and that the insensitive portrayal of the woman made a mockery of African culture." The court ordered the advertiser, at its own cost, to place ads containing the ASA ruling in all the publications where the original ads appeared. Land Rover placed the ads, which were seen as a humiliating apology, in over 20 publications at a cost that exceeded $50,000. Apparently this was the first time the ASA had enforced a disciplinary measure that involved additional costs to the advertiser (Koenderman 2001).

*Culture-Bound: Individuality:* In Chapter 4 we noted that the majority of the world's cultures tended toward collectivism rather than individualism. Thus, while ads appealing to individuality may prove quite persuasive in some markets, the messages may not resonate with consumers in others. For example, showing models alone in an advertisement in a highly collectivistic society may be interpreted to mean that they have no identity, because their identity lies in the group. A number of years ago Levi Strauss ran a campaign for its 501 Blues that was highly successful in the United States. However, the ads didn't click with Hispanic youth. "Why is that guy walking down the street alone?" they asked. "Doesn't he have any friends?" As a result, Levi's changed the advertising for the Hispanic market, downplaying individualism (Mitchell and Oneal 1994, 38). Above and beyond the visual portrayal of individuals versus groups in a commercial message, advertisers must consider whether the product is pitched as appealing to individuality versus conformity. In individualistic cultures, products are often promoted as assisting consumers in their goal of standing out from the crowd. Examples abound of campaigns that suggest that consumers demonstrate their individuality simply by purchasing the advertised product. Such messages should be used with caution in collectivistic cultures. Consider the Lee jeans ad in Figure 6.15 targeting Filipino youth. The headline sends the mixed message "Fit in—Stand out." According

**Figure 6.15:** Lee Jeans tells Filipino youth to both "Fit in" and "Stand out."

to Hofstede (1980), the Philippines ranks quite low on individualism (with a score of 32). In contrast, the United States ranks highest of all countries (with a score of 90).

*Culture-Bound: Comparative Advertising:* Comparative advertising is generally used to claim superiority over competing brands regarding some aspect of the product. In the United States, not only is comparative advertising legal, but the Federal Trade Commission actually encourages comparative campaigns because they are seen as providing consumers with much-needed information for making purchase decisions. International marketers must understand that the technique may be banned in some markets, and in a process of change in others.

Within the European Union, comparative advertising had been allowed in the United Kingdom for more than a quarter of a century (and nearly 30 percent of all ads were comparative in nature), but for many years, comparative messages were all but banned in other European countries. In an attempt to harmonize advertising regulation on the continent, a European Union directive was passed whose aim is to promote honesty and fair play by regulating ads that compare one product with another. Any ads, anywhere in Europe, that in any way, either explicitly or implicitly, identify a competitor or goods and services offered by a competitor are subject to strict legal regulation. Among other things, ads must not create confusion in the marketplace, discredit or denigrate competitors, or take unfair advantage of the reputation of a rival (Staheli 2000).

In some markets, while not banned, comparative appeals simply are not employed. In Japan, for example, cultural norms reflect Japanese advertisers' reluctance to use comparative advertising, which connotes a confrontational practice that could make a competitor lose face (Lin 1993, 40). In Arabic cultures, behavior toward others is influenced by messages in the Shari'a, the Islamic code, as well as the more collectivistic nature of Arabic people. Arabic culture, in general, encourages people not to compete, to avoid the cost of harming others (Al-Olayan and Karande 2000).

*Culture-Bound: Role of Women:* How women are depicted in advertising messages—as housewives, mothers, domestic workers, consumers, or professionals—is strongly influenced by culture. In the United States, advertisers have been strongly criticized for condoning traditional, outdated sex roles. In other markets, particularly in Islamic countries, women may only be portrayed in traditional roles—as mothers or as caregivers. One study (Milner and Collins 2000, 67) examined television ads from Japan, Russia, Sweden, and the United States. Consistent with Hofstede's framework, which suggests that countries may be characterized along a continuum from masculine to feminine, the study found that television ads from feminine countries featured more depictions of relationships between male and female characters than did those from masculine countries. For the most part, in feminine cultures, there is minimal social differentiation between the sexes. Women are free to take assertive roles, while men can feel comfortable taking more relationship-oriented, caring roles. Stereotypic roles in feminine cultures are frowned upon. Sweden's Marketing Council, composed of a panel of legal and advertising industry professionals, ruled that a McDonald's television spot was gender discriminating and out of order with the country's strict gender equality legislation. The spot, by Publicis Groupe's Leo Burnett Worldwide, ran on three Swedish networks but was not allowed to air again after the council's decision. McDonald's apologized to the council and confirmed that it would follow Sweden's gender equality laws in future television and print advertising. In the controversial commercial, a woman helps a man prepare for work. She hands him a cup of coffee and helps him fasten his tie. In the background, the couple's son and daughter imitate their behavior. According to the council's ruling, the commercial conveyed stereotypical gender roles, with the woman taking care of the home and the man as the family breadwinner. This imbalance violates Sweden's gender equality laws (O'Dwyer 2003).

*Culture-Bound Humor:* In general, humor tends not to travel well because it employs cultural conventions that generally are understood only by members of a particular culture. For example, a leading French banking firm, BNP Paribas, launched a campaign that compared bugs and bankers in a cheeky takedown of stereotypes about the financial services industry. Created by Havas-owned BETC Euro RSCG, Paris, the bugs-versus-bankers campaign used unconventional images of insects to demonstrate the strength of relationships BNP Paribas formed with its clients. One ad in the campaign, which depicted a cartoonish sculpted model locust dressed as a banker photographed next to a luxury sedan parked near a drought-stricken cornfield, asked the question, "What do you want, a banker or a locust?" Accompanying text explained that the staff at BNP Paribas "don't hop from place to place, serving our own interests, like the rapacious locust, but rather seek to build mutually beneficial, long-term relationships." The agency hoped the humor would set BNP Paribas apart from other advertisers in the financial services sector (Speer 2002). Clearly, while the French might find the humor in this message, it would be lost on most consumers in other markets. Interestingly, in individualistic cultures, humorous appeals related to very small groups or individuals tend to be more appropriate, while in collectivistic cultures such as Japan, research has shown that humorous dramatizations of situations involving group members—family, office colleagues or superiors, neighbors, landlords, and so on—are most prevalent (Di Benedetto et al. 1992, 39). However, a study examining commercial messages in Korea, Germany, Thailand, and the United States has shown that one type of humor does appear to have potential across markets. Apparently, creatives in all four countries had developed ads employing incongruity as a humorous appeal. Incongruity, as defined by the researchers (Alden et al. 1993), is based on the contrast between the expected and the unexpected. Thus it is possible that incongruity may appeal to consumers. See Figure 6.16 for a German ad employing humor to sell body wash. The headline reads "Caution! Showering with this product causes 'Muchas Maracas.' Are you ready?"

*Culture-Bound: Opinions and Attitudes:* Themes based on cultural opinions and attitudes generally do not travel well across borders. Opinions regarding feminine attractiveness provide an excellent example. As de Mooij explains, "in many countries a slim figure is considered attractive, while in others, including some African countries, a plump figure is preferable. In some Asian countries, Caucasian faces are acceptable or even highly valued for some brands, in others not" (de Mooij 1994, 247). Indeed, a major criticism leveled at Western advertising by non-Western nations is that the global messages suggest not only which products to purchase, but how one should look. Western models, by definition, tend to be tall, blond, blue-eyed, and extremely thin. This is an ideal that most women in the world simply cannot live up to—yet continue to aspire to. Consider the message being sent by Pond's in an advertisement that ran in women's magazines in the Philippines:

> I can't believe my rosy white skin caught their eye. It started when I used Pond's skin whitening vitamin cream. I called the Pond's Institute (telephone number is provided) and they told me all about it. It has vitamin B-3 that whitens skin naturally from within and double sunscreen to protect my skin from the sun's harmful rays. Getting rosy white skin was a lot simpler and safer than I thought.

With messages such as these encouraging women in the Philippines to whiten their skin in order to appear more Caucasian, it is no wonder that many nations have imposed mandates that commercial messages be produced domestically, employing local talent rather than Western models. On much stronger footing is a campaign for Avon Basics, a skincare line specially designed for Filipinas. The

**Figure 6.16:** German ad for Axe body wash employing humor.

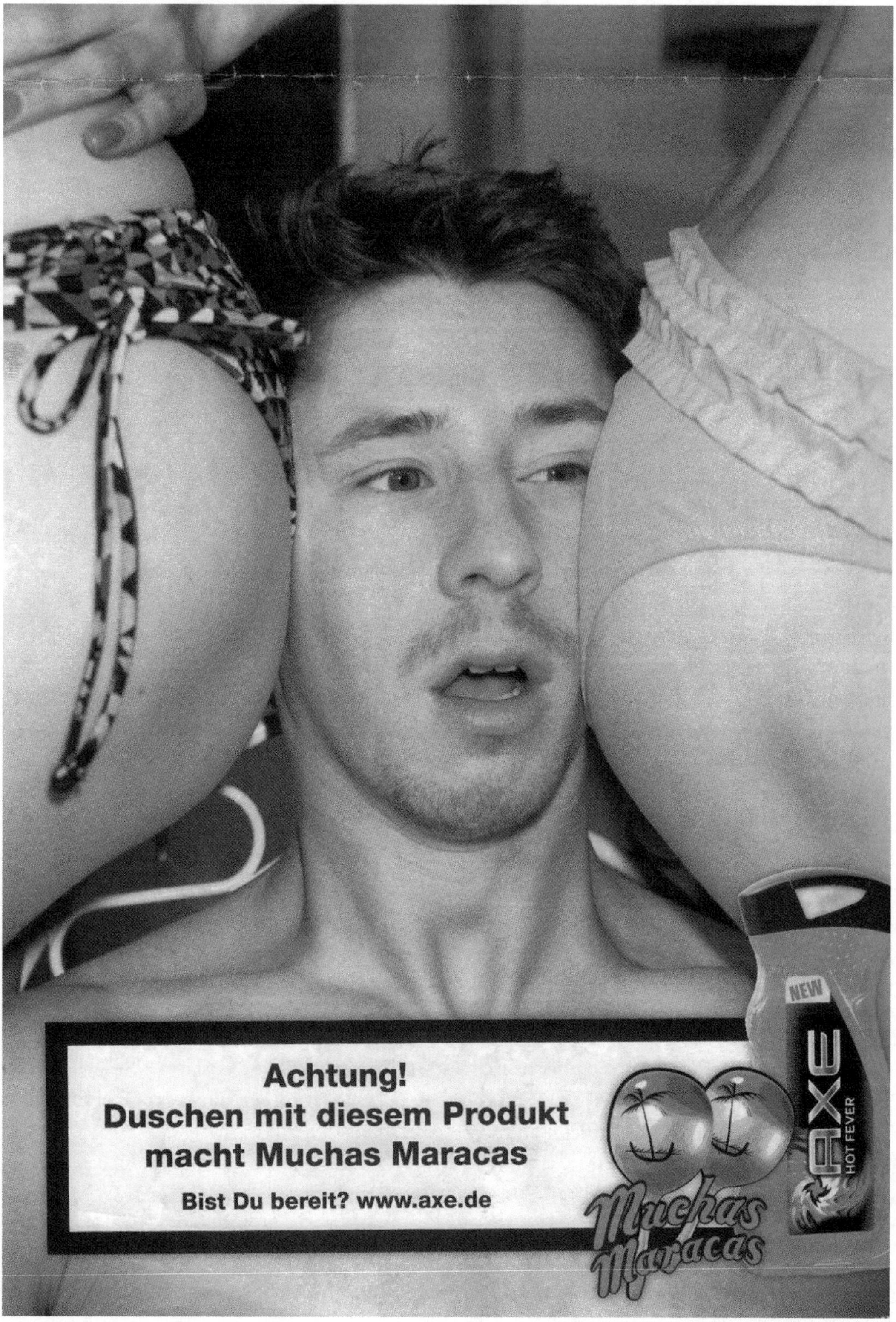

product line was customized for the Filipina skin, taking into consideration its special needs and characteristics. Advertising created by Jimenez D'Arcy featured four local, brown-skinned models, as opposed to the fair-complexioned women who traditionally appear in commercials. "We want simple, beautiful models—those that young Filipinas can identify with. No Unreachables please," noted Avon's marketing director (*Advertising Age* 1999).

## Verbal Communication: Copy and Dialogue

In Chapter 4 we addressed the cultural aspects of verbal communication. Here we will focus on challenges in the translation of advertising copy and dialogue. As Barney Raffield points out: "Seemingly harmless brand names and advertising phrases can take on unintended or hidden meanings when translated into other languages, but such errors can make a marketer look somewhat like a buffoon to foreign consumers" (Raffield 1987). While numerous translation blunders have already been highlighted, several more examples drive home the point that even when quickly corrected, such mistakes, at best, result in embarrassment to the company, and, at worst, may lead to long-term losses of sales, market credibility, and international goodwill. Ford Motor goofed when it named its low-cost third world truck Fiera, which means "ugly old woman" in Spanish. Market research showed that American Motor's Matador meant virility and excitement, but when the car was introduced in Puerto Rico, it was discovered that the word meant "killer"—an unfortunate choice for Puerto Rico, which has an unusually high traffic fatality rate. An ad in a Middle Eastern country featured an automobile's new suspension system that, in translation, said the car was "suspended from the ceiling" (Cateora 1990, 468).

The disasters just cited should make advertisers aware that the most effective translation for advertising purposes is not likely to be the most literal one. The task of the advertising translator is to translate thoughts and ideas rather than words. Yuri Radzievsky, president of Euroamerica Translations, notes with amazement that advertisers spend thousands on what something says in one language, but only pennies to ensure that it says the same thing, the same way, when put into another language (Radzievsky 1983/1984).

The most effective approach in preparing copy for foreign markets is to begin from scratch and have all verbal communications entirely rewritten by a speaker of the foreign language who understands the complete marketing plan—including objectives, strategies, and tactics. With regard to translations from one language to another, says Robert Roth, "As far as can be determined, there has never been a 100 percent acceptable translation—certainly not of advertising or public relations material" (Roth 1982, 135). For copy to be translated, advertisers should be aware of some linguistic and managerial guidelines (Roth 1982, 135; Miracle 1988, RC-51).

*Linguistic Guidelines*

1. Think multilingual. Remember from the start that copy will be translated. Copy should contain neither slang and idioms nor puns, rhymes, figures of speech, similes, or metaphors—all of which are extremely difficult and sometimes impossible to translate.
2. Remember that language is alive and changing. The dictionary should be avoided as a translation tool because the language of the dictionary is not necessarily the language of the people.
3. Recognize that translated words may have different shades of meaning. Some words simply cannot be translated, and others can only be translated in lengthy or awkward forms.
4. Use English at the fifth- or sixth-grade level to ensure ease of translation. Overly technical terms and industry jargon should be avoided.

5. Keep copy for translation relatively short, because many foreign languages invariably take more time or space to say the same thing the English-language copy says.

6. Remember that some languages distinguish between the familiar and the formal (*du/Sie* for "you" in German and *tu/usted* for "you" in Spanish). Others employ honorific expressions depending on the relationship between speakers (inferior/superior in Japanese). Such differences can make translating from one language to another difficult.

*Managerial Guidelines*

1. Choose translators with care. Use only professional translators, preferably those with advertising copy translation experience. Translators may have specialties—medical, legal, or technical.

2. Use native speakers of the language into which the copy is being translated. Ideally, the translator should currently live in the country in which the advertising will appear to ensure both familiarity and currency. Because language evolves, even a native tends to lose track of slang and idioms after being away from home for several years.

3. Examine the region in which translators were born, educated, and resident for significant periods of time. Such exposure may impact dialects. Within Germany, for example, each region speaks its own dialect. Similarly, the French spoken in France, Canada, Belgium, and Switzerland differs significantly.

4. Provide translators with full background on marketing and advertising objectives and strategies.

5. Give translators access to all necessary reference materials dealing with the appropriate subject and industry. Ensure that the translator has an adequate understanding of any required technical terms.

6. Settle on style issues before translation begins. American advertising copy is often considered brusque or staccato, which may not be appropriate for some markets.

7. Allow sufficient time for translations. Forcing translators to work under pressure benefits no one.

8. Don't be stingy—hire the best translators available.

9. Employ the back-translation technique. Here, one individual is responsible for the initial translation of the message, and a second individual then translates the message back into the original language. If the message does not translate back, there is likely a translation problem. Back-translation is a helpful tool; however, it's no guarantee against translation bloopers.

The same translation guidelines apply to both print and broadcast messages. In the production of advertisements for television, it may be preferable to design a spot that does not employ on-camera sound. While it is possible to dub spots for use in the international arena, the result almost always sounds unnatural, and the technique is not inexpensive.

Clearly, translation done well is both costly and time consuming. International marketers have at their disposal machine translations. The primary benefit of machine translations is that they are speedy and, generally, significantly less expensive. However, caution must be exercised, as the translations are not 100 percent accurate. The slogans highlighted in Table 6.1 were fed into an automatic translator—and then translated back into English—with less than successful results. Most translation software has accuracy rates hovering between 70 and 80 percent. However, as of 2009, there was a new entrant in the field—Google Translate. Google Translate is a statistical machine translation system, which means

that it doesn't try to unpick or understand anything. Instead of taking a sentence to pieces and then rebuilding it in the "target" tongue as older machine translators do, Google Translate looks for similar sentences in already translated texts somewhere out there on the Web. Having found the most likely existing match through an incredibly clever and speedy statistical reckoning device, Google Translate coughs it up, raw or, if necessary, slightly cooked. That's how it simulates—but only simulates—what we suppose goes on in a translator's head. But a target sentence supplied by Google Translate is not and must never be mistaken for the "correct translation." That's not just because no such thing as a "correct translation" really exists. It's also because Google Translation gives only an expression consisting of the most probably equivalent phrases as computed by its analysis of an astronomically large set of paired sentences trawled from the Web. (Bellos 2010)

For routine utterances, Google Translate is considered by many to be a fabulous tool. For anything more complex, the program is very patchy. For example, the opening sentence of Proust's *In Search of Lost Time* came out as an ungrammatical "Long time I went to bed early." Currently Google Translate can handle 52 languages. The quality of Google Translate in the different language pairings available is quite variable, due in large part to the disparity in the quantities of human-engineered translations between those languages on the Web. The real benefit of Google Translate and other machine translations appears to be that they significantly reduce the time it takes for humans to translate copy—and sometimes an approximate translation will do. With each passing year, accuracy rates keep inching up.

**TABLE 6.1:** Accuracy of Machine Translations

| ENGLISH PHRASE | AUTOMATIC TRANSLATION |
| --- | --- |
| Ring around the collar (Wisk Detergent) | Ring around the tension ring (German) |
| You deserve a break today (McDonald's) | You deserve a rupture today (French and Portuguese) |
| Silly Rabbit, Trix are for kids (Trix) | Asinine bunny, Trix are prior babies (Swedish) |
| Pork—the other white meat (Pork Council) | Pig—the other white woman meat (Italian) |
| Time to make the donuts (Dunkin' Donuts) | Time to form the foam rubber rings (German) |
| Good to the last drop (Maxwell House) | Bonny to the last bead (Russian). |

*Source:* Recksieck (2003).

## Music

Music seems to travel across borders quite well—due, no doubt, to the immense popularity of many international music stars. Table 6.2 presents the United World Chart for the week of April 8, 2010. The chart ranks the top-selling albums according to global sales figures and national album charts. The popularity of these musicians is a fact that has not gone unnoticed by international marketers, who are increasingly employing popular singers and groups in regional and global ad campaigns. No. 7 on the list, the Black Eyed Peas, was featured in an advertising campaign in the United Kingdom for Pepsi Max in 2007. The advertisement built on Pepsi's successful "Max Your Life" platform and included music written exclusively for Pepsi Max by the group. Running on television, in cinemas, and online, the ad shows a Pepsi Max vending machine user who crashes through the floor into the Black Eyed Peas' recording studio, a house party, and an aerobics studio. More recently, the Black Eyed Peas kicked off Samsung Electronics' global campaign to raise awareness for its 3D television technology leadership, which includes worldwide launch events and a global television advertising campaign. In March 2010, Samsung celebrated the worldwide availability of the first-ever full HD 3D LED televisions with a one-of-a-kind performance by the music group in Times Square. The performance was filmed in 3D and streamed live via Dipdive.com, the popular lifestyle engine for music, arts, action, and more. Samsung also announced that footage from the Black Eyed Peas' hugely popular The E.N.D world tour would be exclusively available in 3D for Samsung customers. The centerpiece of the campaign was a global television commercial filmed by renowned director Sam Brown that translated the immersion of 3D onto a 2D screen. The campaign also aggressively utilized print and out-of-home advertising, as well as in-depth social media. Ads ran on every continent except Antarctica (*Marketwire* 2010). Also among the top 20, Madonna's first single from her 2008 album debuted in a Sunsilk hair products television spot. The track, called "4 Minutes (to Save the World)" is from the singer's album "Hard Candy." The spot depicts how Madonna has continuously reinvented her image over the years (Cassidy 2008). And Rihanna (No. 20 on the list) partnered with Nokia in 2009 to promote the firm's new X6 phone and other entertainment offerings. The R&B singer and her label, Island Def Jam Music Group, Universal Music Group International, helped kick off Nokia's "Nokia Play 2010" campaign while promoting Rihanna's latest album, "Rated R." The partnership includes a live streaming concern, exclusive music offerings, and a mobile application. A concert that took place in London was broadcast across Nokia mobile music, video, and online. The singer was also integrated into Nokia's broader marketing campaign and appeared in a range of advertising materials including retail, outdoor,

**Table 6.2:** Top-Selling Albums According to Global Sales Figures and National Album Charts (April 2010)

| RANK | ARTIST | ALBUM | NUMBER SOLD |
|------|--------|-------|-------------|
| 1. | Justin Bieber | My Worlds (My World + My World 2.0) | 449,000 |
| 2. | Usher | Raymond V Raymond | 348,000 |
| 3. | Lady GaGa | The Fame (Monster) | 172,000 |
| 4. | Aiko | Baby | 136,000 |
| 5. | Erykah Badu | New Amerykah Part 2 | 124,000 |
| 6. | Lady Entebellum | Need You Now | 96,000 |
| 7. | Black Eyed Peas | The E.N.D. | 96,000 |
| 8. | Madonna | Sticky & Sweet Tour | 93,000 |
| 9. | Sade | Soldier of Love | 83,000 |
| 10. | Monica | Still Standing | 83,000 |
| 11. | Alan Jackson | Freight Train | 77,000 |
| 12. | Gorillaz | Plastic Beach | 77,000 |
| 13. | V6 | Ready? | 68,000 |
| 14 | Christophe Mae | On Trace La Route | 60,000 |
| 15. | Ke$ha | Animal | 58,000 |
| 16. | Amy MacDonald | A Curious Thing | 54,000 |
| 17. | Jimi Hendrix | Valleys of Neptune | 54,000 |
| 18. | Michael Buble | Crazy Love | 54,000 |
| 19. | Alicia Keys | The Element of Freedom | 51,000 |
| 20. | Rihanna | Rated R | 49,000 |

*Source:* United World Chart (2010).

and television (Palmer 2009). Without a doubt, top-ranked musicians will continue to play large in global advertising campaigns in the years to come.

## Nonverbal Communication: Visuals and Illustrations

According to several experts, including Martin Mayer, sight, sound, and motion are the future of international advertising: "Words will become very much less important, especially if the product is standardized, like Coca-Cola, Levi's or Marlboro" (Mayer 1991, 213). The growing use of visual presentation (pictures and illustrations) minimizes the need for translations. Vern Terpstra and Ravi Sarathy write: "More and more European and Japanese ads are purely visual, showing something, evoking a mood and citing the company name. Emphasis on such simple illustrations also avoids part of the problem of illiteracy in poorer nations" (Terpstra and Sarathy 1991). As an example, the many different languages spoken in Europe posed a formidable barrier to Levi's in selling its jeans on the continent. Therefore, the company and its advertising agency created broadcast and movie advertisements that consisted solely of moving pictures and music. Unworried by problems of language or complicated dubbing procedures, Levi's advertising agency in London was able to utilize the Levi's 501 spots for use throughout Europe (Rijkens 1992, 79). Care should be taken in the selection of visual backgrounds and settings employed in both print and broadcast advertisements destined for foreign markets. These nonverbal communications should either reinforce the local culture in adapted campaigns or remain neutral enough to be accepted in all markets for those campaigns employing a standardized strategy. The creative team must attend to every visual detail in an advertisement. For example, according to Marieke de Mooij and Warren Keegan:

> Landscapes, buildings, traffic signs, etc., must all be neutral. Dutch, Danish and Belgian houses may look similar to the Japanese or Americans, but they look different to the Dutch, the Danish and the Belgians! As soon as they cross each other's borders, they feel they are in a foreign country, not only because of the language, but because of the landscape, houses and churches. (de Mooij and Keegan 1991)

## CREATIVITY IN THE INTERNATIONAL ARENA

The International Advertising Festival, also known as the Cannes Lions Festival, is the largest gathering of international marketing and advertising professionals in the world. In 2009, more than 6,000 delegates from the advertising and allied disciplines attended the event to celebrate the best creative work in all major media. The festival showcased over 22,652 ads representing 86 countries. Winning ads are awarded the highly coveted Gold, Silver, and Bronze Lions, and the Grand Prix are reserved for the most outstanding creative work in each category. Awards for advertisements in a total of 11 disciplines, including film (both television and "other screens" including computers and phones), radio, press (print), outdoor, cyber, direct, design, media, promo, public relations, titanium & integrated are presented. In 2009, the top film award—the Grand Prix—went to Tribal DDB, based in Amsterdam for its interactive film "Carousel" for Philips. The ad is for a line of movie-theatre-proportioned televisions unfolding in one long take that can be turned into a film-within-a-film with the flick of the cursor (Wentz 2009). Table 6.3 lists the Grand Prix winners by category.

See Figure 6.17 for the ad that won the press Grand Prix. The ad for Wrangler jeans is entitled "We are Animals" and is part of Wrangler's European print campaign. Winners of the Grand Prix

**Table 6.3:** Cannes 2009 Grand Prix Winners by Category

| CATEGORY | ADVERTISER/CLIENT | AGENCY | COUNTRY |
|---|---|---|---|
| FILM | Philips | Tribal DDB, Amsterdam | Netherlands |
| RADIO | Virgin Atlantic Airlines | Network BBDO | Japan |
| PRESS | Wrangler Jeans | Fred & Farid | France |
| OUTDOOR | The Zimbabwean | TBWA/Hunt/Lascaris | South Africa |
| MEDIA | Nestlé/Kit Kat | JWT | Japan |
| PROMO | Yubari | Beacon Communications | Japan |
| TITANIUM/ INTEGRATED | Obama/Biden 2008 | | USA |
| PR/DIRECT/ CYBER | Tourism Queensland | Cummins Nitro | Australia |
| DESIGN | Nike | McCann Worldgroup | Hong Kong |

*Source:* Wentz (2009).

and Gold Lions receive more than just the praise of their peers. Donald Gunn, director of creative resources worldwide for Leo Burnett, notes:

> Research shows that commercials that win awards are at least twice as likely to be successful in the marketplace as commercials on average. My theory…is that there is some definite link between what pleases juries and what pleases viewers when they see advertising in their homes. (Jaffe 1994)

**Figure 6.17:** 2009 Cannes Grand Prix winner for print: Wrangler jeans.

Cannes winners are significantly more likely to report dramatic increases in market shares, sales, volume growth, brand awareness, and favorable image ratings during and after the campaigns' flights" (Tilles 1994).

Two additional Cannes awards should be noted: Agency of the Year and Advertiser of the Year. In 2009, DDB Brazil, located in São Paulo, received the honor of Agency of the Year. The award is given to the agency that obtains the highest score for entries in the press, outdoor, film, and radio Lions sections, irrespective of whether these have been entered by the agency or another party. Table 6.4 lists the contenders for 2009's Agency of the Year award in rank order and by country. Volkswagen, Europe's largest auto manufacturer, was named 2009 Advertiser of the Year in Cannes. Volkswagen has been presented with some 150 "advertising Oscars" in Cannes since 1961. The Cannes Festival has frequently commended Volkswagen's advertising for its innovative and inspiring approach.

Of course, the Cannes awards are not the only ones received for outstanding creativity in advertising. A multitude of other international, national, regional, and local awards are available as well. DDB Worldwide London's office was the most-awarded advertising agency in the world in 2009, according to the 11th annual Gunn Report, widely recognized as the authoritative source on agency awards. This is the third time in the history of the Gunn Report that DDB London has been ranked No. 1. Gunn

**Table 6.4:** Cannes 2009 Agency of the Year (Film, Press, Outdoor, and Radio)

| RANK | AGENCY | COUNTRY |
|------|--------|---------|
| 1. | DDB Brazil, São Paulo | Brazil |
| 2. | AlmapBBDO, São Paulo | Brazil |
| 3. | DDB&CO, Istanbul | Turkey |
| 4. | DDB London | United Kingdom |
| 5. | Marcel Paris | France |
| 6. | BBDO New York | United States |
| 7. | CLM BBDO, Boulogne-Billancourt | France |
| 8. | Ogilvy Johannesburg | South Africa |
| 9. | DDB Paris | France |
| 10. | Saatchi & Saatchi New York | United States |
| 11. | Saatchi & Saatchi Australia, Sydney | Australia |
| 12. | Saatchi & Saatchi NZ, Wellington | New Zealand |
| 13. | Del Campo/Nazca Saatchi & Saatchi Buenos Aires | Argentina |
| 14. | TBWA\Hunt\Lascaris Johannesburg | South Africa |
| 15. | Jung von Matt, Hamburg | Germany |
| 16. | Grey Paris | France |
| 17. | Grey Argentina, Buenos Aires | Argentina |
| 18. | Net#WorkBBDO Johannesburg | South Africa |
| 19. | Ogilvy & Mather, Bangkok | Thailand |
| 20. | Abbott Mead Vickers BBDO London | United Kingdom |

Source: *The Cannes Report* (2009, 9).

ranks agencies based on wins in the most important international and national creative contests. Table 6.5 presents the Gunn Report for 2009, listing the most-awarded agencies in the world. Table 6.6 lists the most-awarded agency networks in the world in the same year. The most-awarded advertisers are listed in Table 6.7. Note that the Gunns Blazing category is for campaigns that don't easily fit into the other categories.

For decades, New York was known as the center of U.S. advertising creativity. Indeed, the rest of the advertising world took lessons from Madison Avenue. Consumers around the globe read U.S.-

**Table 6.5:** The Most-Awarded Agencies in the World in 2009 (Traditional Media)

| | | TV & CINEMA | PRINT | OTHER | TOTAL |
|---|---|---|---|---|---|
| 1. | DDB London | 17 | 23 | 1 | 41 |
| 2. | Almap BBDO (São Paulo) | 13 | 17 | — | 30 |
| 3. | Dentsu (Tokyo & Osaka) | 23 | 1 | 4 | 28 |
| 4. | Goodby, Silverstein & Partners (San Francisco) | 12 | — | 15 | 27 |
| 5. | Del Campo/ Nazca Saatchi & Saatchi | 11 | 13 | 2 | 26 |

*Source:* Gunn Report (2009).

**Table 6.6:** The Most-Awarded Agency Networks in the World in 2009

| | | TV & CINEMA | PRINT | INTERACTIVE | GUNNS BLAZING | TOTAL |
|---|---|---|---|---|---|---|
| 1. | BBDO | 64 | 73 | 33 | 15 | 185 |
| 2. | DDB | 65 | 55 | 16 | 6 | 142 |
| 3. | Ogilvy & Mather | 49 | 45 | 11 | 4 | 109 |
| 4. | Leo Burnett | 52 | 33 | 4 | 18 | 107 |
| 5. | Saatchi & Saatchi | 46 | 44 | 5 | 8 | 103 |

*Source:* Gunn Report (2009).

**Table 6.7:** The Most-Awarded Advertiser in the World in 2009

| | | TV & CINEMA | PRINT | INTERACTIVE | GUNNS BLAZING | TOTAL |
|---|---|---|---|---|---|---|
| 1. | Volkswagen | 34 | 13 | 9 | 2 | 58 |
| 2. | Nike | 20 | 5 | 25 | 3 | 53 |
| 3. | Axe/Lynx | 14 | 2 | 14 | — | 30 |
| 4. | Sony | 12 | 6 | 10 | — | 28 |
| 5. | Adidas | 6 | 12 | 5 | 4 | 27 |
| | Burger King | 2 | 1 | 15 | 9 | 27 |

*Source:* Gunn Report (2009).

produced print advertisements and viewed U.S.-produced television spots. However, during the past two decades, a gradual shift has been taking place. As a creative force, the United States no longer stands alone. As Table 6.8 reveals, while the United States still ranks in first place, Great Britain, Argentina, Germany, and Japan are close behind. And highly creative agencies hail from Argentina to Turkey, and from South Africa to Thailand.

**Table 6.8:** The Most-Awarded Countries in the World in 2009

|   | | TV & CINEMA | PRINT | INTERACTIVE | GUNNS BLAZING | TOTAL |
|---|---|---|---|---|---|---|
| 1. | U.S. | 156 | 37 | 123 | 71 | 387 |
| 2. | Great Britain | 134 | 55 | 60 | 12 | 261 |
| 3. | Argentina | 98 | 22 | 9 | 12 | 141 |
| 4. | Germany | 49 | 34 | 22 | 12 | 117 |
| 5. | Japan | 46 | 2 | 56 | 7 | 111 |

*Source:* Gunn Report (2009).

# SUMMARY

As a strategy, advertising globalization may work well for some products, marketers, and audiences, and in some situations. In other instances, localization or adaption will prove to be more effective. And sometimes, something in between will be most appropriate (Quelch and Hoff 1986, 59). International marketers must carefully evaluate where along the globalization–localization continuum a campaign destined for a specific foreign market should fall. Advertisers also must employ appeals suited to each culture and understand how cultural differences impact advertising content. Finally, advertisers must exercise caution in the use of both verbal and nonverbal messages. Translations must be conducted with care, and every aspect of the illustration or visual must be analyzed to ensure a proper cultural fit. And whatever the product, advertisers must select the best media—the subject of Chapter 7.

REFERENCES

*Advertising Age.* 1998. Nokia launches biggest ever campaign in Asia. 8 July. <www.adageglobal.com/cgi-bin/ daily. pl?daily_id=1681&post_date=1998–07–08>.

———. 1999. Avon breaks skincare ad in Philippines. 21 October. <www.adageglobal.com/cgi-bin/ daily. pl?daily_id+2661&post_date=1999–10–21>.

———. 2000. Coke Turkey launches kids soft drink in Eastern Europe, South Africa. 8 September. <www.adageglobal.com/ cgi-bin/daily.pl?daily_id=3645&post_date=2000–09–08>.

———. 2001. Coke hopes Chinese clay dolls will bring it luck. 17 January. <www.adageglobal. com/ cgi-bin/daily. pl?daily_id=4216&post_date=2001–01–17>.

Alden, Dana, Wayne Hoyer, and Chol Lee. 1993. Identifying global and culture-specific dimensions of humor. *Journal of Marketing,* 57(2): April, 64.

Al-Olayan, Fahad, and Diran Karande. 2000. A content analysis of magazine advertisements from the United States and the Arab world. *Journal of Advertising,* 29(3): Fall, 69.

Arens, William. 2002. *Contemporary advertising.* Boston: McGraw-Hill Irwin.

Ashford. L., D. Clifton, and T. Kaneda. 2006. *The world's youth 2006.* Washington, DC: Population Reference Bureau.

ASIATravelTips.com. 2005. InterContinental Hotels & Resorts to launch new global advertising campaign. 22 September. <http://www.asiatraveltips.com/news05/229-Advertising.shtml.> Retrieved 19 April 2010.

Balakrishna, P., and B. Sidharth. 2003. Selling to India: Lessons for MNCs, BusinessLine, Chennai. <http://proquest.umi.com.ezproxy.lib.rmit.edu.au/pqdweb?did+313046621&sid=2&Fmt=3&clientId=16532&RQT=309&Vname=PQD.>

Banoo, Sreerema. 1999. TAG Heuer tells what makes its campaigns tick. *Business Times* (Kuala Lampur), 11 August, 15.

*Beauty Packaging.* 2008. <http://www.beautypackaging.com/articles/2008/11/top-20-Loreal.php>.

Belch, George E., and Michael A. Belch. 1993. *Introduction to advertising and promotion: An integrated marketing communications perspective.* Homewood, IL: Irwin.

Bellos, David. 2010. I, translator. *New York Times,* 20 March. <http://www.nytimes.com/2010/03/21/opinion/21 bellos.html?pagewan...>. Retrieved 14 April 2010.

Biswas, Abhijit, Janeen E. Olsen, and Valerie Carlet. 1992. A comparison of print advertisements from the United States and France. *Journal of Advertising,* 21(4): December, 73–81.

Bowes, Elena. 1992. From cookies to appliances, pan European efforts build. *Advertising Age,* 22 June, 11, 129.

BusinessLine. 2003. *Coca Cola ad blitz targets urban youth.* Mumbai: The Hindu Business Line.

The Cannes Report. 2009. Agency of the year. 9.

Cassidy, Anne. 2008. Madonna single accompanies Sunsilk ad. *Campaign,* 18 March. <http://www.campaignlive.co.uk/news/793996/Madonna-single>. Retrieved 26 April 2010.

Cateora, Philip. 1990. *International marketing.* Homewood, IL: Irwin.

de Mooij, Marieke. 1994. *Advertising worldwide.* New York: Prentice Hall.

de Mooij, Marieke K., and Warren Keegan. 1991. *Advertising worldwide.* New York: Prentice Hall.

Di Benedetto, C. Anthony, Maiko Tamate, and Rajan Chandran. 1992. Developing creative advertising strategy for the Japanese marketplace. *Journal of Advertising Research,* 32(1): January/February, 39–48.

Ellison, Sarah. 2000. About advertising: Agencies find that sexual innuendos don't travel well across cultures. *Wall Street Journal Europe,* 27 March, 36.

Faiola, Anthony. 2007. U.S. movie stars shine once again in Japan. *Washington Post,* 15 January. <http://www.courierpress.com/news/2007/jan/15/us-movie-stars-shine...>. Retrieved 14 April 2010.

Fannin, Rebecca. 1984. What agencies really think of global theory. *Marketing and Media Decisions,* December, 74–82.

*Financial.* 2010. It's my time—Benetton launches the global interactive multimedia campaign, 8 February. <http://www.finchannel.com/Main_News/Business/57761_IT%27S...>. Retrieved 12 April 2010.

Frazer, Charles. 1983. Creative strategy: A management perspective. *Journal of Advertising,* 12(1): 36–41.

Freeman, Laurie. 1990. Colgate axes global ads, thinks local. *Advertising Age,* 26 November, 1, 51.

Giacomotti, Faboma. 1993. In Europe, there's no place like home. *Adweek,* 7 June, 13.

Green, Robert, William Cunningham, and Isabella Cunningham. 1975. The effectiveness of standardized global advertising. *Journal of Advertising,* 4(3): 25–30.

Gunn Report. 2009. American Association of Advertising Agencies, 11 November. <http://www2.aaaa.org/news/agency/Pages/111909_gunn.aspx>. Retrieved 19 April 2010.

Harris, Greg. 1984. The globalization of advertising. *International Journal of Advertising,* 3: 223–234.

Head, David. 1988. Ad slogans and the made-in concept. *International Journal of Advertising,* 7: 237–252.

Hofstede, Geert. 1980. *Culture's consequences: International differences in work related values.* Beverly Hills, CA: Sage Publications.

Hornik, Jacob. 1980. Comparative evaluation of international vs. national advertising strategies. *Columbia Journal of World Business,* Spring, 36–45.

Jaffe, Andrew. 1994. Burnett's Donald Gunn on what wins at Cannes. *Adweek,* 6 June, 46.

Kaplan, Rachel. 1994. Ad agencies take on the world. *International Management,* 49(3): April, 50.

Kar, Sayantani. 2008. Setting the platter right. *Business Standard,* 12 August. <http://www/business-standard.com/india/storypage.php?leftnm=6&au...>. Retrieved 14 April 2010.

Kaye, J. 2004. Coca Cola India. Tuck School of Business, Dartmouth. <http://www.tuck.dartmouth.edu/pdf/pr20050309_case.pdf>.

Kaynak, Erdener. 1989. *The management of international advertising: A handbook and guide for professionals.* New York: Quorum Books.

Kilburn, David. 1992. Kao enters Australia, but its detergent is no attack. *Advertising Age,* 22 June, 13.

Koenderman, Tony. 2001. Record punishment: Land Rover forced to advertise apology in South Africa. 6 April. www.adage-global.com/cgi-bin/daily.pl?daily_id=4604&post_date=2001-04-06.

Levitt, Theodore. 1983. Globalization of markets. *Harvard Business Review,* May/June, 92–102.

Lin, C. A. 1993. Cultural differences in message strategies: A comparison between American and Japanese TV commercials. *Journal of Advertising Research,* July/August, 40–47.

Lipman, Joanne. 1988. Marketers turn sour on global sales pitch Harvard guru makes. *Wall Street Journal,* 12 May, 1.

Lyman, Eric J. 2001. Barilla cooks up first global ads. 5 July. <www.adageglobal.com/cgi-bin/daily.pl?daily_id=5283&post_date=2001-07-05>.

*Marketwire.* 2010. Samsung celebrates the global launch of full HD 3D LED TV at Times Square with The Black Eyed Peas and "Avatar" Director James Cameron. 11 March. <http://finance.yahoo.com/news/Samsung-Celebrates-the-Global-iw-2...>. Retrieved 26 March 2010.

Matlack, Carol. 2009. Nespresso pitches "luxury" coffee for lean times. *BusinessWeek,* 24 March. <http://businessweek.com/globalbiz/content/mar2009/gb20090...>. Retrieved 29 January 2010.

Mayer, Martin. 1991. *Whatever happened to Madison Avenue: Advertising in the 90s.* Boston: Little, Brown.

Milner, Laura, and James Collins. 2000. Sex-role portrayals and the gender of nations. *Journal of Advertising,* 29(1): Spring, 67–79.

Miracle, Gordon E. 1988. An empirical study of the usefulness of the back-translation technique for international advertising messages in print media. In *Proceedings of the 1988 Conference of the American Academy of Advertising,* ed. John D. Leckenby, American Academy of Advertising. Austin, Texas, RC51–61.

Mitchell, R., and M. Oneal. 1994. Managing by values. *Business Week,* 12 September, 38–43.

Monjaras, Jorge A. 2003. Unilever makes dib for Mexican fabric softener market. 19 February. <www.adageglobal.com/cgi-bin/daily.pl?daily_id=9160&post_date=2003-02-19>.

Mueller, Barbara. 1987. Reflections of culture: An analysis of Japanese and American advertising appeals. *Journal of Advertising Research,* 27(3): June/July, 51–59.

Neff, Jack. 2002. P&G flexes muscle for global branding. *Advertising Age,* 3 June, 53.

Nelson, Bob. 1994. High tech firms lead the way with global campaigns. *Advertising Age,* 11 August, 22.

Nevett, Terence. 1992. Differences between American and British television advertising: Explanations and implications. *Journal of Advertising,* 21(4): December, 61–71.

O'Dwyer, Gerald. 2003. Swedish ad council says McDonald's spot violates gender law. 25 February. <www.adageglobal.com/cgi-bin/daily.pl?daily_id=9171>.

Palmer, Alex. 2009. Rihanna gives voice to Nokia's new push. *Brandweek,* 9 November. <http://brandweek.com/bw/content_display/news-and-features/>. Retrieved 26 April 2010.

Parmar, Arundhati. 2002. Global youth united. *Marketing News,* 28 October, 1, 49.

Quelch, John A., and Edward J. Hoff. 1986. Customizing global marketing. *Harvard Business Review,* 64(3): May/June, 59–68.

Radzievsky, Yuri. 1983/1984. The invisible idiot and other monsters of translation. *Viewpoint: A Publication "By, For, and About Ogilvy & Mather,"* Fall.

Raffield, Barney T., III. 1987. Marketing across cultures: Learning from U.S. corporate blunders. EMU Conference on Languages and Communication for World Business and the Professions, Ann Arbor, MI.

Recksieck, Charlie. 2003. Fun with automatic translation advertising edition. <www.shtick.org/ Translation/translation 48.htm>.

Rijkens, Rein. 1992. *European advertising strategies.* London: Cassell.

Roberts, Jo. 2009. *Marketing Week* (London), 17 December, 20.

Roth, Robert F. 1982. *International marketing communications.* Chicago: Crain Books.

Rutigliano, Anthony. 1986. The debate goes on: Global vs. local advertising. *Management Review,* 75(6): June, 27–31.

Speer, Lawrence. 2002. It's bugs versus bankers in new global ads for BNP Paribas. *Advertising Age*, 11 June. <www.adageglobal.com/cgi-bin/daily.pl?daily_id=7713&post_date=2002–06–11>.

Staheli, Paul. 2000. We're the best, but we're not allowed to tell you. *Evening Standard* (London), 26 April, 59.

Taylor, Charles R. 2008. Lifestyle matters everywhere. *Advertising Age* (Midwest region edition, Chicago), 79(20): 19 May, 21.

Terpstra, Vern, and Ravi Sarathy. 1991. *International marketing*. Hinsdale, IL: Dryden Press.

Tilles, Danie. 1994. Commercials do win awards and sales. *Adweek*, 11 July, 16.

TRU. 2009. 2 March. <www.tru-insight.com/pressrelease.cfm?page_id=758>.

United World Chart. 2010. Album chart. 17 April. <http://www.mediatraffic.de/albums.htm>. Retrieved 14 April 2010.

———. 2009. Cannes swept by PR, integrated, Internet winners. *Advertising Age*, 29 June, 1.

Wong, Elaine. 2009. Unilever's true grit. *Mediaweek* (New York), 19(21): 25 May, A8.

Wroughton, Lesley. 2000. Beer ad boosts Canadian pride. *San Diego Union-Tribune*, 29 April, A-17.

Xinhua News Agency. 2007. 2,000 sex-related ads dropped from Chinese television and radio. 11 October. <http://www.china.org.cn/english/MATERIAL/227557.htm>. Retrieved 16 April 2010.

# CHAPTER SEVEN

# Advertising Media in the International Arena

An area that proves to be particularly challenging and often quite frustrating for most international marketers is that of the media function. The basic goals of media planning and purchasing are generally the same whether the planner is operating in New York or New Delhi: to select those media and vehicles that most efficiently and effectively reach the target audience. However, the application of these principles will vary from one market to the next.

The intention of this chapter is not to provide an overview of the media situation in each of the numerous markets around the world. Not only is a complete survey beyond the scope of this text, but such information would soon be outdated. Rather, the goal here is to outline the media options available to international media planners and to highlight the diversity in the various media environments.

## NATIONAL/LOCAL VERSUS INTERNATIONAL MEDIA

Media planners zeroing in on foreign markets have the option of using national/local media or employing media that cross national borders—better known as international media. Using a combination of the two is clearly an alternative as well. The decision of whether to employ national/local or international media is impacted by a number of factors, including but not limited to: (1) how much centralized control the firm has, (2) what target audience the advertiser is attempting to reach, (3) whether the firm has chosen to employ a localized or globalized campaign, and (4) whether the firm works with national or multinational advertising agencies.

The tendency toward decentralized decision making, the use of campaigns tailored to the local market, and the preference for domestic agencies generally result in more extensive employment of local media than international media. Even where a standardized campaign is employed, media planning and buying usually is conducted on a local basis. Decentralizing this aspect allows for greater input from local advertising experts, which greatly simplifies the execution of media plans. While the amount of advertising in national media is still vastly greater than that appearing in international media, this may well change significantly in the years to come.

# NATIONAL/LOCAL MEDIA

National or local media offer advertisers a greater variety of vehicles—television, radio, newspapers, magazines, outdoor, direct mail, and transit, as well as many rather unique forms. They also permit use of the local language, which is generally more effective in reaching the local market. However, there are drawbacks to using local media. The practice of media planning and buying at the local level is quite complex, because the media environments rarely resemble one another. These differences can take the form of media availability, viability, coverage, cost, quality, and the role of advertising in the media.

## Media Availability

Advertisers in the United States are accustomed to the availability of a wide variety of media vehicles. Yet media that commonly are employed in domestic campaigns may quite simply be unavailable in foreign markets. Until rather recently, for example, Denmark and Sweden did not allow broadcast advertising. And although the United Kingdom does have commercial television networks, the BBC television network—attractive because it is hugely popular among the British—still does not accept advertising. In Saudi Arabia, public cinemas were shut down in the late 1970s, as the country's deeply conservative leaders feared they would lead to the mixing of sexes and undermine Islamic values. In 2009, for the first time in three decades, 300 men crowded the King Fahd Cultural Centre in Riyadh to view a film entitled *Menahi*, a comedy about a naïve Bedouin who leaves the country to face the dangers of the big city. However, outside the center, religious radicals shouted slogans about the moral decay caused by movies, how small steps in favor of an open society were bringing disaster on the country, citing a series of minor earthquakes in western Saudi Arabia (AsiaNews.it 2009). It will likely be a good many years before cinema plays a dominant role in the media scene in Saudi Arabia.

As a result of such limitations, a firm marketing its products in a number of nations may well find it impossible to employ the same media mix in all markets. Even when the same media are available, commercial time may be severely restricted. In Germany, commercial time is limited to 20 minutes a day and is banned on Sundays as well as holidays on each of the government-owned stations. In addition, advertisements are shown in three or four blocks approximately five minutes in length, and, as a result, viewership tends to be rather low. However, Germany's privately owned stations, as those in other EU countries, are considerably more liberal. As of 2009, EU legislation allows 12 minutes (20 percent) of commercial time per hour (Hall 2010). However, this is a maximum limit, so regulations differ widely from country to country, and indeed from network to network within the EU. For example, in France, the Conseil supérieur de l'audiovisuel allows up to 9 minutes of advertising per hour on average in a day. The U.K. broadcasting regulator Ofcom allows even less commercial time—an overall average of 7 minutes of commercial time per hour, with limits of 12 minutes for any particular clock hour (8 minutes per hour between 6 p.m. and 11 p.m.). Such restrictions typically result in high levels of demand and require that commercial time and space be both booked and paid for well in advance—sometimes up to a year or more. Conversely, where regulation is more limited, the resulting invasion of advertising often translates into clutter. According to a survey conducted by Magna Global in 2007, U.S. networks offer about 69 percent of program content in a given hour, with the rest being national commercials, local ads, and program promos. CBS has the least clutter, with 70 percent content per hour, and CW had the most, with only 67 percent program content per hour. Dramas averaged 16 minutes and 52 seconds of non-program time, reality shows, 16:57. The most clutter came from the marketing-friendly show *The Apprentice*, which clocked in with 19:57 of non-program content (Friedman 2007). Over the past few years, networks have increased their use of product placement. When branded appearances are added to network ad messages, some programs (such as late-night shows) are nearly half commercial content. The concern is that such clutter may be driving off television viewers.

Canada has taken a different approach. The Canadian Radio-Televison and Telecommunications Commission announced that as of 2009, there would be no restrictions on advertising for the country's conventional, over-the-air television broadcasters, who had complained loudly about a shrinking advertising base as viewers migrated to cable, satellite, and the Internet. The move was meant to give the big networks, reliant on advertising for revenues since the programming is beamed free over the airways, an edge over the flood of specialty television channels, generally limited to 12 minutes per hour of ads based on individual license agreements. While the change ostensibly opens the door to wall-to-wall commercials on the major networks, industry observers predict that conventional broadcasters are unlikely to lob dozens of extra ads at their audiences. "The whole reason the broadcasters are in trouble is because consumers now have a whole plethora of television choices available to them," said Jeff Leiper, an Ottawa-based communications analyst. "So, if the broadcasters program more ads than the consumers are willing to watch, they're going to slit their own throats" (Sorenson 2007). Time will tell the impact of the easing of the restrictions.

Table 7.1 presents the global percentage share of advertising spending by medium for the period 2009 to 2011, according to Carat, the leading independent media communications agency (2010). As the figures show, television continues to receive the highest share of ad spend. In spite of a continued decline in circulation figures, newspapers should retain the second-highest share of spend. Table 7.2 highlights the differences among countries with regard to how extensively specific media are used, and thereby reveals the relative importance of various media from one market to the next. Such variation necessitates adaptation to the local media environment.

## Media Viability

Beyond media availability, Dean Peebles and John Ryans note the importance of media viability. They suggest that the international advertiser look beyond simple media availability and also explore whether the medium is "available in the quality and quantity and at a cost that will permit the international advertiser to successfully employ it" (1984). While commercial television is available in Malaysia to the international advertiser, governmental restrictions require local production of commercials. The added cost of producing a commercial in Malaysia may well preclude the use of the medium of television if the international advertiser sees a limited market for the product in this country or had planned to use a commercial produced in the domestic market. Also, while a given medium may be available, the cost may be so high in certain markets that the international advertiser's budget prohibits the use of the medium.

**Table 7.1:** Global % Share of Advertising Spend by Medium

| MEDIUM | 2009 | 2010 | 2011 |
|---|---|---|---|
| Television | 43.9 | 45.2 | 46.1 |
| Newspapers | 21.6 | 20.3 | 19.4 |
| Magazines | 10.7 | 10.0 | 9.6 |
| Radio | 6.9 | 6.9 | 6.7 |
| Cinema | 0.5 | 0.5 | 0.6 |
| Outdoor | 6.3 | 6.3 | 6.3 |
| Online | 10.1 | 10.8 | 11.3 |

*Source:* Carat (2010).

## Media Coverage

Media coverage also varies from one market to the next. Table 7.3 presents data on numbers of newspapers, television sets, and computers in countries around the world. Newspapers are heavily read in Finland, which has 431 papers per 1,000 people. And there are an amazing 551 papers per 1,000 Japanese. At the other end of the spectrum, there are just 30 papers per 1,000 South Africans, and even fewer (just 5) in Ethiopia. Turning to the broadcast media, in the United States over 95 percent of households have television sets, and 99 percent of Japanese households have sets. This stands in sharp contrast to the 43 percent of households in Bangladesh and Cambodia that have televisions. These figures clearly suggest that the issue of receiver ownership is particularly relevant in developing countries, where a large percentage of the population simply cannot afford individual ownership of television sets. Regarding access and use of personal computers, 80 out of every 100 Americans have access to and use personal computers. The figures are similar for the United Kingdom. Again, developing countries fare poorly, with just 9 out of every 100 Argentinians and 5 out of every 100 Chinese having access to a computer (World Bank 2009).

Coverage of print media is impacted by both national literacy levels and subscription levels to publications, because illiterate consumers generally do not subscribe to newspapers or magazines. Levels of illiteracy vary significantly from country to country. Differences also exist in the illiteracy levels between males and females. In nearly every instance, illiteracy levels are higher among females, and in some instances the illiteracy rate is over 25 percent higher among women. As highlighted in Chapter 3, at the high end, 41 percent of men and 52 percent of women in Bangladesh, and 32 percent of men and 60 percent of women in Pakistan, are functionally illiterate. At the low end, less than 1 percent of men and women in Italy are illiterate. This suggests that in many countries it is still the male who receives formal education and that, as a result, print may be a more appropriate medium for targeting males in many markets. Another factor that comes into play in terms of media coverage is income. In countries with a low per capita income, consumers probably cannot afford to subscribe to print publications. In certain markets a wide variety of media and numerous media vehicles may be required in order to reach the majority of the market. The international advertiser faced with such a situation may no longer find it profitable to attempt to reach the mass market, particularly in many less-developed countries.

**TABLE 7.2:**Total World Advertising Expenditures by Medium, Purchasing Power Parities, PPP(m), 2007

| COUNTRY | NEWSPAPERS | MAGAZINES | TV | RADIO | OUTDOOR |
|---|---|---|---|---|---|
| Australia | 3,041.1 | 800.3 | 2,920.4 | 766.5 | 339.9 |
| Austria | 1,383.8 | 494.3 | 660.2 | 187.8 | 190.8 |
| Belgium | 778.6 | 339.7 | 959.1 | 321.7 | 178.4 |
| Canada | 3,098.9 | 1,079.7 | 3,129.3 | 1,257.2 | 408.1 |
| Czech Republic | 224.3 | 192.5 | 627.4 | 91.2 | 69.3 |
| Denmark | 739.3 | 172.9 | 295.2 | 33.4 | 55.5 |
| Finland | 774.7 | 238.3 | 304.2 | 54.5 | 48.4 |
| France | 3,003.5 | 2,226.3 | 3,803.0 | 843.2 | 1,211.5 |
| Germany | 8,531.1 | 3,542.2 | 5,274.3 | 878.4 | 1,041.2 |
| Greece | 412.3 | 943.2 | 1,266.1 | 117.2 | – |
| Hungary | 241.7 | 288.3 | 586.3 | 82.5 | 161.1 |
| Ireland | 862.6 | 31.7 | 372.9 | 139.7 | 137.8 |
| Italy | 2,041.3 | 1,727.1 | 5,357.6 | 548.1 | 231.0 |
| Japan | 7,247.8 | 3,496.1 | 15,401.7 | 1,260.3 | 6,389.9 |
| Luxembourg | 46.2 | 26.1 | 10.9 | 25.8 | 4.2 |
| Mexico | 1,358.6 | 866.4 | 20,306.4 | 6,123.3 | – |
| Netherlands | 1,748.0 | 914.8 | 975.9 | 310.3 | 190.4 |
| New Zealand | 536.0 | 166.8 | 424.4 | 177.8 | 50.6 |
| Norway | 836.2 | 136.5 | 343.0 | 62.4 | 55.0 |
| Poland | 593.9 | 511.9 | 1,797.3 | 304.7 | 292.4 |
| Portugal | 662.1 | 332.0 | 1,707.5 | 144.5 | 189.6 |
| Slovak Rep. | 88.8 | 123.7 | 275.0 | 41.1 | 71.7 |
| South Korea | 4,833.3 | 471.3 | 2,938.7 | 311.6 | 1,057.0 |
| Spain | 2,661.3 | 947.2 | 4,550.0 | 889.9 | 745.4 |
| Sweden | 1,205.0 | 270.7 | 513.3 | 69.8 | 112.7 |
| Switzerland | 1,054.8 | 431.5 | 386.0 | 81.3 | 396.2 |
| Turkey | 1,033.1 | 128.4 | 1,836.6 | 115.8 | 245.2 |
| U.K. | 7,135.1 | 2,681.5 | 6,124.3 | 757.5 | 1,488.1 |
| U.S. | 40,012.9 | 16,620.0 | 61,630.8 | 17,428.3 | 5,761.6 |

*Source: World Advertising Trends* (2008).

## Media Cost

Advertising rates in all markets tend to be cyclical. During periods of economic prosperity, media tend to inflate their rates. During economic downturns, when many marketers slash their advertising budgets, media rates typically drop significantly. Between 2008 and 2009, ad prices came down at

**TABLE 7.3:** Newspapers (per 1,000 people), Televisions (% of Households) and Computers (use and access per 100 people)

| COUNTRY | NEWSPAPERS | TELEVISION | COMPUTERS | COUNTRY | NEWSPAPERS | TELEVISION | COMPUTERS |
|---|---|---|---|---|---|---|---|
| Algeria | – | 91 | 1.1 | Japan | 551 | 99 | – |
| Argentina | 36 | 95 | 9.0 | Kenya | – | 32 | 1.4 |
| Australia | 155 | 99 | – | Kuwait | – | 95 | 23.7 |
| Austria | 311 | 98 | 60.7 | Lebanon | 54 | 95 | 10.4 |
| Bangladesh | – | 48 | 2.2 | Libya | – | 50 | 2.2 |
| Belgium | 165 | 99 | 41.7 | Malaysia | 109 | 95 | 23.1 |
| Bolivia | – | 63 | 2.4 | Mexico | 93 | 98 | 14.4 |
| Brazil | 36 | 91 | 16.1 | Morocco | 12 | 78 | 3.6 |
| Bulgaria | 79 | 92 | 8.9 | Netherlands | 307 | 99 | 91.2 |
| Cambodia | – | 43 | 0.4 | New Zealand | 182 | 99 | 52.6 |
| Canada | 175 | 99 | 94 | Nicaragua | – | 60 | 4.0 |
| Chile | 51 | 97 | 14.1 | Nigeria | – | 26 | 0.8 |
| China | 74 | 89 | 5.7 | Norway | 516 | 97 | 62.9 |
| Colombia | 23 | 84 | 8.0 | Pakistan | 50 | – | – |
| Costa Rica | 65 | 94 | 23.1 | Paraguay | – | 79 | 7.8 |
| Cuba | 65 | 70 | 3.6 | Peru | – | 73 | 10.3 |
| Czech Republic | 183 | 83 | 27.4 | Philippines | 79 | 63 | 7.3 |
| Denmark | 353 | 96 | 54.9 | Poland | 114 | 89 | 16.9 |
| Dominican Republic | 39 | 78 | 3.5 | Portugal | – | 99 | 17.2 |
| Ecuador | 99 | 87 | 13.0 | Puerto Rico | – | 97 | 0.8 |
| Egypt | – | 96 | 4.9 | Romania | 70 | 90 | 19.2 |
| El Salvador | 38 | 83 | 5.2 | Russia | 92 | 98 | 13.3 |
| Ethiopia | 5 | 5 | 0.7 | Saudi Arabia | – | 99 | 14.8 |
| Finland | 431 | 87 | 50.0 | Singapore | 361 | 98 | 74.3 |
| France | 164 | 97 | 65.2 | South Africa | 30 | 59 | 8.5 |
| Germany | 267 | 94 | 65.6 | Spain | 144 | 96 | 39..3 |
| Ghana | – | 26 | 0.6 | Sri Lanka | 26 | 32 | 3.7 |
| Greece | – | 100 | 9.4 | Sudan | – | 16 | 11.2 |
| Guatemala | – | 50 | 2.1 | Sweden | 481 | 94 | 88.1 |
| Honduras | – | 61 | 2.0 | Switzerland | 420 | 86 | 91.8 |
| Hong Kong | 222 | 100 | 68.6 | Syria | – | 105 | 9.0 |
| Hungary | 217 | 101 | 25.6 | Thailand | – | 92 | 7.0 |
| India | 71 | 53 | 3.3 | Tunisia | 23 | 93 | 7.5 |
| Indonesia | – | 65 | 2.0 | Turkey | – | 112 | 6.0 |
| Iran | – | – | 10.6 | Ukraine | 131 | 97 | 4.5 |
| Iraq | – | – | – | United Kingdom | 290 | 98 | 80.2 |
| Ireland | 182 | 119 | 58.2 | United States | 193 | 95 | 80.5 |
| Israel | – | 92 | – | Venezuela | 93 | 90 | 9.3 |
| Italy | 137 | 98 | 36.7 | Vietnam | – | 89 | 9.6 |
| Jamaica | – | 70 | 6.8 | Zimbabwe | – | 32 | 6.5 |

*Source:* World Bank (2009, 310–312).

many media outlets worldwide as advertisers pulled back as a result of the economic downturn. Savvy marketers take advantage of such media recessions.

In other instances, advertising rates continue to escalate. Often, it is the popularity of the vehicle or program that drives up rates. For example, in 1972, the price of a 30-second Super Bowl commercial, which reached over 56 million U.S. consumers, was $86,000. By 2010, a 30-second Super Bowl commercial cost between $2.5 and $2.8 million and reached an average of 106.5 million Americans. It is expected that for 2011, the cost will jump to between $2.8 and $3 million, as just five months into 2010, Fox had already sold as much as 80 percent of its inventory for Super Bowl 2011 (Steinberg 2010c).

## Media Quality

Even if a particular medium is available, the quality may vary from that in the home market. For example, newsprint quality is so poor in many countries—such as India—that it is nearly impossible to obtain adequate halftone reproduction. Many markets still have very limited access to color television, which may play a central role in a visually oriented campaign.

## Role of Advertising in the Mass Media

As in the United States, advertising is the principal source of revenue for mass media throughout much of the world. However, the international advertiser should be aware that in numerous markets one or more of the media may be government-owned or -controlled. For example, in many European countries, television is subsidized or owned by the government. In Germany, Italy, and Sweden, as well as a number of other countries, television owners pay annual fees to the government for television viewing, and these fees subsidize programming. With regard to the print media, in many countries readers pay a significantly greater percentage of the cost of subscription rates than do consumers in the United States. As a result, these media are much less dependent on advertising revenues in those countries. In some instances they may choose not to accept commercial messages or to severely restrict the time and space allotted to advertising.

Throughout the world, however, the overall trend is toward privatization and commercialization of both the broadcast and print media. In 1997, Hungary fulfilled its much-delayed plans for media privatization. Hungary was one of the last countries in the former Eastern bloc to liberalize broadcast media, in large part due to fears that the country would be swamped with foreign programming at the expense of local traditions and the Hungarian language. A law was passed to prevent this by requiring 51 percent of programs to be made in Hungary, with a further 30 percent to come from other parts of Europe. Ownership of both radio and television stations must be at least 26 percent Hungarian. In 2001, the Nigerian Bureau of Public Enterprises (BPE) reiterated its commitment to carry out the privatization and commercialization of government media outfits. The government media to be privatized include Nigerian Television Authority (NTA), News Agency of Nigeria (NAN), Federal Radio Corporation of Nigeria (FRCN), and the *New Nigerian* and *Daily Times* newspapers. Privatization Act No. 28 states that NTA, FRCN, and NAN are to be commercialized, while the *New Nigerian* and *Daily Times* are to be privatized outright. Since Nigeria's former President Olusegun Obasanjo took office in 1999, privatization has been regarded as the administration's core policy.

## Media Spillover

There are two kinds of media spillover—incidental and deliberate. *Incidental spillover* refers to those cases in which a local television channel, for example, may be viewed by individuals in other countries as well. Canada provides a prime example of such spillover. Three-quarters of Canadians are clustered within 100 miles of the U.S. border, and more than 95 percent are within 200 miles. Thus, nearly all Canadians are within the broadcast range of U.S. radio and television stations. Similarly, the Netherlands receives broadcasts from Germany, Belgium, and other countries.

*Deliberate spillover* refers to media created with the specific objective of crossing national borders. An example of deliberate spillover is Rupert Murdoch's British Sky Broadcasting, originally a British satellite service, which has taken its Sky News channel to nearly every continent. A country's broadcasts may spill over into another nation via cable, terrestrial stations, or satellite dishes. However, spillover is not limited to the broadcast media. For example, some German publishers promote significant circulation of their magazines and newspapers in Austria and Switzerland because German is also spoken in those markets.

Certain problems are associated with media spillover as well. If a marketer is running both international and local campaigns for the same product, media spillover can expose consumers to multiple campaigns, resulting in confusion about product positioning, pricing, and promotions. Media spillover may disregard differences in regulations and restrictions. For instance, India's state-run Doordarshan Television bans the advertising of a number of product categories, including liquor, baby food, and foreign banks. However, Hong Kong–based Star TV, the pan-Asian network (owned by Rupert Murdoch), reaches millions of households in India and accepts ads for the products banned on Doordarshan TV.

## Local Broadcast Media

*Television:* The medium most commonly employed in attempting to reach broad national markets in both developed and many developing countries is television. Television reaches over 90 percent of people in developed countries and even over 80 percent in many developing countries, including China (Balnaves et al. 2001, 46). Household penetration of television is 100 percent in Hungary, Japan, and Singapore, and over 95 percent in Australia, Austria, France, Hong Kong, Italy, New Zealand, Spain, Sweden, Turkey, the United Kingdom, and the United States. However, all consumers do not watch television in the same fashion. In the more industrialized countries, many children and teens have television sets in their own rooms, and each member of the family watches programming individually. In the United States, television sets are found in the bedrooms of 24 percent of those under the age of 6. Among children 6 to 11, that proportion was 41 percent, and for those ages 8 to 18, a full 68 percent viewed televison in their bedrooms without adult supervision (Rideout et al. 2005). In contrast, those with access to television in rural Africa and Asia often watch television in a public venue or as part of a large family or group.

Television is one of the most highly regulated communications media. Even in developed markets, the availability of television advertising time may be quite limited or even nonexistent. This is often true in cases where television is government owned and controlled. What can be advertised, and how, is also restricted in most every country. Much as in the United States, many countries prohibit the advertising of cigarettes and alcohol other than beer, while other countries also forbid advertising by financial institutions and baby food producers. Regulation of this medium will be discussed in greater detail in Chapter 9.

## Radio

Generally perceived as a secondary medium in the United States, in many countries radio plays a much more dominant role. Radio as an advertising medium enjoys relative popularity in countries such as Colombia, Mexico, the Philippines, and South Africa. A major plus associated with the medium is its ability to reach illiterate customers; moreover, in many countries it is the only medium capable of delivering to large segments of the population. Radio is also popular because sets are affordable, even among the poor. As Onkvisit and Shaw note, it is a virtually free medium for listeners, and the cost of operating and maintaining a set are negligible (Onkvisit and Shaw 1997, 572). However, the medium's popularity is not limited to developing countries. A study examining media use in five European countries revealed that the greatest percentage of Europeans listened to radio on the previous day and also spent the most minutes per day listening to radio. In the United States, radio has become a very specialized medium, with stations adopting a particular format: contemporary hit radio, rock, easy listening, news/talk, classical, religious, and so on. In many other markets, stations vary their programming throughout the day, and audience demographics vary accordingly. In addition, radio networks are much less common in developing markets.

## Local Print Media

The role that print media will play in the media advertising plan is generally correlated directly with the literacy level of the target audience in each country. The more highly developed the nation, the more heavily newspapers and magazines will be used by consumers in those countries. Overall, the print media tend to receive the lion's share of advertising dollars in almost every country in the world. However, the extent of market saturation that can be obtained via newspapers or magazines will vary from one country to the next.

*Newspapers:* In some countries, such as Britain, Japan, and the United States, one or more newspapers can be said to have a truly national circulation. It wasn't until 1983 that the first general-readership national newspaper began being circulated in the United States. *USA Today* has a circulation of over 1.8 million in the United States (the international edition reaches more than 2.8 million readers annually and is available in more than 60 countries). *Wall Street Journal* and *New York Times* are two additional examples of successful nationally distributed newspapers in the United States; however, both are read by a predominantly business-oriented audience. For instance, an advertisement promoting *Wall Street Journal*'s 2.02 million U.S. readers to media planners notes that the publication "outperforms all competitors (combined print and online) in reaching top management" (see Figure 7.1).

International advertisers must be aware of national newspapers that may be available as an advertising medium in each market. Table 7.4 lists the top 25 newspapers by circulation in 2008. Japan, for example, has 11 national newspapers on the list, the largest of which reaches over 14 million readers.

A Dutch firm, PEPC Worldwide, is making it easier than ever for readers to obtain whichever newspaper they desire, no matter where they happen to be. PEPC's digital kiosks have popped up in more than 100 airports, business centers, and hotel lobbies around the world. The kiosks can deliver the latest editions of more than 100 hometown papers. For about $5 a copy, customers can select a paper and, within two minutes, lift out a black-and-white edition complete with photos and advertisements. Newspapers from the *Los Angeles Times* to Reykjavik's *Morgunbladid* have signed up to participate in the service. The papers transmit their latest editions as Adobe PDF files to PEPC, which sends them by satellite to each kiosk (Passariello 2002).

**Figure 7.1:** Advertisement promoting *Wall Street Journal* to media planners.

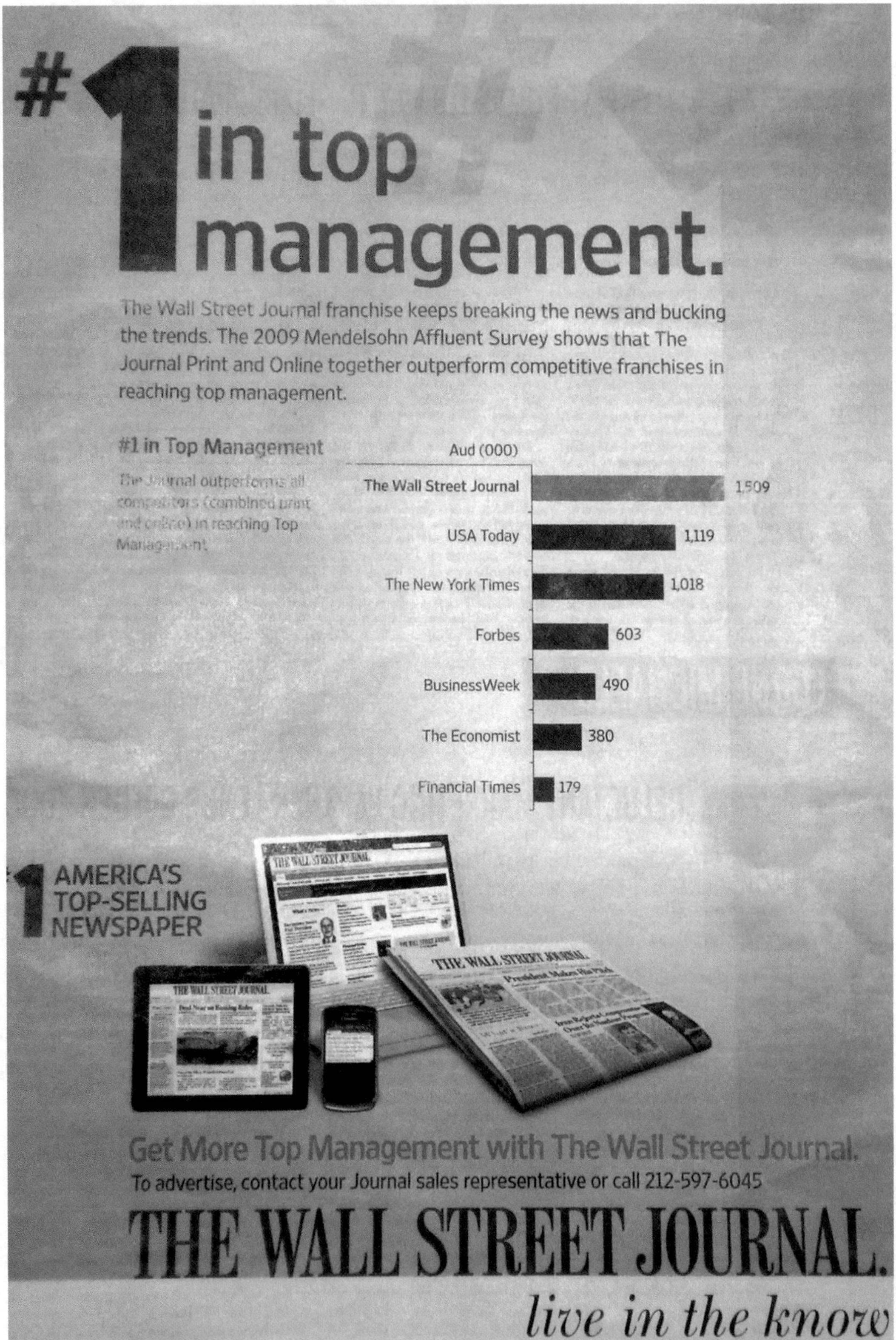

**TABLE 7.4:** Top 25 Global Newspapers by Circulation (in thousands)

| RANK | PUBLICATION | COUNTRY | CIRCULATION (IN THOUSANDS) |
|------|-------------|---------|----------------------------|
| 1. | Yomiuri Shimbun | Japan | 14,067 |
| 2. | Asahi Shimbun | Japan | 12,121 |
| 3. | Mainichi Shimbun | Japan | 5,587 |
| 4. | Nihon Keizai Shimbun | Japan | 4,635 |
| 5. | Chunichi Shimbun | Japan | 4,512 |
| 6. | Bild | Germany | 3,548 |
| 7. | Reference News | China | 3,183 |
| 8. | The Times of India | India | 3,146 |
| 9. | The Sun | England | 2,986 |
| 10. | People's Daily | China | 2,808 |
| 11. | Daily Mail | United Kingdom | 2,311 |
| 12. | The Chosun Ilbo | South Korea | 2,300 |
| 13. | USA Today | United States | 2,293 |
| 14. | Tokyo Sports | Japan | 2,230 |
| 15. | Sankei Shimbun | Japan | 2,204 |
| 16. | JoongAng Ilbo | South Korea | 2,200 |
| 17. | Dainik Jagran | India | 2,168 |
| 18. | Dong-a Ilbo | South Korea | 2,100 |
| 19. | The Wall Street Journal | United States | 2,012 |
| 20. | Nikkan Sports | Japan | 1,868 |
| 21. | Yangtse Evening Post | China | 1,810 |
| 22. | Sports Nippon | Japan | 1,800 |
| 23. | Shimbun Akahata | Japan | 1,680 |
| 24. | Guangzhou Daily | China | 1,680 |
| 25. | Yukan Fuji | Japan | 1,514 |

*Source:* World Press Trends (2008).

In many countries, newspapers tend to be predominantly local or regional rather than national and, as such, serve as the primary medium for local advertisers. Attempting to use a series of local papers to reach a national market is considerably more complex and costly. Unlike in the United States, in many nations there is heavy competition among local newspapers, which tends to benefit advertisers by holding advertising costs down. Indeed, in some markets, up to 200 daily papers may vie for the reader's attention, as is the case in Lebanon. Advertisers must examine several issues when considering the use of local papers. For instance, some publications are sponsored by a particular political party, and the international advertiser must exercise caution in placing advertisements in particularly controversial papers. Content—both editorial and commercial—may very well be limited to what the party in power deems appropriate. Also, many foreign papers have a fixed and much smaller number of pages than typical U.S. papers, thus limiting advertising space. Many foreign national papers run no more than 16–20 pages, often because equipment or paper is limited. Finally, the quality of newspapers may not be consistent from one country to the next. Therefore, for each market, the international advertiser must investigate whether the publication offers high-quality, four-color production or low-quality, black-and-white.

In the United States most newspapers clearly distinguish between editorial and advertising content. Such is not the case in many other countries, where editorial space is regularly sold for advertising purposes, occasionally making it difficult for readers to distinguish between the two. Advertisements even crop up on the front page of many newspapers around the world. For example, in Mexico, advertising space is sold in the form of news columns—without any indication to readers that the "story" is, in fact, a paid advertisement. Indeed, if a marketer pays for a full-page message in this market, he is likely to find his product advertised on the publication's front page.

*Magazines:* In general, magazines have nowhere near the broad readership of newspapers, although readership levels are considerably higher in many foreign markets than in the United States. Rarely, however, can a single magazine reach a majority of a market. In most countries magazines serve to reach specific segments of the population dependent on their subject matter or area of emphasis. It is this selectivity—or ability to reach narrowly targeted audiences—that is one of the main benefits of this medium in many advertisers' eyes. For example, for fashion and beauty tips, young women in Germany read *Freundin*, in France they read *Marie Claire*, and in the United States they read *Glamour*. International marketers should also note that there is a great deal of variation in terms of the number of magazines available from one market to the next.

## Other Local Media

*Billboards:* Billboards are an important medium in many markets, both developed and developing. In crowded metropolitan areas, literally millions of consumers may be exposed to a single billboard message, and in countries with high levels of automobile ownership, billboards located along highways also prove an effective medium. Outdoor billboards in the Netherlands are even using interactive techniques to attract attention in a crowded media environment. As Derek Suchard reports, an increasing number of outdoor billboards in this country are

> taking on elements not usually associated with the medium, including live models sitting in board-mounted displays and the use of boards to offer free samples. In one example, Westimex, a Belgian potato chip marketer, attached bags of Croky chips on 100 boards along streets across the country, inviting sampling with the headline "Bet these are the best-tasting chips in Holland." Passersby accepted the offer, pulling down individual sized bags that were within reach. (Suchard 1993).

Apparently, both consumers and the trade responded positively to the approach.

Alaris, a Norwegian outdoor advertising company, introduced a roadside marketing concept in the United States that captures data from motorists' radio-listening habits to adjust ads or electronic billboards along the highway. Highway electronic billboards (HEBs) are equipped to profile commuters as they whiz by in their cars, using data captured from the radio-listening habits of drivers to instantly personalize freeway messages. For example, if the highway has a large number of drivers listening to country music channels, the billboard would screen ads for casinos. On the other hand, if a large number of drivers using the highway at a particular time of day are tuned to National Public Radio, the billboards would change to ads for a luxury automobile or a gourmet grocery retailer. The

Alaris billboards use a consumer monitoring system to pick up radio waves, which are "leaked" from the antennas of passing cars while pinpointing the stations being played. The system assesses the most popular radio station during a given hour and targets ads to those drivers (O'Dwyer 2003).

In developing markets, where high levels of illiteracy are common, billboards, with their heavy emphasis on visuals and limited use of advertising copy, are a dominant medium. The primary disadvantage related to the use of the billboard medium encountered by international advertisers lies in the different standard sizes offered in different markets. It should be noted that while outdoor advertising is a tightly regulated medium in some markets—such as the United States—in other markets "outdoor" advertising consists of advertisers simply placing posters on any available wall, bus stop, or fence, without cost. The practice encourages one advertiser to replace another advertiser's posters with its own (Onkvisit and Shaw 1997, 580).

*Transit:* Transit advertising is playing an increasingly significant role in many markets. For example, transit advertising is the most effective advertising medium in Romania, according to a survey conducted by the Economic University in Bucharest. Of all consumers surveyed, 91 percent said they remembered the content of transit ads, compared with 82 percent who remembered the content of television ads and only 44 percent who remembered the content of print ads. Transit ad space there is available on 200 buses, and advertisers have included R. J. Reynolds, Colgate-Palmolive, PepsiCo, Rank Xerox, and Philip Morris. Transit advertising may well rank higher than television because of the few television stations in Romania. In addition, magazines and newspapers are not nearly as sophisticated as Western publications and therefore are less attractive to advertisers (Kelly 1992).

The use of transit media is expanding rapidly in China as well. A small firm in Singapore acquired the worldwide rights to sell space on buses, trains, ferries, and airports throughout the vast territory of China. Until rather recently, little transit advertising has been sold in this market. However, observes Ian Stewart, the potential for the development of this medium is enormous: "More than half a million people are carried up and down Changan Avenue in central Beijing every day and in Shanghai more than 160 ferries operate daily" (Stewart 1993). Moscow provides an example of an innovative use of transit media. Mandara—a Swedish firm—signed an agreement with the Moscow Post Office for exclusive 20-year rights to broker advertising on the sides of Moscow's 800 postal vehicles and on the walls of the city's 660 post offices. Under the agreement the Swedish firm also used postal vehicles for client deliveries and outfitted 10,000 Moscow postal carriers in uniforms highlighting a client's logo. The first marketer signed by the company was a Stockholm-based brewery, which bought rights to advertise on 100 postal trucks and one post office wall. Mandara also targeted companies such as Japanese electronics manufacturers and European food companies (Bartal 1993).

*Cinema:* Cinema advertising is commonly overlooked by U.S. marketers because the medium is—comparatively—in its infancy in this country. In many countries, however, where it is common to subsidize the cost of showing movies by running advertising messages, cinema advertising has become an important medium. A common practice is to begin the program by showing slides of advertised products, followed by commercials. Newsreels and documentaries might also be shown. Then, prior to the feature, filmgoers might be exposed to a promotion for coming attractions. For example, India has the highest film audience and the highest level of per capita movie attendance of any country in the world, and as a result, cinema ads play a much greater role in India than in the United States. Indeed, this medium offers access to market segments that would be impossible to reach through any other medium.

*Direct Marketing:* Direct marketing is a way of doing business that employs a wide spectrum of media, including direct mail, telephone, broadcast, and print media. The use of direct mail, the most popular form of direct marketing, varies significantly around the world, and depends on the level of acceptance of this approach, literacy rates, and a number of additional variables. In some countries, for example, sending consumers a direct mail piece is considered an invasion of privacy. Clearly, direct mail would not be an appropriate medium in markets with high illiteracy rates. Direct mail campaigns are also difficult to implement due to dramatic variations in postal rates and service. In Chile, for example, letter carriers collect additional postage from recipients for every item delivered because senders pay only part of the postage. Clearly, the use of the direct mail medium is quite limited in this country—customers generally do not take kindly to paying for unsolicited advertisements. In addition, various national regulations impact the viability of this medium for many international marketers. For instance, in Germany, if an addressee has a label on their mailbox refusing direct mail, mail carriers are prohibited by law from delivering such advertisements. Finally, the necessary infrastructure may not be available to an international marketer. In the United States, marketers have access to a wide selection of mailing lists, which allow them to target their audience. In comparison, list generation and management are still relatively primitive abroad, both in developed and developing markets.

*Mobile Phones:* According to recent statistics, by the end of 2010 there will be 4.6 billion mobile phones in use (Communities Dominate Brands 2010). Table 7.5 presents a ranking of the top 40 countries in terms of number of mobile phones per 100 people. As the table reveals, mobile phone ownership is becoming increasingly common in both developed and developing markets —with countries such as Japan and Mexico both making the list (Srinivasan 2010). In 2000, mobile telephone service was available primarily in developed economies. By 2008, more than two-thirds of mobile phone users lived in the developing world. Eastern Europe and Latin America have reached mobile phone penetration levels similar to that of Western Europe and North America, while Asia Pacific, the Middle East, and Africa still have large potential for expansion (Banjanovic 2009). The global spread of mobile phones has been spectacular. No other technology has narrowed the gap between the developed and developing world so rapidly.

It is estimated that the world passed 5 billion mobile subscribers in November 2010 and that the year ended with 5.1 billion total subscribers. Another truly astonishing statistic is that this reflects 75 percent of the population on the planet. But do keep in mind that as the world approaches 100 percent penetration, in the emerging world, a large part of the population is children—not mobile phone customers. Further, many consumers in developing countries still cannot afford a mobile phone, as the costs are high relative to their income. In 2008, mobile phone costs equalled 20.3 percent of per capita GNI in Cameroon and 36.8 percent in Uganda, compared with 1.8 percent of GNI per capita in China, according to the International Telecommunications Union (ITU) (Banjanovic 2009). Clearly, a 100 percent penetration rate means that many people have two accounts and, increasingly, two mobile phones. For purposes of comparison, the world has 1.1 billion fixed landline phones, but these are heavily concentrated in developed markets. In much of the developing world, fixed telephone infrastructure is poor. In 2008, India had only 3.3 fixed telephone lines per 100 people, and Nigeria had just 0.9 lines per 100 inhabitants. Fixed telephone infrastructure is costly to set up, while wireless technology is cheaper to deploy—hence the explosion of mobile phones in developing markets. In the developed world, fixed telephony is in decline as consumers adopt mobile phones as their main communication medium. Between 2003 and 2008, the number of fixed telephone lines has declined by 17.7 percent in the United States and 5.7 percent in Western Europe (Banjanovic 2009).

**Table 7.5:** Ranking of Top 40 Countries in Terms of Mobile Phones per 100 People

| RANK | COUNTRY | # OF PHONES PER 100 PEOPLE | RANK | COUNTRY | # OF PHONES PER 100 PEOPLE |
|---|---|---|---|---|---|
| 1. | Taiwan | 106.45 | 21. | Germany | 71.67 |
| 2. | Luxembourg | 101.34 | 22. | S. Korea | 67.95 |
| 3. | Hong Kong | 92.98 | 23. | France | 64.7 |
| 4. | Italy | 92.65 | 24. | Hungary | 64.64 |
| 5. | Iceland | 90.28 | 25. | Australia | 63.97 |
| 6. | Sweden | 88.5 | 26. | Japan | 62.1 |
| 7. | Czech Rep. | 84.88 | 27. | New Zealand | 61.84 |
| 8. | Finland | 84.5 | 28. | Slovakia | 54.36 |
| 9. | U.K. | 84.89 | 29. | USA | 48.81 |
| 10. | Norway | 84.33 | 30. | Brunei | 40.06 |
| 11. | Greece | 83.86 | 31. | Canada | 37.72 |
| 12. | Denmark | 83.33 | 32. | Poland | 36.26 |
| 13. | Austria | 82.85 | 33. | Malaysia | 34.88 |
| 14. | Spain | 82.28 | 34. | Turkey | 34.75 |
| 15. | Portugal | 81.94 | 35. | Thailand | 26.04 |
| 16. | Singapore | 79.14 | 36. | Mexico | 25.45 |
| 17. | Switzerland | 78.75 | 37. | Philippines | 17.77 |
| 18. | Belgium | 78.63 | 38. | China | 16.09 |
| 19. | Ireland | 75.53 | 39. | Indonesia | 5.52 |
| 20. | Netherlands | 72.24 | 40. | Vietnam | 2.34 |

*Source:* Srinivasan (2010).

*Note:* The above does not exactly translate into mobile phone users, since in many families in developing markets, one mobile phone can be used by more than one person.

Short messaging services (or SMS) allow mobile phone users to transmit text messages quickly and cheaply. Cell phone subscribers sent about 4.5 trillion text messages globally in 2009, and that number is expected to jump to 5.5 trillion by the end of 2010. Person-to-person texting accounted for most of the traffic, particularly among youth, but marketing applications are becoming more common. SMS is especially popular in Asia, where mobile phone penetration outstrips that of fixed lines and even personal computers in some areas. In China, for instance, McCann-Erickson Worldwide, part of Interpublic, partnered with Siemens to create an SMS contest for Coca-Cola. Cell phone users were invited to guess the next day's temperature in Beijing, a correct guess could win a Siemens phone or a one-year supply of Coke. Contestants who didn't win were invited to download Coke's jingle as a free ring-tone. The result: 4 million messages were exchanged during the 40-day promotion, and nearly 50,000 people downloaded the Coke jingle. Coca-Cola has already decided to repeat the contest. Most advertising agencies have set up interactive divisions to handle SMS campaigns, including Ogilvy & Mather (Madden 2002).

Today, beyond mobile messaging, mobile advertising campaigns can include mobile Web sites, mobile applications, and mobile video. Browsing the mobile Web is similar to traditional PC-based Web browsing and provides users with access to news, sports, weather, entertainment—and shopping sites. Mobile applications are software that consumers download to, or find pre-installed on their mobile phone, and the applications then reside on the phone. Mobile video includes both video and television delivered over a mobile network to the mobile phone's media player. Videos may be downloaded or streamed and are usually accessed from a mobile Web site or contained in an MMS message. Mobile video is accessible to consumers with Mobile Web- and mobile video-enabled phones and data plans. Mobile television is accessible through mobile television-enabled phones. Each of these can be employed by advertisers. One example here is a campaign for Kraft Foods employing an iPhone application. Enough Kraft food devotees are actually paying to be marketed to on their iPhones that the company iFood Assistant is now one of the device's 100 most popular paid apps, and number two in the lifestyle category. Consumers pay a one-time, 99-cent fee for the app and are apparently willing to sit through ads on it. Kraft's app, which it launched in late 2008, is a helpful tool for consumers looking to make dinners faster, easier, and more convenient. iFood Assistant's rich interface works well with the handset, and its navigation is similar to that of the iPod. The app offers a host of recipes, browsable by ingredients, meal type, or prep time. Consumers can register at KraftFoods.com to save recipes and build shopping lists. Recipes come with simple instructions, and daily featured recipes try to tempt the uninspired. Of course, the dishes incorporate Kraft products. There are also a number of instructional videos, with guides to portion sizes and knife skills, as well as step-by-step directions for making dishes. Kraft also runs ads throughout the app, some before the instructional videos and some with searches. The moral: when marketers create something that's actually useful, consumers don't really see it as straight marketing, or at least they're willing to accept advertising as the payoff (York 2009).

Mobile advertising can also be combined with other media. For instance, the push to make magazine pages more interactive is building momentum as major publishers and advertisers adopt technologies centered on mobile phones. Hearst Magazines began an experiment in 2008 incorporating a text-messaging system called ShopText into the pages of *CosmoGirl*. Readers have the opportunity in both editorial promotions and in ads to make purchases, request samples, or enter sweepstakes, just by sending brief text messages. Hearst has adopted the technology across its portfolio, which includes publications from *Esquire* to *Good Housekeeping*. Magazines including Rodale's *Men's Health* and Wenner Media's *Rolling Stone* are pushing ahead with a potential rival system called SnapTell, which allows readers to take camper-phone photos of ads, send in the shots, and receive whatever message a marketer has arranged. If readers continue to respond positively, digital technology may be poised to support traditional ad sales more directly than ever (Ives 2008). The number of people worldwide who received at least one advertisement on their phones passed 2 billion in 2010. But mobile advertising is still a tiny part of all digital advertising, and digital advertising is a small part of all advertising, so while the reach of mobile is the widest on the planet by far, in terms of total ads served and total revenues, mobile advertising is still a baby industry learning to walk (Communities Dominate Brands 2010).

*Unique Media: Low Tech:* In developing countries, which tend to lack the media resources of advanced nations, marketers often adopt unusual promotional strategies. For example, Group Africa, a firm based in Johannesburg, developed Roots Television (RTV), an innovative means for reaching South Africa's rural population. Through a network of 550 television sets and VCRs in country stores, ladies clubs, and traveling shows mixing advertising and entertainment, RTV claims it reaches 3.2 million rural Africans each month—consumers who could not easily be reached via more traditional media. Every four to six weeks, RTV representatives visit rural stores and deliver videotapes featuring six hours of entertainment along with 18 minutes of commercials per hour. The entertainment is tailored to the local village—RTV representatives tape weddings, initiations, coming-of-age ceremonies, gospel music, and sporting events. The raw footage is edited, and commercials are inserted in RTV's Durban studios. On the next trip through the village, a premiere of the local tape is held, which remains with the storeowners. The ladies clubs are included to help draw customers to participate in a day of fun and games, songs and contests, and free samples once every three months. Up to several thousand villagers come from far and wide for an opportunity to see themselves on screen. Group Africa's clients include Lipton, Colgate-Palmolive's Stay Soft fabric softener, Nestlé's Nespray baby-milk formula and Gold Cross condensed milk, and Unilever's Van Den Bergh Foods' Rama margarine. Shop owners pay RTV $42 a month for television and VCR rentals (Barnes 1993).

The best way to see Cairo, according to many, has always been from a felucca—the ancient sailboats that travel up and down the Nile. These days, it is also the best way to see the latest multinational doing business in Egypt. The potential of a market 61 million strong, combined with recent government reforms designed to spur the economy, is drawing in major corporations looking for ways to grab the attention of Egyptians. "In Egypt, there's no better place," says Douglas A. Jackson, senior regional manager in Egypt for Coca-Cola Co., the firm that started the felucca-advertising craze. "Except maybe if we put a neon Coke sign on top of the pyramids." At Cairo's advertising agencies, feluccas are considered hot. Feluccas, which had been used to transport goods since the time of the pharaohs, work because they blend a local custom with a great location. Most Egyptians live along the Nile and often rent a felucca for an evening's entertainment. Some feluccas are built to hold 50 people and, with their triangular-shaped white sails, are also a main draw for tourists. Coke signed a two-year contract with Cairo's most popular felucca operator for around $8,000, plus new sails. Nestlé has also used the sails to promote its Perrier brand. Not everyone is fond of using feluccas to advertise. Some Egyptians criticize the commercialization of the Nile. Others say there is no limit to the craze. Indeed, there is also talk of sponsoring camel races (Dockser Marcus 1997).

Unique low-tech media are not limited to developing countries. Two recent examples illustrate this point. Nytmedie, a Danish media marketing agency, introduced the "Push Pram" outdoor marketing concept. Push Pram is based on a simple idea—provide Danish parents of newborn babies with a new baby carriage if parents agree to accept the buggy complete with a corporate sponsor's logo or brand ad. Swedish fashion retailer Hanes & Mauritz and Scandinavian finance group Nordea Bank are among the first multinational brands to have signed on to this new marketing concept. Nytmedie's goal is to sign up the parents of 10 percent of all babies born in Denmark. A company spokesperson states that ads placed on prams are no less appropriate than on the sides of taxis or athletes' shirts. Under the marketing scheme, parents who enter a contractual agreement with Nytmedie can choose the model of the pram they would like on the company's Web site. The prams may then be used for up to 2.5 years. The company already has a lengthy waiting list for "branded baby buggies" and plans to expand the concept to the rest of Europe and the United States (O'Dwyer 2002). The Netherlands boasts a truly unusual low-tech medium—sheep. In 2006, Hotels.nl, a Dutch online reservations company, began displaying its corporate logo on royal blue waterproof blankets worn by sheep (see Figure 7.2). The company spent 1 euro (about $1.20) per day, per sheep, and sponsored about 144 sheep in flocks throughout the Netherlands. But the commercially branded sheep roaming the meadows of northern Netherlands prompted a negative reaction. The town of Skarsterlan began fining Hotels.nl 1,000 euros

**Figure 7.2:** Hotels.nl counts on sheep to sell hotel rooms.

a day for putting the branded blankets on sheep. Advertising on livestock violates the town's ban on advertising along highways. Hotels.nl paid the fines but planned to fight the ban in court. Since the start of the campaign, sales by Hotels.nl grew 15 percent, and visits to the company's Web site were up significantly. The company increased the number of sheep sporting its logo and focused on locations where there were frequent traffic jams. Hotels.nl did not originate the idea of sheep as billboards, but it was the first company to use the technique in the Netherlands. A Dutch horse breeder dreamed up the concept, and Easy Green Promotions, based in Leiden, created what it called "lease a Sheep Shirt-Sponsoring." Easy Green designs and owns the blankets, which include Velcro strips that allow the logos to be changed. The company plans to expand by offering blankets for horses and cows and is negotiating with neighbors in France and Britain (Carvajal 2006).

*Unique Media: High Tech:* Japanese advertisers are finding dramatic spaces and new techniques for ads, including talking retail shelves, giant outdoor video screens, and train tunnels. Shelf TV, originating from Japan, utilizes a small television monitor affixed to a shelf providing shoppers with additional product information that normally could not be introduced in conventional television ads. The sets are strategically placed in store areas where the particular product being promoted is located. While clients can choose to feed their regular commercials into the sets, specially produced infomercials tend to have a greater impact on brand identity. With this new tool, stores can literally become mini-classrooms, where shoppers can instantly learn more details and hands-on tips regarding the advertised product. The sets are equipped with sensors that shut off the infomercials when there is no shopper nearby. Once the scanner detects movement, the set switches on automatically and attracts the attention of the respective shopper. Shelf TV has also been introduced to Thailand, Hong Kong, Singapore, and Malaysia.

Units of major Japanese agency giants such as Dentsu are at the forefront in developing new media forms. David Kilburn and Julie Skur-Hill report: "Dentsu PROX, for instance, developed a commercial purpose for the sky. With Search Vision, images can be freely suspended by using projectors and aircraft or balloons as screens." Dentsu PROX also developed Tunnel-Vision, using train tunnels as an ad medium. A series of images behind boards placed at 10-meter intervals are lit when the train passes, creating images like those made by flip cards. Tunnel-Vision is increasingly common in metro areas around the globe.

Interactive kiosks and interactive television are examples of two unusual, high-tech media forms. *Paris Vogue* and French department store Le Printemps sponsored the world's first multimedia interactive kiosk called Sensaura that helps customers select perfumes. Sixteen fragrances from such companies as Chanel and Estée Lauder participated in the promotion, which ran for two weeks in Le Printemps. The kiosk uses a touch screen to guide customers through a series of questions about what they like to do or wear. After answering the questions, customers receive a short analysis of their personality and the names of two perfumes that might suit them. The customer can then go to the fragrance counter and request a sample of one of the perfumes. Consumers responded favorably to the promotion, waiting in line up to 30 minutes to use Sensaura. In addition, the promotion was a traffic builder for Le Printemps and netted extra ad pages for *Vogue*. The system has been marketed to cosmetics, apparel, and computer companies.

After years of false starts, interactive television advertising finally became a reality in the fall of 2009, when Cablevision became the first cable operator to offer the technology across its full footprint of 3.1 million subscribers in New York, Connecticut, and New Jersey. The interactive advertising product, Optimum Select, attracted launch advertisers including Gillette, Benjamin Moore paints, realty firm Century 21, Unilever, and Colgate-Palmolive Co. Each marketer signed up for two-week flights in which viewers could click on their remote controls to receive more information, product samples, or gift certificates from the advertisers. But the ads weren't customized or addressed to certain viewer demographics or household incomes, so the only targeting had to come from strategic buys on certain cable networks. But consumer responses were nonetheless positive. Responses were so strong that the campaigns had to be taken off the air after an average of half their scheduled runs after advertisers were caught low on promotional inventory, according to Cablevision marketers. For Benjamin Moore paints, the Cablevision campaign yielded more than 25,000 requests for product samples. Colgate-Palmolive saw similar results from the test, converting 70 percent of the consumers who requested more information into actual recipients of the product giveaway. Optimum Select campaigns, on average, got 40 percent of the people who pressed buttons on their remotes to complete requests for information or other actions. The campaign's results suggest that television can deliver interactive opportunities and that consumers are willing to use their televisions like computers. Indeed, hundreds of Optimum Select campaigns are in the works for 2010 and beyond (Hampp 2010).

Addressable television spots are nearer than ever to becoming a reality. Marketers have long dreamed of a day when they can stop broadcasting ads to the world at large and instead send television commercials for Pampers just to new moms, and Chevrolet ads only to those in the market for a new car. Though so-called addressable advertising has been proclaimed for years as their holy grail, advertisers have continued to face a host of technology issues and resistance against moving away from older ways of doing business. Now, however, as more digital media are able to run video, there is greater impetus for the television industry to push the process. By providing a method to beam ads to smaller groups of consumers who are more interested in the product or service being promoted, television networks and cable operators hope to bring back dollars to the medium that have begun drifting away from it (Steinberg 2010a). But hurdles remain. Advertisers are wary of making consumers feel they are giving up private data about themselves. Further, current technology uses data from set-top boxes and demographic information to ensure that the right ads get to the correct household. Creating a uniform process that allows the ads to be distributed nationally remains a work in progress, owing to the fact that the cable, satellite, and telecommunications concerns whose content-distribution pipes make the technology function often have very different ways of operating. However, Invidi Technologies Corp. says it has been awarded a number of patents that give it the ability to license to others the technology that delivers specific ads to particular households or viewers, and also ascertains the response of the viewers who see them (Steinberg 2010b). Invidi announced that it has secured over $23 million in financing, led by Google, with GroupM (the worlds largest media investment company and a unit of holding company WPP), Motorola Ventures (a leading set-top box manufacturer), and leading venture capital firms Menlo Ventures, InterWest, and EnerTech as participants. "Google and GroupM share our vision that addressability will transform television advertising by increasing effectiveness and eliminating wasted reach," says Invidi CEO David Downey. "They want to play an active role in shaping this revolution. This financing will accelerate our current efforts to deliver the functionality advertisers crave and the ability for operators and networks to increase the value of their advertising inventory" (*BusinessWire* 2010). Indeed, results of some recent tests are encouraging. Homes that received addressable ads tuned out 32 percent less often than homes that saw a normal group of commercials. Data suggest that sending ads only to relevant groups of consumers is 65 percent more efficient in terms of eliminating undesirable audiences than sending ads en masse (Steinberg 2010a). Notes Bruce Anderson, chief technology officer at Invidi, "Our technology is not limited to just cable television. The patent is broad enough to encompass video on cell phones, to regular television viewing, to viewing on your computer. No matter how video is viewed in the future, this intellectual property will come into play" (Steinberg 2010b).

## INTERNATIONAL MEDIA

While television, through satellites and cable, can send royal weddings, Olympic games, and space shots into the homes of consumers in literally hundreds of countries, no single network controls this global transmission. However, international media that provide nearly global market coverage offer a means for international advertisers to reach consumers across many markets. The number of international media and the expenditures on them are rising rapidly.

### International Print Media

*International Magazines:* Print remains the dominant international medium, and magazines rank at the top. A number of U.S.-based magazines have international editions, including *Reader's Digest*, *National Geographic, Time, Newsweek,* and *Cosmopolitan,* among others. *Reader's Digest,* which produced its first non-U.S. edition in 1938 for the U.K. market, is now the world's most widely read magazine, with 50 editions available in over 170 countries. *National Geographic* has a worldwide circulation of 7.8 million—and a U.S. circulation of just over 6 million. *Time* magazine—with a circulation of over 5

**Figure 7.3:** Advertisement promoting the Turkish edition of *Marie Claire* magazine.

million—offers advertisers 133 different editions, enabling precise targeting of audiences around the globe. *Newsweek* publishes editions in Japanese, Korean, Polish, Russian, Spanish, Rioplatense Spanish, Arabic, and Turkish. *Newsweek* also publishes *Newsweek International* in three English-language editions—Atlantic, Asia, and Latin America—and is part of *The Bulletin* with *Newsweek* in Australia. The magazine appears in more than 190 countries around the world. *Cosmopolitan* has 36 international editions. When the magazine first launched Russian *Cosmo* in 1994, it sold a mere 60,000 copies each month. Today, the magazine sells about 480,000 copies monthly—more than in any country outside the United States. In 1998 *Cosmopolitan* arrived in the Philippines, Indonesia, Hungary, Lithuania, and mainland China, where there are approximately 300 million women between the ages of 18 and 30. Estimates are that *Cosmo* will top out at 50 foreign editions. With a circulation of about 2.7 million in the United States and another 4.5 million abroad, *Cosmo* is already the best-selling women's magazine in the world. Thanks in part to the ads, *Cosmo* looks virtually the same in every market. All editions share the same style, format, and supermodel cover girls—as well as staple articles on career advancement, dieting, and dating. But most foreign editions employ local editors and staff, who tailor each issue to their particular market. Chinese editor Gao Xiaohong, for instance, shuns all stories about sex—because Chinese people are modest and women aren't yet at a point where they can talk about sex (Greenberg 1998).

It is not only U.S. magazines that make their way across foreign borders. *Marie Claire*, a French monthly magazine with 29 editions in 15 languages and more than 15 million readers worldwide, debuted in the United States in 1993, becoming a member of the Hearst Magazine family. Figure 7.3 shows the covers of the Turkish editions of *Marie Claire*. In many markets *Marie Claire* competes with the international editions of *Cosmopolitan* and *Elle*. *Elle*, another French publication, has a combined global circulation of nearly 5 million, with 39 editions in 60 countries worldwide. *Elle China* was launched in 1988, and today, with a circulation of about 280,000, it is the best-selling foreign magazine on the mainland.

While many of these publications are translated into many different languages and are available in many different markets, their foreign readers are a quite different group in terms of demographics from those who read these publications in their country of origin. In foreign markets these publications appeal predominantly to international travelers and upscale, high-income consumers. However, the publications are generally less effective in reaching mass consumer markets and thus are of less value in promoting mass consumption items.

Business-oriented publications that reach businesspeople on a worldwide basis include *Forbes*, *Fortune*, and *Harvard Business Review*. A major plus associated with such publications is that they provide verified circulation and audience data. In addition, they tend to lend the magazine's prestige to advertised products. One of the drawbacks of such publications, however, is that they generally offer only English, French, and Spanish editions. *Forbes Korea* debuted in 2002. Local-language editions were also introduced in China (2003); Russia, Dubai, Israel, and Poland (2004); and Turkey (2005). In 2005, *Forbes* also launched *Forbes Asia*. *Forbes* is read by more than 5 million people. In addition to its flagship magazine, the company produces Forbes.com, which claims to be the Web's leading business site.

*International Newspapers:* A number of international newspapers exist that provide opportunities for global advertisers. Among the most well known is the *International Herald Tribune*, a global edition of the *New York Times*. Based in Paris, the newspaper is printed simultaneously via satellite at 37 locations worldwide and distributed in more than 180 countries. Most recently, the *International Herald Tribune* teamed up with the *New York Times* to launch the new online global edition at global.nytimes.

com. The *New York Times* has a weekday circulation of 1.0 million and Sunday circulation of over 1.4 million. A Russian-language edition of the *New York Times* was introduced in Moscow in 1993—the first foreign-language edition of the 141-year-old paper. The *Times* of London and the *Guardian*, also a British newspaper, are also considered global newspapers. Many publishers realize that similar lifestyles and interests in many different markets can be catered to by using the same or similar publishing formulas. The fact that launching multi-local editions of newspapers spreads costs across several markets is not lost on international publishers.

Many international newspapers are directed toward the business community. For example, the *Wall Street Journal*, a Dow Jones Company publication, boasts that it has more top management circulation than any other global business publication. With the *Wall Street Journal Europe*, published in Brussels, the *Asian Wall Street Journal*, published in Hong Kong, and the *Wall Street Journal Americas*, targeting Latin America, the publication reaches over 1.8 million businesspersons around the globe. the *Financial Times* (London) is another prestigious global business newspaper, though its circulation is significantly smaller than that of the *Wall Street Journal*.

## International Broadcast Media

*International Television:* In 1962, AT&T launched Telstar I, the first communication satellite capable of receiving, amplifying, and returning signals. Telstar was able to process and relay telephone and television signals between the United States and Europe. Today's satellites—orbiting 22,000 miles above earth—have greatly enhanced the ability of global marketers such as Sony, Coca-Cola, McDonald's, and Gillette to use television to reach consumers around the globe. Cable has served to bring satellite television into the homes of consumers and will probably remain the major means of receiving satellite transmissions. Those satellites with stronger transmitters allow households to receive signals directly through their own small dish antenna; however, penetration of such satellite dishes in many markets is still rather limited. Developments in high-powered direct broadcast satellites (DBS) have made reception even easier. DBS is likely to have a significant impact for those regions lagging in cable infrastructure. For example, STAR (Satellite Televisions Asian Region) TV sends both U.S. and BBC programming to millions of Asian households. STAR TV is headquartered in Hong Kong, with regional offices in India, mainland China, Taiwan, and Singapore, as well as other South Asian countries. According to the STAR Web site, its service has more than 300 million viewers in 53 countries and is watched by approximately 120 million viewers every day. The worldwide distribution of cable and satellite infrastructure and services is not simply due to market demand. Terrain, demography, economic uncertainty, politics, and regulations are all factors in national and local decisions to promote these forms of television delivery.

In Iran, the desire to exclude "politically inappropriate" content—especially that which contradicts the religious and moral beliefs of the country's government—informs strong regulatory decisions against satellite television, although satellite dishes are bought on the black market. In China, the huge growth of cable services is due in part to the vast size of the country: cable is a relatively cheap way to connect people in rural areas to local provincial television stations. However, the growth of cable is also due to the government's desire to restrict what Chinese citizens are exposed to (Balnaves et al. 2001). Since January 1, 2002, in a bid to tighten control over what residents view on Western media channels, China's government has instructed foreign broadcasters to transmit their channels through a centralized platform, which encrypts them and beams them out over a state-run satellite (Madden

2001). Foreign broadcasters were warned by the Chinese government that if they did not comply, they would be banned. The new system allows the government to block programming it finds objectionable from Chinese living rooms, as well as hotels, embassies, and expatriate housing compounds.

Satellite technology has made the emergence of global television networks possible. Viacom bills its combined MTV Networks (MTVN) as the largest television network in the world. MTV reaches almost 562 million households on its 150 channels worldwide. MTV boasts that it entertains and educates in 33 languages in 161 countries and territories around the globe. The network owes its success to a number of factors. First, demographics: the network appeals to young people between the ages of 10 and 34. Increasingly, this age group is acquiring the bucks to buy CDs, jeans, acne cream—whatever brands are hot in each country. This means advertisers increasingly love MTV. Second, music: the claim that music is the universal language is true, and rock is the universal language of the global teen. Third, television: the number of sets in the world's living rooms—especially in places such as China, Brazil, Russia, and India—is exploding. The folks at MTV are shrewd enough to realize that while the world's teens want American music, they really want local music as well. So MTV's producers and veejays scour their local markets for top talent. The result is an endless stream of overnight sensations that keep MTV's global offerings fresh.

In 1980, Ted Turner launched Cable News Network (CNN), a 24-hour news channel. Two years later, Turner also launched Headline News. Early on, the two cable services lost nearly $80 million before turning a profit. Gradually the network built up a strong audience and advertiser base. The turning point for CNN came in 1991, with the network's coverage of the Persian Gulf War. Two CNN reporters were able to maintain live phone links from a Baghdad hotel during the U.S. bombing of the Iraqi capital. Major networks and newspapers around the world quoted CNN, and audiences have since learned to count on CNN for breaking news. During the Gulf War, the network presented a uniform global feed that presented the war largely though U.S. eyes, but since then CNN International (CNNI) has increasingly worked to tailor its programming to international as well as regional audiences and advertisers, with business programs, local anchors, and the like. Expatriate Americans make up only 1.5 percent of this audience. "The other 98.5 percent of our audience around the world require us to be relevant to their lives," notes Chris Cramer, president of CNN International (Flint and Goldsmith 2003).

There are six variants of CNNI:

- CNN International North America based in Atlanta, Georgia
- CNN International in Latin America based in Atlanta, Georgia
- CNN International Europe/Middle East/Africa, based in London, England
- CNN International Middle East, based in Abu Dhabi, UAE
- CNN International Asia Pacific based in Hong Kong, SAR, China
- CNN International South Asia based in Hong Kong SAR, China

CNNI reports that its broadcast agreement with mainland China includes an arrangement that its signal must pass through the Chinese-controlled satellite mentioned previously. Thus, Chinese authorities have been able to black out CNNI segments at will. The majority of CNNI broadcasts are not generally available in mainland China, but rather are limited to certain diplomatic compounds, hotels, and apartment blocks. Currently, CNNI reaches more than 200 million households and hotel rooms in over 200 countries and territories around the globe. Indeed, CNN promises media planners in advertisements that it "Delivers more news to more people in more ways." CNNI is distributed via satellite, cable, IPTV, and DTT. Its slogan is "The worldwide leader in news" (see Figure 7.4). The success of CNN proved that there is both a need and a lucrative market for 24-hour news. Spawning

**Figure 7.4:** Advertisement promoting CNN to international advertisers.

a host of competition in the United States and worldwide, CNN now battles for viewers with other 24-hour news providers, such as MSNBC, CNBC, and Sky Broadcasting, among others.

Introduced in 1979 as the flagship sports television network, ESPN properties now include ESPN2 (the second-most-popular sports network behind ESPN, featuring MLB, NHL, college football, and basketball), ESPN Classic (a 24-hour, all-sports network featuring the greatest games, stories, and heroes in the history of sports), ESPNEWS (the only 24-hour sports news network), ESPN Radio Network, ESPN The Magazine, ESPN.com (the leading sports Web site since its inception), ESPN Zone (a sports-themed dining and entertainment facility), ESPN Enterprises (which develops products and businesses using the ESPN brand and assets), and ESPN International. ESPN began distributing programming internationally in 1983. ESPN International was formed in 1988, helping ESPN establish a global footprint on all seven continents. ESPN's 46 international networks reach over 200 countries and territories in 16 languages. The network acquires major sporting events for distribution worldwide and local sports for regional distribution, and distributes ESPN domestic programming. Beyond the three networks highlighted above, global consumers can tune into BBC Worldwide, CNBC, the Discovery Channel Network, the Cartoon Network, and Animal Planet, among many others. Channels available to all of Europe include Euronews and Eurosport.

*International Radio:* International radio broadcasting has been performed primarily by government-run stations. Two such stations have established their credibility as reliable sources of news to listeners worldwide. The BBC World Service broadcasts to an international audience of over 140 million listeners in English, plus 32 additional languages. The Voice of America reaches listeners worldwide in 44 languages—from Albanian to Uzbek. VOA English has an estimated global weekly radio audience of more than 11 million people. Both the BBC World Service and Voice of America are available on the Internet. Other major international broadcasters include Deutsche Welle Radio (German), Radio France International, Radio Nederland, Radio Moscow, Radio Beijing, and All India Radio. Kamalipour explains:

> Several decades of research on international radio audiences show that listening to BBC, VOA, and the others is highest among people who have few domestic operations, like those in isolated areas. The numbers of such people have been steadily reduced by the increasing advance of domestic AM and FM radio in most countries. International radio is also sometimes sought by those who do not trust the local or national media that are available to them. That is still the case in a number of countries, but the number has been reduced by the fall of authoritarian regimes that exercised tight control over media contents in the former USSR, Eastern Europe, Asia, Africa, and Latin America. (Kamalipour 2002, 135)

"Regional" radio stations are those that are capable of reaching several nations. Regional stations tend to be most common in Europe, where stations have transmitting power up to five times that allowed in the United States, enabling them to cover much of the continent. A prime example of such a regional station is Radio Luxembourg, which broadcasts in five languages, with over 40 million listeners from the British Isles to Germany, Austria, and Switzerland.

*The Internet:* Unlike the media discussed previously, the Internet truly is global in nature. It can provide the marketer with literally instantaneous worldwide communication. As Keegan noted, the Internet defies a narrow marketing classification. It can be used as a market research vehicle, an advertising vehicle, a public relations vehicle, a sales vehicle, and more. Market researchers can conduct database searches and find information about competition on their Web pages. Surveys, given the right demographics, can be conducted via the computer. Advertising and consumer promotions regularly appear on screens. Public relations in the form of Web pages can readily be presented. The computer can even replace retail outlets and sales personnel if so desired by a company. But while the number of Internet users around the globe is growing exponentially, distribution of the world's online population is still rather uneven. Based on 2009 data, there are 1,802 million Internet users in the world, representing 26.6 percent of the global population. China represents the largest online audience in the world with 404 million users (see Table 7.6), but analysts predict that the Internet's international audience will grow even faster in the coming years (Internet World Stats 2009).

Internet advertisers can take advantage of a variety of different formats: Web sites, banner ads, pop-up windows, pay-per-click messages, among many others. Literally, hundreds of thousands of corporations have Web sites. Some companies use their Web site much like an extended brochure in promoting their goods and services; others act as information and entertainment publishers and try to create a place that people will visit often; and still others treat their Web site as an online catalog store, conducting business on the Internet. The most important difference between Web sites and other forms of online advertising is that consumers actively and voluntarily seek out a company's Web site (to learn more about a company or product, to place an order, and so forth). Another important difference is that much more information about the product or service can be provided on the Web site than through any other form of online advertising. The most valuable Web sites tend to be those that fulfill the consumer's goal-seeking needs by providing useful information. Consumers around the globe are increasingly using the Internet to shop online. When The Nielsen Company conducted its first global survey of Internet shopping in 2005, approximately 10 percent of the world's population (627 million) had shopped online. Within two years that number had increased by approximately 40 percent (to 875 million). Among Internet users, the highest percentage shopping online is in South Korea, where 99 percent of those with Internet access have used it to shop, followed by the U.K. (98 percent), Germany (97 percent), and Japan (97 percent). The United States is eighth at 94 percent. Globally, the most popular and purchased items over the Internet are books, clothing/accessories/shoes, videos/DVDs/games, airline tickets, and electronic equipment (see Table 7.7) ( MC Marketing Charts 2008).

By far the most common form of Internet advertising is the banner ad—typically a static rectangular message that appears across the top or bottom of a Web page. Users who click their mouse pointer on

**TABLE 7.6:** Internet Users by Country 2009

| RANK | COUNTRY | NUMBER OF USERS (MILLION) | RANK | COUNTRY | NUMBER OF USERS (MILLION) |
|------|---------|--------------------------|------|---------|--------------------------|
| 1. | China | 404.0 | 11. | Iran | 32.2 |
| 2. | United States | 234.3 | 12. | Mexico | 30.6 |
| 3. | Japan | 95.9 | 13. | Italy | 30.0 |
| 4. | India | 81.0 | 14. | Indonesia | 30.0 |
| 5. | Brazil | 72.0 | 15. | Spain | 29.0 |
| 6. | Germany | 61.9 | 16. | Turkey | 26.5 |
| 7. | United Kingdom | 46.6 | 17. | Canada | 25.0 |
| 8. | Russia | 45.2 | 18. | Philippines | 24.0 |
| 9. | France | 43.1 | 19. | Nigeria | 23.9 |
| 10. | South Korea | 37.4 | 20. | Vietnam | 22.7 |

*Source:* Internet World Stats (2009).

**Table 7.7:** Most Popular Online Purchases Worldwide

**Q:** *In the past three months, what items have you purchased on the Internet? (Global Average)*

| | |
|---|---|
| Books | 41% |
| Clothing/Accessories/Shoes | 36 |
| Videos/DVDs/Games | 24 |
| Airline Tickets/Reservations | 24 |
| Electronic Equipment (TV/Camera, etc.) | 23 |
| Music | 19 |
| Cosmetics/Nutrition Supplies | 19 |
| Computer Hardware | 16 |
| Tours/Hotel Reservations | 16 |
| Event Tickets | 15 |
| Computer Software | 14 |
| Groceries | 14 |
| Toys/Dolls | 9 |
| Sporting Goods | 8 |
| Automobiles & Parts | 4 |
| Sports Memorabilia | 3 |
| Other | 20 |

*Source:* MC Marketing Charts (2008).

the banner are transported to the advertiser's site. Research has shown, however, that the vast majority of these banner ads are ignored by Internet users—with a "click-through" rate of less than one-half of 1 percent. As a result of the paltry click-through rate of banner ads, Internet advertisers turned to increasingly aggressive means to grab users' attention, such as pop-ups. Pop-ups are ads that appear in a separate window that materializes on the screen, seemingly out of nowhere, while a selected Web page is loading. When pop-ups first became available a number of years ago, they were almost twice as effective in catching users' attention as simple banner ads. Today, however, pop-ups are often a source of irritation to Web site visitors.

Today, search engines such as Google and Yahoo! offer what is called pay-per-click advertising. In this type of advertising, a company will bid on a particular keyword or keyword phrase. If it is the highest bidder for that keyword or phrase, and a visitor to that search engine performs a query using that particular word or phrase, the company's advertising will come up on top of that search result page. Search engines maintain specially designated areas on their pages for this type of ad. In this way, a visitor who is placing the query will not confuse the ads with the normal results of the query. This type of ad tends to do very well.

Issues that must be addressed when using the Web for international business include exchange rates and language. International marketers must determine whether to offer prices in their own currency or the local currency. Some advertisers have made different price offers in different markets. Savvy Internet customers who discover such discrepancies may become frustrated with marketers. English is currently the dominant language on the Internet. However, projections are that in the near future, the majority of Web users will be non-English speakers. As a result, Internet marketers will increasingly need to tailor their Web sites to the language of a specific market. Translating Web pages is no less difficult than translating the copy for any other medium. An example of a Web site that employs the local language is eBay.

Other critical issues concern regulation of the Internet and privacy concerns. Balnaves and colleagues argue that it is a myth that the Internet is not regulated, cannot be regulated, and should not be regulated:

> For the first 15 years of its existence, funding from the U.S. government and military made the Internet possible, and they called the shots. Since the early 1990s, an informal regime of commercial regulation has emerged. To gain access to the Internet, we must subscribe to Internet Service Providers (ISPs) such as America Online or Compuserve. Then to track down a specific site, we use search engines such as Excite, Infoseek, Lycos or Yahoo. These service providers and search engine companies play an increasingly powerful role in determining what information is available and the paths by which we can reach it. The regulation of these *de facto* regulators will, primarily, be national governments and national courts—although international bodies such as the UN's World Intellectual Property Organization (WIPO)—are beginning to have some impact too. Net police squads have been formed in Germany, France, Canada, Italy, U.K., U.S., Japan and Russia. Though some of these governments use the pretext of protecting citizens from subversive ideas or defending national security and unity to deny access to the Internet, usually by forcing them to subscribe to a state-run ISP. Nevertheless, there are certain types of conduct that are properly regarded as being unacceptable on the Internet as they are elsewhere. The argument is not really about whether or not the Internet is regulated. It is. The question is, who does the regulating—private, mostly U.S.-owned companies or national governments and international organizations—and where should the limits of acceptable conduct be drawn? (Balnaves et al. 2001, 86)

Currently, advertising and sales promotion laws related to the Internet vary from country to country. Privacy issues are of concern, both within the United States and internationally. The Internet has been successfully used in the United States to develop profiles of Web visitors, collecting information such as e-mail addresses, purchase preferences, and more. Such information is obtained through online surveys—for example, an ESPN.com contest required users to fill out a survey to be eligible to win sports tickets—or through such sites as Nytimes.com, which required users to provide demographic information for free access to the newspaper's site. Internet firms argue that such tracking is not personal, as it is typically collected anonymously, and assists them in customizing their sites and the content of those sites to better match users' interests. However, most Internet users feel that such tracking is inappropriate, and many believe that sites should ask permission prior to collecting personal information. In light of the above concerns, the International Chamber of Commerce has outlined principles for responsible advertising and marketing over the Internet. The guidelines cover a range of ethical issues, including protection of users' personal data. A guideline entitled "Users' Rights" states that advertisers and marketers should disclose the reason for collecting personal information on users and confine their use of the information to their stated purpose. The guidelines also say that marketers should take reasonable precautions to safeguard the security of these data files. The ICC guidelines state that users should have the opportunity to refuse transfer of their personal data to other advertisers and marketers, except where required by law. Advertisers are also encouraged to post their privacy policy statements clearly on their online sites. Unsolicited commercial messages should not be sent to those users who request not to receive them. Other guidelines address messages directed at children, and the varied sensitivities of global audiences. The ICC guidelines suggest that online advertising and marketing be conducted in accordance with the laws of the country from which the message originates. However, ICC points out that there is currently no international unanimity on legal jurisdiction, and that certain countries may claim jurisdiction over messages posted online from abroad. Interested readers may go to the ICC's Web site for more information (www.iccwbo.org). It should be noted that the Organization for Economic Cooperation and Development (OECD), a multinational trade organization that promotes global trade and economic development, has also drafted guidelines for the international trade in personal information. "Guidelines on the Protection of Privacy and Transborder Flows of Personal Data" addresses the international exchange of information and suggests guidelines for the collection and exchange of such information. The information highway is still under construction—and so, too, are the rules. The ICC recognizes that advertising and marketing in the interactive media is at a relatively early stage of development and acknowledges that the relevant principles and guidelines may have to change and evolve as we learn more about the new technologies and their specific uses.

*Social Media:* Social networking has become a global consumer phenomenon. According to the Nielsen Company (2009), two-thirds of the world's Internet population visits a social network or blogging site, and the sector now accounts for almost 10 percent of all Internet time (note: Nielsen uses the terms "global" or "world" to encompass the following countries in which Nielsen Online has a NetView panel: the United States, the United Kingdom, Brazil, France, Germany, Italy, Spain, Switzerland, and Australia). Indeed, "member communities" have overtaken personal e-mail to become the world's fourth-most-popular online sector after search, portals, and PC software applications. Nielsen reports that the story is consistent across the world: "member communities" have taken a foothold in every major market from 50 percent of the online population in Switzerland and Germany to 80 percent in Brazil. In 2007, "Member communities" accounted for one in every 15 online minutes globally; 12 months later it accounted for one in every 11. In Brazil, member communities account for almost one in every 4 minutes. In the U.K., they account for one in every 6 minutes—and in Italy, one in every 7 minutes (The Nielsen Company 2009).

Global media and advertising industries are faced with both challenges and opportunities that this new consumer medium creates. Social networks provide competition to traditional media for consumers' attention, and simultaneously facilitate new ways for media and advertisers to connect with consumer audiences. Facebook has the greatest reach in the United Kingdom, being visited by 47 percent of Britons online, and actually has a greater online reach in both Italy (44 percent) and Australia (38 percent) than it does in its country of origin, the United States (33 percent). Facebook started out as a service for university students, but now almost one-third of its global audience is aged 35 to 49, and another one-quarter is over age 50. Part of Facebook's extraordinary subscriber growth is because of the lack of advertising clutter. That is, in part, due to the fact that social networkers serve a dual role as both the suppliers and consumers of content. Thus, members have a greater sense of "ownership" around the content they provide and are less inclined to accept commercial messages. Also important to note is the fact that content supplied by the social network members is often of a highly personal nature. While this makes Facebook highly attractive to advertisers, it also proves a major obstacle in generating revenue. As the site becomes more attractive to advertisers, it becomes less appealing to members, who see highly targeted ads as an invasion of privacy. Thus marketers must walk a fine line: engage in a relevant conversation with consumers rather than simply push ads on them. Consider a recent campaign for Splenda Mist, a pocket-sized spray form of the sweetener, which had yet to hit the market. Facebook offered Splenda the opportunity not only to advertise with a brand message, but also to solicit feedback and to have the target audience raise their hands and say, "I want to sample this product." The campaign used engagement ads to direct consumers to the Splenda Mist page, where through a custom sampling application, they could sign up for a first look at the new product. Splenda grabbed names, shipping addresses, and e-mail addresses, but also demographic data including gender and age range. When a consumer signed up for a sample or became a fan of the product, it showed up in his or her feeds, which helped the campaign spread virally. The result: 1,500 product surveys were completed, 16,000 samples were distributed in two weeks, and 3,100 fans professed their admiration for the new product (Zmuda 2009). While other brands have offered samples to fans or promoted giveaways through Facebook, the Splenda campaign differed in that it cultivated a group specifically for the purpose of sampling a prototype—and gathering feedback. Rollout details are being finalized, but a limited amount of the product is available through Splenda's Web site. Clearly, this case proves Facebook is an effective tool in exposing a product idea—or actual product—to a particular audience in a very efficient manner.

While marketers may not be spending huge dollars on social media yet, they know that they should be. A Coremetrics' "Face of the New Marketer" study found that 78 percent of marketers see social media as a way to gain a competitive edge, but fewer than 8 percent have budgets devoted to it. However, that is likely to change. Some 88 percent of the marketers who use social media plan to spend more on it in the coming years, and 31 percent note they will spend significantly more, according to Prospero Technologies research (Bulik 2008). Interactive agency SmashLab has created a white paper on social media designed as a primer for those who want to learn more about it. The paper notes that those who have been least successful in social media have often been so as a result of applying traditional messaging to an environment in which it doesn't resonate. Just as in real life, these communities tend to respond best to authentic, honest dialogue and conduct. SmashLab suggests that marketers should concentrate on delivering value to interested parties without immediately concerning themselves with a need to sell. Instead, advertisers should give their audience a good reason to be the brand's advocate. Companies can invite discussion, allow users to share experiences, or involve them in adventures. Effective social media efforts build relationships between companies and consumers (*Advertising Age* 2008).

## International Media Data

Audience profiles and circulation data are closely monitored in most highly developed nations. Advertisers in these markets have come to expect and rely on data supplied by large, independent, syndicated research services in making virtually all media decisions. One such service is The Nielsen Co., the top U.S. research firm, which operates in more than 100 countries around the globe. A number of additional services conduct research for specific media and in specific regions, including the Pan-European Television Audience Survey (PETAR), the European Business Readership Survey (EBRS), the International Financial Management in Europe Survey (IFME), the Pan-European Survey (PES), the European Media and Marketing Survey (EMS), the European-based Satellite Television Audience Measurement Partnership (STAMP), the Asian Businessman Readership Survey (ABRS), and Asian Profiles 5.

For data in many other countries, comparable services tend simply not to be available, particularly in developing countries. What data are made available in most developing markets are generally supplied by the media themselves, and such unaudited statistics are often viewed by international marketers as rather suspect. Verification of such figures is clearly a difficult task. When data are available, local differences in auditing procedures may make country-by-country comparisons nearly impossible. Data provided are also often outdated and quite simplistic. For example, figures with regard to pass-along circulation are typically not provided, yet such secondary circulation can be quite substantial in many markets. This lack of accurate media information presents one of the primary headaches for media

**TABLE 7.8:** Top 10 Media Specialists by Worldwide Revenue, 2009

| RANK | COMPANY | HEADQUARTERS | WORLDWIDE REVENUE (IN U.S. MILLION $) |
|------|---------|--------------|----------------------------------------|
| 1. | Starcom MediaVest Group (Publicis) | Chicago | 809 |
| 2. | ZenithOptimedia (Publicis) | New York | 779 |
| 3. | OMD Worldwide (Omnicom) | New York | 730 |
| 4. | Mindshare Worldwide (WPP) | New York | 713 |
| 5. | MEC (WPP) | New York | 595 |
| 6. | MediaCom (WPP) | New York | 570 |
| 7. | Carat (Aegis Group) | New York | 550 |
| 8. | MGP (Havas) | New York | 534 |
| 9. | UM (Interpublic) | New York | 368 |
| 10. | Interactive (Interpublic) | New York | 248 |

Source: The Agency Issue, *Advertising Age*, 26 April, 2010, 28.

planners operating in foreign markets. Media data will be discussed in greater detail in Chapter 8, which deals with research in the international arena.

## International Media-Buying Services

There are a number of ways in which the media-planning or -buying function can be handled in the international setting. The traditional model has all planning and buying conducted by the client's domestic or lead agency. Another option is to conduct media planning centrally but to handle media buying on a local basis in each country in which the international advertiser operates. A third option is to turn the function (either all or part) over to an international media agency; such specialists have been cropping up over the past few years. These firms work either directly for international clients or for their advertising agencies. They are generally responsible for finding the local media best suited to the client's needs and the target audience to be reached, providing accurate media data, handling negotiations and obtaining the best rates, making the purchase, and monitoring placement. These media-buying agencies are able to obtain significant media discounts by purchasing time and space on behalf of groups of clients instead of on the basis of single companies or brands. Such agencies can also afford to hire highly trained personnel, conduct multinational audience research, and establish databases that would be beyond the financial reach of most individual advertising agencies (Lane et al. 2008, 732). Kantar Media is one such firm. Its advertisement (see Figure 7.5) promises: "At Kantar, we think of media as your palette. As your global partner, we understand the powerful digital, social and traditional media opportunities changing every day. By providing a full spectrum of solutions to help you master this new media momentum, we optimize audience and brand connections. Moving them together. Our insight. Your mixed media masterpiece." Table 7.8 outlines the world's top-10 media specialists by worldwide billings for 2009.

**Figure 7.5:** Advertisement for Kantar Media promising marketers a "Mixed Media Masterpiece."

## SUMMARY

In this chapter, only some forms of local and international media available to the international advertiser were addressed. A media planner may also turn to autowraps on cars, toilet stall messages, and even advertisements in outer space, among a multitude of other media that in many cases may be specific to a particular market. An advertiser planning on entering a specific market must undertake an in-depth analysis of the media situation particular to that country. Basic questions that must be asked relate to the availability and viability of both traditional and unique media; the coverage, costs, and quality of various media; the role of advertising in the media of a specific country; the selection of local or international media or a combination of the two; the availability of reliable media data; and the decision whether the client, agency, or independent media service should be responsible for media planning and buying. It should also be understood that media change in the international arena is rapid and that many of the facts and statistics presented here may well be out of date in just a few years. Therefore, in Chapter 8 we discuss research in the international arena as a means of ensuring the best data possible.

**REFERENCES**

———. 2008. Need a primer on social media? Read on. 5 May, 13.

———. 2010. The agency issue. 26 April, 28.

AsiaNews.it. 2009. Despite fundamentalist anger Saudis go to the movies for the first time in 30 years. 6 September. <http://www.asianews.it/index.php?l=en&art=15470&size=A>.

Balnaves, Mark, James Donald, and Stephanie Donald. 2001. *The Penguin atlas of media and information.* New York: Penguin Putnam.

Banjanovic, Adisa. 2009. Special report: Towards universal global mobile phone coverage. 8 December. <http://www.euromonitor.com/Articles.aspx?folder=Special_Report...>. Retrieved 7 June 2010.

Barnes, Kathleen. 1993. Reaching rural S. Africa. *Advertising Age,* 19 April, I3.

Bartal, David. 1993. Ads leave stamp on Moscow mail. *Advertising Age,* 3 July, 8.

Bulik, Beth Snyder. 2008. Is your consumer using social media? *Advertising Age,* 5 May, 12.

*BusinessWire.* 2010. INVIDI Technologies completes $23 million= "D" financing round. 5 May. <http://www.marketwatch.com/story/invidi-technologies-completes-2...>. Retrieved 10 June 2010.

Carat Press Release. 2010. Carat forecasts 2.9% global advertising spend growth for 2010 and 4% for 2011. 26 March.

Carvajal, Doreen. 2006. They're counting on these sheep to sell hotel rooms. *San Diego Union-Tribune,* 26 April, A-2.

Communities Dominate Brands. 2010. Dispatches from the near future: Headlines to come in mobile stories in 2010. 31 March. <http://communities-dominate.blogs.com/brands/2010/03/dispatches-from-the-near-future-headlines-to-come-in-mobile-stories-in-2010.html>. Retrieved 12 August 2010.

Dockser Marcus, Amy. 1997. Advertising breezes along the Nile River with signs for sales. *Wall Street Journal,* 18 July, A-I.

FIPP. 2003. Number of magazine titles in selected markets. <www.fipp.com/Data/NoMagTitles.html>.

Flint, Joe, and Charles Goldsmith. 2003. CNN International takes a wider view than U.S. programs—with viewers in 200 countries. *Wall Street Journal Europe,* 11 April, A-5.

Friedman, Wayne. 2007. Odd pods: Agency finds inconsistencies in commercial breaks, ratings. 3 April. <http://www.mediapost.com/publications/index.cfm?fa=Articles.show>. Retrieved 2 June 2010.

Greenberg, Susan. 1998. Your very own Cosmo; Don't judge a mag by its cover. *Newsweek,* 18 May, 24.

Hall, Emma. 2010. Spain blurs the line between programs and ads with extended telepromotions. *Advertising Age,* 28 January. <http://adage.com/print?article_id=141789>. Retrieved 28 January 2010.

Hampp, Andrew. 2010. Interactive commercials show stong early results. *Advertising Age,* 14 January. <http://adage.com/print?article_id=141501>. Retrieved 15 January 2010.

Internet World Stats. 2009. Internet users, update for 2009. <http://www.internetworldstats.com/stats.html>. Retrieved 17 May 2009.

Ives, Nat. 2008. Text messaging makes magazines interactive. *Advertising Age*, 9 June, 10.

Kamalipour, Yahra R. 2002. *Global communication*. Belmont, CA: Wadsworth Publishing.

Kelly, Janice. 1992. Bus ads ride high in Romania. *Advertising Age*, 27 April, 136.

Lane, W. Ronald, Karen Whitehill King, and Russell, J. Thomas. 2008. *Kleppner's advertising procedure*. 17th ed. Upper Saddle River, NJ: Prentice Hall.

Madden, Normandy. 2001. China could censor foreign channels using screening platform. 5 November. <www.adageglobal.com/cgi-bin/daily.pl?daily_id=6146&post_date=2001–11–05>.

———. 2002. Text messaging ads on fast track in Asia. *Advertising Age*, 2 December, 12.

MC Marketing Charts. 2008. 875MM consumers have shopped online—Up 40% in two years. Nielsen Company, 29 January. <http://www.marketingcharts.com/direct/875mm-consumers-have-shopped-online-up-40-in-two-years-3225/>. Retrieved 12 August 2010.

The Nielsen Company. 2009. Global faces and networked places: A Nielsen report on social networking's new global footprint. March.

O'Dwyer, Gerald. 2002. Danish company sells advertising space on prams. 9 August. <www. adageglobal.com/cgi-bin/daily.pl?daily_id=8163&post_date=2002–08–09>.

———. 2003. Norway's Alaris launches interactive billboards along U.S. highways. 9 January. <www.adageglobal.com/cgi-bin/daily.pl?daily_id=9078&post_date=2003–01–09>.

Onkvisit, Sak, and John Shaw. 1997. *International marketing: Analysis and strategy*. Upper Saddle River, NJ: Prentice Hall.

Passariello, Christina. 2002. The Podunk post on sale at the Eiffel Tower. *Business Week*, 16 December, 125.

Peebles, Dean M., and John K. Ryans. 1984. *Management of international advertising: A marketing approach*. Boston: Allyn & Bacon.

Rideout, Victoria, Donald Roberts, and Ulla Foehr. 2005. Generation M: Media in the lives of 8–18 year olds. A Kaiser Family Foundation Study, March, 1–49.

Sorensen, Chris. 2007. TV ad limits lifted. 18 May. <http://www.thestar.com/Business/article/215335>. Retrieved 2 June 2010.

Srinivasan, Anand. 2010. Mobile phone penetration: Country rankings. 23 March. <http://gorumors.com/crunchies/mobile-phone-penetration-country-rankings/>. Retrieved 7 June 2010.

Steinberg, Brian. 2010a. Car ads that are served just to car buyers? It's in the works. *Advertising Age*, 15 February. <http://www.drewkerrpress.com/2010/02/break-invidi-technologies-a…>. Retrieved 10 June 2010.

———. 2010b. Long quest for addressable ads moves forward. *Advertising Age*, 7 June. <http://adage.com/mediaworks/article?article_id=144298>. Retrieved 9 June 2010.

———. 2010c. Fox sells 80% of Super Bowl. *Advertising Age*, 7 June. <http://adage.com/mediaworks/article?article _id=144304>.

Stewart, Ian. 1993. Chinese ad space open to new world. *Advertising Age*, 8 November, 114.

Suchard, Derek. 1993. Netherlands boards get added dimensions. *Advertising Age*, 17 May, 119.

*World advertising trends*. 2008. Oxon, UK: World Advertising Research Center (WARC), 28.

World Bank. 2009. World development indicators, 310–312.

World press trends. 2008. World Association of Newspapers. <http://www.wan-press.org/articles17377.html>. Retrieved 2 June 2010.

York, Emily Bryson. 2009. Kraft hits on killer app for iPhone marketing. *Advertising Age*, 19 January, 3.

Zmuda, Natalie. 2009. Facebook turns focus group with Splenda product-sample app. *Advertising Age*, 13 July. <http://proquest.umi.com.libproxy.sdsu.edu/pqdweb?index=84&did=…>. Retrieved 30 April 2010.

# CHAPTER EIGHT

# Research in the International Arena

The role of research is equally important in domestic and international marketing and advertising. Its basic purpose is to assist advertising and marketing managers in making more informed, and therefore better, decisions. When planning to sell goods to foreign consumers, each element of the marketing mix must be investigated. As noted in Chapter 2, the product must be appropriate for a given market. In some cases the same product can be marketed around the globe; in others modifications may be required. The marketer must determine the most appropriate price, which may be influenced by the firm's short- and long-term objectives, the competitive environment, and a variety of other factors. The marketer must establish the availability of various channels and select the most efficient means of distribution. Marketing research can address each of these areas. Finally, the international marketer must consider promotion of the product: personal selling, sales promotion, direct response, public relations efforts, and, of course, advertising. Advertising research may involve lifestyle studies, concept testing, message pre- and post-testing to determine reactions to different types of advertising appeals and executions, and determination of appropriate media vehicles. Each of the marketing-mix decisions will be influenced by the international marketing environment outlined in Chapter 3. Marketers must familiarize themselves with demographic factors such as market size and population growth; economic factors, including degree of urbanization and income distribution; geographic characteristics such as topography and climate; and the political-legal climate in terms of potential political risk and regulatory restrictions. In addition, the marketer must understand the cultural environment—verbal and nonverbal language, values and attitudes, and religion and ethical standards, as well as customs and consumption patterns, as explored in Chapter 4. "The complexity of the international marketplace, the extreme differences from country to country, and the frequent lack of familiarity with foreign markets accentuate the importance of international market research" (Jeannet and Hennessey 1988, 203). Research can help prevent a multitude of marketing blunders.

Despite the importance of undertaking such research, it is not as frequently employed internationally as it is domestically. Indeed, for many reasons, a significant number of both consumer and industrial goods firms conduct little or no research in most of the foreign markets in which their products are sold. The dominant reason is the high cost associated with conducting research, particularly if primary research is deemed essential. Many companies for which foreign markets represent a relatively low profit potential find it difficult to justify such an investment. In addition, conducting international research is no easy task. Coordinating research and data collection across a number of countries can prove quite challenging, and there is the associated difficulty of establishing comparability and equivalence (Douglas and Craig 1983, 18). Finally, all too many marketers have a rather limited appreciation for the significantly different character of foreign marketing environments. As a result, management relies on little more than casual observations or generalizations drawn from other markets rather than basing their marketing and advertising decisions on solid research. In this chapter we outline the basic steps in international marketing and advertising research.

Currently, the vast majority of research related to marketing and advertising, both commercial and academic, is conducted within the nations of the Industrial Triad—North America, Europe, and Japan. This reflects the current size and attractiveness of these markets. However, this imbalance is likely to change in the future. The countries with the highest growth potential are the emerging market economies in Asia, Latin America, Africa, and Eastern Europe. Firms that wish to succeed in the global markets of the 21st century will need to pay greater attention to examining markets in these regions of the world and developing or acquiring the capabilities to conduct research in these markets. As businesses continue to expand in international markets, the role of timely and accurate marketing and advertising research to guide decision making becomes increasingly critical.

## STEPS IN RESEARCH DESIGN

The procedures and methods related to conducting marketing and advertising research in the international arena are conceptually and methodologically similar to conducting such research in domestic markets. Most research studies involve a common series of tasks: (1) define the research problem, (2) identify information sources, (3) design the research, (4) collect data, and (5) analyze and report the research data.

### Problem Definition

Subhash Jain defines marketing research as the process of

gathering, analyzing and presenting information related to a well-defined problem. The focus of the research is a specific problem or project with a beginning and an end. Marketing research differs from marketing intelligence, which is information gathered and analyzed on a continual basis. (Jain 1984, 550)

Defining the problem is the most important task in international research, because at this stage the researcher determines precisely what information is required. Problems may even vary from one market to another. This may reflect differences in socioeconomic conditions, levels of economic development, cultural forces, or the competitive market structure (Douglas and Craig 1983, 39).

## Determination of Information Sources

Next, the researcher must determine where necessary information can be found. In some instances research may be limited to the collection of *secondary data*. Secondary data refer to information that has previously been collected and is available from another source—for example, governmental bodies, trade associations, or syndicated research suppliers. The collection of secondary data is generally considered the appropriate starting point for all international investigations, as it is most easily accessible and least expensive to obtain. Secondary data can assist in identifying areas of interest not adequately addressed and therefore deserving of additional attention. Marketers may then collect *primary data*. Presumably, primary data provide more relevant information because it has been collected for the sole purpose of addressing the researcher's stated problem. Both qualitative and quantitative methods can be employed in the collection of primary data. The advantages and disadvantages of both secondary and primary data will be discussed in detail later in the chapter.

## Research Design

As Brian Toyne and Peter Walters explain:

> A research design is simply a framework or plan adopted to study a particular research problem. It is the blueprint followed when collecting and analyzing data. Its dual purpose is to ensure that the study is relevant to the problem and that it employs economic, effective procedures. (Toyne and Walters 1989)

The research design typically entails determination of research techniques and instruments to be employed as well as the sampling plan. Each of these areas will be discussed in greater detail later in this chapter. The researcher may choose among several research techniques: observation, focus-group interviews, experimental techniques, and surveys. The most commonly employed instrument for gathering primary data is the survey questionnaire. Issues critical to the design of survey questionnaires include functional equivalence, instrumental equivalence, measurement, scaling, and wording. For surveys, the investigator must know how to draw a sample from the population to be studied that is both representative and comparable.

## Data Collection

Tracking down secondary data sources can be both time consuming and labor intensive. Further, the marketer must realize from the outset that secondary data is unlikely to be available for all variables or in all markets. With regard to secondary data, the issues of accuracy, comparability, and timeliness will be of concern. In the case of primary data collection, the sample must be drawn and the survey instrument must be administered, generally via telephone, mail, or in-person interviews. Here, the researcher must watch for and guard against nonresponse bias, topic bias, and social bias, as well as researcher and respondent bias. Again, each of these issues will be discussed in greater detail in a later section.

## Data Analysis and Reporting

Because secondary data were originally collected to serve other purposes, analyzing requires combining and cross-tabulating various data sets in order for the information to be of use to the researcher. In the case of primary data, the information collected must first be edited and coded. Care must be taken in applying those analytical tools appropriate to the quality of the data collected. Only then can interpretation take place. Finally, the researcher compiles a report that highlights how the research results relate to the originally stated research problem. This report is generally presented to headquarters management as well as local subsidiaries.

# SECONDARY DATA

Secondary data, or pre-existing statistics or information gathered for a purpose other than that of the immediate study, offer some real advantages to the international marketer (Toyne and Walters 1989). Collection and analysis of secondary data are typically the first step in market research for most firms, because a tremendous amount of information can be obtained in this fashion. In addition, secondary data generally can be collected fairly quickly and easily, and, most important, relatively inexpensively—most secondary sources provide the information free or for only a minimal fee. The primary cost, then, for accessing this information can be viewed in terms of the time and energy spent by the research staff. Secondary data are particularly valuable for firms planning on entering smaller markets, because their more limited profit potential may permit only modest research expenditures.

## Problems with Secondary Data

A major problem international marketers face with regard to secondary research is data availability. While the United States is unmatched in terms of the abundance of demographic and economic information available to marketers, this is certainly not the case in every country. In developing markets in particular, secondary data are relatively scarce. Indeed, a direct relationship seems to exist between the availability of secondary data in a country and its level of economic development. Further, while much demographic or economic information may be accessible, more specific types of data, such as information regarding consumer needs or lifestyles, are nearly impossible to obtain from secondary sources. Available data must be evaluated in terms of accuracy, comparability, and timeliness.

Secondary data are often less accurate than the international marketer would prefer. The data available in developing markets in particular tend to be a good deal less accurate than information from developed nations. Industrially advanced countries typically tend to be quite skilled in market research and to possess well-developed data collection mechanisms. In less sophisticated markets, data collection is generally rather rudimentary, and experienced research personnel are not abundant. This directly impacts the quality of the data. For example, if a sample has not been randomly drawn, the results cannot be assumed to be representative of the total population. Data collection methods should always be examined to determine whether proper research methods were employed. More often than not, statistics available in less developed nations represent little more than estimates or even, in some cases, wishful thinking. International marketers should be wary of who collected the data and for what reason. In many countries the primary data-gathering organization is the government, which may have reason to under- or over-represent certain statistics. For instance, a specific country may wish to downplay statistics that might be associated with a negative image, such as high levels of illiteracy or disease; or politicians may overemphasize favorable items, such as industrial production levels, in an attempt to attract foreign investment. Such manipulation of the data is often associated with a country's attempt to obtain assistance from various donor organizations, nations, or agencies.

Even when secondary data are available and accurate, it may not be comparable. If the international marketer is to evaluate foreign countries, the data collected must be comparable. Items of interest to the international marketer may be defined differently from one country to the next. For instance,

Susan P. Douglas and C. Samuel Craig explain how the definition of the term "urban" varies from market to market:

> In Japan, for example, urban population is defined as a shi (city) with 50,000 inhabitants or more, or shis (population usually 30,000 inhabitants) with urban facilities. In India it includes all places with 5,000 inhabitants or more. In Nigeria, it includes the forty largest towns; and in Kenya and Zaire, agglomerations with at least 2,000 inhabitants. Similarly, in France and West Germany, it includes communities with 2,000 or more inhabitants, while in Norway and Sweden it goes down to localities or built-up areas with as few as 200 inhabitants. (Douglas and Craig 1983, 80)

Likewise, one researcher attempted to collect international data on the number of women in the work force in different countries. She obtained wildly conflicting estimates, depending on the source. In Brazil, the percentage of women in the work force ranged from a low of 20 percent to a high of 39 percent—a 19-point difference. In Canada, percentages ranged from 46 to 62 percent. Even within the United States, depending on the source, percentages ranged from 54 to 63 percent. Explanations for the diversity in figures are myriad. For instance, some figures are based on different age parameters. Some are gathered by survey rather than census, and censuses and surveys do not always collect the same information. Some figures represent estimates, while others represent hard data. Finally, different definitions of what constitutes the "work force" impact the ultimate number (Bartos 1989, 205). Regarding such differences in definitions, ESOMAR (The European Society for Opinion and Marketing Research) produced a working paper on the harmonization of demographics within the European Union. ESOMAR noted that with the Common Market now firmly in place, it is possible to conduct marketwide research, rather than having to do separate studies in each country. To that end, it recommended that a common set of definitions of demographic terms be employed by all member countries.

There is also the question of the *timeliness* of the data. In some countries data may be collected annually, while in others, literally decades pass before a survey is again undertaken. For example, Bolivia hasn't had a census since 1950 and Congo since 1958. In 1980, when China was opening up to dealings with Western firms, some of the first figures on the Chinese economy were made public. Officials admitted that some of the figures were drawn from CIA studies. China's first official census was conducted in 1986 (Terpstra and Russo 2000). There is often a very good reason for this lag in data collection activity. Information gathering is an expensive endeavor, so that in a country with limited resources, data collection may simply not be a priority. Few countries—developed or not—can match the frequency of U.S. data collection efforts.

Data from secondary sources from any country (including the United States) must be checked and interpreted carefully. As a practical matter, the following questions should be asked in order to judge the reliability of the data sources:

- Who collected the data? Would there be any reason for purposely misrepresenting the facts?
- For what purposes were the data collected?
- How was it collected (methodology)?
- Are the data internally consistent and logical in light of known data sources or market factors? (Cateora and Hess 1979, 262)

International marketers may turn to both domestic and foreign sources of secondary data.

## Domestic Sources of Secondary Data

*The U.S. Government:* More information is collected by the U.S. government than any other agency in the world. The data, which are characterized by its timeliness and accuracy, is generally available to the public either at no cost or for a minimal fee. The Department of Commerce is heavily involved in promoting the expansion of U.S. business in the international arena through its International Trade Administration. The International Trade Administration regularly publishes a variety of materials of interest to the international marketer, and this data can be accessed at field offices in every major city in the country. Most of this data is also available on CD-ROM as well as online. Publications include: *Top U.S. Export Markets; International Trade Updates; Annual Report of the Foreign-Trade Zones Board;* and *Export Programs Guide.* Also, the Department of Commerce keeps firms abreast of developments in Washington that might impact international business undertakings. Many other governmental agencies and departments—including the State Department, the Federal Trade Commission, the Department of Labor, the Bureau of the Census, the Department of the Treasury, and the Department of Agriculture—also publish information pertaining to international trade.

*Foreign Embassies and Consulates:* As Subhash Jain notes, virtually all foreign nations have embassies in Washington, D.C., as well as United Nations mission offices in New York City. In addition, foreign governments may have one or more consulate offices in the United States. Jain writes:

> For example, the government of Brazil maintains consulate offices in New York, Chicago, Dallas, San Francisco, and Los Angeles in addition to their embassy in Washington, D.C. Usually an embassy has a commercial attaché who may be a good source of secondary information on a country. The consulate and U.N. mission usually have basic information on their country to offer the researcher. (Jain 1984, 562)

*Foreign Trade Offices:* A number of governments also maintain foreign trade offices (FTOs) in the United States—mostly in Washington, D.C., and New York. The function of these FTOs is to assist U.S. exporters and importers, the end goal being the stimulation of trade. These offices can provide the international marketer with brochures, booklets, and newsletters outlining various aspects of doing business in their countries. One example of such an FTO is the Japan External Trade Organization, which has available over 100 complimentary publications on doing business in Japan.

*Industry and Trade Associations:* Industry associations are generally formed to represent entire industry segments. For example, the industry associations for the automotive and pharmaceutical industries gather both national and international data from their members and publish them in aggregate form. A variety of business groups, such as chambers of commerce, the Conference Board, and the National Foreign Trade Council, also can provide marketers with counsel and information on local markets.

*Banks and Other Service Institutions:* Major U.S. banks that operate multinationally (such as Citigroup), foreign banks with branches in the United States (such as Sanwa), and national banks located abroad (such as the Bank of England) provide assistance to their client companies engaging in marketing efforts around the globe. Marketers may find these banks' annual reports or yearbooks to be useful sources of information. In addition, many of these banks maintain libraries accessible to both current and potential customers. These banks may also provide a variety of services, including suggesting overseas markets for goods and services, locating potential foreign investors, contacting distributors, and obtaining information on foreign exchange regulations. In addition to banks, the international marketer can turn to accounting firms and transportation companies (such as major airlines and freight services) for information on business practices in foreign markets as well as basic trade data.

*Universities:* Universities in general and schools of business administration in particular, both in the United States and abroad, are excellent sources of information. For example, Harvard has an abundance of case studies on almost every country worldwide. The University of Texas has published over

100 case studies on foreign markets. Similarly, libraries at the University of Washington, Pennsylvania State University, and the University of Southern California all house relevant bodies of information.

*Research Firms:* Marketing research firms can provide relevant secondary data—however, at a cost to users. While they are a more expensive source of secondary data than published (e.g., government) information, such services are still much less expensive for a company than if it were to gather its own primary data. Some market research firms simply retrieve previously printed materials requested by clients, while others also collect primary data. Not unlike U.S. advertising agencies, U.S. research firms have followed in the footsteps of their clients and turned to foreign soil for growth. These organizations are devoted to the gathering and selling of marketplace information, specializing in data related to consumer behavior so difficult to obtain from other sources. Table 8.1 lists the world's 25 largest marketing, advertising, and public opinion research organizations, which in 2008 had total revenues of $18.9 billion. Over half (13) of the top 25 organizations call the United States home. Four are based in the United Kingdom, three each in France and Japan, and one each in Germany and Brazil (Honomichl 2009). The top-ranked firm, the Nielsen Co., is based in both New York and Haarlem, the Netherlands, and has operations in 108 countries. Nielsen is the world leader in marketing information, media measurement and information, business media, and directories. Among just a few of the services Nielsen provides to its clients are retail measurement (including data on product movement, market share, distribution, and price), consumer panels (used to explore consumer behavior and identify new markets), customized research (to support decision making at each state of product marketing—from the identification of market opportunities, the development of product concepts, and product positioning to sales forecasting, advertising testing, and tracking), and test marketing (including live/in-store test marketing of new and existing products as well as simulated test marketing).

Listings of international market research firms can be found in the Market Research Society's *International Directory of Market Research Organizations*; the American Marketing Association's *Worldwide Directory of Marketing Research Companies and Services* (also known as the Green Book); and *Bradford's Directory of Marketing Research Agencies and Management Consultants in the United States and the World*.

*Consulting Firms, International Advertising Agencies, and Other Sources:* A number of consulting firms gather, organize, and make available information of value to international marketers. For example, the Economist Intelligence Unit (EIU), which is based in London and associated with the *Economist* magazine, bills itself as the world's leading provider of country intelligence. The unit draws on a global network of over 500 analysts to assess and forecast political, economic, and business conditions in 195 countries. EIU publishes a large number of special reports offered through a full range of print and electronic delivery channels, and also conducts customized market studies for international firms.

Major international advertising agencies, through their overseas offices, can provide clients with guidance in marketing goods in foreign countries. In a nod to globalization and the purchasing power of kids, a number of agencies have developed youth-related market research consultancies. Among them are WPP Group's Geppetto Group and Saatchi & Saatchi's Youth Connection. Geppetto's focus is on consumers ages 12–24, and the group provides marketing solutions via branding, advertising, promotions, web design, new product development, strategic planning and research, as well as character development and design. Youth Connection's mission is to go beyond trend spotting to observe children, tweens and teenagers in their environments and understand how they feel and interact with others, including mothers. This is achieved through a process called "Xplor," in which planning executives

**TABLE 8.1:** Top Global Market Research Organizations (in U.S. million $)

| RANK | ORGANIZATION | GLOBAL RESEARCH REVENUES | REVENUES FROM OUTSIDE PARENT COUNTRY | % GLOBAL REVENUES FROM OUTSIDE HOME COUNTRY |
|---|---|---|---|---|
| 1. | The Nielsen Co. (US) | 4,575.0 | 2,344.0 | 51.2% |
| 2. | The Kantar Group (UK) | 3,615.1 | 2,722.6 | 75.3 |
| 3. | IMS Health Inc (US) | 2,329.5 | 1,487.5 | 63.9 |
| 4. | GfK SE (Germany) | 1,797.2 | 1,389.1 | 77.3 |
| 5. | Ipsos Group S.A. (France) | 1,442.1 | 1,283.5 | 89.0 |
| 6. | Synovate (UK) | 961.0 | 817.3 | 85.1 |
| 7. | IRI (US) | 725.0 | 271.0 | 37.4 |
| 8. | Westat Inc (US) | 469.5 | — | — |
| 9. | Arbitron Inc (US) | 368.8 | 4.4 | 1.2 |
| 10. | INTAGE Inc (JAPAN) | 332.2 | 3.8 | 1.1 |
| 11. | J.D. Power & Asso (US) | 272.2 | 83.6 | 30.7 |
| 12. | Maritz Research (US) | 230.7 | 33.3 | 14.4 |
| 13. | Opinion Research Corp. (US) | 227.7 | 82.4 | 36.2 |
| 14. | The NPD Group Inc (US) | 226.1 | 57.6 | 25.5 |
| 15. | Harris Interactive Inc (US) | 221.8 | 84.7 | 38.2 |
| 16. | Video Research Ltd. (Japan) | 188.3 | 0.2 | 0.1 |
| 17. | IBOPE Group (Brazil) | 158.9 | 35.7 | 22.5 |
| 18. | ComScore Inc (US) | 117.4 | 16.5 | 14.1 |
| 19. | Cello Research & Consulting (UK) | 98.8 | 39.3 | 39.8 |
| 20. | Market Strategies International (US) | 92.2 | 14.7 | 15.9 |
| 21. | Lieberman Research Worldwide (US) | 90.1 | 16.4 | 18.2 |
| 22. | Mediametrie (France) | 85.4 | 9.4 | 11.0 |
| 23. | BVA Group (France) | 83.9 | 9.0 | 10.7 |
| 24. | You Gov plc. (UK) | 82.9 | 58.8 | 71.0 |
| 25. | Dentsu Research Inc (Japan) | 68.2 | 0.3 | 0.3 |

*Source:* Honomichl (2009).

spend a month hanging out with kids and their moms (McMains 2006). The race to establish youth units is a reaction to clients' needs. Marketers have begun to flood shelves with kid-friendly versions of products—everything from soap to shampoo to soup.

Finally, the international marketer should also investigate a number of trade journals and other periodicals as potential sources of secondary information. For example, *Business Week, Business International,* the *Economist,* the *New York Times,* and *Advertising Age* often publish special reports on specific countries or regions as well as data reflecting global marketing trends.

## International Sources of Secondary Data

Simply because secondary data are not available domestically does not mean it may not be available abroad. Various international organizations as well as regional bodies (such as the European Union) and even the governments of individual countries can be tapped for international marketing data.

*International Organizations:* International organizations such as the United Nations, the World Bank, the International Monetary Fund (IMF), and the Organization for Economic Cooperation and Development (OECD) all provide extensive data of value to the international marketer.

The UN—and its affiliated organizations—is the official source of many international statistics. UN data are carefully compiled and generally acknowledged to be quite accurate. It should be noted, though, that UN statistics are not always completely reliable because the UN must occasionally depend on unsubstantiated statistics provided by member countries. The UN publishes the *Statistical Yearbook of the United Nations* (which provides demographic and economic development data plus political, geographic, and cultural information on over 200 countries). A monthly statistical supplement to the *Yearbook* is available as well. The UN also publishes *The Demographic Yearbook*, which covers population, natality, mortality, and other important demographic statistics. The *World Trade Annual* provides data from the principal trading nations by commodity and country. The UN Industrial Development Organization's (UNIDO) primary objectives are the advancement of developing nations and the fostering of industrial cooperation between regions and countries of the world. As part of these efforts, UNIDO, in collaboration with the Organization for Economic Cooperation and Development (OECD), compiles, stores, and disseminates global statistics. UNIDO collects national data directly from all countries and areas that are not members of OECD, while OECD collects data for its member states and provides them to UNIDO in order to complete the global coverage of UNIDO's industrial statistics databases.

The World Bank is an important source of information on economic, social, and natural resource indicators. The World Bank publishes *Development Data: Country Data* and the *World Development Report.* The former provides data covering key indicators of social and economic development, including population, poverty levels, illiteracy, structure of the economy, and trade. The latter focuses on a different topic each year and contains selected indicators for over 200 countries. Statistics cover quality-of-life issues, poverty, role of the government in the economy, distribution of income, education, health, communications, and science and technology.

The IMF publishes *International Financial Statistics* on a monthly basis to provide information on the financial status of over 100 countries. In addition, the IMF makes available data on a variety of national economic indicators, such as GNP, industrial production, inflation rate, and money supply.

The OECD conducts studies on the economic performance of its member countries, publishing both quarterly and annual data. Two publications in particular will be of interest to those conducting business internationally: the *OECD Economic Outlook,* which provides statistics from a semiannual survey of trends in member nations, and the *OECD Economic Surveys,* which contains information on the economic standing of each member country.

*International Marketing and Market Research Organizations:* A number of international organizations, including the International Advertising Association (IAA), the World Federation of Advertisers (WFA), the American Marketing Association (AMA), the American Academy of Advertising (AAA), and the European Society for Opinion and Marketing Research (ESOMAR), publish a wealth of marketing- and advertising-related information. In addition, ESOMAR, together with the International Chamber of Commerce, has established an international code of ethical practices and professional standards for conducting market research, which is endorsed by the major national professional bodies around the world (www.esomar.nl). Some organizations also regularly undertake surveys—for example, the International Advertising Association conducts an annual survey of all international advertising agencies. Other organizations also organize conferences where delegates from around the globe present papers and exchange experiences. Conference proceedings also serve as valuable resources.

*Regional Organizations:* The European Union is an excellent resource for statistics specific to European countries. Eurostat, the statistical office of the EU, publishes *Eurostat Yearbook,* which provides, as the name implies, basic demographic information on member countries. Euromonitor, headquartered in London, publishes two volumes on European markets as well as an additional volume on all other markets. An incredible amount of detailed information is available in these publications, from population, employment, production, trade, and economic data to statistics on consumption, housing, health, education, communications, and standard of living. With regard to standard-of-living data, Euromonitor provides information on comparative wages and earnings, consumer prices, comparative costs, consumer durables, household expenditures, and ownership of radios, televisions, and autos.

*Foreign Governments:* The governments of the countries that the international marketer is planning to enter can be an important source of secondary information, although both the quantity and the quality of the data are likely to vary from one market to the next. Even if the requested information is not on hand, governmental employees are generally able to direct the international marketer to the appropriate source. Unfortunately, much of the data available in foreign markets may be published only in the native language. Another drawback is that political bias may potentially skew the data.

The preceding provides just a brief overview of major sources of secondary data. Clearly, it is impractical to include a complete listing of all secondary sources available for all international markets. However, for an expanded discussion of the topic, see C. Samuel Craig and Susan P. Douglas's discussion of secondary data sources (Craig and Douglas 2005).

## PRIMARY DATA

Although secondary data are likely to reveal most basic demographic and economic information needed by international marketers in order to conduct business in a specific country, many marketing and advertising decisions require more specific kinds of information. As Philip Cateora and Susan Keaverney point out:

> Consumer buying behavior, attitudes about products or promotional messages, relevance of product attributes, product positioning and other manifestations of cultural and societal norms are usually product- or industry-specific and must be gathered by primary research. This information may be critical to sound tactical decisions and usually warrants the time, energy, creativity and expense required to collect it. (Cateora and Keaverney 1987, 47)

This statement highlights the major advantage of conducting primary research—the fact that the data collected are specific to the firm's needs.

The greatest disadvantage associated with primary data collection is that it can be quite expensive. The international researcher's golden rule should be to exhaust all secondary sources before doing primary research, and then to obtain only the data that are absolutely necessary (Peebles and Ryans 1984, 156). Research conducted abroad is generally a good deal more costly than comparable research conducted in the domestic market. Even in developing markets, research tends to be expensive. This

**Figure 8.1:** Advertisement for Maritz Market Research, encouraging advertisers to employ their services.

increased cost stems from a number of factors, including limited availability of marketing research firms abroad and differences in the level of sophistication of such firms. For this reason the use of primary research in the international arena is a good deal less widespread than it should be, particularly in less industrialized markets. Yet it is precisely in these countries that management is likely to be less familiar with market conditions and more prone to making marketing errors. Dean Peebles and John Ryans provide the following advice:

> We recommend one particular criterion when considering the value of a research project: will the benefits obtained from the information be greater than the cost of conducting the research. In answering the question, the advertising manager must recognize both the short-term and long-term value of the information and its potential use across markets. (Peebles and Ryans 1984, 145)

As might be expected, larger companies are more likely to conduct primary research in foreign markets than smaller or even medium-sized firms. As the Maritz market research organization (ranked No. 12 in Table 8.1) notes in the advertisement touting their services, "Nine of the top 10 Fortune 100 rely on it. You can too."

## PRIMARY RESEARCH METHODS

The manner in which primary data is collected is strongly influenced by culture. U.S. managers tend to prefer methods allowing them to collect large quantities of data that can then be manipulated statistically. Quantitative methods are generally the tool of choice. In fact, suggests Joseph T. Plummer, "American marketers are number crazy and need numbers or scores to make decisions" (Plummer 1986, 11). This is not to say that qualitative techniques do not have a place in Western research. Focus-group and in-depth interviews are commonly employed in advertising investigations. The preoccupation with numbers is not nearly so prevalent in other countries. For example, Japanese-style market research depends to a greater extent on nonquantitative approaches, including both soft data (obtained from visits to dealers and other distribution channel members) and hard data (dealing with shipments, inventory levels, and retail sales). Indeed, many Japanese managers express disdain for large-scale consumer surveys and other scientific research tools so commonly employed in the West. Johny K. Johansson and Ikujiro Nonaka write: "As the head of Matsushita's videocassette recorder division once said: Why do Americans do so much marketing research? You can find out what you need by traveling around and visiting the retailers who carry your product" (Johansson and Nonaka 1987, 16).

Qualitative and quantitative research methods include observation, focus-group and in-depth interviews, experimental techniques, and surveys. Because each method has certain strengths and weaknesses when used in foreign markets, international marketers and advertisers are increasingly relying on triangulation studies. Here, two or more entirely different methods are employed to study the same research question. If similar results are obtained by the various techniques, the researcher can feel relatively confident that the findings are both valid and reliable.

### Observation

Observational or ethnographic research can take a number of forms. Typically, an anthropologist or other trained observer is sent into the field to chart the hidden recesses of consumer behavior, or behaviors may be videotaped. Subjects may be either aware or unaware that they are being observed. The traditional view of observation as a data-collecting technique was that it was simply too cumbersome and snail-like in its pace to be of any real value. However, over the past decade, an increasing number of international marketers and advertisers have adopted this approach. For example, in the early 1990s, Nissan Motor Co. redesigned its Infiniti car after anthropologists helped it to see that Japanese notions of luxury-as-simplicity were very different from Americans' yen for visible opulence. A few years later, Volkswagen's ad agency, Arnold Communications, used the approach to reposition the brand toward active users with its "Drivers wanted" campaign. These days, plenty of other companies are hiring anthropologists who are trained to observe without changing the outcome. Though often more expensive than traditional focus groups, such ethnographic research is quickly becoming a standard agency offering. As products mature and differences diminish, marketers are anxious to hook into subtle emotional dimensions that might give them an edge. The approach enables the marketer to know the individual consumer on an intimate basis. It is also useful in helping marketers figure out how different demographic and ethnic groups react to their products. For example, Best Western International paid 25 over-55 couples to tape themselves on cross-country journeys. Their goal was to learn how seniors decide when and where to stop for the night. The videotapes of the older couples on three-to-seven-day-long drives revealed that the hotel chain didn't need to boost its standard 10 percent senior discount. The tapes showed that seniors who talked the hotel clerk into a better deal didn't need the lower price to afford the room; they were after the thrill of the deal. Instead of attracting new customers, bigger discounts would simply allow the old customer to trade up to a fancier dinner down the street, doing absolutely nothing for Best Western. Indeed, Best Western captured such a wealth of customer behavior on tape that it delayed its marketing plan in order to weave the insights into its core strategy. "The process definitely opened our eyes," said Tom Dougherty, manager of programs, promotions, and partnerships for the Phoenix-based chain. "Unfortunately for seniors, that means the rooms won't be getting any cheaper" (Khermouch 2001).

## Focus-Group Interviews and In-Depth Interviews

In focus-group interviews, some seven to ten members of the target audience are invited to discuss a specific topic related to the marketer's or advertiser's research question, typically in a home or laboratory setting. A focus-group moderator guides the discussion, which can last from two to four hours. Participants may be more willing to discuss certain issues in such a group setting than they would be in a one-on-one interview. While attendees of focus groups are generally randomly selected, even here, researchers must be sensitive to cultural differences. For example, various aspects of Chinese culture de-emphasize the open expression of one's thoughts, feelings, beliefs, and values. Naturalistic groups can be particularly effective in overcoming Chinese participants' reluctance to share. Rather than bringing together a group of strangers, here already-existing, naturally formed social groups are tapped to participate in focus-group sessions, leading to more naturalistic discussions, according to a study by Eckhardt and Bengtsson (2010).

While focus-group interviews do not provide statistically significant data because of their small sample size, they help provide insights into underlying consumer motives and attitudes. Focus-group interviews are effective in studying everything from product development to advertising strategy and execution. Indeed, it was a focus group that led to the 2009 blockbuster Hyundai Assurance program. Since coming on board as Hyundai Motor America's head of marketing in 2007, Joel Ewanick has gone directly to the people, asking consumers what they want through focus groups. Ewanick leads about six focus groups a year. He notes, "You can only learn so much by reading research numbers. It's another thing to have them look you in the eye and say how they feel—'I lost my job; I'm worried about my house.' These are the kinds of deep things that come out. That's how Assurance came about" (Jackson 2009). Insights from focus groups helped Hyundai understand that consumers were fearful. The Hyundai Assurance plan, ushered in with splashy Super Bowl commercials, made a simple promise: If you finance or lease a new Hyundai, and then lose your job, you can return it. The company later upped the ante in Academy Award ads by offering to make loan payments for three months if consumers financed or leased a Hyundai and subsequently lost their jobs. Later that year, Hyundai kicked into fifth gear with the Assurance Gas Lock offer, which promised that if the owner of certain new models pays more than $1.49 a gallon at the pump, Hyundai would pony up the difference for a year. Apparently, listening to consumers works. Between January and July 2009, Hyundai sold some 250,000 vehicles—only about 20,000 shy of results during the same period in 2008. Though that reflects about an 8 percent drop, it's miles better than the 32 percent average decline that the overall market experienced during the same period, according to Autodata (Stilson 2009). And, Hyundai's U.S. market share rose more than any other brand's in 2009. Another measure of Assurance's success is the number of copycat programs from Sears and Hewlett-Packard, among others.

In-depth interviews are basically unstructured means of collecting information from either individuals or small groups. They can be applied across a very wide range of areas and types of study including exploratory, broad market studies; diagnostic studies; creative development (advertising, packaging); and tactical research studies (Birn 2000). Both focus-group interviews and in-depth interviews, while still huge in the research arsenal, have a number of limitations. They tend to be time consuming and costly. Stronger personalities can wield undue influence, and participants often won't admit in public—or may not even recognize—their behavior patterns and motivations. Also, there are significant cultural differences in the willingness of respondents to discuss their feelings openly. Because of this, a highly skilled interviewer or moderator capable of stimulating discussion is essential. Note, too, that neither focus-group sessions nor in-depth interviews are amenable to statistical analysis.

## Experimental Techniques

On the topic of experimental techniques, Susan P. Douglas and C. Samuel Craig state:

> Experimental techniques are, at least in theory, potentially applicable to all cultural and socio-economic backgrounds. In practice, however, it is often difficult to design an experiment that is comparable or equivalent in all respects in every country or socio-cultural context. Experiments, particularly field experiments, typically incorporate certain elements of the specific socio-cultural context in which they are conducted. (Douglas and Craig 1983, 40)

## Surveys

Surveys are employed where quantitative data are desired. Collection of primary data in foreign markets via survey methods presents a variety of challenges generally not encountered when conducting research in the domestic market. These include, but are not limited to, problems relating to data comparability, instrument design, sampling, data collection, and infrastructure limitations. Note Brian Toyne and Peter Walters: "At best, failure to recognize these problems results in findings that are of no value to the decision maker. At worst, it results in decisions that may prove extremely costly for the firm" (Toyne and Walters 1989).

*Challenges Relating to Data Comparability:* The issue of comparability was discussed previously with regard to secondary data. However, it also plays a significant role in the collection of primary data. A researcher may examine a particular phenomenon in just a single market or undertake an investigation in a number of countries. For example, the research objective may be to explore the potential effectiveness of a specific advertising theme in Germany or to determine the feasibility of employing the same theme across the European Union. If cross-cultural research is being conducted, every effort must be made to ensure that the findings from different test markets can indeed be compared. The challenge of comparability increases with the number of markets under investigation. Even when the research program initially focuses only on a single country, similar research may be required for markets that the firm subsequently enters—again reinforcing the importance of comparability.

In order to achieve comparability, researchers engaging in cross-cultural investigations must deal with the external environmental factors of *functional equivalence* and *conceptual equivalence*. In addition, researchers must concern themselves with the internal measurement issue of *instrument equivalence* (which will be addressed in the next section). The researcher must be sensitive to functional equivalence, which refers to whether a concept, behavior, or product serves the same or a different function in the markets under consideration. For example, while refrigerators are used to store frozen foods in some countries and to chill water and soft drinks in others, in certain markets they serve as status symbols and are prominently displayed in the home—often in the living room rather than the kitchen. If similar products have different functions in different societies, their parameters cannot be used for comparative purposes (Choudhrey 1977, 18). Consider the example of hot milk-based chocolate drinks. While in the United States and United Kingdom they are primarily considered an evening drink, best before going to sleep, in much of Latin America a "chocolate caliente" is a morning drink. Functional equivalence is realized neither in the consumption time period nor in the purpose for use (waking/energizer versus sleep/relaxer) (Usunier 1996, 144).

A second consideration in cross-cultural research is conceptual equivalence. Explains Yusuf A. Choudhrey:

> Sometimes concepts have totally different meanings in different cultures and are thus inappropriate for use on an international scale. This means that proper care has to be exercised to ensure that the words used to elicit response carry similar meanings to individuals in different cultures. (Choudhrey 1977, 20)

For example, the word "family" has very different connotations in different parts of the world. In the United States it generally refers to the nuclear family consisting of mother, father, and children, whereas in other countries it could also include grandparents, aunts, uncles, cousins, and so on.

*Instrument Design Challenges:* For purposes of comparative evaluation, the international researcher also must strive for instrument equivalence, which Choudhrey defines as "the necessity of an instrument that measures a phenomenon uniformly in different cultures.... Unfortunately, the most popular instrument for collecting consumer data, the survey questionnaire, is susceptible to considerable bias in cross cultural applications" (Choudhrey 1977, 21). Fortunately, however, instrument design is one element over which the researcher does have some control.

The issues of measurement, scaling, and wording are central to the design of the research instrument. Asking the right question—in the right way—is always a challenge in marketing research, whether conducted in domestic or foreign markets. In designing the survey instrument, the researcher must ensure that the questions are measuring the same thing in each market. Susan P. Douglas and C. Samuel Craig note that the "most significant problems in drawing up questions in multicountry research are likely to occur in relation to attitudinal, psychographic, and lifestyle data. Constructs such as aggressiveness, respect for authority or honor may not be relevant in all countries and cultures" (Douglas and Craig 1983, 176). W. Fred Van Raaij provides an excellent example of a totally inappropriate questionnaire statement designed to measure social responsibility in a foreign market: "'A good citizen is responsible for shoveling the sidewalk in front of his home.' This statement assumes private owner-ship of houses, one-family housing, and a climate with snow in winter, and is clearly not applicable in an African country" (Van Raaij 1977, 693). Here, social responsibility would need to be measured with a completely different statement or perhaps even a series of statements.

The appropriateness as well as the effectiveness of various scales and response categories is depen-dent on the market in which the research is to be conducted. The semantic differential is one type of scale that is widely believed to be pan-cultural. However, even here the international researcher must exercise caution. While the 5- or 7-point semantic differential scale is commonly employed in the United States to rate objects and other items, in some countries consumers are much more familiar with 10- or even 20-point scales, while in still others respondents are most comfortable with a 3-point scale. When confronted with a verbal 7-point scale ranging from "excellent" to "terrible," Westerners tend to start from the extreme positions and then work inward, whereas Japanese tend to take a neutral position and move outward, seldom reaching the extremes (Fields 1980, 52). Thus, the range of Japanese scores is generally much more limited than that of Westerners, making the use of such scales problematic. This seems to be a cultural phenomenon—Japanese tend to arrive slowly at a fixed position, carefully weighing all known facts and consequences before responding.

Response categories may need to be expanded or collapsed depending on the specific market. For instance, in a study that required the determination of marital classification in Gabon, the standard categories of "married," "single," "divorced," and "widowed" were used. The category of "concubine" was not included, even though about 20 percent of the female respondents fell into this category. This is a typical case of applying Western classifications and assuming that they will be inclusive in other cultures (Mueller 1990, 194). On the other hand, some categories may need to be dropped. When ask-ing Third World customers where they purchase an item, it may be advisable to delete "supermarkets" as a possible response if a particular area is not blessed with this institution.

In an interesting situation, a category that was dropped from market research in South Africa was later reinstated. The South African Advertising Research Foundation (SAARF), an organization that is responsible for managing surveys covering newspapers, magazines, television, radio, and the Internet, reversed a decision to remove all reference to the race of the market research respondents. The original decision, which was made in an attempt to defuse accusations that market and media research was racist, led to a heated debate. Previously, race was included in survey questionnaires because it was seen as a fact of life, which surveys needed to reflect. However, explained Paul Haupt, SAARF chief executive:

> Race is not essential for media planning or target marketing, so its presence is not only unnecessary but harmful. The basis of racial segmentation is inherently unsound as it accepts that all people in a specific population group are similar and that they differ from those in other groups, which is patently untrue.

The foundation argued that other demographics, such as age, gender, language, and education, were adequate to achieve target marketing and media selection. But many people in the research industry were appalled by SAARF's decision. Erik du Plessis, managing director of Millward Brown Impact, noted the decision was a

> big step backward for market research. We will have no means to measure the progress of the black community. We will be reliant on anecdotal information about our largest community, which is the one growing in terms of wealth and consumer spending power.

Mr. Haupt concedes that the "removal of race might lead people to believe all problems have been resolved and inhibit the debate." He said, "We will return to the practice of asking respondents for the racial group to which they belong" (Koenderman 2002).

With regard to wording, the translation of a survey instrument into a foreign language can pose significant problems for the international researcher. While some questions are relatively easy to translate (for instance, those dealing with such demographic information as age, sex, or education), if the goal is to collect data regarding motivations and attitudes, the researcher must ensure that questions are understood by foreign respondents. Some questions simply cannot be translated into another language because the words do not exist to express precisely the same thought (Cundiff and Hilger 1988, 245). The problem of survey instrument translation is compounded in multilingual societies—for example, 14 different languages are spoken in India. Here, the researcher may be tempted to use the official language (say, English or French), only to find that just a fraction of the population speaks that language (Terpstra 1988).

In order to minimize translation errors, many experts suggest that researchers employ the back-translation technique. Back-translation, as noted in Chapter 6, involves independent translators translating the questionnaire into the foreign language and then back into the original language and comparing the two versions for equivalence. Even when using the same language, care must be taken in transporting the survey from one country to the next. Translation difficulties were experienced in a questionnaire designed for the United Kingdom. A question aimed at business executives was to have read: "Should advertising practitioners be certified?" but instead was understood as: "Should advertising practitioners be confined to an insane asylum?" The British word "certificated" should have been employed because it is the equivalent of the American "certified" (Mueller 1990). It is generally advisable to pilot-test all survey instruments prior to undertaking the investigation, ideally with a subset of the population under investigation.

Problems with equivalence can be encountered in other areas of international research as well, including sampling, data collection procedures, and the analysis and interpretation of results.

*Sampling Challenges:* After designing the survey instrument and translating it into the foreign language(s), the researcher must determine the appropriate respondents and the procedures best suited to selecting a sample from the population. Respondents selected for a survey may, in fact, vary significantly from one market to the next. For example, in examining purchase behavior of major household durables, researchers in the United States are likely to focus on women in their survey. In some foreign markets, however, men may be the primary decision makers. And in still others, several family members might be involved in the decision; thus, the focus would most appropriately be on the group rather than on an individual.

*Sampling* refers to the selection of a subset or group from a population that is representative of the entire population (Keegan 1984, 233). Most commonly employed sampling methods were developed for use in economically advanced markets, such as the United States, and, as a result, these methods are not always transferable to other nations (Cundiff and Hilger 1988, 183). For instance, in most Western countries researchers prefer to employ a *probability sample* because it allows an accurate prediction of the margin of error. Since the size of the population in a probability sample is known, data collected from the sample (if it is of adequate size) can be projected to the entire population. In a *random probability sample* each unit selected has an equal chance of being included in the sample. In a *nonrandom probability sample* each unit has a known probability of being selected.

In any probability sampling the researcher must have access to reliable information that can be used as sampling frames—such as census data, census maps, electoral lists, telephone listings, and mailing lists. While such data are readily available in industrialized countries, they may simply not exist in many poorer markets—or, if available, they may be sorely out of date. As Philip Cateora and

Susan Keaverney point out, "Neither Cairo nor Tehran have telephone books. Saudi Arabia has neither street names nor house numbers. Street maps are frequently unavailable in parts of South America" (Cateora and Keaverney 1987, 47). A lack of infrastructure may further complicate sampling procedures. In many less developed countries, only a small percentage of the population may own telephones, and it may be nearly impossible to access rural areas if adequate transportation is not available. In short, it is often extremely difficult to obtain a proper random sample in developing markets. The researcher's only viable alternative may be to employ nonprobability sampling procedures, such as convenience sampling or judgment sampling. A convenience sample involves selecting any respondent who happens to be readily available. A judgment sample involves selecting respondents based on the assumption that certain individuals are likely to be better informed than others or possess expert knowledge in a given area. Researchers might focus on village elders or local authority figures (Douglas and Craig 1983, 212). Such nonprobability samples generally do not lend themselves to inferential statistical analysis, and, as a result, the data collected cannot be assumed to be representative of the entire population.

The researcher must also consider whether the same sampling procedures should be employed across markets. Sampling procedures may vary in their reliability from one country to the next; thus, employing identical procedures is no guarantee of comparability. Instead, it may be preferable to utilize different methods that have equivalent levels of accuracy or reliability.

*Data Collection Challenges:* A variety of data collection methods can be employed, including mail, telephone, and in-person surveys. Each has its advantages and disadvantages, and the method ultimately employed depends largely on individual market conditions. The international marketing researcher must also consider the various forms of respondent bias, which may be related to the specific survey method selected, the country under investigation, the topic being explored, or a combination of these variables. One form is *nonresponse bias,* which refers to the fact that in some cultures individuals are more reluctant to answer questions posed by a stranger. While Americans are quite familiar with market surveys and generally willing to answer even the most personal questions, this is not the case in every country. In some markets respondents may be unwilling to share information because they suspect that the interviewers might, in fact, be government agents or perhaps tax auditors. Tax evasion is a way of life in some countries, and respondents are hesitant to answer any questions related to income or expenditures. The international researcher must also recognize that it may be extremely difficult to obtain responses from some segments of the population. For example, in Muslim countries women aren't allowed to speak with male interviewers, and the number of female interviewers is still quite limited, because this is not considered an appropriate career choice for women.

Willingness to respond to questions dealing with certain topics is likely to vary from country to country as well. Some topics in certain cultures are simply perceived as more sensitive than others. For example, the subject of sex is considered taboo in India. Even in the United States many individuals are wary of responding to questions about their income. Therefore, potential areas of *topic bias* must be identified during the design of the research instrument. The international researcher is also likely to face some form of *social bias.* For instance, social acquiescence bias refers to the increased tendency for respondents in some markets—particularly in Asian countries, where courtesy is highly valued—to provide the response they believe will most please the interviewer, rather than stating their true beliefs. In societies with a collective orientation, respondents are not used to making individual decisions; therefore, questions demanding individual answers may be problematic. Likewise, respondents may attempt to give an answer they think reflects popular opinion so as not to appear to deviate from the norm. This social desirability bias is a particular danger in group interviews, where a participant might look to others for the "appropriate" response.

When researchers from one country conduct an investigation in another country, they also must deal with what is termed *researcher bias*—the tendency to observe phenomena or behavior in the host country and define it in home-country terms (Cateora and Keaverney 1987, 47). One way to counter researcher bias is to incorporate the perspectives of researchers from a variety of different cultural backgrounds.

Finally, there is the danger of *researcher–respondent bias*, which refers to the interaction that may take place between the interviewer and respondent, thus tainting the survey results. For example, sexual bias may result in a reluctance to grant interviews. In many traditional countries, housewives may be reluctant to provide information to male interviewers. Ethnic bias may also exist. A Chinese person, for instance, may refuse to be interviewed by a Malay. Often, ethnic membership between interviewer and interviewee must be shared for the interview to take place. If the interviewer is perceived to be a foreigner, there may be an increased level of mistrust, further contaminating the data collected.

Mail surveys are quite popular in industrialized markets for a number of reasons. First, the cost of administering mail surveys tends to be relatively low on a per-questionnaire basis. Respondents may also be more willing to respond to sensitive questions via a mail survey, and there is no potential for researcher–respondent bias. On the downside, nonresponse may be higher than with other survey methods, which can bias the results of the investigation. Also, all control over responses to the survey instrument is lost in mail surveys. For instance, the respondent may fail to answer some questions and respond incorrectly to others. The use of a mail survey may be inappropriate in many developing markets due to a lack of available mailing lists or poor mail service. Surprisingly, even some developed markets—such as Italy—are notorious for their unreliable mail delivery. In addition, many developing countries are characterized by high levels of illiteracy (up to 50 percent in some Asian and African markets); clearly, where illiteracy prevails, written questionnaires are of little use.

Much like mail surveys, costs per respondent are relatively low for telephone surveys—at least in developed markets. Telephone surveys are an extremely fast way of obtaining necessary data, and nonresponse rates tend to be low. A major disadvantage associated with telephone surveys is that the interview itself cannot take too long, and questions cannot be overly complicated. In addition, respondents may be rather reluctant to answer certain types of questions over the telephone. Researcher–respondent bias can also come into play with telephone surveys. Even in economically advanced markets, the researcher must exercise caution when attempting to employ telephone surveys. For instance, Germany's laws are such that, if followed to the letter, telephone interviews would not be permitted unless the interviewee had previously agreed to be interviewed. This would, in effect, require two interview attempts—one to gain permission and one to conduct the interview. In addition, telephone numbers are not a fixed length, making random-digit dialing almost impossible. Developing countries pose a number of additional challenges. If levels of telephone ownership are low, as they are in many less developed markets, other survey methods may be more appropriate, unless the researcher is limiting data collection to urban areas. Telephone numbers may be difficult to access given that telephone books are nonexistent in some developing markets, which is the case, for example, in Cairo and Tehran. Further, telephone costs tend to be higher in many developing countries, making this a rather expensive means of obtaining data.

With in-person interviews, nonresponse rates are particularly low. Given data and infrastructure limitations, this approach may be the most viable means of data collection in poorer markets. Yet even this method is not without its disadvantages. With a largely rural population in many developing countries, reaching potential respondents becomes a major challenge. Roads are likely to be poor, and reliable public transportation may simply not be available. In addition, in-person interviews are the most expensive method of administering a questionnaire to a sample population in any market. Finally, interviewer bias is a very real problem.

In much the same way that sampling procedures vary from one country to the next in terms of comparability, so, too, do data collection procedures. For example, in one country, telephone surveys may be known to offer a certain level of reliability, while in another market, mail surveys offer the equivalent level of reliability. In collecting data, international researchers must be sensitive to such cross-cultural variations because they directly impact the comparability of the research results.

*Infrastructure Limitations:* Skilled marketing and advertising researchers can be found in primary over-seas markets as well as a number of developing markets. However, the researcher should be aware that obtaining facilities, field staff, and other resources will probably be a significantly greater challenge in less developed countries. Not only must these individuals be well trained in the area of marketing research, they should be familiar with the local culture and conversant in the local language(s). In addition, they should recognize that infrastructure limitations pose a major stumbling block in many international investigations. As noted above, mail surveys are not feasible without reliable postal service. Similarly, telephone surveys are not possible if ownership of telephones is limited. Finally, undertaking research abroad becomes a good deal more difficult without adequate roads and transportation systems.

## RESEARCH RELATING TO MESSAGE DESIGN AND PLACEMENT

Message research can help marketers to avoid promotional blunders in the international arena. For instance, research allows the marketer to determine whether creative strategies should vary by country or whether a single strategy can be adopted for all markets in which the firm plans to operate (the issue of globalization versus localization was addressed in detail in Chapters 5 and 6). Message research must be conducted in each market, as findings do not necessarily cross borders. Just because a particular advertisement tests well in Austria does not ensure that it will be equally successful in Germany or Switzerland.

Some of the same tools employed in domestic markets are also used in international advertising research. Lifestyle data is of particular value to marketers, yet it can be exceptionally difficult to access, especially in developing markets. The researcher should begin by exploring secondary data, as the anthropological literature is ripe with detailed studies of lifestyle patterns and cultural values in a large number of countries. In order to select concepts and position brands, international marketers may find it necessary to conduct lifestyle research to determine which patterns are similar across markets. For example, MTV and Nickelodeon, in association with Microsoft Digital Advertising Solutions, launched a major children's lifestyle survey on how kids and young people interact with digital technology, called "Circuits of Cool/Digital Playground." Both qualitative and quantitative methodologies were employed to examine how technology has changed youth culture. The survey included 18,000 "tech embracing" young people in 16 countries, including China, India, Japan, Sweden, Poland, Australia, Canada, and the United States. Notes Chris Dobson, Vice President, Global Advertising Sales, Microsoft Digital Advertising Solutions, "Digital communications—from IM, SMS, social networking to e-mail—have all revolutionized how young people communicate with their peers. We wanted to understand more deeply how young people interact with these technologies and consequently what this means for our advertising partners focused on reaching this highly engaged and influential audience" (Microsoft Advertising 2007). The study found that, globally, the average young person connected to digital technology has 94 phone numbers in his or her mobile, 78 people on a messenger buddy list, and 86 people in a social networking community. Yet despite their technological immersion, digi-kids are not geeks: 59 percent of kids aged 8 to 14 still prefer their television to their PCs, and only 20 percent of young people aged 14 to 24 globally admitted to being "interested" in technology. They are, however, expert multi-taskers and able to filter different channels of information. But the report also found that while many young people have access to similar digital technologies, they use them in very different ways. For example, Japan's reputation as a land enthralled with technology is different from the reality. Japanese young people live in small homes with limited privacy and generally don't possess their own PC until they go to college. As a result, their key digital device is the mobile phone, because it offers privacy and portability. Unlike young people in other countries, Japanese kids and young people have few online friends. Japanese teens also used IM and e-mail the least out of the 16 countries surveyed. In contrast, China has lower mobile use among young people, a less evolved print media market, and a family life of no siblings with parents and multiple grandparents. As a result, the Internet provides a rare opportunity for only—and lonely—children to reach out and communicate using social networks, blogs, and instant messaging. Northern European youth are perhaps most immersed in technology. Out of all nationalities surveyed, young Danes are most likely to say they can't live without their mobiles or televisions, and young Dutch are also most likely to say they can't live without e-mail. Even climate impacts digital technology. In countries with strong outdoor cultures, such as Italy, Brazil, and Australia, young people use mobiles for arranging to meet and to take pictures of their friends. Despite the plethora of new communications tools, the majority in almost every nation expressed a preference for meeting in person, though Japanese, Chinese, Poles, and Germans scored higher than others when it came to wanting to communicate online. Only Chinese youth actually expressed a majority preference for texting over face-to-face meetings. Such insights are of value to advertisers and content companies wishing to evolve and engage with kids and youth audiences in markets around the globe.

If advertisers wish to know whether foreign consumers understand the basic selling idea or product benefit highlighted and whether the message elicits the desired response, they may employ concept testing. The use of concept testing in international advertising research is growing rapidly because—although it employs qualitative methods such as focus-group discussions or in-depth interviews—it can provide considerable insights quickly and relatively cheaply (Peebles and Ryans 1984, 144). For example, a U.S. manufacturer of dishwashers introduced its product to the Swiss market using the same product benefit employed in the United States: convenience. The firm did not research the effectiveness of the convenience appeal and assumed (incorrectly) that the Swiss consumer would respond much as U.S. consumers had. What the firm did not realize was that Swiss homemakers are much more involved in their role than their U.S. counterparts. Swiss homemakers rejected the idea of being replaced by a machine, and, consequently, sales were dismal. Later, in-depth interviews revealed the source of the problem, and the product was successfully repositioned in terms of hygiene. The Swiss apparently place great value on cleanliness and responded favorably to a "kills bacteria and germs" appeal (Douglas and Craig 1983, 13). Ideally, concept testing should take place in the early stages of creative development. The logic behind this approach, explains Joseph Plummer, is that "if the basic selling idea has little relevance or appeal in a significant number of the markets, there is no value…to proceeding further by testing executions" (Plummer 1986, 15).

Once there is agreement on the strategy, the international marketer must determine whether the message execution will be appropriate. Pre-test research focuses on the potential effectiveness of an advertising execution prior to its full-scale use in a market or markets. The typical industry rationale for pre-testing "rough" or animatic commercials before they become a final film version can be summed up in five words: screen out bad ideas economically. Rough pre-testing has traditionally been used as a "go/no go" early-warning system to minimize waste and limit the time and expense allocated to fully produce an execution. Considering that the average cost of an animatic is roughly one-tenth the cost of a fully finished commercial, a pre-test can be a cost-effective solution. However, this is only half of the value of pre-testing. The other important benefit of working with rough commercials is the ability to use diagnostic information from the test in order to optimize the performance of the final film. Kastenholz and colleagues (2004) describe a Suave Hair Care ad that was improved as a result of pre-testing. Analysis of the animatic for this brand revealed that there was no initial hook to engage viewers at the outset of the commercial. To compound this problem, the animatic had music but no voice-over for the first 12 of its entire 30 seconds. Based on these findings, engaging close-ups of a child having fun on a merry-go-round were inserted at the beginning of the commercial to enhance viewer interest and generate positive emotion. Additionally, the voice-over narrative started seven seconds earlier in the final version of the ad. Finally, the key discriminator, "You don't have to spend a lot to get a lot," was added to the copy to more clearly communicate the Suave point of difference. As a result of the modifications, attention scores for the final film increased by a dramatic 21 percent. With regard to pre-testing, many in the industry suggest, the earlier, the better. This is not to say that researching a finished ad isn't valuable. But the earlier an idea can be explored, the less likely it is that the creative themes, or even final ads, will need to be changed, or tossed. Consider the case of a recent Cadbury's campaign that had to be scrapped (*Daily Mail* 2010). For more than 40 years, Cadbury's racy ads for its Flake chocolate bars have walked a fine line between the suggestive and the overtly sexual. But, apparently, a recently produced Flake television spot, which was scripted around the theme of temptation and showed a beautiful woman being seduced by a devil-like character, finally went too far. Research revealed that it polarized opinion in focus groups, and the ad was ultimately deemed too racy for Cadbury to show on television. Cadbury had invested nearly $2 million in producing the spot. Agency professionals know that if the strategy is right, and the central idea strikes a chord with the audience, the chance of producing an effective campaign is increased manifold. An analysis of 70 ads submitted to Millward Brown for pre-testing proves the point about early-stage research. It showed that when an ad is researched at an early stage and the creative team given guidance, the final version is far more effective. It is estimated that pre-testing ads earlier made them 50 percent more efficient (White 2007).

Focus groups and in-depth interviews are commonly employed techniques in pre-test research. Post-test research, on the other hand, is employed to determine whether the advertisement or campaign has achieved its objective—whether that be to build awareness, convey knowledge, generate liking, or create preference for the brand in each market. Not only is such research necessary in determining the success or failure of a campaign, but insights garnered through post-testing can suggest how the message might be modified or adapted in the future. While focus-group interviews may be employed here as well, telephone, mail and—increasingly—online surveys are more commonly conducted to measure recognition and recall as well as changes in attitude ascribed to the advertising.

International advertisers are increasingly employing ad-tracking studies—the continual monitoring of brand awareness, image, trials, and usage trends. For instance, TNS recently introduced a new influence-based consumer tracking model. Larry Friedman, chief research officer at TNS, notes: "For more than a generation, the research community has relied on survey-based methods that attempt to gauge how consumers are reacting to marketing stimuli. The marketing landscape has fundamentally changed, which requires the paradigm for tracking research to change as well" (*PR Newswire* 2010). TNS partnered with Emory University to introduce the new tracking model that incorporates social media to yield better results and makes observation the central focus of tracking. The model is based on the three S's: See, Seek, and Say. The See component is based on brand-generated media, while Seek is focused on the interactions between brands and the target audience. The Say component is the newest part of the marketing equation and is based on consumer-generated media (CGM). These can take the form of traditional word of mouth, blogs, Internet postings, and so forth—all of which allow consumers to share their unfiltered product experience in real time with the goal of influencing potential buyers in ways that were not available just a few years ago. To demonstrate how the new influence-tracking model works in practice, Friedman and his colleagues developed a case study based on Tiger Woods that examined how his brand image was impacted by events in late 2009 and early 2010. In late 2009, Tiger Woods earned over $100 million as spokesperson for a variety of brands including Gatorade, EA Sports, Gillette, Accenture, Nike, and others. On November 27, 2009, the media announced his car accident. On December 11, Woods announced that he was taking an indefinite leave from golf to address personal issues. Then, on February 18, 2010, he delivered his public apology, which received extensive media coverage. For the period January 2008 through December 2008, total Tiger Woods–related ad expenditures surpassed $131 million. For the period December 2009 through February 2010, ad expenditures had dropped to a little more than $1 million, the bulk of which was magazine ads that were likely placed prior to his accident. The research examined the effectiveness of two Tiger Woods Gillette ads, pre- and post-accident. The spot for Gillette Fusion with tennis star Roger Federer experienced a 37 percent decline in effectiveness, while a commercial with baseball star Derek Jeter saw a 47 percent decline in effectiveness. This stage represents the "See" component of the tracking model. The "Seek" component covers the public's Internet searches related to Tiger Woods, which spiked shortly after his accident and significantly outnumbered those for any other athlete. Indeed, at one point Tiger Woods searches eclipsed 3 million on a weekly basis. In contrast, no other athlete surpassed more than half a million for the entire year of 2009. Similar trends were seen on Tiger Woods–specific Web sites. The "Say" component of the tracking model was the more than 24,000 mentions of Tiger on various social media sites for the period November 30 to December 29, 2009, the bulk of which were negative in nature. "The Tiger Woods scandal brought the Influence Tracking model to life in terms that people could relate to, given the extensive media coverage. Using traditional research methods, it would not have been possible to gauge the impact of how consumers' perception of Tiger Woods had changed," noted Friedman. While not every brand will experience such dramatic changes, the influence of social media clearly cannot be ignored by marketers. It should be noted that different conditions in different markets make comparison of tracking study results difficult. These conditions include: (1) the size of advertising expenditures, (2) the nature of the brands, (3) the differences in advertising styles and cultures, (4) media differences in advertising practice, and (5) differences in legal restrictions (de Mooij and Keegan 1991).

With regard to message placement, marketers will require information relating to the availability of media for commercial purposes as well as data relating to advertising readership, listenership, and viewership and audience characteristics. The individual media in established markets are capable of providing such information to the marketer. This is increasingly true of the media in developing markets as well. In addition, media-generated research—such as audience profiles, product perception surveys, and brand preference or awareness studies—may be available without cost from various foreign print and broadcast media. A number of general resources are likely to be of value to the international marketer, including the *World Radio and Television Handbook,* the *Media Guide International for Business and Professional Publications and Newspapers,* and Euromonitor's *European and International Marketing Data.* The number of quality international media placement services is also on the increase.

## TECHNOLOGICAL ADVANCES AND RESEARCH

The Internet has dramatically changed the way in which international marketing research is conducted, both in providing ready access to secondary data, and in providing a new means of collecting primary data. Omar (2009) notes that for those researchers with access to fee-based databases of periodicals, journals, and company-based information, such as ABI/Inform, Dow Jones Interactive, and LexisNexis, background research can be accomplished with new power. For those without access to such fee-based databases, free-access sites remain extremely useful. Primary data can also be collected via the Internet, either by tracking visitors to a Web site or through administering electronic questionnaires over the Net. To the extent that Web sites are increasingly likely to be accessed by users worldwide, information on an international sample can be gathered. Behavior at the site can be tracked (such as the number of times a Web page is visited, and the amount of time spent on the page), revealing interest relating to the products and services or information offered, as well as response to promotional materials or offers.

The Internet can also be used to collect primary data in a more systematic fashion. Subject to the availability of suitable Internet sampling frames, questionnaires can be administered directly over the Internet. Questionnaires can be sent via e-mail to respondents, and responses are returned via e-mail. Birn (2000) highlights both the advantages and disadvantages of using the Internet to conduct research. On the plus side, responses tend to be objective, as respondents are typing in their own feedback; the use of the Internet is unintrusive, because respondents typically complete surveys at their own pace; responses tend to be speedy; there are no international boundaries, and so questionnaires can be completed as easily on the opposite side of the world as at a more local address; and, because data is collected in a predefined electronic format, there is no need to re-enter responses manually, making for considerable cost savings. In addition, the anonymity of the Internet provides a comfort level that cannot be achieved with telephone or mall research, particularly when the subject matter is about income, medical issues, lifestyle, or sensitive or controversial issues. Internet surveys tend to draw more honest responses. On the downside, the target audience is currently still somewhat narrow—the vast majority of users are based in the developed markets, and the system is biased toward more affluent individuals, although the balance is changing. There may also be technical restrictions that vary from one market to the next (some users may be using high-speed modems over a digital telephone network, while others may have something far more basic). The random-digit dialing method of sampling commonly used in telephone research is not easy to achieve online, as e-mail addresses are not published in the same way that phone numbers are, and are considered private to each Web user. Other challenges include determining whether survey takers are real people, ensuring survey takers don't rush through surveys just to get incentives, and weeding out chronic survey takers driven by such incentives. Fortunately, steps are being taken to address these issues. For example, Peanut Labs Inc. is one of several firms that draw survey respondents only from social networks like Facebook and LinkedIn, and then use their profile information to confirm that they are not only real people (as opposed to bots), but also the age and gender they say they are. Peanut Labs also combats the incentive problem by giving out only "virtual currencies," things like points for a Scrabble application in Facebook, for example. And MarketTools Inc. recently debuted an offering called TrueSample that uses a three-layered technique to catch duplicate or false respondents and also weeds out those who are disengaged or are simply rushing though answers to finish a survey. TrueSample monitors respondents' behavior to determine whether they are actually taking time to consider the questions or simply checking off answers in order to finish quickly. Anyone who doesn't pass the system's filters is kept out of the final results (Quenqua 2009). As the use of the Internet becomes more commonplace in developing, as well as developed, markets, online surveys will increasingly replace mail and phone surveys.

In 2009, ACE Metrix, a Los Angeles consulting firm, unveiled an online advertising diagnostic, which it calls the "first on-demand TV advertising creative measurement service" (Neil 2009). The firm's subscription-based service (costing $100,000 and up annually) essentially diagnoses every new commercial that hits the airwaves using 500 online respondents. This is a vastly larger sample size than all but the most ambitious agency focus groups. The survey-takers answer nine questions that deal with the ads' persuasiveness and "watchability." These results, parsed by age and gender, are then fed into the ACE Analyzer's proprietary algorithms that produce scores of 1 to 1,000 in categories such as "desire," "relevance," "change," "attention," "information," and the all-important "likability." For comparison's sake, the system also generates a category segment average—for example, the average ACE score for all automotive or beer and wine advertisers. Clients can then log on, usually within 24 hours of their ad airing, to see how well it was received—and by whom. This instant feedback feature is one of ACE Metrix's selling points. If advertisers know what the response is early on, they can do something about it. For instance, if in the data-mining process advertisers realize their ad is working with a non-targeted demographic—say, a fast-food commercial resonates with older females as opposed to young males—the advertiser can reallocate ad dollars, chasing the more receptive audience. In addition, the system allows advertisers to keep tabs on their competition's advertising, the ratings for which they can follow on the ACE Analyzer. Consider how two ads for import beers fared. One is the Heineken ad called "Men Scream in Cooler" (Wieden & Kennedy), in which a group of friends visit a couple's home to see their current renovations. While the women are admiring the wife's shoe closet, the men are in another part of the house, screaming, crying, and hugging each other with delight over the man's walk-in "beer" closet, stocked with ice-cold Heineken. The other ad is a Dos Equis spot called "A Man's Reputation Expands Quickly" (Euro RSCG Worldwide), featuring the "most interesting man in the world" character. According to the ACE scores, the Heineken ad absolutely trounces the Dos Equis ad, 565 to 310; and in the key demographic, males aged 21 to 35, the Heineken ad scores a stunning 703 compared with Dos Equis at 583. Without question, in the years to come, the Internet will continue to revolutionize how marketing and advertising research is conducted.

## Control of International Research

There are three major approaches to organizing international marketing and advertising research: (1) centralized control, (2) decentralized control, and (3) coordinated control. Each has its advantages as well as disadvantages. The approach ultimately adopted is largely influenced by the overall manner in which the marketer's organization is structured, as well as by the size of the firm's international operations in general and specific markets.

Where a centralized mode of control is employed, headquarters is responsible for all aspects of the investigation to be conducted in each market. This includes determining data sources, outlining the research design and sampling procedures, and specifying the data analysis to be performed. Fieldwork may be undertaken by either headquarters staff or an outside organization. One of the major benefits of the centralized approach is that it ensures maximum comparability of studies conducted across a number of markets. It is also a good deal less expensive to coordinate research design and data processing and analysis in the home office, particularly if the firm is doing research on a regular basis. In addition, it is an excellent way for a firm to gain familiarity with a particular market. The primary drawback of this approach is that local conditions may not be taken into consideration. Too often, headquarters will prefer a uniform research design that may not be sensitive to host-country differences. Also, headquarters staff may be too limited in size or lack the necessary skills in the areas of marketing and advertising research to conduct multicountry investigations.

Where research efforts are decentralized, headquarters establishes the research objectives but assigns supervision of the research program to local personnel. Local units may then opt to hire domestic research firms to assist in the design and implementation of the investigation. Data collection and analysis are handled in the host market, and upon completion of the study, a representative from the research firm or local management presents a report to corporate headquarters. This is often the mode of choice when a firm is completely unfamiliar with a particular country or is undertaking a specialized or one-time-only investigation. It may also be employed in cases where the volume of business in a particular market is limited and does not warrant headquarters' full attention. The major advantage of this approach is that researchers can adapt to differences in the local culture and infrastructure. In addition, local management may be more likely to implement changes based on research in which they were involved. The use of an outside research firm may also provide an added degree of objectivity, which is often of great importance to management. The potential danger associated with a decentralized approach is that the research design and data collection techniques may not be comparable with efforts undertaken in other markets, thus limiting the usefulness of the findings.

With a coordinated approach, headquarters maintains its involvement in defining the research objectives, but turns over the coordination of the research efforts in different countries to either an international research agency or the corporation's regional headquarters. The research agency or regional headquarters generally involves, to varying degrees, both headquarters and staff in the local operating units in the research endeavor. As a result, local operating units may be less likely to object to plans based on such research. The coordinated approach increases, but does not guarantee, the comparability of research results between markets, particularly if modifications are incorporated based on local input.

## SUMMARY

As companies increase their involvement in foreign markets, they recognize the importance of conducting international marketing and advertising research. This process involves defining the research problem, identifying information sources, collecting data, and analyzing and reporting the data. The two means of obtaining marketing information are collecting secondary data and conducting primary research. Secondary data are quick and inexpensive to obtain, so almost all international research begins with the collection of previously compiled data. However, as the extent of a firm's international involvement increases, so does its recognition of the importance of primary research. While secondary data can provide the marketer with a wealth of information, only primary data can truly address the marketer's more specific questions. Data collection methods include observation, focus-group interviews, in-depth interviews, and surveys—telephone, mail, in-person, and e-surveys. Firms must also recognize that conducting research in the international setting differs from that in domestic settings, and must decide on a centralized, decentralized, or coordinated approach to research efforts. A sincere commitment by management to conduct both secondary and primary research in each of the foreign markets in which their firm operates is sure to reduce the potential for marketing blunders. We now turn our attention to regulatory considerations in the international arena.

## REFERENCES

Bartos, Rena. 1989. International demographic data? Incomparable! *Marketing and Research Today*, 17: November, 205–212.

Birn, Robin. 2000. *The handbook of international market research techniques*. London: Kogan Page.

Cateora, Philip R., and John M. Hess. 1979. *International marketing*. Homewood, IL: Irwin.

Cateora, Philip R., and Susan M. Keaverney. 1987. *Marketing: An international perspective*. Homewood, IL: Irwin.

Choudhrey, Yusuf A. 1977. Pitfalls in international marketing research: Are you speaking French like a Spanish cow? *Akron Business and Economic Review*, 17(4): Winter, 18–28.

Craig, C. Samuel and Susan P. Douglas. 2005. *International marketing research*. 3rd ed. Chichester, England: John Wiley & Sons.

Cundiff, Edward, and Marye Tharpe Hilger. 1988. *Marketing in the international environment*. Englewood Cliffs, NJ: Prentice Hall.

*Daily Mail* (London). 2010. Axed, Flake's raciest TV advertising campaign. 6 March, 45.

de Mooij, Marieke, and Warren Keegan. 1991. *Advertising worldwide*. New York: Prentice Hall.

Douglas, Susan P., and C. Samuel Craig. 1983. *International marketing research*. Englewood Cliffs, NJ: Prentice Hall.

Eckhardt, Giana, and Anders Bengtsson. 2010. Naturalistic group interviewing in China. *Qualitative Market Research* (Bradford), 13(1): 36.

Fields, George. 1980. Advertising strategy in Japan. *Dentsu's Japan Marketing/Advertising*, Fall/ Winter, 52–56.

Honomichl, Jack. 2009. Global top 25, 2009 Honomichl Report. *Marketing News*, 30 August, 23.

Jackson, Kathy. 2009. Hyundai marketer Ewanick goes face to face with the customer. *Automotive News* (Detroit), 26 October, 16.

Jain, Subhash. 1984. *International marketing management*. Boston: PWS-Kent.

Jeannet, Jean-Pierre, and Hubert Hennessey. 1988. *International marketing management: Strategies and cases*. Boston: Houghton Mifflin.

Johansson, Johny K., and Ikujiro Nonaka. 1987. Market research the Japanese way. *Harvard Business Review*, 65: May/June, 16–22.

Kastenholz, John, Charles Young, and Tony Dubitsky. 2004. Roughing it. *Marketing Research*, Winter, 23–27.

Keegan, Warren J. 1984. *Multinational marketing management*. Englewood Cliffs, NJ: Prentice Hall.

Khermouch, Gerry. 2001. Consumers in the mist. *Business Week*, 26 February, 92.

Koenderman, Tony. 2002. Unilever claims innovation with aloe vera sensitive detergent. 6 May. <www.adageglobal.com/cgi-bin/daily.pl?daily_id=7502&post_date=2002–05–06>.

McMains, Andrew. 2006. Saatchi revamps Youth Connection. *AdWeek*, 7 August. <http://www.allbusiness.com/marketing-advertising/4165788-1.html>. Retrieved 2 May 2010.

Microsoft Advertising Press Release. 2007. New global study from MTV, Nickelodeon and Microsoft. 24 July. <http://advertising.microsoft.com/asia/NewsAndEvents/PressRelease>. Retrieved 28 April 2010.

Mueller, Barbara. 1990. Cultural pitfalls in international advertising research. In *Proceedings of the 1990 Conference of the American Academy of Advertising*, ed. Patricia Stout. American Academy of Advertising, Austin, Texas. RST 194–196.

Neil, Dan. 2009. Company town: Do TV ads measure up? Survey says..." *Los Angeles Times*, 30 June, B-1.

Omar, Ogenyi. 2009. *International marketing*. New York: Palgrave Macmillan.

Peebles, Dean M., and John K. Ryans. 1984. *Management of international advertising: A marketing approach*. Newton, MA: Allyn & Bacon.

Plummer, Joseph T. 1986. The role of copy research in multinational advertising. *Journal of Advertising Research*, 26(5): October/November, 11–15.

*PR Newswire*. 2010. TNS presenting new influence-based consumer tracking model at ARF. 23 March. <http://proquest.umi.com.librpoxy.sdsu.edu/pqdweb?index=3&did=1...>. Retrieved 30 April 2010.

Quenqua, Douglas. 2009. Survey says: New tools aim to ensure the integrity of online surveys. *Marketing News*, 30 November, 20–21.

Stilson, Janet. 2009. Joel Ewanick: Grand marketer of the Year 2009. *AdWeek*, 14 September, 12.

Terpstra, Vern. 1988. *International dimensions of marketing*. Boston: PWS-Kent.

Terpstra, Vern, and Lloyd Russow. 2000. *International dimensions of marketing*. Cincinnati, OH: South-Western College Publishing.

Toyne, Brian, and Peter Walters. 1989. *Global marketing management: A strategic perspective*. Boston: Allyn & Bacon.

Usunier, Jean-Claude. 1996. *Marketing across cultures*. London: Prentice Hall.

Van Raaij, W. Fred. 1977. Cross-cultural research methodology: A case of construct validity. *Advances in Consumer Research*, 5: 693–710.

White, Dan. 2007. Earlier the better. *Marketing* (London), 3 October, 17.

# CHAPTER NINE

# Advertising Regulatory Considerations in the International Arena

Much as the media scene of a particular country changes rapidly, so, too, does the regulatory situation. In fact, the two are often related. As new media forms evolve, such as the Internet and mobile phone advertising, new regulations also develop regarding advertising messages that may appear in those media. Currently, advertising regulations differ significantly among nations. A message considered perfectly acceptable in one market might well be deemed inappropriate in another. Product categories that can be advertised freely in one country may be banned altogether elsewhere. In this chapter we will highlight the various types of advertising regulations and regulatory agencies the international advertiser may encounter when promoting goods and services in foreign countries. We will also discuss the role of self-regulation in both national and international markets and the implications of advertising regulation for the international marketer. Each of these points is relevant, regardless of whether the international marketer plans to undertake a standardized campaign or anticipates localizing promotional efforts for each country. Because it is beyond the scope of this text to provide a complete overview of the regulatory environment of each and every market, examples will be provided instead to reinforce the variety of advertising regulations worldwide.

## INFLUENCES ON NATIONAL REGULATIONS

Much in the same way international marketers must familiarize themselves with the foreign marketing environment, as discussed in Chapter 3, so, too, must they investigate the regulatory environment. Indeed, demographic, economic, geographic, political-legal, and cultural factors may all directly influence the regulatory situation. In particular, the degree to which advertising is regulated, as well as the forms that regulations take, is inextricably intertwined with the political system and the dominant religion of a country. The political environment in a nation shapes the prevalent attitudes toward business. Edward Cundiff and Marye Tharp Hilger explain: "Differences in attitudes may be due to different political structures or to party philosophies, history and tradition, the roles of interest groups or the political elite, an unstable political environment and forces of nationalism" (Cundiff and Hilger 1988, 196). For instance, less than 20 years ago, foreign investment was forbidden by law, and foreign investors were considered agents of treason in Albania. The Stalinist totalitarian regime that had ruled Albania since 1944 fell apart with the collapse of communism in Eastern Europe. Coca-Cola became the first major foreign investor in 1994, opening a $10-million bottling plant just outside the capital (Tagliabue 1994). Since then, Albania has joined NATO and, in April 2009, formally applied for EU membership. Today the country has implemented a number of fiscal and legislative reforms to improve the business climate and thereby further increase foreign direct investment.

Legal restrictions are often based on religious foundations, and particular religions may frown on certain business practices. For example, writes Katherine Toland Frith:

> Islam is the national religion in Malaysia and there have been cases where commercials have been withdrawn from the media because of complaints from religious authorities. The Seiko watch company had been running a worldwide campaign using the theme: "Man Invented Time, Seiko Perfected It." A series of commercials with this theme ran on RTM networks…until RTM received a complaint from the Head of Islamic Studies at University Malaya charging that this commercial should be withdrawn because God, not man, invented time. RTM complied. The agency was told that if they wanted to advertise in Malaysia they must change their slogan. After lengthy consultations with the client, a new slogan was developed: "Man Invented Timekeeping, Seiko Perfected It." The agency had to change all television commercials, as well as outdoor and press ads. (Frith 1987)

In some countries, regulation may be quite limited, and the laws that reinforce such regulation quite lax, particularly in developing markets. In others, advertising regulation may be perceived as quite extensive and often may be stringently enforced. As Barbara Sundberg Baudot points out, "International law accords the host country sovereignty over all peoples, resources and activities within their territorial limits. The capacity, willingness and effectiveness of the host countries to perform such roles vary considerably" (Baudot 1989, 31).

At the national level, deceptive advertising practices are considered a crime in every country. The U.S. criteria for defining deception include determining whether the claim is false, whether the information presented is partially true and partially false, whether the message lacks sufficient information, whether the claim is true but the proof is false, and whether the message creates a false implication. Similar standards hold in other countries and have been adopted by international regulatory bodies as well. Clearly, such deceptive practices should be avoided because they are harmful not only to the consumer but also to honest advertisers and the public image of advertising in general.

Beyond deception, advertising regulation also focuses on the type of products that may be advertised, the audience the advertiser may address, the content or creative approach that may be employed in advertising, the media that all advertisers (or different classes of product/service advertisers) are permitted to employ, the amount of advertising that a single advertiser may employ in total or in a specific medium, the use of advertising materials prepared outside the country, and the use of local versus international advertising agencies. Each of these areas will be addressed in turn.

## Types of Products That May Be Advertised

*Alcohol:* In the United States, alcoholic beverage ads are restricted in terms of where the messages can appear, as well as what they can say. But guidelines differ depending upon the type of alcoholic beverage: beer, wine, or spirits. In 1936 the makers of distilled spirits agreed collectively not to air ads on radio, and a decade later followed suit for television. For eight decades, American television was free of liquor ads. However, in the mid 1990s, the Distilled Spirits Council—the industry trade group—announced that it would reverse the decades-old voluntary ban and would begin purchasing commercial time on radio and television stations willing to accept the messages. In 1996, Joseph E. Seagram & Sons ran a series of advertisements for its Crown Royal Canadian whiskey brand on local television stations in Texas and the northeastern United States. Initially rebuffed by broadcast network television, the distilled spirits industry aggressively turned to cable television. Indeed, the number of distilled spirits ads on cable networks grew 5,687 percent between 2001 and 2004—from 645 advertisements to 37,328. Distilled spirits spending on cable networks grew 3,392 percent, from $1.5 million to $53.6 million (Center on Alcohol Marketing and Youth 2005). Since then, distilled spirits ads have aired on hundreds of cable stations and networks, including CNN, Fox Sports Network, Discovery, A&E, Comedy Central, and USA Network. Slowly, the networks have begun to open their doors as well. In December 2001, NBC, now part of the NBC Universal division of General Electric, tried to bring liquor commercials onto national broadcast programs by running spots for Smirnoff vodka during *Saturday Night Live.* The plan called for spots that promoted responsible drinking to be followed by product commercials, but widespread outcry against the concept led NBC to end the experiment in March 2002. Distilled spirits ads began airing in November 2007 on WNBC in New York, the NBC local flagship. The network said at the time that the decision to carry the spots, for brands like Bacardi rum and Grey Goose vodka, was made by the station. In 2009, viewers in New York City who watched the CBS network's national coverage of the Grammy Awards on WCBS, the local affiliate, saw a 30-second spot for Absolut vodka. CBS also said that the decision to accept or decline liquor commercials is made by the executives at local stations. The Absolut spot, part of the "In an Absolut World" campaign, ran after 10 p.m. on stations that, in addition to WCBS in New York, included stations owned by CBS in cities such as Boston, Chicago, Denver, Los Angeles, Miami, Philadelphia, and San Francisco (Elliott 2009). Today, heavy television and radio advertising for the beer segment continues. Moderate amounts of electronic advertising for the wine segment of the industry appear to be developing in certain markets throughout the United States, though in significantly smaller levels relative to beer. And the distilled spirits industry devotes approximately 25 percent of its advertising to television—in comparison to the 54 percent it devotes to magazines. The Distilled Spirits Council of the United States updated its Code of Responsible Practices for Advertising and Marketing in 2003, and now requires a 70 percent adult demographic for ad placements, transparency through semi-annual public reports on advertising complaints, post-audits of ad placements, and the establishment of an outside code advisory board.

Some countries have more lenient guidelines for the marketing of alcoholic beverages than does the United States, while others have restrictions that are significantly more stringent. In Japan, advertising for wine, spirits, and beer is allowed in all major media vehicles. In fact, practices that would not be deemed acceptable in the United States are common practices in Japan. For example, Anheuser-Busch introduced Buddy's, a beer created for the Japanese market that contains less malt but more alcohol than most other beers. This allows Anheuser-Busch to advertise the product's lower price and to promote it as "extra strong," a claim backed up by its alcohol content, which is 20 percent higher than Budweiser's.

The use of celebrities to advertise hard liquor on television is also common. Within the EU, alcohol advertising is regulated differently everywhere. Austria and Belgium have banned spirits from television. In Italy, there is no alcohol advertising on television between 4 P.M. and 9 P.M.—the time when children might be watching. German alcoholic beverage manufacturers cannot show sports stars drinking alcohol or air television ads before 8 P.M. The Czech Republic forbids the pouring of alcoholic drinks in ads or the depiction of anyone enjoying such a drink. In the United Kingdom, a recent study by the British Medical Association entitled "Under the Influence" is recommending a complete ban on all alcohol advertising and sponsorships in that country, a call the Irish Medical Association has also backed (Hall 2009). Perhaps the strictest country in the EU is France. Back in 1991, an increasingly health-obsessed French government passed a law named after its legislative proponent, Claude Evin, banning alcohol advertising on television and at sporting events and severely limiting advertising in print. Under the Evin law, wine producers were forbidden to make any claims about quality. Indeed, they couldn't mention anything relating to smell, taste, or color. Just the name, manufacturer, alcohol content, and appellation of origin were allowed. Only in 2005 was the law modestly amended to allow "references to the qualitative characteristics of the product." President Nicolas Sarkozy says he is in favor of softening the Evin law but so far has taken no legislative action (Kramer 2008). And while France may be home to some of the world's finest wines, it could be about to join the tiny club of Muslim states that also prohibit their promotion on the Internet. Winemakers and other players in the drinks industry are fighting to avert a ban on advertising, sales, and even vineyard Web sites that has been looming ever since a court ruled that the Internet should be included in France's strict laws regarding alcohol advertising. The Heineken Beer Company was forced by the ruling to block French access to its corporate site. Since then, some of the biggest drinks brands have shut out French visitors for fear of prosecution (Bremner and Tourres 2008).

While the regulation of alcohol advertising is strict in France, it is even stricter in Thailand. In 2007, the Thai government announced that it would enforce a total ban on alcohol advertising in the kingdom. The Alcohol Control Act provides, in part, that advertising alcohol products is prohibited by all means of advertising media or by any other method. This extremely broad prohibition extends, but is not limited to, all forms of traditional and non-traditional electronic and print media, as well as to advertising through sponsorships, promotions, or in the staging of public events and displays. In addition, the use of established logos or branding, or those confusingly similar, in the promotion of non-alcoholic brands is strictly prohibited. Further, advertisements containing the names or trademarks of alcohol manufacturers, importers, or distributors are prohibited. The only exceptions to these strict prohibitions are for print media and live television broadcasts originating abroad and not intended for specific distribution in Thailand (Ramirez and Hauserman 2007).

*Tobacco:* In the United States, broadcast ads for cigarettes were officially outlawed under the Federal Cigarette Labeling and Advertising Act in 1971—but cigarette ads proliferated in most other media. In 1994, the heads of seven top U.S. tobacco companies swore before Congress that nicotine was not addictive. This blatant lie ushered in a wave of litigation on the addictive nature of tobacco products. In November 1998, tobacco producers and 46 states came to a $246 billion settlement to resolve state claims for health costs related to smoking. As part of the settlement, stricter guidelines related to the marketing of cigarettes were imposed. Gone were outdoor billboard messages; advertisements on the sides of buses, in subways, and on top of taxis; stadium advertising; branded merchandise such as caps and T-shirts; payment for product placement in movies and on television; and point-of-sale advertising excessive in size.

In 1999, representatives of the tobacco firms recanted their statements and finally admitted that nicotine is indeed addictive. And in late 1999, the U.S. Justice Department filed a sweeping civil lawsuit against the nation's largest tobacco companies. It sought to force cigarette makers to give up profits that were "ill-gotten" through what it said were efforts to conceal the dangers of smoking that go back to the 1950s. The suit alleged that beginning in 1954, tobacco executives met at the Plaza Hotel in New York to plan a long-term campaign to conceal the health risks of smoking. The lawsuit accused the tobacco industry of promoting biased research, wrongly asserting that nicotine was not addictive, and falsely denying that they were targeting their products to children. The federal suit did not specify how much would be sought in damages.

The lawsuit sought to recover billions of dollars the federal government spent on smoking-related healthcare for elderly Medicare patients, military veterans, and federal employees, expenses not covered by the settlement that the industry reached in 1998. The defendants included Philip Morris, The Liggett Group, American Tobacco, British-American Tobacco, R.J. Reynolds Tobacco, Brown & Williamson Tobacco, and Lorillard Tobacco. Along with these companies, which sell 98 percent of the cigarettes in the United States, the suit also named two industry groups, the Council for Tobacco Research USA and the Tobacco Institute (the *New York Times* News Service 1999). The Clinton Administration and the Food and Drug Administration proposed very strict regulations regarding the promotion and advertising of tobacco, including a ban on magazine advertisements that have a 15 percent or greater readership among those under 18, a ban on billboard ads within 1,000 feet of a school or playground, a ban on the sponsorship of sporting or entertainment events, as well as a ban on cigarette machines in stores or restaurants. The Bush Administration inherited the lawsuit from the previous administration and proposed even more stringent regulation, including banning terms such as "low tar" and "light," requiring that health warnings cover 50 percent of cigarette packs and advertisements, and even eliminating cigarette vending machines (Zuckerbrod 2002). In 2008, the U.S. Supreme Court ruled that tobacco companies that marketed "light" and "low tar" cigarettes may indeed be sued for fraud. The 5–4 ruling is expected to open the way for dozens of lawsuits claiming billions of dollars in damages.

Tobacco firms in the United States are likely to face increased regulation yet again. Many proponents of tobacco regulation have urged government to grant the U.S. Food and Drug Administration (FDA) authority over tobacco products. On April 2, 2009, anti-smoking forces won a long-awaited victory as the House passed legislation (voting 298–112) to give the federal government key controls over the tobacco industry for the first time. The measure gives the FDA broad authority to regulate—but not ban—cigarettes and other tobacco products. The White House supports the legislation, a shift from the Bush Administration, which had threatened to veto a House-passed measure in 2008. The measure will allow the agency to regulate the contents of tobacco products, make ingredients public, prohibit flavoring, require much larger warning labels, and strictly control or prohibit marketing campaigns, especially those geared toward children. Most important, it will grant the FDA the authority to impose additional marketing restrictions and counter tobacco companies' efforts to get around specific restrictions (Werner 2009).

While U.S. tobacco firms are lamenting long and loud about the federal government's restrictions on their promotional activities, the U.S. government is comparatively lenient in the realm of tobacco advertising. Consider Malaysia, where virtually all forms of tobacco advertising have been banned for nearly two decades—though cigarette manufacturers were able to sponsor sporting events and advertise their brand name at the point of sale, as long as no product images were used. But regulations introduced in 2002 even put a stop to that. The restrictions also prohibited scenes in movies and television shows that depicted people smoking. Further, such scenes were edited out of existing movies and television programs (Vance 2002, 1). And Russia, one of the world's top markets for tobacco sales, plans to ban all cigarette advertising by 2013.

Of course, there are also markets with significantly fewer restrictions. Japan remains among the least restrictive industrialized nations with respect to cigarette advertising. Indeed, it has been dubbed a "smoker's paradise," where over 60 percent of males smoke. Despite the high consumption rate of tobacco, Japan has just recently begun to address the public health issues related to smoking. The Tobacco Institute of Japan announced a voluntary ban on all television, radio, cinema, and Internet advertising. While the Tobacco Institute's policies are much more restrictive than was the case in the past, it is worth noting that self-regulation is the dominant force behind the restrictions—cigarette ads are not formally banned in any medium—and that advertising in magazines and newspapers and on billboards remains legal (Taylor and Raymond 2000, 289). Even today, smoking is common in restaurants, vending machines abound, and free samples are frequently given out. Japan's only true prohibition is that cigarette advertising should not target women (Hadenfeldt 2008). And Indonesia—with virtually no bans on cigarette advertising—has the weakest anti-smoking regulation in Southeast Asia. Some 63 percent of Indonesian men smoke, with an estimated 200,000 dying each year of smoking-related illnesses. The country has been called a "cash cow" for Philip Morris International (PMI), the owner of Indonesia's PT HM Sampoerna Company, which last year claimed a 30 percent share of the Indonesian market and estimated revenues of $1 billion (*Earth Times* 2009).

*Pharmaceuticals:* Nonprescription drugs have been advertised through various media to consumers around the globe for decades. However, commercial messages promoting prescription drugs were typically directed at physicians and generally appeared only in trade journals. Then, in August 1997, the Food and Drug Administration relaxed the rules of pharmaceutical product promotion in the United States. Under the new guidelines, companies needed only mention significant side effects in television messages, referring viewers to magazine ads, toll-free phone numbers, Internet sites, or to medical professionals for specific details. The result? The American Medical Association reported that in 1998, $1.3 billion was spent on direct-to-consumer (DTC) pharmaceutical advertising (Pirisi 1999). In the first half of 1999 alone, companies spent $905 million, a 43 percent increase over the same time period the previous year, according to the industry research company IMS Health (Neergaard 1999). Between 2000 and 2004, prescription drug advertising surged 70 percent, to nearly $4.5 billion (Jordan 2007). In 2008, spending on DTC advertising totaled $4.7 billion, nearly one-fourth of pharmaceutical manufacturers' expenditures for all promotional activities (Congressional Budget Office 2009). Television continues to be the medium of choice, accounting for 59 percent of all direct-to-consumer advertising spending. Indeed, the average American sees about 30 hours of drug commercials a year (McGowan 2008). Magazines represent about 34 percent of total ad spending on DTC medications, while newspapers account for only 3 percent of total spending (*Wall Street Journal* 2006). However, industry experts predict that pharmaceutical manufacturers will increasingly turn to the Web as well as digital and cable alternatives, since these options offer better-targeted and cost-effective advertising returns. The FDA vets all marketing communications for DTC before the ads hit the media (Schmit 2008). They are empowered by Congress to impose fines as high as $250,000 for ads it deems misleading. However, the organization has insufficient staff to handle the thousands of promotional pieces submitted by the drug companies and ad agencies for review. So the FDA is asking doctors and health care professionals across the country to serve as "Big Brothers" in an initiative designed to catch misleading drug ads. The program allows doctors and medical professionals to report false or deceptive ads to the FDA and to do so anonymously via e-mails to badad@fda.gov (Thomaselli 2010). The FDA also launched a new Web site, "Be Smart about Prescription Drug Advertising, A Guide for Consumers" (www.fda.gov/cder/ethicad). The goal of the site is to educate consumers about how to view DTC advertisements, prepare them for discussion with health care professionals, and help improve patient understanding and medical care.

The United States is on the cutting edge of this trend. New Zealand and China, to a more limited extent, are the only other countries where direct-to-consumer advertising is currently legal. In the past, however, the policing of pharmaceutical advertising in China was clearly insufficient. Chinese consumers were annually inundated with hundreds of messages for medicines and medical devices purported to diagnose, cure, or prevent illness, or regulate body functions (many of them variations on traditional Chinese herbs and methods of treatment). While some of the ads for these products were harmless, others were outrageous, such as a television spot for an anti-aging tea that showed older people becoming young and virile. Other messages were potentially dangerous. Love Solution, a "sterilizing spray," claimed it could protect the user from contracting AIDS; print ads claimed the product was approved by the Virus Institute of the Chinese Academy of Preventative Medicine. The Chinese government has since clamped down on the promotion of pharmaceutical products. According to current guidelines, all pharmaceutical messages are now subject to review. The advertisements must be true, accurate, and scientific. When advertising pharmaceuticals, manufacturers must back up any statistical claims with recognized research. Pharmaceutical ads may not make extravagant claims or feature names or images of medical or research units, academic institutions, medical experts, or testimony from doctors or patients (Taylor and Raymond 2000, 292).

DTC is being considered in Australia, Canada, and the United Kingdom. Until quite recently, European consumers were protected from or deprived of (depending on one's point of view) such blandishments. Interestingly, the Internet may ultimately force the issue. The thousands of medical sites worldwide are all accessible from a European desktop, and many of them name branded products. Also, many branded prescription drugs have their own Web sites, such as the one for Pfizer's best-selling cholesterol drug Lipitor. The site features an endorsement from Robert Jarvik, who invented the artificial heart and who also appears in Lipitor's television ads in the United States. The sites usually have disclaimers saying the product information is intended only for U.S. citizens, but anyone around the world can view them. For some U.S. drug Web sites, up to 30 percent of visitor traffic comes from outside the United States, estimates Mark Bard, president of Manhattan Research LLC, a health market research firm (Loftus 2007). However, most U.S. product Web sites are in English, limiting their usefulness to non-English speakers. Nonetheless, health chat rooms, virtual pharmacies, and self-diagnosis sites are mushrooming. This flood of information makes a ban on regulated advertising hard to justify. "Consumer pressure is going to become more and more important," says Jean-Pierre Garnier, chief operating officer at SmithKlineBeecham. "You can mobilize a group of patients through the internet. That will start to create pressure on what governments can or cannot forbid" (Pilling 1999). In 2001, the EU proposed allowing direct-to-consumer advertising for three specific conditions—AIDS, respiratory problems such as asthma, and diabetes—allowing pharmaceutical companies to communicate with patients via the Internet (*Marketing Week* 2001). If direct-to-consumer advertising were to be legalized, it is predicted that it would have an even bigger impact on the nationalized health services of Europe than it has already had on the private ones of the United States. Some are concerned that the Nationalized Health Services won't be able to cope with the financial implications of patients' demand for expensive drugs. Soaring drug sales are less of a government concern in the United States, where the bulk of health care is paid by private insurance. In Europe, an advertising-led boom in sales would have to be met by public expenditure (Thornton 2000). But because of cultural as well as health-system differences between the United States and Europe, most don't expect to see a lifting of the DTC ban on the continent any time soon.

*Other Products:* Although most international marketers are accustomed to some form of restriction on the products noted above, there are numerous unanticipated restrictions as well. While South Africa has allowed the advertising of condoms for nearly two decades now, after years of hesitation, China lifted its ban in 2002. The ban was based on a regulation passed in 1989 that outlawed the advertising of "sex products." China's Industrial and Commercial Bureau, the government department that rules on advertising, said that this included condoms. It argued that the public was not ready for such ads. A campaign by one condom maker on buses in Guangzhou brought a flood of complaints from the public that it was poisoning the minds of young people. But the spread of AIDS finally changed the government's mind. According to official figures, there are more than 1 million people infected with the virus in China. By 2010, there will be more than 10 million. An Baohan, who works at the Yi Dian Health Center, hailed the decision: "As a doctor, I strongly support this. It will help us in controlling the population, is a symbol of modern thinking, and will help to prevent sexual diseases, especially AIDS" (*South China Morning Post* 2002).

In Vietnam, municipal authorities announced restrictions on feminine hygiene products and even lingerie, noting that depictions of these products are inappropriate for the public arena. An official from Ho Chi Minh City's Culture and Information Department explained that the restrictions were the result of complaints that some advertisements did not respect Vietnamese culture and traditions. State-owned Vietnam television (VTV) has informed advertisers that manufacturers of feminine hygiene products and underwear would not be allowed to sponsor films or programs on television. Nor would these ads be allowed on billboards or buses (Timms 2001).

Saudi Arabia implemented a new law in 2008 that banned the advertising of infant milk formulas, food substitutes, baby bottles, and pacifiers. The Ministries of Health and Commerce enforce the law, which was designed to encourage new mothers to breastfeed their infants. Islam, the dominant religion, encourages natural feeding of infants from the mother's breast milk. The Quran specifically mentions a weaning period of two full years, for those who wish to breastfeed. Indeed, the special bond created by breast feeding a child is also recognized under Islamic law: two unrelated children who are breastfed by the same mother are considered to be "milk siblings" with applicable rights. Saudi Arabia's law does not limit a mother's choice to use alternative milk products if she chooses. Various brands of formula are available within the country. The ban is on the advertisements of these products (About.com: Islam 2008).

Among restricted product categories around the world, undoubtedly the most unusual is Thailand's restriction on the promotion of energy drinks containing caffeine. Rules prohibit athletes and blue-collar workers from being featured in the ads in order to avoid associating the drinks with increased energy—the main promise of the energy drinks. In addition, warnings must be printed clearly on both ads for the products and on product packaging. The warnings cite that not more than two bottles of the energy drinks should be consumed in a day, and that pregnant women and children should avoid the caffeine-laden beverages altogether (Schmid 2002).

## The Audiences That Advertisers May Address

In many Western countries, and particularly in the United States, kids and teens are perceived by advertisers as an increasingly lucrative market. The primary body involved in the oversight of advertising to children in the United States is a self-regulatory one. In 1974 the National Advertising Division (NAD) of the Council of Better Business Bureaus set up a group charged with helping advertisers deal with children's advertising in a manner sensitive to children's special needs. The Children's Advertising Review Unit (CARU) was established to review and evaluate advertising directed at children under the age of 12. The CARU general guidelines address the following nine areas: deception; product presentations and claims; disclosures and disclaimers; endorsements; the blurring of advertising and editorial/program content; premiums, kids' clubs, sweepstakes, and contests; online sales; sales pressure; unsafe and inappropriate advertising to children. A complete overview of these guidelines can be found at http://www.caru.org. As excellent as these guidelines are, the primary problem is that CARU doesn't have the power to enforce them, while the Federal Trade Commission, which has the power, cannot issue sweeping regulations. The FTC can only respond to complaints on a case-by-case basis. It should be noted that the United States is one of the most lenient countries in the developed world when it comes to marketing to children.

Other countries have been more aggressive in regulating marketing to children. The Canadian province of Quebec has long banned advertising to children on television and radio. Recently a bill was introduced seeking to extend the ban across the entire country (*Today's Parent* 2008). New Zealand's government has indicated it intends to eliminate advertising during all children's programs. While advertising to children is allowed in Malaysia, guidelines are very strict. Advertising in Malaysia is self-regulated by what is referred to as the Malaysian Code of Advertising Practices (Mirandah 2005). In addition to guidelines quite similar to those of CARU in the United States, the code stipulates:

- Use of children in advertisements is discouraged unless the products that are advertised have a direct bearing on them.
- No advertisement is allowed that encourages children to enter strange places or to converse with strangers in an effort to collect coupons, wrappers, labels, or the like. The details of any collecting scheme must be submitted for investigation to ensure the scheme contains no element of danger to children.
- No advertisement dealing with the activities of a club is allowed without the submission of satisfactory evidence that the club is carefully supervised, and there is no suggestion of the club being a secret society.
- Children seen in advertisements must be reasonably well mannered and well behaved.

To date there are no continent-wide rules regarding marketing to children in Europe, but in Norway, Austria, and the Flemish part of Belgium, no advertising is allowed around children's programs. Greece does not allow advertisements for toys to be screened between 7:30 A.M. and 10 P.M., and the Republic of Ireland restricts advertisements in its preschool programming. In France, children are not allowed to endorse products, thus a spot produced in the United Kingdom with a scene showing a child wearing a Kellogg's T-shirt in a Corn Flakes commercial had to be edited for French audiences. Italy, Poland, Denmark, and Latvia are studying plans for tighter regulation. Sweden has taken the strongest line on this issue. Recognizing that children under 10 are incapable of telling the difference between a commercial and a program, and cannot understand the purpose of a commercial until the age of 12, Sweden has banned all advertisements during children's prime time television programming,

**Table 9.1:** "Guideposts" from The International Chamber of Commerce's Framework for Responsible Food and Beverage Marketing Communications

- Marketing Communications must not encourage excess consumption
- Portion sizes must suit the occasion
- Health and nutrition claims must be backed by sound science
- Foods not intended as meal substitutes should not be presented as such
- Food and drink promotions must not undermine the importance of a healthy lifestyle
- Using fantasy and animation to market to children are acceptable, but must not mislead them about nutritional benefits
- Marketing should not lead a child to believe a product will make him or her more popular, smarter or more successful in school or in sports
- Sales promotions must present the conditions of a premium offer or contest in language a child can understand, spelling out the products that must be purchased to receive the offer, the terms of entry, the prizes and chance of winning

*Source:* www.iccwbo.org

and commercials featuring characters children are familiar with are prohibited until 9 P.M. during the week and 10 P.M. on weekends. This rules out not just advertising for toys and candy, but also many ads for products with wider family appeal: McDonald's in Sweden, for instance, cannot employ the clown Ronald McDonald in any of its television ads. Sweden would like other European countries to follow suit, and several have come out in favor of strengthening regulations related to marketing to children, but most other states are satisfied with the status quo, which allows each country to decide on its own measures. It remains to be seen whether an EU-wide ban on broadcast ads aimed at children will be imposed in the near future.

The debate over advertising to children continues to be one of the most controversial topics in advertising discourse. Criticisms of advertising to children are many and varied. Most recently, critics have blamed food and beverage marketers who target young consumers for the negative trends in children's health. Obesity rates in kids around the globe have indeed skyrocketed. The statistics—in both developed and developing countries—are hard to argue with. In the United States, the prevalence of childhood obesity has risen significantly over the past three decades. In 1971 only 4 percent of children aged 6 to 11 were obese; by 2004, the number had leaped to 18.8 percent. In the same period, the figure rose from 5 percent to 13.9 percent among children aged 2 to 5, and from 6.1 percent to 17.4 percent in the 12-to-19-year-old group. If overweight children are included, 32 percent of all U.S. children today carry more pounds than they should (Kluger 2008). The situation does not look much better across the pond. A European Union report shows that one in five EU schoolchildren is now overweight—a total of 14 million—a figure that includes at least 3 million youngsters who fall into the obese category (European Report 2005). But childhood obesity is not unique to Western countries. It appears that China has not only entered the era of obesity, but is also "super-sizing its children as fast as its economy" (MacLeod 2007, 1). The prevalence of overweight and obese children increased by 28 times between 1985 and 2002 (Walsh 2006). Today, 8 percent of childred aged 10 to 12 in China's cities are obese, and an additional 15 percent are overweight (MacLeod 2007). The prevalence of childhood obesity has also rapidly increased in countries as diverse as Brazil, Egypt, Ghana, and Haiti. Indeed, worldwide, 10 percent of children are now estimated to be obese or overweight (Hawkes 2007).

Of all known and suspected risk factors for obesity—and there are many, ranging from rising incomes and falling food prices, to the challenges of preparing healthy meals in households where both parents work, and a dramatic increase in sedentary behavior—the finger has been pointed directly at food marketers. The food industry's global ad budget is a whopping $40 billion, a figure greater than the GDP of 70 percent of the world's nations (*Nutrition and Food Science* 2004). Children in the United States and around the world are clearly being bombarded with an unprecedented avalanche of food advertisements. Television advertising remains marketers' prime tool for selling food to kids (Spake 2003). Research has revealed that kids see an average of more than 10 food ads every hour they watch television, and that fast foods and sweets comprise 83 percent of the advertised foods (Harrison and Marske 2005). Ads for healthier options, such as fruits, vegetables, dairy products, meats, poultry, and fish are seldom seen. Beyond television, there are a multitude of other promotional practices designed to make children desire specific food products, including Web sites, in-school marketing, sales promotions, product placement, event sponsorships, and movie tie-ins.

To assist in the worldwide effort to foster improved diet and health and curb childhood obesity, the International Chamber of Commerce issued a global framework that promotes high ethical standards for the marketing of foods and beverages. The framework's "guideposts" for food and beverage marketers is outlined in Table 9.1. In the United States, the Children's Advertising Review Unit announced intentions to enforce a new level of oversight for food ads. While outright bans on marketing food to children have been debated in many countries, it is notable that both Sweden and Quebec, which have banned most advertising to children, still face high obesity rates. Time will tell whether proposed bans on ads for all unhealthy foods and drinks—set to take effect in Korea and in Russia at the end of 2010—will have the intended effect of slimming down kids in these countries.

In response to criticisms of the U.S. food industry for advertising's role in childhood obesity, an alliance of major food manufacturers pledged to introduce new, more healthful options, cut portion sizes, and trim calories in existing products. The Healthy Weight Commitment Foundation, which includes Campbell's Soup, General Mills, Kellogg, and Kraft Foods vowed to slash 1 trillion calories by the end of 2010 and 1.5 trillion calories by the end of 2015. The 16 members make 20 percent of the food consumed in the United States (Black 2010). Further, many of the companies have agreed to either stop aiming ads at kids or to promote only what are termed "better-for-you products" in ads targeting children. And in Europe, Nestlé, Mars, Coca-Cola, and PepsiCo are among 11 food and beverage companies that signed an EU pledge to stop marketing unhealthful foods to children on the continent. The group promised to stop running junk food ads on television, in print, and on the Internet aimed at those under 12. Altogether, the 11 companies represent more than 50 percent of the food and beverage marketing budgets aimed at kids across Europe (Hall 2007). Clearly these steps are an effort to ward off stricter government regulation. Critics of the self-regulatory approach are concerned by the lack of industry-wide definitions of exactly what "advertising to children" entails and what exactly "better foods" means. Currently, each company defines for itself what these terms mean.

## The Content or Creative Approach That May Be Employed

Many countries have restrictions on the types of claims advertisers can make, the manner in which products can be presented, and the appeals that may be employed in advertisements.

*Comparative Claims:* In the United States, the Federal Trade Commission encourages advertisers to employ comparative claims, as they are seen as providing consumers with relevant product information. Indeed, it is estimated that nearly one-third of commercial messages incorporate some form of comparative claim. Until quite recently, some European nations allowed comparative ads, while others did not. An EU directive was passed that addressed guidelines for the appropriate use of comparative claims in advertising. While the directive compels member states to legalize comparative advertising, it allows each country to ban comparative advertising for certain goods, as well as for professional services. Thus, each member state must obey the directive but can tailor legislation to be more restrictive (Cunningham 2000). South Africa's Advertising Standards Authority, the industry's self-regulatory body, is also considering loosening its strict policy against comparative ads. Marketers are currently prohibited from naming competitors, showing rival brands, or making any comparisons that would identify a specific brand. Advertisers in the country favor relaxation of the policy and have made their opinions known to the Authority (*Advertising Age* 1993).

In Japan, comparative ads remain a rarity, not because of specific regulations, but rather because in Japanese culture direct confrontation and actions that cause another to lose face are considered taboo. Unaccustomed to comparative claims, Japanese consumers were astonished by a newspaper ad for the Ford Motor Co. that criticized Volkswagen's Golf by questioning why the model was so expensive in Japan. Some thought the provocation would spark an ad war or force foreign automakers to cut prices, but, unlike in the United States, such aggressive campaigns do not easily take root. Comparative ads in Japan are mainly the domain of foreign firms. But even so, to go so far as to mention the names of rivals or their product, as Ford did, is extremely rare (*Daily Yomiuri* 1996). Direct-comparison advertising is not allowed in the Philippines. Indirect-comparison ads may be permitted provided they do not use symbols, slogans, titles, or statements that are clearly identified or directly associated with competing brands. Finally, comparative claims simply aren't permitted in Chinese advertising.

*Health and Nutrition Claims:* Most countries have guidelines in place regarding nutrition and health claims made for foods. Marketers who do not comply with these guidelines will likely face censure. The British Advertising Standards Authority ruled that both GlaxoSmithKline (GSK) and Nestlé made unfounded nutritional claims about their products. Television spots for both brands included suggestions that the products could make children taller, stronger, and more intelligent, and give them more powerful muscles. The GSK ad for Horlicks showed an experiment where half the children at a boarding school were given Horlicks and the other half an unnamed health drink. Those drinking Horlicks emerged from the test "taller, stronger and sharper." The ad ended with the line: "The Horlicks challenge, now proven. Now see for yourself." Meanwhile, the Nestlé ads featured a mother saying: "Maggie is best because it has essential protein and calcium that help to build stong muscles and bones. There is no comparison…. Amazing nutrition!" Graphics showed an arm with a yellow glow over the bicep and a knee with a yellow glow over the kneecap. EU law states that "nutritional and health claims which encourage consumers to purchase a product, but are false, misleading, or not scientifically proven are prohibited." Neither GSK nor Nestlé demonstrated to the ASA evidence of the claims they made, and both were banned from showing the ads again. The companies claimed the ads were shown by accident and were intended for audiences in developing markets, not Europe. The case has brought calls for new global advertising regulations and highlighted some of the extraordinary claims brand owners make for their products in developing countries that they would struggle to get approved in Europe (*Marketing Week* 2008).

*Use of Unattainable Body Images:* France has joined the United Kingdom, Italy, and Spain in signing an agreement to end the distribution of images that could encourage anorexia in young women.

Advertising agencies, fashion houses, modeling agencies, and media companies have signed an accord to stop the use of overly thin models. Such images have been blamed for promoting an unattainable and unhealthy ideal for female beauty that has resulted in young girls starving themselves and developing long-term psychological problems related to their weight and body size. Adherence to the pact is voluntary (*Web in France Magazine* 2008). In yet another attempt to fight unrealistic and unattainable body images, France has begun to regulate airbrushed and photo-shopped images (*Clean Cut Media* 2009). Apparently, even after hours of hair and makeup styling, photos used in print advertisements typically go through hours of photo-manipulation. Common practices include slimming waistlines and hips, lengthening neck and legs, altering facial structures, fixing nose shape, moving eyebrows, erasing freckles, and enhancing breasts. French lawmakers decided to require disclaimers on photos that are photo-shopped or enhanced in any way. Disclaimers need to be included in newspaper and magazine ads, as well as product packaging and any situation in which there is a re-touched photograph aimed at changing a person's physical appearance. Some advertisers, notably Unilever, have embraced the value shift, promoting a new ideal of female beauty that is not as thin, not as young, and not as uniformly pretty as has been the standard in the past. Indeed, Unilever has adopted new global guidelines that will require that all its future marketing communications should not use models or actors who are either excessively slim or promote "unhealthy slimness." All brand directors and agencies would be expected to use a Body Mass Index (BMI) of between 18.5 and 25 as a guideline for models and actors (Reuters. com 2007). BMI is a measure expressed as a ratio of weight to height. The World Health Organization considers anyone with a BMI below 18.5 underweight. A BMI below 17.5 is one of the criteria for the diagnosis of anorexia nervosa, and a BMI nearing 15 is used as an indicator of starvation. Consider Unilever's advertising for its Dove brands. Figure 9.1 features a French ad from its "campaign for Real Beauty." The copy reads "Ronde? Rayonnante?" and can be loosely translated as Round or Radiant?

*Other Limitations:* Multinational marketers must be aware of more obscure restrictions on advertising content. The Vietnamese Ordinance on Advertising strictly prohibits advertising that discloses state secrets or that harms national independence and sovereignty, defense, and security or the safety of society; advertising that is contrary to the traditions, history, culture, ethics, or customs of the Vietnamese people; and advertising that arouses violence, that is shocking, or that uses unhealthy language. In China, certain superlatives—"the best," "the most"—are not allowed. Marketers cannot use the word "national," show China's flag, or use its official song or images of its politicians (alive or dead, e.g., Mao is forbidden). Certain statistics or data, such as sales volume, cannot be used (O'Leary, 2007). In Mongolia, a law prohibits advertisers from defaming and slandering the state emblem and symbols, historical personalities, the national currency banknote, religion and faith, and any tradition that needs to be revered by every Mongolian (*BBC Monitoring* 2002). In Greece, ads are prevented from making humorous references regarding national monuments. And in Britain, ads referring to death or religion, and those containing bad language, are considered a "no-no" (*Dominion* 1998).

## The Media That Advertisers Are Permitted to Employ

Media availability is severely limited in many markets. Many countries have banned advertising from state-run television. Britain's BBC is famous for being advertising-free. French president Nicolas Sarkozy created quite a stir in 2009 when he banned ads from prime-time on all state-owned television channels in an attempt to create, in his own words, a public television service to "rival the quality of the BBC." Sarkozy argued that the two terrestrial, state-owned channels, France 2 and France 3, spent too

**Figure 9.1:** No stick-thin models in the French ad for Unilever's line of Dove beauty products.

much money and energy chasing ratings and copying the lowest-common-denominator quiz shows and police serials on the main (private) channel, TF1. By lifting them out of the ratings and advertising game, they will, he argued, be freed to produce more cultural programs, documentaries, and higher-brow television dramas. Monies lost by the state channels in prime time advertising are refunded by a tax on the ad revenue of private channels and a small levy on mobile phone calls. From the end of 2011 onward, the state channels will also have to give up advertising in the morning, afternoon, and early evenings (Lichfield 2009).

With regard to outdoor advertising, while Italian marketers know that billboard ads are banned on highways, they must also comply with a code that bans the outdoor messages from panoramic roads, inside parks, and within 50 meters of bus shelters. The code imposes strong limits on the colors that billboards can employ—only 20 percent of a poster's surface can be red (the only exception is for registered trademarks). In China, city planning officials have segmented the capital into areas where outdoor advertising is permitted—including commercial zones where only well-known Chinese and foreign ads can be displayed—and where it is not. Areas such as Tiananmen Square, Zhongnanhai, Changan Street, the Palace Museum, and Diaoyutai State Guest House are officially off limits to marketers. The guidelines also forbid outdoor advertising within 200 meters of historical and cultural sites, government offices, foreign embassies and consulates, and offices for international trade organizations. However, limited advertising will be allowed in scenic areas, the city's airport, and Zhonggauncun Science and Technology Park (Madden 2001). The Chinese government said the ruling was imposed to improve safety and clear streets and passageways of obstructions. Some media are banned outright. In early 2007, São Paulo—South America's largest city—officially banned all outdoor advertising. Billboards, neon signs, bus-stop ads, even the Goodyear blimp, all were suddenly illegal. The ban on what the mayor called "visual pollution" was the culmination of a long battle between the city's politicians and the advertising industry, which had blanketed Brazil's economic capital with all manner of commercial messages. In Saudi Arabia, direct mail is considered an invasion of privacy, and is thus not used.

Media bans may also be related to specific product categories—in particular, tobacco and alcohol. In China, there is regulation banning the television advertising of spirits with over 40 percent alcohol content. In Taiwan, the government only allows companies to advertise alcohol on network television from 9:30 P.M. until 6:00 A.M. In South Korea, alcoholic beverages may be advertised on television after 10:00 P.M. and on radio after 1:00 P.M. Interestingly, ads for undergarments in this country are only allowed on broadcast media on weekdays between 8:30 A.M. and 4:00 P.M., or after 10:00 P.M.

How the media are used for advertising purposes also differs from market to market. U.S. television viewers are accustomed to having their programming interrupted at regular intervals with commercial messages. The EU's Television Without Frontiers Directive, which aims to harmonize regulation of television across Europe, is significantly more strict. The directive includes strict rules on commercial-break frequency. Commercial breaks must occur not more than every 20 minutes for dramas and documentaries and every 45 minutes for movies (Bowes 2002). A Russian law prohibits the interruption of children's, religious, or educational programs by advertisers. All other programs must not be interrupted more frequently than every 15 minutes. Programs shorter than 15 minutes in length are not to be interrupted with commercial messages. During transmission of the ads, the volume must not be louder than the volume of the program that has been interrupted. Finally, laws also stipulate that ads of similar content for one and the same product must not be transmitted more than twice per hour, and their overall duration must not exceed two minutes (*BBC Monitoring* 2001).

## The Use of Advertising Materials Prepared Outside the Country

A growing number of markets around the globe restrict foreign-produced ads or the use of foreign talent in commercial messages. In an effort to reduce the use of elements of foreign culture in advertising, the Malaysian Ministry of Information has, since the early 1970s, imposed the Made-in-Malaysia (MIM) rule, which requires all advertisements to be produced locally. The talent, creative team, and the production staff must also be Malaysians. Foreign scenes or technologies can only be used after prior approval from the Ministry of Information. This approval is only granted when the technologies or footage are unavailable in the country. If the language used in the commercials is English, then it must be "Malaysia-English," as the use of "British- or American-English" is prohibited. Only the Internet has escaped this governmental regulation. Even if ads are locally produced, they must still refrain from depicting "ways of life that are against or totally different from the ways of life followed by the Malaysians. The government instituted this regulation because of the belief that not all its citizens are prepared to fully accept all aspects of Western culture. Banned are clothing imprinted with words or symbols conveying undesirable messages or impressions; scenes of an amorous, intimate, or suggestive nature; and kissing between adults (Waller, 2000). In 2007, the Indonesian government passed a similar ruling. Regulations issued by the Indonesian Ministry of Communication prohibit advertisers in this country from using foreign models, directors, producers, camera operators and crew, animation artists, musicians, songwriters, stuntmen, and even voice-overs in their ads or from airing foreign-produced commercials on radio and television. The only exceptions, officials say, will be made for brands that carry a "global image," such as the Marlboro man, or for commercials that tout foreign vacations, properties, or events. All other ads must be made locally, using only Indonesian personnel (Yuniar 2007). Peru also bans foreign-inspired models and materials in advertisements appearing in that country, and it appears likely that Vietnam may also follow suit. Beyond nationalistic and cultural objectives, restrictions on foreign-prepared materials are often motivated by economic considerations—such as the desire to provide jobs for the local print production and film industry (Boddewyn and Mohr 1987, 21). There is also the fear that multinational ad agencies will hamper the development of the local advertising businesses.

## The Use of Foreign Languages in Advertising and Marketing Materials

Some countries are quite sensitive about the use of foreign words in commercial communications as well. France, Vietnam, Korea, and Russia are examples of countries that resist the foreignization or anglicization of the local language in advertising messages. The 1994 Toubon Law, put through by Justice Minister Jacques Toubon, required that all goods advertised in France be translated into French names if there were an adequate word available (e.g., the Walkman became le Baladeur; the answering machine, le Répondeur). The law is part of a series of legislative efforts dating back to 1539 to protect the French language from foreign influences. The Toubon law mandates that only the French language can be used on television and radio, in all advertising, schools, and work places. Minister Toubon and his supporters fear that France is becoming overly Americanized and that the French language is dying out. Such language restrictions cost companies extra time and money to change their Americanized labels and themes; thus the law has become another form of trade barrier (Klebnikov 1995, 292). "If someone uses foreign words in publicity or consumer information on products, they will be fined," notes Brigitte Peyrou, an official with the General Delegation for the French Language. "Repeat offenders will pay double" (Waxman 1994). However, the Toubon law cannot require the translation of registered brand names. This means that companies such as Nike that have registered ad slogans as international trademarks may find themselves exempt (Crumley 1993). On the Internet's global computer links, about 90 percent of communication is in English and only 5 percent in French. Toubon believes that here, too, the survival of the French culture is at stake and that the predominantly English Internet is "a new form of colonialism" (Coleman 1997, 57). Thus, the Toubon law also affects the Internet by sparking new laws that will require that information on the Internet from Web sites in France also be in French. Despite these measures to preserve the French language, many French firms find it more profitable to conduct their business in English because more of their customers connected to the Web understand that language. Moreover, many companies do not have the resources to translate sites into other languages.

While some areas of advertising regulation in Vietnam are vague and hard to enforce, others, such as the use of the Vietnamese language, are strictly enforced. The spoken or written text of an advertisement must be in Vietnamese, except in the case of internationally known words, commercial names, or words that cannot be translated into Vietnamese. However, ads in print media, as well as radio and television, may employ foreign or ethnic minority languages if the vehicles target those particular audiences. Article 22 of Korea's regulations on broadcast advertising stipulates that

> commercial advertisements shall not unnecessarily use foreign languages except for the brand names, corporate names or corporate slogans of foreign companies. Any brand names, corporate names or corporate slogans, etc in a foreign language shown shall also be expressed in Korean letters. Furthermore, commercial advertisements shall not use foreign language commercial jingles. (*Korea Herald* 2001)

The rationale behind such restrictive use of foreign languages in aired advertisements lies in the desire to protect the Korean language as a cultural asset. But this reasoning is perplexing, given that many other foreign broadcast programs, including movies, sitcoms, and documentaries, are fully aired in the original languages (with subtitles), and recent technological advances in television sets now allow viewers to switch off the Korean language voice-overs. A law in Russia attempts to purge advertising and media of Westernized words. Under the law, anyone caught employing Westernisms such as "biznes," "menedgment," or "merchendaizing" faces up to two months of "corrective work"—the Russian term for community service. Variations of English words have become common since the country was flooded with Western culture after the break-up of the Soviet Union (Walsh 2003).

Regulations regarding the language employed in the labeling of products can be very complex as well. A commonly asked question regarding packaging and labeling in Belgium is: "What language am I required to use?" Belgium recognizes three official languages: Flemish (Dutch), French, and German. The prevailing Belgian law is simply that the consumers of the targeted market must be able to read the product information. Typically, this has meant that Dutch (Flemish) is employed in the northern half of Belgium (Flanders), French in the southern half of the country (Wallonia), and German in the two small communities of German-speaking Belgians on the Belgian border with Germany. Typically, both Flemish and French appear on all products sold in the Belgian market.

## The Use of Local versus International Advertising Agencies

An increasing number of advertising agencies are positioning themselves as "global," or capable of providing services to clients worldwide. J. J. Boddewyn notes that "such a reach requires that they be allowed to establish themselves, or to merge with and acquire others, rather freely around the world" (Boddewyn 1988). However, the degree to which foreign countries allow foreign ownership of advertising agencies varies significantly. For example, in the Philippines, foreign ownership of up to only 30 percent is allowed. In Jordan, non-Jordanian investor ownership of agencies shall not exceed 50 percent. And the year 2008 saw several new developments regarding advertising in China. Initially, the only way for foreign enterprises to invest in the ad industry in China was through joint advertising ventures; advertising was deemed a restricted area of investment, and wholly foreign-owned enterprises were not allowed to operate in the country. This changed in 2004 with China's WTO commitments, under which wholly foreign-owned advertising ventures were permitted beginning December 10, 2005. However, applications needed to be approved by two state-level bodies—the Ministry of Commerce and the State Administration of Industry and Commerce. The requirements were onerous, and approval was difficult to obtain. The 2008 regulations made several changes, and while they may seem nuanced, they are indeed significant. Applications are now reviewed by local offices of Ministries of Commerce, rather than the state-level Ministry of Commerce. In practice, provincial-level authorities are often more willing to grant approval in order to bring foreign investment to their province. Furthermore, the application procedures have been streamlined. Provincial-level Administrations of Industry and Commerce have joined state-level authorities in the approval procedure, making approvals more local and reducing the role the State Administration plays in the decision. The reasoning behind this change in law was twofold: to stimulate the domestic advertising market and to better implement China's WTO commitment to fully open China's advertising market to foreign investment (Lehman 2008).

## INTERNATIONAL AND REGIONAL REGULATION

International and regional regulations consist of those rules and guidelines that states and nations consider to be binding upon themselves. Among the major bodies or organizations that have developed or are developing international or regional regulations related to marketing and advertising are the various United Nations agencies, the World Trade Organization (WTO), and the Organization for Economic Cooperation and Development (OECD), as well as a number of regional bodies, including the European Union and the Gulf Cooperation Council.

### The United Nations

The United Nations and its various agencies influence advertising regulation in member countries. The most important of these agencies are the World Health Organization (WHO), the Commission on Transnational Corporations, the United Nation's Educational, Scientific and Cultural Organization (UNESCO), and the UN Conference on Trade and Development (Dunn 1982, 29). Barbara Sundberg Baudot explains their functions:

> These organizations lack the attribute of sovereignty, or the legislative authority of a world government to legislate enforceable regulation. Thus their roles are restricted to the development of voluntary codes and guidelines whose effectiveness depends on moral suasion and public acceptance. However, these codes may be translated through national legislation into laws. By consensus, members also may decide to adopt regulations by treaty, which becomes enforceable law in ratifying countries. Alternately, countries may decide to adopt conventions or resolutions binding members in accordance with voting rules in organizational charters. (Baudot 1989, 31)

Several issues appear to have top priority at the various UN agencies. First, the UN perceives market data as a type of national resource. In a report on transborder data flow that highlighted the significant expansion in this area as well as the great value of such data to international marketers, the UN expressed concern over whether such data flow helps or hinders developing countries. The report implies that developing countries should limit the flow of information from their country to the headquarters of international firms, and that they should use their data to negotiate advantageous contracts and agreements. Second, the various UN agencies have all targeted pharmaceutical advertising for special attention. The UN is particularly concerned with international firms that may be dumping substandard or hazardous pharmaceutical products on unsuspecting developing markets as well as with the costly, high-pressure marketing and promotional methods employed by many international pharmaceutical firms. Third, the UN agencies acknowledge that media depend on advertising for much of their financial support and are concerned that media dollars may not always support those media of greatest importance to developing countries. Unfortunately, the developing nation's most critical media forms may not provide the proper target audience coverage for the international marketer.

## World Trade Organization

The World Trade Organization is the regulatory body with the broadest impact on international business activities. First mentioned in Chapter 3, the WTO is the international body concerned with fair trade and open markets, as well as intellectual property protection. Apart from trade liberalization, the WTO addresses a number of subjects relevant to consumers. In recent rounds of trade negotiations, WTO discussions covered labeling, product safety, and deceptive practices. The WTO serves as a permanent, comprehensive forum to address new or evolving issues in the global market.

## The Organization for Economic Cooperation and Development

The Organization for Economic Cooperation and Development is the international organization of the industrialized, market-economy countries—including those of Europe and North America, and Australia, New Zealand, and Japan. The OECD regularly gathers statistical information on foreign trade and makes the statistics internationally comparable by converting the information into uniform units (Onkvisit and Shaw 1997, 174). In addition, the OECD addresses a wide range of issues relevant to international business, in particular through its Committee on Consumer Policy. A primary focus of this committee is on cross-border consumer transaction issues. As such, it has established guidelines in the following areas: consumer protection in the online marketplace, disputes arising out of business-to-consumer electronic commerce, and the use of credit and debit cards online.

## The European Union

Despite efforts to standardize EU advertising regulation, advertising differences across the European Union have been legion. Though minimum criteria regarding truth in advertising were established by the European Commission (EC), specific laws against misleading advertising differ widely from member state to member state. Audiences that may be appealed to, and approaches that may be employed in advertisements, are not uniform, causing endless headaches for international marketers. The European Union has continued to work toward a legal framework to govern promotional marketing across the 27 member states. The Unfair Commercial Practices (UCP) Directive was passed in 2005 and went into effect on December 12, 2007. The UCP Directive substantially reinforces existing EU standards on misleading advertising and sets new EU standards against aggressive commercial practices. The directive is designed to benefit both business and consumers. Businesses benefit because the directive seeks to harmonize different rules among member states. European citizens benefit from the increased level of consumer protection. An extensive blacklist of schemes—the so-called the "dirty dozen"—are banned by the directive (see Table 9.2 for the list). As with any European directive, it requires national rules to incorporate it in each national legal system (German, French, Italian law, and so forth). It is difficult to predict the exact impact of the directive in any given market without consulting the national laws.

## The Gulf Cooperation Council

The Gulf Cooperation Council (GCC) consists of six member countries: Saudi Arabia, Qatar, Kuwait, Oman, the United Arab Emirates, and Bahrain. Among them, they control nearly half of the world's known oil reserves, and by the end of 2007 had accumulated $1.8 trillion in foreign assets—the equivalent of 13 percent of the U.S. economy. The GCC was established in 1981, according to its charter, to "effect coordination, integration and inter-connection among the Member States in all fields in order

**Table 9.2:** The European Union's Unfair Commercial Practices Directive "Dirty Dozen"

1. Bait Advertising: Lures the consumer into buying from a company by advertising a product at a very low price without having a reasonable stock available.

2. Fake "Free" Offers: Falsely creating the impression of free offers by describing a product as "gratis," "free," "without charge," or similar if the consumer has to pay anything other than the unavoidable cost of responding to the commercial practice and collecting or paying for delivery of the item.

3. Direct Exhortations to Children to buy advertised products or to persuade their parents or other adults via "pester power" to buy advertised products for them. Direct exhortation was banned for television, but the black list extends it to all media, most importantly to Internet advertising.

4. False Claims about Curative Capacity—from allergies to hair loss to weight loss.

5. Advertorials: Using editorial content in the media to promote a product where an advertiser has paid for the promotion without making that clear.

6. Pyramid Schemes: A pyramid promotional scheme where compensation is derived primarily from the introduction of other consumers into the scheme, rather than from the sale or consumption of products.

7. Prize Winning: Creating the false impression that the consumer has won a prize when there is no prize, or if taking action to claim the prize is subject to the consumer paying money or incurring cost.

8. Misleading Impression of Consumers' Rights: Presenting rights given to consumers in law as a distinctive feature of the advertiser.

9. Limited Offers: Falsely stating that a product will only be available for a very limited time to deprive consumers of sufficient opportunity to make an informed choice.

10. Language of After-Sales Service: Undertaking to provide after-sales service to consumers and making such service available only in another language without clear disclosure before the consumer is committed to the transaction.

11. Inertia Selling: Demanding immediate or deferred payment for or the return or safekeeping of products supplied by the advertiser, but not solicited by the consumer.

12. Europe-Wide Guaranteed: Creating the false impression that after-sales service in relation to a product is available in a member state other than the one in which the product is sold.

to achieve unity and stress the special relations, common qualities and similar systems founded on the creed of Islam, faith in a common destiny and sharing one goal defined by the Arab identity" (Tristam 2008). The GCC is making a very committed attempt to become an effective trading bloc to rival the European Union. To this end, it is forging a common consumer and trade policy to ensure economic integration. A common currency is planned for 2010. An understanding of the advertising regulatory environment of the member states is essential for marketers interested in this region. Because Saudi Arabia is the largest and economically strongest member of the GCC, it is playing a dominant role in shaping the regulations that will govern all commercial activity among member states.

With regard to the marketing environment, religion takes precedence over all other cultural considerations in Saudi Arabia. Mushtaq Luqmani and colleagues (1989) explain: "The Saudi legal system is unique in that it identifies law with the personal command of the 'one and only one God, the Almighty.'" The Islamic legal code known as the "Sharia" is the master framework to which all legislation is referred and with which it must be compatible. The Sharia is a comprehensive code governing the duties, morals, and behavior of all Muslims in all areas of life, including commerce. Sharia is derived from two basic sources, the *Koran* or Holy Book and the *Hadith*, based on the life, sayings, and practices of the Prophet Muhammad. The implications of religion on advertising regulation in Saudi Arabia are far-reaching (Luqmani et al. 1989).

Several sets of Koranic messages hold special significance for advertisers and advertising regulators. The most important have to do with strict taboos dealing with alcohol, gambling, and immodest exposure. For example, according to the Koran, at no time may alcoholic beverages be consumed, and games of chance are illegal. Religious norms in several Islamic nations require that women cover themselves in advertising messages as well as in public. Therefore, international print messages may need to be modified by superimposing long dresses on models or by shading their legs with black. In addition, advertisers may not picture a sensuous-looking female. Instead, a pleasant-looking woman in a robe and headdress with only her face showing is the typical model. Cartoon characters are often employed to present women in messages, because they are less likely to violate the Islamic codes on exposure. Advertising messages may also be considered deceptive by religious standards. For example, according to Islam, fraud may occur if the seller fails to deliver everything promised, and advertising may need to use factual appeals based on real rather than perceived product benefits.

No specific governmental agency is responsible for controlling advertising behavior in Saudi Arabia. No self-regulatory industry group exists, and there is no evidence of plans to develop one. Companies are, however, involved in self-compliance, which may eventually lead to self-regulation. As Luqmani and colleagues state:

> Possible violations are monitored in two ways. The government is involved through the Ministry of Commerce, which ensures that ads remain within legal bounds, and the Ministry of Information, which approves television commercials. Less formal oversight is provided by a voluntary religious group, the Organization for the Prevention of Sins and Order of Good Deeds. Members observe public and commercial behavior (including promotions) for any violations of Islamic law. (Luqmani 1989)

Obviously, advertisers must take great care to ensure that advertising content is compatible with the Islamic religion and its laws.

In addition to the European Union and the Gulf Cooperation Council, there are a number of other major regional economic organizations:

- North American Free Trade Agreement (NAFTA)
- Asia-Pacific Economic Cooperation (AEPC)
- Central American Common Market (CAMC)
- Andean Group
- Southern Cone Common Market (Mercosur)
- Caribbean Community and Common Market (CARICOM)
- Association of Southeast Asian Nations (ASEAN)
- Central European Free Trade Association (CEFTA)
- Economic Community of West African States (ECOWAS)
- South African Development Coordination Conference (SADCC)

International and regional codes and guidelines contribute to the harmonization of national laws and, in doing so, pave the way for global advertising campaigns. International marketers planning on promoting their products or services in a particular region may be faced with a multitude of advertising regulations—many of which may conflict with one another—and therefore have little choice but to employ a localized campaign for each country. However, with increasingly standardized advertising regulation in the European Union or the Persian Gulf region, marketers have the option of employing the same or similar message strategy.

## SELF-REGULATION

### The Trend toward Self-Regulation

As noted by de Mooij:

> Self regulation started in the USA at the beginning of the 20th century with the foundation of local clubs consisting of agents, advertisers, and media representatives. The American Advertising Federation (AAF), the American Association of Advertising Agencies), and the Association of National Advertisers (ANA) joined to form the central organization for the regulation of advertising. This is the National Advertising Review Board (NARB). The NARB, together with the Federal Trade Commission (FTC) has helped in setting standards for developing the regulation of advertising in other parts of the world. (de Mooij 1994, 498)

During the past several decades, both consumer groups and governments around the globe have increasingly turned their attention toward the control of advertising, and advertising, trade, and industry associations, as well as the media in many countries, have realized the importance of voluntary self-regulation. In addition to avoiding government-mandated regulation, self-regulation in advertising generally has three objectives:

1.  to protect consumers against false or misleading advertising and against advertising that intrudes on their privacy through its unwanted presence or offensive content;
2.  to protect legitimate advertisers against false or misleading advertising by competitors;
3.  to promote the public acceptance of advertising so that it can continue as an effective institution in the marketplace. (Rijkens and Miracle 1986, 40)

Consumer protection laws in the United Kingdom are among the strongest in the world. Self-regulation of advertising in the United Kingdom dates back to 1961, when the Advertising Association established what became the Committee of Advertising Practice (CAP), the industry body that sets the rules for advertisers, agencies, and the media. CAP revises and enforces the British Code and Advertising, Sales Promotion and Direct Marketing. The basic principles of the code are that advertising, sales promotions, and direct-marketing efforts should be: (1) legal, decent, honest, and truthful, (2) prepared with a sense of responsibility to consumers and to society, and (3) in line with the principles of fair competition generally acceptable in business. In 1962, the industry established the Advertising Standards Authority (ASA) to adjudicate complaints about advertising that appeared to breach the code. The ASA is independent of both government and the advertising industry. Its advertising standards codes are separated into codes for television, radio, and all other types of ads. There are also rules for Teletext ads, Interactive ads, and the scheduling of television ads (the codes can be read in full at http://www.asa.org.uk). The codes include specific rules for product categories, specific audiences, and marketing techniques (for instance, the use of environmental claims and prize promotions). Much as in the United States, advertisers must be able to prove the claims they make if challenged. The ASA regulates the content of advertisements, sales promotions, and direct marketing both by monitoring ads to spot problems and by investigating complaints received. Consequences for advertisers who flout the rules can be quite serious—adverse publicity may result from the rulings published by the ASA weekly on its Web site. Further, advertisers can be denied access to newspapers, magazines, poster sites, direct mail, or the Internet. The ASA may also mandate that a marketer's ads must be pre-cleared prior to dissemination to the media. Since 1988, self-regulation has also been backed up by statutory powers under the Control of Misleading Advertisements Regulations. The ASA can refer advertisers who refuse to cooperate with the self-regulatory system to the Office of Fair Trading (OFT) or Ofcom for legal action. For instance, the ASA might refer an advertiser, agency, or publisher to the OFT if it persistently runs misleading ads that breach the Codes. Or, it can refer a broadcaster to Ofcom if a licensee is not abiding by the rules. However, this is considered a last resort and is rarely employed. The partnership between the CAP, which writes the Code, and the ASA, which adjudicates complaints, is the strength of the United Kingdom's self-regulatory system. CAP interprets ASA rulings to the industry and helps advertisers to comply with the Code through "Copy Advice" and "Help Notes." Today, almost five decades after CAP was established, advertisers in the United Kingdom overwhelmingly comply with the code. Several additional bodies help keep advertising standards high in the United Kingdom. Clearcast (previously the Broadcast Clearance Centre) pre-checks ads on behalf of television broadcasters before they go on the air, eliminating almost all problems before transmission. The Radio Advertising Clearance Centre pre-checks national radio ads and ads for specific categories before they are aired. And the CAP Copy Advice Team provides a pre-publication advice service for the industry to avoid problems with ads in other media.

The European Advertising Standards Alliance (EASA) was founded in 1992 to support self-regulatory efforts across Europe. EASA brings together national advertising self-regulatory organizations and bodies (such as the U.K.'s Advertising Standards Authority) representing the advertising industry in Europe. Based in Brussels, the alliance is the European voice for advertising self-regulation. It exists to help ensure that cross-border complaints are resolved as quickly and effectively as possible. The EASA's Blue Book, published every 2–3 years, provides practitioners and regulators with a comprehensive overview of the scope and activities of the self-regulation systems in place and provides detailed analyses of the role of self-regulation; global self-regulatory codes; national, European, and cross-border complaints statistics; and an overview of European legislation affecting advertising. For more information about EASA, visit www.easa-alliance.org.

Advertising Standards Canada (ASC) is the national, not-for-profit industry body committed to creating and maintaining community confidence in advertising. ASC membership includes Canada's leading advertisers, advertising agencies, and media organizations. The ASC administers the Canadian Code of Advertising Standards, the industry's principal self-regulatory code. The ASC accepts written complaints from consumers who have a concern about an advertisement they see or hear. In 2009, the ASC received 1,228 complaints about 760 ads. Of these, 80 complaints regarding 56 ads were deemed to violate the standards code. Total complaints were up from 2008, when 1,119 complaints were made about 778 ads. The category with the most complaints was the food category, including ads by food manufacturers, food retailers, and restaurants, which combined for 163 of the total. The most popular reasons for complaints fell under the code's Clause 14—for "unacceptable depictions or portrayals." Although the food category had the highest number of complaints, it actually had one of the fewest that were later upheld by the ASC. The majority of the upheld complaints fell under Clause 1—for accuracy and clarity. "Someone can find something personally distasteful and not like it, but that doesn't mean the ad raises an issue under Clause 14, which would have to promote violence or be derogatory to a particular group," said Janet Feasby, vice-president, standards for the ASC (Beer 2010).

While voluntary self-regulation plays a dominant role in markets such as the United Kingdom and Canada, its role is significantly more limited in other countries. For example, the China Advertising Association, the only national advertising trade organization in the country and an affiliate of the state, does not monitor compliance or handle complaints. Rather, it functions as a liaison between the government and the advertising industry. It does, however, provide compliance consulting services to advertisers and agencies, charging a fee for reviewing whether an advertisement violates the law (CAA 2007). In a sense, self-regulation in China takes the form of "mandated self-regulation" (Boddewyn 1989b), as ad agencies and media companies are required by law to censor advertisements under their commission (Gao 2008). The Chinese advertising market is, however, still at a comparatively early stage of its development. It remains to be seen whether self-regulation of advertising will play a more important role in the future.

It should be noted that national media are also involved in the monitoring of advertising content. Both media associations and individual media are concerned about advertising messages that may be deceptive, offensive, or even contrary to public standards. In addition to advertising-association, industry, and media codes, individual firms, including Procter & Gamble, General Foods, and Revlon, have begun to develop their own guidelines.

## THE INTERNATIONAL CHAMBER OF COMMERCE

The International Chamber of Commerce (ICC) was established in 1919 to promote the interests of international business. The ICC, which today is represented in over one hundred countries, is the most important international body influencing the self-regulation of advertising. With the support of advertisers, agencies, and the media, the ICC has developed a formal, internal self-regulatory code for advertising. The ICC Code of Advertising Practice states that all advertisers have an overall duty

**Figure 9.2:** Banned Dolce & Gabbana advertisement.

to be "decent, honest, legal and truthful." The code goes on to state that advertisements "should be prepared with a due sense of social responsibility...and not be such as to impair public confidence in advertising." With these words, the ICC code moved away from addressing only "hard" matters that center on the deceptive character of advertisements and on proper substantiation of advertising claims. The code also encompassed "soft" issues, including matters of sex and decency in advertising. Jean J. Boddewyn notes: "Reflecting these ICC principles, various clauses on decency, taste, public opinion and social responsibility are usually found in advertising self-regulatory codes and guidelines around the world" (Boddewyn 1991, 25).

Sex and decency can be broken into five major subcategories:

- tasteless/indecent ads, which do not conform to recognized standards of propriety, good taste, and modesty;
- sexy ads, which use sexual imagery or suggestiveness;
- sexist ads, which diminish or demean one sex in comparison with the other—particularly through the use of sex-role stereotypes;
- objectification-of-women ads, which use women primarily as decorative or attention-getting objects with little or no relevance to the product advertised;
- violence-against-women ads. (Boddewyn 1991, 25)

An IAA survey inquired about the salience of these five advertising issues. Table 9.3 reveals that a larger number of developing countries (15) than of developed ones (11) rated one or more of these issues as "major." Lebanon and the United States appeared to be most concerned with these issues, and these countries are the only ones represented in at least three columns. The subcategory of tasteless/indecent ads generated the most mentions, particularly in developing countries.

**TABLE 9.3:** Countries Rating Advertising Taste/Decency Issues as "Major"

| TASTELESS/ INDECENT | SEXY | SEXIST | OBJECTIFICATION OF WOMEN | VIOLENCE AGAINST WOMEN |
|---|---|---|---|---|
| Bahrain* | Austria | India* | Argentina* | Chile* |
| Canada | Bahrain* | Ireland | Austria | Lebanon* |
| Chile* | Indonesia* | Lebanon* | Brazil* | New Zealand |
| Indonesia* | Ireland | Peru* | Lebanon* | Spain |
| Kenya* | Italy | Sweden | Portugal | Trinidad & Tobago* |
| Lebanon* | Kenya* | Switzerland | Singapore* | United States |
| Malaysia* | Lebanon* | United States | Spain | |
| Philippines* | Norway | | Sweden | |
| Taiwan* | Philippines* | | Switzerland | |
| Trinidad & Tobago* | | | | |
| United States | | | | |

* = countries that are usually classified as "developing" or "less developed."

*Source:* Boddewyn (1989a).

Some self-regulatory bodies refuse to handle soft issues, limiting themselves to the hard issues of truth and accuracy. This is true of the United States's National Advertising Review Board. Other bodies, including those in Spain and Italy, readily deal with "taste and opinion" complaints. For example, after Spain's Women's Institute (a government organization linked to the Labour Ministry) branded a Dolce and Gabbana print ad (see Figure 9.2) as "glorifying chauvinist violence," the ad was outlawed in that country. The offending ad shows a bare-chested man pinning a woman to the ground by her wrists while other men look on passively. In response, the Italian fashion house said it would stop advertising in Spain to protect its "creative freedom." "Recently, Spain, with its climate of censorship, has shown itself willing to negatively interpret all messages even when there is no reason to do so," the company said in a statement. The ad was later banned by Italy's self-regulatory advertising body IAP, and subsequently pulled from all world markets (*BBC News Business* 2007).

Most bodies, however, stand in-between, occasionally agreeing to handle soft cases on the basis of the general principles they apply—particularly when gross breaches of social standards occur, as in matters of obscenity, racism, and denigration (Boddewyn 1991, 25).

The primary problem with indecency is that what is considered improper in one country is deemed perfectly acceptable in another. For example, the mere use of the word "erection" is enough to get consumers up in arms in some markets. Dozens of consumers in South Africa lodged complaints with their Advertising Standards Authority (ASA) for the liberal use of that word in a Pfizer campaign for its impotence pill, Viagra, charging the campaign would lead to the destruction of South Africa's moral fiber (Koenderman 2002). Britain's regulatory bodies have also become notorious for their Victorian mind-set when it comes to issues of decency in advertising. Los Angeles-based American Apparel's self-described "provocative advertising" has gotten it in trouble with the British Advertising Standards Authority (ASA). The ad in question read: "Ryan wears a classic unisex Fleece Zip Hoody" and showed a young-looking blond girl modeling the sweatshirt, open and sans shirt in a series of photographs. The self-regulatory body ruled that the ad breached the "Taste and Decency" clause of the code. ASA did note that while the model was in various states of undress, it wasn't bothered by the partial nudity, saying that showing skin was acceptable given the publication in which the ad ran (targeted to 18- to 34-year-olds with editorial content that was of an adult nature). Instead, the ASA found the ad "could be seen to sexualize a model who appeared to be a child, under the age of 18." American Apparel disagreed, arguing that "Ryan" didn't look 16 and was actually 23. Nonetheless, the ASA concluded that the ad was inappropriate and could cause serious offense to some readers, and banned the ad from running in U.K. media outlets (Chang 2009).

To demonstrate the variety of definitions of "decent" even within the European Union, consider the case of France, which has developed a reputation for bare-all ads. Indeed, research has shown that French women do not see nudity as sexist; instead they think of it as aesthetic (Nelson and Paek 2005). The ads in this nation have become so risqué that they have been dubbed "porno-chic." But apparently a number of campaigns crossed the invisible barrier that had previously prevailed against the use of zoophilic and sadomasochistic images in advertising (Speer 2001). The campaign for La City, a French clothing retailer, provides a good example of one that overstepped the bounds of what even French consumers were willing to accept. Consumers found it degrading to depict a nearly naked woman in a sexually suggestive position next to a sheep with the tagline "I need a sweater." Then there was the Weston Shoes ad, which portrayed a woman lying on the ground fondling the moccasin of a muscular male who was virtually treading on her. As a result of the offensive campaigns, France introduced a new self-regulatory code that replaced the outdated standards on the image of women in advertising first drafted in 1975. Authorities emphasized that nudity in and of itself is not under attack, because bare breasts are used to promote everything from pullovers to Parmesan cheese. Rather, the new standards insist that ads must respect human dignity and refuse any "degrading" or "humiliating" portrayals of human beings (Galloni 2001). But supporters of porno-chic are adamant that censorship must not prevail over the liberty to use sex and fantasy in ads. "You must not mix up sexism with sexuality," said Paola Paoletti, advertising director with Sisley, a fashion retailer. Referring to a Sisley campaign in which a woman's breast is being groped by a male, Paoletti notes, "The woman in our ad is not a sexual object; she accepts the game of seduction. People can read into an ad what they want to, just like in life—either you can be a victim, or you can be someone who is making a strong sexual choice" (TheAge.com 2004). Other French marketers fear that such explicit ads will prompt the government to replace the existing system of industry self-regulation with laws pertaining to what can and cannot be portrayed in ads.

In developing self-regulatory guidelines, many countries have turned to the ICC codes. Because latecomers often borrow from the ICC codes as well as from codes outlined by U.S., U.K., and Canadian associations, voluntary codes often appear to resemble one another. In addition to a code of advertising practices, the ICC also outlines codes of practice in marketing, market research practice, sales promotion practices, and interactive marketing. The ICC's voluntary guidelines on interactive marketing and advertising are designed to promote worldwide consumer confidence and minimize the need for regulatory intervention (International Chamber of Commerce 1998). The revised guidelines on advertising and marketing on the Internet cover such ethical issues as protection of a user's personal data, messages directed at children, and the different sensitivities of global audiences. ICC recommendations to marketers include: revealing their identity when posting a message; disclosing the reason for collecting personal information on users; not sending unsolicited commercial messages to those who request not to receive them; and providing information to parents on ways to protect children's online privacy. The guidelines also caution marketers to ensure that their messages are not perceived as pornographic, violent, racist, sexist, or otherwise offensive. Online advertising and marketing should be conducted according to the laws of the country from which the message originates, the ICC code stipulates. "If business successfully adheres to this set of guidelines...we may well preclude the imposition of restrictive bureaucratic legislation at the national, regional, and global levels," says John Manfredi, chairman of the ICC Commission on Marketing, Advertising and Distribution, which drafted the guidelines (*Advertising Age* 1998). Ad associations around the world are expected to incorporate the main provisions of these guidelines into their codes covering online advertising. Additional information about the ICC, as well as the complete code, can be accessed at http://www.iccwbo.org.

Industry, trade, and advertising associations have developed codes of ethics and guidelines in more than 50 nations, and the number is increasing every year. This is particularly true of developed markets and countries where advertising expenditures are relatively large. Increasingly, we are seeing movement toward self-regulation in developing markets as well.

## Implications for International Advertisers

Although it is nearly impossible for international advertisers to be familiar with the regulation of advertising worldwide, they are still responsible for making every effort to inform themselves of the regulatory environment of markets they plan to enter. Because of the changing regulatory environment, advertisers must develop a system for keeping abreast of new developments. Often, advertisers will retain the services of an attorney familiar with the local laws of the market or markets they are planning to enter.

Beyond the impact of the regulatory environment on a single campaign, the global regulatory climate will influence how successfully international advertisers can conduct their business in years to come. In the meantime, international advertisers should do the following:

1. Have their in-house and external legal counsels check and double-check the true nature of advertising restrictions in relevant foreign markets.

2. Monitor and oppose the spread of regulations, taxes, and other obstacles that hamper international advertising. In particular, advertisers should support U.S. and other governments' efforts to liberalize trade and investment in services through GATT and other bilateral agreements. Defending the freedom of commercial expression and communication at home and abroad is part of this agenda.

3. Support and assist the development of advertising self-regulation around the world. Advertising self-regulation exists in a relatively small number of countries and is well developed in even fewer. It is largely nonexistent or ineffective in most of the developing countries where the spread of regulation is imminent. (Boddewyn 1991, 29)

Local and national resources should be tapped for current information on legislative or self-regulatory efforts. National advertising associations can provide invaluable assistance. In the United States the American Advertising Association (AAA), the American Association of Advertising Agencies (AAAA), and the American Advertising Federation (AAF) are all excellent resources. Most developed countries have similar associations. For example, in Europe the international advertiser may contact the European Association of Advertising Agencies (EAAA), the Institute of Practitioners in Advertising (IPA), or the European Advertising Tripartite (EAT). Likewise, the Asian Federation of Advertising Agencies (AFAA) provides current data to advertisers entering Asian markets.

Finally, the International Advertising Association (IAA) conducts numerous surveys that deal with governmental regulations as well as specific industry guidelines. In addition, the IAA publishes a variety of reports on government regulation and industry self-regulation in more than 50 countries.

## SUMMARY

Some experts propose that the extent and severity of advertising regulation worldwide is likely to increase; others predict it will decline. However, many governments currently are developing tougher regulations with regard to advertising in general as well as stronger restrictions relating to specific product categories such as cigarettes, alcohol, and pharmaceuticals.

On the other hand, many governments—particularly those in developed markets—are moving toward deregulation. Especially in markets facing slow- or no-growth economies, politicians are questioning the wisdom of further increasing the costs associated with doing business.

Regardless of the regulatory environment in which international marketers find themselves, every effort should be made to comply with both national and international rules and guidelines. In addition, international marketers should strive to operate abroad in a socially responsible fashion. Such efforts can assist in avoiding legal entanglements and stemming any erosion of consumer confidence in advertising worldwide. The issue of social responsibility and ethical standards in the international arena will be addressed in the next chapter.

## REFERENCES

About.com: Islam. 2008. Saudi Arabia: Ban on baby formula advertising. 25 May. <http://islam.about.com/b/2008/05.25/saudi-arabia-ban-on-baby-formula...>. Retrieved 21 May 2010.

*Advertising Age.* 1993. *Advertising Age* legal briefs: Comparative advertising mulled. 15 March, I6.

———. 1998. ICC draws up new code of international online advertising. 22 April, 24.

TheAge.com. 2004. Sex and shopping—it's a French thing. 6 March. <http://www.theage/com.au/articles/2004/03/05/1078464638343.html>. Retrieved 21 May 2010.

Baudot, Barbara Sundberg. 1989. *International advertising handbook: A user's guide to rules and regulations.* Lexington, MA: Lexington Books.

*BBC Monitoring.* 2001. Russia: Duma bids to curb advertising on TV, radio. 15 November, 1.

———. 2002. Mongolian parliament passes advertising law. 31 March, 1.

*BBC News Business.* 2007. Censored ad sparks row in Spain. 13 March. <http://news.bbc.co.uk/2/hi/business/6448421.stm>. Retrieved 18 May 2010.

Beer, Jeff. 2010. Ad complaints rise slightly in 2009: ASC. *Marketing,* 12 March. <http://www.marketingmag.ca/english/news/marketer/article.jsp?conte...>. Retrieved 23 May 2010.

Black, Jane. 2010. Food makers vow to cut 1.5 trillion calories. *The San Diego Union–Tribune,* 19 May, A-4.

Boddewyn, J. J. 1988. The one and many worlds of advertising: Regulatory obstacles and opportunities. *International Journal of Advertising,* 7(1): 13.

———. 1989a. *Sexism and decency in advertising: Government regulation and industry self-regulation in 47 countries.* New York: International Advertising Association.

———. 1989b. Advertising self-regulation: True purpose and limits. *Journal of Advertising,* 18(2): 19–27.

———. 1991. Controlling sex and decency in advertising around the world. *Journal of Advertising* 20(4): December, 25–35.

Boddewyn, Jean J., and Iris Mohr. 1987. International advertisers face government hurdles. *Marketing News,* 8 May, 20–22.

Bowes, Elena. 2002. No change to EU TV directive until 2004 after all. 31 May. <www. adageglobal.com/cgi-bin/daily. pl?daily_id=7668&post_date=2002–05031>.

Bremner, Charles, and Marie Tourres. 2008. France ban on Internet alcohol advertising hits industry. *TimesOnline,* 19 September. <http://www.timesonline.co.uk/tol/life_and_style/fppd_and_drink/win...>. Retrieved 19 May 2010.

CAA. 2007. Consultation on the legality of advertisements. <http://www.cnadtop.com/china_aa/chk_index.asp>. Retrieved 29 May 2007.

Center on Alcohol Marketing and Youth. 2005. Alcohol advertising on television, 2001–2004: The move to cable. December. <http://camy.org/research/tvl205)>. Retrieved 19 May 2010.

Chang, Bee-Shyuan. 2009. American Apparel ad banned in the UK for potentially sexualizing a model who "appears to be a child." 3 September . <http://www.stylelist.com/2009/09/03/american-apparel-ad-banned-in...>. Retrieved 21 May 2010.

*Clean Cut Media.* 2009. France to regulate airbrushed & photoshopped pictures. 29 September. <http://www.cleancutmedia.com/advertising/france-to-regfulate-airbrush...>. Retrieved 21 May 2010.

Coleman, Fred. 1997. A great lost cause: French vs. the Internet: The language of kings doesn't have a prayer on the net. 21 April. *U.S. News & World Report,* 12(15): 57–59.

Congressional Budget Office. 2009. Economic and budget issue brief: Promotional spending for prescription drugs. <http://www.cbo.gov/ftpdocs/105xx/doc10522/Drug Promo_Brief.shtml>.

Crumley, Bruce. 1993. Un-French ad copy: Is it fine or fini? *Advertising Age,* 64(10): 7 March, 16.

Cundiff, Edward, and Marye Tharp Hilger. 1988. *Marketing in the international environment.* Englewood Cliffs, NJ: Prentice Hall.

Cunningham, Anne. 2000. Advertising self-regulation in a broader context: An examination of the European Union's regulatory environment. *Journal of Promotional Management,* 15(2): 61–83.

*Daily Yomiuri* (Tokyo). 1996. Comparative advertising fails to take off in Japan. 22 March, 1.

de Mooij, Marieke. 1994. *Advertising worldwide.* Hemel, Hempstead, U.K.: Prentice Hall International.

*Dominion* (Wellington, New Zealand). 1998. Forum told of overseas taboos in advertising. 5 May, 7.

Dunn, S. Watson. 1982. United Nations as a regulator of international advertising. In *Proceedings of the 1982 Conference of the American Academy of Advertising*, ed. Alan Fletcher. Lincoln, NE: American Academy of Advertising, 29–32.

*Earth Times*. 2009. Indonesia is "cash cow" for cigarette industry says SEATCA. 4 May. <http://www/earthtimes.org/articles/show/267221,indonesia-is-cash-...>. Retrieved 19 May 2010.

Elliott, Stuart. 2009. More liquor ads pour onto broadcast TV. *Media Decoder*, 9 February. <http://mediadecoder.blogs.nytimes.com/2009/02/09/more-liquor-ads...>. Retrieved 19 May 2010.

European Report. 2005. Consumers: Kyprianou launches EU platform against obesity. <http://web.lexis-nexis.com.libproxy.sdsu.edu/universe/document?_m=db84139b84376b8c46>. Retrieved 16 March 2005

Frith, Katherine Toland. 1987. The social and legal constraints on advertising in Malaysia. *Media Asia* 14(2): 103.

Galloni, Alessandra. 2001. Clampdown on "porno-chic" ads is pushed by French authorities. *Wall Street Journal*, 25 October, B-4.

Gao, Zhihong. 2008. Controlling deceptive advertising in China: An overview. *Journal of Public Policy & Marketing*, 27(2): Fall, 165–177.

Hadenfeldt, Seth. 2008. Humor in the media. *Associated Content*, 5 August. <http://www/associatedcontent.com/article/918705/humor_in_the_me...>. Retrieved 19 May 2010.

Hall, Emma. 2007. Food marketers pledge no more kids' ads in the European Union. *Advertising Age*, 78(50): 17 December, 2.

———. 2009. Europe faults alcohol marketers for binge drinking; U.K. proposes $286M ad ban. *Advertising Age*, 12 October, 6.

Harrisson, Dristen, and Amy Marske. 2005. Nutritional content of foods advertised during the television programs children watch most. *American Journal of Public Health*, 95(9): 1568–1574.

Hawkes, Corinna. 2007. Regulating food marketing to young people worldwide: Trends and policy drivers. *American Journal of Public Health*, 97(11): November, 1962–1973.

International Chamber of Commerce. 1998. *ICC Guidelines on advertising and marketing on the Internet*. <http://www.iccwbo.org/home/statements_rules/rules/1998/internet_guidelines.asp.>. Retrieved 10 August 2002.

Jordan, George. 2007. After lull, drug firms' direct-to-consumer ads surge. *Newhouse News Service* (Washington, DC), 18 July, 1. <http://proquest.umi.com.libproxy.sdsu.edu/pqdweb?index=37&did>. Retrieved 20 October 2008.

Klebnikov, Paul. 1995. Minister Toubon, meet General Gamelin. *Forbes*, 155(11): 22 May, 292–293.

Kluger, Jeffrey. 2008. How America's children packed on the pounds. *Time*, 23 June, 66–69.

Koenderman, Tony. 2002. Viagra ad causes offence in South Africa. 2 April. www.adageglobal. com/cgi-bin/daily.pl?daily_id-7282&post_date=2002–04–02.

*Korea Herald*. 2001. Irrational regulations hindering global branding strategies. 19 December, 1.

Kramer, Matt. 2008. The folly that is France. *New York Sun*, 23 January. <http://www.nysun.com/food-drink/folly-that-is-france/70044/>. Retrieved 19 May 2010.

Lehman, Edward. 2008. Procedures for the establishment of wholly foreign owned advertising ventures simplified with new regulations. <http://www/gala-marketlaw.com/joomla4/index.php?option=com_con...>. Retrieved 21 May 2010.

Lichfield, John. 2009. Fury in France as Sarkozy bans adverts from state TV. *Independent*, 5 January. <http://www.independent.co.uk.news/world/europe/fury-in-france-as...>. Retrieved 21 May 2010.

Loftus, Peter. 2007. Drug ads don't tempt Europe. *Wall Street Journal*, 7 November, B5D.

Luqmani, Mushtaq, Ugur Yavas, and Zahir Quraeshi. 1989. Advertising in Saudi Arabia: Content and regulation. *International Marketing Review* 6(1): 59–72.

MacLeod, C. 2007. *Obesity of China's kids stuns officials*. 9 January. <http://www.usatoday.com/news/world/2008-01-08-chinese-obesity_x.htm>. Retrieved 28 July 2008.

Madden, Normandy. 2001. Beijing reinforces out-of-home ad restrictions. 29 August. <www.adageglobal.com/cgi-bin/daily.pl?daily_id=5623&post_date=2001–08–29>.

*Marketing Week*. 2001. Side effects of an EU drug ads rethink. 19 July, 21.

———. 2008. Global campaigns: Brands behaving badly. 30 October <http://proquest.umi.com.libproxy.sdsu.edu/pqdweb?index=0&did=...>. Retrieved 23 January 2009.

McGowan, Kathleen. 2008. There's a pill for that. *Redbook*, March 210(3):158.

Mirandah, Patrick. 2005. Advertising to children in Malaysia. *Young Consumers*, World Advertising Research Center, 74–76.

Neergaard, Lauren. 1999. Consumers tune out drug ads, expert says. *Arizona Republic*, 17 November, A13.

Nelson, M. R., and H. J. Paek. 2005. Cross-cultural differences in sexual advertising content in a translational women's magazine. *Sex Roles*, 53(5–6): 371–383. Retrieved 11 October 2009, from Psychology Module (Document ID: 926150711).

*New York Times* News Service. 1999. US files king-size tobacco lawsuit. *San Diego Union-Tribune*, 23 September, A1.

*Nutrition and Food Science*. 2004. Health groups warn: Children at risk for junk food marketing 34(1): 42.

O'Leary, Noreen. 2007. The lay of the land. *AdWeek*, 48(6): 5 February, 14–21.

Onkvisit, Sak, and John J. Shaw. 1997. *International marketing: Analysis and strategy*. Upper Saddle River, NJ: Prentice Hall.

Pilling, David. 1999. Just what the patient ordered: The practice of advertising drugs is spreading. *Financial Times* (London), 11.

Pirisi, Angela. 1999. Patient-directed drug advertising puts pressure on US doctors. *Lancet* (London), 27 November, 1887.

Ramirez, Michael, and Joshua Hauserman. 2007. A guide to the alcohol ad ban. May. Tilleke & Gibbons International Ltd. Thailand: Level Developments.

Reuters.com. 2007. Unilever bans super slim models from advertising. 9 May. <http://uk.reuters.com/article/idUKL092898020070510>. Retrieved 21 May 2010.

Rijkens, Rein, and Gordon E. Miracle. 1986. *European regulation of advertising*. New York: North-Holland.

Schmid, Thomas. 2002. Thailand to limit advertising of energy drink. 26 November. <www.adageglobal.com/cgi-bin/daily.pl?daily_id=8844&post_date=2002–11–26>.

Schmit, Julie. 2008. Drug ads to get more FDA scrutiny. *USA Today*, 24 February. <http://www.usatoday.com/money/industries/health/drugs/2008-02-24>. Retrieved 20 October 2008.

*South China Morning Post*. 2002. Beijing Mark O'Neill advertising condoms. 2 December, 16.

Spake, A. 2003. Hey kids! We've got sugar and toys. *U.S. News and World Review*, 17 November, 62.

Speer, Lawrence. 2001. France sets code on portrayal of women in advertising. 17 October. <www.adageglobal.com/cgi-bin/daily.pl?daily_id=6018&post_date=2001–10–17>.

Tagliabue, John. 1994. Albania, Europe's poorest state, gets big Coca-Cola bottling plant. *San Diego Union-Tribune*, 20 May, A24.

Taylor, Charles, and Mary Anne Raymond. 2000. An analysis of product category restrictions in advertising in four major East Asian markets. *International Marketing Review*, 17: 287–304.

Thomaselli, Rich. 2010. FDA deputizes doctors to police "bad" Rx drug ads. *Advertising Age*, 24 May. <http://adage.com/print?article_id=144039>. Retrieved 24 May 2010.

Thornton, Jacqui, 2000. Should drug ads be legal? The ban on DTC pharmaceutical ads looks to be coming to an end. *Marketing*, 4 May.

Timms, Jonathan. 2001. Ho Chi Minh officials restrict ads for lingerie, sanitary towels. 18 December. <www.adageglobal.com/cgi-bin/daily.pl?daily_id=6651&post_date=2001– 12–18>.

*Today's Parent* (Toronto, Canada). 2008. The media and the message. 25(8): August, 88, 90.

Tristam, Pierro. 2008. *Glossary: Gulf Cooperation Council*. <http://middleeast.about.com/od/oileneergy/g/me080117.htm>. Retrieved 23 January 2009.

Vance, Deborah. 2002. Match game. *Marketing News*, 11 November, 1.

*Wall Street Journal*. 2006. Drug makers raise ad spending. 6 October, B-4.

Waller, David S. 2000. Cultural values and advertising in Malaysia: Views from the industry. *Asia Pacific Journal of Marketing and Logistics*, 12(1): 3–16.

Walsh, Bryan. 2006. No longer starving in China. *Time*, 18 August. <http://time.blogs.com/global_health/2006/08/no-longer_starv.html>. Retrieved 18 July 2008.

Walsh, Nick Paton. 2003. "Biznesmen" face fine for lapses into English. *Guardian* (Manchester), 7 February, 1.

Waxman, Sharon. 1994. French tell English users: Just say "Non." *Chicago Tribune*, 14 June, 1.

*Web in France Magazine*. 2008. In France, advertising, fashion and media companies sign accord to stop use of overly thin models. 10 April. <http://www.webinfrance.com/france-advertising-fashion-media-comp...>. Retrieved 21 May 2010.

Werner, Erica. 2009. House votes to give FDA authority over tobacco. *San Diego Union-Tribune*, 3 April, A-3.

Yuniar, Yayu. 2007. Indonesia circles the wagons; Ad market expands, but new rules demand homemade productions. *Wall Street Journal*, 25 October, B-4.

Zuckerbrod, Nancy. 2002. Bush seeks tough, new rules on nation's tobacco industry. *Charleston Gazette*, 12 March, 3A.

# CHAPTER 10

# Ethics and Beyond: Corporate Social Responsibility and Doing Business in the Global Marketplace

Back in the 1970s, renowned economist Milton Friedman argued that while it was important for businesses to "stay within the rules of the game" and "operate without deception or fraud," businesses did the most for society by just maximizing shareholder profits (*Reason* 2005). And many corporations bought into this philosophy. But much has changed in the corporate landscape over the last four decades. Increasingly, firms have recognized that it takes something more than engaging in ethical business practices and generating profits to navigate the mines of today's global marketplace. That something is the realization that companies are beholden not just to shareholders, but also to their customers and employees, the environment, and even society in general (Grow et al. 2005). Marketers must sell the message that they are "doing well by doing good" and simultaneously create high-level awareness of the connection between their brands and the social issues they support (Harris 2005). Today, more than ever, a company's reputation in the global marketplace is related to its social, as well as its ethical, performance.

## BUSINESS ETHICS IN THE GLOBAL MARKETPLACE

Corporations and their advertising agencies are required to make many difficult decisions when operating both in domestic markets and abroad. Granted, numerous laws govern what can and cannot be done. However, not every issue is covered by a written rule, and even where laws exist, there is a good deal of room for interpretation. With regard to business behavior, most marketers would agree that it is important to maintain high ethical standards, whether operating at home or in international markets. Determining exactly what is meant by "high ethical standards" is a good deal more complex. While interest in the ethical issues pertaining to international business has grown enormously in the past few decades, research on the ethical dimensions of international business and marketing has been relatively limited and generally non-empirical in nature (Taylor et al. 1989).

*Determining What's Ethical:* Ethical standards are often perceived as difficult to define. However, taking or offering bribes, cheating, stealing, lying, and spying are generally considered unacceptable business behaviors. Researchers surveyed American international business managers to determine the aspects of international marketing that pose the most difficult ethical or moral problems. The most frequent ethical problem faced was, in fact, bribery; the next most salient ethical problems faced related to governmental interference, customs clearance, transfer of funds, and cultural differences (Mayo et al. 1991). Apparently, other marketers around the globe find bribery to be similarly challenging. In a study comparing Australian and Canadian managers' perceptions of international marketing ethics problems, Chan and Armstrong (1999) found that "gifts/favors/entertainment" and "traditional small scale bribery" are among the top challenges. The researchers define "gifts/favors/entertainment" as including items such as lavish gifts, opportunities for travel at the company's expense, and gifts received after the completion of a transaction, as well as extravagant entertainment. "Traditional small scale bribery" was defined as payment of somewhat small sums of money, typically to a foreign official in exchange for violating some official duty or responsibility to speed routine government actions. Interestingly, both Australian and Canadian managers also noted "cultural differences" to be a critical problem. Here the managers expressed concern about cultural misunderstandings related to the traditional requirement of the exchange process—in other words, transactions regarded in one culture as bribery may be perceived as acceptable business practices in another. Indeed, the issue of bribery is often more than merely an ethical question, because the offering or taking of bribes is illegal in some countries. The U.S. Congress passed the Foreign Corrupt Practices Act (FCPA) in 1977, making it illegal for U.S. firms to bribe foreign officials, candidates, or political parties. The act provides for fines of up to $1 million for offending firms, and company executives, directors, and employees may be fined up to $10,000 and face five years in prison (Mayo et al. 1991). Other countries, however, may not have laws against bribery. It is estimated that foreign companies use bribes to eliminate U.S. competitors on approximately $45 billion in international business each year (*Globe and Mail* 1997). Because of the great concern regarding bribery in the global business community, the International Chamber of Commerce (ICC) published its *Rules of Conduct to Combat Extortion and Bribery*. As with its codes related to marketing and advertising, the ICC's rules on extortion and bribery are intended to complement existing international and national laws. For more information on these rules, see www.iccwbo. org/id914/index.html.

Many firms engage in what is euphemistically called "competitive analysis" but in reality is nothing more than corporate spying. Indeed, corporate security experts say that gathering information on competitors is both commonplace and necessary. "All companies keep their eyes on their competitors," according to Stephen Miller, spokesman for the Society of Competitive Intelligence Professionals, which is, in fact, an association for corporate spies. Competitive intelligence, the process of legally gathering information on competitors, has grown into a $2-billion-a-year industry. Practiced by America's largest companies since the 1960s, competitive intelligence is now increasingly being used by small- and mid-sized businesses as they try to seek ways to survive and grow in their industries. "What you don't know can hurt you," noted Alden Taylor, of Kroll Inc., a New York-based security consulting company. "If you're foolish enough not to be alert about your competitors, you are giving your competitors an advantage. It allows them to move deftly without being concerned about you because you're not paying attention" (Stammen 2001).

Procter & Gamble is one major marketer that employs competitive intelligence. However, it is how P&G gathered its information that ultimately got the firm into trouble. The consumer goods giant said that while it did nothing illegal, the methods it used, which included going through Unilever's trash, violated even P&G's own internal policies. Fierce rivals with Unilever in the hair care business, P&G's goal was to glean competitive data on Unilever's product line, which includes Salon Selectives, Finesse, Thermasilk, and Helene Curtis, in order to bolster P&G's own brands, which include Pantene, Head & Shoulders, and Pert. P&G said it fired three employees involved in the operation and informed Uniliver as soon as it discovered what was going on. The two companies reached a settlement in the amount of $10 million over the incident. In addition, an independent, third-party auditor was appointed to review P&G's entire business plan in the hair care area and report back to Unilever to ensure that any trade secrets stolen from Unilever would not be used (Barnes 2001). Undoubtedly, any attempt to conceal the truth would have done even greater damage to P&G in the long term. Experts agree that the vast majority of information collected in competitive intelligence is public information, and the rest is typically gained through interviews. Competitive intelligence experts give P&G high marks for promptly going to Unilever and admitting what it had done. "Being responsible and behaving responsibly is, in fact, good business," notes Professor Rajan Kamath, who teaches competitive analysis at the University of Cincinnati. "In the long run, you are going to get more hurt by doing things which could be represented in the public eye as unethical, irresponsible, or not in the best interests of the consumer. I'm pretty sure that even before P&G went to Unilever and said 'We fess up to what we did,' they put a dollar value on what would happen if this got out there" (Stammen 2001). Experts say that increased global competition has ratcheted up pressure on companies to find ways to gather information on their competitors. Companies now need to know what's going on with competitors half-way around the globe. The espionage case involving P&G is apparently only the tip of the iceberg. For example, China has thousands of technology intelligence analysts, and France has even developed master's degree programs to train intelligence specialists. The question, then, is not whether a company will gather competitive research, but how. Apparently, there are plenty of gray areas concerning acceptable methods of such information gathering.

There appears to be little agreement as to what principles should be used to guide business behavior in the international arena. For example, should the international marketer or advertiser adhere to the ethical mores of the home country, the host country, or the international marketplace? Advertisers likely will operate in markets that reflect a wide spectrum of ethical standards—standards that may well be in conflict. For example, an American marketer may adhere to the United States' Foreign Corrupt Practices Act and refrain from engaging in bribery in markets where such behavior is considered perfectly acceptable. However, many business people believe such strict adherence to home country laws would place U.S. companies at a distinct disadvantage in foreign markets.

Another perspective is that the legal and political system of the host country should set the parameters for ethical behavior; that is, "When in Rome, do as the Romans do." The fundamental idea here is that as long as the international marketer and advertiser operate within the confines of these parameters, they need not be concerned with ethical issues. Yet just because a given foreign country deems a particular business behavior acceptable does not necessarily make it ethical. Indeed, a number of American firms have been criticized for engaging in business practices abroad that are quite legal in the host country, but that are frowned on or even illegal in the United States. Moreover, this philosophy does not address the fact that in many developing countries the legal system may not sufficiently protect consumers or the environment.

There are numerous examples of multinational marketers who behave highly irresponsibly in foreign markets but break no laws. Swiss-based Nestlé, the world's largest food company, provides a classic example. In the late 1970s, the firm was heavily criticized for its aggressive marketing of infant milk formula in developing countries. In selling the formula to consumers in less-developed markets, Nestlé failed to address a number of factors that resulted in an international scandal. First, illiteracy rates in many developing markets were quite high, and a large percentage of consumers in the target audience were unable to understand the instructions on the product packaging. As a result, many mothers diluted the formula improperly, and children in developing countries suffered from malnutrition. Consumers also did not know of the need to sterilize the bottles, often mixing the formula with impure water, thereby feeding their infants contaminated milk. Another problem was related to price. To purchase a one-week supply of the formula, the typical Nigerian family spent up to 67 percent of its household income. To afford the product, mothers diluted the formula—resulting in malnutrition among formula-fed babies. Studies revealed that the overall death rate of formula-fed babies was three times higher than among those who were breastfed. Consumer outrage around the globe led to boycotts of Nestlé products. During the same period a Swiss court ruled that Nestlé had to undertake fundamental reconsideration of its promotional efforts if it wished to avoid charges of immoral and unethical behavior. The boycott ended after seven years when Nestlé finally complied with the infant formula marketing codes established by the World Health Organization (WHO). The code banned all promotional efforts, including advertising, sampling, and any direct contact with consumers. Nestlé was required to limit its activities simply to taking orders for the product from distributors (Post 1985). The marketing code has since been used as a basis for advertising regulation in numerous countries. Unfortunately, infant milk formula manufacturers are still aggressively marketing their wares in developing countries. In response to ads claiming that breast milk substitutes are equal to or better than breast milk, officials in Vietnam have drafted legislation forbidding the advertising of all breast milk substitutes for infants younger than six months. Vietnam says it is banning the ads to promote breast feeding among young mothers and to reduce infant malnutrition (*Advertising Age* 2000). Even more recently, makers of breast milk substitutes have been accused of violating international marketing codes in poor African countries. In a report in the *British Medical Journal*, researchers said that firms are still advertising directly to the public, often suggesting that their products will improve an infant's health. Further, they fail to provide sufficient information about the health hazards of such substitutes. Nestlé was named in the report, along with French firm Danone and U.S.-based Wyeth. It is clear that better monitoring mechanisms to curb violations of the code are needed (*Irish Times* 2003).

The third perspective holds that the responsibility for ethical behavior rests squarely in the hands of international marketing managers and practitioners. Companies and agencies should apply high standards of ethical behavior regardless of what a particular system might allow. Universal standards should be outlined in codes of behavior to be followed in each and every market. The primary criticism of this philosophy is that cultures differ so greatly that the creation of a viable set of worldwide ethical standards becomes nearly impossible. Despite cultural differences, a number of firms operating in the international arena have developed worldwide codes of ethics and expect the rules outlined therein to be followed in all areas of operation and in all markets. Such progressive firms include IBM, Caterpillar, S. C. Johnson, and Citigroup. For example, Citigroup's code states:

> We must never lose sight of the fact that we are guests in foreign countries. We must conduct ourselves accordingly. We recognize the right of governments to pass local legislation and our obligation to conform. Under these circumstances, we also recognize that we can survive only if we are successful in demonstrating to the local authorities that our presence is beneficial. We believe that every country must find its own way politically and economically. Sometimes we believe that local policies are wise; sometimes we do not. However, irrespective of our views, we try to function as best we can under prevailing conditions. We have also felt free to discuss with local governments matters directly affecting our interests, but we recognize that they have final regulatory authority. (Naor 1982).

The goal of a code of ethics is to give expression to the actual core values of an organization and then to use these to guide management and marketing decisions. Core values are beliefs that are so fundamental to the organizational structure that they will not be compromised. Codes may also embody peripheral values, which may be adjusted according to the local customs of various markets (Laczniak and Murphy 1990). The most effective codes of ethics recognize the importance of all individuals, agencies, and institutions relevant to the operation of the firm or agency, including customers, employees, the host community, relevant governmental agencies, the population at large, and so forth. A company must consider the impact of each of its decisions on these various publics. Such guides to ethical behavior may well assist international marketers and advertisers in avoiding some of the costly ethical mistakes of the past. Even the most detailed code, however, cannot cover each and every morally difficult situation. While most marketers and advertisers typically have little difficulty in making the "correct" decision with regard to health and safety issues, many other situations have no easy solutions and must be handled on a case-by-case basis. In some instances, when the gap between the values of the multinational corporation or advertising agency and the host country is too wide, voluntary suspension of all marketing and promotion activities must be considered.

## APPLYING ETHICS TO THE MARKETING MIX

Because of growing concern on the part of consumers, consumer organizations, and governments with the practices of international marketers and advertisers, the highest standards of marketing behavior must be applied to each of the marketing mix elements—product, price, distribution, and promotion. With regard to product responsibility, firms should strive to produce high-quality goods that are safe for both consumers and the environment, as well as being culturally sensitive. The right product targeted to the right audience can benefit both marketer and consumer. Hammond and Prahalad (2004) provide an excellent example. In rural India, only 4 of 10 households use iodized table salt, even though iodized salt provides a critical and convenient nutritional supplement. Due to India's environmental conditions, much of the iodine in salt is lost during transport and storage. The remainder often disappears in the cooking process. To overcome this problem, Hindustan Lever, Ltd., a subsidiary of Europe's Unilever Corp., has developed a way to encapsulate iodine, protecting it from transportation, storage, and cooking, and releasing the iodine only when salted food is ingested. The new salt required Hindustan Lever to invest in two years' worth of advanced research and development, but successful sales of the product would sharply reduce iodine deficiency disorder, a disease that affects more than 70 million people in India and is the country's leading cause of mental retardation. Hammond and Prahalad note that successful product development requires a deep understanding of local circumstances, so that critical features and functionality—salt with protected iodine—can be incorporated into the product's design.

Of course, "products"—broadly defined—also include services. Citibank's campaign to broaden its traditional base of rich clients exemplifies its approach to emerging markets. In Bangalore, India, it launched a program called Suvidha—Hindi for "ease." It persuaded mid-sized companies to set up retail bank accounts for their entire staffs, from janitors to top managers. To open accounts, customers needed just $22. Employees then received a card, which they could use to obtain cash, take out loans, pay bills at local ATMs, and purchase groceries. In just three years, Citibank (now Citigroup) gained 200,000 retail clients, doubling its base in India, for about $10 million (Engardio et al. 2001).

Pricing responsibility refers to charging only what consumers can afford. At the bottom of the world economic pyramid is a market of 5 billion people who live on less than $2 a day. These consumers are invisible to most large corporations, because too few executives can conceive of a market among people so poor (Prahalad 2004). But developing markets have proven successful for advertisers responsive to their needs. In 2003, Thailand's Information and Communications Technology Minister Surapong Suebwonglee was looking for ways to extend the benefits of technology to the masses, so he challenged Thailand's computer industry to come up with a $260 personal computer and a $450 laptop. In return, Suebwonglee guaranteed a market of at least 500,000 machines. The Thai computer industry met that price. But to do so, it had to omit Microsoft's widely used (and costly) Windows and Office operating software and offer the open-source Linux operating system. In response, Microsoft cut the price for its software to just $38 in Thailand, dramatically below normal retail prices. The "people's PCs" sold briskly throughout Thailand, and in 2004 Microsoft announced plans for a tailored and limited Thai-language version of its Windows XP Home software at reduced prices (Hammond and Prahalad 2004).

Additionally, goods must be distributed in a responsible fashion, and international marketers must ensure that products are made available to consumers where they require them. For over a decade, Hindustan Lever—the Indian subsidiary of Unilever—has been selling products geared to low-income Indians in rural areas. Research revealed that these consumers tend to shop at small, decentralized outlets. So, rather than ship truckloads of Lever products to supermarkets—primarily concentrated in the urban areas—which would have proven prohibitively expensive as well as ineffective, the company employed locals to deliver small quantities of their products to kiosks in the village markets (James 2001). Lever has also put together a rural selling network, Shakti (meaning "strength"), which employs about 31,000 women to sell soap, shampoo, detergent, and other products door-to-door in more than 100,000 villages (Onstad 2007). Similarly, appliance retailers are not common in rural India. This hasn't stopped Whirlpool from reaching every nook and cranny of the vast nation. The company uses local contractors, conversant in India's 18 languages, to collect payments in cash and deliver appliances by truck, bicycle, or even oxcart. Since 1996, Whirlpool's sales in India have jumped 80 percent, and the company is now the leading brand of India's fast-growing market for fully automatic washing machines (Engardio et al. 2001).

Promotion responsibility refers not just to advertising message content, but rather to all promotional activities. Advertising's high visibility, however, makes it particularly vulnerable to criticism. Writes Jack Neff (2008) in *Advertising Age*: "With no obvious connection, Häagen-Dazs' support for the effort to curb the declining honeybee population might cause suspicion that it is attaching its name to a timely cause to generate some positive, um, buzz. But upon further inspection, it becomes clear the brand has a reason for backing the cause." Indeed, it has 30 reasons. That's how many of Häagen-Dazs's 73 flavors contain ingredients pollinated by honeybees. The company refers to them as honeybee-dependent flavors and is tagging them with an "HD Loves HB" icon. Katty Pien, brand manager at Häagen-Dazs, said this marks the first time the brand has ever lent its support to a cause.

**Figure 10.1:** Print Ad from the "Häagen-Dazs Loves Honey Bees" campaign.

"From a brand perspective it was important to take on a cause that was integrally linked to who we are," she said. "We didn't want to be another brand profiting from the latest cause of the day" (Neff 2008b). The company is so serious about the campaign that it has devoted support in the area of "seven-figures" to it. The initial push began with a press release in early 2008 that was picked up in the United States by the Associated Press and sparked coverage in parts of Europe, as well as Japan and China. That was followed by national cable TV spots and one network TV spot that aired during *60 Minutes*, which had done a story on the honeybee population. Print ads ran during the spring of that year in magazines such as *Gourmet* and *National Geographic*. All promotional materials directed consumers to helpthehoney-bees.com, where they could make donations and learn more about how to help. In a June 2008 green-themed issue of *Newsweek*, Häagen-Dazs ran an ad printed on 100 percent recycled linen paper embedded with flower seeds that consumers could rip out of the magazine and plant. The company next launched a Vanilla Honey Bee flavor. A portion of the proceeds from the new flavor and all the HD Loves HB-labeled flavors went to the effort. Häagen-Dazs also donated $250,000 to UC Davis and Penn State University to fund Colony Collapse Disorder research, as well as honeybee-sustainability research. In addition, the firm visits community gardening groups with the hope of issuing more than a million plant seeds to be used to grow honeybee-friendly gardens. It produced a huge public relations payoff. Ms. Pien noted that the campaign generated more than 186 million media impressions is less than four months—shattering its goal of 125 million impressions for the entire year. And, while she had no exact figures, Ms. Pien noted that the campaign had resulted in "a very healthy increase in our baseline volume in retail sales" (Neff 2008b). See Figure 10.1 for a print ad from the Häagen-Dazs campaign.

Key questions facing marketing and advertising practitioners on a day-to-day basis include the following:

- Who should and who should not be advertised to?
- What should and should not be advertised?
- What should and should not be the content of the advertising message?
- What should and should not be the symbolic tone or actual character of the advertising message?
- What should and should not be the relationship among clients, agencies, and the mass media?
- What should and should not be advertising's business obligations versus its societal obligations? (Rotzoll et al. 1986).

## BEYOND ETHICS: CORPORATE SOCIAL RESPONSIBILITY

It can be said that ethical behavior deals primarily with "doing no harm." In contrast, socially responsible behavior has more to do with "doing good." Jeffrey R. Immelt, chairman and chief executive officer of General Electric, ranked both the world's most valuable *and* most admired company by *Fortune* magazine in 2004 (Gunther 2004) puts it this way: "Think about your neighbours," he says. "If they obey the law, if they pay their taxes, if they don't park their Winnebago on the street, are they just compliant? Now what about the neighbor who organizes the block party? Or, the one who picks the kids up after school? That's a good neighbor." GE wants to be known as a good company, not just in the United States, but also around the world. And expectations about what it means to be a good company are rising. Companies are increasingly expected to engage in corporate social responsibility.

A number of factors are driving corporate social responsibility: the unending parade of corporate wrongdoing—from the Bhopal disaster in 1984 (when a Union Carbide plant in Bhopal, India, leaked tons of toxic gas, killing thousands) to the Enron scandal of 2001 (in which the company engaged in systematic accounting fraud as well as bribed foreign government to win contracts abroad)—that has rocked the business world, the resulting increase in regulatory scrutiny, intense 24-hour-a-day, world-wide media coverage, and, in particular, consumers' critical view of corporate scandals and their increasing expectations of big business. Today, more than ever, a company's reputation in the global marketplace is related to its social, as well as its ethical, performance.

In late 2009, a survey was conducted in 10 countries (the United States, the United Kingdom, Brazil, Canada, Italy, Germany, India, China, France, and Japan) of 6,000 consumers by Edelman goodpurpose, a consultancy, to examine global consumer attitudes toward corporate social responsibility. The survey revealed that a firm's social actions play a far greater role than originally anticipated in forming consumers' *impressions* of companies. Specifically:

- 56 percent of global consumers feel the interests of society and the interests of business should have equal weight in business decisions.
- 65 percent are more likely to trust a company that addresses social concerns.
- 59 percent have a better opinion of corporations that integrate good causes into their business, regardless of the reasons why they do so.

Higher expectations are being placed on businesses to integrate good causes into their day-to-day operations. Of the countries surveyed, Brazilian consumers are most likely to agree with the statement that "It is no longer enough for corporations to simply give money away to good causes,; they need to integrate good causes into their day-to-day business" (see Table 10.1). The survey also asked consumers which causes they cared most about. Protecting the environment tops the list (see Table 10.2).

More important, consumers' impressions of corporations influence their *behavior*. The Edelman goodpurpose survey revealed the following:

**Table 10.1:** Higher Expectations Being Placed on Businesses to Engage in Corporate Social Responsibility on a Day-to-Day Basis

**% Agreeing**: "It is no longer enough for corporations to simply give money away to good causes; they need to integrate good causes into their day-to-day business."

| | |
|---|---|
| Brazil | 82% |
| India | 69 |
| U.S. | 67 |
| Canada | 67 |
| France | 67 |
| Italy | 66 |
| China | 63 |
| Japan | 61 |
| U.K. | 59 |
| Germany | 57 |

*Source*: Edelman goodpurpose Report (2009).

**Table 10.2:** Causes Global Consumers Care Most About

Question: How much do you personally care about...?

| | |
|---|---|
| Protecting the environment | 91% |
| Improving the quality of healthcare | 89 |
| Reducing poverty | 87 |
| Alleviating hunger and homelessness | 86 |
| Equal opportunity to education | 86 |
| Promoting societal health and wellness | 85 |
| Disaster Relief | 85 |
| Supporting human and civil rights | 83 |
| Building understanding/respect for other cultures | 81 |
| Supporting labor rights | 81 |
| Fighting the spread of global disease | 80 |
| Helping to raise people's self-esteem | 78 |
| Supporting animal rights | 76 |
| Supporting the creative arts | 68 |

*Source:* Edelman goodpurpose Report (2009).

- Two out of three people globally (67 percent) stated they would switch brands if a competitor of a similar quality supported a cause (country breakdown in Table 10.3).
- When choosing between two brands of the same quality and price, social purpose is what would most affect consumers' decisions (43 percent), ahead of design and innovation (34 percent) and their loyalty to the brand (24 percent).
- Globally, 64 percent of consumers say they would recommend a brand that supports a good cause (a 12-point increase from 2008).
- Over half (59 percent) of those surveyed would help a corporation "promote" a product if a good cause were behind it (a 6-point increase from 2008).
- Global consumers say they would be prepared to pay more for a brand that supports a good cause they believe in. Indeed, 61 percent of people have purchased a brand that supports a good cause even if it wasn't the cheapest.
- 63 percent of global consumers are looking to global brands to make it easier for them to make a positive difference in the world.

"People are demanding social purpose, and brands are recognizing it as an area where they can differentiate themselves and in many parts of the world, not only meet governmental compliance requirements, but also build brand equity," notes Mitch Markson, Edelman's chief creative officer, and president of its brand consulting group and founder of goodpurpose. "This year's survey shows that if companies respond intelligently to the sea of change in consumer attitudes, brand loyalty among consumers—even during seriously challenging economic times—will actually grow. Even better, consumers will want to share their support for these brands with others" (Edelman goodpurpose Report 2009).

**Table 10.3:** Consumers Would Switch Brands to Help Support a Good Cause

% Agree: "I would switch brands if a different brand of similar quality supported a good cause."

| | |
|---|---|
| Brazil | 83% |
| Italy | 74 |
| India | 73 |
| China | 70 |
| France | 67 |
| U.S. | 63 |
| Canada | 62 |
| Germany | 61 |
| U.K. | 58 |
| Japan | 57 |

*Source:* Edelman goodpurpose Report (2009).

Executives and investors alike are paying attention. A world-wide survey of senior executives and institutional investors found that 85 percent of respondents ranked corporate responsibility as "central" or "important" to business decisions, compared with a mere five years earlier, when only 44 percent of respondents answered similarly (*PR News* 2005). Globally, there are around 2,000 companies that report on their corporate social responsibility activities, though this is still only a fraction of the 60,000 multinational corporations operating world-wide (Blyth 2005). Over half of the top 250 companies on the Fortune 500 list publish separate reports on corporate social responsibility. Corporate social responsibility reporting rose particularly strongly in Italy, Spain, Canada, and France, where the number of companies issuing such reports almost doubled. However, Britain and Japan remain the countries most strongly wedded to the concept (Buck 2005). By one count, there are more than 100,000 pages on corporate Web sites dealing with the topic, and more than 200 mutual funds specialize in socially responsible investing (Pearlstein 2005). But the attention doesn't stop there. Amazon lists more than 600 books related to the topic. Increasingly business schools, both in the United States and in Europe, offer courses in it. A survey of 166 European academic institutions in 20 countries revealed that fully 80 percent of the respondents indicated that they were "undertaking activities of some kind to bring corporate social responsibility into their business teaching mainstream" (Gardiner and Lacy 2005). Corporate social responsibility consultancies have cropped up around the globe. In fact, London alone boasts over 400 such consulting firms, and at least one conference or seminar per week is devoted to the topic in that country (Doane 2003). The United Nations has even hosted a summit on it.

While corporate social responsibility is certainly the current buzzword, it is hardly a new concept. Indeed, it has been around since the 18th century, when anti-slavery groups appealed to the public to buy sugar that had been produced in a country where unpaid labor was not enforced (*Strategic Direction* 2002). And, over the decades, numerous companies have prided themselves in looking out for their employees. However, it was only relatively recently that the term "corporate social responsibility" was coined. In the 1990s it was primarily equated with environmental concerns, but today the expression has expanded to encompass a range of issues. Beyond a firm's commitment to its consumers (providing a quality product at a fair price, promoted in an ethical fashion) and its commitment to stockholders, businesses today must consider the interests of all of their employees, their impact on the environment, and, finally, their greater role in society.

*A Firm's Responsibility to All Its Employees:* After years of allegations that it is a poor employer with sexually and racially discriminatory hiring and employment practices, as well as being a destroyer of local businesses, Wal-Mart, in 2005, was on the receiving end of the largest class action lawsuit ever filed, with more than 1.5 million present and former employees taking part in the suit. To add to its woes, the Center for Community and Corporate Ethics ran a full-page ad in *The New York Times* that accused Wal-Mart of costing U.S. taxpayers some $1.6 billion a year. The ad said that Wal-Mart's low pay and benefits forced tens of thousands of employees to seek government aid in the form of Medicaid, food stamps, and housing assistance. The group included union leaders, environmentalists, and academics among its directors, and said on its Web site that it aims to "fight Wal-Mart on the streets, in the media, and in the customer's mind" (*Marketing Week* 2005). Fair treatment of employees can become a matter of life and death. Foxconn, a Taiwanese electronics company with factories in China, has been buffeted by a spate of employee suicides. The basic salary at the China plants of Foxconn Technology Group (which makes iPhones and other popular gadgets) is currently about 900 yuan ($130) per month. Labor activists have accused the company of also having a rigid management style, an excessively fast assembly line, and forced overwork. In just the first six months of 2010, 10 workers have killed themselves, and 3 have attempted suicide at the company's operations in southern China. Another Foxconn worker in northern China also committed suicide. Foxconn announced it would raise the pay of workers by an average of 20 percent. A company official, speaking on condition of anonymity because he wasn't authorized to talk to the press, noted that the big jump in pay could help to lift worker morale. "Feeling sad is contagious and so is feeling happy," he said. "We hope the workers will have a positive attitude toward their lives" (Huang 2010). The company, part of Taiwan's Hon Hai Precision Industry Co., is the world's largest contract maker of electronics, and its long list of big-name customers includes Apple Inc., Sony Corp., Dell Inc., Nokia Corp., and Hewlett-Packard Co. Manufacturers are not only responsible to employees in their domestic factories, but also in factories abroad. Nike, Disney, and many others have all had to deal with negative publicity surrounding their arrangements for foreign manufacturing at one time or another. Sub–minimum-wage pay, child labor, and unsafe working conditions all occur in developing countries, and local governments may not have the resources to stop these practices. Multinational corporations are ultimately responsible for insuring humane working conditions in their foreign manufacturing operations, as well as their domestic operations.

In contrast to the above case, some companies have received recognition for their treatment of employees. SAS, a software company, ranked #1 on *Fortune's* 2010 list of "100 Best Companies to Work For." Some of the benefits SAS offers its employees include a 35-hour work week; a 401(k) matching program; generous healthcare benefits, as well as on-site clinics staffed with physicians, nurse practitioners, registered dieticians/nutritionists, medical laboratory technicians, psychologists, and physical therapists; wellness and fitness programs (employees have access to gyms and pools); child care centers; summer day camps; and even a hair salon, nail salon, and auto detailing service. Facilities are located on a campus that features nature trails, lakes, soccer and baseball fields, and racquetball and tennis courts. SAS's legendary devotion to its employees makes it a model for other corporations. To compile the list, *Fortune* surveyed more than 81,000 employees from 353 companies. Rounding out the top ten were, in rank order, Edward Jones (investment advisors), Wegman's Food Markets, Google, Nugget

Markets, DreamWorks Animation, NetApp, Boston Consulting Group, Qualcomm, and Camden Property Trust (*Fortune* 2010).

Increasingly, firms are giving their employees opportunities to give back to the community, and Home Depot provides an excellent example. Every year Home Depot associates invest millions of hours of service through Team Depot, their volunteer corps. Home Depot has become involved with Habitat for Humanity and Rebuilding Together, which allows Home Depot not only to use its materials and products, but also its associates' working knowledge. In 2009, Home Depot and Habitat for Humanity announced a $30-million green building program that would provide funds and resources over a five-year period to help Habitat affiliates build 5,000 homes for low-income families that meet Energy Star guidelines or nationally recognized green building standards. These features incorporate the use of energy-efficient equipment and water-conserving fixtures and help ensure good indoor air quality. Benefits of homes built to these standards include: up to 50 percent less energy use than their conventional counterparts; reductions of up to one-third in indoor water consumption as a result of high-efficiency plumbing fixtures; and approximately 11 tons less carbon and greenhouse gas emissions per household annually—the equivalent of taking 250 cars off the road. "The Home Depot believes green building techniques are not a luxury—they aren't exotic or expensive," said Kelly Caffarelli, president of The Home Depot Foundation. "By embracing the practical principles of green building, our partnership with Habitat for Humanity is demonstrating that these techniques can actually make homes more affordable to own, maintain, and live in from day one and for the long term" (Habitat for Humanity Press Release 2009). As part of Rebuilding Together, Home Depot associates teach homeowners, particularly the elderly and disabled, to make simple home repairs. Home Depot volunteers have also responded to the military's needs. In 2003, the company created Project Homefront as a way to support the more than 1,800 employees who were called upon for military service. Through the program, Home Depot assists military families with home repairs and maintenance while family members are deployed. To help those who were affected by Hurricane Katrina (in addition to giving financial aid, donating goods and services, or establishing matching-gift programs that encourage and enhance employees' individual contributions to charities such as the American Red Cross), many firms allowed workers the flexibility to assist with relief efforts. According to Environics' CSR Monitor, 80 percent of employees of large companies say that the more socially responsible their companies become, the more motivated and loyal they are as employees (*PR News* 2005). Robert Nardelli, CEO of Home Depot, concurs:

> The ultimate payoff of our good citizenship is its impact on our corporate culture. Volunteering creates a culture of character, a set core of values that are both a natural extension of us, as individuals, and also the way we conduct our business. It also allows for greater associate gratification, which is key to building loyalty and morale. As measured in our most recent employer-of-choice survey, we've seen significant improvement in associate morale and a reduction in attrition. Moreover, having this dual initiative of building value and sharing values can become one of a company's best recruiting tools. When we go out on campus or do direct recruiting, most people comment on the values of the Home Depot. That provides us with a true competitive advantage in our ability to attract, motivate and retain the right kinds of people. (Nardelli 2004)

*A Firm's Responsibility to the Environment:* Globally, consumers are increasingly concerned about the environment. Since 2006, WPP agencies Cohn & Wolfe, Landor Associates, and Penn, Shoen & Berland Associates have partnered to conduct a "Green Brands" Survey. The 2009 survey (in which Esty Environmental Partners, a corporate environmental strategy consulting firm also participated) was the largest yet, with over 5,000 consumers in seven countries participating (Brazil, China, France, Germany, India, the United Kingdom, and the United States). The study revealed that while many

**Table 10.4:** Global Consumer Perceptions of the Importance of Being Green

Question: When you think about what brands to buy, how important is it to you that a company is green?

| | Very Important | Somewhat Important | Somewhat Unimportant | Very Unimportant |
|---|---|---|---|---|
| Brazil | 54% | 39% | 5% | — |
| China | 45 | 52 | 3 | — |
| France | 41 | 48 | 9 | 1 |
| Germany | 20 | 57 | 19 | 3 |
| India | 58 | 40 | 1 | — |
| U.K. | 15 | 62 | 16 | 4 |
| U.S. | 23 | 54 | 13 | 6 |

*Source:* Landor Staff (2009).

environmental beliefs and behaviors are shared across different consumer cultures, others vary widely. Key findings of the 2009 survey include:

- Globally, consumers report that it is important for companies to be green. At least 77 percent of consumers in all seven countries say it is somewhat or very important for a company to be green. Consumers distinguish between firms that produce green products (in the United States, for example, Clorox Green Works, which makes "natural" cleaning and laundry products, and Burt's Bees, which specializes in "natural" personal-care products) and those who engage in green corporate actions (in the United States, Wal-Mart and Dove). Interestingly, consumers in Brazil, China, and India report being more inclined to seek out green products and to favor companies they consider green, while their counterparts in France, Germany, the United States, and United Kingdom are less inclined to do so (see Table 10.4).

- Despite economic concerns, consumers say they will spend more on green products in the coming year. In particular, Chinese, Indians, and Brazilians show significant support for plans to increase their green spending.

- Consumers trust a variety of sources to inform their green-purchase decisions. Worldwide, consumers identify television and the Internet as their primary sources of information for environmental issues. And respondents—especially those in developing countries—say they trust advertising to inform them about green products. Attitudes toward green advertising for products vary by country (see Table 10.5).

- In order to gauge which firms are communicating their green initiatives or values most effectively, the survey asked participants in each country to rate a predetermined set of brands. No company established itself as a dominant global green brand, but several—Idea, Dove, The Body Shop, and Microsoft—are recognized in several markets. See Figure 10.2 for a Clorox Green Works ad, ranked No. 1 in the United States. Very few countries identified the same categories as the greenest, though personal care was in the top three for all countries except China (see Table 10.6).

**Table 10.5:** Global Consumer Perceptions of Green Advertising

**Question**: What do you think about advertising for green products? Responses below:

| | Advertising for green products helps consumers make informed purchase decisions and understand benefits of the product. | There is so much advertising for green products that it makes consumers tune out. | Undecided |
|---|---|---|---|
| Brazil | 90% | 5% | 5% |
| China | 80 | 18 | 2 |
| France | 46 | 43 | 11 |
| Germany | 49 | 36 | 15 |
| India | 81 | 15 | 4 |
| U.K. | 60 | 27 | 13 |
| U.S. | 62 | 25 | 13 |

*Source*: Landor Staff (2009).

**Table 10.6:** Green Brands by Country for 2009

| RANK | BRAZIL | CHINA | FRANCE | GERMANY |
|---|---|---|---|---|
| 1. | Natura | Haier | Le Petit Marseillais | Frosch |
| 2. | O Boticario | Li Ning | Yves Rocher | Weleda |
| 3. | Johnson & Johnson | Lenovo | Center Parcs | Dr. Hauschka |
| 4. | Unilever | Daidu | Decathlon | Ikea |
| 5. | Azaleia | Apple | Ikea | dm Drogerie |
| 6. | Hering | Shangri-La Hotels | E.Leclerc | Nivea |
| 7. | Pao de Acucar | Adidas | Belambra VVF | Tegut |
| 8. | Grendene | Liushen | Nivea | REWE |
| 9. | Nivea | Microsoft | Dove | The Body Shop |
| 10. | Microsoft | Ikea | Citroen | Vileda |

| | INDIA | U.K. | U.S. |
|---|---|---|---|
| 1. | Dettol | The Body Shop | Clorox Green Works |
| 2. | Tata Indicom | M & S | Burt's Bees |
| 3. | Infosys | Sainsbury's | Tom's of Maine |
| 4. | Taj Hotels & Resorts | Waitrose | S.C. Johnson |
| 5. | Wipro | Tesco | Toyota |
| 6. | Microsoft | E.ON | P&G |
| 7. | Reva | EDF | Wal-Mart |
| 8. | Maruti | Google | Ikea |
| 9. | Colgate | Dove | Disney |
| 10. | Lifebuoy | Honda | Dove |

*Source*: Landor Staff (2009).

- Consumers around the globe expect companies to take comprehensive environmental action. The survey indicates that consumers have clear ideas about the steps that companies should take to be viewed as green. Reducing toxins leads the list of consumer priorities. Consumers also expect companies to recycle, use energy efficiently, reduce packaging, and pursue green innovation. To gain loyalty, the company's environmental strategy must be comprehensive.

The 2009 Green Brands survey "findings in both developed and developing countries reinforce consumers' desires to be green by using products that are green," notes Russ Meyer, chief strategy officer of Landor Associates. "However, we're also beginning to see a strong positive correlation between greenness and more traditional brand attributes like honesty and trustworthiness. This creates an incentive for global brands faced with the challenge of expanding the reach of pre-existing products while introducing green ones, as the presence of one attribute can have a halo effect on others" (Landor Staff 2009).

Increasingly, firms are committing to environmentally sound practices—not only within, but also among their suppliers. In 2010, Procter & Gamble, the world's largest advertiser and ranked #6 as the greenest brand in America (see Table 10.6), unveiled its Supplier Environmental Sustainability Scorecard, and neither advertising agencies nor media companies appear to be off the hook. The scorecard "represents the next step in P&G's commitment to environmental sustainability," Chairman-CEO Bob McDonald noted. "Keeping sustainability at the core of our business fuels innovation and strengthens our results" (Neff 2010). P&G announced that suppliers will have a full year to prepare their data before their scores can adversely affect their supplier ratings. Eventually, though, P&G will use the scorecard to determine sustainability ratings as part of its annual performance reviews. Getting a top rating on the scorecard requires reporting on and improving all applicable-to-the-industry P&G core environmental impact measures, working collaboratively on all applicable P&G sustainability initiatives, jointly developing several ideas adopted by P&G, and reporting on all additional feasible measures of environmental impact requested by P&G. The environmental measures include a broad range of energy use, waste disposal, reduction and recycling, and environmental regulatory compliance factors. P&G will offer "extra credit" for providing sustainability ideas. Clearly, ad agency holding companies and media players rank among P&G's biggest suppliers. Publicis Group alone earns around $900 million annually in P&G business. Many TV networks and other media companies also top nine figures in annual P&G business. How can agencies possibly help their clients help the environment? In a special report on green marketing, *Advertising Age* (Frazier 2008) profiled dozens of agencies' efforts to help "fuel the green machine." For example, the Omnicom Group media shop launched PHD Sustain, aimed at reducing the environmental impact of media plans. PHD Sustain teamed up with a researcher from the University of California, Berkeley, to measure the environmental impact of each media channel—for instance, the amount of electricity required to power a 30-second TV spot. Using those data, an Environmental Media Sustainability Index is created for media planners. The software tool shows how green options, such as solar panel billboards, can lessen a media plan's environmental impact. Horizon Media slashed the amount of paper used in media buys when it started applying a system called Eleven, which is totally paperless, to maintain buys for local TV, cable, and radio. WPP Group's "Tackling Climate Change" is a company-wide initiative to reduce energy consumption. The company has identified four areas for conservation: office, IT, travel, and procurement. WPP says that up to 70 percent of the electricity used in its U.K. offices comes from renewable sources. The company plans to decrease the energy used by computers in its offices worldwide by 30 percent. And Omnicom's BBDO Worldwide tied the greening of its agency to clients through the new "Project Greener Light"

**Figure 10.2:** Ad for Clorox Green Works—perceived as the greenest brand in the United States.

initiative. BBDO New York, for example, replaced all incandescent light bulbs in the office with client GE's compact fluorescent lights and, to bring the idea home, made the lights available to employees at a discounted price at another client, Lowe's. It appears even agencies can be greener.

Because of the growing importance of environmental issues and the complexity of judging and verifying environmental claims, the International Chamber of Commerce (ICC) issued a Framework for Responsible Environmental Marketing Communications in 2010 to help businesses make responsible use of green advertising. The code is intended to complement the existing frameworks of national and international law (see www.iccwbo.org/policy/marketing/id30752/index.html), and it applies to all ads containing environmental claims. It covers any form of advertising in which, explicitly or implicitly, references are made to environmental aspects relating to production, packaging, distribution, use/consumption, or disposal of goods and services. The code recognizes that environmental claims can be made in any medium, including labeling, package inserts, promotional and point-of-sale materials, product literature, as well as telephone, digital, or electronic media such as e-mail and the Internet. The code is a practical tool to be used by all concerned with environmental advertising.

*A Firm's Responsibility to Society:* Good leaders, in companies large and small, are looking for ways to "give back." In ranking the "World's Most Admired Companies" for 2010, *Fortune* surveyed thousands of directors, executives, and managers at more than 650 companies from 33 countries around the world. Table 10.7 presents the World's 50 Most Admired Companies. Of the 50 companies listed, 38 were mentioned by at least one other corporate social responsibility ranking or sustainability index (Dow Jones Sustainability Index, Corporate Knights, Ethisphere, RiskMetrics Group, or CRO). Indeed, four firms had the honor of appearing on at least four of the rankings: Procter & Gamble, Starbucks, Nike, and Hewlett-Packard. Number 6 on *Fortune's* list for 2010 is Procter & Gamble. While the company has an excellent reputation for taking care of it employees (P&G's profit-sharing program, introduced in 1887, is the oldest in the United States) and the environment (one of the company's strategies is to deliver an additional 20 percent reduction [per unit production] in $CO_2$ emissions, energy consumption, water consumption, and disposal waste from P&G plants by 2012, leading to a total reduction over a decade of at least 50 percent). P&G takes it as a given that it has an obligation not just to make money and obey the law, but also to help solve the world's problems. To that end, P&G has at least eight brands that have active ad campaigns touting environmental and philanthropic efforts (Neff 2008b). Just a few examples are provided here.

- Every year, 128,000 people die from maternal and neonatal tetanus, a completely preventable disease. So, for the past four years, Pampers has teamed up with UNICEF to deliver the vaccines that vulnerable women and their children need. This effort involves consumers. With the purchase of one pack of Pampers, one dose of the vaccine is donated. Since the start of the campaign, 45.5 million women and their babies have been protected against maternal and neonatal tetanus. P&G's goal is to eliminate the disease by 2012. Pampers has committed to providing the vaccine to target and protect an additional 33 million women and their babies in at least 32 countries around the world.
- Establishing good hygiene habits early is essential to protecting children from disease. So Safeguard, in partnership with the Red Cross and China's Ministry of Health, launched the "Safeguard Health Great Wall" campaign on October 15, 2008—Global Hand Washing Day. Hand washing is one of the most effective and affordable health interventions, but water alone is not enough. Using soap and water can help reduce the incidence of diarrheal disease by almost half and cut respiratory infections by nearly 25 percent. It is also recommended as a

critical action to prevent the spread of influenza. Despite its life-saving potential, hand washing with soap is seldom practiced in some parts of the world. So the Safeguard Health Great Wall campaign, using the slogan "Clean hands save lives," aims to engage school children as effective agents for change. The program's goal is to educate 10 million children over an eight-year period. Consumer purchases of Safeguard help to fund the program. Beyond China, Safeguard delivers hand hygiene education to children in Mexico, Pakistan, and the Philippines.

■ More than six million children are hospitalized each year in the United States and forced to confront the challenges of overcoming illness while being away from home in an unfamiliar environment. In order to bring a little comfort and security back to some of these children, Downy fabric softener, in partnership with Quilts for Kids, Inc., has launched the "Downy Touch of Comfort" program to provide quilts to those children while hospitalized. See Figure 10.3 for a Spanish-language ad promoting the Downy Touch of Comfort program. For addi-

**Table 10.7:** *Fortune's* "World's 50 Most Admired Companies" for 2010

| | | | |
|---|---|---|---|
| 1. | Apple | 26. | Starbucks |
| 2. | Google | 27. | Singapore Airlines |
| 3. | Berkshire Hathaway | 28. | Exxon Mobil |
| 4. | Johnson & Johnson | 29. | American Express |
| 5. | Amazon.com | 30. | Nordstrom |
| 6. | Procter & Gamble | 31. | Intel |
| 7. | Toyota Motor Corp. | 32. | Hewlett-Packard |
| 8. | Goldman Sachs Group | 33. | UPS |
| 9. | Wal-Mart Stores | 34. | Nestlé |
| 10. | Coca-Cola | 35. | Caterpillar |
| 11. | Microsoft | 36. | Honda Motor |
| 12. | Southwest Airlines | 37. | Best Buy |
| 13. | Fedex | 38. | Sony |
| 14. | McDonald's | 39. | Wells Fargo |
| 15. | IBM | 40. | Ebay |
| 16. | General Electric | 41. | Nokia |
| 17. | 3M | 42. | Samsung Electronics |
| 18. | J.P. Morgan Chase | 43. | Deere |
| 19. | Walt Disney | 44. | L'Oréal |
| 20. | Cisco Systems | 45. | AT&T |
| 21. | Costco Wholesale | 46. | Lowe's |
| 22. | BMW (tied with Target) | 47. | General Mills |
| 22. | Target | 48. | Marriott International |
| 24. | Nike | 49. | Dupont |
| 25. | PepsiCo | 50. | Volkswagen |

*Source:* Bernasek (2010).

**Figure 10.3:** Spanish-language ad promoting the "Downy Touch of Comfort" program.

tional examples of P&G's corporate social responsibility activities, visit http://www.pg.com/en_US/sustainability/Social_responsibility.

Starbucks was recognized by *Fortune* as number 42 on its list of "most admired companies" in 2010. Central to Starbucks's success is its commitment to corporate social responsibility. Starbucks was among the first companies to provide health care benefits and stock options even to part-time employees. The company pays poor Colombian and Ethiopian farmers more for "fair trade" coffee beans. In terms of the environment, it has created relationships with suppliers in developing countries who meet environmental criteria. However, Starbucks also has a broader social vision: helping to bring clean water to children and their communities in developing countries. In 2005, the company purchased Ethos, an ethical bottled-water company. With the launch of Ethos water in nearly 5,000 U.S. Starbucks stores, Starbucks hopes to inspire and empower customers to play a personal role in helping children and their communities around the world to get clean water. By purchasing Ethos water, customers can help to make a difference. Five cents from the sale of each bottle of Ethos water supports the nonprofit organizations that are helping to alleviate the world water crisis (*Business Wire* 2005). The bottom line: to date, more than $6 million has been raised to help support water, sanitation, and hygiene education programs in water-stressed countries, benefiting more than 420,000 people around the world. See Figure 10.4 for an advertisement promoting Ethos water and $H_2O$ Africa. When the recession hit in 2008, Starbucks stock lost more than half its value. CEO Howard Schultz responded quickly, outlining more than $400 million in cost reductions for the 2009 fiscal year. But there was one area that escaped relatively unscathed: corporate responsibility. "Short-term thinking in a recession can lead to the false belief that investments in people and training can wait, that corporate social responsibility can be put on the back burner," Schultz noted. "Now is the time to invest, truly and authentically, in our people, our corporate responsibility and in our communities. The argument—and opportunity—for companies to do this has never been more compelling" (Delevingne 2009).

While the good deeds of big corporations may receive media attention, even small companies are aligning their brands with the causes and concerns of their market. Canadian firm Olly Shoes, a children's shoe retailer with just 11 stores, started a "gently used shoes" donation program when it opened in 2000. To date, it has sent thousands of customer-donated, used shoes to charities in Canada, the United States, and overseas. "Everything we do tends to focus around the well-being of children and it's a perfect match for Olly," explains Christine Siewete, marketing manager of the Toronto-based retailer. "Often you see programs, and the customers don't understand it because it doesn't relate to what the corporation is" (Harris 2005). And in Tucson, Arizona, entrepreneur Bob Schlesinger decided to move away from running ads for his business, Bookman's Used Books, Music and Software. Instead, he earmarked those funds for charitable causes. Bookman's five stores, which pull in $14 million annually, have sponsored mailings for literacy volunteers, purchased shoes for more than 100 kids, and donated hundreds of thousands of books to halfway houses, jails, nonprofit groups, and schools (Relly 2000). Small firms like Olly Shoes and Bookman's are increasingly building community service into their business plans.

But corporate social responsibility is not divorced from a company's bottom line. Based on a survey of the 250 top companies in the Fortune 500 survey, as well as the 100 largest companies in 16 countries, researchers have revealed that businesses cited a variety of reasons for their involvement in corporate social responsibility, though by far the greatest number pointed to economic considerations. "The economic reasons were either directly linked to increased shareholder value or market share, or

**Figure 10.4:** Advertisement promoting Ethos water and H$_2$O Africa.

indirectly linked through increased business opportunities, innovation, reputation and reduced risk," the survey noted (Buck 2005). In short, corporate social responsibility makes good business sense.

## COMMUNICATING CORPORATE SOCIAL RESPONSIBILITY TO THE PUBLIC

Corporate social responsibility isn't only about how companies behave; it is also about how they communicate their actions to key audiences. Firms should formalize social responsibility policies and disseminate them widely within the organization. Frequent internal communication about core values and socially responsible efforts between upper management and lower-level employees is critical. Equally important is the dissemination of the message externally. Unfortunately, research reveals that the public's knowledge of specific companies' corporate social responsibility performance appears to be limited. When asked to name a socially responsible company, many people across the 21 countries surveyed were unable to answer. Those who did often mentioned companies with strong brand reputations rather than ones particularly active in social activities (*Brand Strategy*, 2005). Despite the fact that companies more often have good stories to tell, and consumers increasingly express interest in firms' socially responsive activities, businesses have not communicated their commitments effectively.

Corporate social responsibility is difficult to communicate. Efforts in this area are often perceived as public relations smokescreens designed to conceal or divert attention from corporate misdeeds. Before attempting to promote themselves as good corporate citizens, firms must ensure that they "walk the talk." For example, when British Petroleum replaced its shield with a green and yellow sunflower logo in 1999, it told the world that it was no longer just in the oil business, but instead was an energy company that wanted to go "Beyond Petroleum." Greenpeace was not impressed, accusing BP of spending more on re-branding than exploring renewable energy sources. It dubbed BP "Burning the Planet" (*Campaign* 2005), and it didn't help when, in 2003, Henderson Global Investors pulled out of BP following health and safety problems in Alaska. Further, a group of non-governmental organizations claimed that BP had evaded labor, tax, and environmental laws in the development of a pipeline running through Azerbaijan, Georgia, and Turkey (Doane 2003). To top off the company's list of woes, BP has received bitter but well-deserved, universal criticism for the 2010 oil spill in the Gulf of Mexico, which not only killed 11 employees but also pumped tens of thousands of gallons of oil into the ocean. Facing both criminal and civil investigations, BP began running full-page ads in major publications such as the *New York Times*, the *Wall Street Journal*, and *USA Today*. In the ads the company has acknowledged that "The Gulf oil spill is a tragedy that should have never happened." The copy reads: "BP will continue to take full responsibility for cleaning up the spill," and explains its efforts so far to do so, including organizing "the largest environmental response in this country's history. More than 3 million feet of boom, 30 planes and more than 1,300 boats are working to protect the shoreline." Finally conceding that oil will in fact come ashore, the ad reads: "When oil reaches the shore, thousands of people are ready to clean it up." The tagline promises: "We will get it done. We will make it right" (Bush 2010). Critics have noted that until PB plugs that hole, it doesn't matter what the company says. BP clearly has much to do to re-position itself as a socially responsible corporation.

A second major challenge to corporate social responsibility is that there are different expectations across different markets that require tailored content and tactics. For example, research conducted by Globescan involving 20,000 consumers, shareholders, and corporate staff across 20 nations reveals that consumers in Brazil, China, Indonesia, the Philippines, South Africa, and the United States are most receptive to formal corporate messages (*Brand Strategy* 2005). Indeed, according to Cone's Corporate Citizenship Study, nine out of ten Americans want companies to tell them what they are doing in terms of corporate social responsibility. But the information consumers are presented with is often lacking. While an increasing number of firms may include social responsibility sections in their annual reports, many such sections consist of little more than glossy photos or promises of more commitment. Too often this is not enough for the public, which—after years of mistrust of "greedy capitalist corporations"—wants to see facts and figures proving that businesses are really giving something back (*Strategic Direction* 2002). Annual reports for such consumers ought to provide numbers and include comparative data on past and present performance, as well as the plans for the future. Starbucks, for example, not only publishes a complete Corporate Social Responsibility Annual Report, but also has an outside auditor verify the figures. Consumers increasingly want evidence of responsible behavior. It is also critical that companies issue detailed reports, even when their performance fails to meet stated targets, since candid disclosure of corporate faults and misdeeds can serve as a basis for both dialogue and negotiations between companies and their critics. Transparency is critical. Beyond the annual report, information about socially responsible efforts can be conveyed through Web sites, through point-of-sale information, by speaking with customers, and even in ad campaigns.

In Mexico, Canada, Australia, and Europe, where skepticism is high, more informal communication may, in contrast, win over consumers more effectively (*Brand Strategy* 2005). Research has revealed that some consumers prefer to find out about such activities from a third-party source, particularly the media (*PR News* 2005). Consumer magazines in more than 10 countries, for example, have already published product tests that include labor, environmental, and social criteria. Rob Harrison, editor of the United Kingdom's *Ethical Consumer* magazine, seeks to satisfy a desire among mainstream consumer groups around the world for information on ethical and social issues (Williamson 2004). In addition, *Test,* Germany's leading guide to consumer products, recently began assessing products to measure whether the practices used in their production complied with international social and labor standards, and whether they are good or bad for the environment. Holger Brackemann, research coordinator for the organization that publishes *Test,* says that the decision was consumer driven. "It is clear from surveys that consumers are increasingly interested in social and environmental issues, so we are responding to that. Products are become more similar in terms of quality, so consumers are looking for other ways of making purchasing decisions" (Williamson 2004). (See Figure 10.5 for a German ad for Ariel laundry detergent. Note the "Testsieger" [Test Winner] ratings highlighted in the lower portion of the ad.) It is the responsibility of firms large and small to inform their audiences as to how they're making the world a better place if they hope to enhance their corporate reputations.

## SUMMARY

Clearly, both ethics and corporate social responsibility matter. They matter to consumers, to employees, to investors, and to governments and activist groups, whose power to influence business is growing. Benjamin W. Heineman, Jr., senior vice president for law and public affairs at General Electric argues that companies must invest in their reputations. "Just as there's goodwill on balance sheets, and just as a brand has value, reputation, broadly defined, has enormous value for companies" (Gunther 2004). In 2008, SABMiller commissioned a survey in association with Henley Management College in the United Kingdom to contribute to a series of debates it was sponsoring regarding globalization. The survey asked which factors might be the hallmarks of successful global consumer brands over the next

**Figure 10.5:** German ad for Ariel laundry detergent highlighting the test ratings the product has received.

decade. The respondents were not just members of the general public whose views could be dismissed as ill-informed, nor were they concerned ethical shoppers with a moral axe to grind. Rather, the survey was conducted among some of the world's most influential figures from business, politics, the media, and public services. They made up research group YouGovStone's "Think Tank" of nearly 4,000 influential "leaders in their field." Top place in the survey went to ethics and sustainability, which was chosen by 68 percent of respondents. Next came competitive pricing. Product innovation polled just 52 percent, and authentic brand personality a mere 37 percent. Clearly, the respondents gave a good deal of credit to ethics and sustainability in terms of building global success (*Marketing Week* 2008).

It is no longer enough for a company to stand for productivity, growth, rising profits, and shareholder returns. In the global marketplace of today—and tomorrow,—the combination of ethics and corporate social responsibility isn't just a "nice thing" but rather a "must have."

## REFERENCES

Advertising Age. 2000. Vietnam to ban ads for breast milk substitutes. 13 June. <www.adageglobal.com/cgi-bin/daily.pl?daily_id= 3198&post_date=2000-06-13>.

Barnes, Julian. 2001. P&G said to agree to pay Unilever $10 million in spying case. *The New York Times*, 7 September, C-7.

Bernasek, Ana. 2010. Who does business trust? *Fortune*, 2 March, 122.

Blyth, Alex. 2005. Business behaving responsibly. *Director* (London), 59(1): August, 30.

*Brand Strategy*. 2005. Corporate social responsibility and its impact on corporate reputation. London, 8 September, 40.

Buck, Tobias. 2005. More companies reveal social policies. *Financial Times* (London), 15 June, 8.

Bush, Michael. 2010. BP print ads promise to "Make this right." *Advertising Age*, 2 June. <http://adage.com/print?article_id=144196>. Retrieved 2 June 2010.

*Campaign*. 2005. Brands that play the green card. Teddington, 15 July, 26–28.

Chan, Robert, and Robert Armstrong. 1999. Comparative ethical report card: A study of Australian and Canadian managers' perceptions of international marketing ethics problems. *Journal of Business Ethics*, 18(1): January, 3–15.

Delevingne, L. 2009. Surprising survivors: Corporate do-gooders. CNNMoney.com. 20 January. <http://money.cnn.com/2009/01/19/magazines/fortune/do_gooder.fortu...>. Retrieved 28 May 2010.

Doane, Deborah. 2003. Let's walk the talk on corporate integrity. *The Independent on Sunday* (London), 11 May, 7.

Edelman goodpurpose Report (2009). Put meaning into marketing & profit through purpose. Retrieved from the Edelman Web site 2 June 2010.

Engardio, Pete, Manjeet Kripalani, and Alysha Webb. 2001. Smart globalization. *Business Week*, 20–27 August, 132.

*Fortune*. 2010. The 100 best companies to work for. 8 February.

Frazier, Mya. 2008. How agencies are helping their clients help the environment. *Advertising Age*, 9 June, S-4.

Gardiner, Louise, and Peter Lacy. 2005. Lead, respond, partner or ignore: The role of business schools on corporate responsibility. *Corporate Governance* (Bradford), 5(2): 174–186.

*Globe and Mail* (Toronto). 1997. OECD nations agree to ban bribery. 24 May, B-3.

Grow, Brian, Steve Hamm, and Louise Lee. 2005. The debate over doing good. *Business Week*, 15 August, 76.

Gunther, Marc. 2004. Money and morals at GE. *Fortune*, 150(10): 15 November, 175–180.

Habitat for Humanity Press Release. 2009. Habitat for Humanity International and The Home Depot Foundation announce national expansion of "Partners in Sustainable Building." 4 August. <http://www.habitat.org/newsroom/2009archive/08_04_2009_HFH...>. Retrieved 27 May 2010.

Hammond, Allen L., and C. K. Prahalad. 2004. Selling to the poor. *Foreign Policy*, May/June, 30–37.

Harris, Rebecca. 2005. Growing responsibilities. *Marketing*, 110(27), 15–2 August, 15-17.

Huang, Annie. 2010. Taiwan firm moves to stop suicides. *San Diego Union-Tribune*, 29 May, C-1.

*Irish Times* (Dublin). 2003. Breaches of baby formula code denied. 18 January, 12.

James, Dana. 2001. B2-4B spells profits. *Marketing News* (Chicago), 35(23): 5 November, 1.

Laczniak, Gene, and Patrick Murphy. 1990. International marketing ethics. *Bridges: An Interdisciplinary Journal of Theology, Philosophy, History and Science*, 2(3,4): Fall/Winter, 155–177.

Landor Staff. 2009. Green brands, global insight: Findings from the 2009 ImagePower Green Brands survey. September. <http://www/landor.co,/index.cfm?do=thinking.article&storyid=749…>. Retrieved 27 May 2010.

*Marketing Week* (London). 2005. America: Who cares wins, but is there a hidden agenda? 28 April, 34.

———. 2008. Global brands: Forcing the ethical issue. 10 July, 18.

Mayo, Michael, Lawrence Marks, and John K. Ryans. 1991. Perceptions of ethical problems in international marketing. *International Marketing Review*, 8(3): 61–75.

Naor, Jacob. 1982. A new approach to multinational social responsibility. *Journal of Business Ethics*, 1: 219–225.

Nardelli, Bob. 2004. Good citizenship builds strong cultures. *Chief Executive* (New York), April, 14.

Neff, Jack. 2008a. Unilever, P&G war over which is most ethical. *Advertising Age*, 13 March, 1.

———. 2008b. Yes, there is an ROI for doing good. *Advertising Age*, 26 May, 14.

———. 2010. Agencies also on hoof for P&G's green scorecard. *Advertising Age*, 12 May. <http://adage.com/print?article_id=143817>. Retrieved 13 May 2010.

Onstad, Eric. 2007. Big firms rush to tap vast market of poor consumers. *Reuters*, 4 June. <http://www.reuters.com/articlePrint?articleId=USL1711076420070604>. Retrieved 22 November 2009.

Pearlstein, Steven. 2005. Social responsibility doesn't much sway the balance sheet. *Washington Post*, 5 October, D-1.

Post, James E. 1985. Assessing the Nestlé boycott. *California Management Review*, 27: Winter, 113–131.

*PR News*. 2005. How CSR is driving the way companies conduct business. 61(22): 1 June, 1.

Prahalad, C. K. 2004. Why selling to the poor makes for good business. *Fortune*, 150(10): 11 November, 70–72.

*Reason*. 2005. Rethinking the social responsibility of business. 37(5): October, 28–38.

Relly, Jeannine. 2000. Charitable work sells at a number of firms. *Arizona Daily Star* (Tucson), 17 July, D-1.

Rotzoll, Kim B., James E. Haefner, and Charles H. Sandage. 1986. *Advertising in contemporary society*. Cincinnati, OH: South-Western.

Stammen, Ken. 2001. Corporate spying common, *Cincinnati Post*, 7 September, 1-A.

*Strategic Direction*. 2002. McDonald's jumps on the CSR bandwagon. 18(9): September, 8–11.

Taylor, R. E., D. Edwards, and J. R. Darling. 1989. The ethical dimensions of trade barriers: An exploratory study. *Columbia Journal of World Business*.

Williamson, Hugh. 2004. Product tests highlight ethics: Corporate social responsibility. *Financial Times* (London), 1 July, 9.

# Index